VISIONARIES: THOR

WALTER SIMONSON

MARVEL COMICS

STAN LEE PRESENTS

VISIONARIES: THOR

WALTER SIMONSON

Collecting The Mighty Thor #s 337-348

Walter Simonson
STORY, PENCILS AND INKS

◆

**Terry Austin and
Bob Wiacek**
ADDITIONAL INKS

◆

John Workman, Jr.
LETTERS

◆

**George Roussos and
Christie Scheele**
COLORS

◆

**Mark Gruenwald and
Mike Carlin**
ORIGINAL SERIES EDITORS

◆

Steve Buccellato
COVER COLOR

◆

**JG and Comicraft's
Eng Wong**
DESIGN

◆

Ben Abernathy
COLLECTION EDITOR

◆

Joe Quesada
EDITOR IN CHIEF

*Special thanks to the crew at
Mighty Marvel Repro, Marie Javins,
and Doreen Mulryan.

CONTENTS ◆ ◆ ◆

INTRODUCTION

...For If The Odinsword Be Drawn!

I wrote that title in 1967 during the worst excesses of my efforts to imitate Stan Lee. Back then, I was a geology major in college, Viet Nam was a looming shadow for every young man of draftable age in America, and Marvel was publishing about 11 comics a month. Which meant that I was measuring strikes and dips on the rocks below the Holyoke Dam, thinking tough thoughts about my future after graduation, and purchasing every comic Marvel published.

Thor was my personal favorite. I'd already had an abiding interest in Norse mythology when I discovered Marvel's version. And Stan and Jack were telling wonderful stories. Stories I read so many times, I can still remember them better than I can my own. Off the top of my head -- the Trial of the Gods, Thor's evolving struggle against Loki, the Norn Stones and the Destroyer, the Absorbing Man, the coming of Hercules, the treachery of Seidring the Merciless (I did think Odin missed the boat there; would you trust an advisor on your staff named Seidring the Merciless?), the titanic battle against Pluto and the forces of the Netherworld, the ultimate fate (at least for the first time) of Jane Foster, and the introduction of Sif coinciding with the War against the Trolls and their hidden ally, Orikal. (I never got the 'Oracle' reference there; I always thought the name sounded like some sort of decay-preventing dentifrice with an accent on the last syllable.)

Inspired by the comic, I wrote my own Thor story, an amalgam of Stan and Jack continuity sprinkled with a little Norse mythology, and overcooked in my heated imagination. The idea grew out of a pair of Thor Annuals Marvel published during the summers of the mid-60's. Somewhere along the way, I thought of doing a BIG Thor story, so big that it couldn't be contained in a single comic, and I structured it out along the lines of Marvel's publishing schedule. My imagined story would come out in the summertime. It would begin in one of the regular monthly issues of Thor, run through all the other Marvel titles the same month (they only had about 11 titles then, remember?), and finish up the following month with a double-length flourish in a Thor Annual!

I cast the fire elemental, Surtur, as my principal villain. Stan and Jack had already introduced him into the Thor comic by then but mostly, he was just one more really large bad guy. I wanted to go back to the mythology and recreate something closer to the Surtur I found there. A great being of fire who, at the end of time during Ragnarok, flings fire across the Nine Worlds with his really big sword, and burns almost everything to ashes. Including himself presumably.

And the Marvel Universe already **had** a really big sword.

In Tales of Asgard, a backup feature that ran in the early issues of Thor, Stan and Jack spun a story around the Odinsword (or Oversword as it was originally called). It was a huge blade fit for a giant that lay in a great sheath enshrined in the middle of Asgard. And it was said that if the sword were ever drawn, Ragnarok would fall.

Hooking the Odinsword up with Surtur didn't seem any great stretch given the prophecy. So I began building a story by assigning the sword an identity. I posited that it was Surtur's weapon, the very Sword with which he was destined to end the Nine Worlds. Odin had at some point in the deeps of time carried the Sword off to prevent Surtur from triggering Ragnarok prematurely. Over the centuries, the actual origin of the Sword had been forgotten and Odin's own name given to the blade. The prophecy was a faint echo of the sword's true nature. But of course, Odin remembered. As did Surtur.

My story began as Surtur magically retrieved his sword, calling it to his side and breaking the protective spells Odin had woven around it. But Surtur still had to set it alight in Asgard in order to bring about the final doom of the gods. And the way to Asgard led through Earth. Surtur's various minions would attack Earth throughout the Marvel Universe in the company's other titles, and finally, Surtur would attack Asgard directly, going up against Thor and then Odin himself in the final chapter, the Annual.

By the summer of 1969, I'd given up geology, failed my draft physical, and entered art school. And I had begun to draw my imaginary Annual. I was about 30 pages of pencils and inks into it before I concluded that my inking wasn't up to snuff. So I put the project aside, thinking I would return to it when my inks had improved.

I got my chance fourteen years later. Editor Mark Gruenwald offered me the chance to write and draw Thor for Marvel. By then, the Odinsword was gone, destroyed in an earlier story. I decided not to try to resurrect it. There didn't seem much point by then. But forging a new weapon wasn't a big story problem and after all those years, I finally got the chance to tell my original story, enlarging its mythological framework, and even layering in a little black-smithing, some science fiction, and a bit of the Celtic fairy faith as well. I'd learned a few things since I'd imagined that original story.

There was an extra benefit from the gap between the story's conception and its execution. By the time I finally had the chance to do it, I'd given up trying to be either Stan Lee or Jack Kirby. Which meant among other things that I could abandon my original title for the saga. Until now. Just as well. I can't imagine what sentence that clause was supposed to be completing. And with luck, I'll never write a dangling phrase beginning with an ellipsis, a preposition, and a conjunction again!

SIMONSON

New York, 2000

CHAPTER ONE

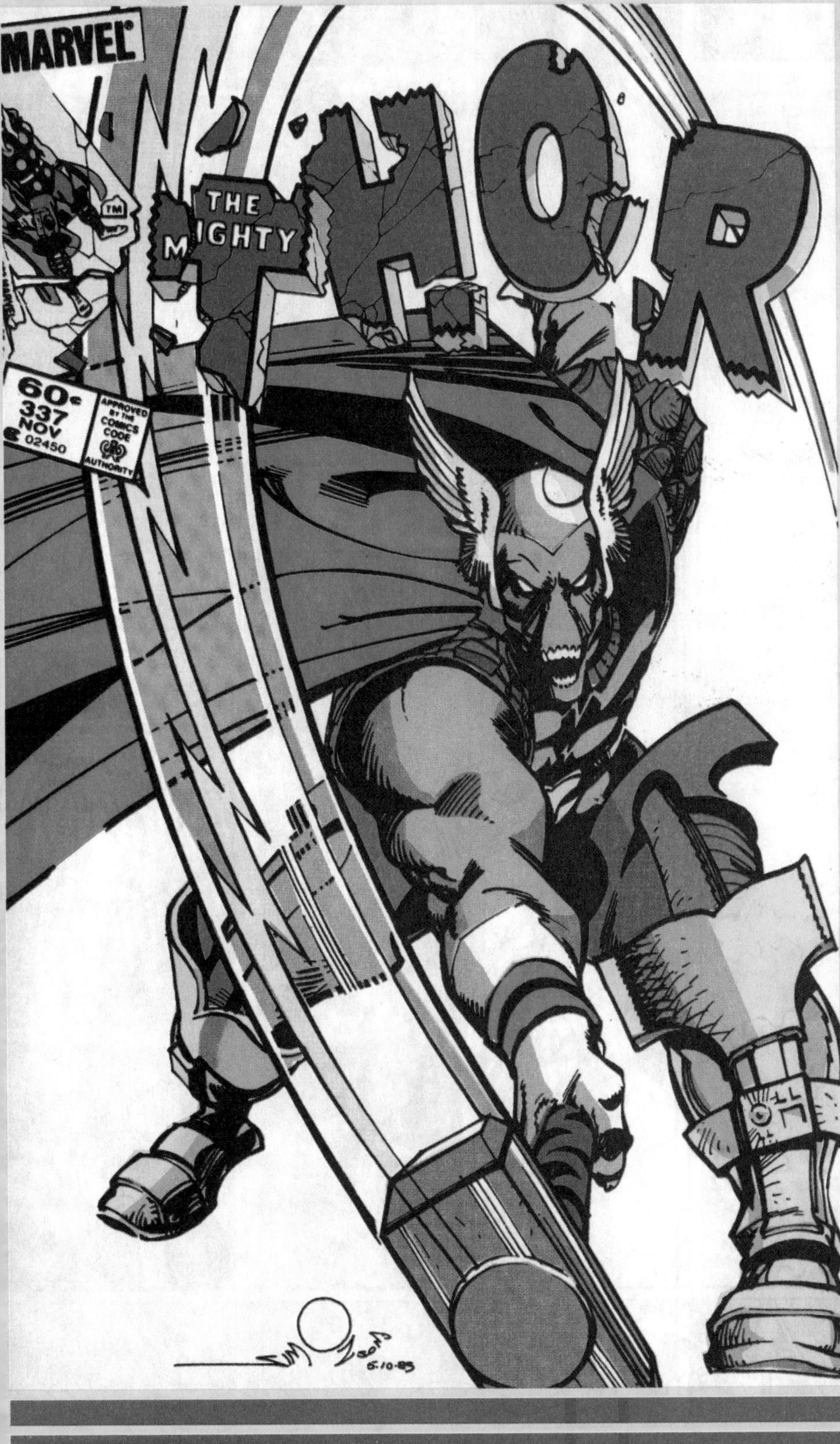
MARVEL
THE MIGHTY THOR
60¢
337
NOV
02450
APPROVED BY THE COMICS CODE AUTHORITY

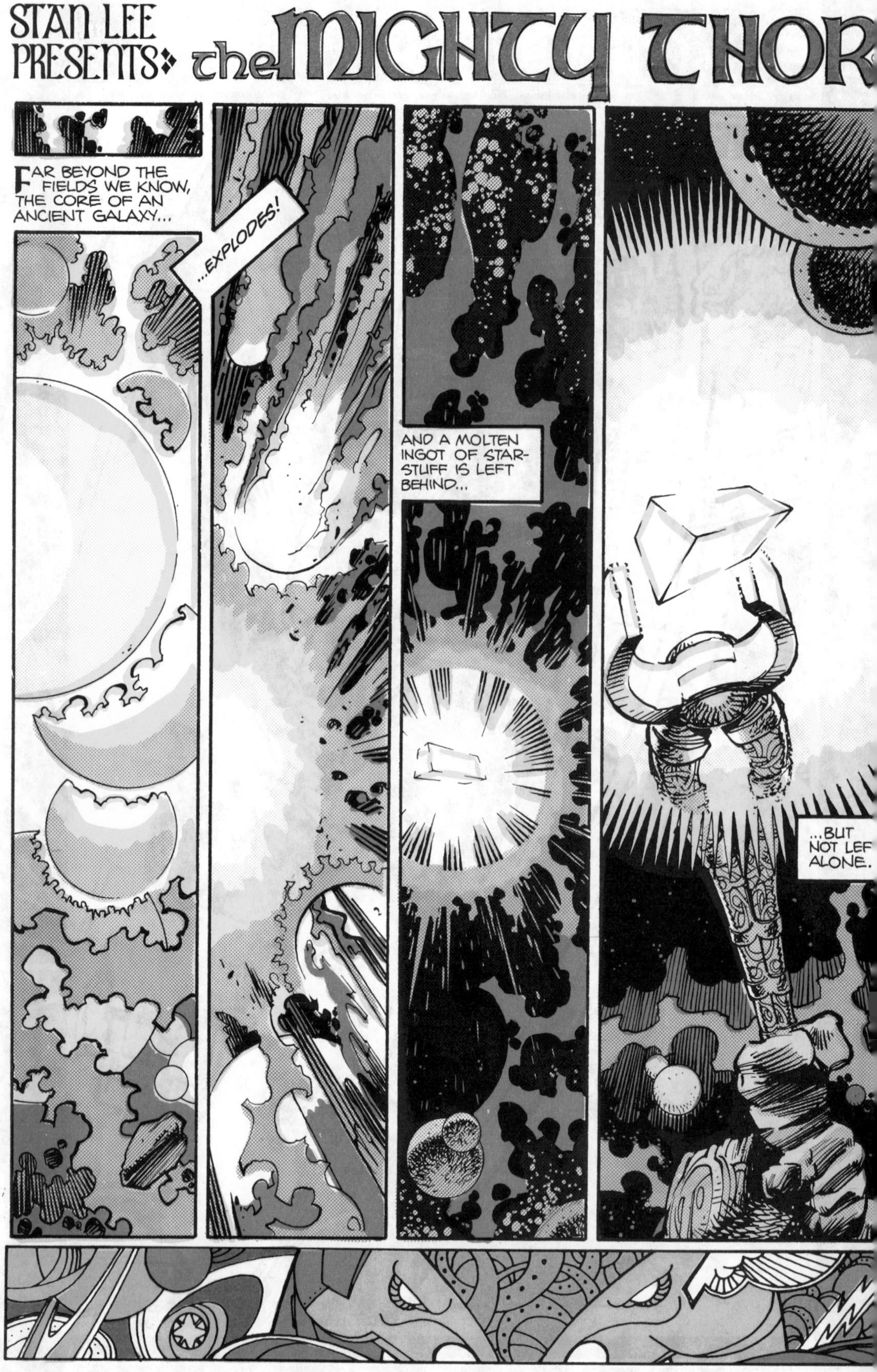
STAN LEE PRESENTS: the MIGHTY THOR
FAR BEYOND THE FIELDS WE KNOW, THE CORE OF AN ANCIENT GALAXY...
...EXPLODES!
AND A MOLTEN INGOT OF STAR-STUFF IS LEFT BEHIND...
...BUT NOT LEF ALONE.

MARK WELL THIS FIGURE AND LISTEN.
LISTEN.
CAN YOU HEAR IT?
THE WIND IS RISING.

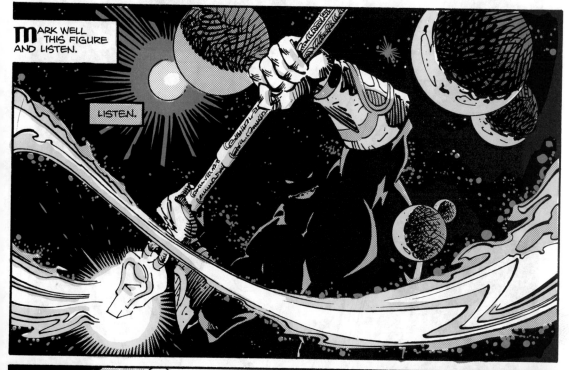

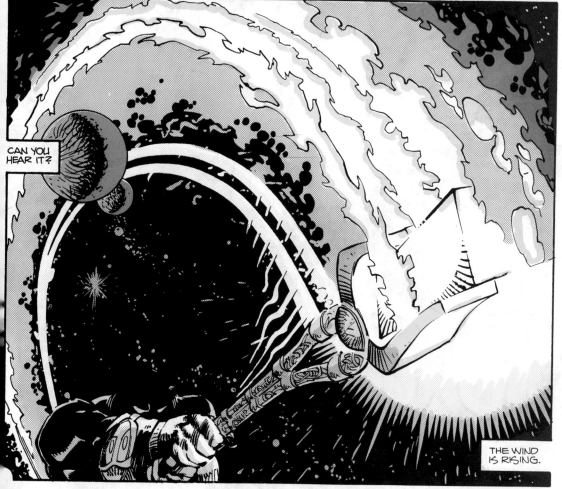

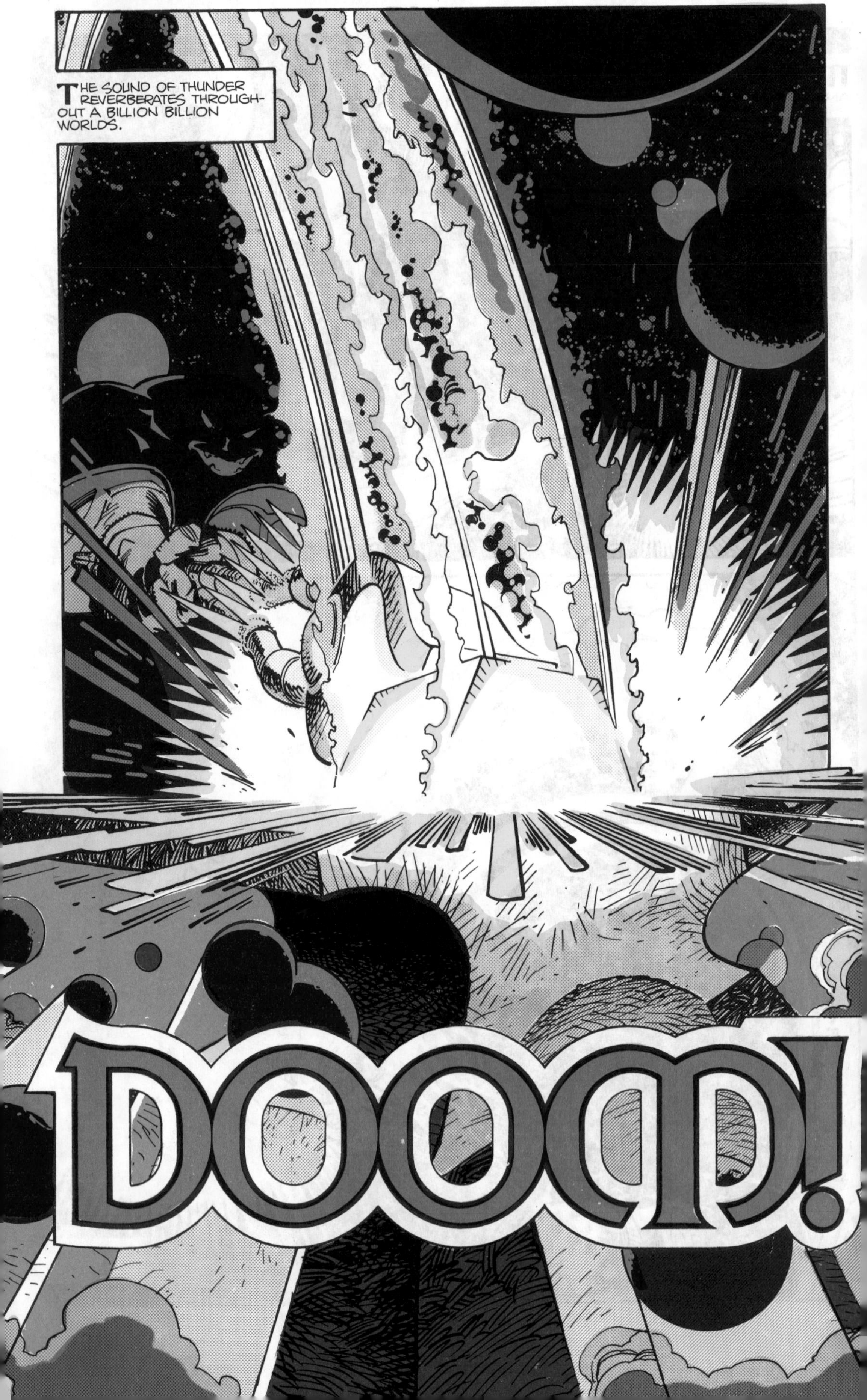
THE SOUND OF THUNDER REVERBERATES THROUGH-OUT A BILLION BILLION WORLDS.
DOOOM!

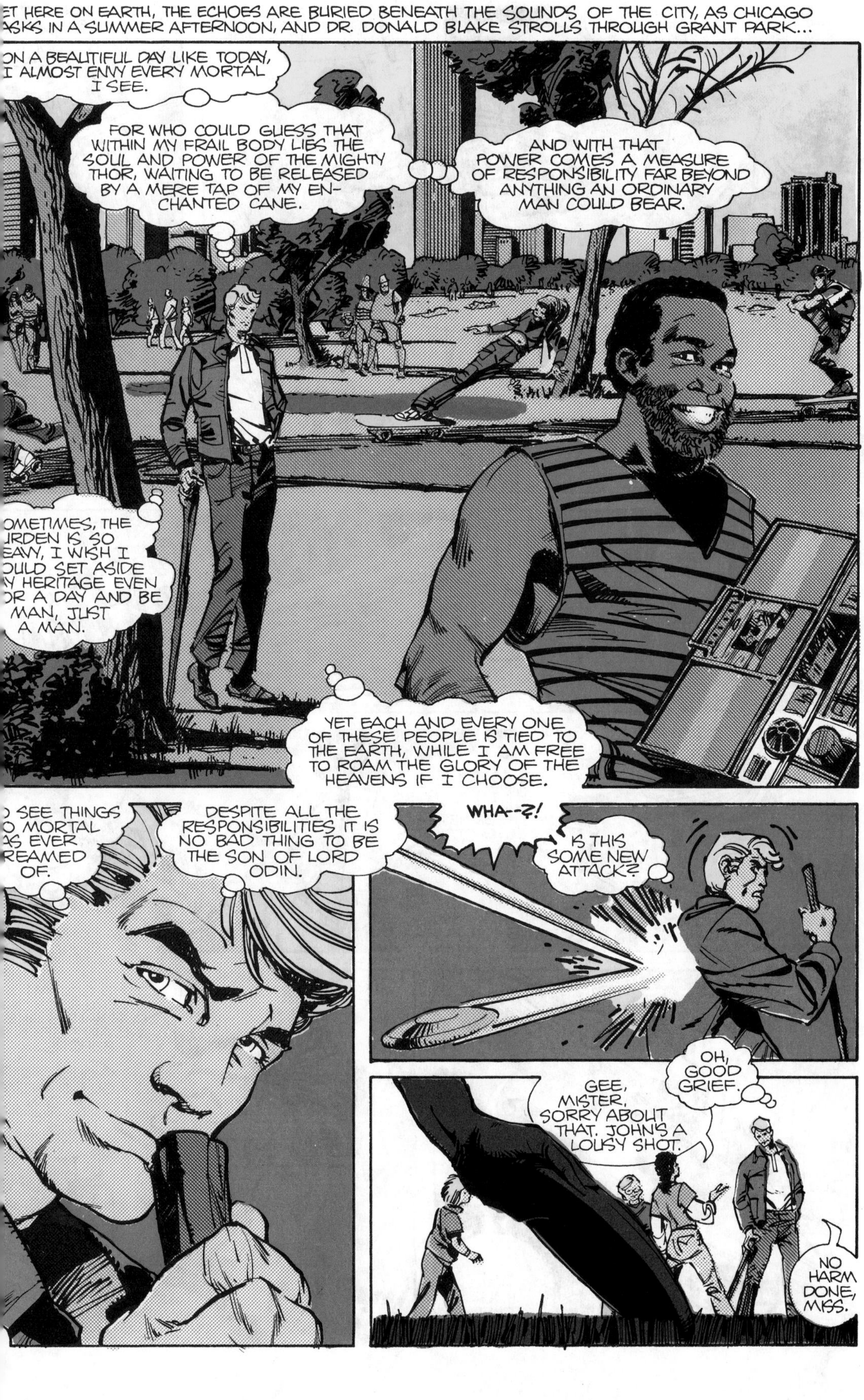
ET HERE ON EARTH, THE ECHOES ARE BURIED BENEATH THE SOUNDS OF THE CITY, AS CHICAGO ASKS IN A SUMMER AFTERNOON, AND DR. DONALD BLAKE STROLLS THROUGH GRANT PARK...
ON A BEAUTIFUL DAY LIKE TODAY, I ALMOST ENVY EVERY MORTAL I SEE.
FOR WHO COULD GUESS THAT WITHIN MY FRAIL BODY LIES THE SOUL AND POWER OF THE MIGHTY THOR, WAITING TO BE RELEASED BY A MERE TAP OF MY ENCHANTED CANE.
AND WITH THAT POWER COMES A MEASURE OF RESPONSIBILITY FAR BEYOND ANYTHING AN ORDINARY MAN COULD BEAR.
OMETIMES, THE URDEN IS SO EAVY, I WISH I OULD SET ASIDE Y HERITAGE EVEN OR A DAY AND BE MAN, JUST A MAN.
YET EACH AND EVERY ONE OF THESE PEOPLE IS TIED TO THE EARTH, WHILE I AM FREE TO ROAM THE GLORY OF THE HEAVENS IF I CHOOSE.
O SEE THINGS O MORTAL AS EVER REAMED OF.
DESPITE ALL THE RESPONSIBILITIES IT IS NO BAD THING TO BE THE SON OF LORD ODIN.
WHA--?!
IS THIS SOME NEW ATTACK?
OH, GOOD GRIEF.
GEE, MISTER, SORRY ABOUT THAT. JOHN'S A LOUSY SHOT.
NO HARM DONE, MISS.

WHY NOT LET US BE THE JUDGES OF THAT, MISTER. A LAME GUY LIKE YOURSELF--YOU LOOK LIKE YOU COULD USE SOME HELP.

LET ME TAKE YOUR CANE.

HEY!

NOT TOO LOUD NOW, BUB. YOU'RE JUST GOING FOR A LITTLE RIDE.

THROW THE STICK IN, TOO, BOYS.

SURE THING, COLONEL.

YOU'RE ALL SE' SIR.

SLAM

ANY IDEA WHAT'S GO-ING ON?

BEATS ME.

VARROOOOM

WHAT DO YOU THINK YOU'RE--

COLONEL NICK FURY!

YOU WIN THE KEWPIE DOLL, DOCTOR BLAKE.

SORRY TA GRAB YA SO DRAMATIC-LIKE, BUT WE NEED YER HELP ...FAST!

HOLD ON TA YER HELMET.

I'M CONVERTIN' TA AERIAL MOD

WHAT IS THIS, FURY? WHY DOES THE DIRECTOR OF SHIELD--

--NEED AN ORDINARY SAWBONES?

I DON'T. I NEED YOUR OTHER HALF!

WHAT DO YOU MEAN?

LOOK, DOC, I'LL LEVEL WITH YA.

WE GOT AN EMERGENCY ON OUR HANDS LIKE WE AIN'T SEEN BEFORE.

ONLY ONE GUY I KNOW OF CAN MAYBE HANDLE IT.

AND HE PACKS A HAMMER THAT MAKES OUR LATEST WEAPONS LOOK LIKE TINKERTOYS!

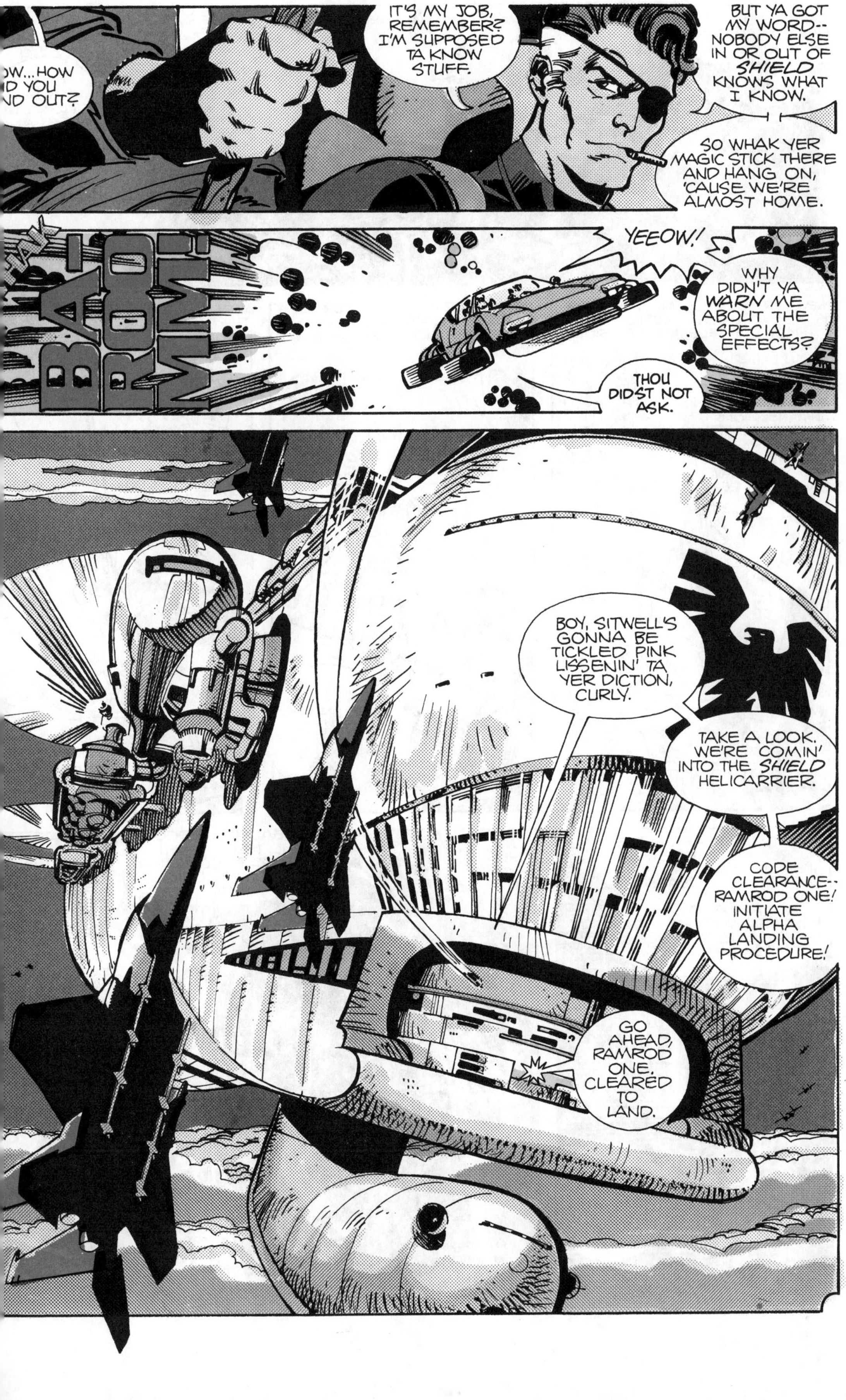

OW... HOW
D YOU
ND OUT?
IT'S MY JOB, REMEMBER? I'M SUPPOSED TA KNOW STUFF.
BUT YA GOT MY WORD-- NOBODY ELSE IN OR OUT OF SHIELD KNOWS WHAT I KNOW.
SO WHAK YER MAGIC STICK THERE AND HANG ON, 'CAUSE WE'RE ALMOST HOME.
BA-ROOOMM!
YEEOW!
WHY DIDN'T YA WARN ME ABOUT THE SPECIAL EFFECTS?
THOU DIDST NOT ASK.
BOY, SITWELL'S GONNA BE TICKLED PINK LISSENIN' TA YER DICTION, CURLY.
TAKE A LOOK. WE'RE COMIN' INTO THE SHIELD HELICARRIER.
CODE CLEARANCE-- RAMROD ONE! INITIATE ALPHA LANDING PROCEDURE!
GO AHEAD, RAMROD ONE, CLEARED TO LAND.

SHORTLY, IN A DARKENED SHIELD SCREENING ROOM...

SITWELL'S OUR LOCAL ENCYCLOPEDIA. IF HE DON'T KNOW IT, IT AIN'T A FACT!

OKAY, SITWELL, FILL IN OUR GUEST AND MAKE IT SNAPPY, HUH?

WELL, SIR, YOUR HONOR... AHEM... THIS IS THE VERY LATEST DEVELOPMENT FROM OUR TELEMETRY DIVISION.

AN EXPERIMENTAL WARP-DRIVEN PROBE CAPABLE OF COVERING UNIMAGINABLE DISTANCES AND TRANSMITTING PICTURES INSTANTANEOUSLY VIA HYPER-WAVE BACK TO A RECEIVER.

NAMELY US.

OPERATING ON AN ASSIGNED CARRIER FREQUENCY OF--

THE GUTS, SITWELL, JUST THE GUTS!

YESSIR! THESE ARE THE LAST PICTURES WE RECEIVED FROM THE PROBE. NOTE THE APPARENT VESSEL IN CENTER SCREEN.

AN ALIEN SHIP, UNLIKE ANYTHING WE'VE EVER SEEN BEFORE.

NOW WATCH THE STAR.

AS THE SHIP PASSED BY IT, THE STAR SUDDENLY FLARED TO LIFE...

...AND WAS SUCKED IN BY THE SHIP.

OUR EXPERTS THINK THE VESSEL WAS REFUELING AND DESTROYED AN ENTIRE STAR TO DO IT.

SHORTLY THEREAFTER, THE PROBE WAS DETECTED BY THE ALIEN SHIP AND ALL TRANSMISSION CEASED.

ACCORDING TO OUR BEST ESTIMATES, THE SHIP IS TRAVELING AT SEVERAL TIMES LIGHT SPEED...

...HEADING DIRECTLY FOR OUR SOLAR SYSTEM.

AND THE PROBE?

DEADER'N A DOORNAIL, THOR. BLOWN APART BY SOMETHING COMING OUR WAY.

SOMETHING REAL POWERFUL! AND DANGEROUS!

WE GOTTA FIND OUT WHAT IT IS! AND YER THE ONLY JOE WHO CAN DO IT!

WILL YA HELP US?

THE ANSWER IS NOT LONG IN COMING...

...YET EVEN AS THE MIGHTY THOR ARCS SKYWARD...

FAR BEYOND THIS REALM OF SPACE AND TIME, IN THE GOLDEN HALLS OF ASGARD, HOME OF THE NORSE GODS, ALL IS NOT WELL.

AH, MILADY SIF, COME AND JOIN BALDER AND MYSELF IN A HEARTY REPAST.

WE'VE HARDLY BEGUN — ONLY *SIXTEEN* COURSES SINCE BREAKFAST—AND BALDER IS LATELY GLUM COMPANY!

I CAN SCARCELY CREDIT IT!

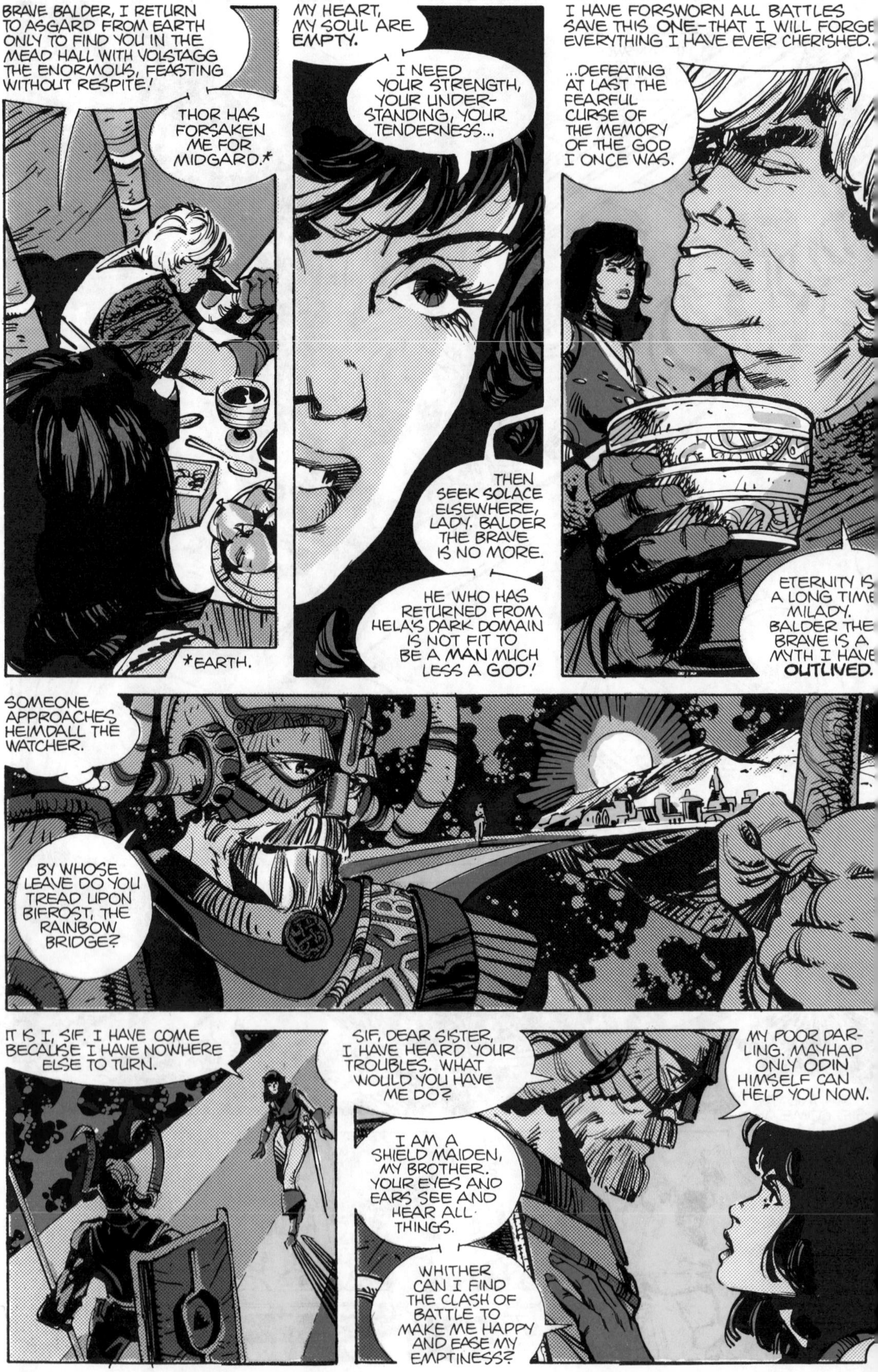
BRAVE BALDER, I RETURN TO ASGARD FROM EARTH ONLY TO FIND YOU IN THE MEAD HALL WITH VOLSTAGG THE ENORMOUS, FEASTING WITHOUT RESPITE!
THOR HAS FORSAKEN ME FOR MIDGARD.*
*EARTH.
MY HEART, MY SOUL ARE EMPTY.
I NEED YOUR STRENGTH, YOUR UNDER-STANDING, YOUR TENDERNESS...
THEN SEEK SOLACE ELSEWHERE, LADY. BALDER THE BRAVE IS NO MORE.
HE WHO HAS RETURNED FROM HELA'S DARK DOMAIN IS NOT FIT TO BE A MAN MUCH LESS A GOD!
I HAVE FORSWORN ALL BATTLES SAVE THIS ONE--THAT I WILL FORGE EVERYTHING I HAVE EVER CHERISHED...
...DEFEATING AT LAST THE FEARFUL CURSE OF THE MEMORY OF THE GOD I ONCE WAS.
ETERNITY IS A LONG TIME MILADY. BALDER THE BRAVE IS A MYTH I HAVE OUTLIVED.
SOMEONE APPROACHES HEIMDALL THE WATCHER.
BY WHOSE LEAVE DO YOU TREAD UPON BIFROST, THE RAINBOW BRIDGE?
IT IS I, SIF. I HAVE COME BECAUSE I HAVE NOWHERE ELSE TO TURN.
SIF, DEAR SISTER, I HAVE HEARD YOUR TROUBLES. WHAT WOULD YOU HAVE ME DO?
I AM A SHIELD MAIDEN, MY BROTHER. YOUR EYES AND EARS SEE AND HEAR ALL THINGS.
WHITHER CAN I FIND THE CLASH OF BATTLE TO MAKE ME HAPPY AND EASE MY EMPTINESS?
MY POOR DAR-LING. MAYHAP ONLY ODIN HIMSELF CAN HELP YOU NOW.

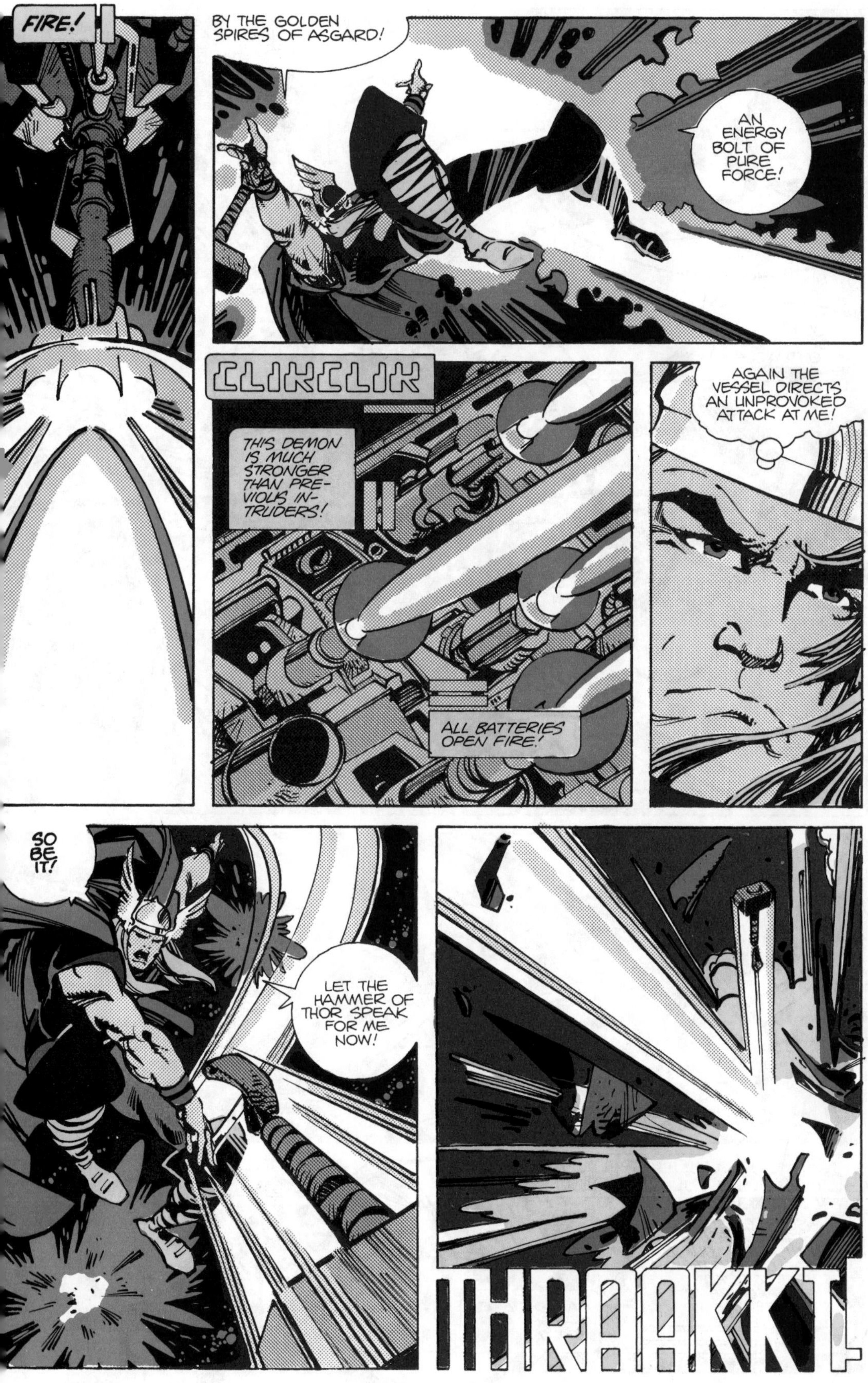

FIRE!
BY THE GOLDEN SPIRES OF ASGARD!
AN ENERGY BOLT OF PURE FORCE!
CLIKCLIK
THIS DEMON IS MUCH STRONGER THAN PREVIOUS INTRUDERS!
ALL BATTERIES OPEN FIRE!
AGAIN THE VESSEL DIRECTS AN UNPROVOKED ATTACK AT ME!
SO BE IT!
LET THE HAMMER OF THOR SPEAK FOR ME NOW!
THRAAKK!

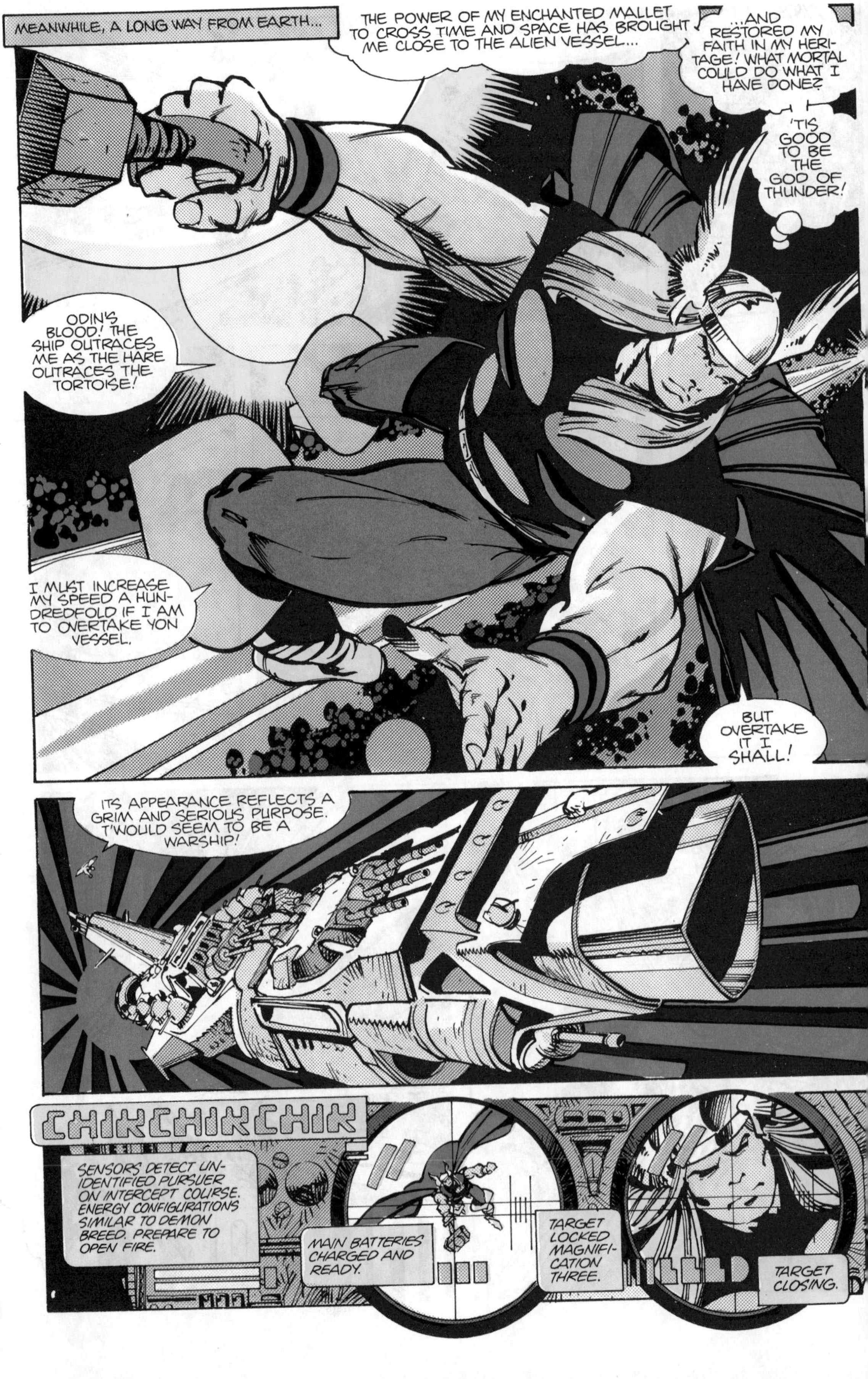
MEANWHILE, A LONG WAY FROM EARTH...
THE POWER OF MY ENCHANTED MALLET TO CROSS TIME AND SPACE HAS BROUGHT ME CLOSE TO THE ALIEN VESSEL...
...AND RESTORED MY FAITH IN MY HERITAGE! WHAT MORTAL COULD DO WHAT I HAVE DONE?
'TIS GOOD TO BE THE GOD OF THUNDER!
ODIN'S BLOOD! THE SHIP OUTRACES ME AS THE HARE OUTRACES THE TORTOISE!
I MUST INCREASE MY SPEED A HUNDREDFOLD IF I AM TO OVERTAKE YON VESSEL.
BUT OVERTAKE IT I SHALL!
ITS APPEARANCE REFLECTS A GRIM AND SERIOUS PURPOSE. T'WOULD SEEM TO BE A WARSHIP!
CHIKCHIKCHIK
SENSORS DETECT UNIDENTIFIED PURSUER ON INTERCEPT COURSE. ENERGY CONFIGURATIONS SIMILAR TO DEMON BREED. PREPARE TO OPEN FIRE.
MAIN BATTERIES CHARGED AND READY.
TARGET LOCKED MAGNIFICATION THREE.
TARGET CLOSING.

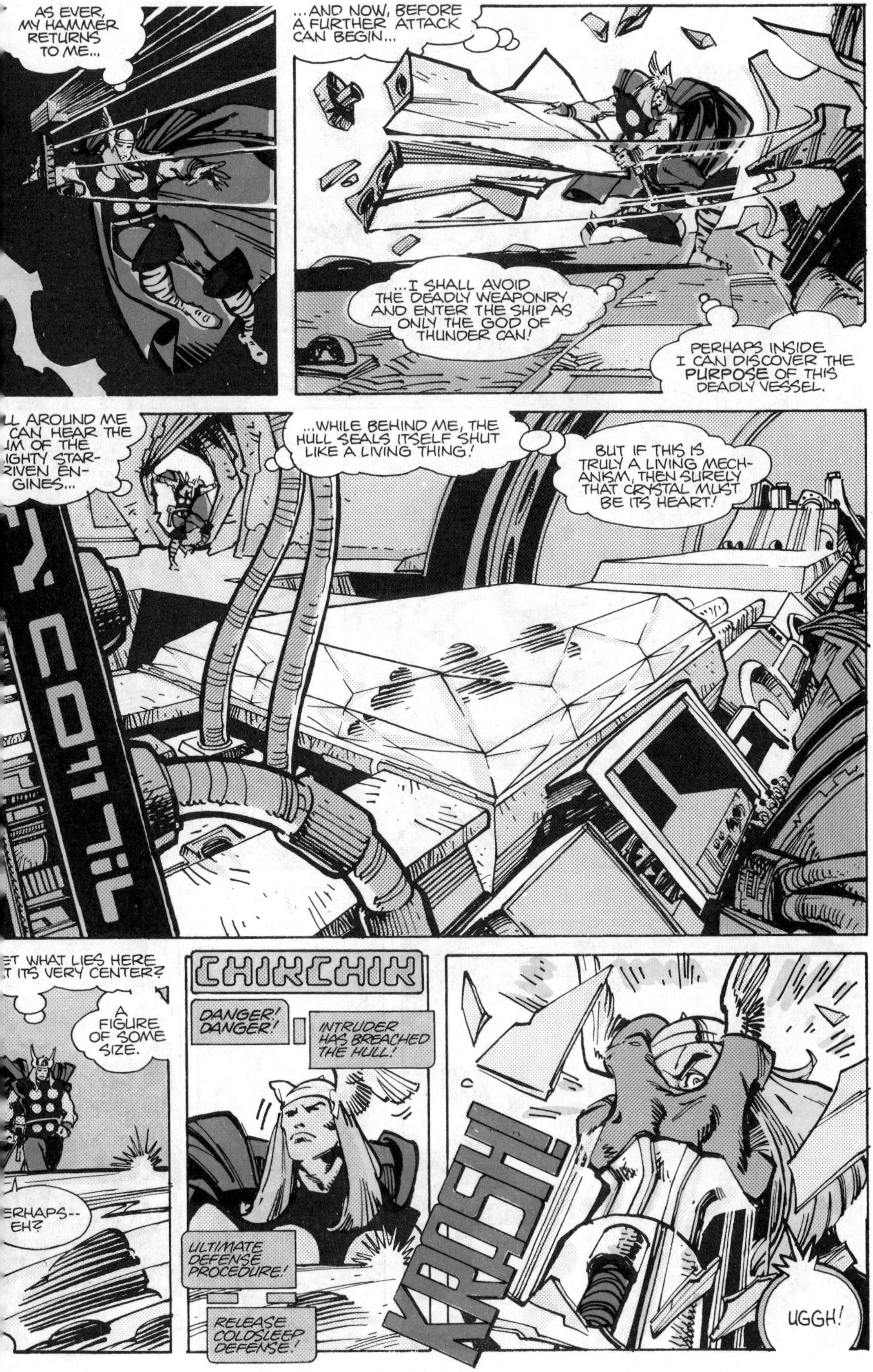
AS EVER, MY HAMMER RETURNS TO ME...
...AND NOW, BEFORE A FURTHER ATTACK CAN BEGIN...
...I SHALL AVOID THE DEADLY WEAPONRY AND ENTER THE SHIP AS ONLY THE GOD OF THUNDER CAN!
PERHAPS INSIDE I CAN DISCOVER THE PURPOSE OF THIS DEADLY VESSEL.
LL AROUND ME CAN HEAR THE M OF THE IGHTY STAR-RIVEN EN-GINES...
...WHILE BEHIND ME, THE HULL SEALS ITSELF SHUT LIKE A LIVING THING!
BUT IF THIS IS TRULY A LIVING MECH-ANISM, THEN SURELY THAT CRYSTAL MUST BE ITS HEART!
ET WHAT LIES HERE T ITS VERY CENTER?
A FIGURE OF SOME SIZE.
ERHAPS-- EH?
CHIKCHIK
DANGER! DANGER!
INTRUDER HAS BREACHED THE HULL!
ULTIMATE DEFENSE PROCEDURE!
RELEASE COLDSLEEP DEFENSE!
KRASH
UGGH!

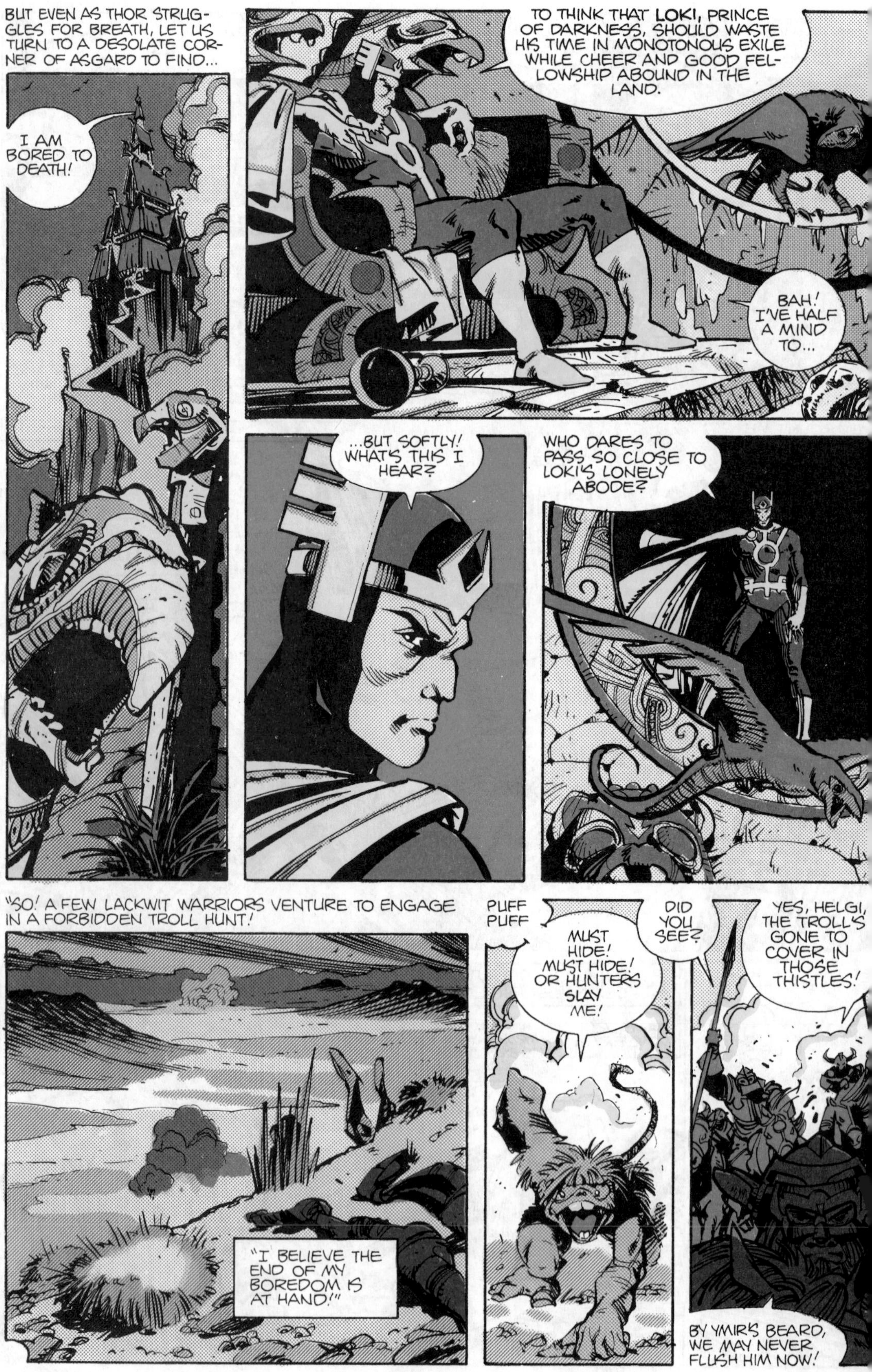

BUT EVEN AS THOR STRUGGLES FOR BREATH, LET US TURN TO A DESOLATE CORNER OF ASGARD TO FIND...
I AM BORED TO DEATH!
TO THINK THAT LOKI, PRINCE OF DARKNESS, SHOULD WASTE HIS TIME IN MONOTONOUS EXILE WHILE CHEER AND GOOD FELLOWSHIP ABOUND IN THE LAND.
BAH! I'VE HALF A MIND TO...
...BUT SOFTLY! WHAT'S THIS I HEAR?
WHO DARES TO PASS SO CLOSE TO LOKI'S LONELY ABODE?
"SO! A FEW LACKWIT WARRIORS VENTURE TO ENGAGE IN A FORBIDDEN TROLL HUNT!
"I BELIEVE THE END OF MY BOREDOM IS AT HAND!"
PUFF PUFF
MUST HIDE! MUST HIDE! OR HUNTERS SLAY ME!
DID YOU SEE?
YES, HELGI, THE TROLL'S GONE TO COVER IN THOSE THISTLES!
BY YMIR'S BEARD, WE MAY NEVER FLUSH HIM NOW!

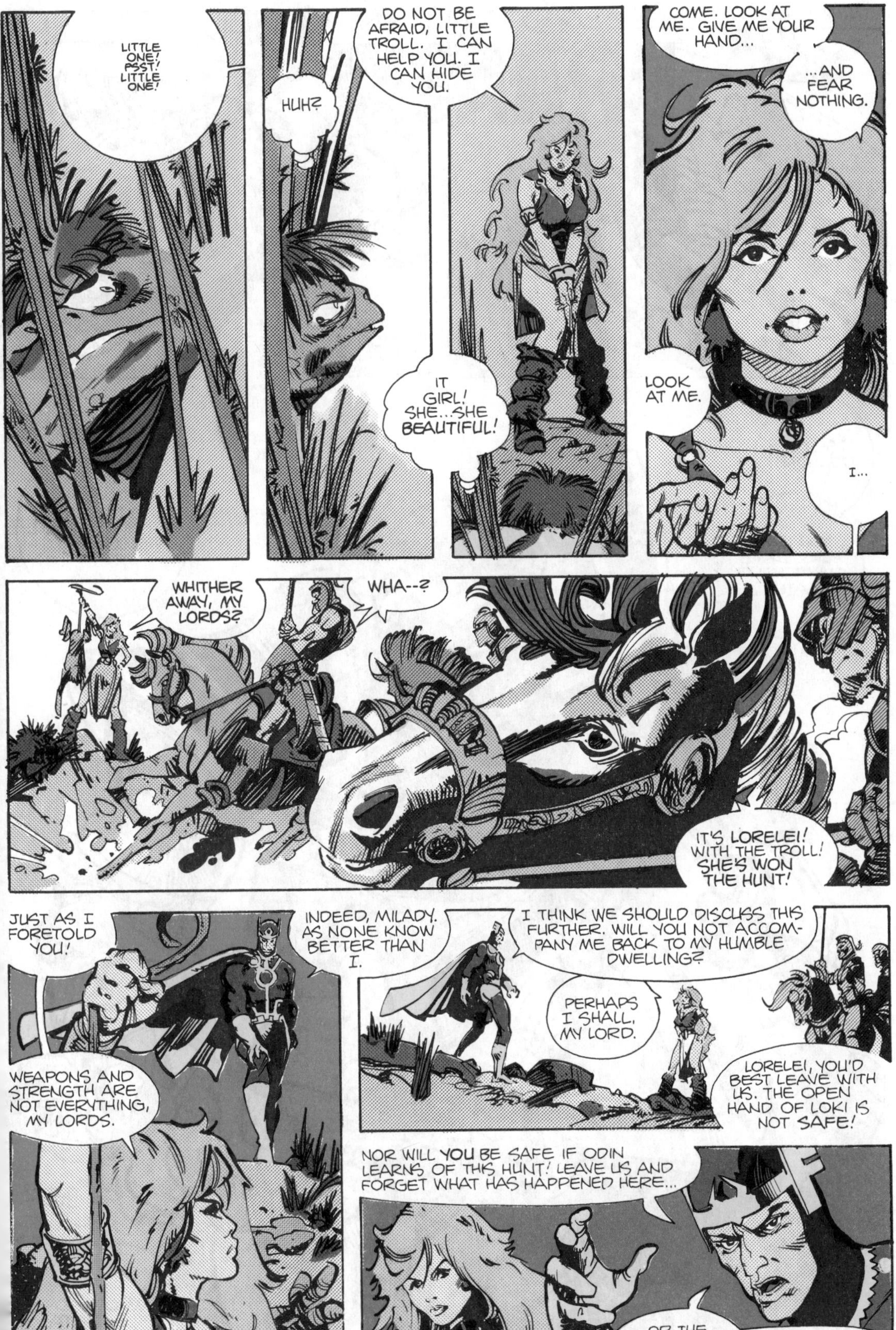

LITTLE ONE! PSST! LITTLE ONE!
HUH?
DO NOT BE AFRAID, LITTLE TROLL. I CAN HELP YOU. I CAN HIDE YOU.
IT GIRL! SHE...SHE BEAUTIFUL!
COME. LOOK AT ME. GIVE ME YOUR HAND...
...AND FEAR NOTHING.
LOOK AT ME.
I...
WHITHER AWAY, MY LORDS?
WHA--?
IT'S LORELEI! WITH THE TROLL! SHE'S WON THE HUNT!
JUST AS I FORETOLD YOU!
INDEED, MILADY. AS NONE KNOW BETTER THAN I.
WEAPONS AND STRENGTH ARE NOT EVERYTHING, MY LORDS.
I THINK WE SHOULD DISCUSS THIS FURTHER. WILL YOU NOT ACCOMPANY ME BACK TO MY HUMBLE DWELLING?
PERHAPS I SHALL, MY LORD.
LORELEI, YOU'D BEST LEAVE WITH US. THE OPEN HAND OF LOKI IS NOT SAFE!
NOR WILL YOU BE SAFE IF ODIN LEARNS OF THIS HUNT! LEAVE US AND FORGET WHAT HAS HAPPENED HERE...
...OR THE NEXT HAND OF LOKI YOU SEE WILL BE FILLED WITH MENACE.

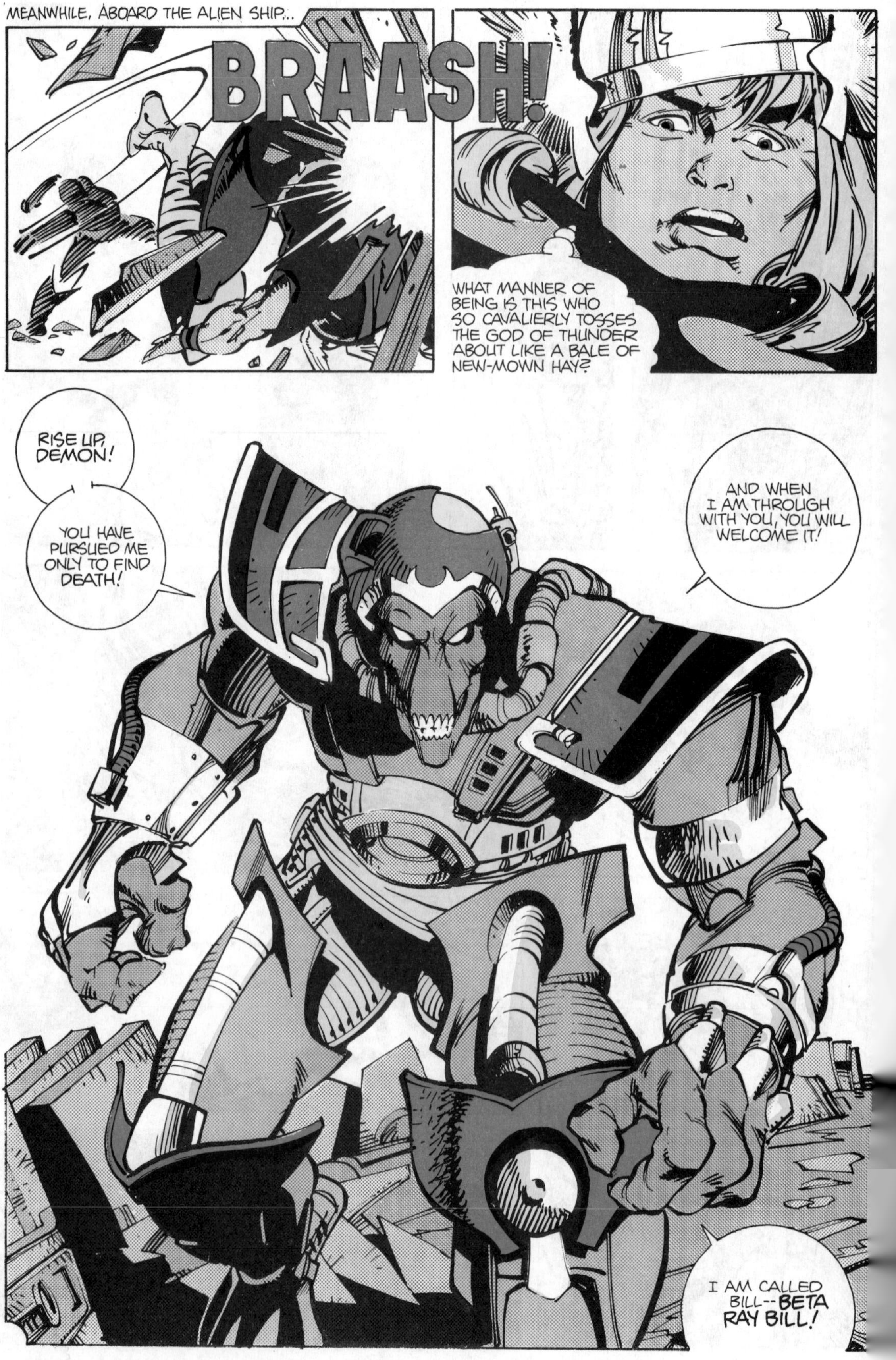
MEANWHILE, ABOARD THE ALIEN SHIP...
BRAASH!
WHAT MANNER OF BEING IS THIS WHO SO CAVALIERLY TOSSES THE GOD OF THUNDER ABOUT LIKE A BALE OF NEW-MOWN HAY?
RISE UP, DEMON!
YOU HAVE PURSUED ME ONLY TO FIND DEATH!
AND WHEN I AM THROUGH WITH YOU, YOU WILL WELCOME IT!
I AM CALLED BILL-- BETA RAY BILL!

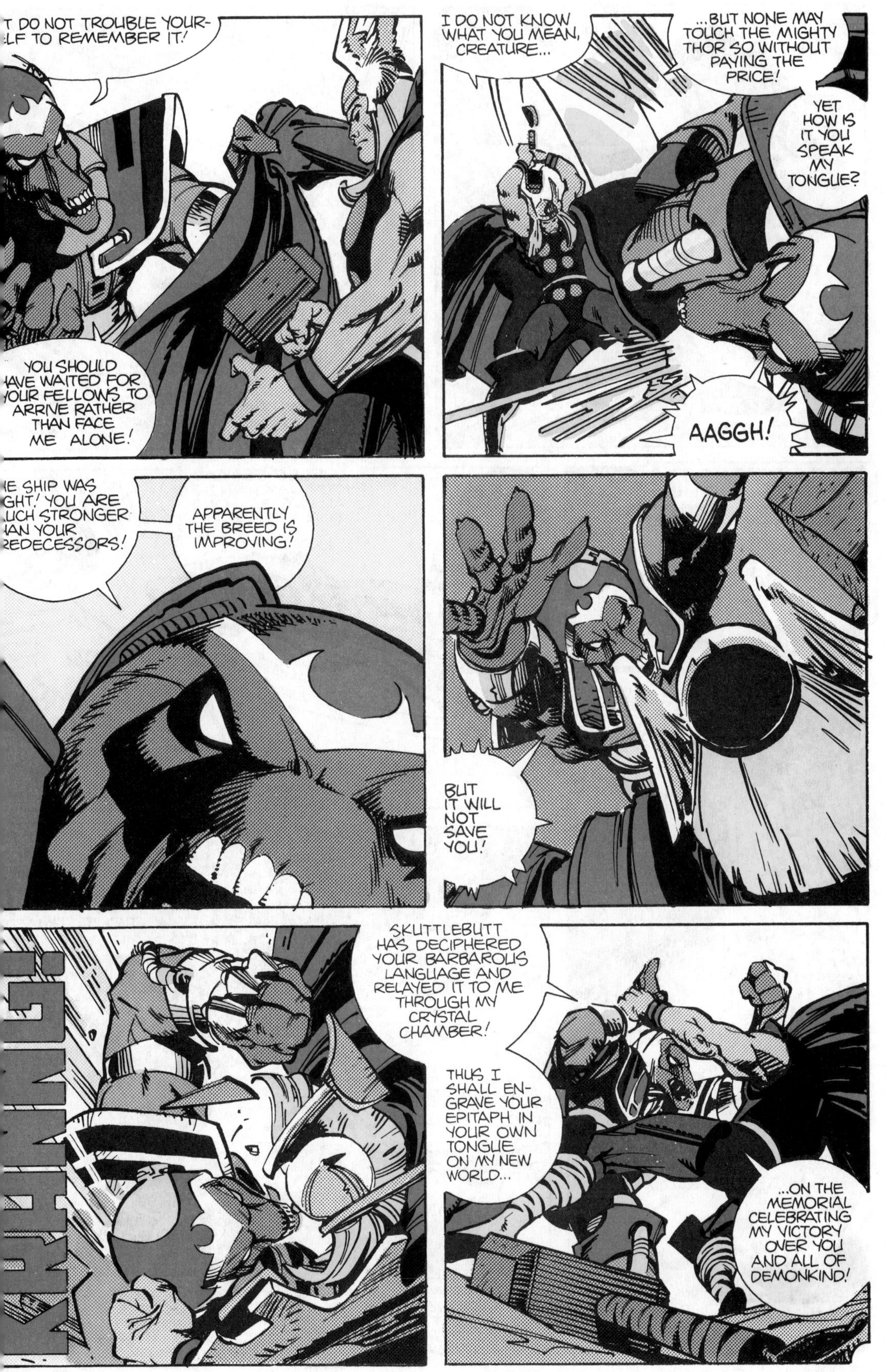
T DO NOT TROUBLE YOUR-
ELF TO REMEMBER IT!
YOU SHOULD
AVE WAITED FOR
YOUR FELLOWS TO
ARRIVE RATHER
THAN FACE
ME ALONE!
I DO NOT KNOW
WHAT YOU MEAN,
CREATURE...
...BUT NONE MAY
TOUCH THE MIGHTY
THOR SO WITHOUT
PAYING THE
PRICE!
YET
HOW IS
IT YOU
SPEAK
MY
TONGUE?
AAGGH!
E SHIP WAS
GHT! YOU ARE
UCH STRONGER
HAN YOUR
REDECESSORS!
APPARENTLY
THE BREED IS
IMPROVING!
BUT
IT WILL
NOT
SAVE
YOU!
KRANG!
SKUTTLEBUTT
HAS DECIPHERED
YOUR BARBAROUS
LANGUAGE AND
RELAYED IT TO ME
THROUGH MY
CRYSTAL
CHAMBER!
THUS I
SHALL EN-
GRAVE YOUR
EPITAPH IN
YOUR OWN
TONGUE
ON MY NEW
WORLD...
...ON THE
MEMORIAL
CELEBRATING
MY VICTORY
OVER YOU
AND ALL OF
DEMONKIND!

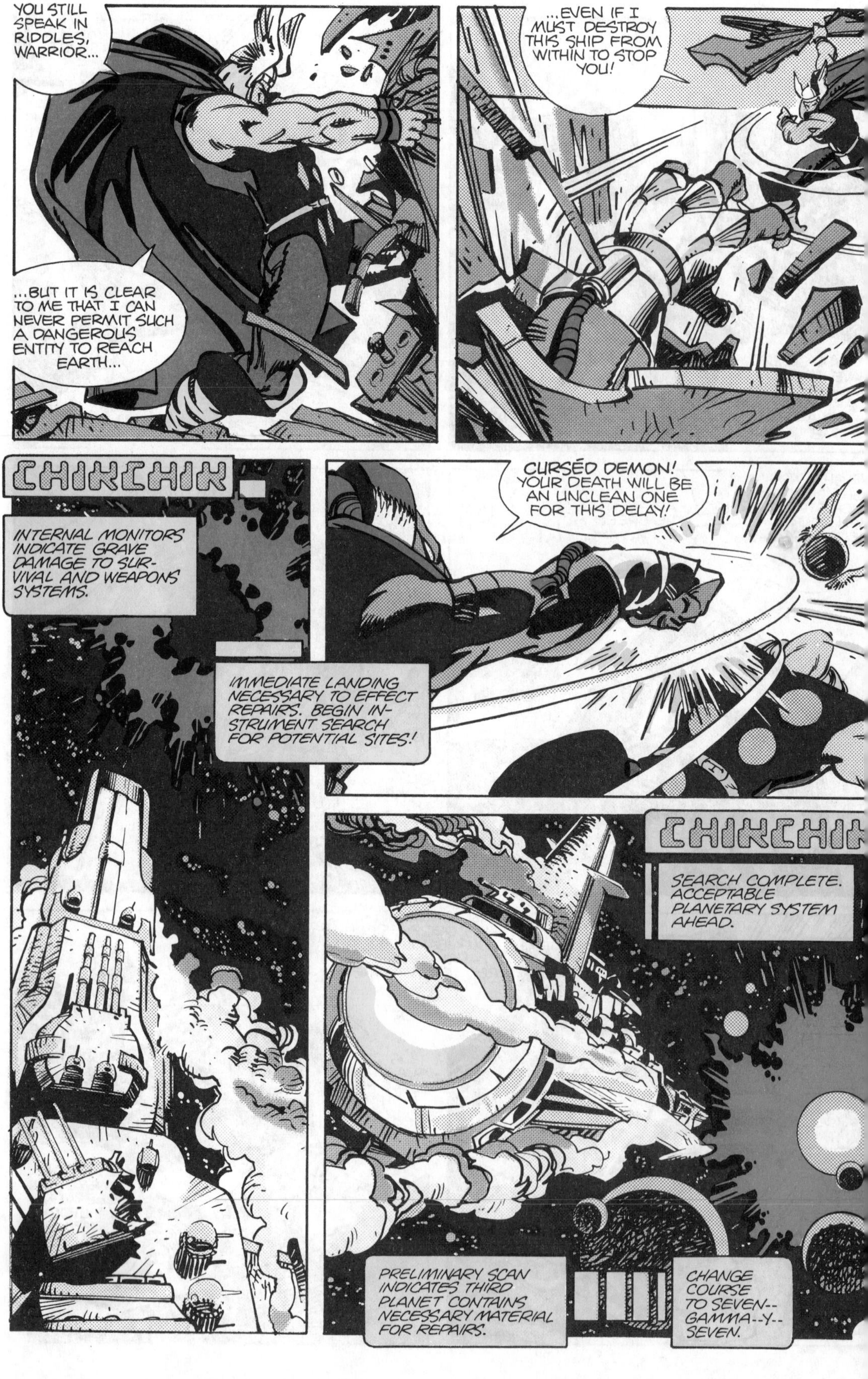
YOU STILL SPEAK IN RIDDLES, WARRIOR...
...BUT IT IS CLEAR TO ME THAT I CAN NEVER PERMIT SUCH A DANGEROUS ENTITY TO REACH EARTH...
...EVEN IF I MUST DESTROY THIS SHIP FROM WITHIN TO STOP YOU!
CHINCHIK
INTERNAL MONITORS INDICATE GRAVE DAMAGE TO SURVIVAL AND WEAPONS SYSTEMS.
IMMEDIATE LANDING NECESSARY TO EFFECT REPAIRS. BEGIN INSTRUMENT SEARCH FOR POTENTIAL SITES!
CURSÉD DEMON! YOUR DEATH WILL BE AN UNCLEAN ONE FOR THIS DELAY!
SEARCH COMPLETE. ACCEPTABLE PLANETARY SYSTEM AHEAD.
PRELIMINARY SCAN INDICATES THIRD PLANET CONTAINS NECESSARY MATERIAL FOR REPAIRS.
CHANGE COURSE TO SEVEN--GAMMA--Y--SEVEN.

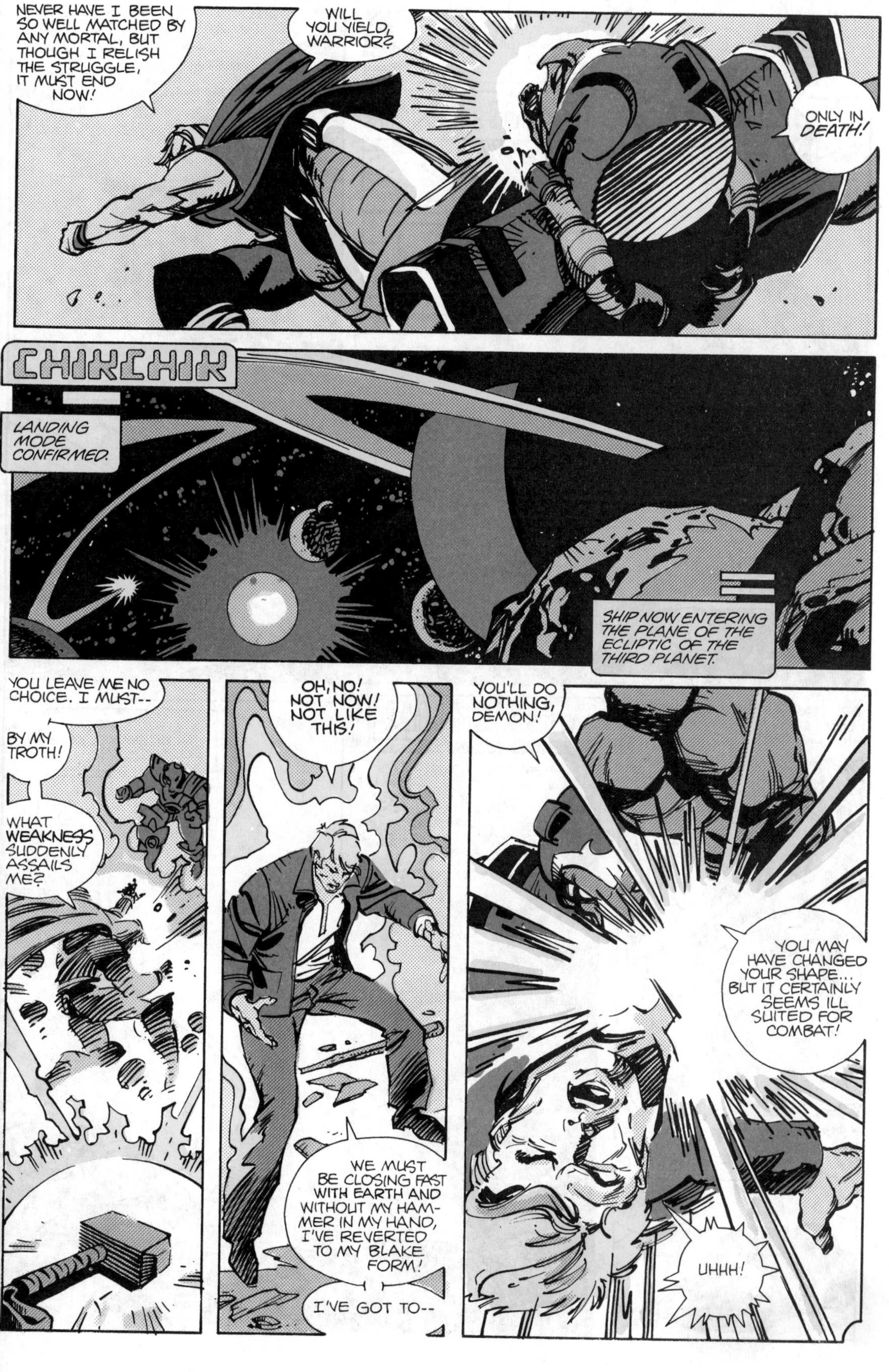
NEVER HAVE I BEEN SO WELL MATCHED BY ANY MORTAL, BUT THOUGH I RELISH THE STRUGGLE, IT MUST END NOW!
WILL YOU YIELD, WARRIOR?
ONLY IN DEATH!
CHIRCHIR
LANDING MODE CONFIRMED.
SHIP NOW ENTERING THE PLANE OF THE ECLIPTIC OF THE THIRD PLANET.
YOU LEAVE ME NO CHOICE. I MUST--
BY MY TROTH!
WHAT WEAKNESS SUDDENLY ASSAILS ME?
OH, NO! NOT NOW! NOT LIKE THIS!
WE MUST BE CLOSING FAST WITH EARTH AND WITHOUT MY HAMMER IN MY HAND, I'VE REVERTED TO MY BLAKE FORM!
I'VE GOT TO--
YOU'LL DO NOTHING, DEMON!
YOU MAY HAVE CHANGED YOUR SHAPE... BUT IT CERTAINLY SEEMS ILL SUITED FOR COMBAT!
UHHH!

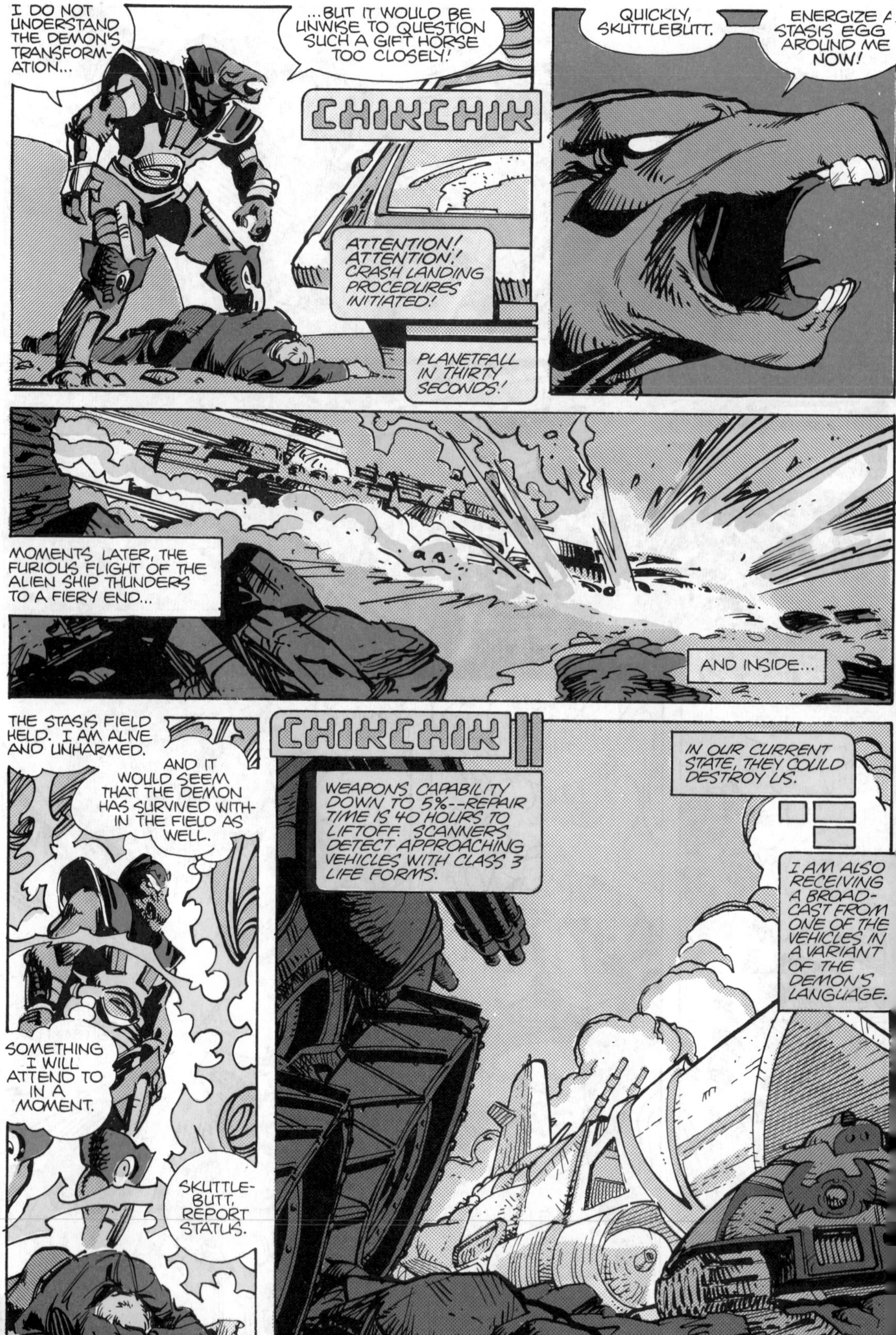
I DO NOT UNDERSTAND THE DEMON'S TRANSFORMATION...
...BUT IT WOULD BE UNWISE TO QUESTION SUCH A GIFT HORSE TOO CLOSELY!
CHINCHIK
ATTENTION! ATTENTION! CRASH LANDING PROCEDURES INITIATED!
PLANETFALL IN THIRTY SECONDS!
QUICKLY, SKUTTLEBUTT.
ENERGIZE A STASIS EGG AROUND ME NOW!
MOMENTS LATER, THE FURIOUS FLIGHT OF THE ALIEN SHIP THUNDERS TO A FIERY END...
AND INSIDE...
THE STASIS FIELD HELD. I AM ALIVE AND UNHARMED.
AND IT WOULD SEEM THAT THE DEMON HAS SURVIVED WITHIN THE FIELD AS WELL.
SOMETHING I WILL ATTEND TO IN A MOMENT.
SKUTTLEBUTT, REPORT STATUS.
CHINCHIK
WEAPONS CAPABILITY DOWN TO 5%--REPAIR TIME IS 40 HOURS TO LIFTOFF. SCANNERS DETECT APPROACHING VEHICLES WITH CLASS 3 LIFE FORMS.
IN OUR CURRENT STATE, THEY COULD DESTROY US.
I AM ALSO RECEIVING A BROADCAST FROM ONE OF THE VEHICLES IN A VARIANT OF THE DEMON'S LANGUAGE.

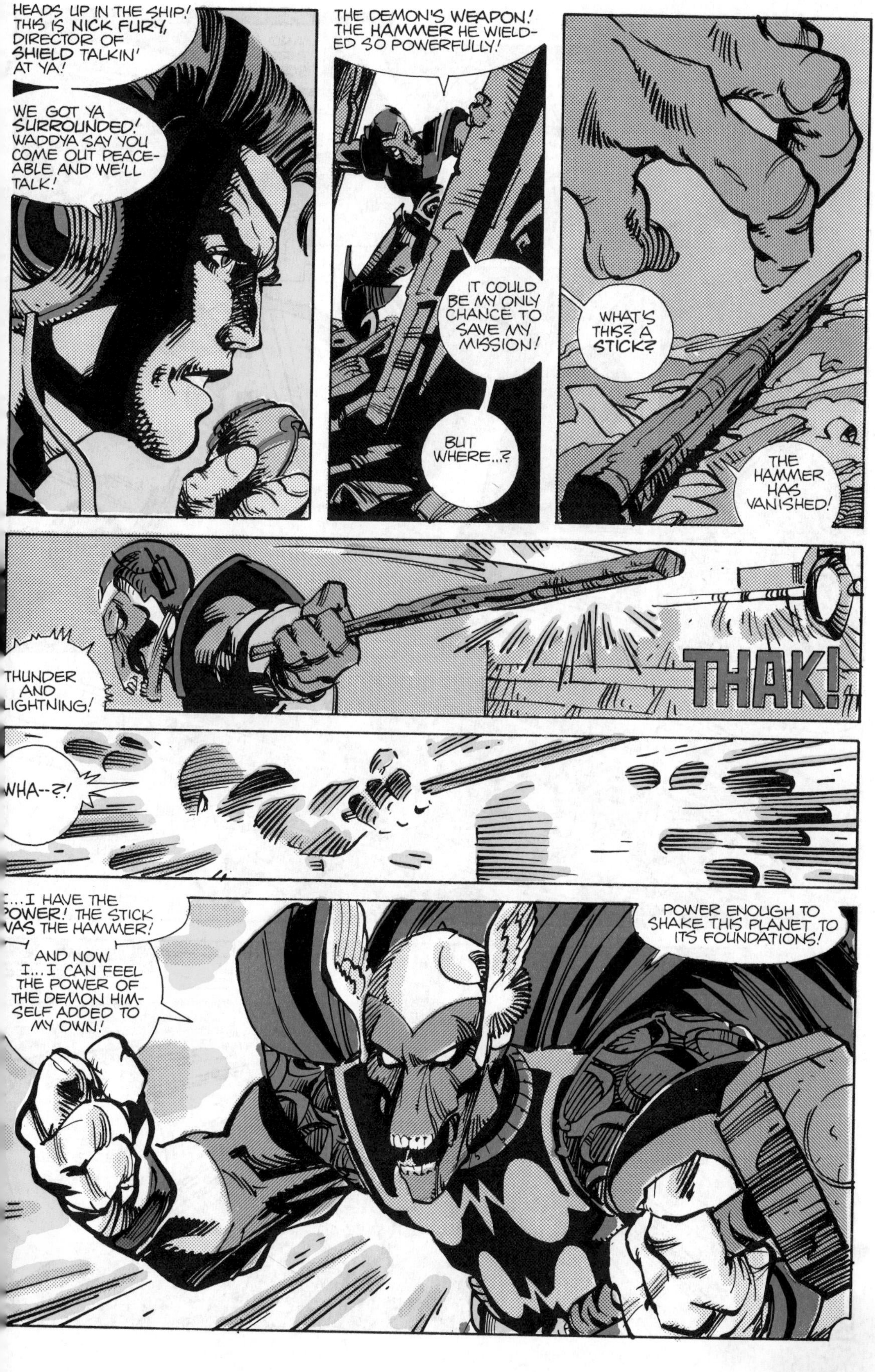

HEADS UP IN THE SHIP! THIS IS NICK FURY, DIRECTOR OF SHIELD TALKIN' AT YA!
WE GOT YA SURROUNDED! WADDYA SAY YOU COME OUT PEACEABLE AND WE'LL TALK!
THE DEMON'S WEAPON! THE HAMMER HE WIELDED SO POWERFULLY!
IT COULD BE MY ONLY CHANCE TO SAVE MY MISSION!
BUT WHERE...?
WHAT'S THIS? A STICK?
THE HAMMER HAS VANISHED!
THUNDER AND LIGHTNING!
THAK!
WHA--?!
...I HAVE THE POWER! THE STICK WAS THE HAMMER!
AND NOW I...I CAN FEEL THE POWER OF THE DEMON HIMSELF ADDED TO MY OWN!
POWER ENOUGH TO SHAKE THIS PLANET TO ITS FOUNDATIONS!

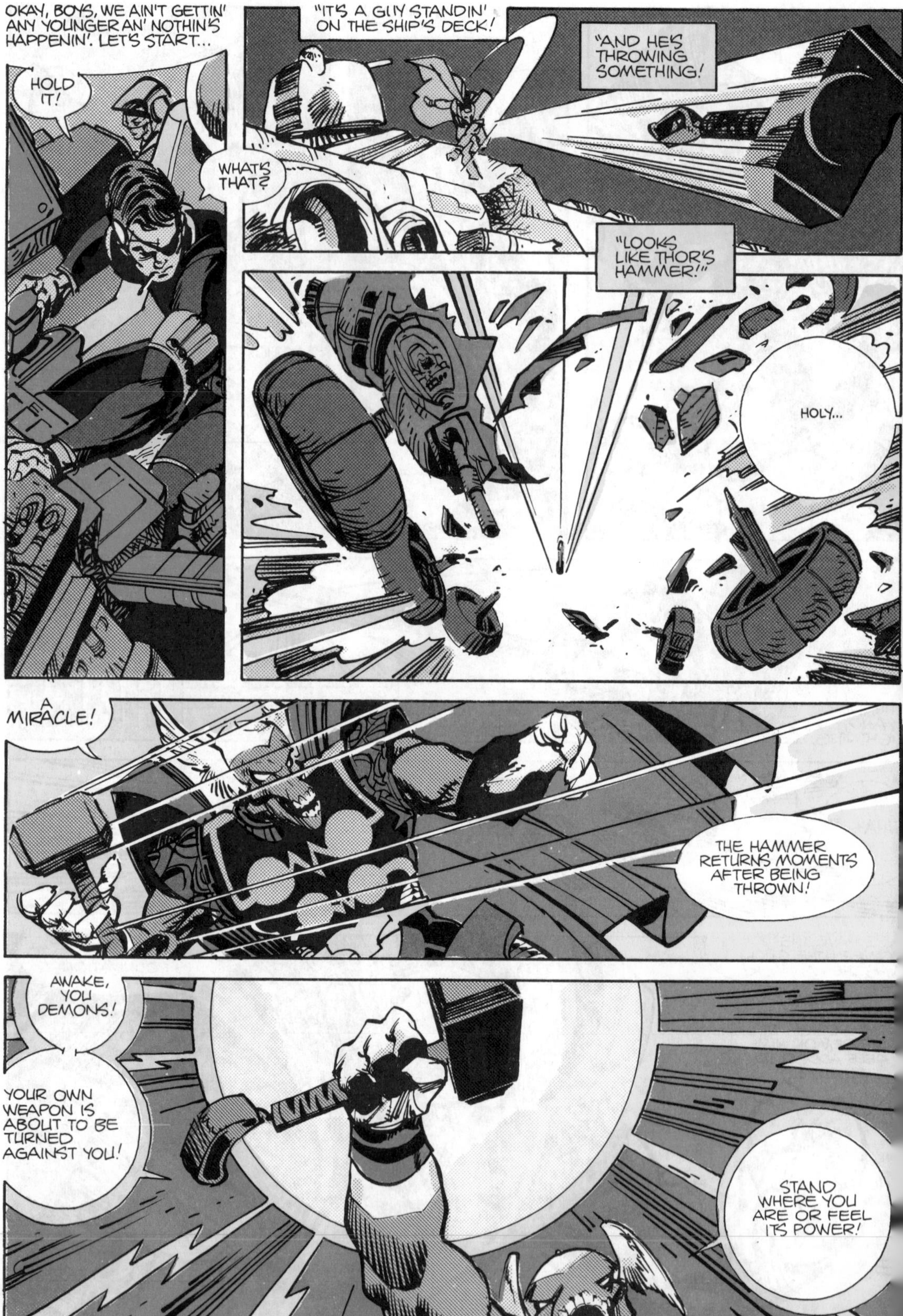
OKAY, BOYS, WE AIN'T GETTIN' ANY YOUNGER AN' NOTHIN'S HAPPENIN'. LET'S START...
HOLD IT!
WHAT'S THAT?
"IT'S A GUY STANDIN' ON THE SHIP'S DECK!
"AND HE'S THROWING SOMETHING!
"LOOKS LIKE THOR'S HAMMER!"
HOLY...
A MIRACLE!
THE HAMMER RETURNS MOMENTS AFTER BEING THROWN!
AWAKE, YOU DEMONS!
YOUR OWN WEAPON IS ABOUT TO BE TURNED AGAINST YOU!
STAND WHERE YOU ARE OR FEEL ITS POWER!

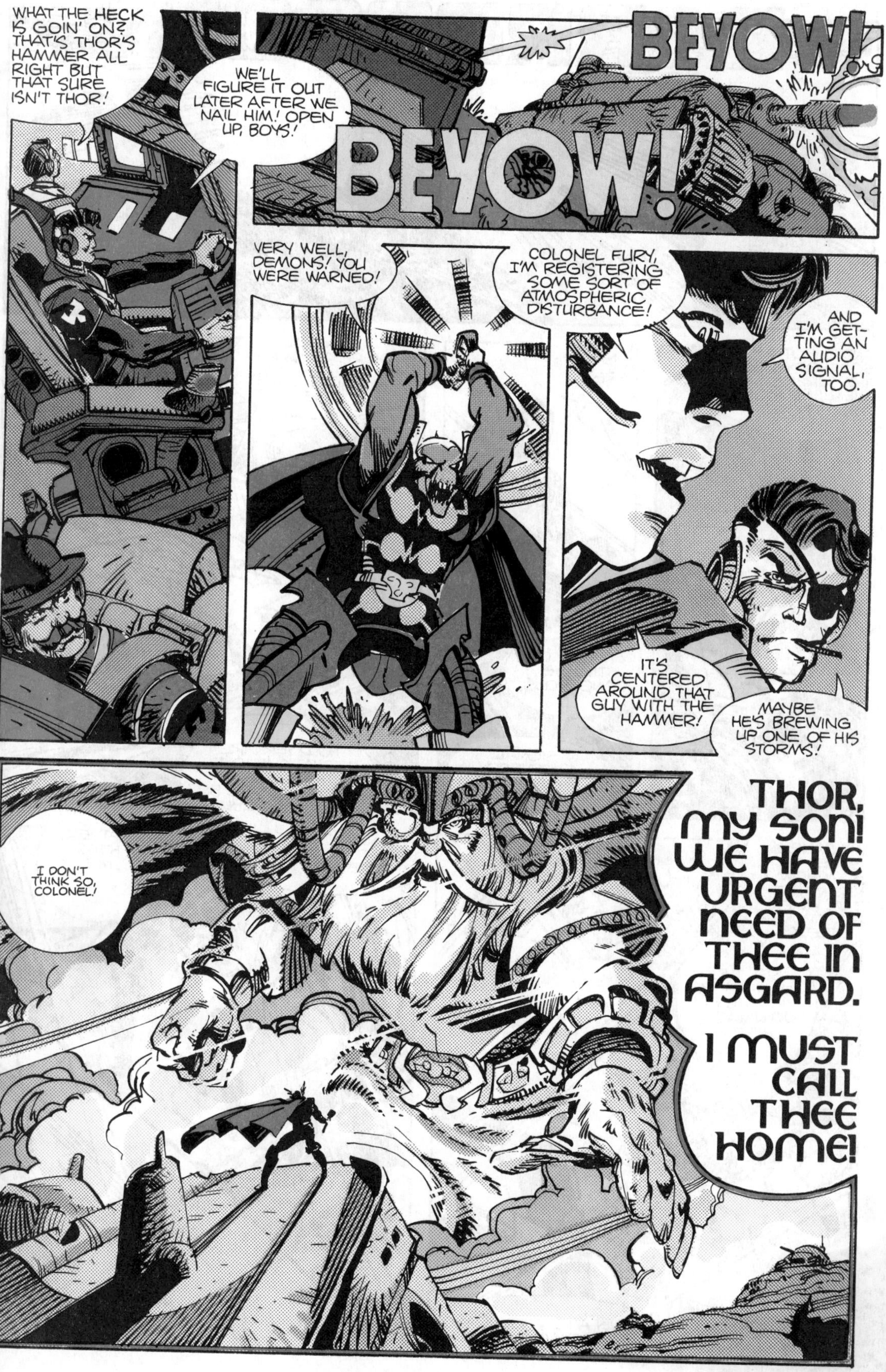
WHAT THE HECK IS GOIN' ON? THAT'S THOR'S HAMMER ALL RIGHT BUT THAT SURE ISN'T THOR!
WE'LL FIGURE IT OUT LATER AFTER WE NAIL HIM! OPEN UP, BOYS!
BEYOW!
BEYOW!
VERY WELL, DEMONS! YOU WERE WARNED!
COLONEL FURY, I'M REGISTERING SOME SORT OF ATMOSPHERIC DISTURBANCE!
AND I'M GETTING AN AUDIO SIGNAL, TOO.
IT'S CENTERED AROUND THAT GUY WITH THE HAMMER!
MAYBE HE'S BREWING UP ONE OF HIS STORMS!
I DON'T THINK SO, COLONEL!
THOR, MY SON! WE HAVE URGENT NEED OF THEE IN ASGARD.
I MUST CALL THEE HOME!

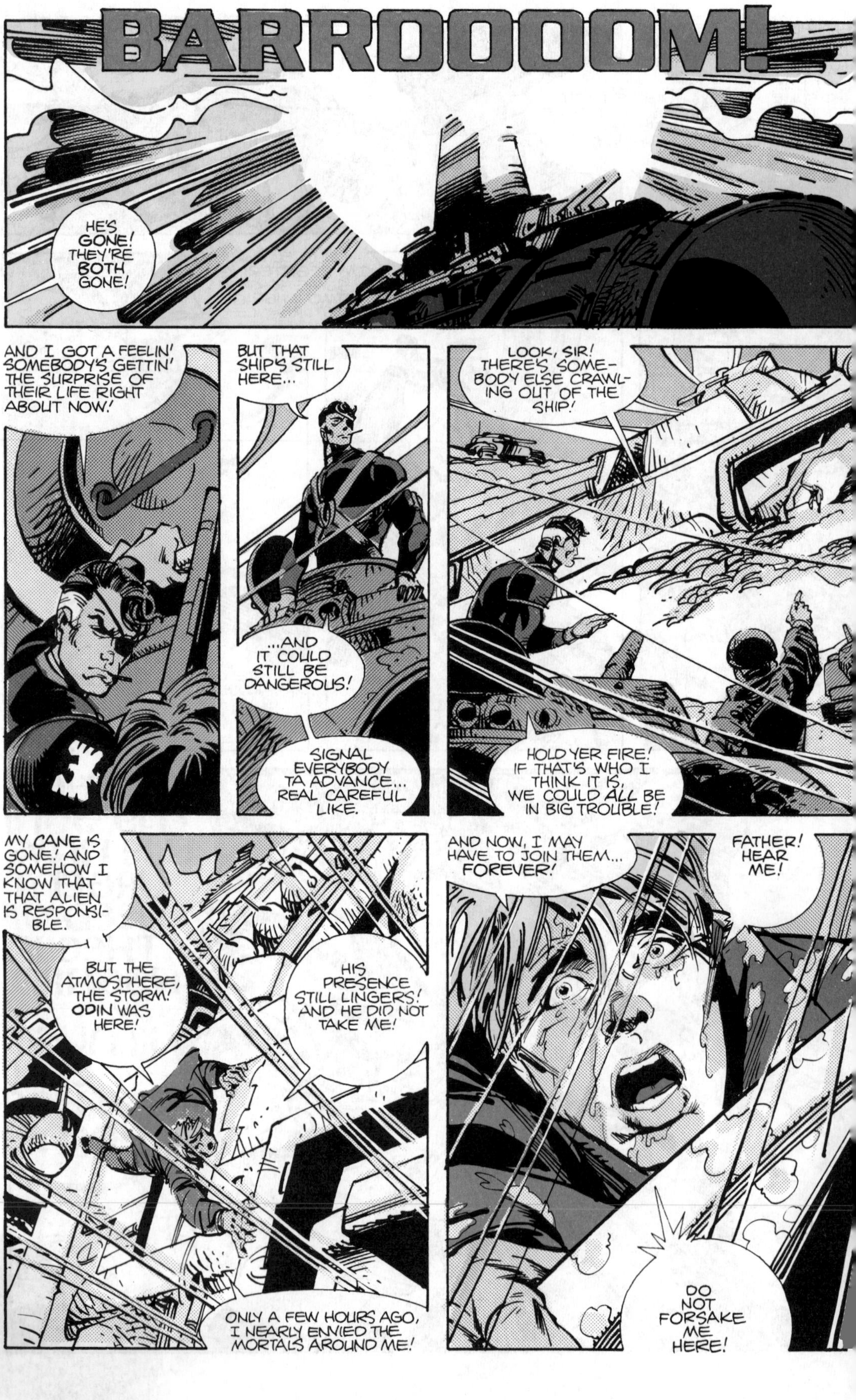
BARROOOOM!
HE'S GONE! THEY'RE BOTH GONE!
AND I GOT A FEELIN' SOMEBODY'S GETTIN' THE SURPRISE OF THEIR LIFE RIGHT ABOUT NOW!
BUT THAT SHIP'S STILL HERE...
...AND IT COULD STILL BE DANGEROUS!
SIGNAL EVERYBODY TA ADVANCE... REAL CAREFUL LIKE.
LOOK, SIR! THERE'S SOMEBODY ELSE CRAWLING OUT OF THE SHIP!
HOLD YER FIRE! IF THAT'S WHO I THINK IT IS, WE COULD ALL BE IN BIG TROUBLE!
MY CANE IS GONE! AND SOMEHOW I KNOW THAT THAT ALIEN IS RESPONSIBLE.
BUT THE ATMOSPHERE, THE STORM! ODIN WAS HERE!
HIS PRESENCE STILL LINGERS! AND HE DID NOT TAKE ME!
ONLY A FEW HOURS AGO, I NEARLY ENVIED THE MORTALS AROUND ME!
AND NOW, I MAY HAVE TO JOIN THEM... FOREVER!
FATHER! HEAR ME!
DO NOT FORSAKE ME HERE!

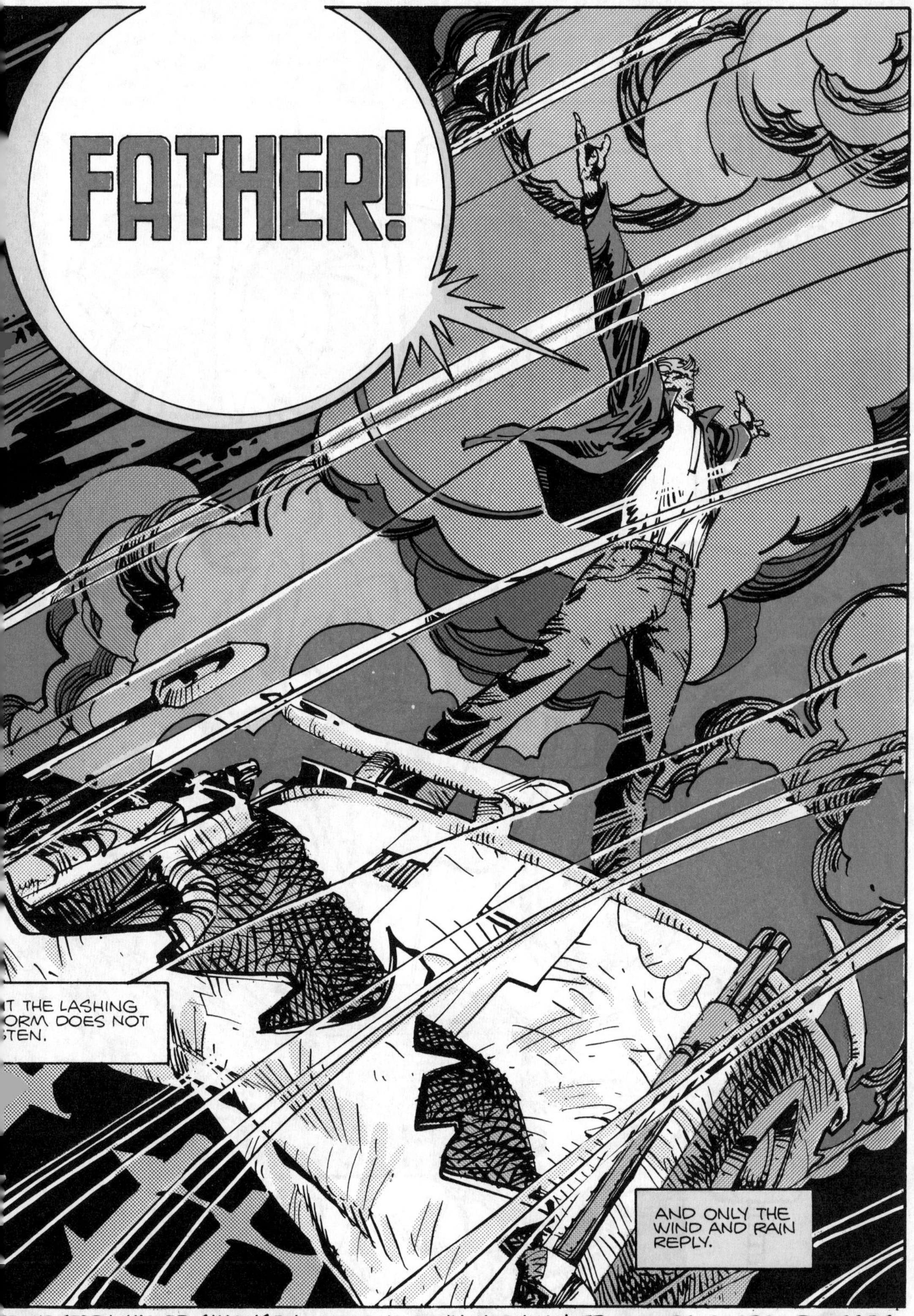
FATHER!
T THE LASHING
ORM DOES NOT
STEN.
AND ONLY THE WIND AND RAIN REPLY.

RT AND STORY: WALTER SIMONSON · LETTERING: JOHN WORKMAN, JR. · COLORS: GEORGE ROUSSOS ·
EDITING: MARK GRUENWALD · EDITOR-IN-CHIEF: JIM SHOOTER

NEXT--A FOOL AND HIS HAMMER...

BE HERE! 'CAUSE WE'LL MISS YOU IF YOU'RE NOT AROUND.

CHAPTER TWO

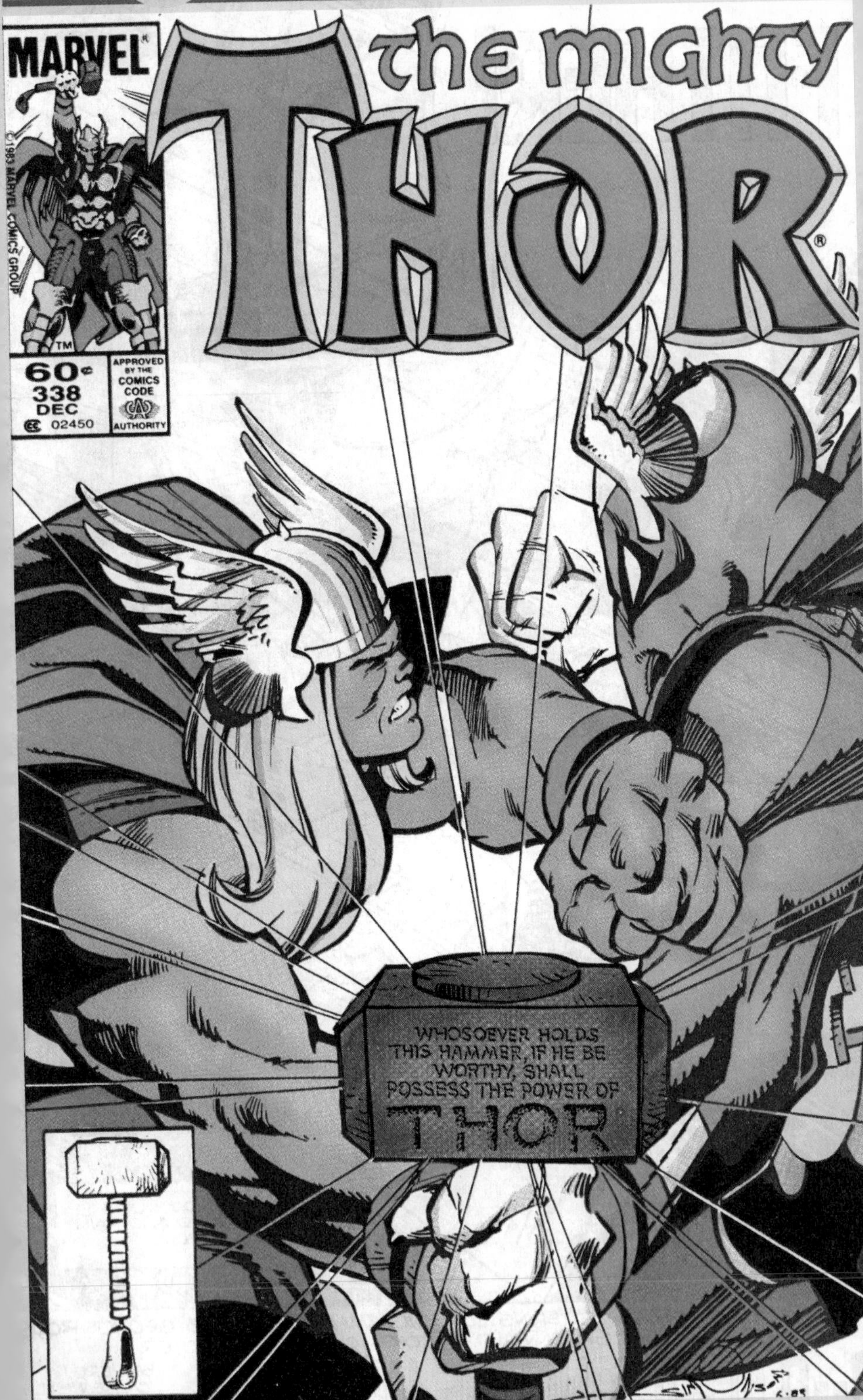
MARVEL
the mighty THOR
60¢
338
DEC
02450
APPROVED BY THE COMICS CODE AUTHORITY
WHOSOEVER HOLDS THIS HAMMER, IF HE BE WORTHY, SHALL POSSESS THE POWER OF
THOR

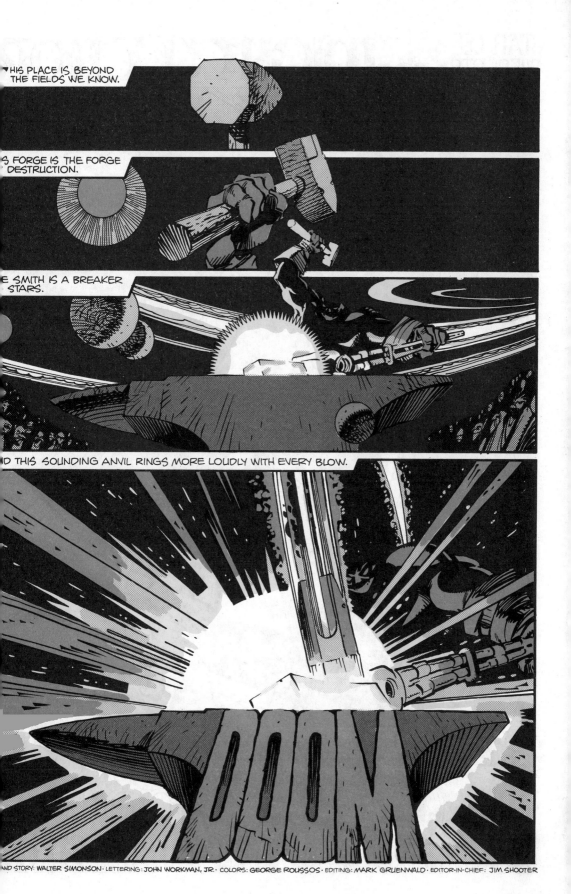

THIS PLACE IS BEYOND THE FIELDS WE KNOW.

S FORGE IS THE FORGE DESTRUCTION.

E SMITH IS A BREAKER STARS.

D THIS SOUNDING ANVIL RINGS MORE LOUDLY WITH EVERY BLOW.

DOOM

D STORY: WALTER SIMONSON · LETTERING: JOHN WORKMAN, JR. · COLORS: GEORGE ROUSSOS · EDITING: MARK GRUENWALD · EDITOR-IN-CHIEF: JIM SHOOTER

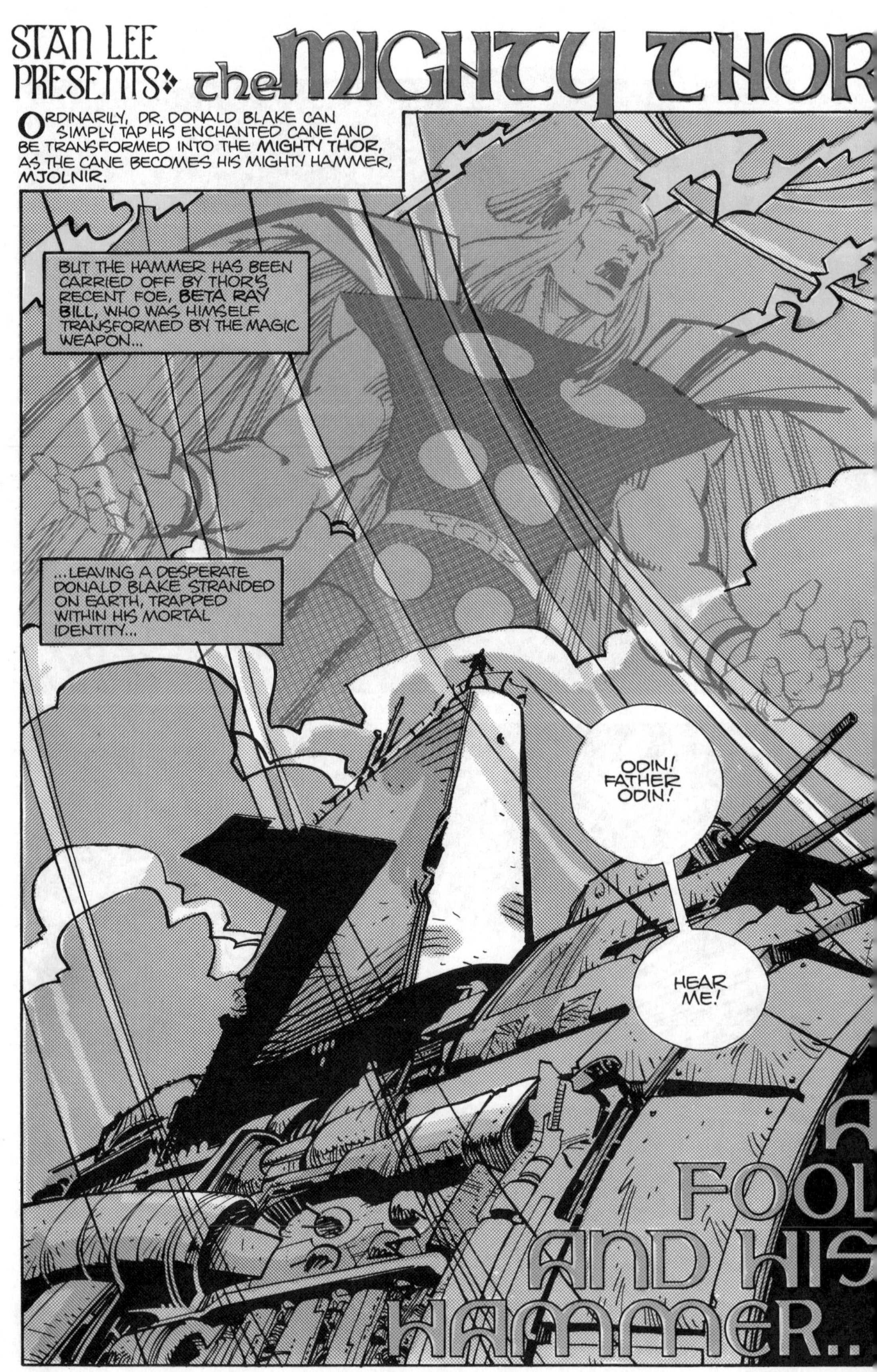
STAN LEE PRESENTS: the MIGHTY THOR
ORDINARILY, DR. DONALD BLAKE CAN SIMPLY TAP HIS ENCHANTED CANE AND BE TRANSFORMED INTO THE MIGHTY THOR, AS THE CANE BECOMES HIS MIGHTY HAMMER, MJOLNIR.
BUT THE HAMMER HAS BEEN CARRIED OFF BY THOR'S RECENT FOE, BETA RAY BILL, WHO WAS HIMSELF TRANSFORMED BY THE MAGIC WEAPON...
...LEAVING A DESPERATE DONALD BLAKE STRANDED ON EARTH, TRAPPED WITHIN HIS MORTAL IDENTITY...
ODIN! FATHER ODIN!
HEAR ME!
FOOL AND HIS HAMMER..

HEAR ME.

IT'S NO USE. THE HAMMER'S GONE AND WITHOUT IT, I'M DOOMED TO REMAIN A MORTAL, UNABLE TO CONTACT ASGARD OR ODIN, MY FATHER.

WHAT WILL I DO? WHAT WILL I DO? ODIN, HELP ME.

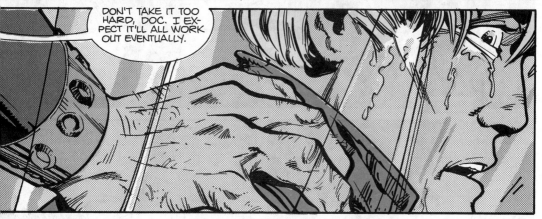

DON'T TAKE IT TOO HARD, DOC. I EXPECT IT'LL ALL WORK OUT EVENTUALLY.

COLONEL FURY! I... I SHOULD HAVE KNOWN YOU'D BE HERE.

I'VE LOST EVERYTHING, NICK! THERE WAS AN ALIEN ON BOARD THIS SHIP. WE FOUGHT AND I TURNED BACK INTO DON BLAKE AT THE WRONG MOMENT.

HE KNOCKED ME OUT AND NOW IT LOOKS AS THOUGH HE'S TAKEN MY HAMMER. THAT'S NEVER HAPPENED BEFORE. AND WITHOUT MJOLNIR, I'M MAROONED HERE, PERHAPS FOREVER.

MAYBE NOT, DOC. AN OLD GUY WITH ONE EYE APPEARED AND THEN VANISHED, TAKING THE ALIEN WITH HIM.

URE THING, DOC. SHIELD'S EEN TRACKIN' THIS SHIP LL THE WAY. THOUGHT YA GHT NEED A LITTLE HELP HEN IT CRASHED ON EARTH.

LOOKS LIKE WE WERE RIGHT. YOU OKAY?

IF THAT WAS YER OLD MAN, HE AIN'T GONNA BE REAL HAPPY TO SEE SOMEBODY ELSE WEARIN' YER THREADS AND HEFTIN' YER HAMMER.

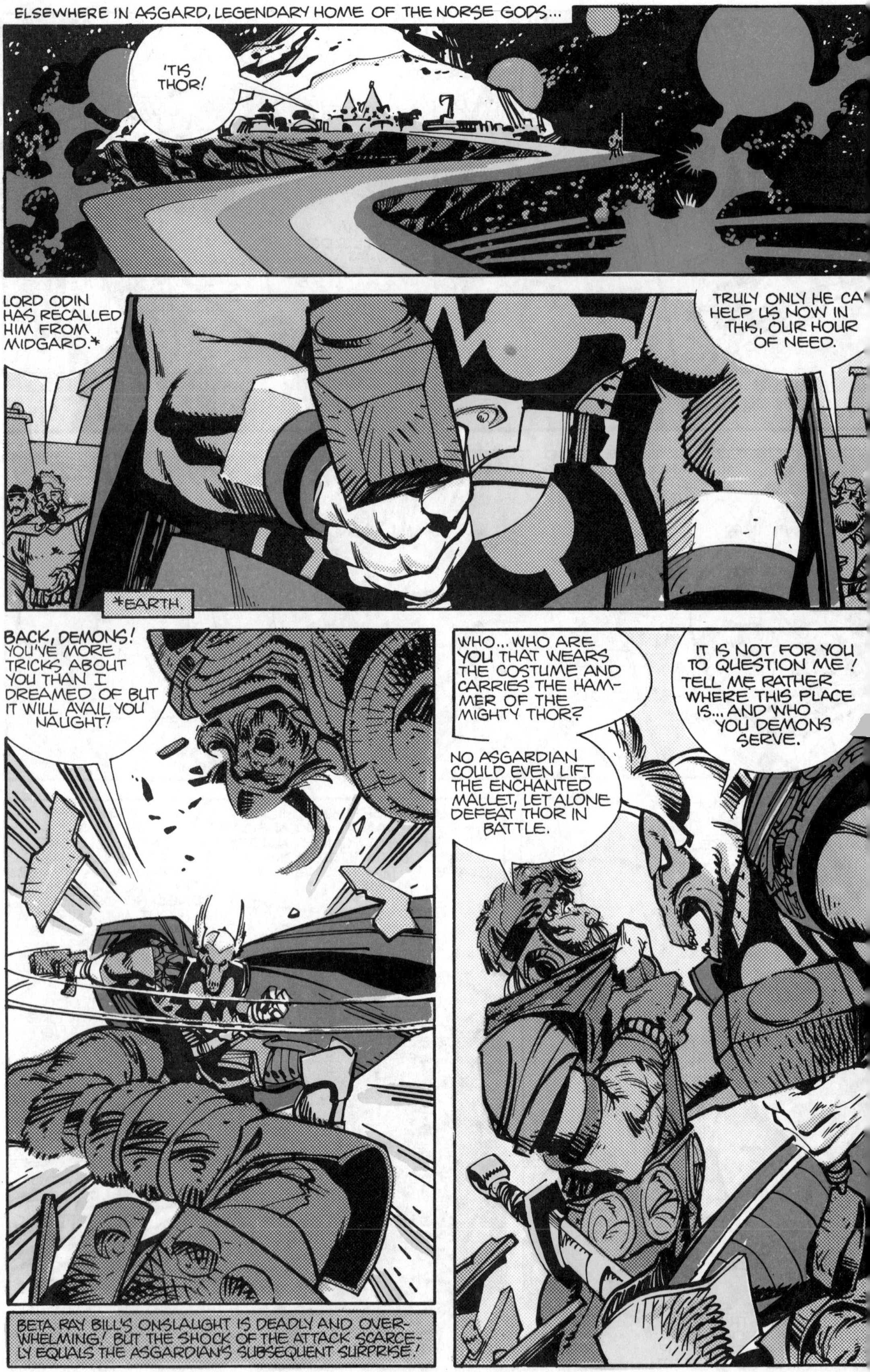
ELSEWHERE IN ASGARD, LEGENDARY HOME OF THE NORSE GODS...
'TIS THOR!
LORD ODIN HAS RECALLED HIM FROM MIDGARD.*
TRULY ONLY HE CA HELP US NOW IN THIS, OUR HOUR OF NEED.
*EARTH.
BACK, DEMONS! YOU'VE MORE TRICKS ABOUT YOU THAN I DREAMED OF BUT IT WILL AVAIL YOU NAUGHT!
BETA RAY BILL'S ONSLAUGHT IS DEADLY AND OVERWHELMING! BUT THE SHOCK OF THE ATTACK SCARCELY EQUALS THE ASGARDIAN'S SUBSEQUENT SURPRISE!
WHO... WHO ARE YOU THAT WEARS THE COSTUME AND CARRIES THE HAMMER OF THE MIGHTY THOR?
NO ASGARDIAN COULD EVEN LIFT THE ENCHANTED MALLET, LET ALONE DEFEAT THOR IN BATTLE.
IT IS NOT FOR YOU TO QUESTION ME! TELL ME RATHER WHERE THIS PLACE IS... AND WHO YOU DEMONS SERVE.

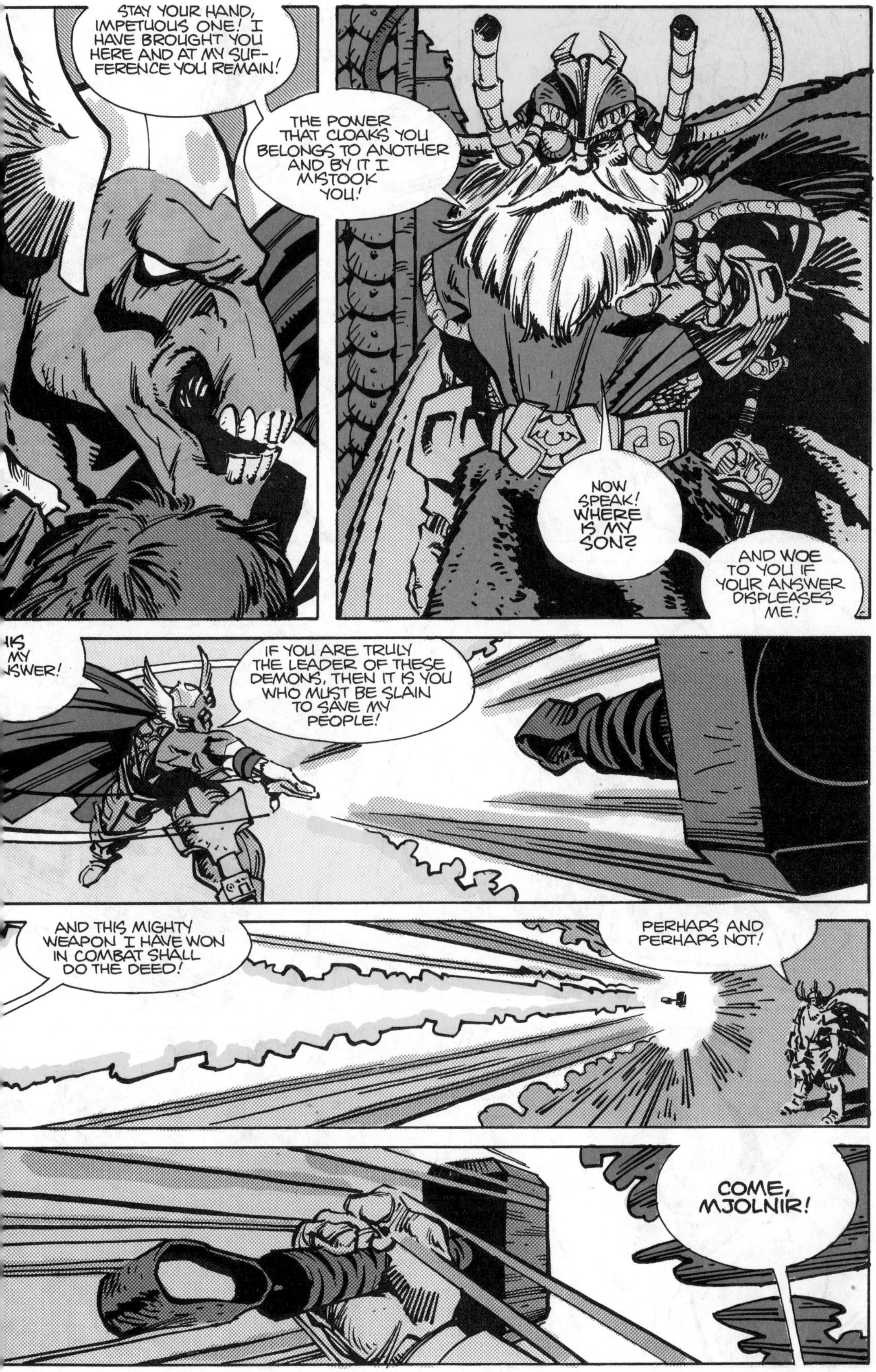
STAY YOUR HAND, IMPETUOUS ONE! I HAVE BROUGHT YOU HERE AND AT MY SUFFERENCE YOU REMAIN!
THE POWER THAT CLOAKS YOU BELONGS TO ANOTHER AND BY IT I MISTOOK YOU!
NOW SPEAK! WHERE IS MY SON?
AND WOE TO YOU IF YOUR ANSWER DISPLEASES ME!
MY
IF YOU ARE TRULY THE LEADER OF THESE DEMONS, THEN IT IS YOU WHO MUST BE SLAIN TO SAVE MY PEOPLE!
AND THIS MIGHTY WEAPON I HAVE WON IN COMBAT SHALL DO THE DEED!
PERHAPS AND PERHAPS NOT!
COME, MJOLNIR!

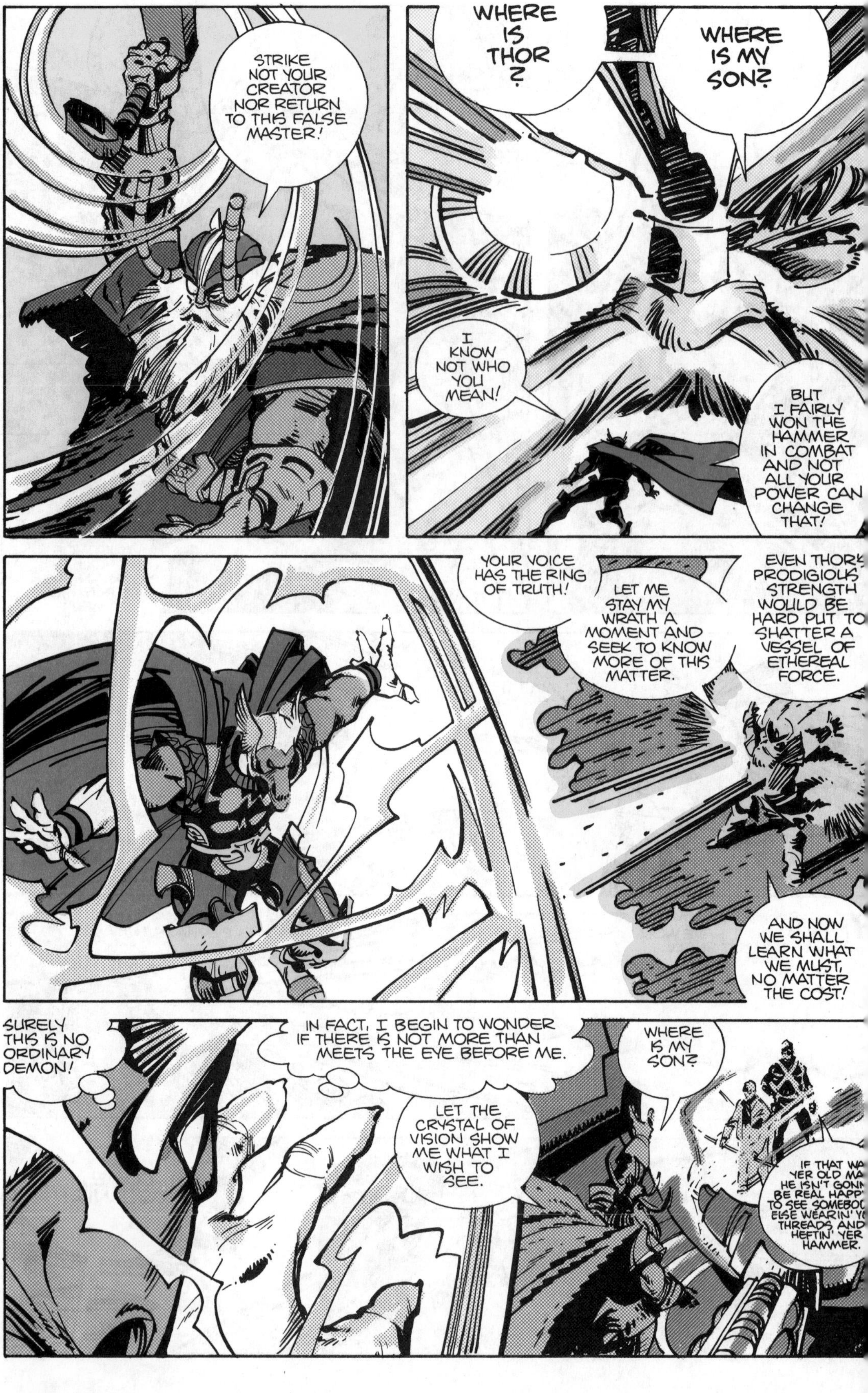
STRIKE NOT YOUR CREATOR NOR RETURN TO THIS FALSE MASTER!
WHERE IS THOR?
WHERE IS MY SON?
I KNOW NOT WHO YOU MEAN!
BUT I FAIRLY WON THE HAMMER IN COMBAT AND NOT ALL YOUR POWER CAN CHANGE THAT!
YOUR VOICE HAS THE RING OF TRUTH!
LET ME STAY MY WRATH A MOMENT AND SEEK TO KNOW MORE OF THIS MATTER.
EVEN THOR'S PRODIGIOUS STRENGTH WOULD BE HARD PUT TO SHATTER A VESSEL OF ETHEREAL FORCE.
AND NOW WE SHALL LEARN WHAT WE MUST, NO MATTER THE COST!
SURELY THIS IS NO ORDINARY DEMON!
IN FACT, I BEGIN TO WONDER IF THERE IS NOT MORE THAN MEETS THE EYE BEFORE ME.
WHERE IS MY SON?
LET THE CRYSTAL OF VISION SHOW ME WHAT I WISH TO SEE.
IF THAT WA YER OLD MA HE ISN'T GONN BE REAL HAPP TO SEE SOMEBOD ELSE WEARIN' YO THREADS AND HEFTIN' YER HAMMER.

FACT IS, I'M SURPRISED HE HASN'T...

...IT MY IMAGINATION OR IS IT GETTIN' DARKER?

...HOPE WASN'T ...OMETHIN' ...SAID.

BARROOM

YEOW! NOT AGAIN!

NOW DOC'S GONE, TOO. BROTHER, THIS IS GONNA MAKE ONE HECK OF A REPORT!

WELL, GOOD LUCK, BLAKE. I THINK YER GONNA NEED IT.

IT LOOKS LIKE IT'S STARTIN' TO RAIN AGAIN, TOO.

SWELL. DON'T THESE GUYS EVER TRAVEL IN DRY WEATHER?

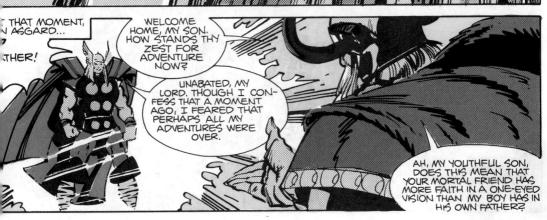

...T THAT MOMENT, ...N ASGARD...

...THER!

WELCOME HOME, MY SON. HOW STANDS THY ZEST FOR ADVENTURE NOW?

UNABATED, MY LORD, THOUGH I CON-FESS THAT A MOMENT AGO, I FEARED THAT PERHAPS ALL MY ADVENTURES WERE OVER.

AH, MY YOUTHFUL SON, DOES THIS MEAN THAT YOUR MORTAL FRIEND HAS MORE FAITH IN A ONE-EYED VISION THAN MY BOY HAS IN HIS OWN FATHER?

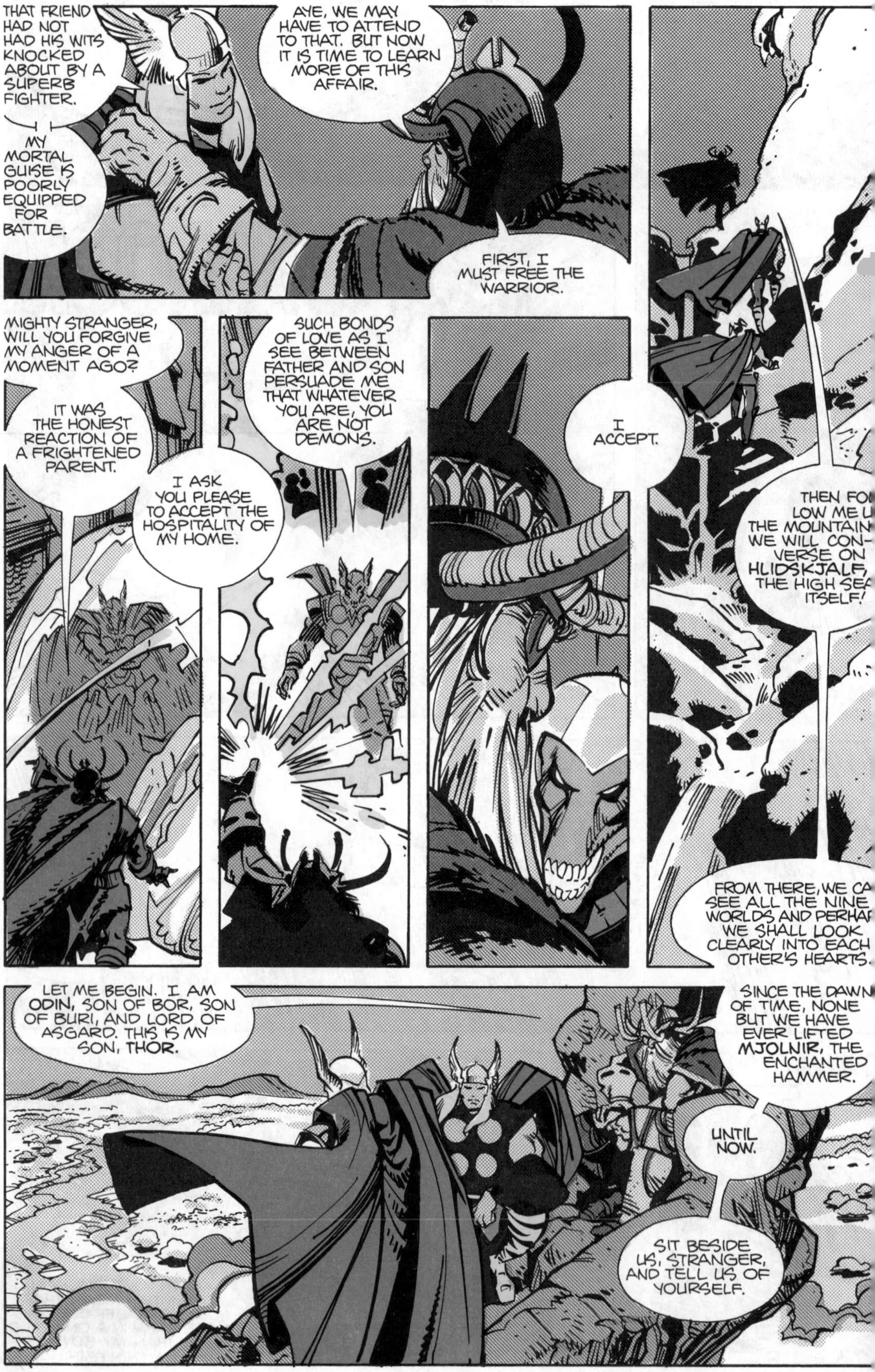
THAT FRIEND HAD NOT HAD HIS WITS KNOCKED ABOUT BY A SUPERB FIGHTER.
MY MORTAL GUISE IS POORLY EQUIPPED FOR BATTLE.
AYE, WE MAY HAVE TO ATTEND TO THAT. BUT NOW IT IS TIME TO LEARN MORE OF THIS AFFAIR.
FIRST, I MUST FREE THE WARRIOR.
MIGHTY STRANGER, WILL YOU FORGIVE MY ANGER OF A MOMENT AGO?
IT WAS THE HONEST REACTION OF A FRIGHTENED PARENT.
SUCH BONDS OF LOVE AS I SEE BETWEEN FATHER AND SON PERSUADE ME THAT WHATEVER YOU ARE, YOU ARE NOT DEMONS.
I ASK YOU PLEASE TO ACCEPT THE HOSPITALITY OF MY HOME.
I ACCEPT.
THEN FO LOW ME U THE MOUNTAIN WE WILL CON- VERSE ON HLIDSKJALF, THE HIGH SEA ITSELF!
FROM THERE, WE CA SEE ALL THE NINE WORLDS AND PERHAP WE SHALL LOOK CLEARLY INTO EACH OTHER'S HEARTS.
LET ME BEGIN. I AM ODIN, SON OF BOR, SON OF BURI, AND LORD OF ASGARD. THIS IS MY SON, THOR.
SINCE THE DAWN OF TIME, NONE BUT WE HAVE EVER LIFTED MJOLNIR, THE ENCHANTED HAMMER.
UNTIL NOW.
SIT BESIDE US, STRANGER, AND TELL US OF YOURSELF.

MEANWHILE, BELOW THE HIGH SEAT, IN THE GARDEN ENTRANCE TO ODIN'S NOBLE HALL, WE FIND THE LADY SIF...

MY BROTHER, HEIMDALL THE WATCHER, MAY BE RIGHT. ONLY ODIN HIMSELF CAN HELP ME EASE MY EMPTY HEART NOW THAT THOR AND I ARE NO LONGER PROMISED TO EACH OTHER.

WOULD THAT ODIN HAD NEVER GIVEN THOR HIS MORTAL IDENTITY SO LONG AGO. I STILL LOVE THE NOBLE WARRIOR BUT HIS HEART MAY EVER BE DIVIDED BETWEEN ASGARD AND MIDGARD.

AND THOUGH MY LOVE SURPASSES UNDERSTANDING, I CANNOT SHARE THOR'S JOY FOR EARTH.

BUT WHAT'S THIS I HEAR?

SURELY MY SENSES DECEIVE ME!

OH, LADY LORELEI, TO FEEL YOUR ARMS ENTWINED ABOUT ME, YOUR SWEET BREATH UPON MY FACE, YOUR LIPS PRESSED TO MINE... 'TIS ALL THAT I DESIRE.

FOR SUCH KISSES, I WOULD FORSAKE EVEN MIDGARD ITSELF!

SO.

I...UH...I... MILADY SIF?

THOUGH MY OWN BREATH IS LESS SWEET, MY LORD THOR, ACCEPT THIS PARTING KISS...

THE KISS OF A WARRIOR BORN AND NO SOFT PLAYTHING!

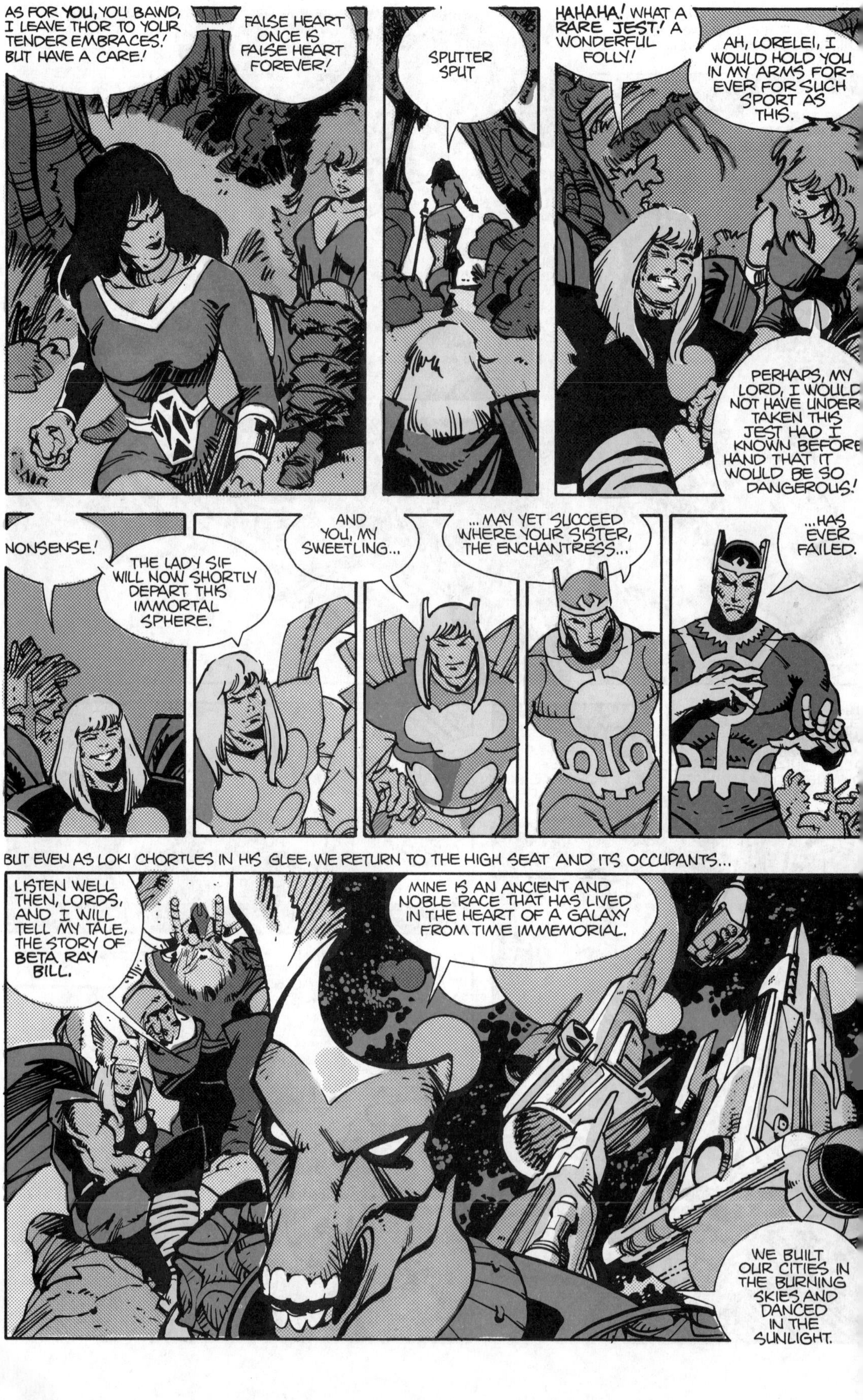

AS FOR YOU, YOU BAWD, I LEAVE THOR TO YOUR TENDER EMBRACES! BUT HAVE A CARE!
FALSE HEART ONCE IS FALSE HEART FOREVER!
SPUTTER SPUT
HAHAHA! WHAT A RARE JEST! A WONDERFUL FOLLY!
AH, LORELEI, I WOULD HOLD YOU IN MY ARMS FOREVER FOR SUCH SPORT AS THIS.
PERHAPS, MY LORD, I WOULD NOT HAVE UNDERTAKEN THIS JEST HAD I KNOWN BEFOREHAND THAT IT WOULD BE SO DANGEROUS!
NONSENSE!
THE LADY SIF WILL NOW SHORTLY DEPART THIS IMMORTAL SPHERE.
AND YOU, MY SWEETLING...
...MAY YET SUCCEED WHERE YOUR SISTER, THE ENCHANTRESS...
...HAS EVER FAILED.
BUT EVEN AS LOKI CHORTLES IN HIS GLEE, WE RETURN TO THE HIGH SEAT AND ITS OCCUPANTS...
LISTEN WELL THEN, LORDS, AND I WILL TELL MY TALE, THE STORY OF BETA RAY BILL.
MINE IS AN ANCIENT AND NOBLE RACE THAT HAS LIVED IN THE HEART OF A GALAXY FROM TIME IMMEMORIAL.
WE BUILT OUR CITIES IN THE BURNING SKIES AND DANCED IN THE SUNLIGHT.

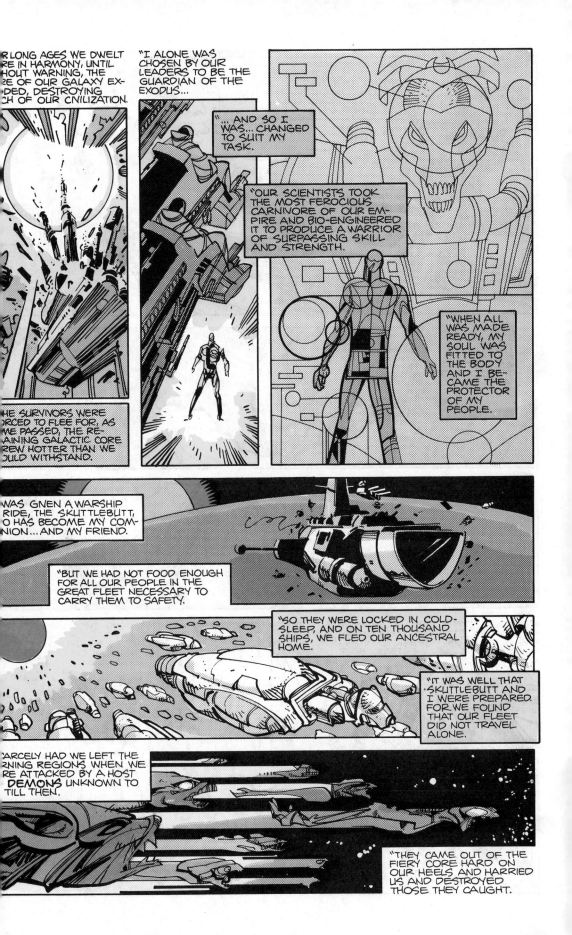

"...OR LONG AGES WE DWELT ...RE IN HARMONY, UNTIL ...HOUT WARNING, THE ...RE OF OUR GALAXY EX-...DED, DESTROYING ...CH OF OUR CIVILIZATION.

"I ALONE WAS CHOSEN BY OUR LEADERS TO BE THE GUARDIAN OF THE EXODUS...

"... AND SO I WAS... CHANGED TO SUIT MY TASK.

"OUR SCIENTISTS TOOK THE MOST FEROCIOUS CARNIVORE OF OUR EM-PIRE AND BIO-ENGINEERED IT TO PRODUCE A WARRIOR OF SURPASSING SKILL AND STRENGTH.

"WHEN ALL WAS MADE READY, MY SOUL WAS FITTED TO THE BODY AND I BE-CAME THE PROTECTOR OF MY PEOPLE.

...HE SURVIVORS WERE ...RCED TO FLEE FOR, AS ...ME PASSED, THE RE-...AINING GALACTIC CORE ...REW HOTTER THAN WE ...OULD WITHSTAND.

...WAS GIVEN A WARSHIP ...RIDE, THE SKUTTLEBUTT, ...O HAS BECOME MY COM-...NION... AND MY FRIEND.

"BUT WE HAD NOT FOOD ENOUGH FOR ALL OUR PEOPLE IN THE GREAT FLEET NECESSARY TO CARRY THEM TO SAFETY.

"SO THEY WERE LOCKED IN COLD-SLEEP, AND ON TEN THOUSAND SHIPS, WE FLED OUR ANCESTRAL HOME.

"IT WAS WELL THAT SKUTTLEBUTT AND I WERE PREPARED. FOR WE FOUND THAT OUR FLEET DID NOT TRAVEL ALONE.

...ARCELY HAD WE LEFT THE ...RNING REGIONS WHEN WE ...RE ATTACKED BY A HOST ... DEMONS UNKNOWN TO ... TILL THEN.

"THEY CAME OUT OF THE FIERY CORE HARD ON OUR HEELS AND HARRIED US AND DESTROYED THOSE THEY CAUGHT.

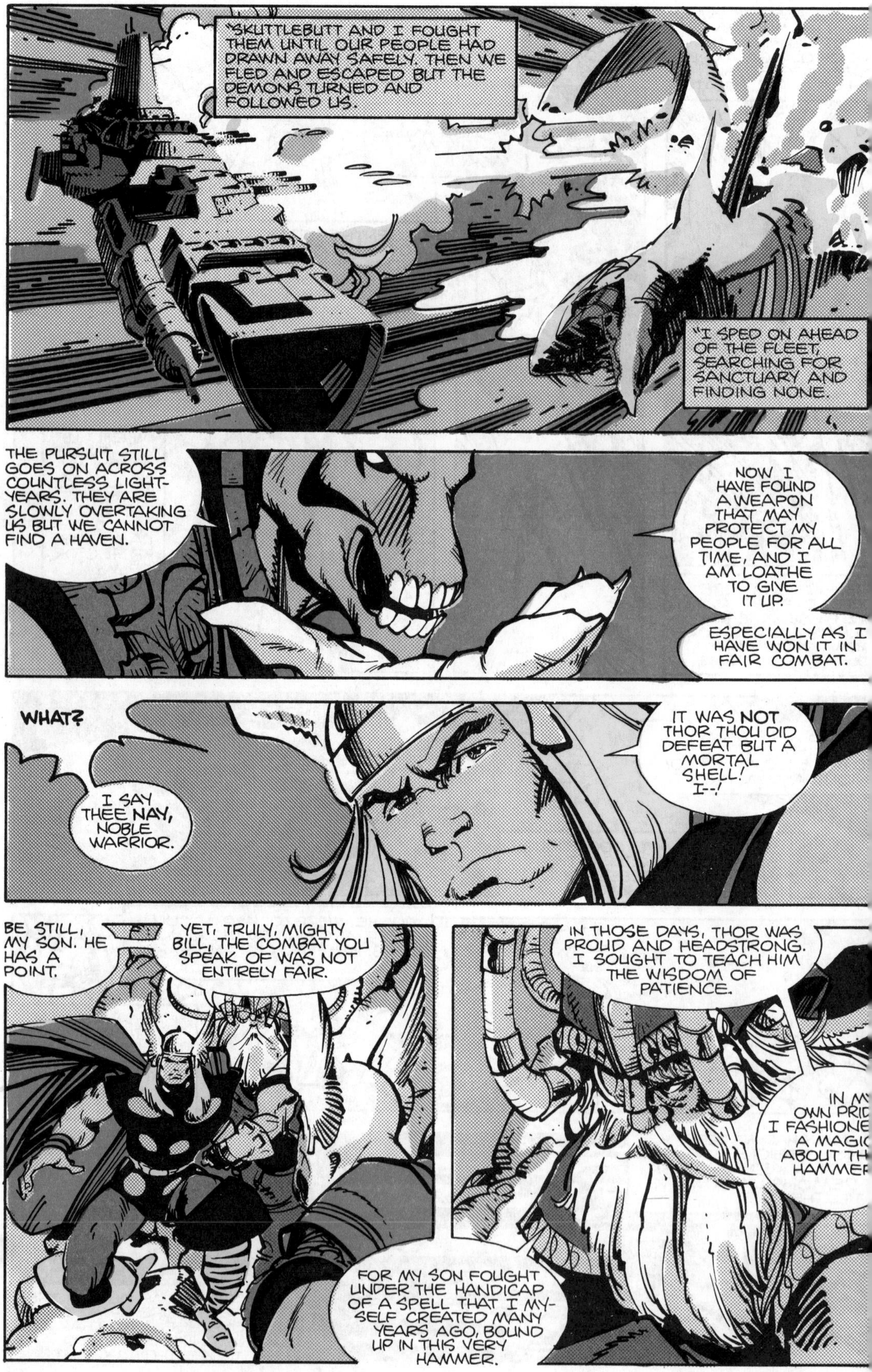
"SKUTTLEBUTT AND I FOUGHT THEM UNTIL OUR PEOPLE HAD DRAWN AWAY SAFELY. THEN WE FLED AND ESCAPED BUT THE DEMONS TURNED AND FOLLOWED US.
"I SPED ON AHEAD OF THE FLEET, SEARCHING FOR SANCTUARY AND FINDING NONE.
THE PURSUIT STILL GOES ON ACROSS COUNTLESS LIGHT-YEARS. THEY ARE SLOWLY OVERTAKING US BUT WE CANNOT FIND A HAVEN.
NOW I HAVE FOUND A WEAPON THAT MAY PROTECT MY PEOPLE FOR ALL TIME, AND I AM LOATHE TO GIVE IT UP.
ESPECIALLY AS I HAVE WON IT IN FAIR COMBAT.
I SAY THEE NAY, NOBLE WARRIOR.
WHAT?
IT WAS NOT THOR THOU DID DEFEAT BUT A MORTAL SHELL! I--!
BE STILL, MY SON. HE HAS A POINT.
YET, TRULY, MIGHTY BILL, THE COMBAT YOU SPEAK OF WAS NOT ENTIRELY FAIR.
FOR MY SON FOUGHT UNDER THE HANDICAP OF A SPELL THAT I MYSELF CREATED MANY YEARS AGO, BOUND UP IN THIS VERY HAMMER.
IN THOSE DAYS, THOR WAS PROUD AND HEADSTRONG. I SOUGHT TO TEACH HIM THE WISDOM OF PATIENCE.

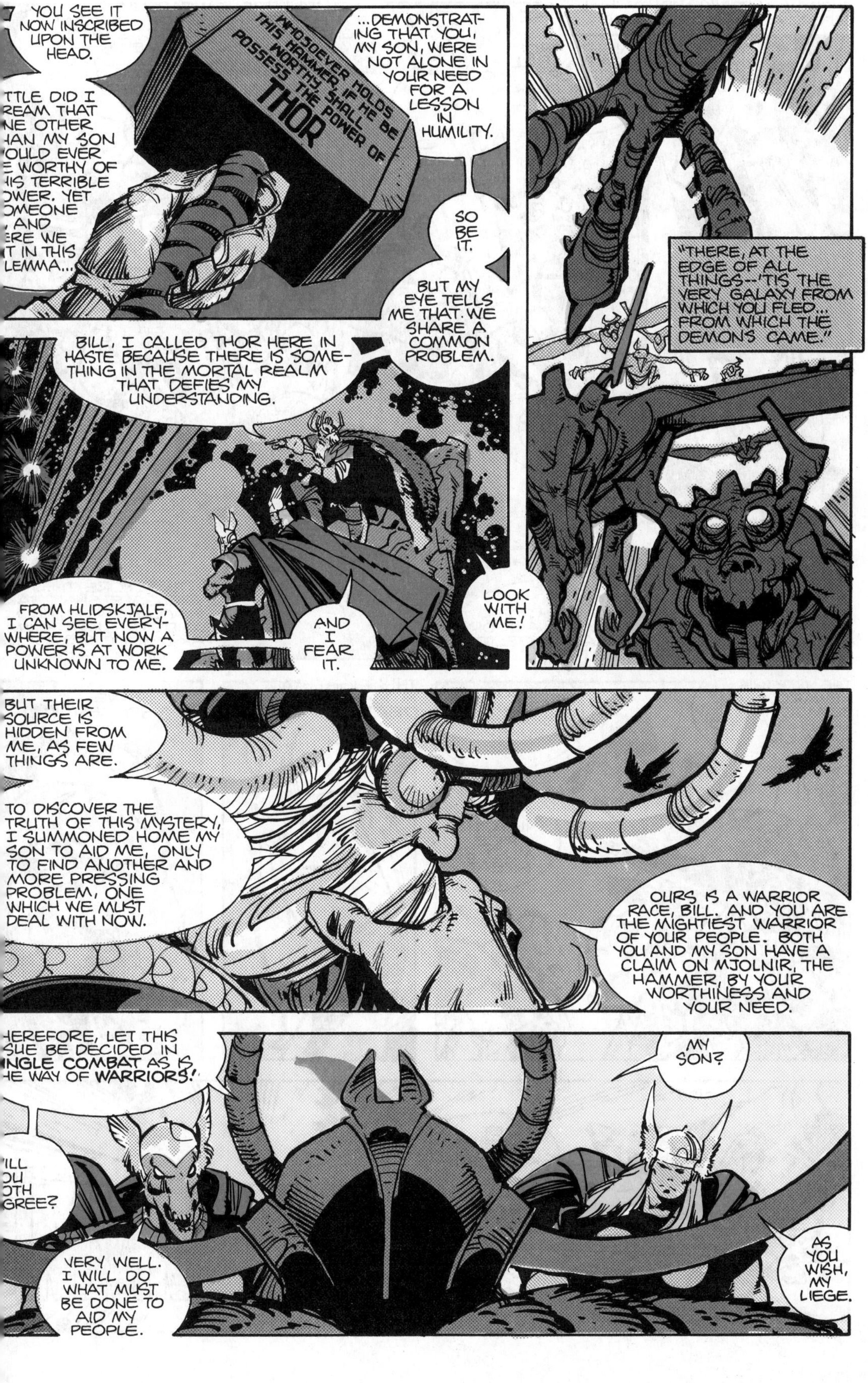

YOU SEE IT NOW INSCRIBED UPON THE HEAD.
WHOSOEVER HOLDS THIS HAMMER, IF HE BE WORTHY, SHALL POSSESS THE POWER OF THOR
TTLE DID I REAM THAT NE OTHER HAN MY SON OULD EVER E WORTHY OF HIS TERRIBLE OWER. YET OMEONE , AND ERE WE T IN THIS LEMMA...
...DEMONSTRATING THAT YOU, MY SON, WERE NOT ALONE IN YOUR NEED FOR A LESSON IN HUMILITY.
SO BE IT.
BUT MY EYE TELLS ME THAT WE SHARE A COMMON PROBLEM.
"THERE, AT THE EDGE OF ALL THINGS--'TIS THE VERY GALAXY FROM WHICH YOU FLED... FROM WHICH THE DEMONS CAME."
BILL, I CALLED THOR HERE IN HASTE BECAUSE THERE IS SOMETHING IN THE MORTAL REALM THAT DEFIES MY UNDERSTANDING.
FROM HLIDSKJALF, I CAN SEE EVERYWHERE, BUT NOW A POWER IS AT WORK UNKNOWN TO ME.
AND I FEAR IT.
LOOK WITH ME!
BUT THEIR SOURCE IS HIDDEN FROM ME, AS FEW THINGS ARE.
TO DISCOVER THE TRUTH OF THIS MYSTERY, I SUMMONED HOME MY SON TO AID ME, ONLY TO FIND ANOTHER AND MORE PRESSING PROBLEM, ONE WHICH WE MUST DEAL WITH NOW.
OURS IS A WARRIOR RACE, BILL. AND YOU ARE THE MIGHTIEST WARRIOR OF YOUR PEOPLE. BOTH YOU AND MY SON HAVE A CLAIM ON MJOLNIR, THE HAMMER, BY YOUR WORTHINESS AND YOUR NEED.
HEREFORE, LET THIS SUE BE DECIDED IN NGLE COMBAT AS IS HE WAY OF WARRIORS!
MY SON?
ILL OU OTH GREE?
VERY WELL. I WILL DO WHAT MUST BE DONE TO AID MY PEOPLE.
AS YOU WISH, MY LIEGE.

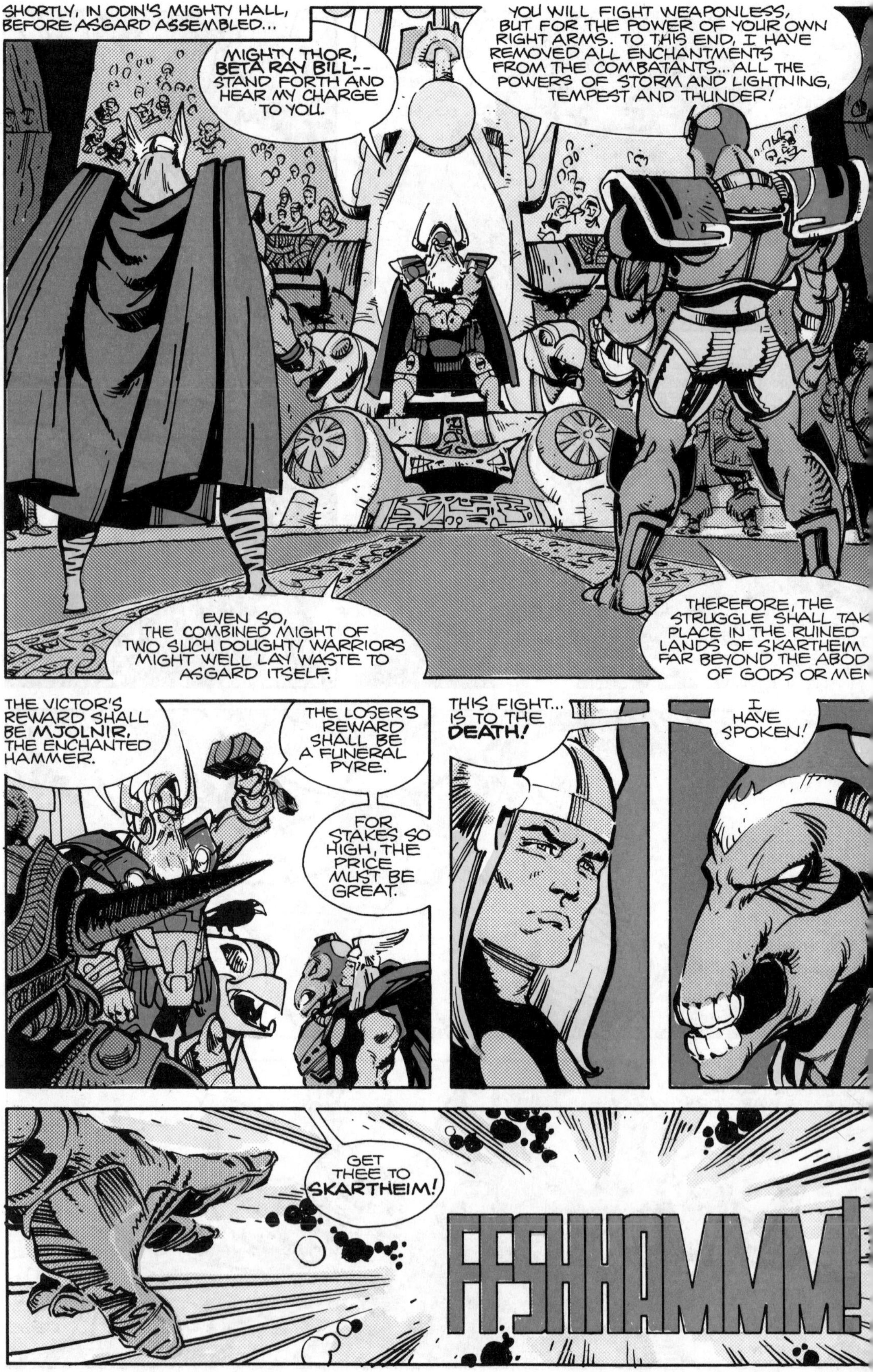
SHORTLY, IN ODIN'S MIGHTY HALL, BEFORE ASGARD ASSEMBLED...
MIGHTY THOR, BETA RAY BILL-- STAND FORTH AND HEAR MY CHARGE TO YOU.
YOU WILL FIGHT WEAPONLESS, BUT FOR THE POWER OF YOUR OWN RIGHT ARMS. TO THIS END, I HAVE REMOVED ALL ENCHANTMENTS FROM THE COMBATANTS... ALL THE POWERS OF STORM AND LIGHTNING, TEMPEST AND THUNDER!
EVEN SO, THE COMBINED MIGHT OF TWO SUCH DOUGHTY WARRIORS MIGHT WELL LAY WASTE TO ASGARD ITSELF.
THEREFORE, THE STRUGGLE SHALL TAK PLACE IN THE RUINED LANDS OF SKARTHEIM FAR BEYOND THE ABOD OF GODS OR MEN
THE VICTOR'S REWARD SHALL BE MJOLNIR, THE ENCHANTED HAMMER.
THE LOSER'S REWARD SHALL BE A FUNERAL PYRE.
FOR STAKES SO HIGH, THE PRICE MUST BE GREAT.
THIS FIGHT... IS TO THE DEATH!
I HAVE SPOKEN!
GET THEE TO SKARTHEIM!
FFSHHAMMM!

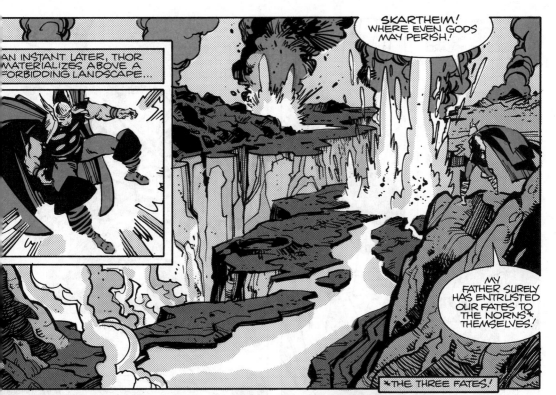

AN INSTANT LATER, THOR MATERIALIZES ABOVE A FORBIDDING LANDSCAPE...

SKARTHEIM! WHERE EVEN GODS MAY PERISH!

MY FATHER SURELY HAS ENTRUSTED OUR FATES TO THE NORNS* THEMSELVES!

*THE THREE FATES!

...BUT I DO NOT SEE MY OPPONENT.

NO DOUBT LORD ODIN CAUSED HIM TO APPEAR ELSEWHERE IN THIS DANGEROUS REALM.

I FEEL THE HEAT OF THE EARTH ITSELF!

THE VERY GROUND ERUPTS BENEATH MY FEET!

I MUST TAKE MYSELF TO A SAFER PERCH!

UHGG!

NAY, THUNDER GOD, THERE IS NO SAFETY IN ALL THIS LAND AS LONG AS ONE OF US REMAINS ALIVE!

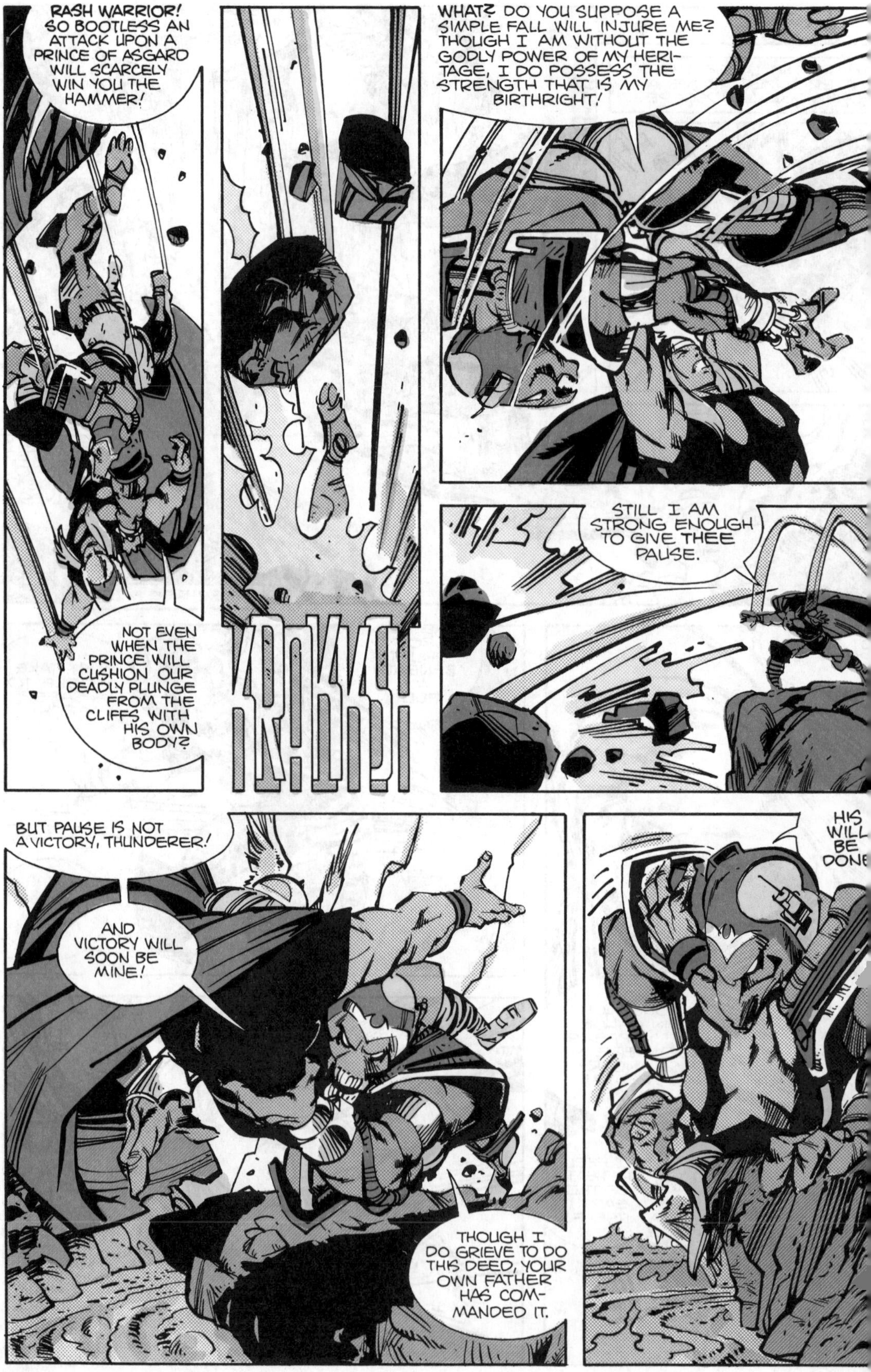
RASH WARRIOR! SO BOOTLESS AN ATTACK UPON A PRINCE OF ASGARD WILL SCARCELY WIN YOU THE HAMMER!
NOT EVEN WHEN THE PRINCE WILL CUSHION OUR DEADLY PLUNGE FROM THE CLIFFS WITH HIS OWN BODY?
KRAKKSH
WHAT? DO YOU SUPPOSE A SIMPLE FALL WILL INJURE ME? THOUGH I AM WITHOUT THE GODLY POWER OF MY HERITAGE, I DO POSSESS THE STRENGTH THAT IS MY BIRTHRIGHT!
STILL I AM STRONG ENOUGH TO GIVE THEE PAUSE.
BUT PAUSE IS NOT A VICTORY, THUNDERER!
AND VICTORY WILL SOON BE MINE!
THOUGH I DO GRIEVE TO DO THIS DEED, YOUR OWN FATHER HAS COMMANDED IT.
HIS WILL BE DONE

T EVERYONE IN ASGARD, HOWEVER, IS ATTENDING THE MIGHTY HALL OF ODIN TO WITNESS THIS
ANIC STRUGGLE. ELSEWHERE IN THE DESERTED BOULEVARDS OF THE GOLDEN CITY...
ALDER, MY RIEND, I EAR YOU DO OT PROPERLY PPRECIATE HE TRUE HILOSOPHY F EATING!
TAKE ME, FOR INSTANCE. SOME SAY I EAT BECAUSE I HAVE A WIFE WHO COULD SINK A LONGSHIP AND EIGHTEEN SCREAMING OFF-SPRING WHOSE FURY WOULD DAUNT NOBLE ODIN HIMSELF!
URRILOUS LIES! EAT BECAUSE I JOY IT. IT IS POS-LY THE GREATEST EASURE IN LIFE! D ONE OF THE W I HAVE LEFT, I MAY SAY SO.
BUT NOBLE FRIEND, EATING SHOULD BE AN AFFIRMATION OF LIFE, NOT AN ESCAPE FROM IT.
SHOULD YOU NOT TASTE MORE KEENLY THE JOYS OF LIVING, BALDER, YOU WHO ALONE AMONG US HAS TASTED DEATH ITSELF?
ONE WOULD THINK SO, VOLSTAGG, MY FRIEND.
BUT THE VISIONS I HAVE SEEN TROUBLE ME CEASE-LESSLY.
THE FACES OF THOSE I HAVE SLAIN IN HONORABLE COMBAT ARE NOW MORE REAL TO ME THAN THE BRIGHT BLUE SKIES OF ASGARD.
D THE SAVOR OF NG SEEMS FOREVER ST TO ME NOW. AN EMPTY DREAM.
THEN PERHAPS THE DREAMER SHOULD RETURN TO HIS FINAL REST!
EH? WHO--?
I AM AGNAR, SON OF HROTHGAR! I HAVE COME FROM VANAHEIM SEEKING BALDER, WHOSE FAME TELLS OF HIS PROWESS IN BATTLE.
I WOULD CHAL-LENGE HIM TO FIGHT IF HE BE NOT A COWARD...
...AND PROVE TO ME THAT HE IS A BETTER WARRIOR THAN I!

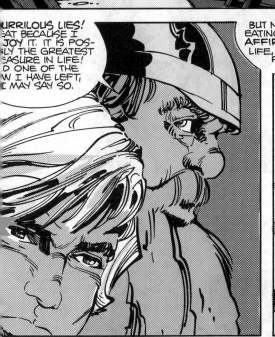

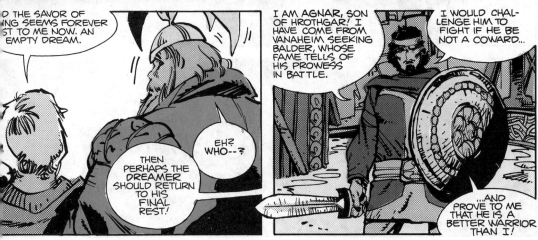

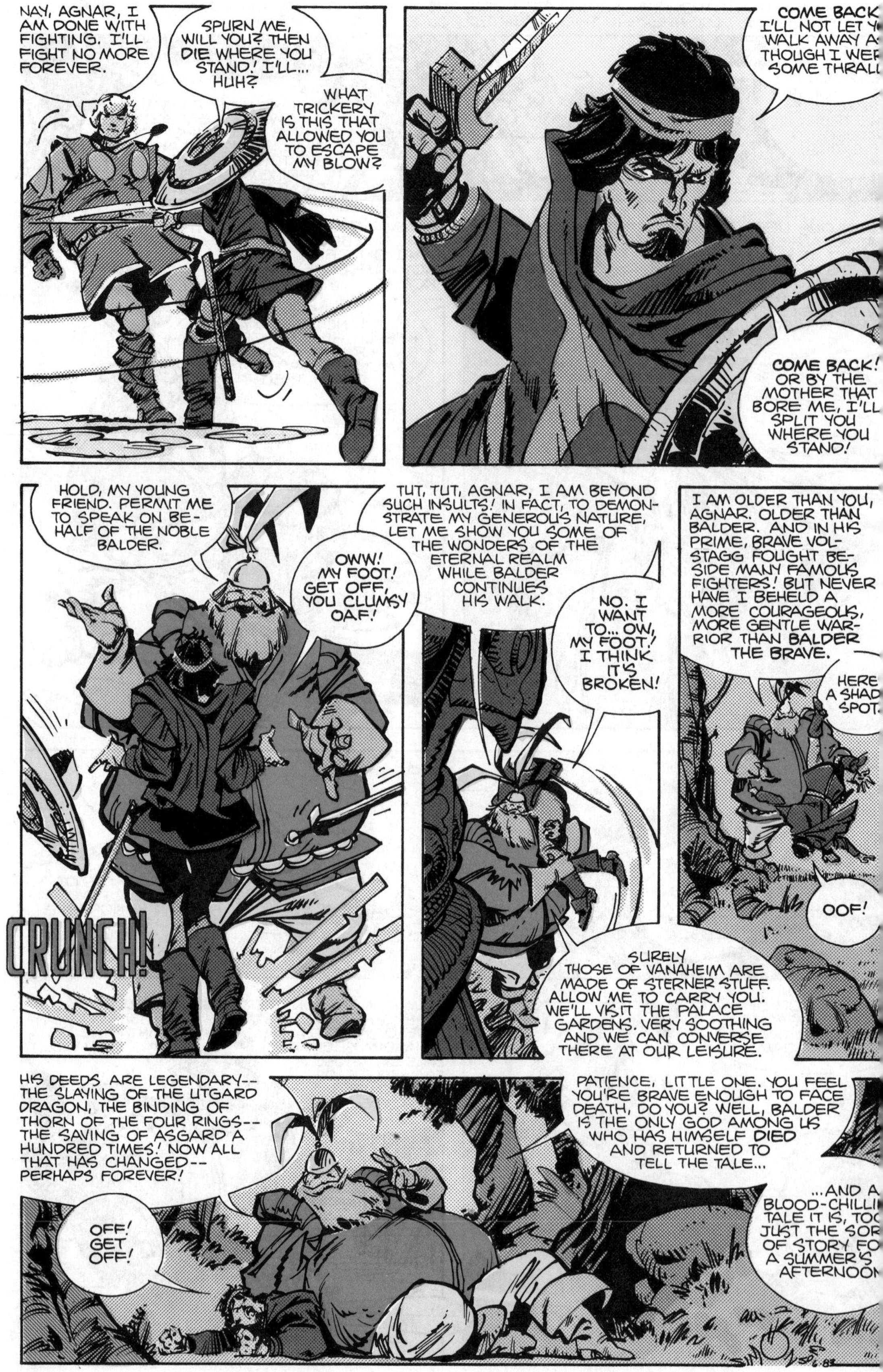
NAY, AGNAR, I AM DONE WITH FIGHTING. I'LL FIGHT NO MORE FOREVER.
SPURN ME, WILL YOU? THEN DIE WHERE YOU STAND! I'LL... HUH?
WHAT TRICKERY IS THIS THAT ALLOWED YOU TO ESCAPE MY BLOW?
COME BACK I'LL NOT LET Y WALK AWAY A THOUGH I WER SOME THRAL
COME BACK! OR BY THE MOTHER THAT BORE ME, I'LL SPLIT YOU WHERE YOU STAND!
HOLD, MY YOUNG FRIEND. PERMIT ME TO SPEAK ON BEHALF OF THE NOBLE BALDER.
OWW! MY FOOT! GET OFF, YOU CLUMSY OAF!
CRUNCH!
TUT, TUT, AGNAR, I AM BEYOND SUCH INSULTS! IN FACT, TO DEMONSTRATE MY GENEROUS NATURE, LET ME SHOW YOU SOME OF THE WONDERS OF THE ETERNAL REALM WHILE BALDER CONTINUES HIS WALK.
NO. I WANT TO... OW, MY FOOT! I THINK IT'S BROKEN!
SURELY THOSE OF VANAHEIM ARE MADE OF STERNER STUFF. ALLOW ME TO CARRY YOU. WE'LL VISIT THE PALACE GARDENS. VERY SOOTHING AND WE CAN CONVERSE THERE AT OUR LEISURE.
I AM OLDER THAN YOU, AGNAR. OLDER THAN BALDER. AND IN HIS PRIME, BRAVE VOLSTAGG FOUGHT BESIDE MANY FAMOUS FIGHTERS! BUT NEVER HAVE I BEHELD A MORE COURAGEOUS, MORE GENTLE WARRIOR THAN BALDER THE BRAVE.
HERE A SHAD SPOT.
OOF!
HIS DEEDS ARE LEGENDARY-- THE SLAYING OF THE UTGARD DRAGON, THE BINDING OF THORN OF THE FOUR RINGS-- THE SAVING OF ASGARD A HUNDRED TIMES! NOW ALL THAT HAS CHANGED-- PERHAPS FOREVER!
OFF! GET OFF!
PATIENCE, LITTLE ONE. YOU FEEL YOU'RE BRAVE ENOUGH TO FACE DEATH, DO YOU? WELL, BALDER IS THE ONLY GOD AMONG US WHO HAS HIMSELF DIED AND RETURNED TO TELL THE TALE...
...AND A BLOOD-CHILLI TALE IT IS, TOO JUST THE SOR OF STORY FO A SUMMER'S AFTERNOON

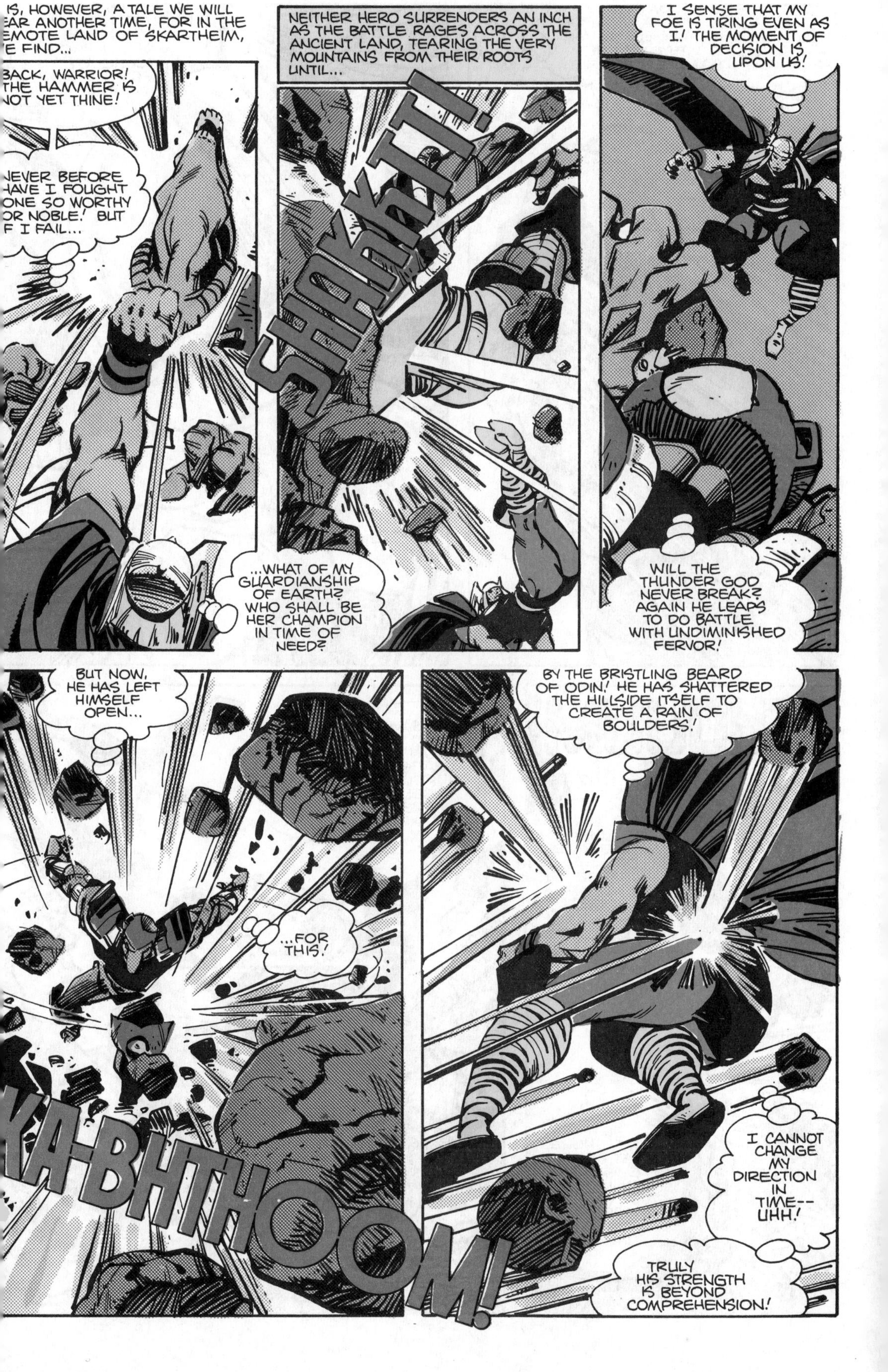

IS, HOWEVER, A TALE WE WILL
EAR ANOTHER TIME, FOR IN THE
EMOTE LAND OF SKARTHEIM,
E FIND...
BACK, WARRIOR! THE HAMMER IS NOT YET THINE!
NEVER BEFORE HAVE I FOUGHT ONE SO WORTHY OR NOBLE! BUT F I FAIL...
NEITHER HERO SURRENDERS AN INCH AS THE BATTLE RAGES ACROSS THE ANCIENT LAND, TEARING THE VERY MOUNTAINS FROM THEIR ROOTS UNTIL...
SHRAKT!
...WHAT OF MY GUARDIANSHIP OF EARTH? WHO SHALL BE HER CHAMPION IN TIME OF NEED?
I SENSE THAT MY FOE IS TIRING EVEN AS I! THE MOMENT OF DECISION IS UPON US!
WILL THE THUNDER GOD NEVER BREAK? AGAIN HE LEAPS TO DO BATTLE WITH UNDIMINISHED FERVOR!
BUT NOW, HE HAS LEFT HIMSELF OPEN...
...FOR THIS!
YA-BHTHOOOM!
BY THE BRISTLING BEARD OF ODIN! HE HAS SHATTERED THE HILLSIDE ITSELF TO CREATE A RAIN OF BOULDERS!
I CANNOT CHANGE MY DIRECTION IN TIME-- UHH!
TRULY HIS STRENGTH IS BEYOND COMPREHENSION!

STILL, I AM PRO-VIDED WITH A WEAPON THAT MAY SERVE ME AS WELL AS THE HAMMER OVER WHICH WE FIGHT!

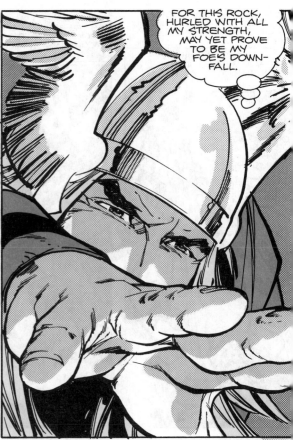

FOR THIS ROCK, HURLED WITH ALL MY STRENGTH, MAY YET PROVE TO BE MY FOE'S DOWN-FALL.

BTHOUUM!

I'M FALLING INTO THE RIVER OF LAVA! CAN THIS BE THE END OF MY QUEST?

BUT WAIT! THERE! THAT RAFT OF OBSIDIAN! IF ONLY I CAN TWIST MYSELF AROUND IN TIME--!

SAVED! YET EVEN NOW, MY FOE LEAPS UPON ME! SURELY, I MUST GIRD MYSELF, FOR THE SUPREME MOMENT IS AT HAND!

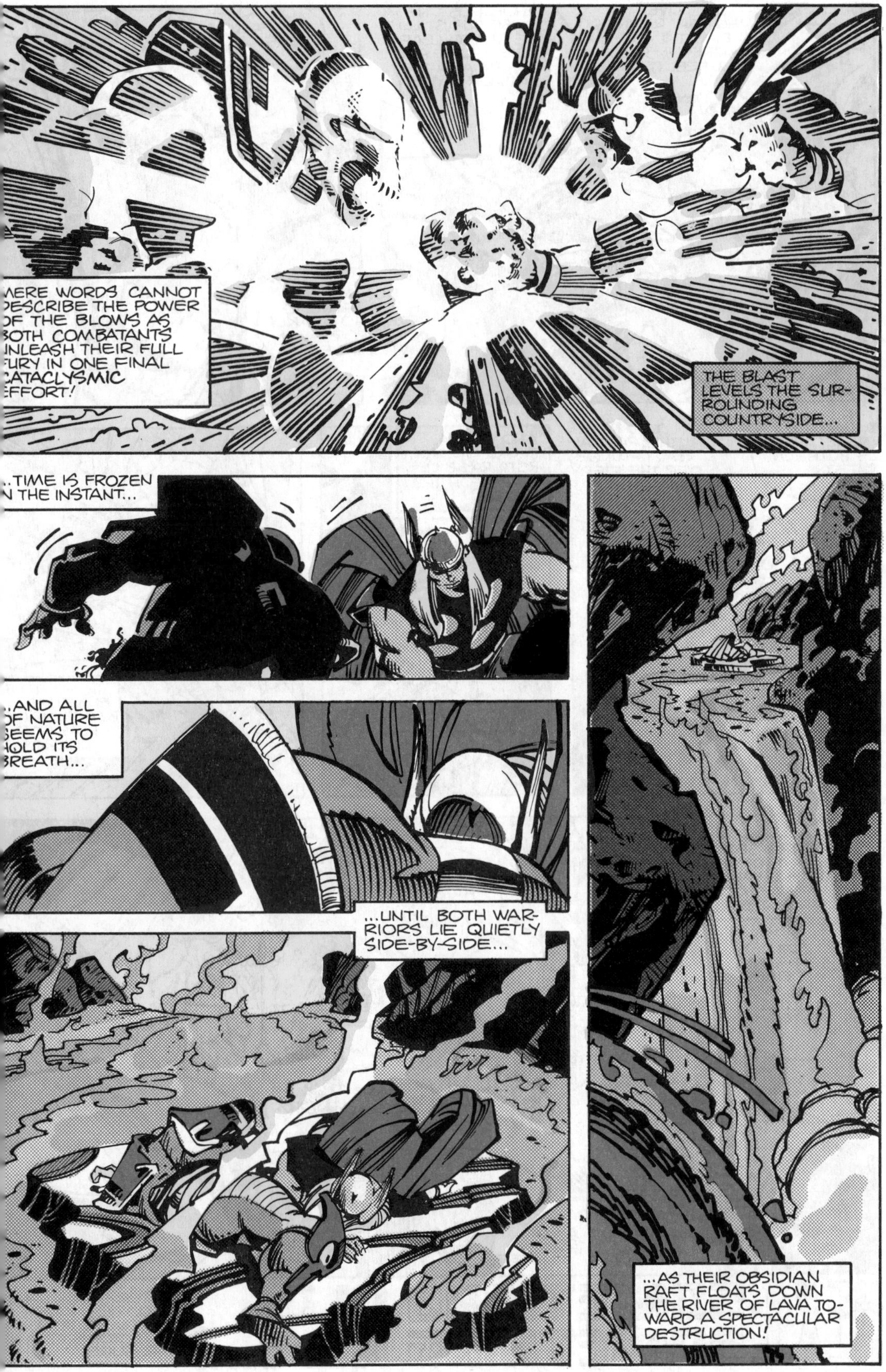
MERE WORDS CANNOT DESCRIBE THE POWER OF THE BLOWS AS BOTH COMBATANTS UNLEASH THEIR FULL FURY IN ONE FINAL CATACLYSMIC EFFORT!
THE BLAST LEVELS THE SURROUNDING COUNTRYSIDE...
...TIME IS FROZEN IN THE INSTANT...
...AND ALL OF NATURE SEEMS TO HOLD ITS BREATH...
...UNTIL BOTH WARRIORS LIE QUIETLY SIDE-BY-SIDE...
...AS THEIR OBSIDIAN RAFT FLOATS DOWN THE RIVER OF LAVA TOWARD A SPECTACULAR DESTRUCTION!

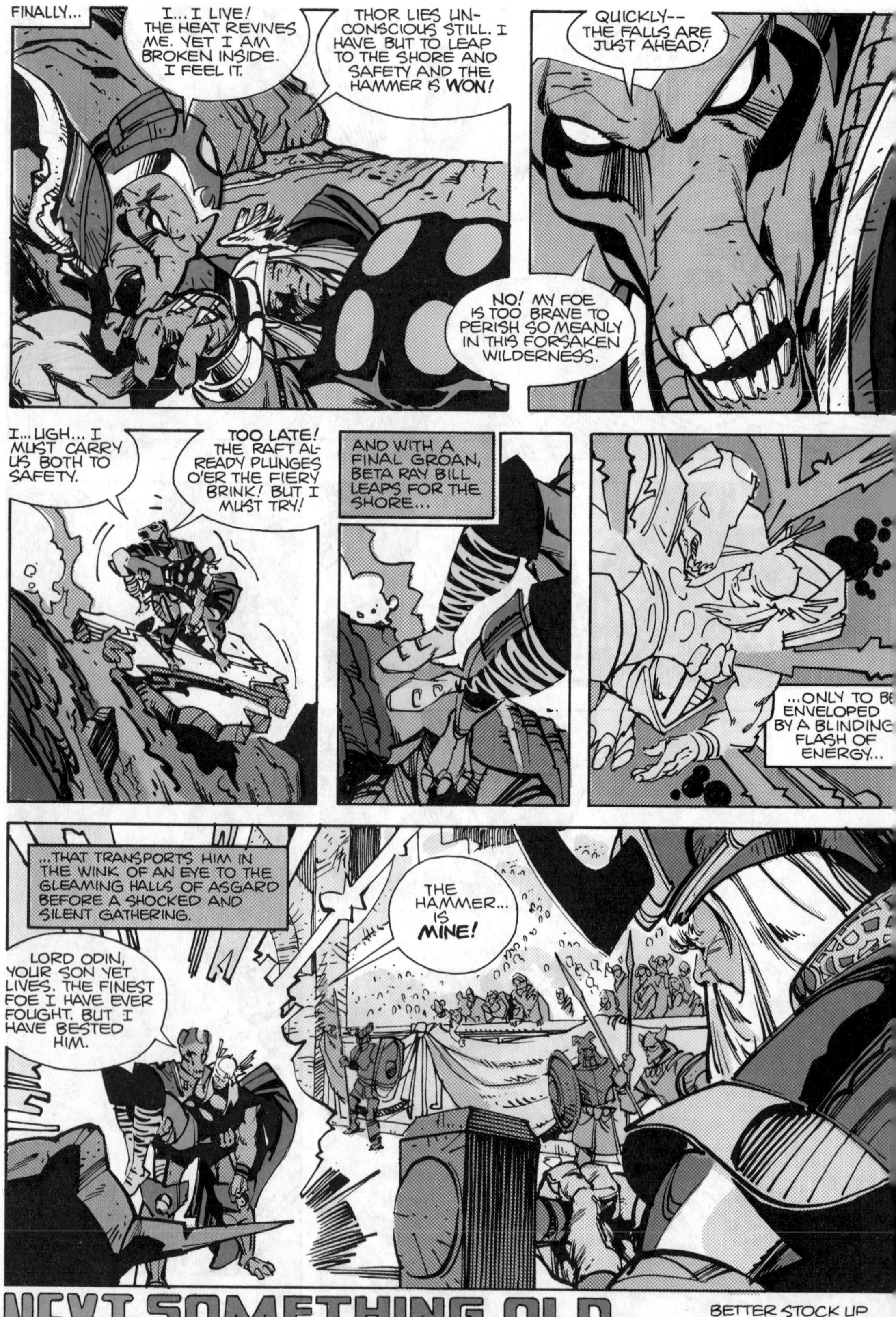
FINALLY...
I... I LIVE! THE HEAT REVIVES ME. YET I AM BROKEN INSIDE. I FEEL IT.
THOR LIES UN-CONSCIOUS STILL. I HAVE BUT TO LEAP TO THE SHORE AND SAFETY AND THE HAMMER IS WON!
QUICKLY-- THE FALLS ARE JUST AHEAD!
NO! MY FOE IS TOO BRAVE TO PERISH SO MEANLY IN THIS FORSAKEN WILDERNESS.
I... UGH... I MUST CARRY US BOTH TO SAFETY.
TOO LATE! THE RAFT AL-READY PLUNGES O'ER THE FIERY BRINK! BUT I MUST TRY!
AND WITH A FINAL GROAN, BETA RAY BILL LEAPS FOR THE SHORE...
...ONLY TO BE ENVELOPED BY A BLINDING FLASH OF ENERGY...
...THAT TRANSPORTS HIM IN THE WINK OF AN EYE TO THE GLEAMING HALLS OF ASGARD BEFORE A SHOCKED AND SILENT GATHERING.
THE HAMMER... IS MINE!
LORD ODIN, YOUR SON YET LIVES. THE FINEST FOE I HAVE EVER FOUGHT. BUT I HAVE BESTED HIM.
NEXT: SOMETHING OLD, SOMETHING NEW...!
BETTER STOCK UP ON COPIES, KIDS! THIS ONE'LL BE A COLLECTOR'S ITEM FOR SURE!

Chapter Three

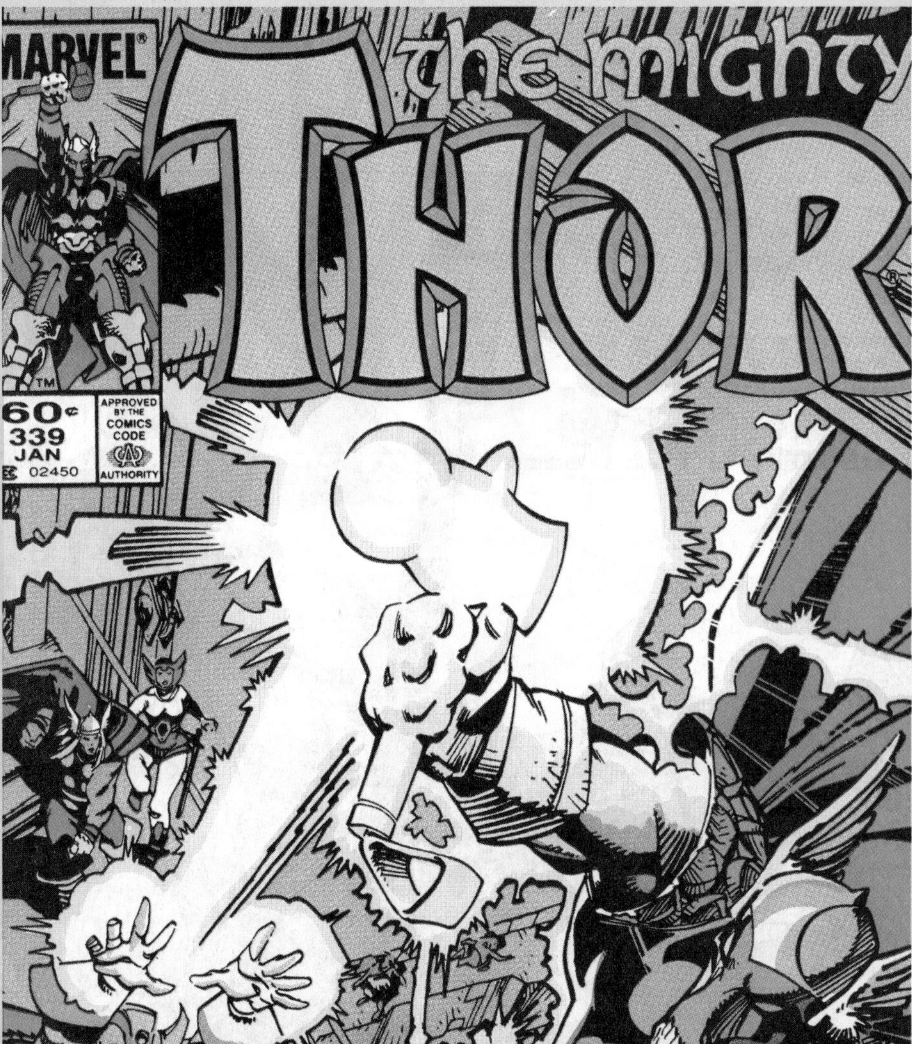
MARVEL
the mighty
THOR
60¢
339
JAN
02450
APPROVED BY THE COMICS CODE AUTHORITY

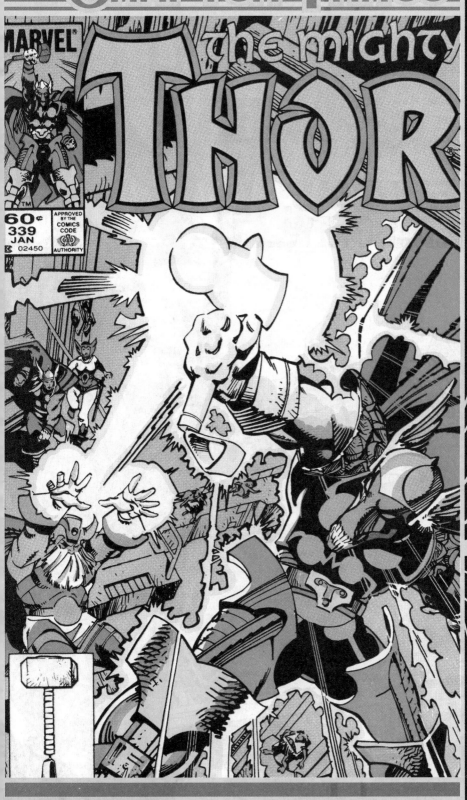

STAN LEE PRESENTS: the MIGHTY THOR®

MOMENTS AGO, **BETA RAY BILL**, A BIONIC ALIEN, BESTED THE MIGHTY THOR IN SINGLE COMBAT AND SO WON THE RIGHT TO POSSESS THOR'S ENCHANTED HAMMER, **MJOLNIR**.*

BUT EVEN AS HE ANNOUNCES HIS VICTORY BEFORE THE STUNNED ASGARDIANS...

SOMETHING OLD, SOMETHING NEW...

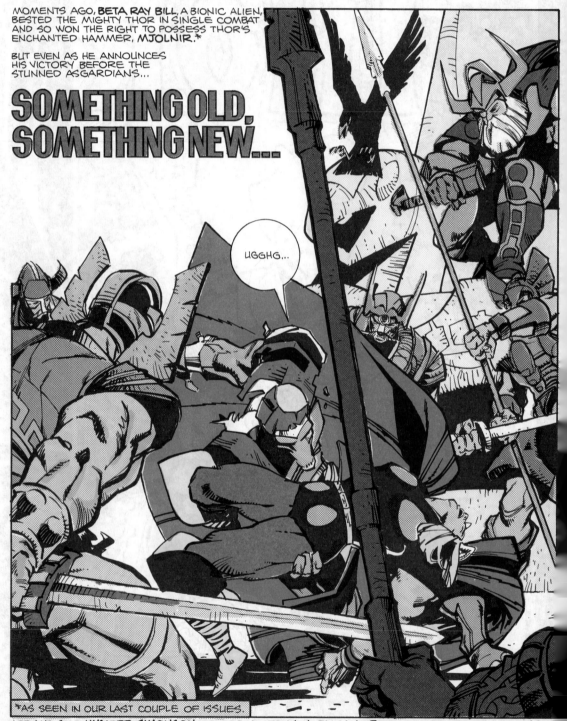

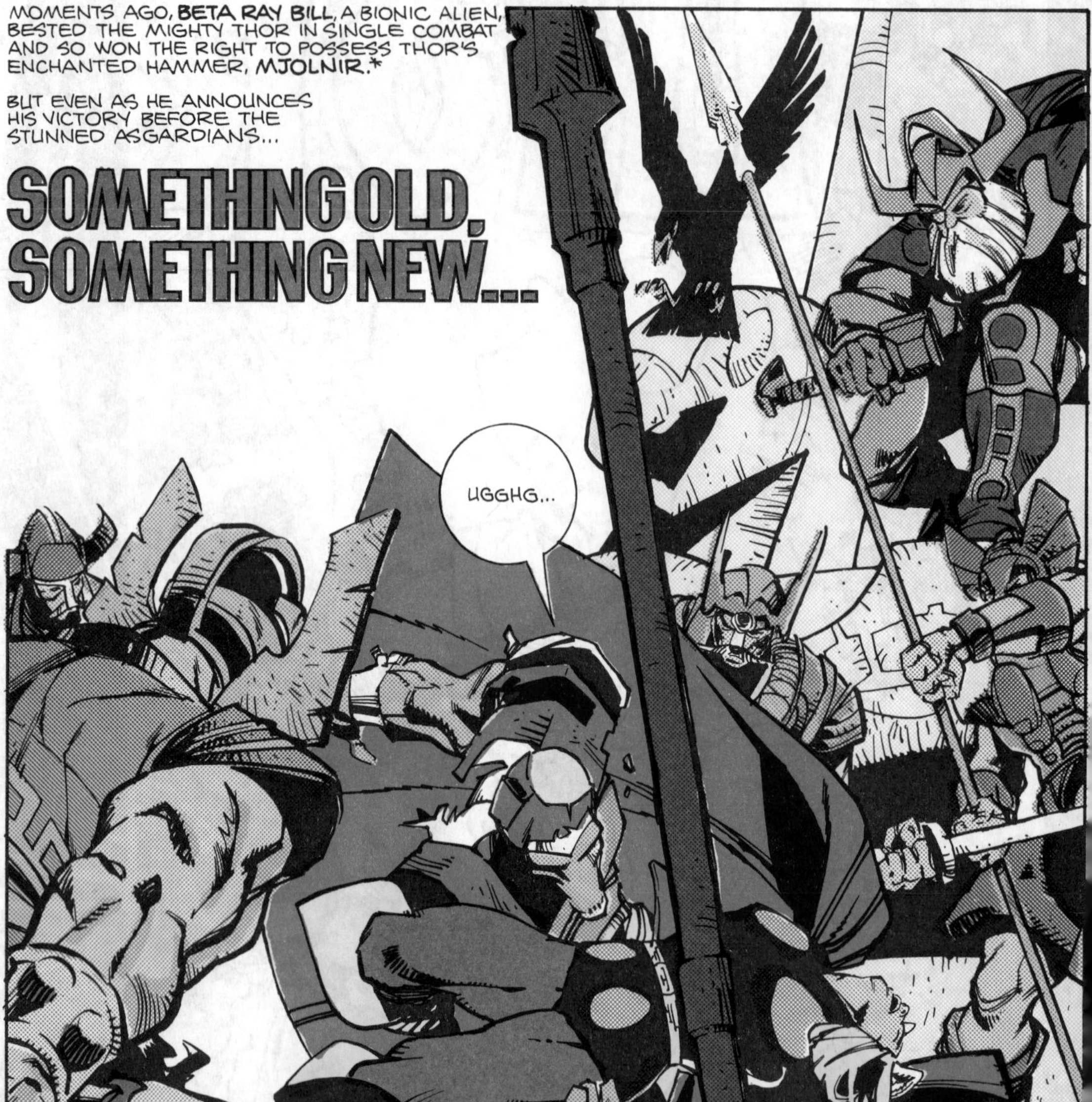
UGGHG...

*AS SEEN IN OUR LAST COUPLE OF ISSUES.

ART AND STORY: **WALTER SIMONSON** • LETTERING: **JOHN WORKMAN, JR.** • COLORS: **GEORGE ROUSSOS**
EDITING: **MIKE CARLIN** • EDITOR-IN-CHIEF: **JIM SHOOTER**

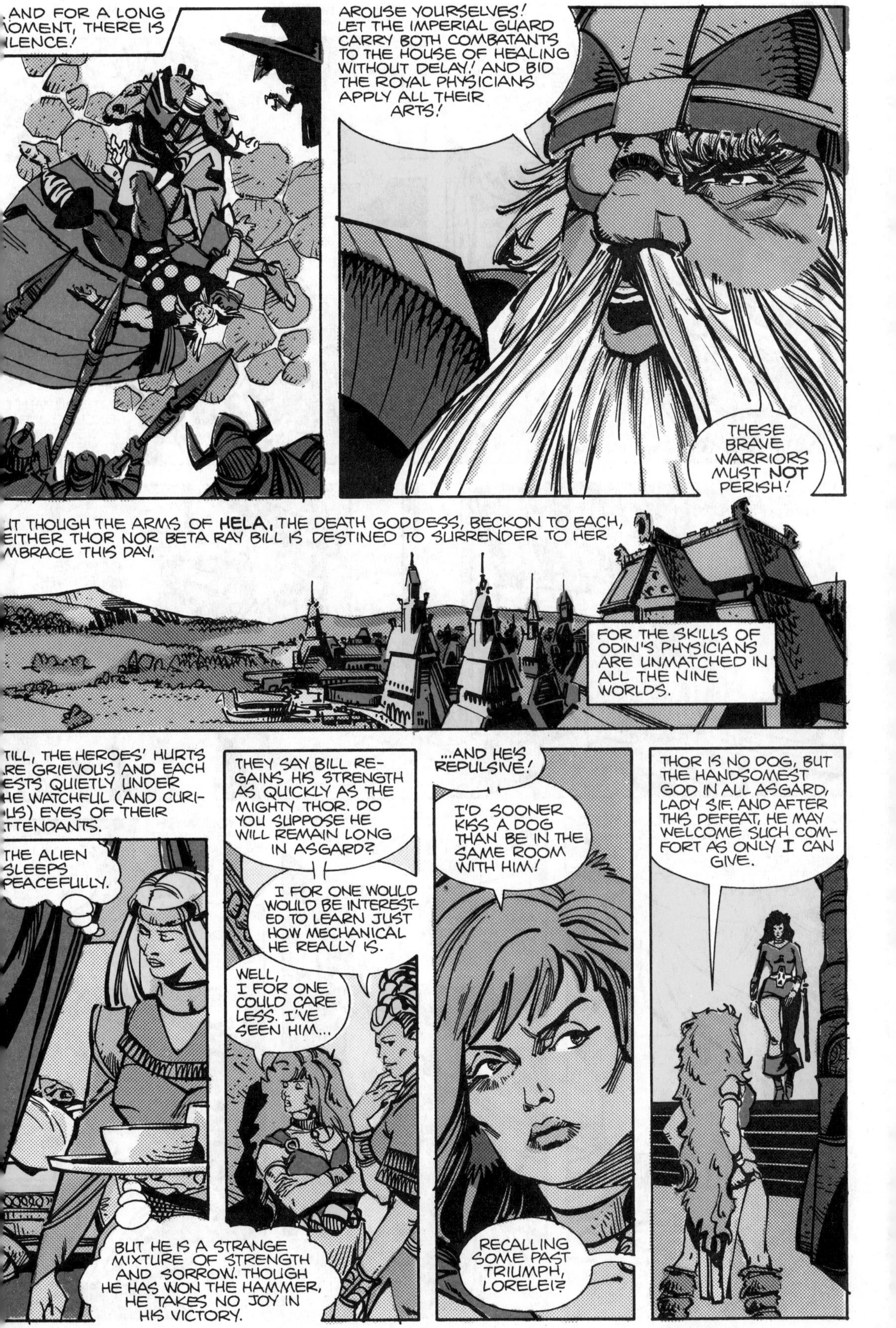

AND FOR A LONG
MOMENT, THERE IS
SILENCE!
AROUSE YOURSELVES! LET THE IMPERIAL GUARD CARRY BOTH COMBATANTS TO THE HOUSE OF HEALING WITHOUT DELAY! AND BID THE ROYAL PHYSICIANS APPLY ALL THEIR ARTS!
THESE BRAVE WARRIORS MUST NOT PERISH!
UT THOUGH THE ARMS OF HELA, THE DEATH GODDESS, BECKON TO EACH, EITHER THOR NOR BETA RAY BILL IS DESTINED TO SURRENDER TO HER MBRACE THIS DAY.
FOR THE SKILLS OF ODIN'S PHYSICIANS ARE UNMATCHED IN ALL THE NINE WORLDS.
TILL, THE HEROES' HURTS RE GRIEVOUS AND EACH ESTS QUIETLY UNDER HE WATCHFUL (AND CURI-US) EYES OF THEIR TTENDANTS.
THE ALIEN SLEEPS PEACEFULLY.
BUT HE IS A STRANGE MIXTURE OF STRENGTH AND SORROW. THOUGH HE HAS WON THE HAMMER, HE TAKES NO JOY IN HIS VICTORY.
THEY SAY BILL REGAINS HIS STRENGTH AS QUICKLY AS THE MIGHTY THOR. DO YOU SUPPOSE HE WILL REMAIN LONG IN ASGARD?
I FOR ONE WOULD WOULD BE INTERESTED TO LEARN JUST HOW MECHANICAL HE REALLY IS.
WELL, I FOR ONE COULD CARE LESS. I'VE SEEN HIM...
...AND HE'S REPULSIVE!
I'D SOONER KISS A DOG THAN BE IN THE SAME ROOM WITH HIM!
RECALLING SOME PAST TRIUMPH, LORELEI?
THOR IS NO DOG, BUT THE HANDSOMEST GOD IN ALL ASGARD, LADY SIF. AND AFTER THIS DEFEAT, HE MAY WELCOME SUCH COMFORT AS ONLY I CAN GIVE.

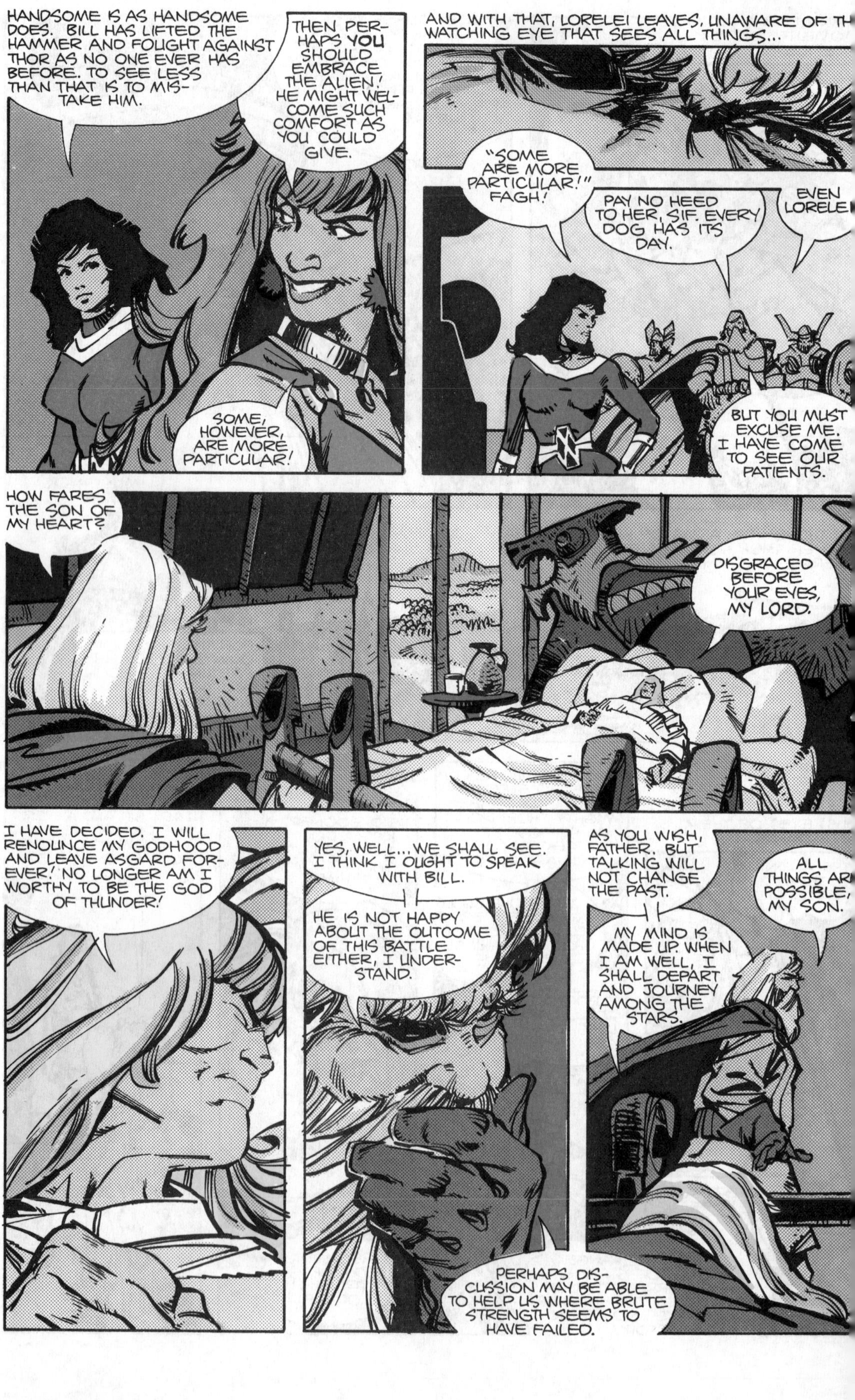

HANDSOME IS AS HANDSOME DOES. BILL HAS LIFTED THE HAMMER AND FOUGHT AGAINST THOR AS NO ONE EVER HAS BEFORE. TO SEE LESS THAN THAT IS TO MISTAKE HIM.
THEN PERHAPS YOU SHOULD EMBRACE THE ALIEN! HE MIGHT WELCOME SUCH COMFORT AS YOU COULD GIVE.
SOME, HOWEVER, ARE MORE PARTICULAR!
AND WITH THAT, LORELEI LEAVES, UNAWARE OF TH WATCHING EYE THAT SEES ALL THINGS...
"SOME ARE MORE PARTICULAR!" FAGH!
PAY NO HEED TO HER, SIF. EVERY DOG HAS ITS DAY.
EVEN LORELE
BUT YOU MUST EXCUSE ME. I HAVE COME TO SEE OUR PATIENTS.
HOW FARES THE SON OF MY HEART?
DISGRACED BEFORE YOUR EYES, MY LORD.
I HAVE DECIDED. I WILL RENOUNCE MY GODHOOD AND LEAVE ASGARD FOREVER! NO LONGER AM I WORTHY TO BE THE GOD OF THUNDER!
YES, WELL... WE SHALL SEE. I THINK I OUGHT TO SPEAK WITH BILL.
HE IS NOT HAPPY ABOUT THE OUTCOME OF THIS BATTLE EITHER, I UNDERSTAND.
PERHAPS DISCUSSION MAY BE ABLE TO HELP US WHERE BRUTE STRENGTH SEEMS TO HAVE FAILED.
AS YOU WISH, FATHER. BUT TALKING WILL NOT CHANGE THE PAST.
MY MIND IS MADE UP. WHEN I AM WELL, I SHALL DEPART AND JOURNEY AMONG THE STARS.
ALL THINGS AR POSSIBLE, MY SON.

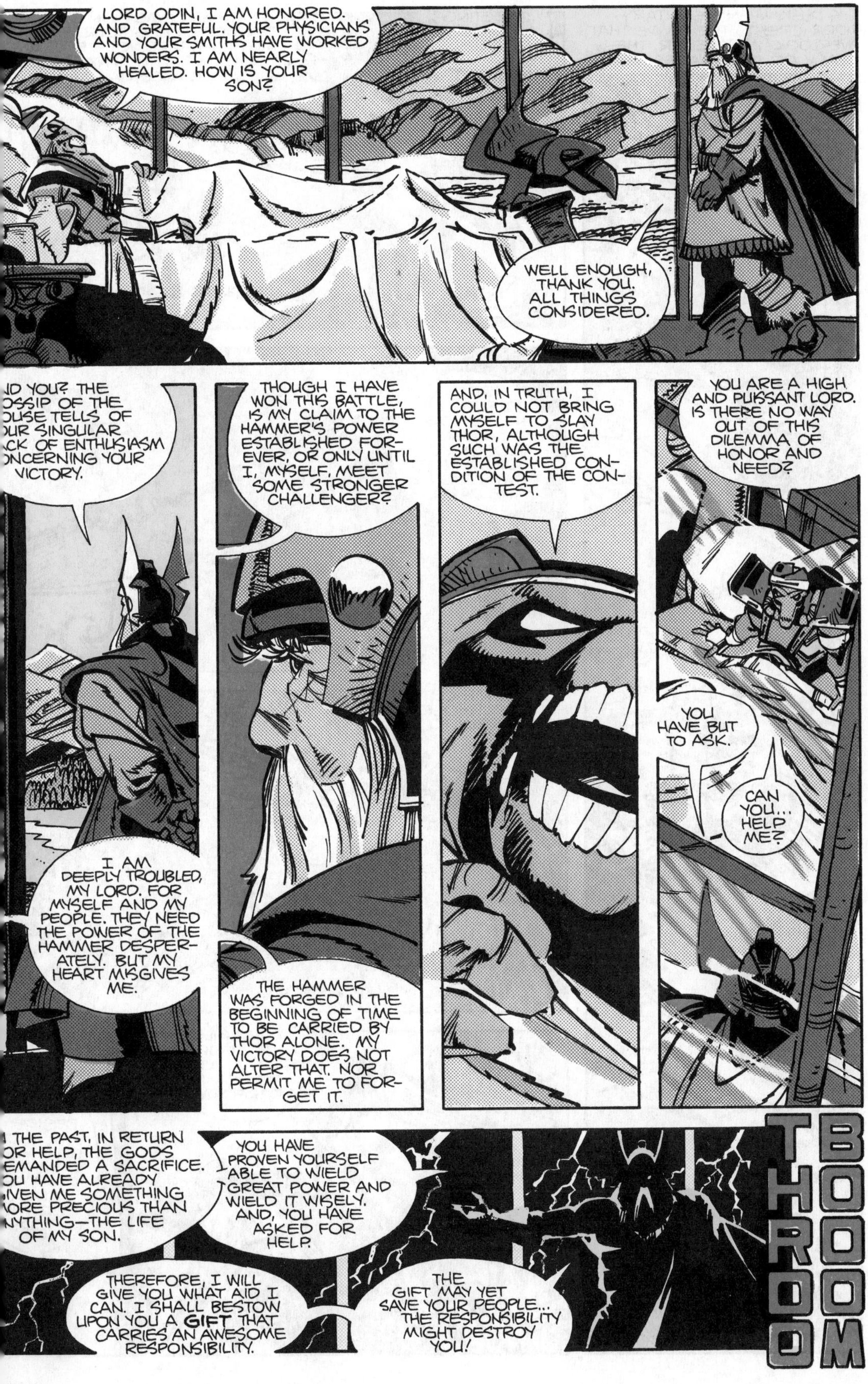
LORD ODIN, I AM HONORED. AND GRATEFUL. YOUR PHYSICIANS AND YOUR SMITHS HAVE WORKED WONDERS. I AM NEARLY HEALED. HOW IS YOUR SON?
WELL ENOUGH, THANK YOU. ALL THINGS CONSIDERED.
ND YOU? THE OSSIP OF THE OUSE TELLS OF OUR SINGULAR CK OF ENTHUSIASM ONCERNING YOUR VICTORY.
I AM DEEPLY TROUBLED, MY LORD. FOR MYSELF AND MY PEOPLE. THEY NEED THE POWER OF THE HAMMER DESPERATELY. BUT MY HEART MISGIVES ME.
THOUGH I HAVE WON THIS BATTLE, IS MY CLAIM TO THE HAMMER'S POWER ESTABLISHED FOREVER, OR ONLY UNTIL I, MYSELF, MEET SOME STRONGER CHALLENGER?
THE HAMMER WAS FORGED IN THE BEGINNING OF TIME TO BE CARRIED BY THOR ALONE. MY VICTORY DOES NOT ALTER THAT. NOR PERMIT ME TO FORGET IT.
AND, IN TRUTH, I COULD NOT BRING MYSELF TO SLAY THOR, ALTHOUGH SUCH WAS THE ESTABLISHED CONDITION OF THE CONTEST.
YOU ARE A HIGH AND PUISSANT LORD. IS THERE NO WAY OUT OF THIS DILEMMA OF HONOR AND NEED?
YOU HAVE BUT TO ASK.
CAN YOU... HELP ME?
N THE PAST, IN RETURN OR HELP, THE GODS EMANDED A SACRIFICE. OU HAVE ALREADY IVEN ME SOMETHING MORE PRECIOUS THAN NYTHING—THE LIFE OF MY SON.
YOU HAVE PROVEN YOURSELF ABLE TO WIELD GREAT POWER AND WIELD IT WISELY. AND, YOU HAVE ASKED FOR HELP.
THEREFORE, I WILL GIVE YOU WHAT AID I CAN. I SHALL BESTOW UPON YOU A GIFT THAT CARRIES AN AWESOME RESPONSIBILITY.
THE GIFT MAY YET SAVE YOUR PEOPLE... THE RESPONSIBILITY MIGHT DESTROY YOU!
THROOOM
BOOOOOM

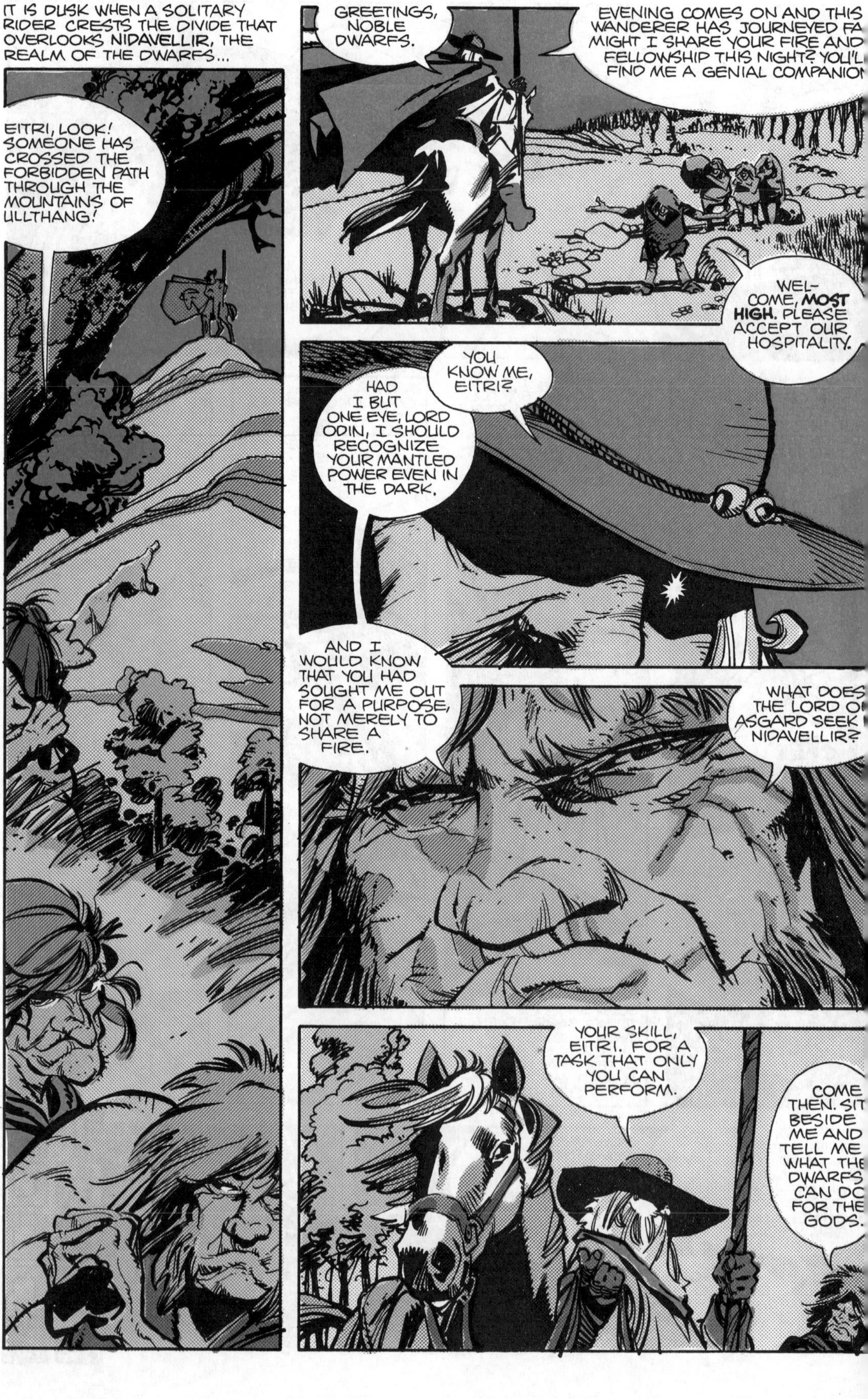
IT IS DUSK WHEN A SOLITARY RIDER CRESTS THE DIVIDE THAT OVERLOOKS NIDAVELLIR, THE REALM OF THE DWARFS...
EITRI, LOOK! SOMEONE HAS CROSSED THE FORBIDDEN PATH THROUGH THE MOUNTAINS OF ULLTHANG!
GREETINGS, NOBLE DWARFS.
EVENING COMES ON AND THIS WANDERER HAS JOURNEYED FA MIGHT I SHARE YOUR FIRE AND FELLOWSHIP THIS NIGHT? YOU'L FIND ME A GENIAL COMPANION
WEL-COME, MOST HIGH. PLEASE ACCEPT OUR HOSPITALITY.
YOU KNOW ME, EITRI?
HAD I BUT ONE EYE, LORD ODIN, I SHOULD RECOGNIZE YOUR MANTLED POWER EVEN IN THE DARK.
AND I WOULD KNOW THAT YOU HAD SOUGHT ME OUT FOR A PURPOSE, NOT MERELY TO SHARE A FIRE.
WHAT DOES THE LORD O ASGARD SEEK NIDAVELLIR?
YOUR SKILL, EITRI. FOR A TASK THAT ONLY YOU CAN PERFORM.
COME THEN. SIT BESIDE ME AND TELL ME WHAT THE DWARFS CAN DO FOR THE GODS.

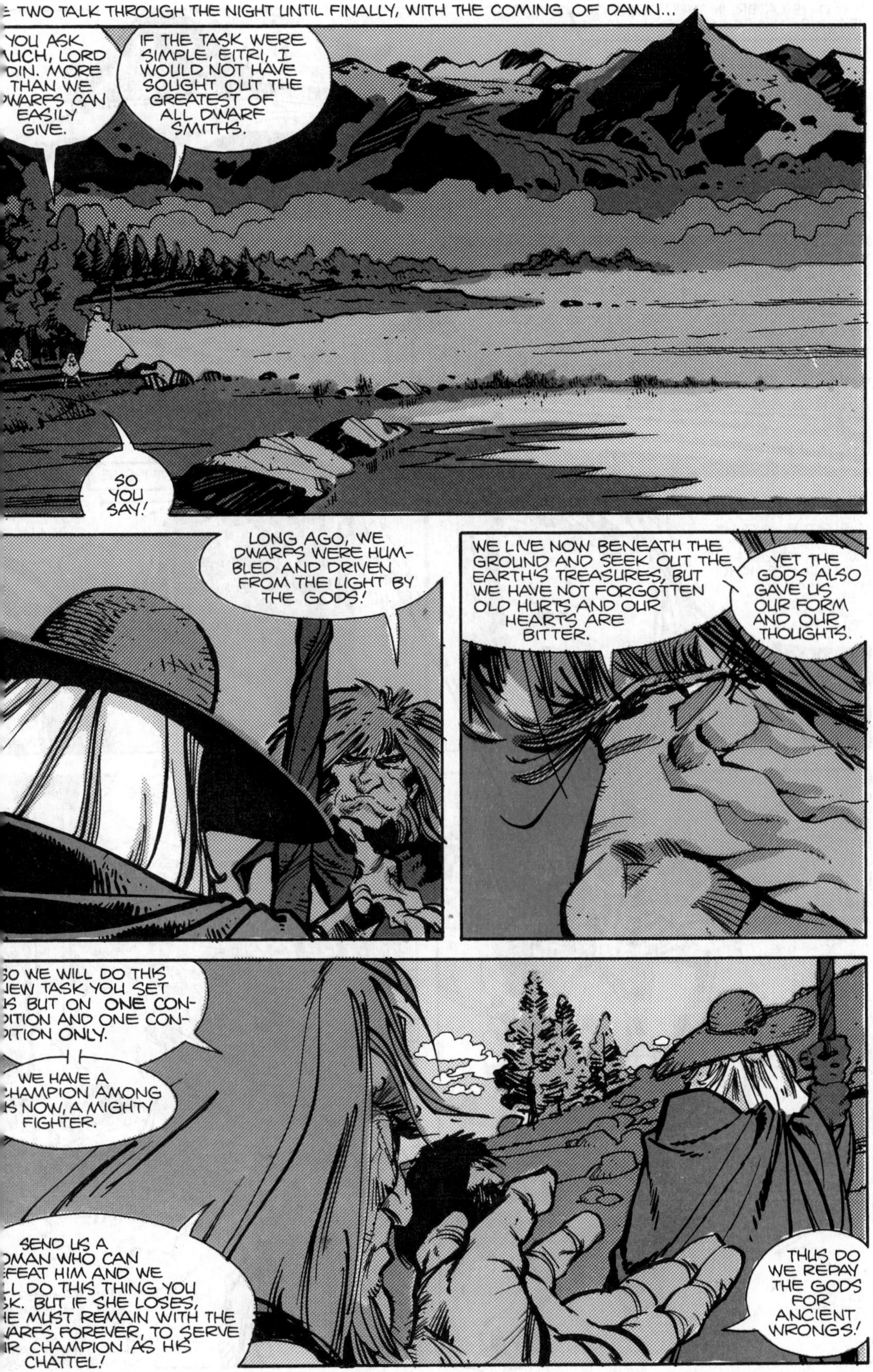
E TWO TALK THROUGH THE NIGHT UNTIL FINALLY, WITH THE COMING OF DAWN...
YOU ASK UCH, LORD DIN. MORE THAN WE WARFS CAN EASILY GIVE.
IF THE TASK WERE SIMPLE, EITRI, I WOULD NOT HAVE SOUGHT OUT THE GREATEST OF ALL DWARF SMITHS.
SO YOU SAY!
LONG AGO, WE DWARFS WERE HUMBLED AND DRIVEN FROM THE LIGHT BY THE GODS!
WE LIVE NOW BENEATH THE GROUND AND SEEK OUT THE EARTH'S TREASURES, BUT WE HAVE NOT FORGOTTEN OLD HURTS AND OUR HEARTS ARE BITTER.
YET THE GODS ALSO GAVE US OUR FORM AND OUR THOUGHTS.
SO WE WILL DO THIS NEW TASK YOU SET S BUT ON ONE CONDITION AND ONE CONDITION ONLY.
WE HAVE A CHAMPION AMONG S NOW, A MIGHTY FIGHTER.
SEND US A OMAN WHO CAN EFEAT HIM AND WE LL DO THIS THING YOU SK. BUT IF SHE LOSES, HE MUST REMAIN WITH THE WARFS FOREVER, TO SERVE R CHAMPION AS HIS CHATTEL!
THUS DO WE REPAY THE GODS FOR ANCIENT WRONGS!

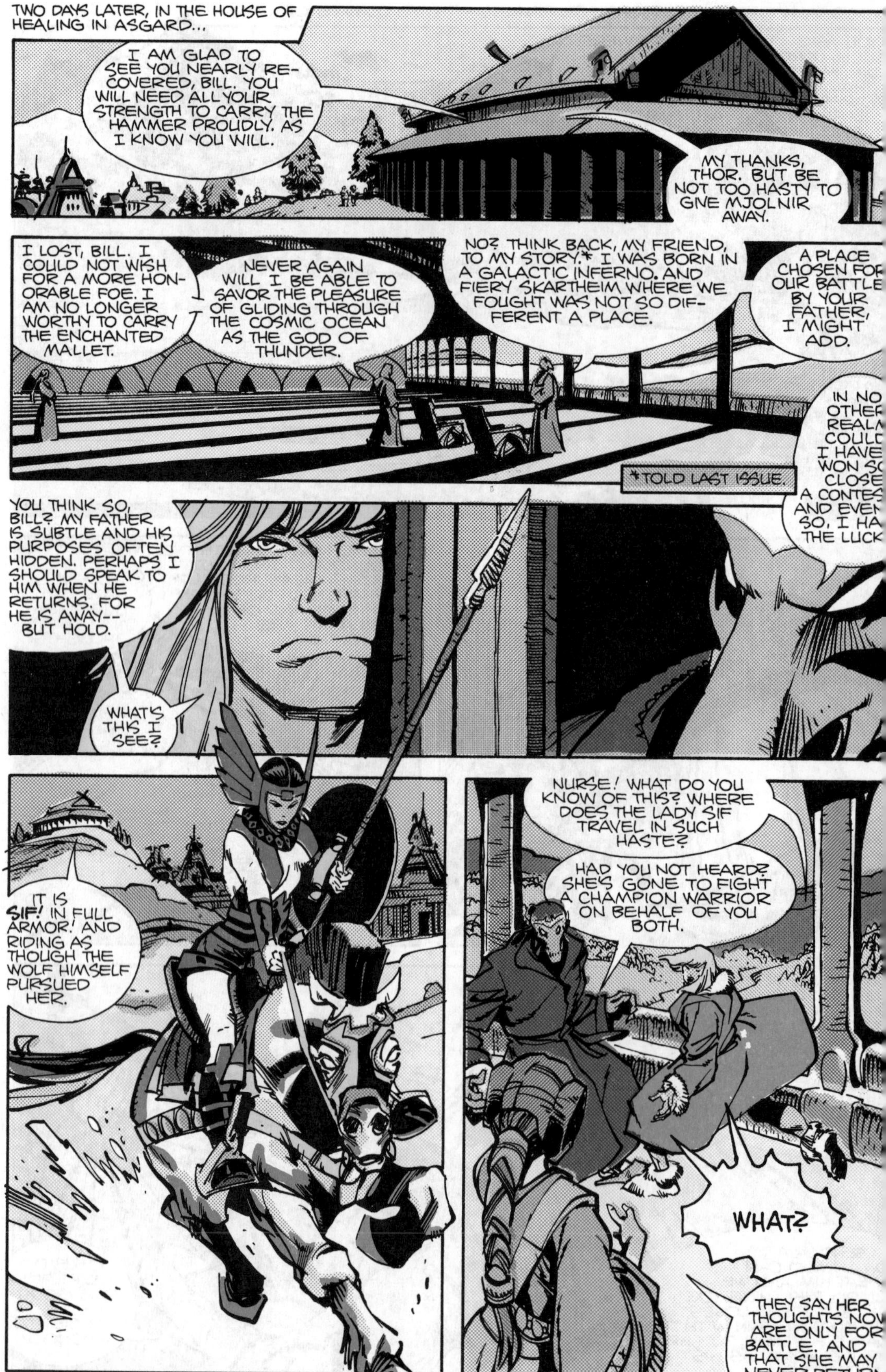
TWO DAYS LATER, IN THE HOUSE OF HEALING IN ASGARD...
I AM GLAD TO SEE YOU NEARLY RE-COVERED, BILL. YOU WILL NEED ALL YOUR STRENGTH TO CARRY THE HAMMER PROUDLY. AS I KNOW YOU WILL.
MY THANKS, THOR. BUT BE NOT TOO HASTY TO GIVE MJOLNIR AWAY.
I LOST, BILL. I COULD NOT WISH FOR A MORE HON-ORABLE FOE. I AM NO LONGER WORTHY TO CARRY THE ENCHANTED MALLET.
NEVER AGAIN WILL I BE ABLE TO SAVOR THE PLEASURE OF GLIDING THROUGH THE COSMIC OCEAN AS THE GOD OF THUNDER.
NO? THINK BACK, MY FRIEND, TO MY STORY.* I WAS BORN IN A GALACTIC INFERNO. AND FIERY SKARTHEIM WHERE WE FOUGHT WAS NOT SO DIF-FERENT A PLACE.
A PLACE CHOSEN FOR OUR BATTLE BY YOUR FATHER, I MIGHT ADD.
*TOLD LAST ISSUE.
IN NO OTHER REALM COULD I HAVE WON SO CLOSE A CONTEST AND EVEN SO, I HAD THE LUCK
YOU THINK SO, BILL? MY FATHER IS SUBTLE AND HIS PURPOSES OFTEN HIDDEN. PERHAPS I SHOULD SPEAK TO HIM WHEN HE RETURNS. FOR HE IS AWAY-- BUT HOLD.
WHAT'S THIS I SEE?
IT IS SIF! IN FULL ARMOR! AND RIDING AS THOUGH THE WOLF HIMSELF PURSUED HER.
NURSE! WHAT DO YOU KNOW OF THIS? WHERE DOES THE LADY SIF TRAVEL IN SUCH HASTE?
HAD YOU NOT HEARD? SHE'S GONE TO FIGHT A CHAMPION WARRIOR ON BEHALF OF YOU BOTH.
WHAT?
THEY SAY HER THOUGHTS NOW ARE ONLY FOR BATTLE. AND THAT SHE MAY NEVER RETURN

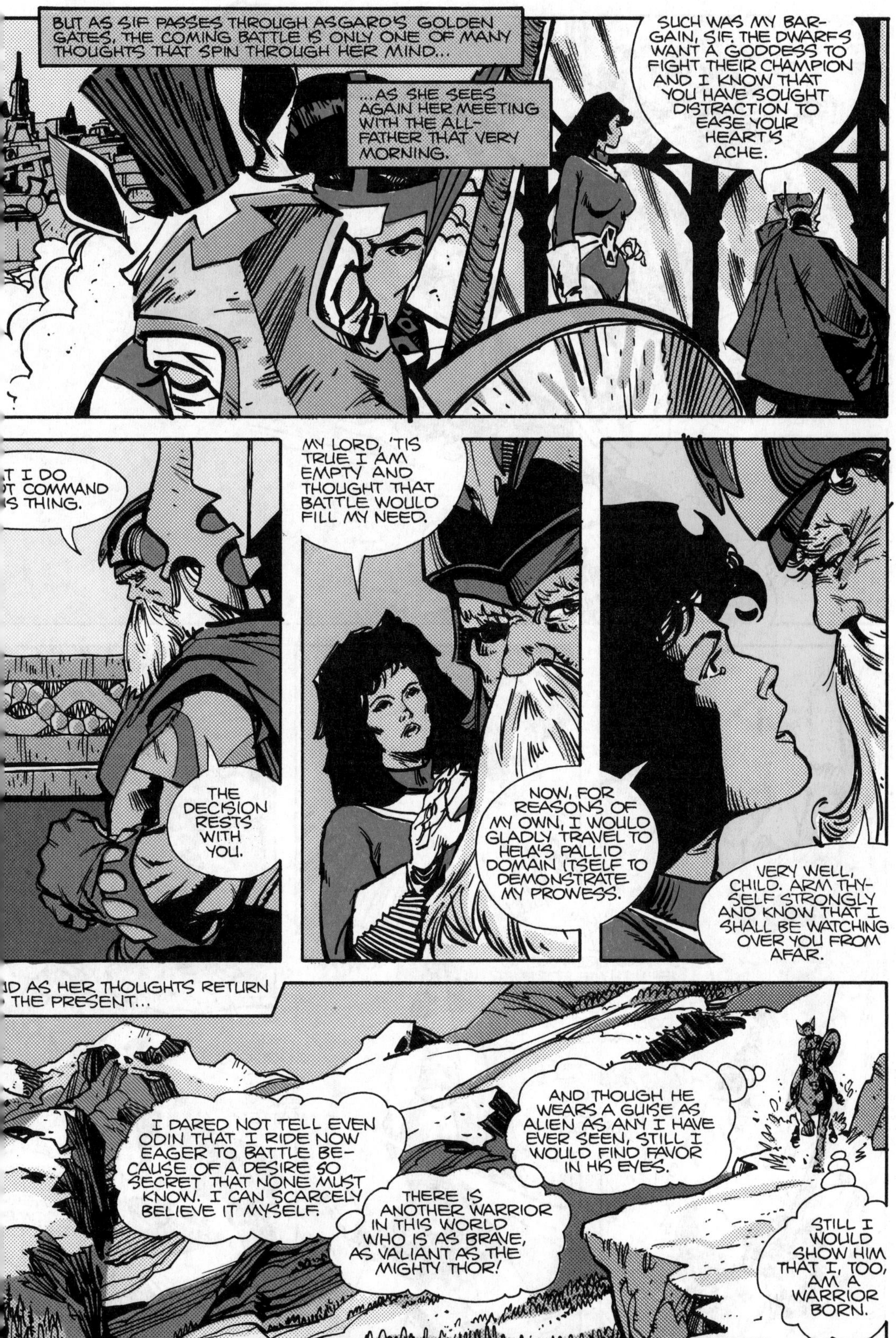
BUT AS SIF PASSES THROUGH ASGARD'S GOLDEN GATES, THE COMING BATTLE IS ONLY ONE OF MANY THOUGHTS THAT SPIN THROUGH HER MIND...
...AS SHE SEES AGAIN HER MEETING WITH THE ALL-FATHER THAT VERY MORNING.
SUCH WAS MY BARGAIN, SIF. THE DWARFS WANT A GODDESS TO FIGHT THEIR CHAMPION AND I KNOW THAT YOU HAVE SOUGHT DISTRACTION TO EASE YOUR HEART'S ACHE.
T I DO T COMMAND S THING.
THE DECISION RESTS WITH YOU.
MY LORD, 'TIS TRUE I AM EMPTY AND THOUGHT THAT BATTLE WOULD FILL MY NEED.
NOW, FOR REASONS OF MY OWN, I WOULD GLADLY TRAVEL TO HELA'S PALLID DOMAIN ITSELF TO DEMONSTRATE MY PROWESS.
VERY WELL, CHILD. ARM THYSELF STRONGLY AND KNOW THAT I SHALL BE WATCHING OVER YOU FROM AFAR.
D AS HER THOUGHTS RETURN THE PRESENT...
I DARED NOT TELL EVEN ODIN THAT I RIDE NOW EAGER TO BATTLE BECAUSE OF A DESIRE SO SECRET THAT NONE MUST KNOW. I CAN SCARCELY BELIEVE IT MYSELF.
THERE IS ANOTHER WARRIOR IN THIS WORLD WHO IS AS BRAVE, AS VALIANT AS THE MIGHTY THOR!
AND THOUGH HE WEARS A GUISE AS ALIEN AS ANY I HAVE EVER SEEN, STILL I WOULD FIND FAVOR IN HIS EYES.
STILL I WOULD SHOW HIM THAT I, TOO, AM A WARRIOR BORN.

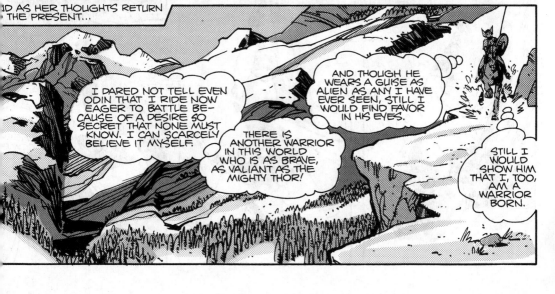

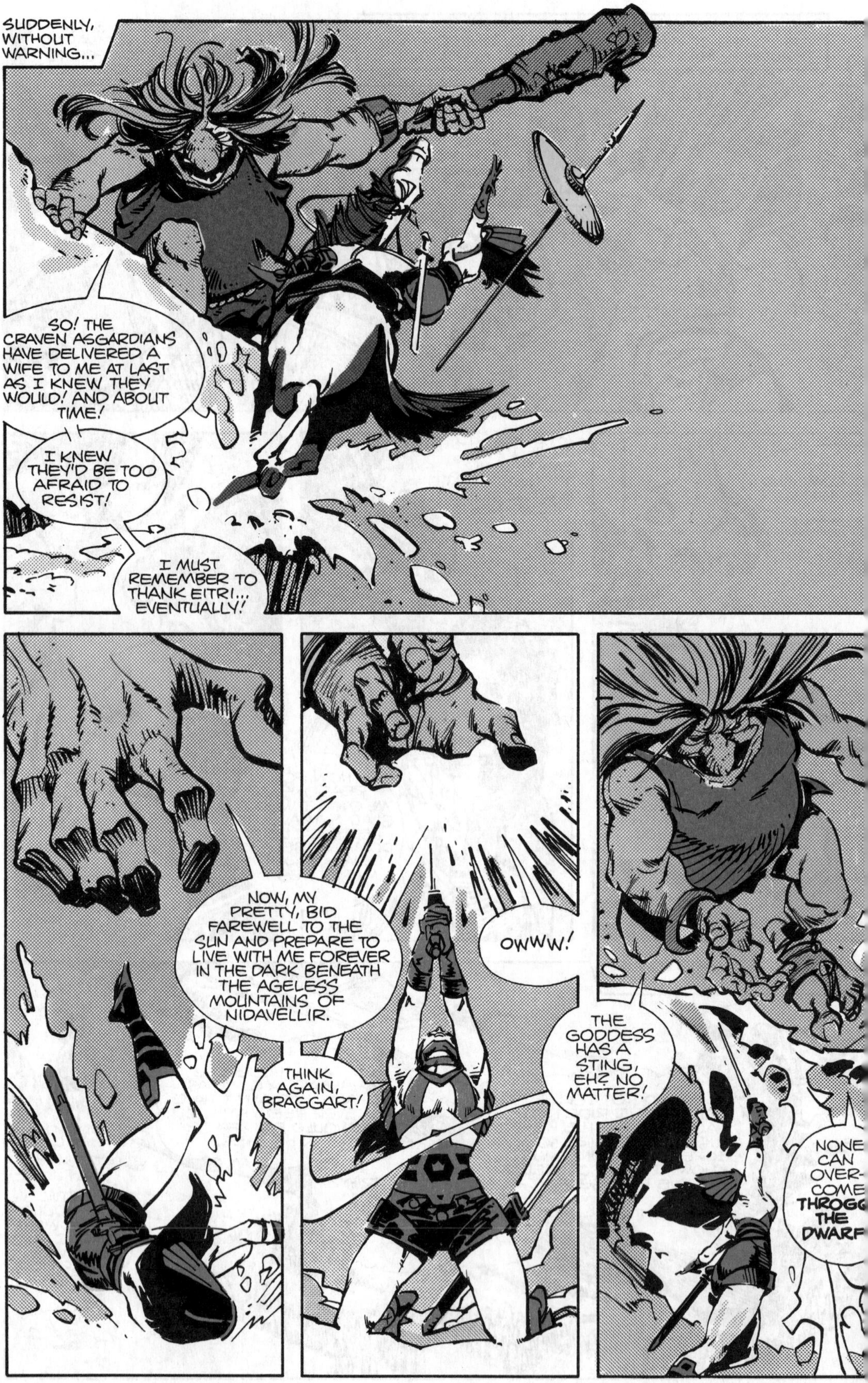
SUDDENLY, WITHOUT WARNING...
SO! THE CRAVEN ASGARDIANS HAVE DELIVERED A WIFE TO ME AT LAST AS I KNEW THEY WOULD! AND ABOUT TIME!
I KNEW THEY'D BE TOO AFRAID TO RESIST!
I MUST REMEMBER TO THANK EITRI... EVENTUALLY!
NOW, MY PRETTY, BID FAREWELL TO THE SUN AND PREPARE TO LIVE WITH ME FOREVER IN THE DARK BENEATH THE AGELESS MOUNTAINS OF NIDAVELLIR.
THINK AGAIN, BRAGGART!
OWWW!
THE GODDESS HAS A STING, EH? NO MATTER!
NONE CAN OVER-COME THROGG THE DWARF

EVEN AS THROGG LEAPS HIGH INTO THE AIR ABOVE SIF, WE TURN ELSEWHERE TO FIND, IN THE GARDENS OF ASGARD, VOLSTAGG THE ENORMOUS CHATTING WITH AGNAR OF VANAHEIM...

MARK WELL THESE WORDS, MY YOUNG FRIEND, AND I WILL TELL THE STORY OF BALDER THE BRAVE AND HIS TRAGIC DEATH AS ONLY VOLSTAGG CAN!

FROM THIS CAUTIONARY TALE, YOU WILL LEARN MORE THAN YOU EVER WISHED TO ABOUT MUCH THAT IS HIDDEN EVEN FROM THE GODS.

"IT BEGAN WITH AN ARROW MAGICALLY CREATED BY THE ARCH DECEIVER LOKI, HIMSELF, MADE OF THE LITTLE PLANT MISTLETOE. AND ON A BLACK DAY FOR ASGARD, THAT ARROW SLEW BRAVE BALDER.

"THOUGH ANOTHER HELD THE BOW, LOKI WAS THE PERPETRATOR OF THE CRIME, AND HE WAS PUNISHED.

"BUT BALDER'S FATE WAS UN- KNOWN TO US, AND ONLY AFTER HE RETURNED TO THESE GOLDEN HALLS DID WE LEARN OF THE DREADFUL DESTINY THAT AWAITED HIM IN THE MISTS OF THE NIFFLEHEIM...

"...THE LAND OF HELA, GODDESS OF DEATH...

"...A DESTINY TO MAKE EVEN VALOROUS VOLSTAGG TREMBLE WITH FEAR."

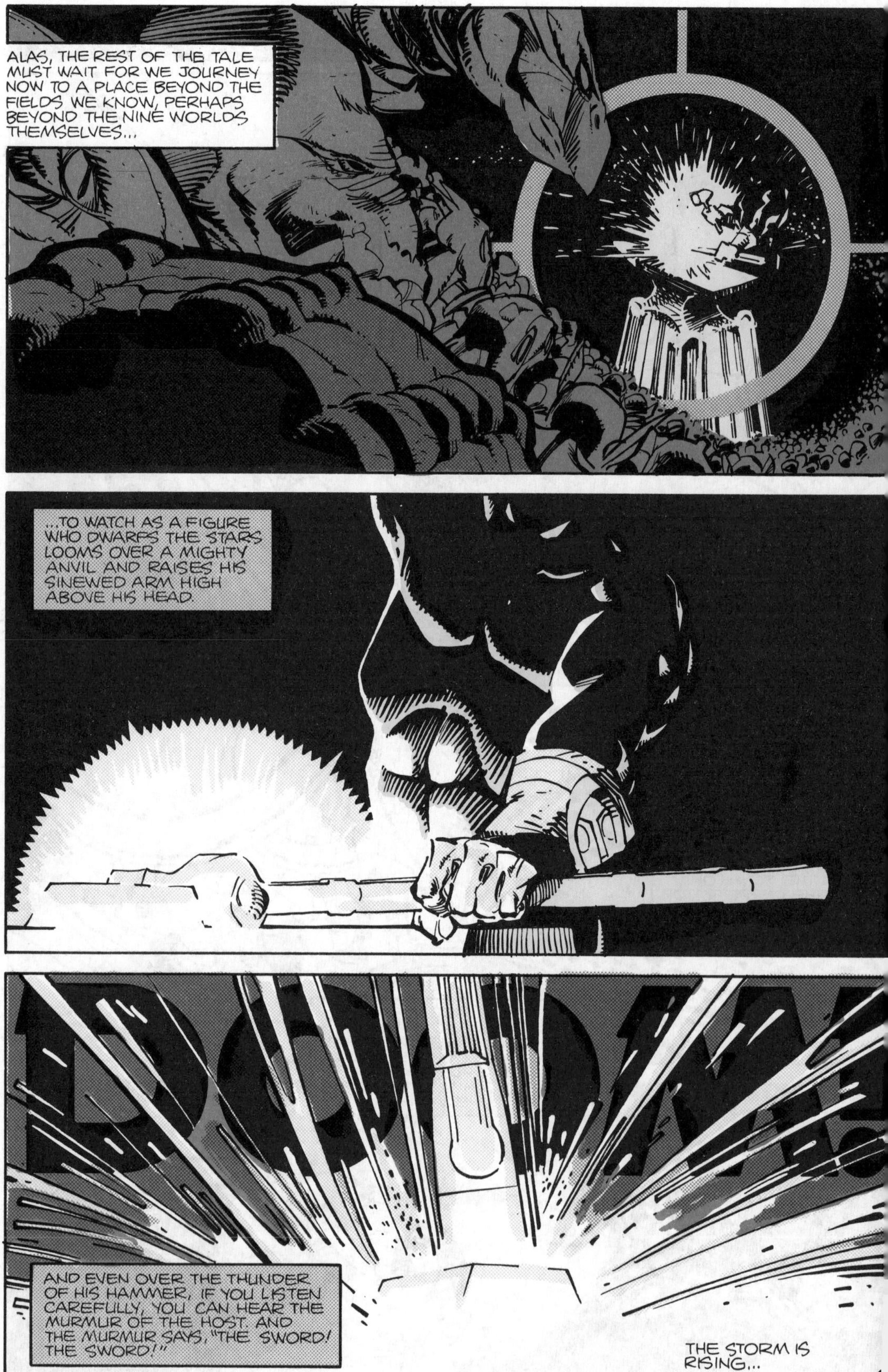
ALAS, THE REST OF THE TALE MUST WAIT FOR WE JOURNEY NOW TO A PLACE BEYOND THE FIELDS WE KNOW, PERHAPS BEYOND THE NINE WORLDS THEMSELVES...
...TO WATCH AS A FIGURE WHO DWARFS THE STARS LOOMS OVER A MIGHTY ANVIL AND RAISES HIS SINEWED ARM HIGH ABOVE HIS HEAD.
AND EVEN OVER THE THUNDER OF HIS HAMMER, IF YOU LISTEN CAREFULLY, YOU CAN HEAR THE MURMUR OF THE HOST. AND THE MURMUR SAYS, "THE SWORD! THE SWORD!"
THE STORM IS RISING...

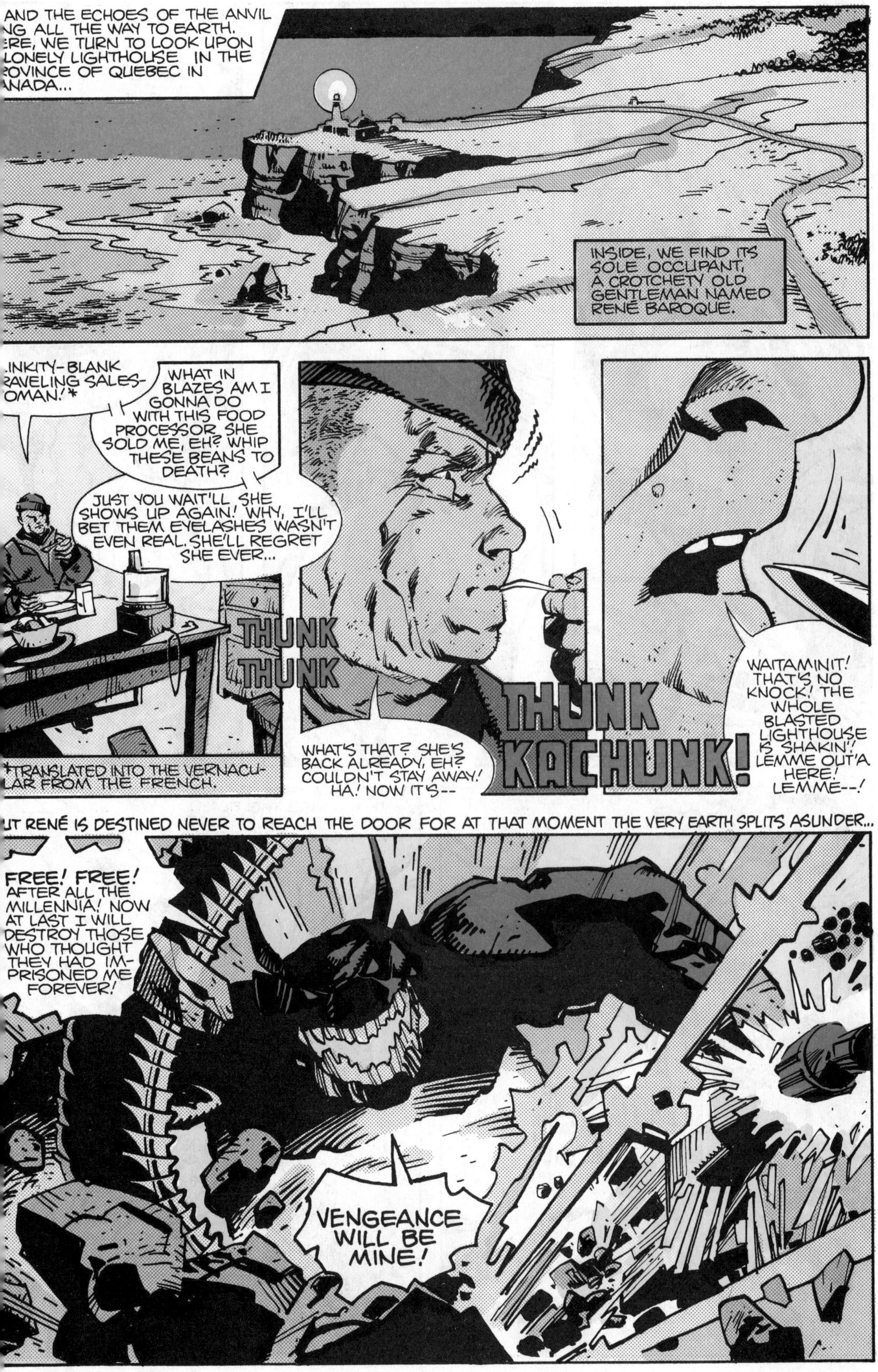
AND THE ECHOES OF THE ANVIL
NG ALL THE WAY TO EARTH.
ERE, WE TURN TO LOOK UPON
LONELY LIGHTHOUSE IN THE
ROVINCE OF QUEBEC IN
ANADA...
INSIDE, WE FIND ITS SOLE OCCUPANT, A CROTCHETY OLD GENTLEMAN NAMED RENÉ BAROQUE.
INKITY-BLANK RAVELING SALES-OMAN!*
WHAT IN BLAZES AM I GONNA DO WITH THIS FOOD PROCESSOR SHE SOLD ME, EH? WHIP THESE BEANS TO DEATH?
JUST YOU WAIT'LL SHE SHOWS UP AGAIN! WHY, I'LL BET THEM EYELASHES WASN'T EVEN REAL. SHE'LL REGRET SHE EVER...
THUNK THUNK
*TRANSLATED INTO THE VERNACU-LAR FROM THE FRENCH.
WHAT'S THAT? SHE'S BACK ALREADY, EH? COULDN'T STAY AWAY! HA! NOW IT'S--
THUNK KACHUNK!
WAITAMINIT! THAT'S NO KNOCK! THE WHOLE BLASTED LIGHTHOUSE IS SHAKIN'! LEMME OUT'A HERE! LEMME--!
UT RENÉ IS DESTINED NEVER TO REACH THE DOOR FOR AT THAT MOMENT THE VERY EARTH SPLITS ASUNDER...
FREE! FREE! AFTER ALL THE MILLENNIA! NOW AT LAST I WILL DESTROY THOSE WHO THOUGHT THEY HAD IM-PRISONED ME FOREVER!
VENGEANCE WILL BE MINE!

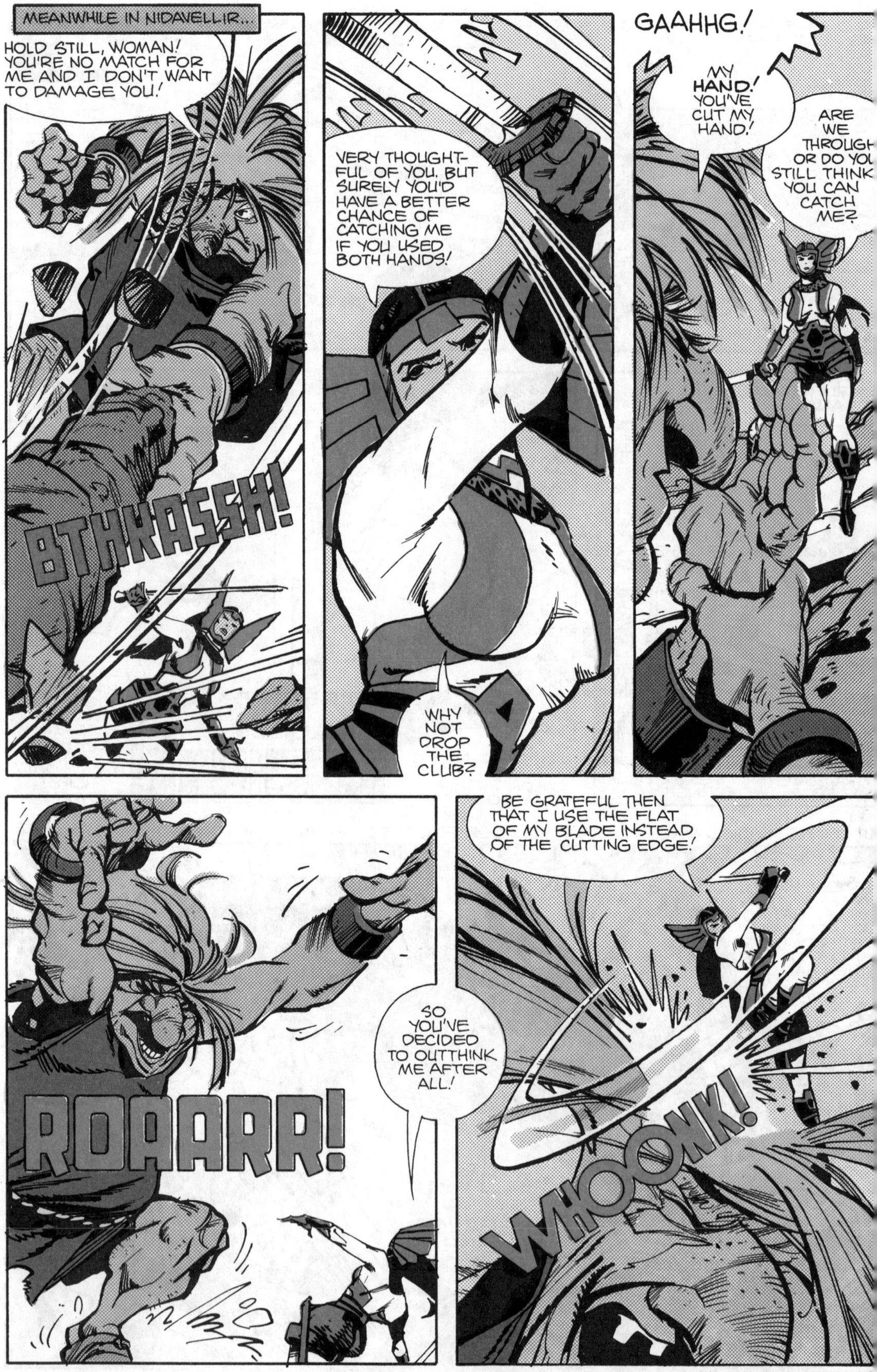

MEANWHILE IN NIDAVELLIR...
HOLD STILL, WOMAN! YOU'RE NO MATCH FOR ME AND I DON'T WANT TO DAMAGE YOU!
BTHRASSH!
VERY THOUGHTFUL OF YOU. BUT SURELY YOU'D HAVE A BETTER CHANCE OF CATCHING ME IF YOU USED BOTH HANDS!
WHY NOT DROP THE CLUB?
GAAHHG!
MY HAND! YOU'VE CUT MY HAND!
ARE WE THROUGH OR DO YOU STILL THINK YOU CAN CATCH ME?
ROAARR!
SO YOU'VE DECIDED TO OUTTHINK ME AFTER ALL!
BE GRATEFUL THEN THAT I USE THE FLAT OF MY BLADE INSTEAD OF THE CUTTING EDGE!
WHOONK!

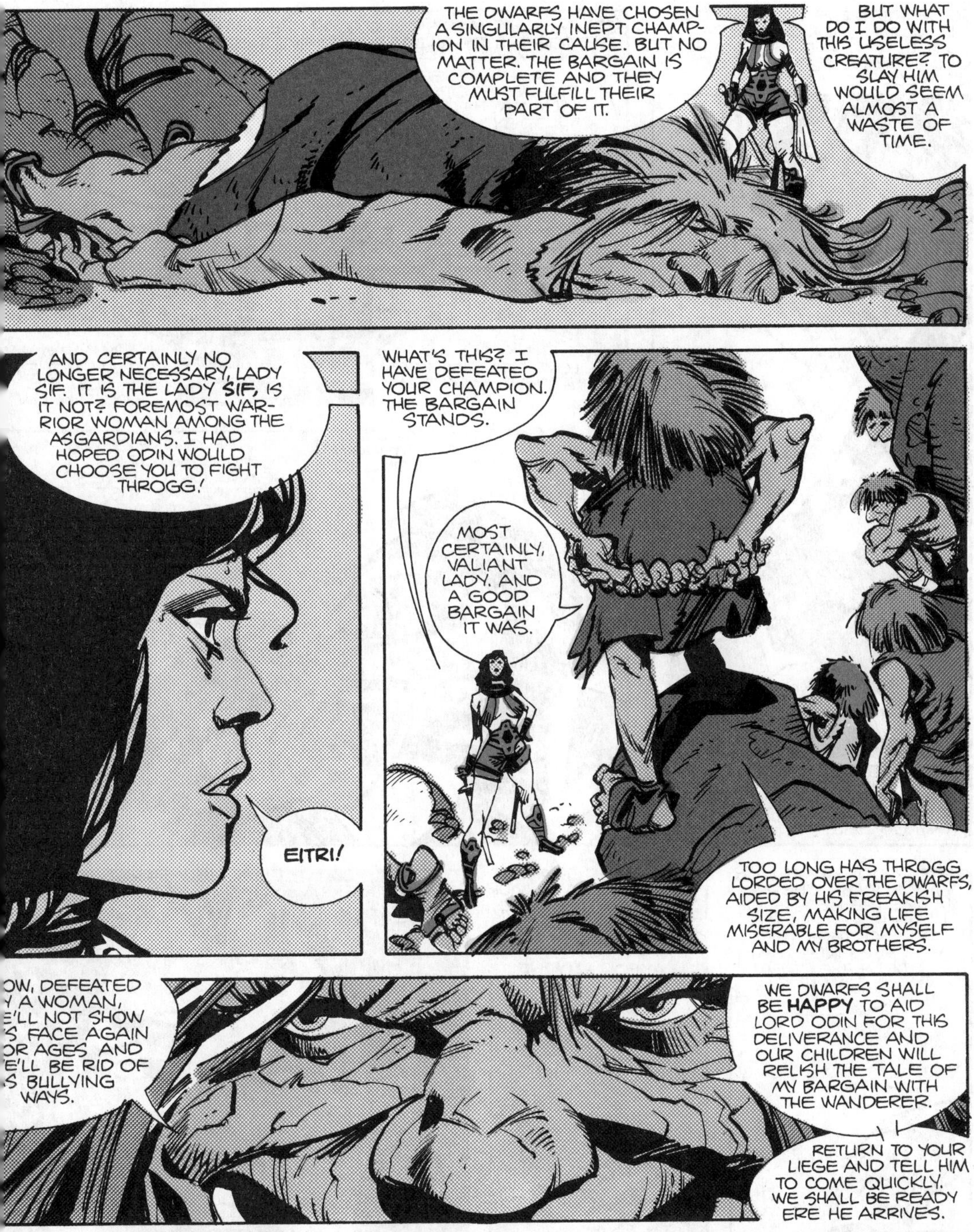

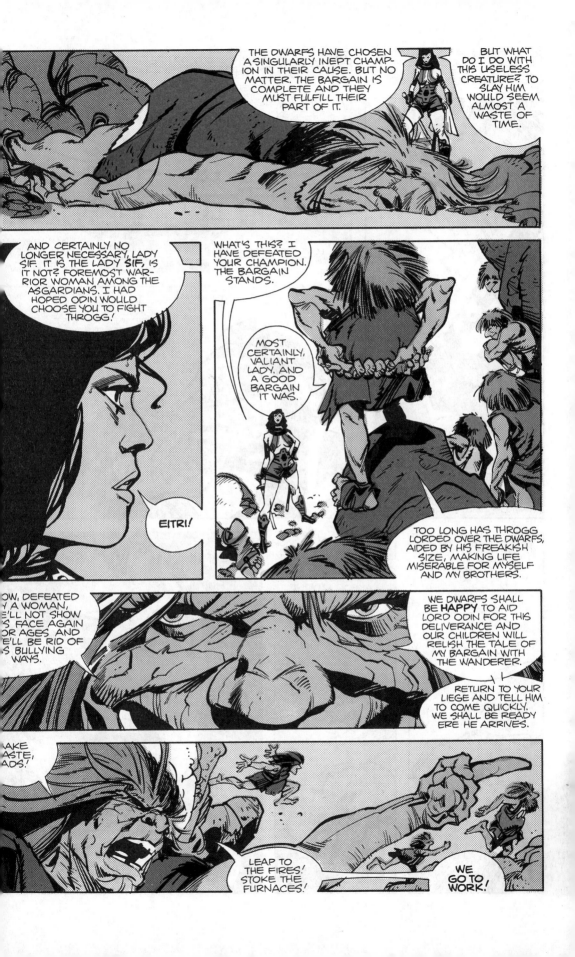

THE DWARFS HAVE CHOSEN A SINGULARLY INEPT CHAMPION IN THEIR CAUSE. BUT NO MATTER. THE BARGAIN IS COMPLETE AND THEY MUST FULFILL THEIR PART OF IT.
BUT WHAT DO I DO WITH THIS USELESS CREATURE? TO SLAY HIM WOULD SEEM ALMOST A WASTE OF TIME.
AND CERTAINLY NO LONGER NECESSARY, LADY SIF. IT IS THE LADY SIF, IS IT NOT? FOREMOST WARRIOR WOMAN AMONG THE ASGARDIANS. I HAD HOPED ODIN WOULD CHOOSE YOU TO FIGHT THROGG!
EITRI!
WHAT'S THIS? I HAVE DEFEATED YOUR CHAMPION. THE BARGAIN STANDS.
MOST CERTAINLY, VALIANT LADY. AND A GOOD BARGAIN IT WAS.
TOO LONG HAS THROGG LORDED OVER THE DWARFS, AIDED BY HIS FREAKISH SIZE, MAKING LIFE MISERABLE FOR MYSELF AND MY BROTHERS.
OW, DEFEATED Y A WOMAN, E'LL NOT SHOW S FACE AGAIN OR AGES AND E'LL BE RID OF S BULLYING WAYS.
WE DWARFS SHALL BE HAPPY TO AID LORD ODIN FOR THIS DELIVERANCE AND OUR CHILDREN WILL RELISH THE TALE OF MY BARGAIN WITH THE WANDERER.
RETURN TO YOUR LIEGE AND TELL HIM TO COME QUICKLY. WE SHALL BE READY ERE HE ARRIVES.
AKE ASTE, ADS!
LEAP TO THE FIRES! STOKE THE FURNACES!
WE GO TO WORK!

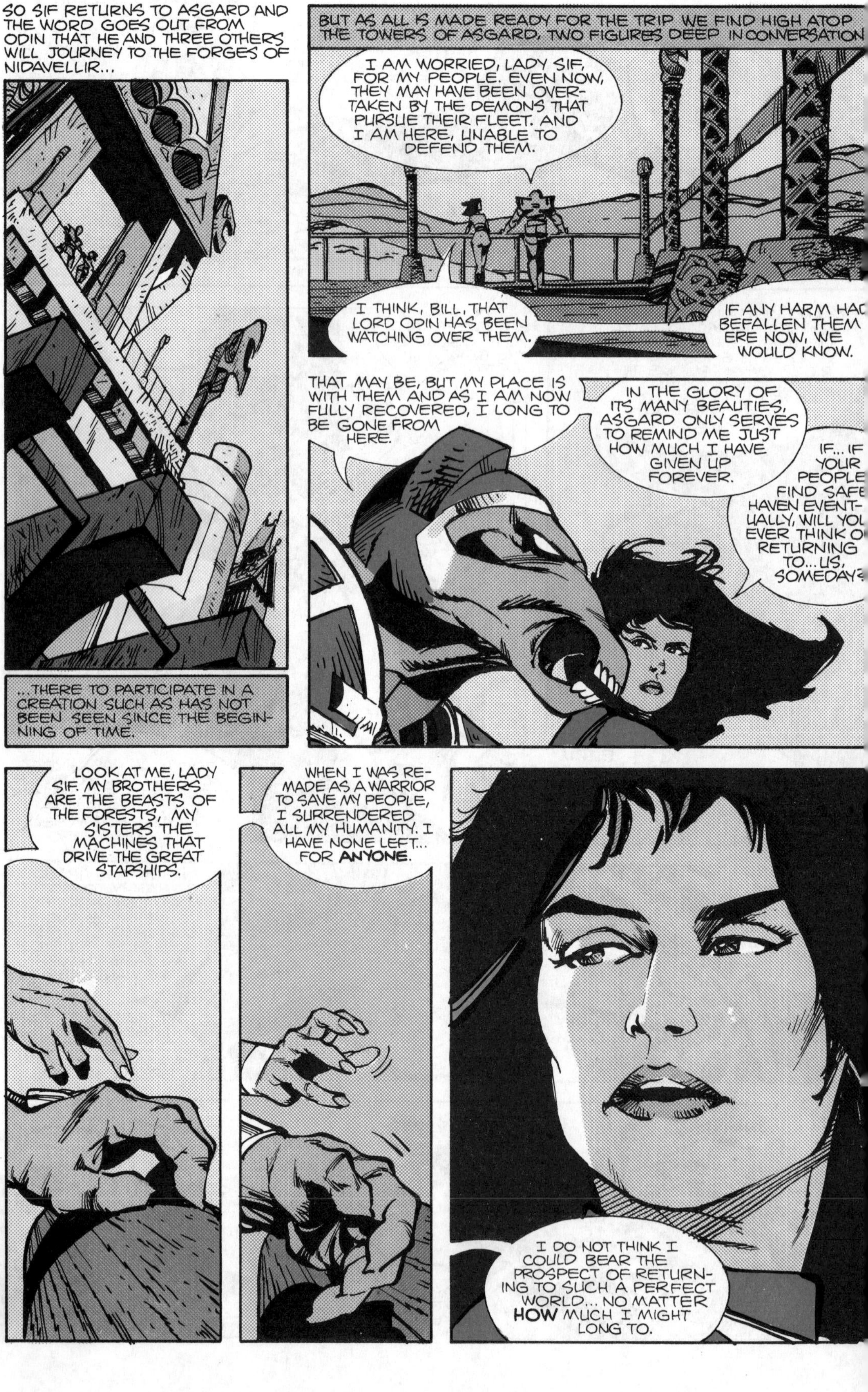
SO SIF RETURNS TO ASGARD AND THE WORD GOES OUT FROM ODIN THAT HE AND THREE OTHERS WILL JOURNEY TO THE FORGES OF NIDAVELLIR...
...THERE TO PARTICIPATE IN A CREATION SUCH AS HAS NOT BEEN SEEN SINCE THE BEGINNING OF TIME.
BUT AS ALL IS MADE READY FOR THE TRIP WE FIND HIGH ATOP THE TOWERS OF ASGARD, TWO FIGURES DEEP IN CONVERSATION
I AM WORRIED, LADY SIF, FOR MY PEOPLE. EVEN NOW, THEY MAY HAVE BEEN OVERTAKEN BY THE DEMONS THAT PURSUE THEIR FLEET. AND I AM HERE, UNABLE TO DEFEND THEM.
I THINK, BILL, THAT LORD ODIN HAS BEEN WATCHING OVER THEM.
IF ANY HARM HAD BEFALLEN THEM ERE NOW, WE WOULD KNOW.
THAT MAY BE, BUT MY PLACE IS WITH THEM AND AS I AM NOW FULLY RECOVERED, I LONG TO BE GONE FROM HERE.
IN THE GLORY OF ITS MANY BEAUTIES, ASGARD ONLY SERVES TO REMIND ME JUST HOW MUCH I HAVE GIVEN UP FOREVER.
IF... IF YOUR PEOPLE FIND SAFE HAVEN EVENTUALLY, WILL YOU EVER THINK OF RETURNING TO... US, SOMEDAY?
LOOK AT ME, LADY SIF. MY BROTHERS ARE THE BEASTS OF THE FORESTS, MY SISTERS THE MACHINES THAT DRIVE THE GREAT STARSHIPS.
WHEN I WAS REMADE AS A WARRIOR TO SAVE MY PEOPLE, I SURRENDERED ALL MY HUMANITY. I HAVE NONE LEFT... FOR ANYONE.
I DO NOT THINK I COULD BEAR THE PROSPECT OF RETURNING TO SUCH A PERFECT WORLD... NO MATTER HOW MUCH I MIGHT LONG TO.

ESE ARE THE **FURNACES** OF **NIDAVELLIR,** THE GREAT FORGES OF THE DWARFS, WHERE FOR
GES, THEY HAVE CREATED THE MOST WONDERFUL DELIGHTS OF THEIR IMAGINATIONS.

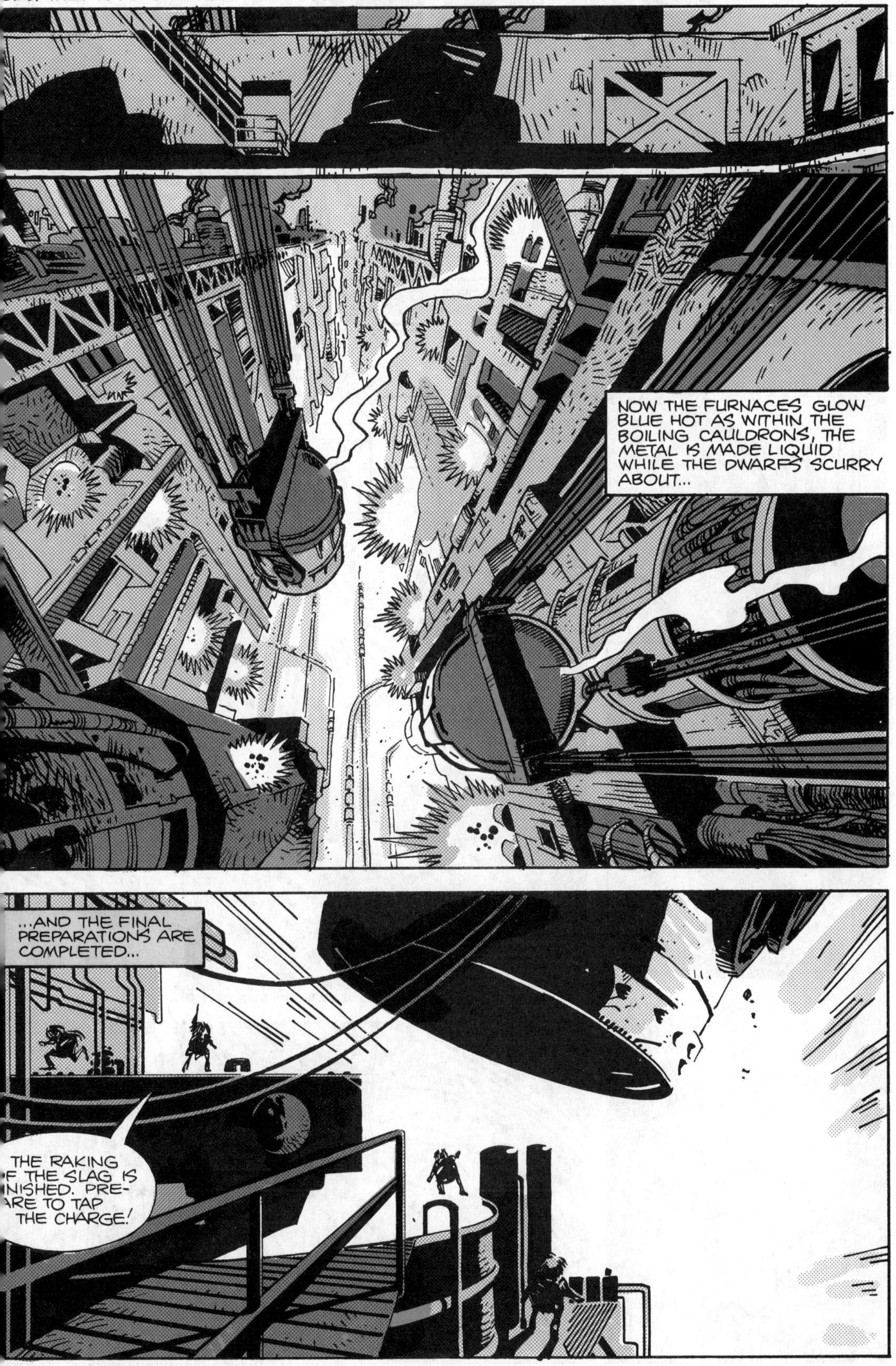

NOW THE FURNACES GLOW BLUE HOT AS WITHIN THE BOILING CAULDRONS, THE METAL IS MADE LIQUID WHILE THE DWARFS SCURRY ABOUT...
...AND THE FINAL PREPARATIONS ARE COMPLETED...
THE RAKING F THE SLAG IS NISHED. PRE- ARE TO TAP THE CHARGE!

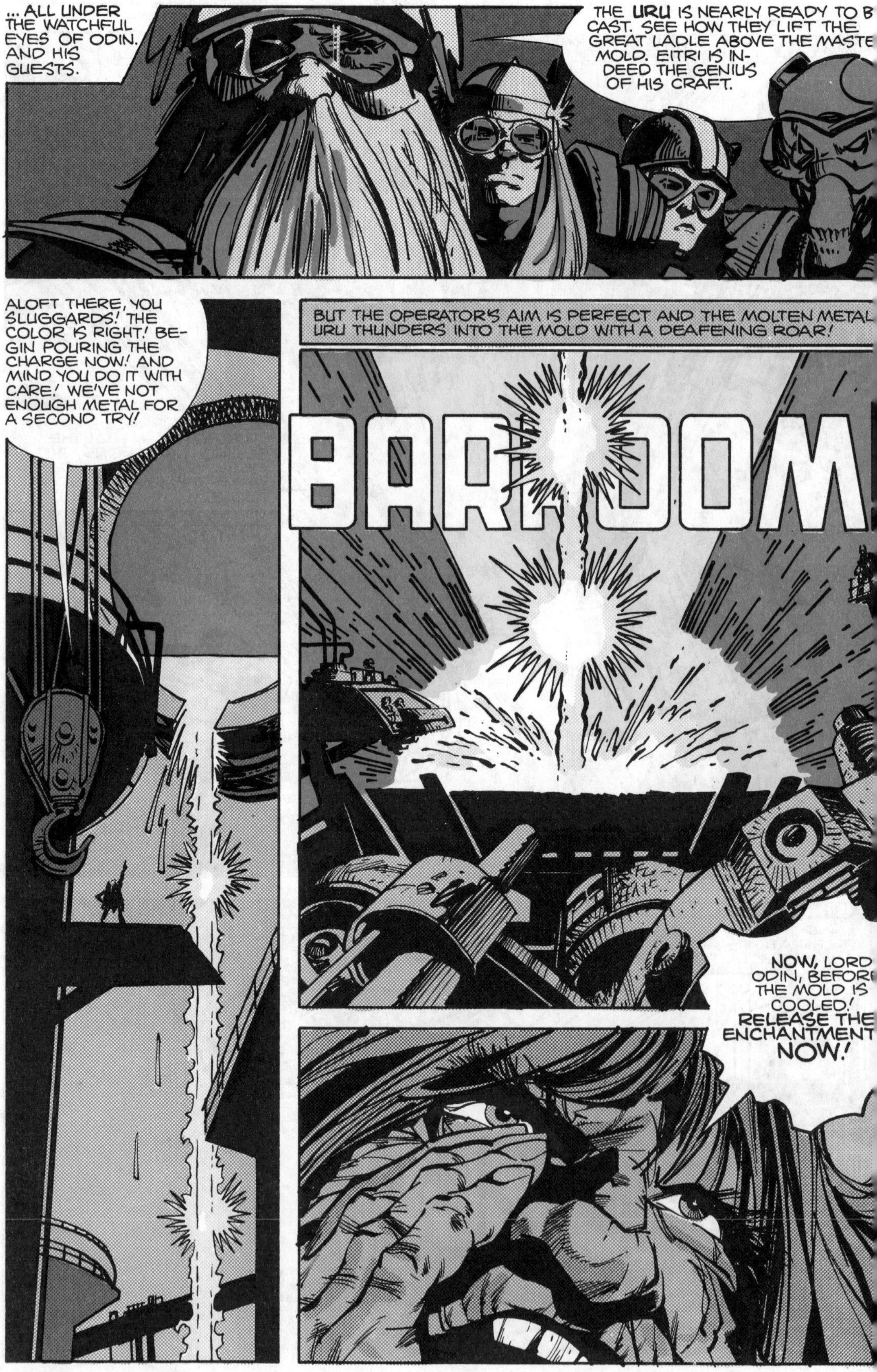

...ALL UNDER THE WATCHFUL EYES OF ODIN. AND HIS GUESTS.
THE URU IS NEARLY READY TO B CAST. SEE HOW THEY LIFT THE GREAT LADLE ABOVE THE MASTE MOLD. EITRI IS INDEED THE GENIUS OF HIS CRAFT.
ALOFT THERE, YOU SLUGGARDS! THE COLOR IS RIGHT! BEGIN POURING THE CHARGE NOW! AND MIND YOU DO IT WITH CARE! WE'VE NOT ENOUGH METAL FOR A SECOND TRY!
BUT THE OPERATOR'S AIM IS PERFECT AND THE MOLTEN METAL URU THUNDERS INTO THE MOLD WITH A DEAFENING ROAR!
BARROOM
NOW, LORD ODIN, BEFOR THE MOLD IS COOLED! RELEASE THE ENCHANTMENT NOW!

STAND BACK! THIS IS THE MOMENT WHEN WE SUCCEED OR FAIL! I MUST STRIKE WITH THE FULL FORCE OF THE ODIN POWER TO ACHIEVE OUR PURPOSE!

ONLY THUS CAN THE MAGIKS WE DESIRE BE LOCKED WITHIN THE URU METAL FOREVER!

SO BE IT!

KA THOOM!

QUICKLY NOW, BILL. DON THIS GAUNTLET AND STEP FORWARD. FOR YOU THIS MAGIC IS PERFORMED AND TO YOU THIS MAGIC SHALL BE BOUND!

EITRI WILL INSTRUCT YOU!

WHAT MUST I DO, EITRI?

AS I RAISE THE DOOR, YOU MUST REACH INTO THE MOLTEN POOL WITHIN AND REMOVE THAT WHICH YOU FIND THERE. THE GAUNTLET WILL PROTECT YOU! MAKE HASTE OR THE MOMENT IS LOST!

NOW!

I...I FEEL NOTHING-- HOLD! I HAVE IT! THE WEIGHT IS ENORMOUS! BUT IT GROWS LIGHTER EVEN AS I PULL IT FROM THE FIRE!

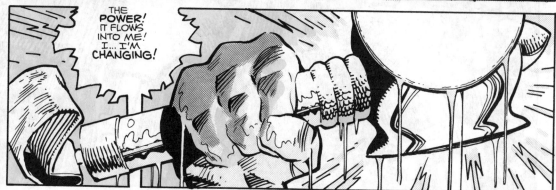

THE POWER! IT FLOWS INTO ME! I... I'M CHANGING!

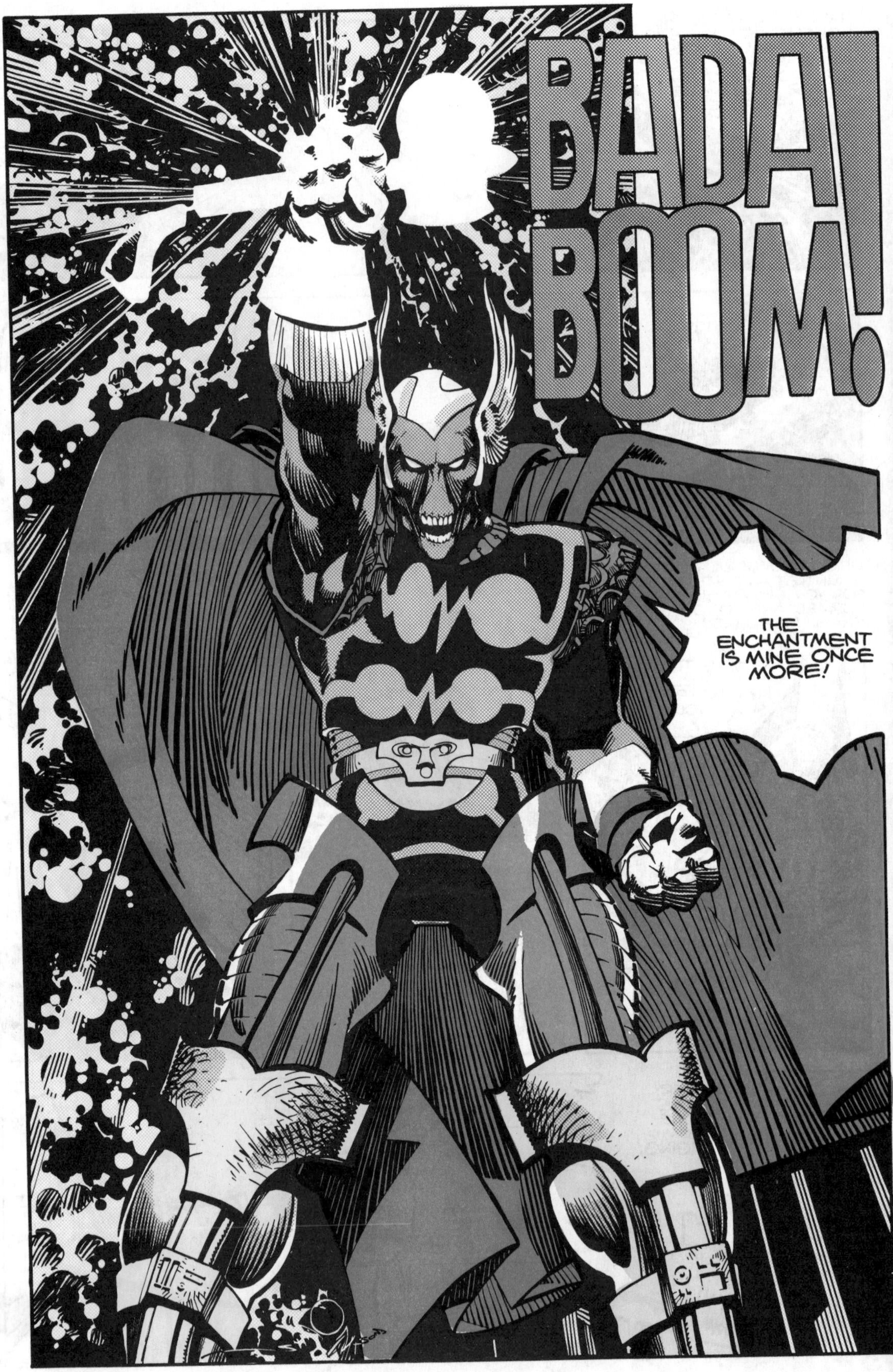
BADA BOOM!
THE ENCHANTMENT IS MINE ONCE MORE!

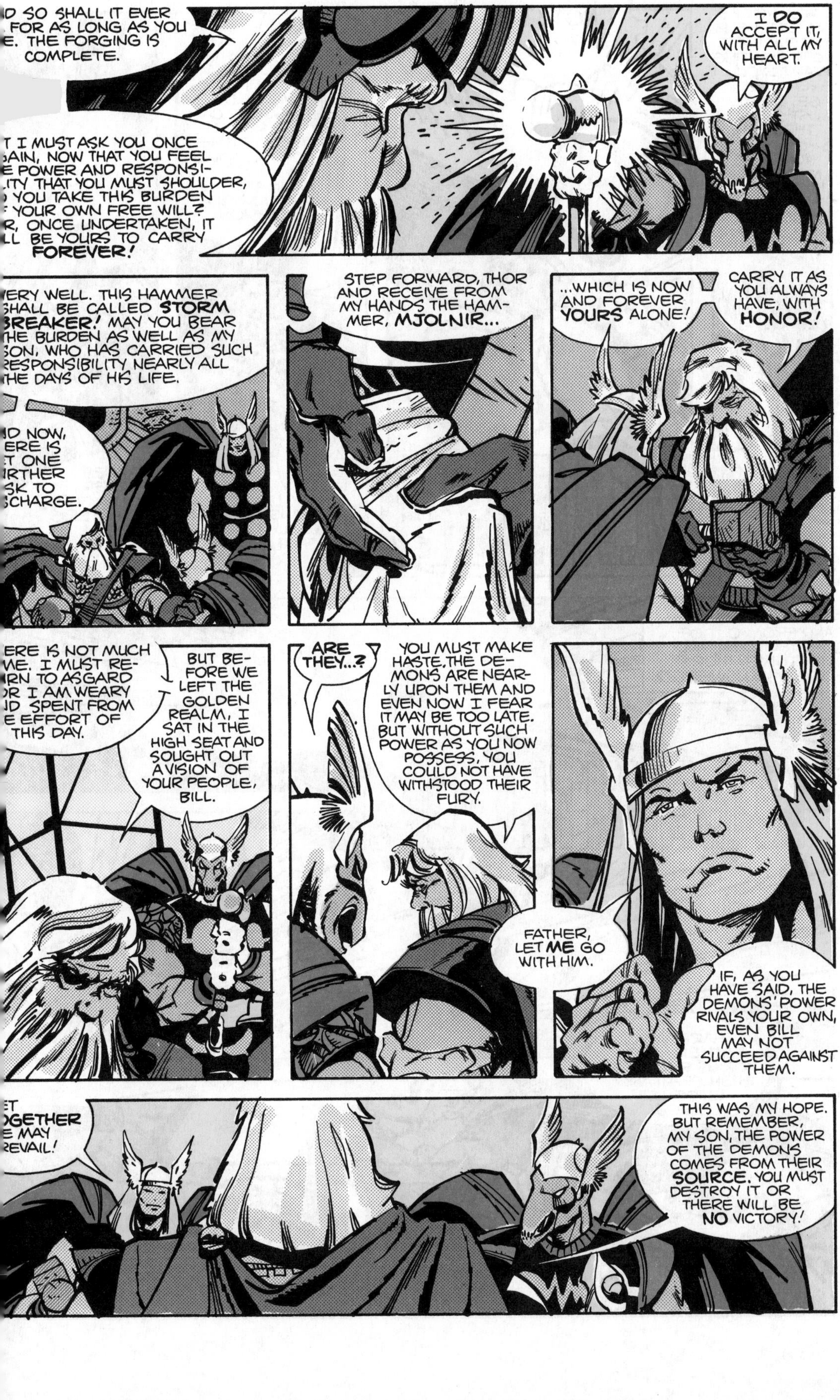

ID SO SHALL IT EVER FOR AS LONG AS YOU E. THE FORGING IS COMPLETE.
T I MUST ASK YOU ONCE GAIN, NOW THAT YOU FEEL E POWER AND RESPONSI-ITY THAT YOU MUST SHOULDER, YOU TAKE THIS BURDEN YOUR OWN FREE WILL? R, ONCE UNDERTAKEN, IT LL BE YOURS TO CARRY FOREVER!
I DO ACCEPT IT, WITH ALL MY HEART.
ERY WELL. THIS HAMMER SHALL BE CALLED STORM BREAKER! MAY YOU BEAR THE BURDEN AS WELL AS MY SON, WHO HAS CARRIED SUCH RESPONSIBILITY NEARLY ALL THE DAYS OF HIS LIFE.
ID NOW, ERE IS T ONE RTHER SK TO SCHARGE.
STEP FORWARD, THOR AND RECEIVE FROM MY HANDS THE HAM-MER, MJOLNIR...
...WHICH IS NOW AND FOREVER YOURS ALONE!
CARRY IT AS YOU ALWAYS HAVE, WITH HONOR!
ERE IS NOT MUCH ME. I MUST RE-RN TO ASGARD R I AM WEARY D SPENT FROM E EFFORT OF THIS DAY.
BUT BE-FORE WE LEFT THE GOLDEN REALM, I SAT IN THE HIGH SEAT AND SOUGHT OUT A VISION OF YOUR PEOPLE, BILL.
ARE THEY...?
YOU MUST MAKE HASTE. THE DE-MONS ARE NEAR-LY UPON THEM AND EVEN NOW I FEAR IT MAY BE TOO LATE. BUT WITHOUT SUCH POWER AS YOU NOW POSSESS, YOU COULD NOT HAVE WITHSTOOD THEIR FURY.
FATHER, LET ME GO WITH HIM.
IF, AS YOU HAVE SAID, THE DEMONS' POWER RIVALS YOUR OWN, EVEN BILL MAY NOT SUCCEED AGAINST THEM.
ET OGETHER E MAY REVAIL!
THIS WAS MY HOPE. BUT REMEMBER, MY SON, THE POWER OF THE DEMONS COMES FROM THEIR SOURCE. YOU MUST DESTROY IT OR THERE WILL BE NO VICTORY!

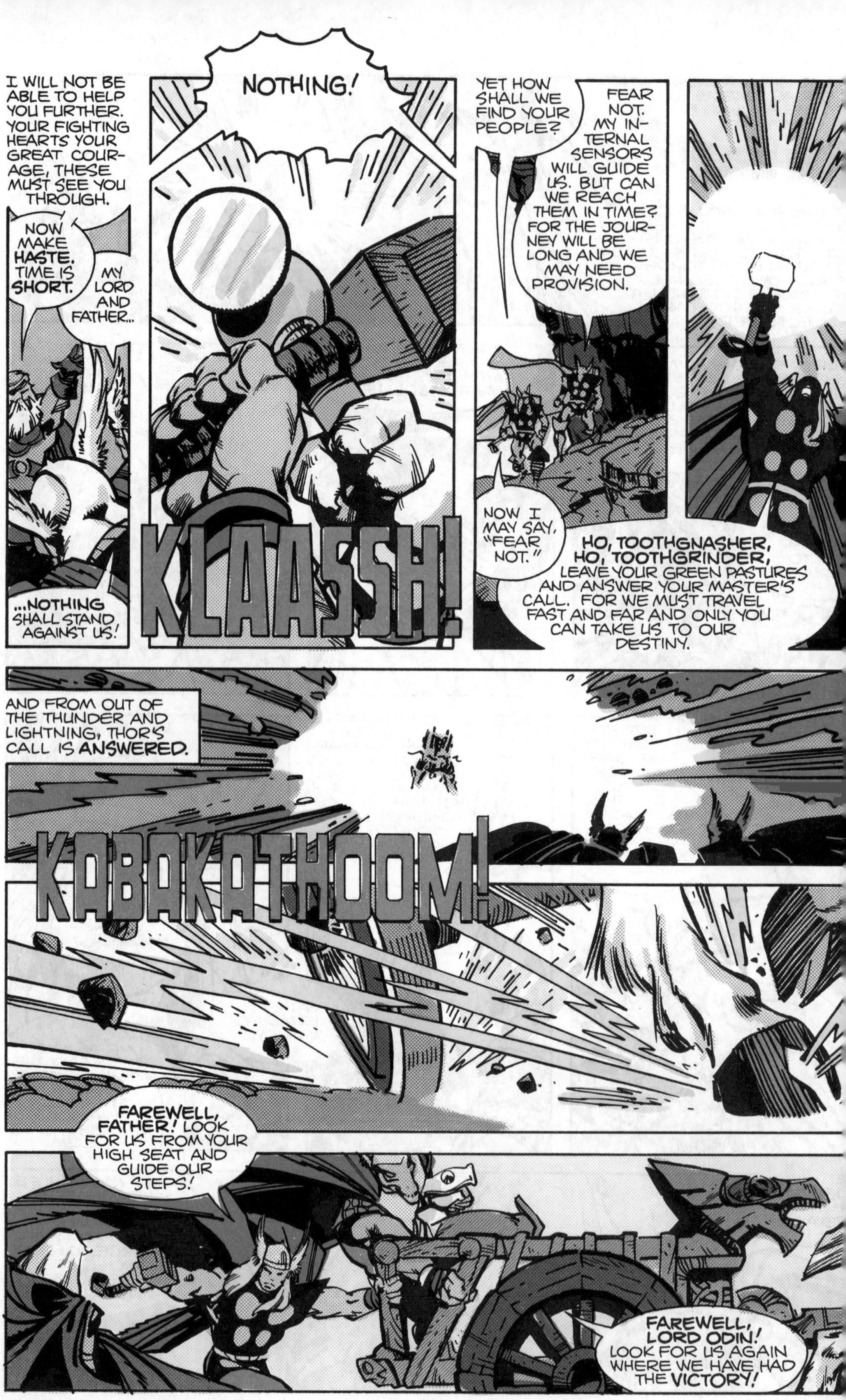
I WILL NOT BE ABLE TO HELP YOU FURTHER. YOUR FIGHTING HEARTS YOUR GREAT COURAGE, THESE MUST SEE YOU THROUGH.
NOW MAKE HASTE. TIME IS SHORT.
MY LORD AND FATHER...
...NOTHING SHALL STAND AGAINST US!
NOTHING!
KLAASSH!
YET HOW SHALL WE FIND YOUR PEOPLE?
FEAR NOT. MY INTERNAL SENSORS WILL GUIDE US. BUT CAN WE REACH THEM IN TIME? FOR THE JOURNEY WILL BE LONG AND WE MAY NEED PROVISION.
NOW I MAY SAY, "FEAR NOT."
HO, TOOTHGNASHER, HO, TOOTHGRINDER, LEAVE YOUR GREEN PASTURES AND ANSWER YOUR MASTER'S CALL. FOR WE MUST TRAVEL FAST AND FAR AND ONLY YOU CAN TAKE US TO OUR DESTINY.
AND FROM OUT OF THE THUNDER AND LIGHTNING, THOR'S CALL IS ANSWERED.
KABAKATHOOM!
FAREWELL, FATHER! LOOK FOR US FROM YOUR HIGH SEAT AND GUIDE OUR STEPS!
FAREWELL, LORD ODIN! LOOK FOR US AGAIN WHERE WE HAVE HAD THE VICTORY!

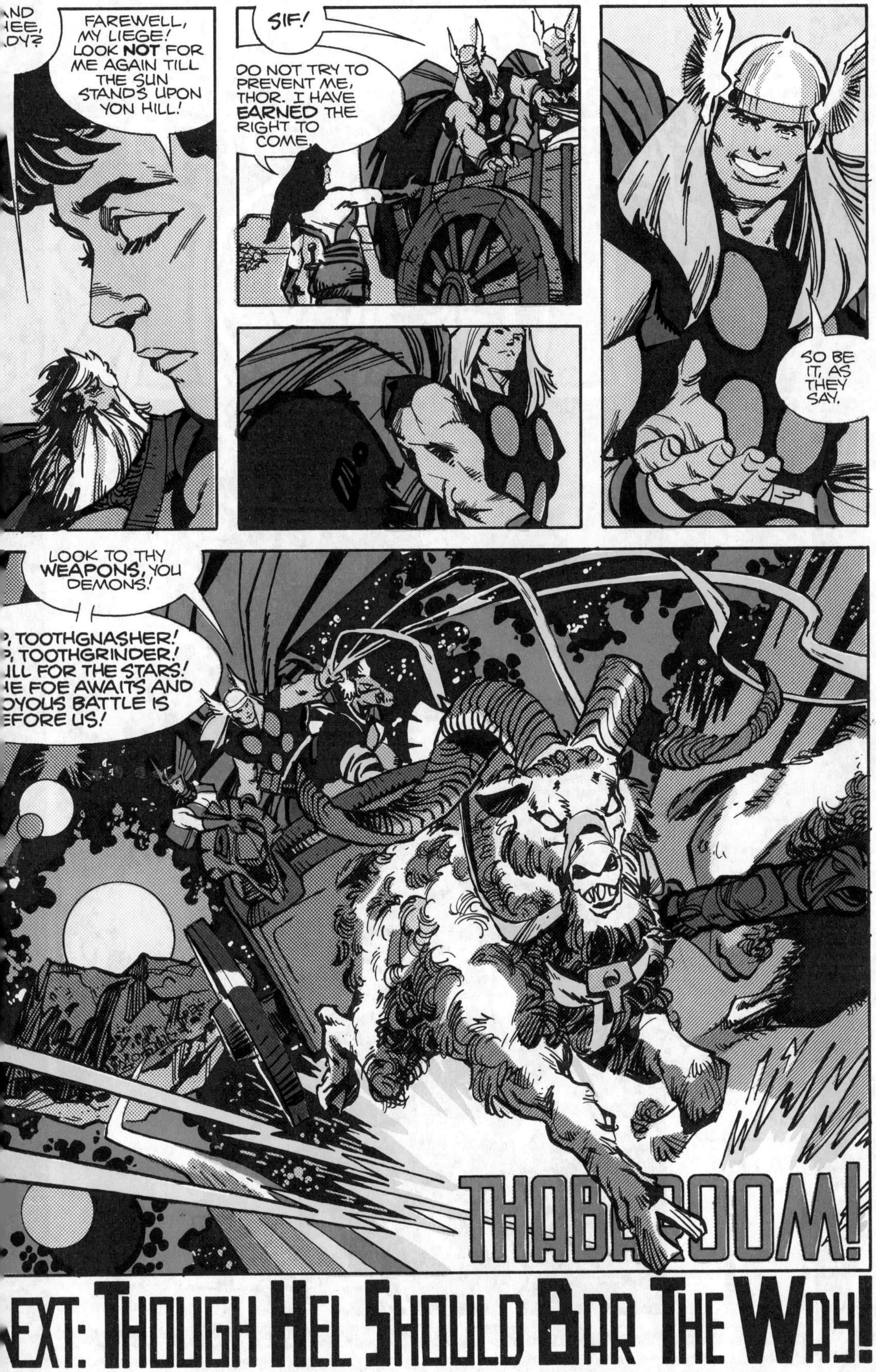

FAREWELL, MY LIEGE! LOOK NOT FOR ME AGAIN TILL THE SUN STANDS UPON YON HILL!
SIF!
DO NOT TRY TO PREVENT ME, THOR. I HAVE EARNED THE RIGHT TO COME.
SO BE IT, AS THEY SAY.
LOOK TO THY WEAPONS, YOU DEMONS!
P, TOOTHGNASHER! P, TOOTHGRINDER! ILL FOR THE STARS! HE FOE AWAITS AND OYOUS BATTLE IS EFORE US!
THABADOOM!

EXT: THOUGH HEL SHOULD BAR THE WAY!

CHAPTER FOUR

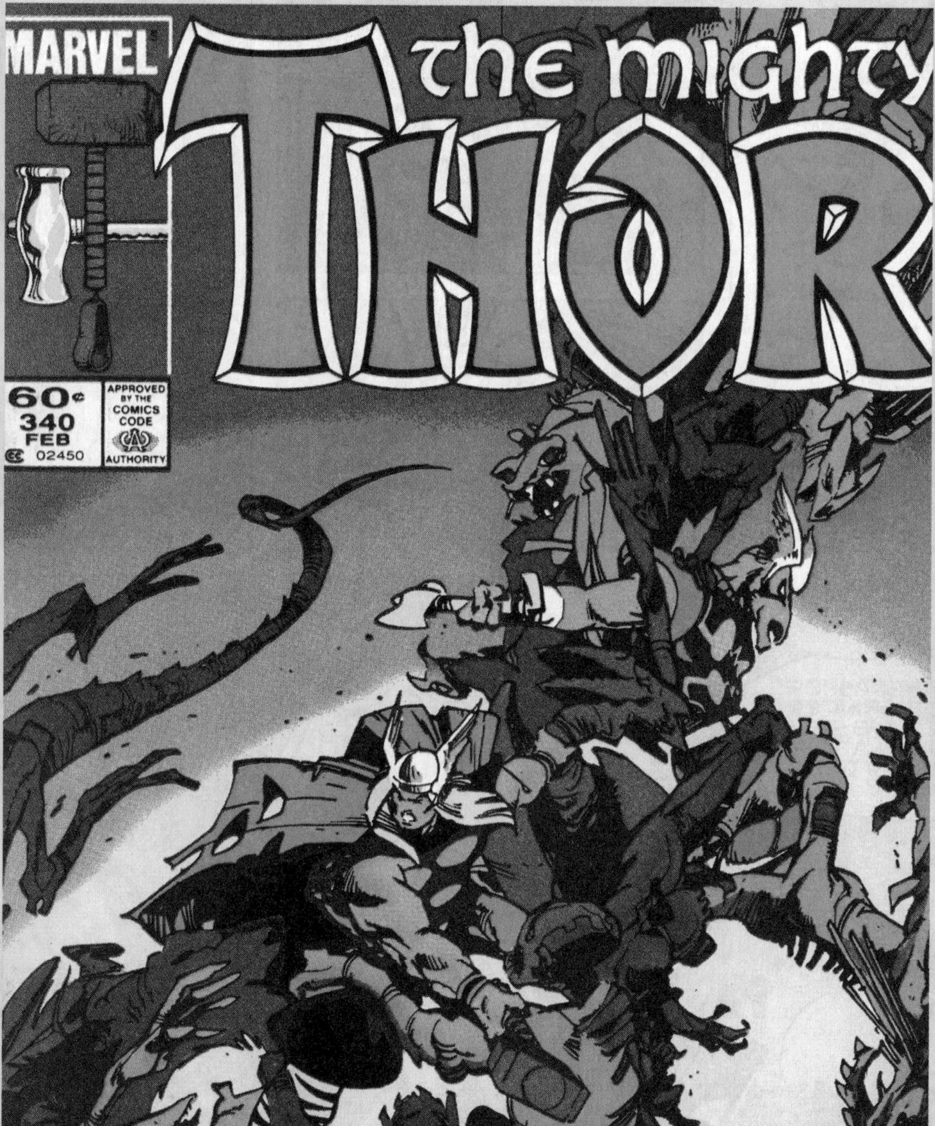

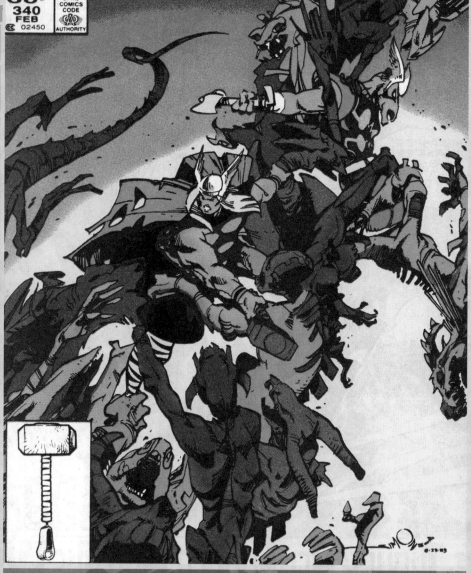

MARVEL
the mighty THOR
60¢
340
FEB
02450
APPROVED BY THE COMICS CODE AUTHORITY

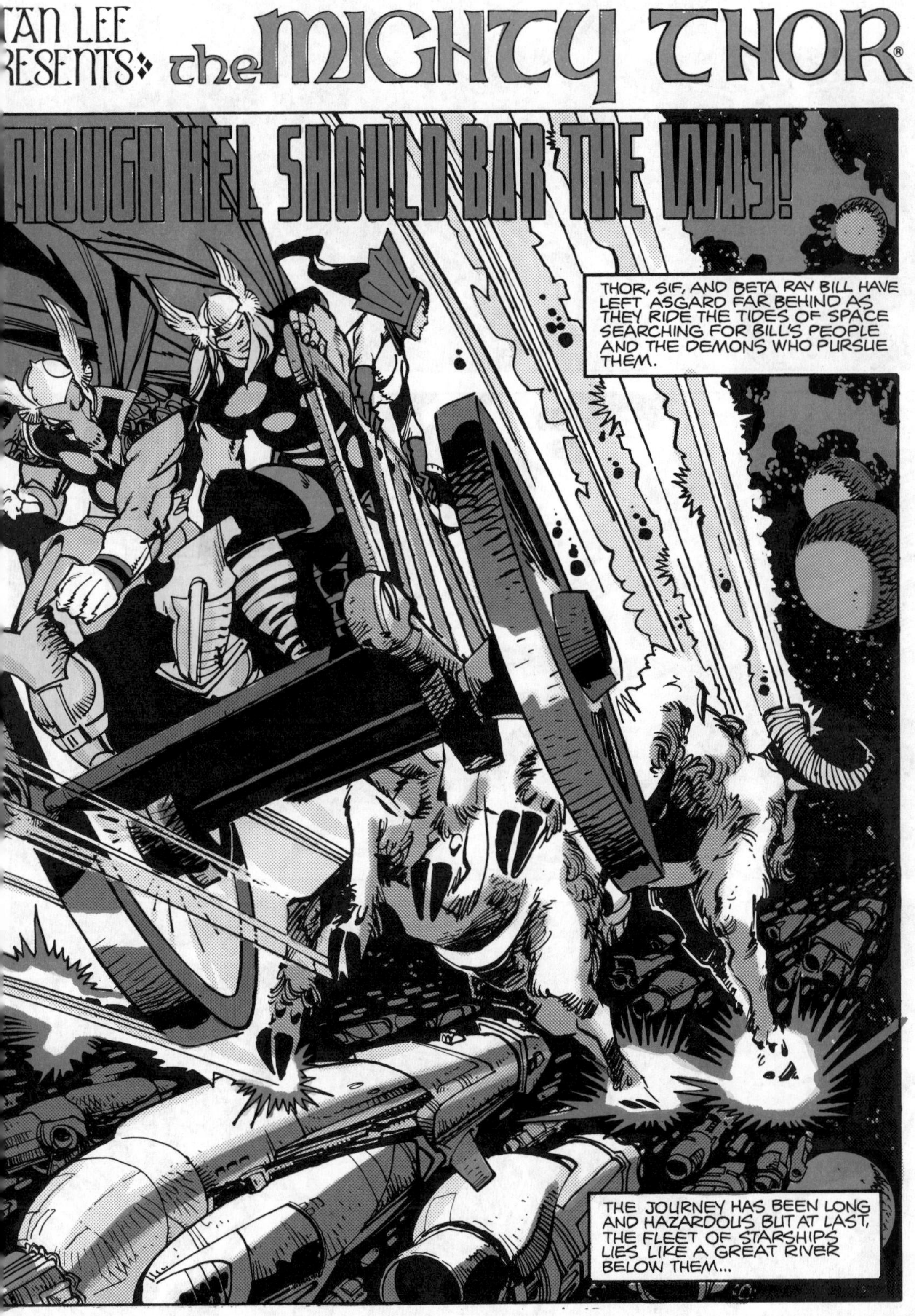

STAN LEE PRESENTS: the MIGHTY THOR®
THOUGH HEL SHOULD BAR THE WAY!
THOR, SIF, AND BETA RAY BILL HAVE LEFT ASGARD FAR BEHIND AS THEY RIDE THE TIDES OF SPACE SEARCHING FOR BILL'S PEOPLE AND THE DEMONS WHO PURSUE THEM.
THE JOURNEY HAS BEEN LONG AND HAZARDOUS BUT AT LAST, THE FLEET OF STARSHIPS LIES LIKE A GREAT RIVER BELOW THEM...

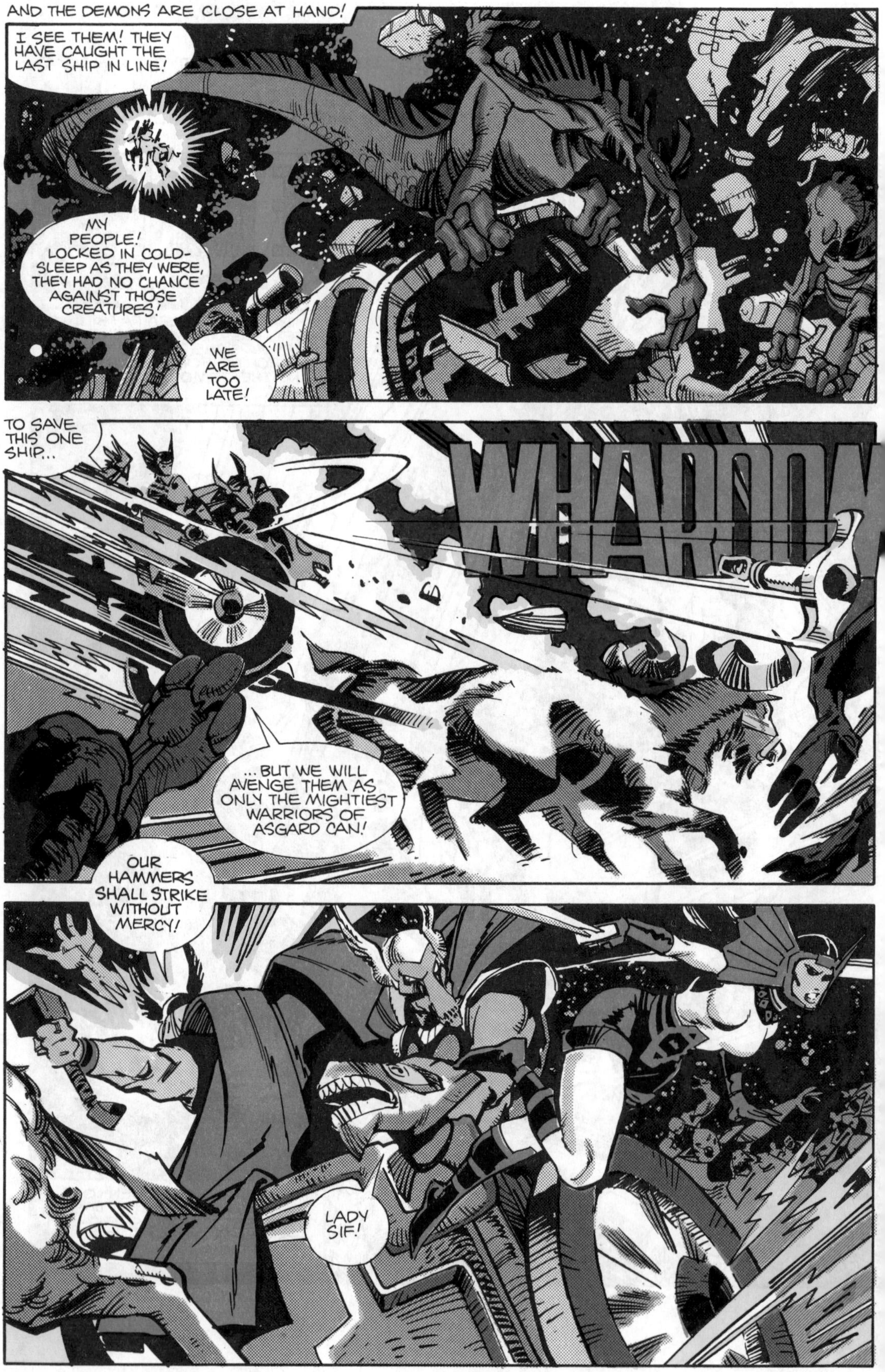
AND THE DEMONS ARE CLOSE AT HAND!
I SEE THEM! THEY HAVE CAUGHT THE LAST SHIP IN LINE!
MY PEOPLE! LOCKED IN COLD-SLEEP AS THEY WERE, THEY HAD NO CHANCE AGAINST THOSE CREATURES!
WE ARE TOO LATE!
TO SAVE THIS ONE SHIP...
WHADOOM
...BUT WE WILL AVENGE THEM AS ONLY THE MIGHTIEST WARRIORS OF ASGARD CAN!
OUR HAMMERS SHALL STRIKE WITHOUT MERCY!
LADY SIF!

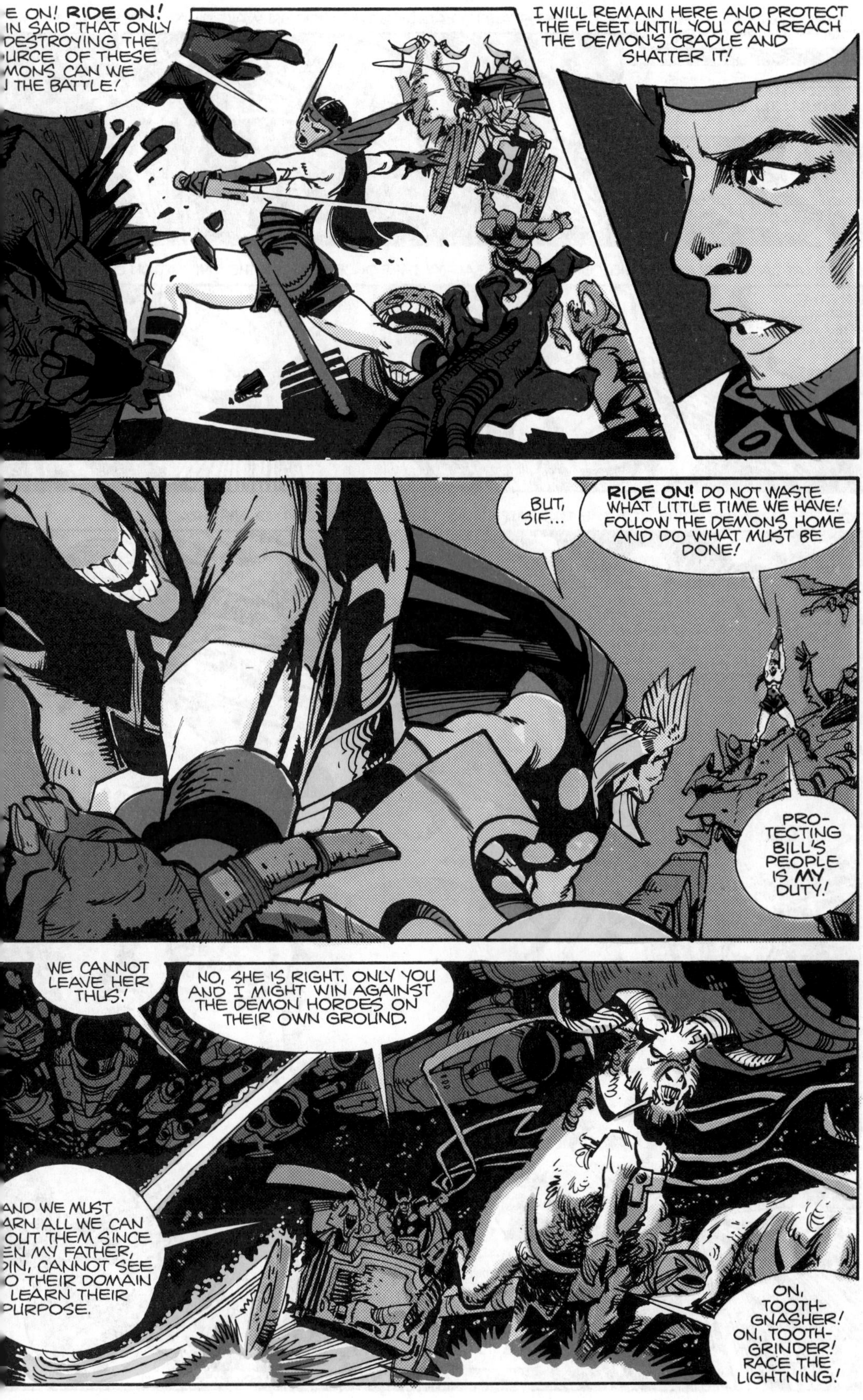
E ON! RIDE ON!
IN SAID THAT ONLY DESTROYING THE URCE OF THESE MONS CAN WE THE BATTLE!
I WILL REMAIN HERE AND PROTECT THE FLEET UNTIL YOU CAN REACH THE DEMON'S CRADLE AND SHATTER IT!
BUT, SIF...
RIDE ON! DO NOT WASTE WHAT LITTLE TIME WE HAVE! FOLLOW THE DEMONS HOME AND DO WHAT MUST BE DONE!
PROTECTING BILL'S PEOPLE IS MY DUTY!
WE CANNOT LEAVE HER THUS!
NO, SHE IS RIGHT. ONLY YOU AND I MIGHT WIN AGAINST THE DEMON HORDES ON THEIR OWN GROUND.
AND WE MUST ARN ALL WE CAN OUT THEM SINCE EN MY FATHER, DIN, CANNOT SEE O THEIR DOMAIN LEARN THEIR URPOSE.
ON, TOOTH-GNASHER! ON, TOOTH-GRINDER! RACE THE LIGHTNING!

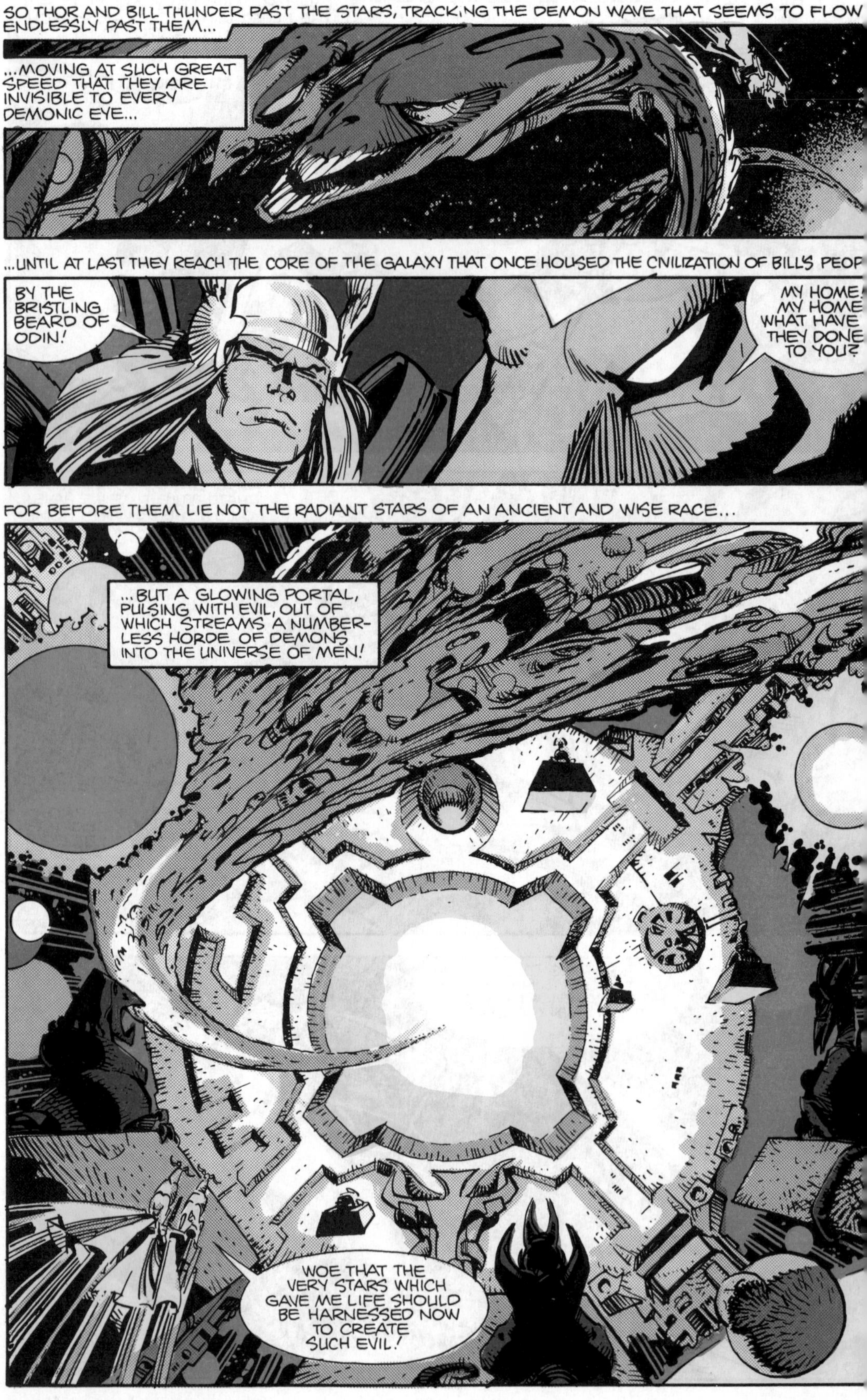
SO THOR AND BILL THUNDER PAST THE STARS, TRACKING THE DEMON WAVE THAT SEEMS TO FLOW ENDLESSLY PAST THEM...
...MOVING AT SUCH GREAT SPEED THAT THEY ARE INVISIBLE TO EVERY DEMONIC EYE...
...UNTIL AT LAST THEY REACH THE CORE OF THE GALAXY THAT ONCE HOUSED THE CIVILIZATION OF BILL'S PEOP
BY THE BRISTLING BEARD OF ODIN!
MY HOME! MY HOME! WHAT HAVE THEY DONE TO YOU?
FOR BEFORE THEM LIE NOT THE RADIANT STARS OF AN ANCIENT AND WISE RACE...
...BUT A GLOWING PORTAL, PULSING WITH EVIL, OUT OF WHICH STREAMS A NUMBERLESS HORDE OF DEMONS INTO THE UNIVERSE OF MEN!
WOE THAT THE VERY STARS WHICH GAVE ME LIFE SHOULD BE HARNESSED NOW TO CREATE SUCH EVIL!

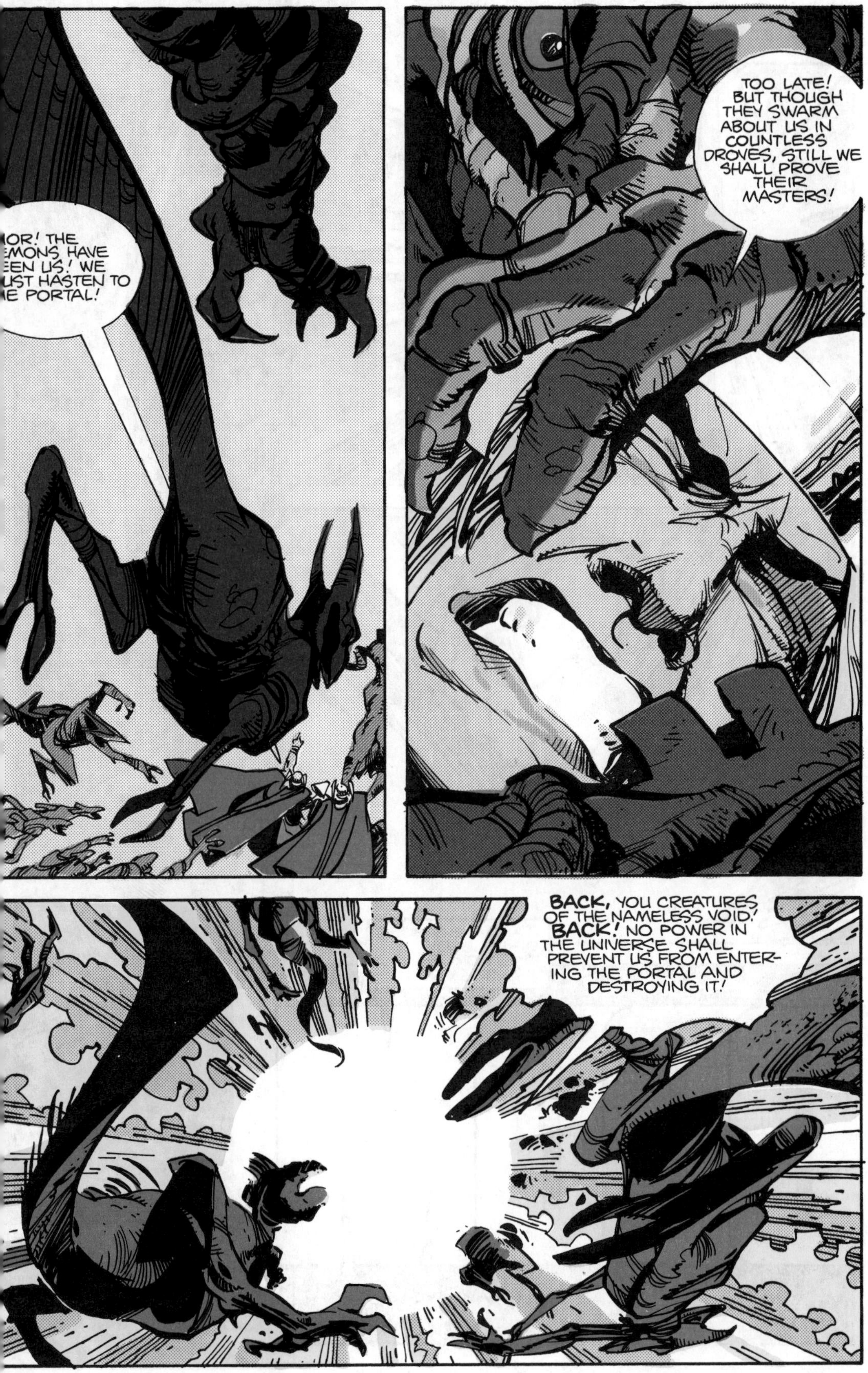

OR! THE EMONS HAVE EEN US! WE UST HASTEN TO E PORTAL!
TOO LATE! BUT THOUGH THEY SWARM ABOUT US IN COUNTLESS DROVES, STILL WE SHALL PROVE THEIR MASTERS!
BACK, YOU CREATURES OF THE NAMELESS VOID! BACK! NO POWER IN THE UNIVERSE SHALL PREVENT US FROM ENTERING THE PORTAL AND DESTROYING IT!

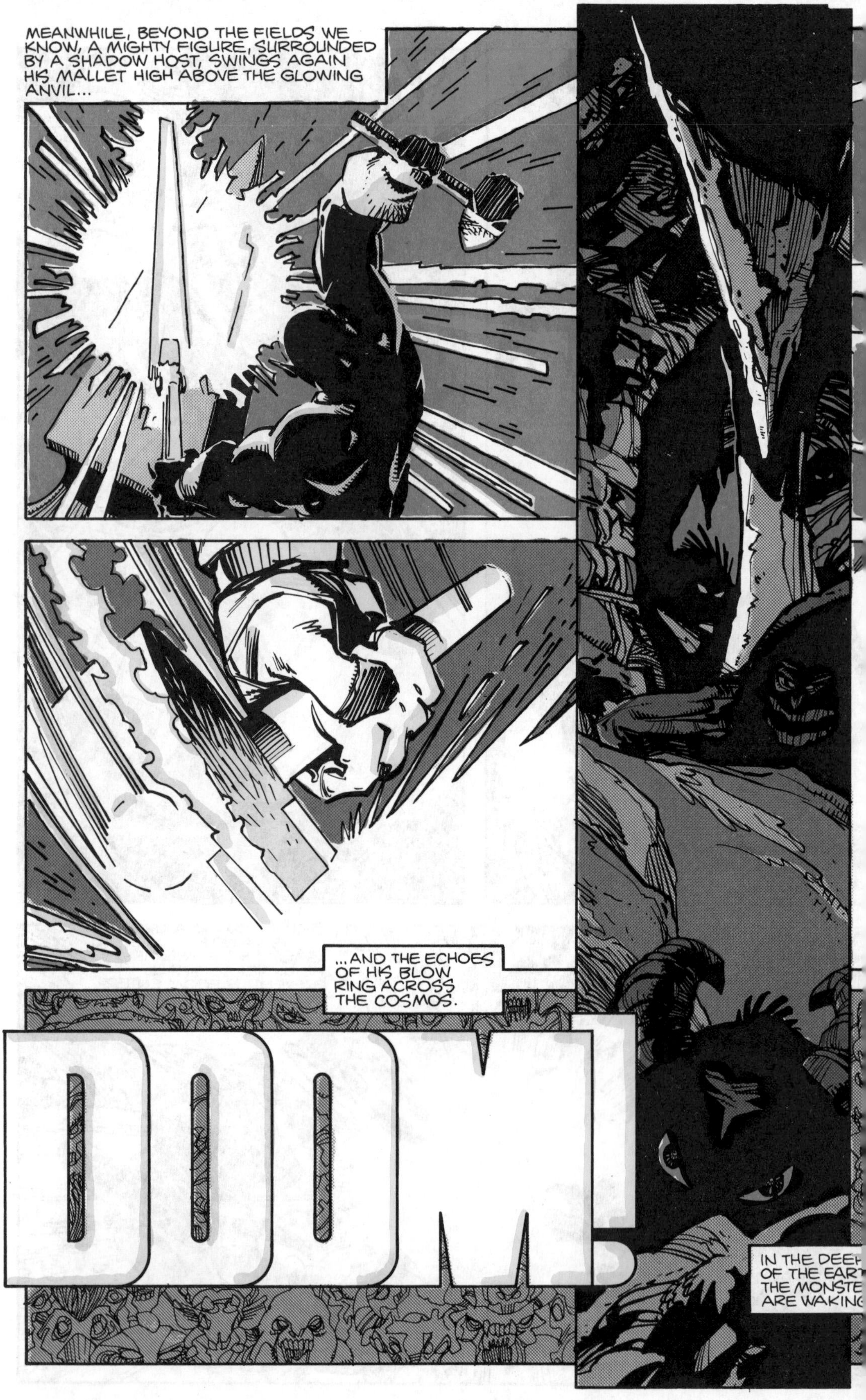
MEANWHILE, BEYOND THE FIELDS WE KNOW, A MIGHTY FIGURE, SURROUNDED BY A SHADOW HOST, SWINGS AGAIN HIS MALLET HIGH ABOVE THE GLOWING ANVIL...
...AND THE ECHOES OF HIS BLOW RING ACROSS THE COSMOS.
DOOM!
IN THE DEEP
OF THE EART
THE MONSTE
ARE WAKING

WHILE FAR AWAY, IN THE GREAT FLEET...

NO DEMON HAS YET GOTTEN PAST ME, BUT THEIR NUMBERS INCREASE WITH EVERY SECOND.

AND NOW THEY HAVE BEGUN TO MASS TOGETHER FOR THEIR FINAL ATTACK!

VERY WELL! IF TODAY I MUST JOURNEY TO THE HALLS OF HELA, I SHALL NOT TRAVEL ALONE!

COME, DEMONS! WHO WILL BE THE FIRST TO TASTE THIS SWEET STEEL?

BADDOOM! BADDOOM!

WHA--!

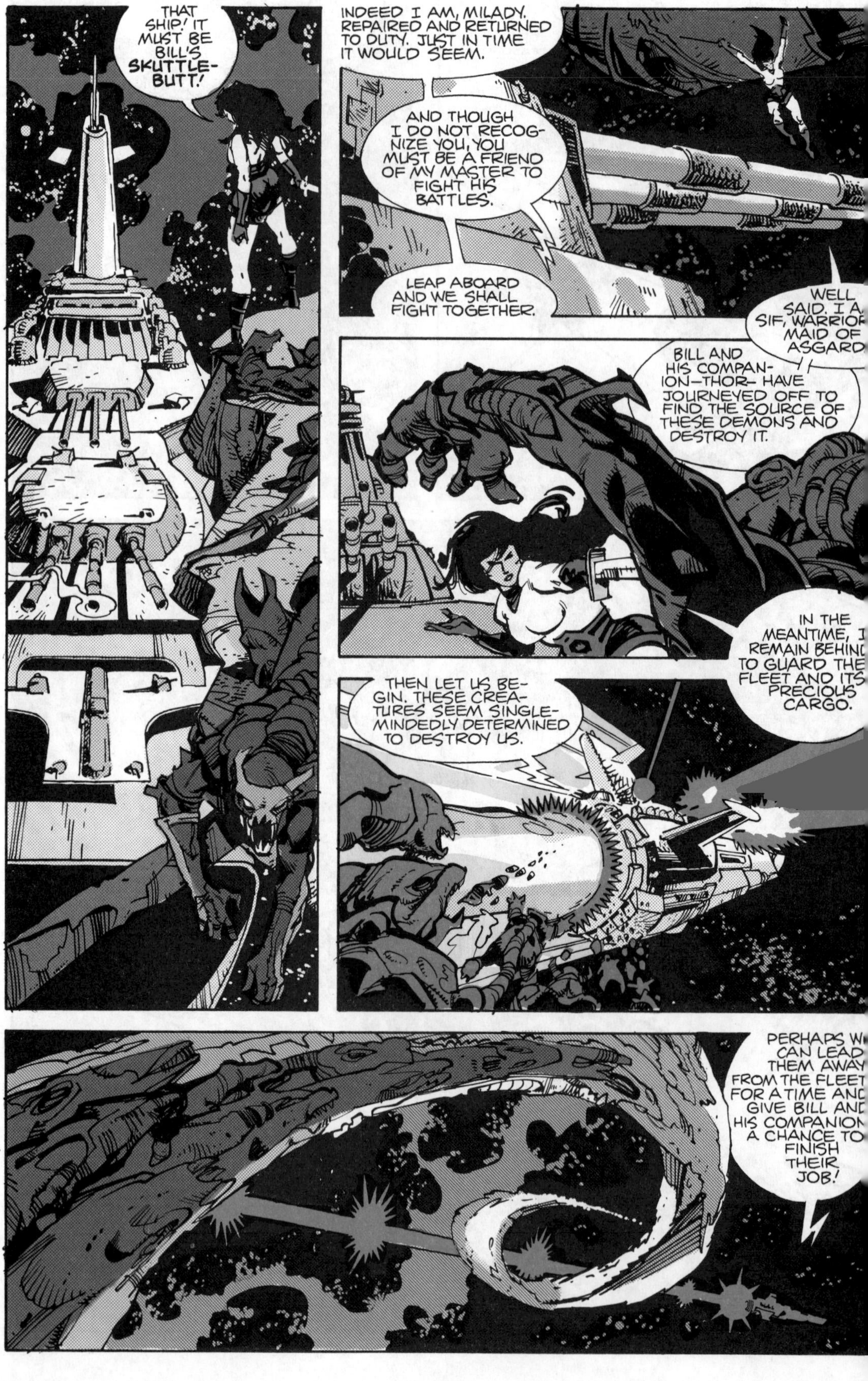

THAT SHIP! IT MUST BE BILL'S SKUTTLEBUTT!
INDEED I AM, MILADY. REPAIRED AND RETURNED TO DUTY. JUST IN TIME IT WOULD SEEM.
AND THOUGH I DO NOT RECOGNIZE YOU, YOU MUST BE A FRIEND OF MY MASTER TO FIGHT HIS BATTLES.
LEAP ABOARD AND WE SHALL FIGHT TOGETHER.
WELL SAID. I A SIF, WARRIOR MAID OF ASGARD
BILL AND HIS COMPANION—THOR— HAVE JOURNEYED OFF TO FIND THE SOURCE OF THESE DEMONS AND DESTROY IT.
IN THE MEANTIME, I REMAIN BEHIND TO GUARD THE FLEET AND ITS PRECIOUS CARGO.
THEN LET US BEGIN. THESE CREATURES SEEM SINGLE-MINDEDLY DETERMINED TO DESTROY US.
PERHAPS W CAN LEAD THEM AWAY FROM THE FLEET FOR A TIME AND GIVE BILL AND HIS COMPANION A CHANCE TO FINISH THEIR JOB!

BUT AS THE DEMONS TURN FROM THE FLEET IN HOT PURSUIT, LET US TURN TO THE GARDENS OF ASGARD TO LISTEN TO VALOROUS VOLSTAGG CONCLUDE HIS CHILLING TALE OF THE DEATH OF BALDER...

SO, MY YOUNG FRIEND, NOBLE BALDER WENT DOWN TO NIFFLEHEIM, HELA'S DARK DOMAIN.

HE FOUND THAT THE LEGENDS OF THE AFTER-LIFE WERE TRUE.

BEFORE HIM, DANK AND CHEERLESS, LAY THE CORPSE STRAND, THE HALLS OF THE TORTURED...

...AND THE DRAGON, NID-HOGG, THE EATER OF THE DEAD...

...CONSUMING THE SOULS OF THOSE WHO HAVE FLED IN TERROR DEEP INTO NIFFLEHEIM PAST THE GREAT WOLF GARM.

...FOR THERE BEFORE HIM WERE THE VERY WARRIORS WHOM HE HIMSELF HAD SLAIN AND SENT TO NIFFLEHEIM IN BATTLES PAST!

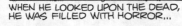
WHEN HE LOOKED UPON THE DEAD, HE WAS FILLED WITH HORROR...

THESE WERE THE FRUITS OF HIS MANY VICTORIES!

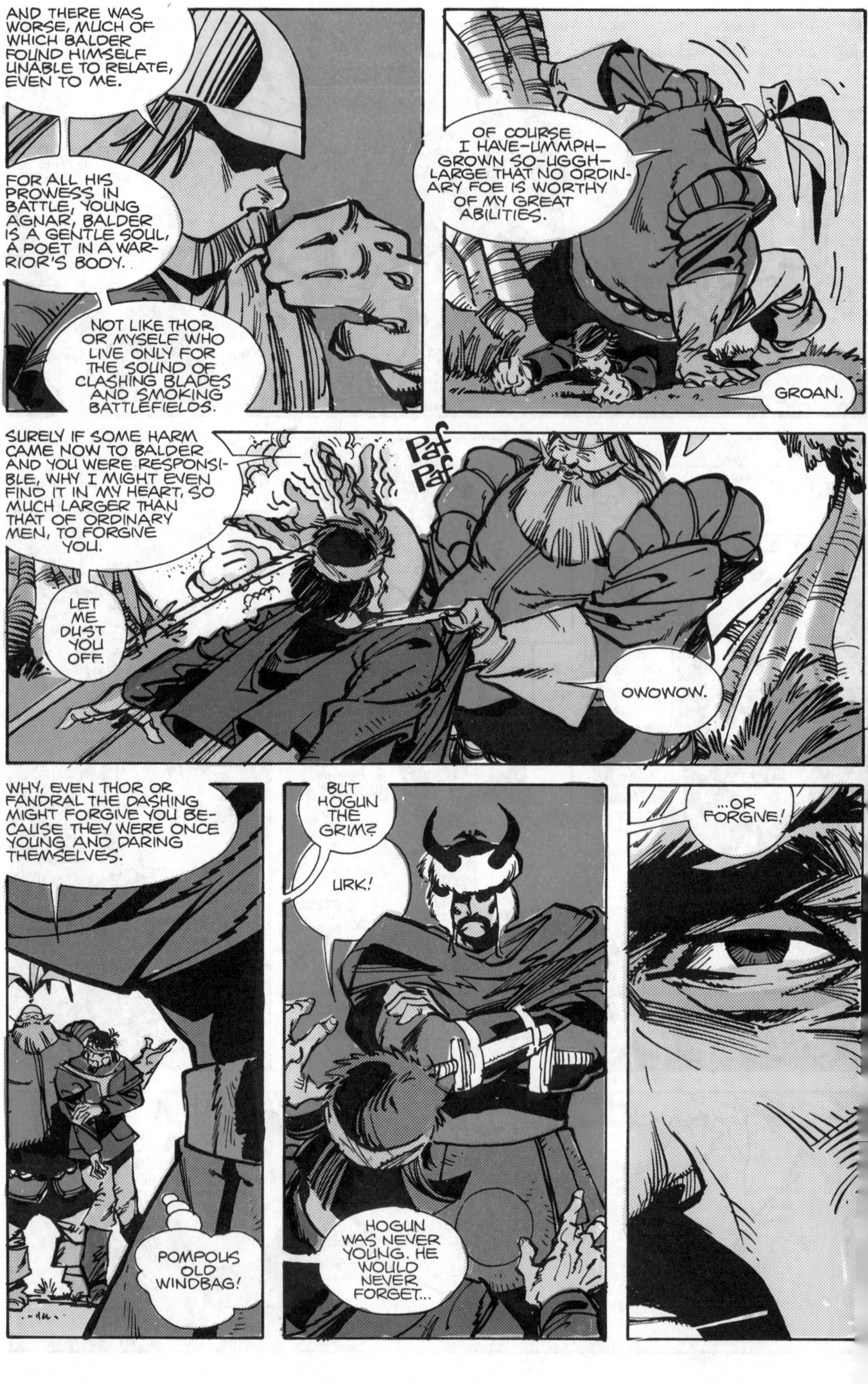
AND THERE WAS WORSE, MUCH OF WHICH BALDER FOUND HIMSELF UNABLE TO RELATE, EVEN TO ME.
FOR ALL HIS PROWESS IN BATTLE, YOUNG AGNAR, BALDER IS A GENTLE SOUL, A POET IN A WARRIOR'S BODY.
NOT LIKE THOR OR MYSELF WHO LIVE ONLY FOR THE SOUND OF CLASHING BLADES AND SMOKING BATTLEFIELDS.
OF COURSE I HAVE-UMMPH-GROWN SO-UGGH-LARGE THAT NO ORDINARY FOE IS WORTHY OF MY GREAT ABILITIES.
GROAN.
SURELY IF SOME HARM CAME NOW TO BALDER AND YOU WERE RESPONSIBLE, WHY I MIGHT EVEN FIND IT IN MY HEART, SO MUCH LARGER THAN THAT OF ORDINARY MEN, TO FORGIVE YOU.
Paf Paf
LET ME DUST YOU OFF.
OWOWOW.
WHY, EVEN THOR OR FANDRAL THE DASHING MIGHT FORGIVE YOU BECAUSE THEY WERE ONCE YOUNG AND DARING THEMSELVES.
POMPOUS OLD WINDBAG!
BUT HOGUN THE GRIM?
URK!
HOGUN WAS NEVER YOUNG. HE WOULD NEVER FORGET...
...OR FORGIVE!

MEANWHILE, IN THE DISTANT GALACTIC CORE...

IT IS NO GOOD, THOR! EVEN OUR COMBINED MIGHT IS UNABLE TO FORCE AN ENTRANCE THROUGH THE PORTAL!

THE POWER WITHIN IS TOO GREAT!

AND THE HEAT IS MORE THAN EVEN I CAN BEAR!

YOU ARE RIGHT, FRIEND BILL!

I NEVER THOUGHT SUCH POWER EXISTED BEYOND THE HALLS OF ODIN IN ASGARD!

YET THOUGH WE CANNOT ENTER, WE MAY STILL BE ABLE TO CLOSE THE PORTAL FOREVER TO THE DEMON HORDE AND SAVE YOUR PEOPLE!

STAND BESIDE THE PORTAL HERE AND AWAIT MY CALL.

I WILL TAKE MYSELF TO THE OTHER SIDE AND TOGETHER, WE MAY DO WHAT NEITHER OF US COULD ACCOMPLISH ALONE!

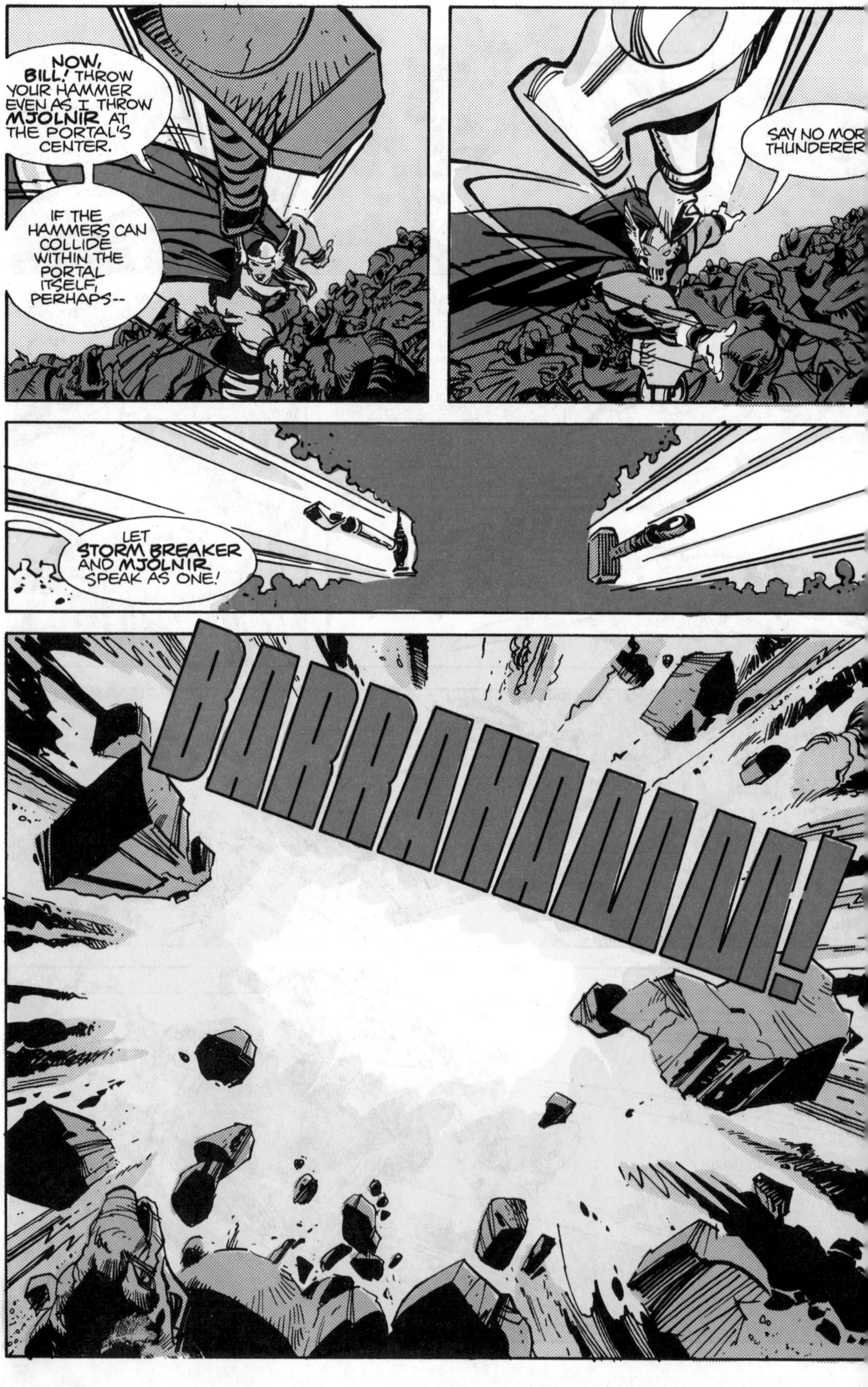
NOW, BILL! THROW YOUR HAMMER EVEN AS I THROW MJOLNIR AT THE PORTAL'S CENTER.
IF THE HAMMERS CAN COLLIDE WITHIN THE PORTAL ITSELF, PERHAPS--
SAY NO MOR THUNDERER
LET STORM BREAKER AND MJOLNIR SPEAK AS ONE!
BARRAHAOOOOM!

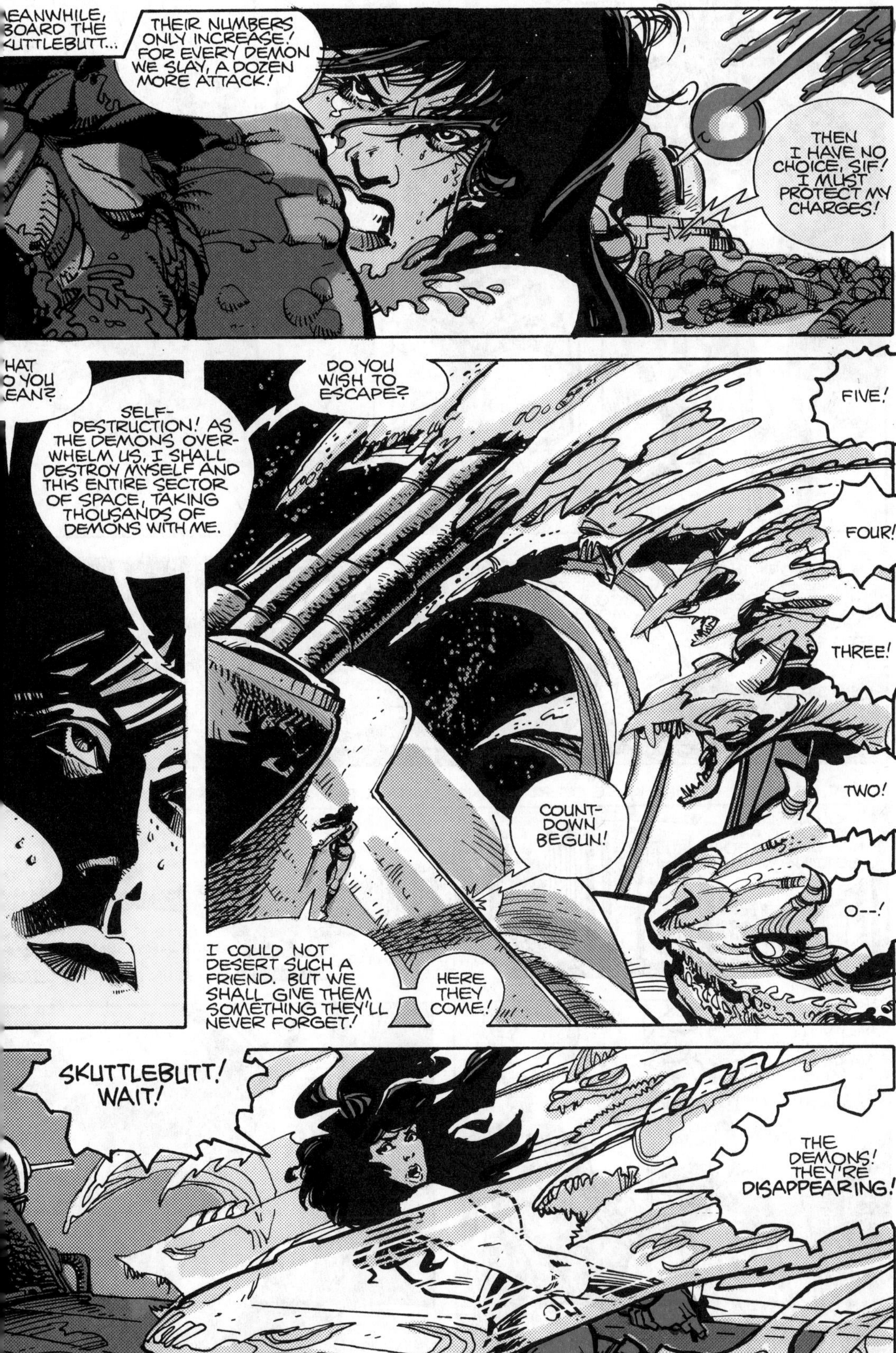

EANWHILE, BOARD THE KUTTLEBUTT...
THEIR NUMBERS ONLY INCREASE! FOR EVERY DEMON WE SLAY, A DOZEN MORE ATTACK!
THEN I HAVE NO CHOICE, SIF! I MUST PROTECT MY CHARGES!
HAT O YOU EAN?
SELF-DESTRUCTION! AS THE DEMONS OVERWHELM US, I SHALL DESTROY MYSELF AND THIS ENTIRE SECTOR OF SPACE, TAKING THOUSANDS OF DEMONS WITH ME.
DO YOU WISH TO ESCAPE?
I COULD NOT DESERT SUCH A FRIEND. BUT WE SHALL GIVE THEM SOMETHING THEY'LL NEVER FORGET!
COUNT-DOWN BEGUN!
HERE THEY COME!
FIVE!
FOUR!
THREE!
TWO!
O--!
SKUTTLEBUTT! WAIT!
THE DEMONS! THEY'RE DISAPPEARING!

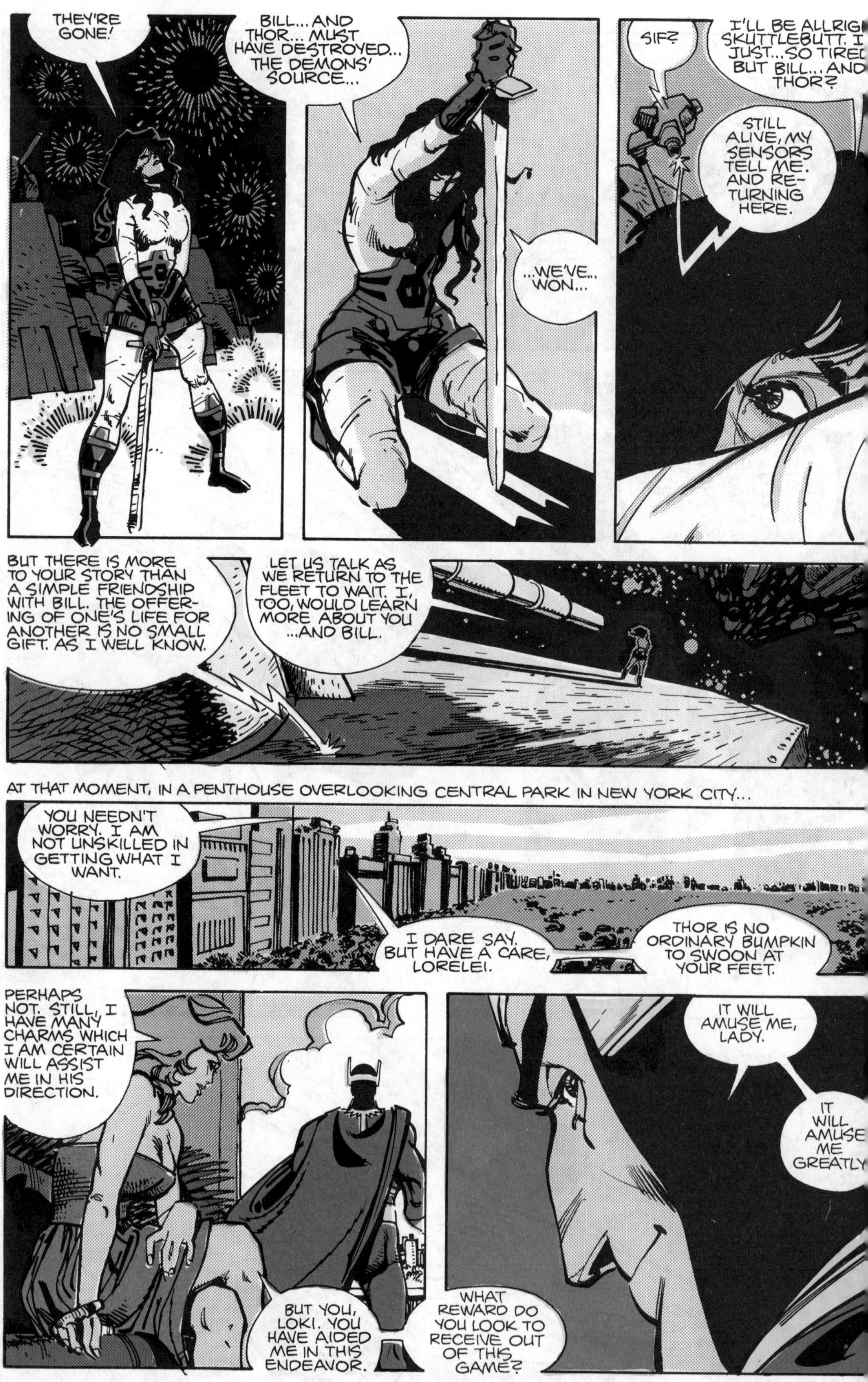
THEY'RE GONE!
BILL... AND THOR... MUST HAVE DESTROYED... THE DEMONS' SOURCE...
...WE'VE... WON...
SIF?
I'LL BE ALLRIG SKUTTLEBUTT. I JUST... SO TIRED BUT BILL... AND THOR?
STILL ALIVE, MY SENSORS TELL ME. AND RETURNING HERE.
BUT THERE IS MORE TO YOUR STORY THAN A SIMPLE FRIENDSHIP WITH BILL. THE OFFERING OF ONE'S LIFE FOR ANOTHER IS NO SMALL GIFT. AS I WELL KNOW.
LET US TALK AS WE RETURN TO THE FLEET TO WAIT. I, TOO, WOULD LEARN MORE ABOUT YOU ...AND BILL.
AT THAT MOMENT, IN A PENTHOUSE OVERLOOKING CENTRAL PARK IN NEW YORK CITY...
YOU NEEDN'T WORRY. I AM NOT UNSKILLED IN GETTING WHAT I WANT.
I DARE SAY. BUT HAVE A CARE, LORELEI.
THOR IS NO ORDINARY BUMPKIN TO SWOON AT YOUR FEET.
PERHAPS NOT. STILL, I HAVE MANY CHARMS WHICH I AM CERTAIN WILL ASSIST ME IN HIS DIRECTION.
BUT YOU, LOKI. YOU HAVE AIDED ME IN THIS ENDEAVOR.
WHAT REWARD DO YOU LOOK TO RECEIVE OUT OF THIS GAME?
IT WILL AMUSE ME, LADY.
IT WILL AMUSE ME GREATLY

THE NIGHT DRAWS ITS VEIL AC-
ROSS NEW YORK CITY, BUT IN
THE MORNING LIGHT OF ASGARD,
WE FIND THE STALWART WATCH-
MAN OF THE GODS...

STAND AND
IDENTIFY YOUR-
SELVES IF YOU SEEK
TO CROSS THE RAINBOW
BRIDGE INTO THE
GOLDEN REALM!

GREETINGS, HEIM-
DALL! WE HAVE RE-
TURNED FROM THE
FAR REACHES OF
SPACE WITH A
VICTORY.

THE LADY SIF,
BETA RAY BILL,
SKUTTLEBUTT, AND
I BRING NEWS
OF THE DE-
STRUCTION OF
OUR FOES!

WELL MET,
MIGHTY THOR!
LORD ODIN HAS
PROCLAIMED YOUR
TRIUMPH ACROSS
THE LAND.

EVEN NOW,
THE FEAST
IS MADE
READY. I
GIVE YOU
LEAVE TO
ENTER.

WHILE SKUTTLEBUTT REMAINS OUTSIDE (FOR THERE ARE NO HALLS IN ASGARD LARGE ENOUGH TO
HOLD HER)...

...THOR AND HIS COM-
PANIONS ENTER THE
CITY TO THE CHEERS
OF THE THRONG!

STILL, EVEN HEROES NEED BATHS AND AS OUR COMRADES CHANGE INTO FRESH CLOTHING TO PREPARE FOR THE FEAST...

YOU ARE STRANGELY SILENT, FRIEND BILL. I HOPE YOU DO NOT FEEL THAT I HOLD A GRUDGE AGAINST YOU FOR YOUR VICTORY EARLIER AGAINST ME.*

AND AS FOR *YOUR* PEOPLE, WE DID WIN, YOU KNOW.

*THOR 338—NO POINTS IF YOU MISSED IT.

FEAR NOT, MY FRIEND. YOUR FRIENDSHIP IS BEYOND RE-PROACH. AS IS OUR VICTORY.

BUT I MUST SHORTLY RETURN TO GUIDE MY PEOPLE TO A NEW HOME AND THOUGH I CAN HARDLY BELIEVE IT, I AM LOATH TO LEAVE ASGARD...

...AND ALL THAT I HAVE FOUND HERE.

THE UNCOMPROMIS[ING] ACCEPTANCE I HAVE HAD WHEN EVEN MY O[WN] PEOPLE CAN SCARCE[LY] LOOK AT ME, THE JOY [OF] COMRADESHIP, EVEN TH[E] TOUCH OF A WOMAN'S HAND...

BUT I SAY TOO MUCH.

I AM WHAT I AM AND CANNOT CHANGE IT.

I SHALL SEE YOU AT DINNER.

ELSEWHERE...

YOU SENT FOR ME, MY LORD.

THANK YOU FOR COMING SO QUICKLY, SIF.

I WOULD LIKE A FEW WORDS WITH YOU... ABOUT BILL.

I KNOW MORE THAN YOU MIGHT THINK, LADY, ABOUT YOUR FEELINGS FOR HIM. I, TOO, FIND HIM A MATCH FOR MY OWN SON IN MORE WAYS THAN ONE.

BUT THERE IS IN BILL A CORE OF MELANCHOLY THAT EVEN I CANNOT FATHOM.

I THOUGH[T] PERHAPS A WOMAN'S HEART WOUL[D] KNOW WHAT [I] DO NOT.

...HEART WOULD KNOW MORE THAN YOU, LORD [ODIN], WERE IT NOT FOR [BILL'S] ...[SHIP] AND I HAVE HAD A ...[LONG] TALK AND SHARED MANY SECRETS.

SHE HAS BEEN WITH HIM ON THEIR ODYSSEY AND KNOWS HIM BETTER THAN ANYONE. SHE KNOWS WHAT HE DID **NOT** TELL US HIMSELF.

FOR THOUGH HIS STORY WAS TRUE, IT WAS IN-COMPLETE!

"WHEN HE WAS CHOSEN TO BE THE GUARDIAN OF HIS PEOPLE, HE NEGLECTED TO TELL US OF THE GREAT GAMES THAT WERE HELD TO PICK THE MIGHTIEST CHAMPION.

"HOW HE WON OVER THOUSANDS OF OTHERS IN GRUELING TESTS OF POWER AND ENDURANCE.

...HOW, FROM AMONG ...[THE] PHYSICALLY [A]CCEPTABLE CANDI-...DATES, THE BEST ...[WERE] CHOSEN IN A ...[S]ERIES OF PSYCHO-...OGICAL EXAMINA-...TIONS...

...[T]HAT LEFT MOST ...[OF] THEM DEAD OR ...[IN]SANE!

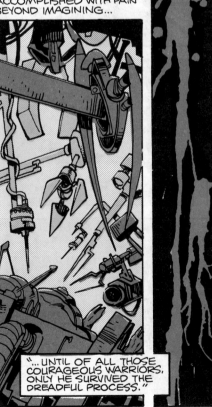

"OR HOW THE CREATION OF BETA RAY BILL WAS ACCOMPLISHED WITH PAIN BEYOND IMAGINING...

"...UNTIL OF ALL THOSE COURAGEOUS WARRIORS, ONLY HE SURVIVED THE DREADFUL PROCESS."

AND THE CHANGE WAS IRREVERSIBLE. HE WILL ALWAYS BE WHAT HE HAS BECOME.

WORST OF ALL, HIS OWN PEOPLE COULD HARDLY BEAR THE SIGHT OF HIM ONCE HE HAD BEEN FINISHED. YET HE WOULD DO IT ALL AGAIN IF NECESSARY.

OH, ALL-FATHER, HOW DO MORTALS ENDURE IT?

BE AT PEACE, SIF. LET US SEE WHAT WE CAN DO.

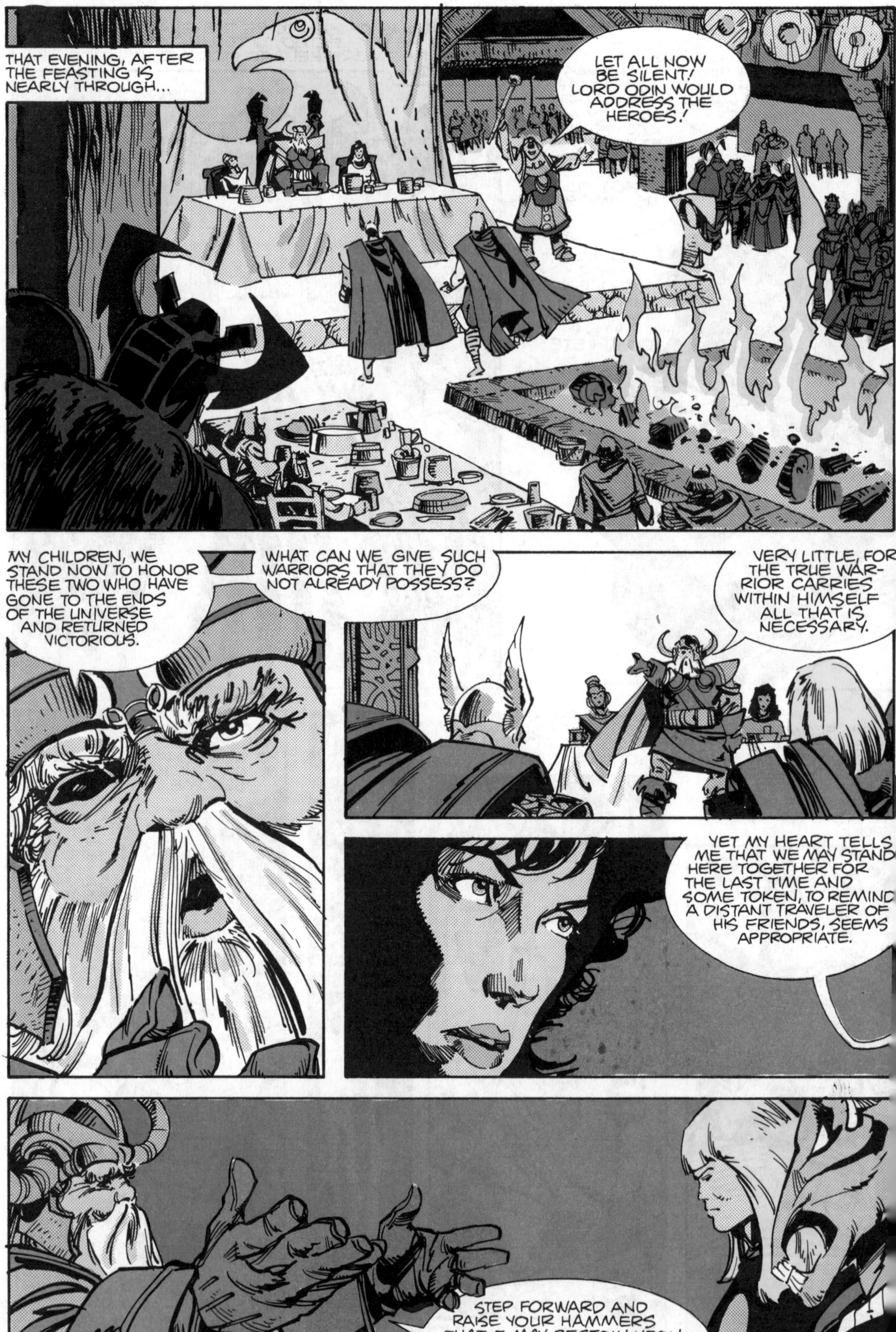
THAT EVENING, AFTER THE FEASTING IS NEARLY THROUGH...
LET ALL NOW BE SILENT! LORD ODIN WOULD ADDRESS THE HEROES!
MY CHILDREN, WE STAND NOW TO HONOR THESE TWO WHO HAVE GONE TO THE ENDS OF THE UNIVERSE AND RETURNED VICTORIOUS.
WHAT CAN WE GIVE SUCH WARRIORS THAT THEY DO NOT ALREADY POSSESS?
VERY LITTLE, FOR THE TRUE WARRIOR CARRIES WITHIN HIMSELF ALL THAT IS NECESSARY.
YET MY HEART TELLS ME THAT WE MAY STAND HERE TOGETHER FOR THE LAST TIME AND SOME TOKEN, TO REMIND A DISTANT TRAVELER OF HIS FRIENDS, SEEMS APPROPRIATE.
STEP FORWARD AND RAISE YOUR HAMMERS THAT I MAY BESTOW UPON YOU EACH A GIFT THAT I HOPE WILL BE WORTHY OF YOU.

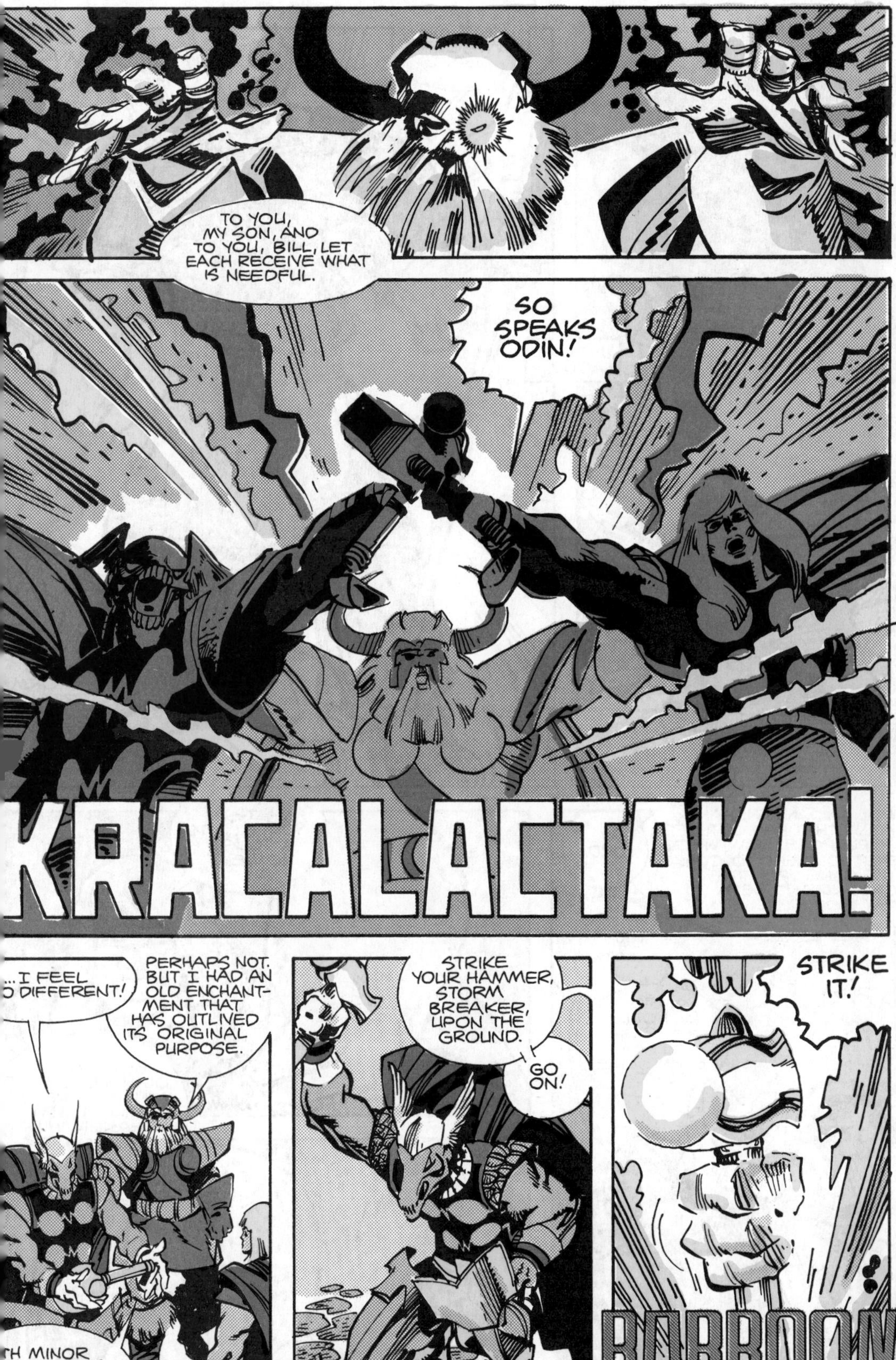

TO YOU, MY SON, AND TO YOU, BILL, LET EACH RECEIVE WHAT IS NEEDFUL.
SO SPEAKS ODIN!
KRACALACTAKA!
...I FEEL O DIFFERENT!
PERHAPS NOT. BUT I HAD AN OLD ENCHANTMENT THAT HAS OUTLIVED ITS ORIGINAL PURPOSE.
TH MINOR TERATIONS, I OUGHT YOU GHT FIND USEFUL.
STRIKE YOUR HAMMER, STORM BREAKER, UPON THE GROUND.
GO ON!
STRIKE IT!
BARROOM!

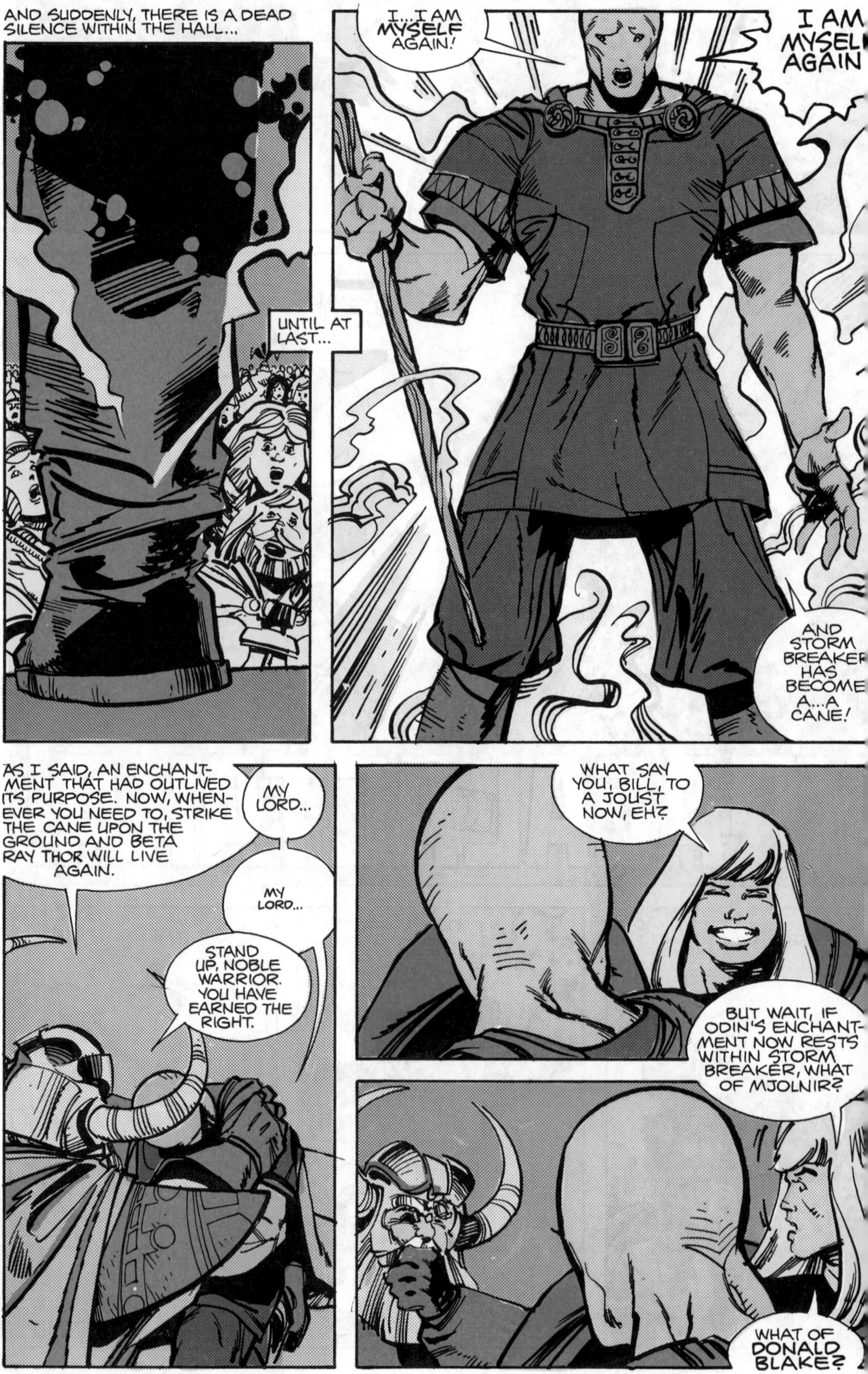

AND SUDDENLY, THERE IS A DEAD SILENCE WITHIN THE HALL...
UNTIL AT LAST...
I...I AM MYSELF AGAIN!
I AM MYSEL AGAIN
AND STORM BREAKER HAS BECOME A...A CANE!
AS I SAID, AN ENCHANTMENT THAT HAD OUTLIVED ITS PURPOSE. NOW, WHENEVER YOU NEED TO, STRIKE THE CANE UPON THE GROUND AND BETA RAY THOR WILL LIVE AGAIN.
MY LORD...
MY LORD...
STAND UP, NOBLE WARRIOR. YOU HAVE EARNED THE RIGHT.
WHAT SAY YOU, BILL, TO A JOUST NOW, EH?
BUT WAIT, IF ODIN'S ENCHANTMENT NOW RESTS WITHIN STORM BREAKER, WHAT OF MJOLNIR?
WHAT OF DONALD BLAKE?

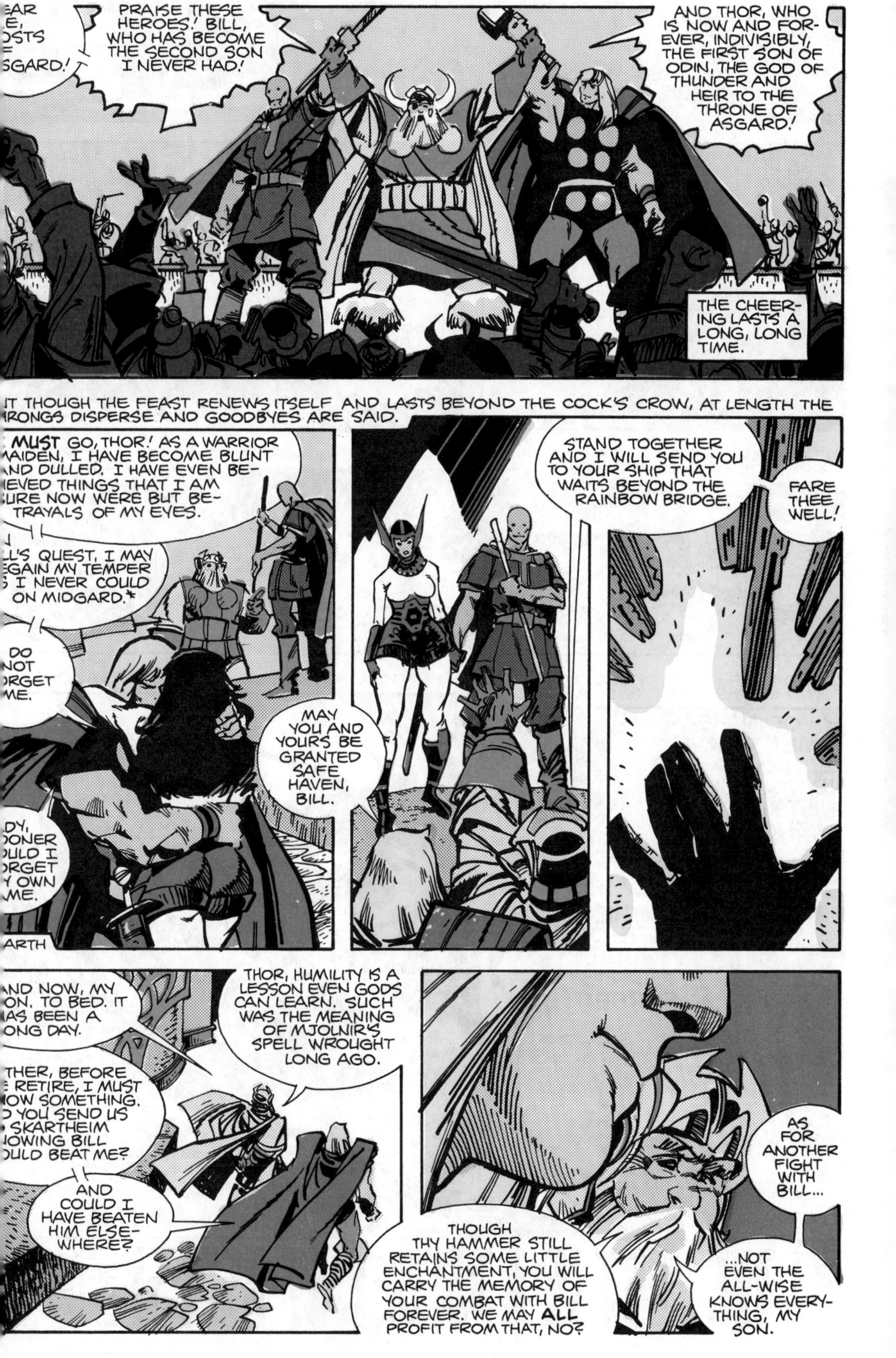

EAR
E,
OSTS
F
SGARD!
PRAISE THESE HEROES! BILL, WHO HAS BECOME THE SECOND SON I NEVER HAD!
AND THOR, WHO IS NOW AND FOREVER, INDIVISIBLY, THE FIRST SON OF ODIN, THE GOD OF THUNDER AND HEIR TO THE THRONE OF ASGARD!
THE CHEERING LASTS A LONG, LONG TIME.
T THOUGH THE FEAST RENEWS ITSELF AND LASTS BEYOND THE COCK'S CROW, AT LENGTH THE
RONGS DISPERSE AND GOODBYES ARE SAID.
MUST GO, THOR! AS A WARRIOR MAIDEN, I HAVE BECOME BLUNT AND DULLED. I HAVE EVEN BE-
IEVED THINGS THAT I AM
URE NOW WERE BUT BETRAYALS OF MY EYES.
N
L'S QUEST, I MAY
EGAIN MY TEMPER
I NEVER COULD
ON MIDGARD.*
DO
NOT
RGET
ME.
DY,
OONER
OULD I
RGET
OWN
ME.
ARTH
MAY YOU AND YOURS BE GRANTED SAFE HAVEN, BILL.
STAND TOGETHER AND I WILL SEND YOU TO YOUR SHIP THAT WAITS BEYOND THE RAINBOW BRIDGE.
FARE THEE WELL!
ND NOW, MY
ON. TO BED. IT
AS BEEN A
ONG DAY.
THOR, HUMILITY IS A LESSON EVEN GODS CAN LEARN. SUCH WAS THE MEANING OF MJOLNIR'S SPELL WROUGHT LONG AGO.
THER, BEFORE
RETIRE, I MUST
OW SOMETHING.
YOU SEND US
SKARTHEIM
OWING BILL
OULD BEAT ME?
AND COULD I HAVE BEATEN HIM ELSEWHERE?
AS FOR ANOTHER FIGHT WITH BILL...
THOUGH THY HAMMER STILL RETAINS SOME LITTLE ENCHANTMENT, YOU WILL CARRY THE MEMORY OF YOUR COMBAT WITH BILL FOREVER. WE MAY ALL PROFIT FROM THAT, NO?
...NOT EVEN THE ALL-WISE KNOWS EVERYTHING, MY SON.

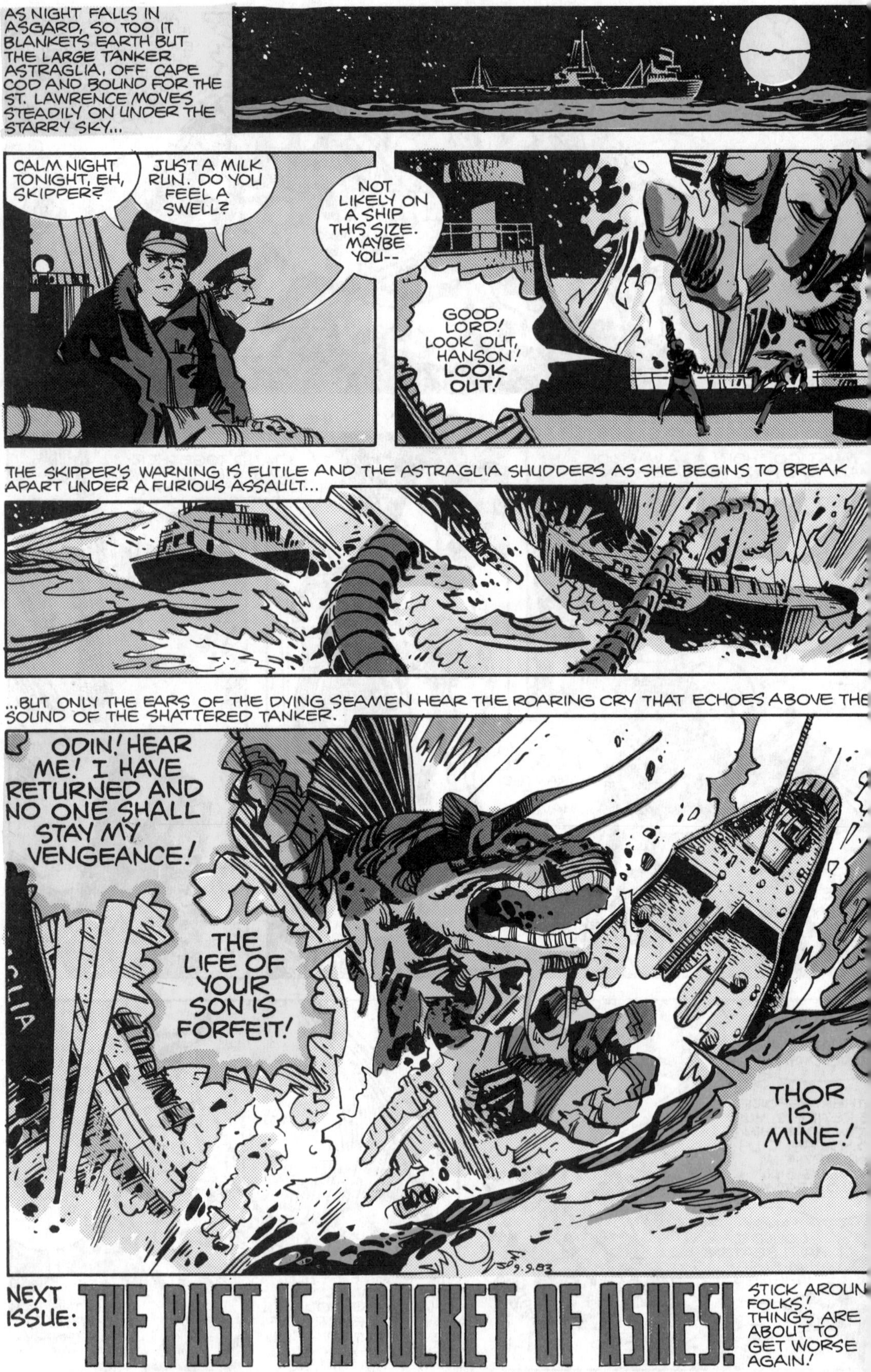
AS NIGHT FALLS IN ASGARD, SO TOO IT BLANKETS EARTH BUT THE LARGE TANKER ASTRAGLIA, OFF CAPE COD AND BOUND FOR THE ST. LAWRENCE MOVES STEADILY ON UNDER THE STARRY SKY...
CALM NIGHT TONIGHT, EH, SKIPPER?
JUST A MILK RUN. DO YOU FEEL A SWELL?
NOT LIKELY ON A SHIP THIS SIZE. MAYBE YOU--
GOOD LORD! LOOK OUT, HANSON! LOOK OUT!
THE SKIPPER'S WARNING IS FUTILE AND THE ASTRAGLIA SHUDDERS AS SHE BEGINS TO BREAK APART UNDER A FURIOUS ASSAULT...
...BUT ONLY THE EARS OF THE DYING SEAMEN HEAR THE ROARING CRY THAT ECHOES ABOVE THE SOUND OF THE SHATTERED TANKER.
ODIN! HEAR ME! I HAVE RETURNED AND NO ONE SHALL STAY MY VENGEANCE!
THE LIFE OF YOUR SON IS FORFEIT!
THOR IS MINE!
9.9.83
NEXT ISSUE: THE PAST IS A BUCKET OF ASHES!
STICK AROUN' FOLKS! THINGS ARE ABOUT TO GET WORSE AGAIN!

Chapter Five
MARVEL
the mighty
THOR
60¢
341
MAR
02450
APPROVED BY THE COMICS CODE AUTHORITY

STAN LEE PRESENTS: the MIGHTY THOR

THE PAST IS A BUCKET OF ASHES

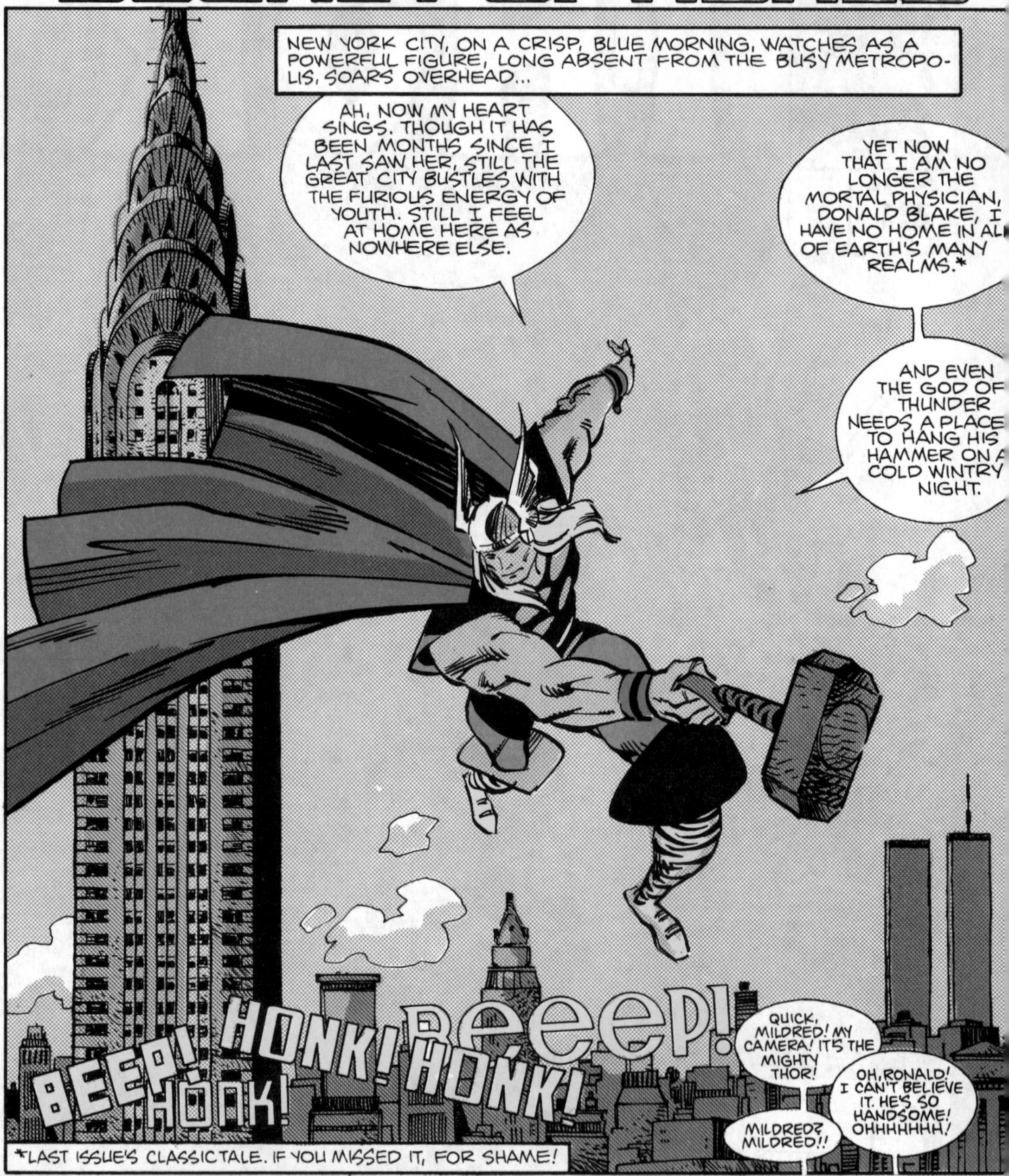
NEW YORK CITY, ON A CRISP, BLUE MORNING, WATCHES AS A POWERFUL FIGURE, LONG ABSENT FROM THE BUSY METROPOLIS, SOARS OVERHEAD...
AH, NOW MY HEART SINGS. THOUGH IT HAS BEEN MONTHS SINCE I LAST SAW HER, STILL THE GREAT CITY BUSTLES WITH THE FURIOUS ENERGY OF YOUTH. STILL I FEEL AT HOME HERE AS NOWHERE ELSE.
YET NOW THAT I AM NO LONGER THE MORTAL PHYSICIAN, DONALD BLAKE, I HAVE NO HOME IN AL OF EARTH'S MANY REALMS.*
AND EVEN THE GOD OF THUNDER NEEDS A PLACE TO HANG HIS HAMMER ON A COLD WINTRY NIGHT.
BEEP! HONK! HONK! HONK! BEEEP!
QUICK, MILDRED! MY CAMERA! IT'S THE MIGHTY THOR!
OH, RONALD! I CAN'T BELIEVE IT. HE'S SO HANDSOME! OHHHHHHH!
MILDRED? MILDRED!!
*LAST ISSUE'S CLASSIC TALE. IF YOU MISSED IT, FOR SHAME!

ART AND STORY: WALTER SIMONSON · LETTERING: JOHN WORKMAN, JR. · COLORS: GEORGE ROUSSOS
EDITING: MARK GRUENWALD · EDITOR-IN-CHIEF: JIM SHOOTER

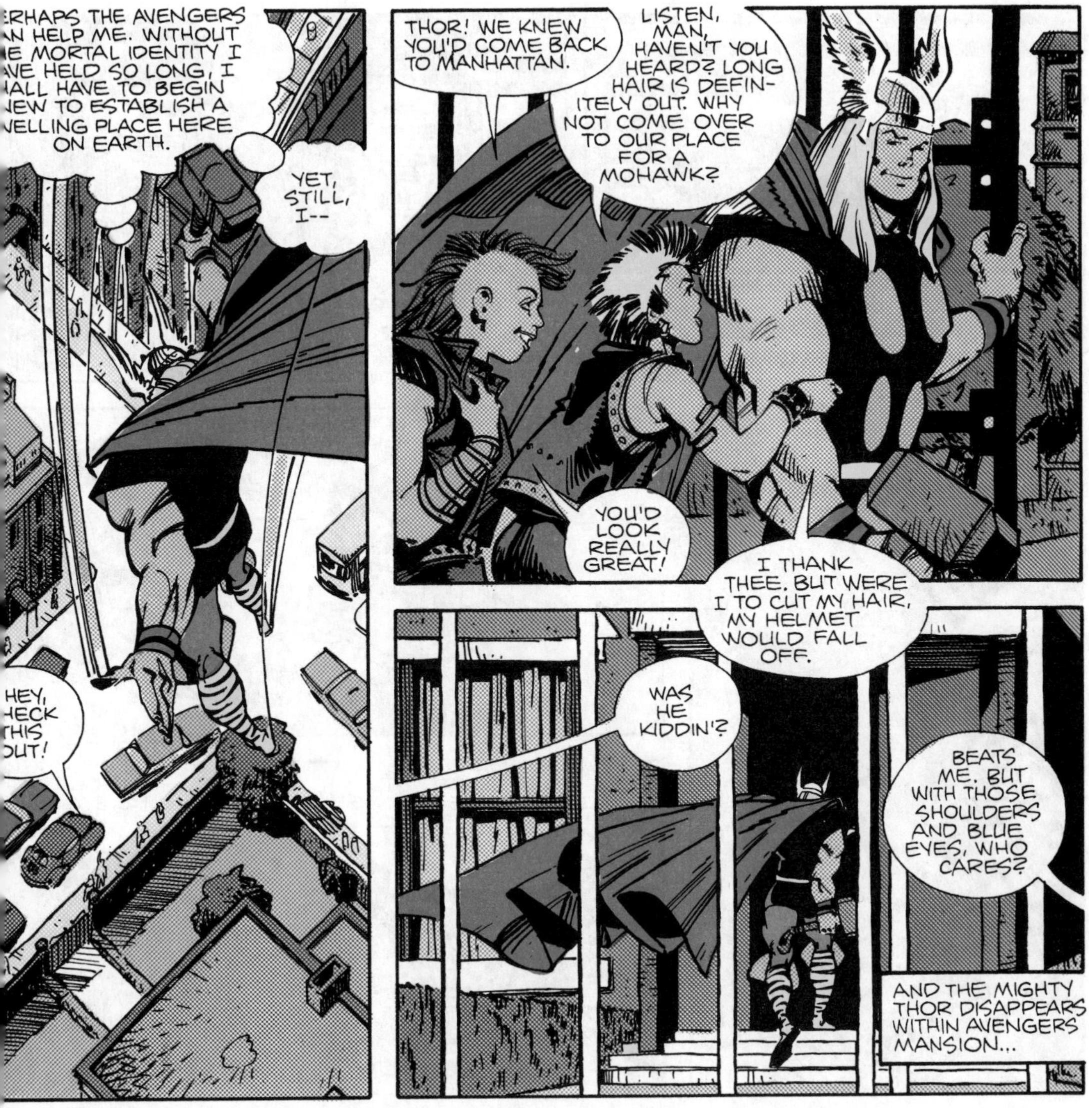
ERHAPS THE AVENGERS AN HELP ME. WITHOUT E MORTAL IDENTITY I VE HELD SO LONG, I HALL HAVE TO BEGIN NEW TO ESTABLISH A VELLING PLACE HERE ON EARTH.
YET, STILL, I--
HEY, HECK THIS OUT!
THOR! WE KNEW YOU'D COME BACK TO MANHATTAN.
LISTEN, MAN, HAVEN'T YOU HEARD? LONG HAIR IS DEFIN-ITELY OUT. WHY NOT COME OVER TO OUR PLACE FOR A MOHAWK?
YOU'D LOOK REALLY GREAT!
I THANK THEE. BUT WERE I TO CUT MY HAIR, MY HELMET WOULD FALL OFF.
WAS HE KIDDIN'?
BEATS ME. BUT WITH THOSE SHOULDERS AND BLUE EYES, WHO CARES?
AND THE MIGHTY THOR DISAPPEARS WITHIN AVENGERS MANSION...

TO FIND HIMSELF ON THE MOST SURPRISING ADVENTURE OF HIS CAREER.*

*SO SURPRISING, IN FACT, THAT WE CAN'T EVEN TELL YOU ABOUT IT UNTIL NEXT MONTH! WATCH THIS SPACE.

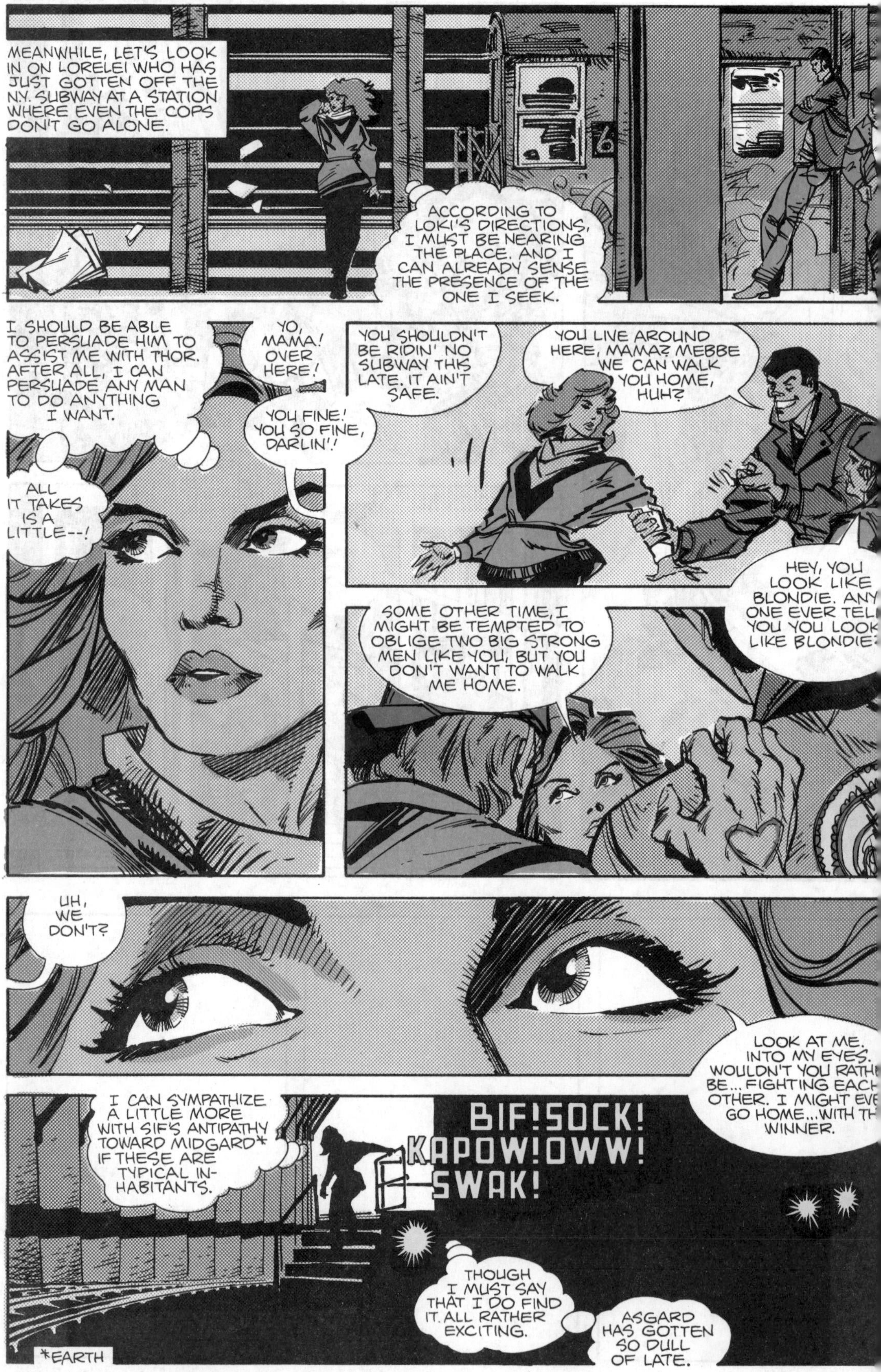

MEANWHILE, LET'S LOOK IN ON LORELEI WHO HAS JUST GOTTEN OFF THE N.Y. SUBWAY AT A STATION WHERE EVEN THE COPS DON'T GO ALONE.
ACCORDING TO LOKI'S DIRECTIONS, I MUST BE NEARING THE PLACE. AND I CAN ALREADY SENSE THE PRESENCE OF THE ONE I SEEK.
I SHOULD BE ABLE TO PERSUADE HIM TO ASSIST ME WITH THOR. AFTER ALL, I CAN PERSUADE ANY MAN TO DO ANYTHING I WANT.
ALL IT TAKES IS A LITTLE--!
YO, MAMA! OVER HERE!
YOU FINE! YOU SO FINE, DARLIN'!
YOU SHOULDN'T BE RIDIN' NO SUBWAY THIS LATE. IT AIN'T SAFE.
YOU LIVE AROUND HERE, MAMA? MEBBE WE CAN WALK YOU HOME, HUH?
HEY, YOU LOOK LIKE BLONDIE. ANY ONE EVER TEL YOU YOU LOOK LIKE BLONDIE?
SOME OTHER TIME, I MIGHT BE TEMPTED TO OBLIGE TWO BIG STRONG MEN LIKE YOU, BUT YOU DON'T WANT TO WALK ME HOME.
UH, WE DON'T?
LOOK AT ME. INTO MY EYES. WOULDN'T YOU RATH BE... FIGHTING EACH OTHER. I MIGHT EVE GO HOME... WITH TH WINNER.
I CAN SYMPATHIZE A LITTLE MORE WITH SIF'S ANTIPATHY TOWARD MIDGARD* IF THESE ARE TYPICAL IN-HABITANTS.
BIF! SOCK! KAPOW! OWW! SWAK!
THOUGH I MUST SAY THAT I DO FIND IT ALL RATHER EXCITING.
ASGARD HAS GOTTEN SO DULL OF LATE.
*EARTH

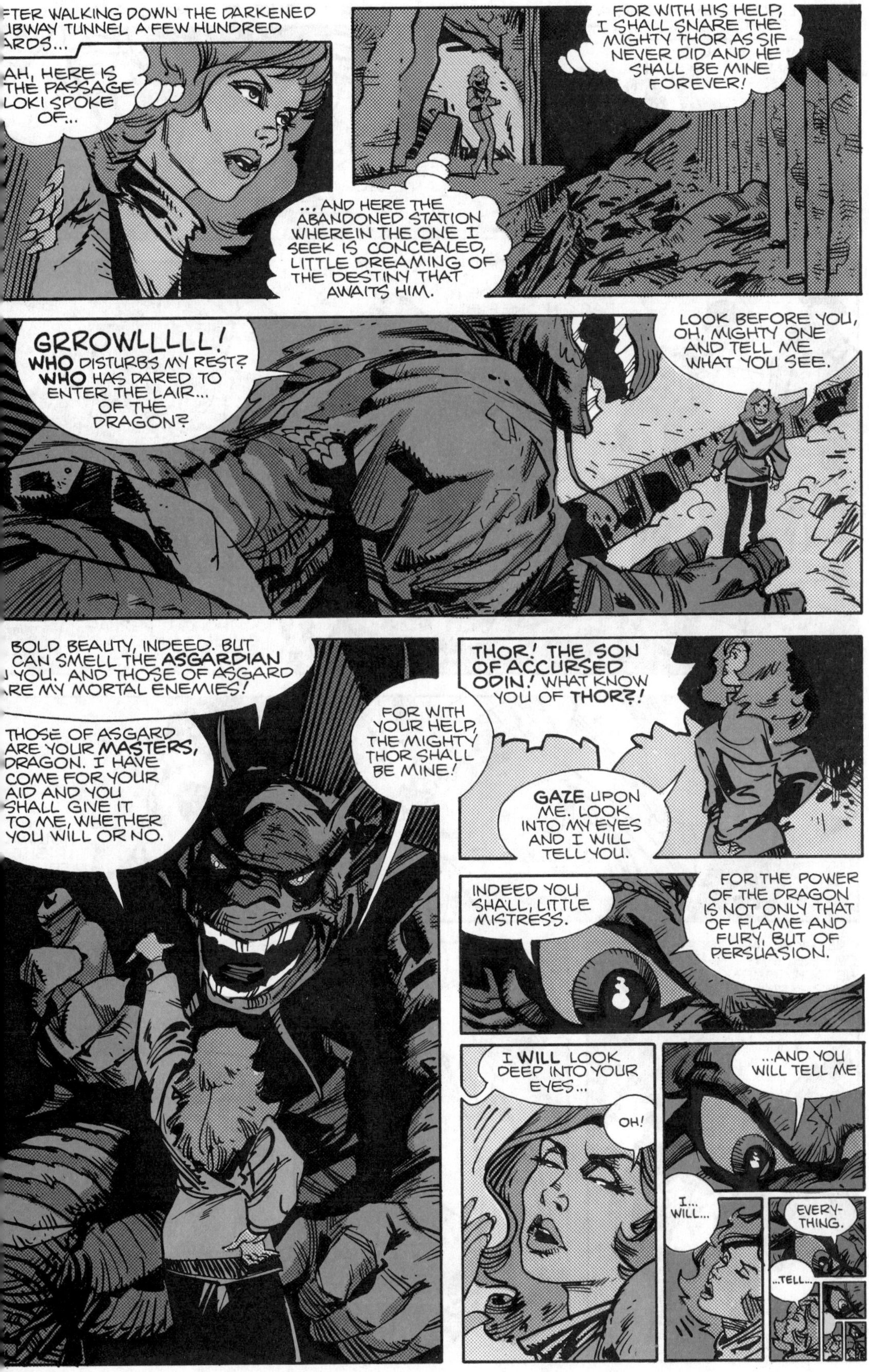

FTER WALKING DOWN THE DARKENED UBWAY TUNNEL A FEW HUNDRED ARDS...
AH, HERE IS THE PASSAGE LOKI SPOKE OF...
...AND HERE THE ABANDONED STATION WHEREIN THE ONE I SEEK IS CONCEALED, LITTLE DREAMING OF THE DESTINY THAT AWAITS HIM.
FOR WITH HIS HELP, I SHALL SNARE THE MIGHTY THOR AS SIF NEVER DID AND HE SHALL BE MINE FOREVER!
GRROWLLLLL! WHO DISTURBS MY REST? WHO HAS DARED TO ENTER THE LAIR... OF THE DRAGON?
LOOK BEFORE YOU, OH, MIGHTY ONE AND TELL ME WHAT YOU SEE.
BOLD BEAUTY, INDEED. BUT CAN SMELL THE ASGARDIAN YOU. AND THOSE OF ASGARD RE MY MORTAL ENEMIES!
THOSE OF ASGARD ARE YOUR MASTERS, DRAGON. I HAVE COME FOR YOUR AID AND YOU SHALL GIVE IT TO ME, WHETHER YOU WILL OR NO.
FOR WITH YOUR HELP, THE MIGHTY THOR SHALL BE MINE!
THOR! THE SON OF ACCURSED ODIN! WHAT KNOW YOU OF THOR?!
GAZE UPON ME. LOOK INTO MY EYES AND I WILL TELL YOU.
INDEED YOU SHALL, LITTLE MISTRESS.
FOR THE POWER OF THE DRAGON IS NOT ONLY THAT OF FLAME AND FURY, BUT OF PERSUASION.
I WILL LOOK DEEP INTO YOUR EYES...
OH!
...AND YOU WILL TELL ME
I... WILL...
EVERY-THING.
...TELL...

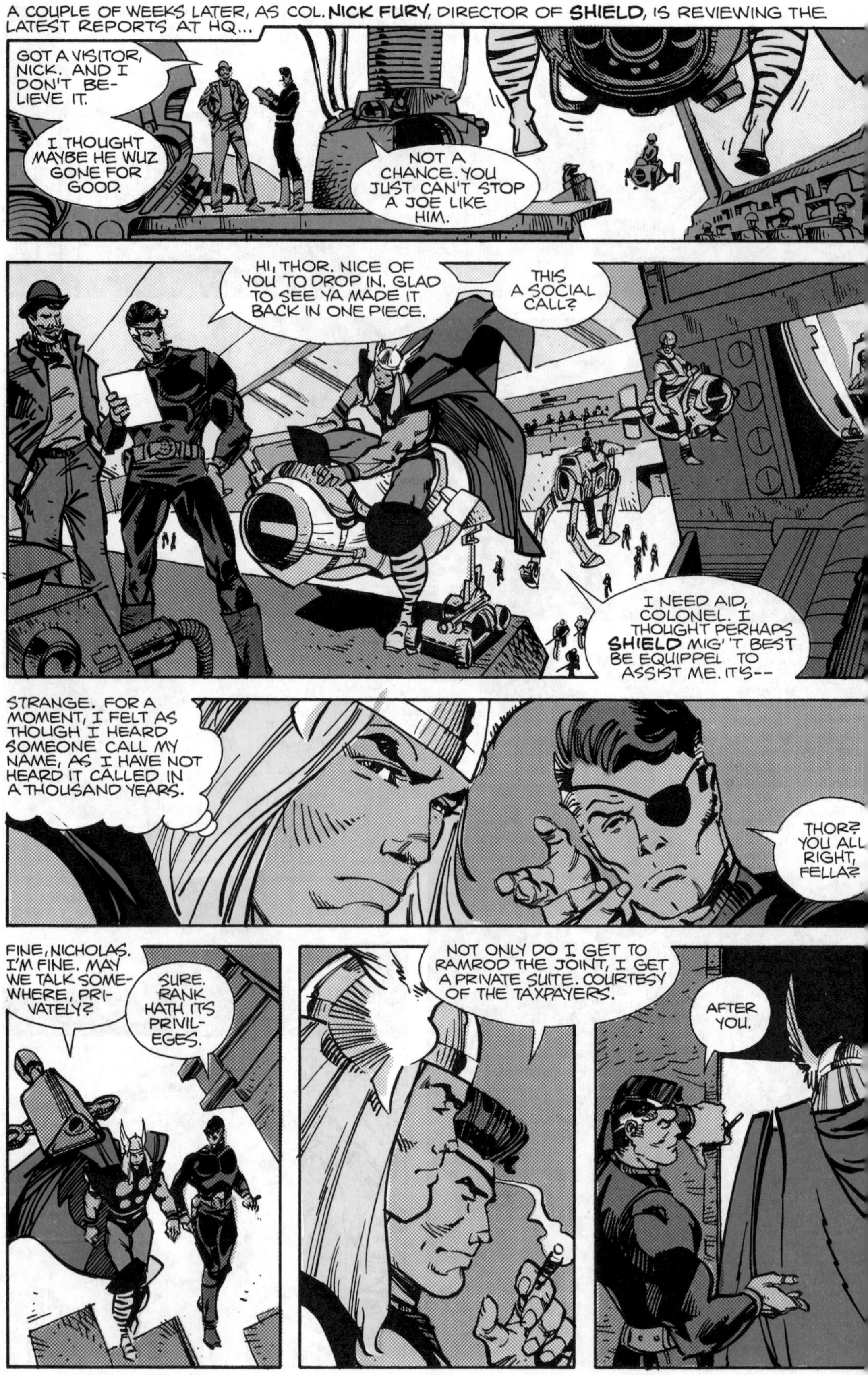
A COUPLE OF WEEKS LATER, AS COL. NICK FURY, DIRECTOR OF SHIELD, IS REVIEWING THE LATEST REPORTS AT HQ...
GOT A VISITOR, NICK. AND I DON'T BE-LIEVE IT.
I THOUGHT MAYBE HE WUZ GONE FOR GOOD.
NOT A CHANCE. YOU JUST CAN'T STOP A JOE LIKE HIM.
HI, THOR. NICE OF YOU TO DROP IN. GLAD TO SEE YA MADE IT BACK IN ONE PIECE.
THIS A SOCIAL CALL?
I NEED AID, COLONEL. I THOUGHT PERHAPS SHIELD MIG'T BEST BE EQUIPPEL TO ASSIST ME. IT'S--
STRANGE. FOR A MOMENT, I FELT AS THOUGH I HEARD SOMEONE CALL MY NAME, AS I HAVE NOT HEARD IT CALLED IN A THOUSAND YEARS.
THOR? YOU ALL RIGHT, FELLA?
FINE, NICHOLAS. I'M FINE. MAY WE TALK SOME-WHERE, PRI-VATELY?
SURE. RANK HATH ITS PRIVIL-EGES.
NOT ONLY DO I GET TO RAMROD THE JOINT, I GET A PRIVATE SUITE. COURTESY OF THE TAXPAYERS.
AFTER YOU.

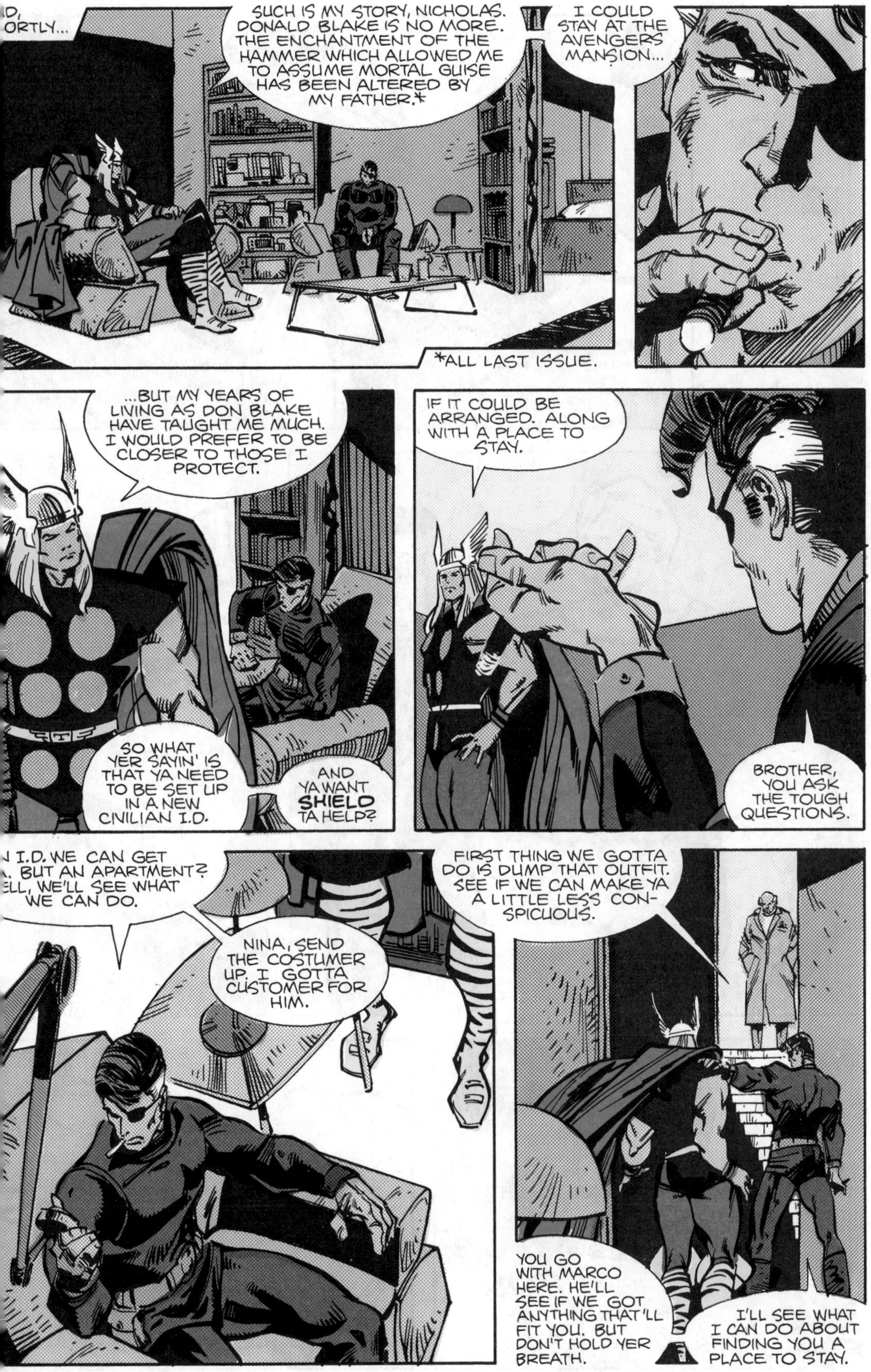
D, ORTLY...
SUCH IS MY STORY, NICHOLAS. DONALD BLAKE IS NO MORE. THE ENCHANTMENT OF THE HAMMER WHICH ALLOWED ME TO ASSUME MORTAL GUISE HAS BEEN ALTERED BY MY FATHER.*
*ALL LAST ISSUE.
I COULD STAY AT THE AVENGERS MANSION...
...BUT MY YEARS OF LIVING AS DON BLAKE HAVE TAUGHT ME MUCH. I WOULD PREFER TO BE CLOSER TO THOSE I PROTECT.
SO WHAT YER SAYIN' IS THAT YA NEED TO BE SET UP IN A NEW CIVILIAN I.D.
AND YA WANT SHIELD TA HELP?
IF IT COULD BE ARRANGED. ALONG WITH A PLACE TO STAY.
BROTHER, YOU ASK THE TOUGH QUESTIONS.
I.D. WE CAN GET . BUT AN APARTMENT? ELL, WE'LL SEE WHAT WE CAN DO.
NINA, SEND THE COSTUMER UP. I GOTTA CUSTOMER FOR HIM.
FIRST THING WE GOTTA DO IS DUMP THAT OUTFIT. SEE IF WE CAN MAKE YA A LITTLE LESS CON-SPICUOUS.
YOU GO WITH MARCO HERE. HE'LL SEE IF WE GOT ANYTHING THAT'LL FIT YOU. BUT DON'T HOLD YER BREATH.
I'LL SEE WHAT I CAN DO ABOUT FINDING YOU A PLACE TO STAY.

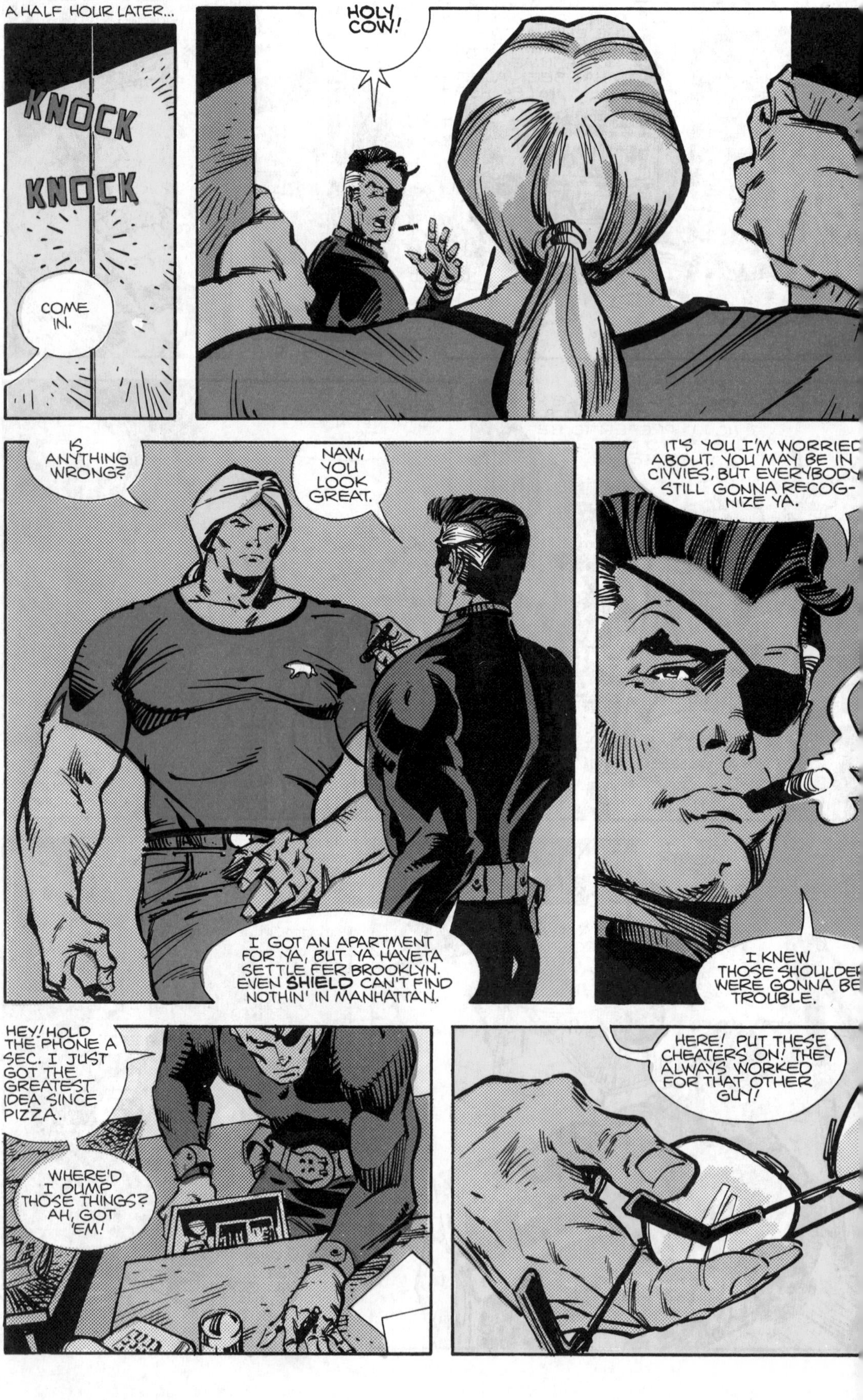
A HALF HOUR LATER...
KNOCK
KNOCK
COME IN.
HOLY COW!
IS ANYTHING WRONG?
NAW, YOU LOOK GREAT.
I GOT AN APARTMENT FOR YA, BUT YA HAVETA SETTLE FER BROOKLYN. EVEN SHIELD CAN'T FIND NOTHIN' IN MANHATTAN.
IT'S YOU I'M WORRIED ABOUT. YOU MAY BE IN CIVVIES, BUT EVERYBODY STILL GONNA RECOG-NIZE YA.
I KNEW THOSE SHOULDERS WERE GONNA BE TROUBLE.
HEY! HOLD THE PHONE A SEC. I JUST GOT THE GREATEST IDEA SINCE PIZZA.
WHERE'D I DUMP THOSE THINGS? AH, GOT 'EM!
HERE! PUT THESE CHEATERS ON! THEY ALWAYS WORKED FOR THAT OTHER GUY!

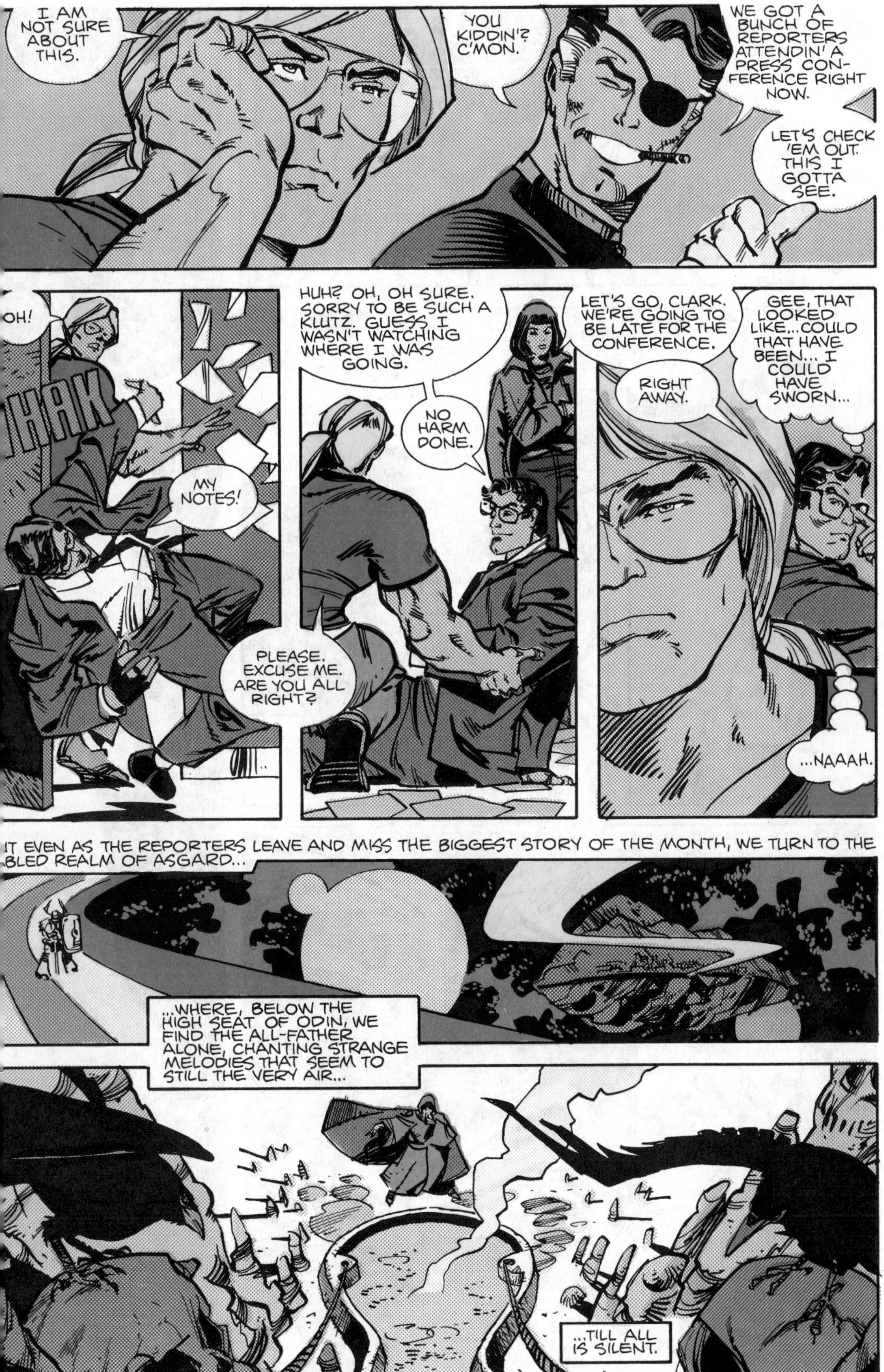
I AM NOT SURE ABOUT THIS.
YOU KIDDIN'? C'MON.
WE GOT A BUNCH OF REPORTERS ATTENDIN' A PRESS CONFERENCE RIGHT NOW.
LET'S CHECK 'EM OUT. THIS I GOTTA SEE.
OH!
HAK
MY NOTES!
HUH? OH, OH SURE. SORRY TO BE SUCH A KLUTZ. GUESS I WASN'T WATCHING WHERE I WAS GOING.
NO HARM DONE.
PLEASE. EXCUSE ME. ARE YOU ALL RIGHT?
LET'S GO, CLARK. WE'RE GOING TO BE LATE FOR THE CONFERENCE.
RIGHT AWAY.
GEE, THAT LOOKED LIKE... COULD THAT HAVE BEEN... I COULD HAVE SWORN...
...NAAAH.
IT EVEN AS THE REPORTERS LEAVE AND MISS THE BIGGEST STORY OF THE MONTH, WE TURN TO THE BLED REALM OF ASGARD...
...WHERE, BELOW THE HIGH SEAT OF ODIN, WE FIND THE ALL-FATHER ALONE, CHANTING STRANGE MELODIES THAT SEEM TO STILL THE VERY AIR...
...TILL ALL IS SILENT.

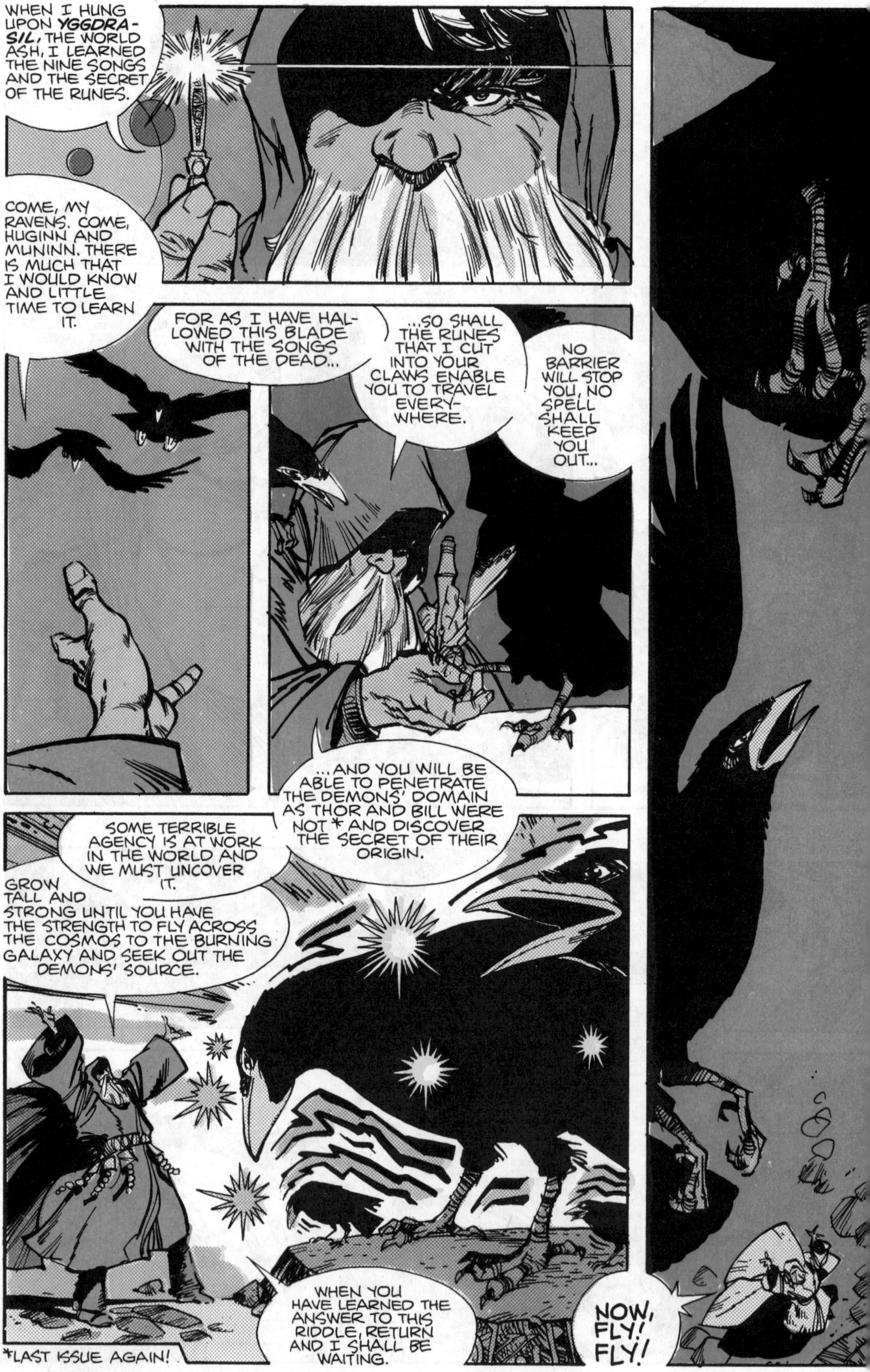
WHEN I HUNG UPON YGGDRASIL, THE WORLD ASH, I LEARNED THE NINE SONGS AND THE SECRET OF THE RUNES.
COME, MY RAVENS. COME, HUGINN AND MUNINN. THERE IS MUCH THAT I WOULD KNOW AND LITTLE TIME TO LEARN IT.
FOR AS I HAVE HALLOWED THIS BLADE WITH THE SONGS OF THE DEAD...
...SO SHALL THE RUNES THAT I CUT INTO YOUR CLAWS ENABLE YOU TO TRAVEL EVERYWHERE.
NO BARRIER WILL STOP YOU, NO SPELL SHALL KEEP YOU OUT...
...AND YOU WILL BE ABLE TO PENETRATE THE DEMONS' DOMAIN AS THOR AND BILL WERE NOT* AND DISCOVER THE SECRET OF THEIR ORIGIN.
SOME TERRIBLE AGENCY IS AT WORK IN THE WORLD AND WE MUST UNCOVER IT.
GROW TALL AND STRONG UNTIL YOU HAVE THE STRENGTH TO FLY ACROSS THE COSMOS TO THE BURNING GALAXY AND SEEK OUT THE DEMONS' SOURCE.
WHEN YOU HAVE LEARNED THE ANSWER TO THIS RIDDLE, RETURN AND I SHALL BE WAITING.
NOW, FLY! FLY!
*LAST ISSUE AGAIN!

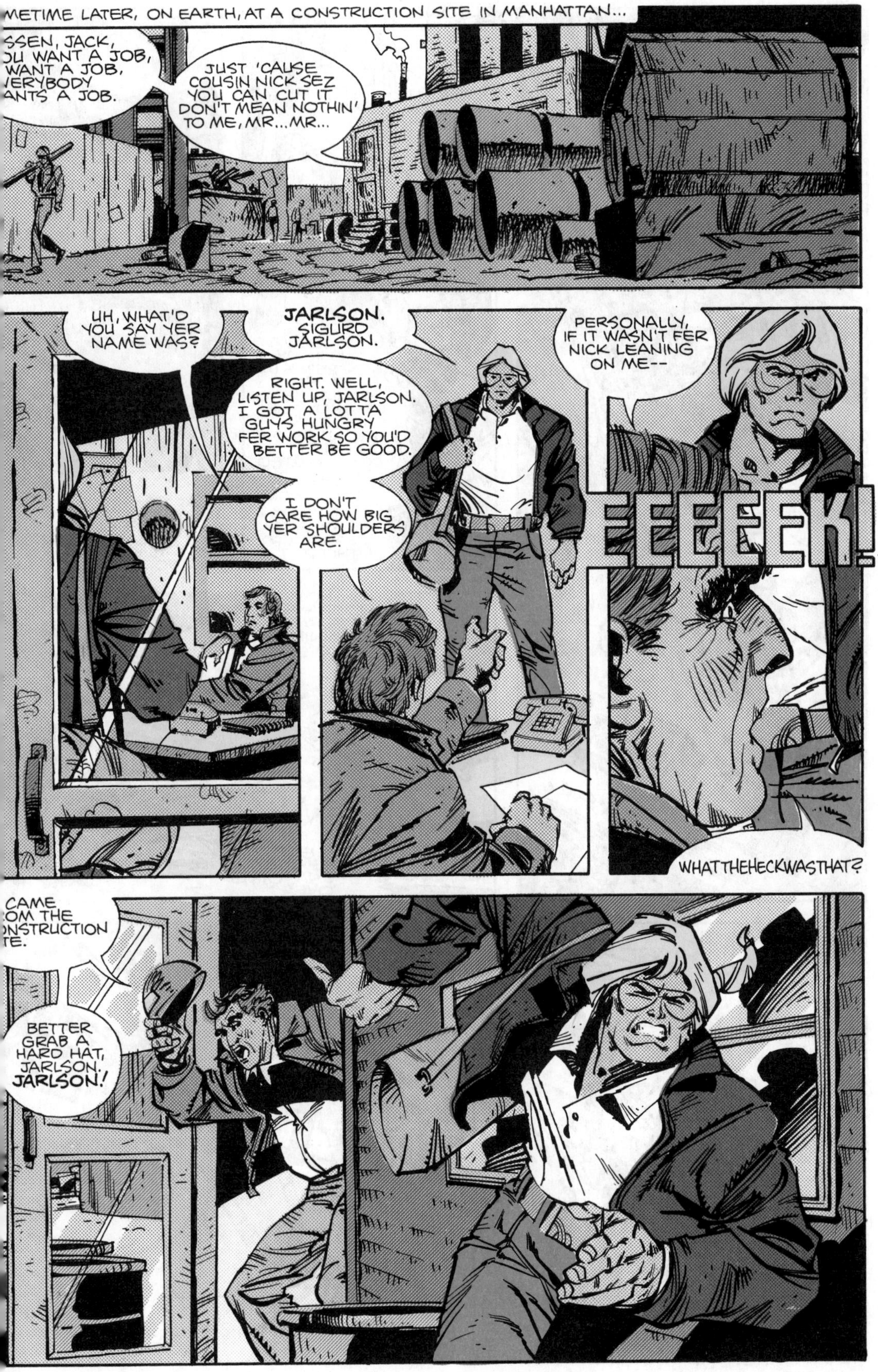
METIME LATER, ON EARTH, AT A CONSTRUCTION SITE IN MANHATTAN...
SSEN, JACK, OU WANT A JOB, WANT A JOB, VERYBODY ANTS A JOB.
JUST 'CAUSE COUSIN NICK SEZ YOU CAN CUT IT DON'T MEAN NOTHIN' TO ME, MR... MR...
UH, WHAT'D YOU SAY YER NAME WAS?
JARLSON. SIGURD JARLSON.
RIGHT. WELL, LISTEN UP, JARLSON. I GOT A LOTTA GUYS HUNGRY FER WORK SO YOU'D BETTER BE GOOD.
I DON'T CARE HOW BIG YER SHOULDERS ARE.
PERSONALLY, IF IT WASN'T FER NICK LEANING ON ME--
EEEEEK!
WHATTHEHECKWASTHAT?
CAME OM THE NSTRUCTION TE.
BETTER GRAB A HARD HAT, JARLSON. JARLSON!

GOOD LORD! THERE'S SOMEBODY HANGING FROM THE CRANE!

SHE'LL BE KILLED!

IT'S A GIRL!

JARLSON! JARLSON, WHERE ARE YOU GOING?

SHE WILL BE KILLED UNLESS I CAN REACH HER IN TIME.

MJOLNIR IS IN MY KNAPSACK BUT TO USE IT WOULD BE TO DESTROY THE IDENTITY NICHOLAS HAS SO CAREFULLY CONSTRUCTED.

I SHOULD BE ABLE TO REACH HER WITHOUT IT.

I DON'T BELIEVE IT! JARLSON'S HALFWAY UP THE BUILDING!

WHAT TH--? THE GROUND'S SHAKIN'! FEELS LIKE AN EARTHQUAKE! BUT THIS IS NEW YORK!

OH, NO! THE CRANE'S PLATFORM IS BEGINNING TO GIVE!

CLEAR THE SITE! SHE'S GOING OVER!

THE CRANE IS INDEED BEGINNING TO TILT!

BUT THIS CABLE SHOULD GIVE ME THE SPEED I NEED!

THE ROPE THAT SECURED HER TO THE CRANE HAS SLIPPED LOOSE! SHE'S FALLING!

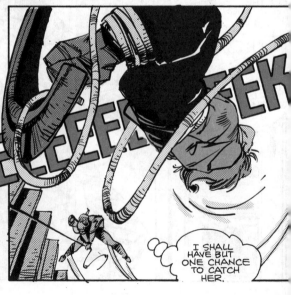

EEEEEEEEK

I SHALL HAVE BUT ONE CHANCE TO CATCH HER.

...ST IN TIME! ...OTHER MOMENT ...D IT WOULD HAVE ...EN TOO LATE.

THOUGH SHE IS SAFE FOR THE MOMENT, THERE IS MORE HERE THAN MEETS THE EYE.

THE LADY SEEMS TO HAVE FAINTED FROM THE SHOCK.

YET HOW CAME SHE TO DANGLE ABOVE THE CITY SO?

AGAIN THE GROUND SHAKES! BUT 'TIS NO EARTHQUAKE!

AY?

AT LAST I HAVE FOUND THEE!

...AND I ...LL BE THY ...EATH!

NAY, IT CANNOT BE! WHAT VISION OF EVIL IS THIS RISING OUT OF THE RIVER?

BEFORE ME STANDS THE LIKENESS OF ONE I DEFEATED AGES AGO, LARGER AND SEEMINGLY MORE DEADLY THAN EVER!

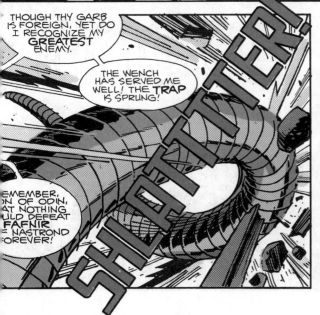

THOUGH THY GARB IS FOREIGN, YET DO I RECOGNIZE MY GREATEST ENEMY.

THE WENCH HAS SERVED ME WELL! THE TRAP IS SPRUNG!

...EMEMBER, ...N OF ODIN, ...AT NOTHING ...ULD DEFEAT ...FAFNIR ...E NASTROND ...FOREVER!

SHATTTER!

AND CARRY THAT THOUGHT TO YOUR GRAVE!

THE VERY BUILDING COLLAPSES AROUND US.

MY HAMMER! I MUST REACH MY HAMMER!

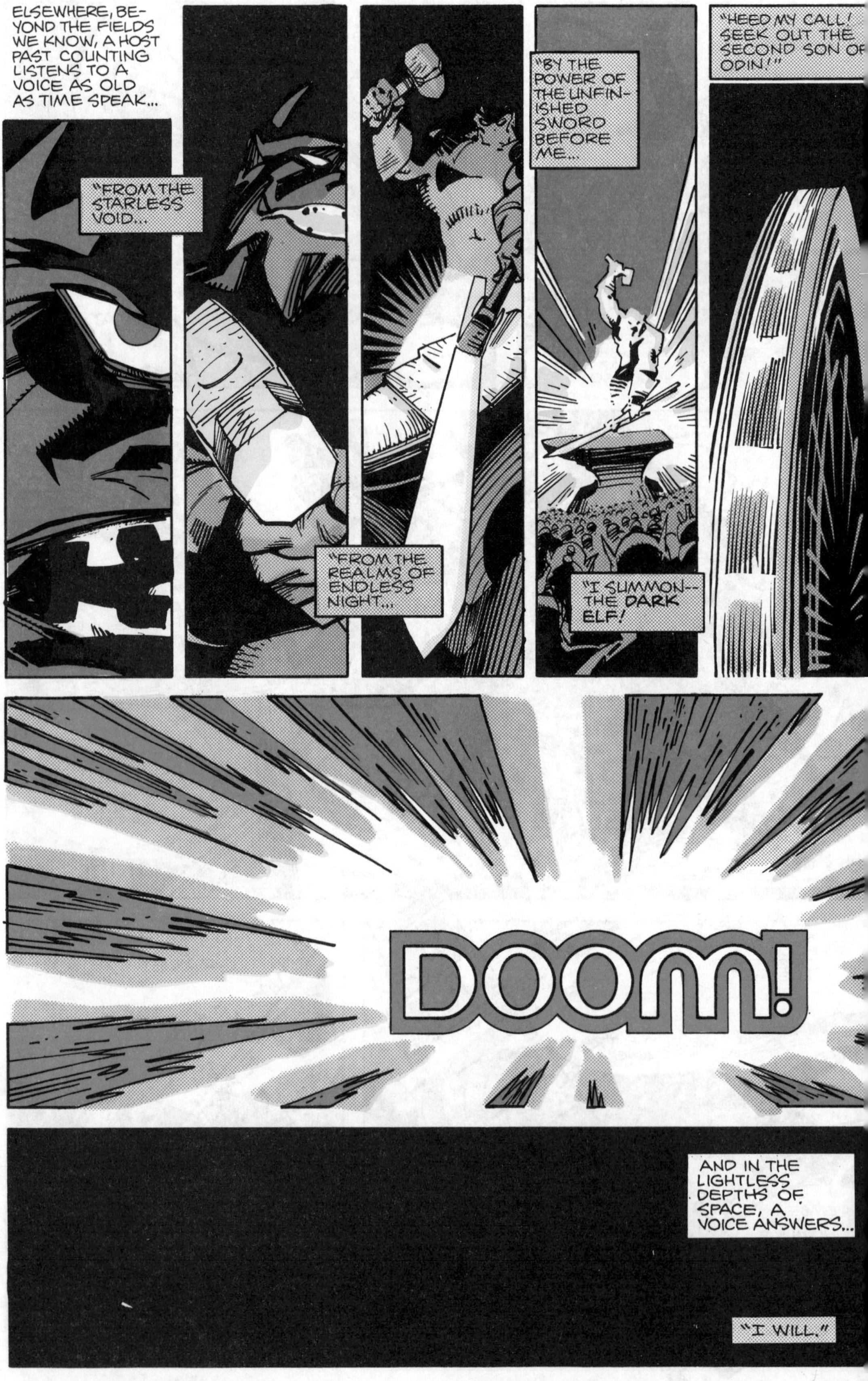
ELSEWHERE, BEYOND THE FIELDS WE KNOW, A HOST PAST COUNTING LISTENS TO A VOICE AS OLD AS TIME SPEAK...
"FROM THE STARLESS VOID...
"FROM THE REALMS OF ENDLESS NIGHT...
"BY THE POWER OF THE UNFINISHED SWORD BEFORE ME...
"I SUMMON-- THE DARK ELF!
"HEED MY CALL! SEEK OUT THE SECOND SON OF ODIN!"
DOOM!
AND IN THE LIGHTLESS DEPTHS OF SPACE, A VOICE ANSWERS...
"I WILL."

MEANWHILE, ON EARTH...

ONLY A WHIRLING VORTEX CREATED BY MY ENCHANTED MALLET CAN SAVE US NOW.

IT WILL PREVENT THE DEBRIS FROM CRUSHING US AS WE LIGHT UPON THE GROUND.

AND WHILE THE RUBBLE SETTLES ABOVE US, I CAN FORM A CAVITY HERE TO HOLD HER SAFELY TILL I DEAL WITH FAFNIR.

BUT WAIT, AGAIN I HEAR MY NAME, AS THOUGH SOMEONE WERE CALLING TO ME FROM A GREAT DISTANCE.

CALLING IN THE TONGUE OF THE NORSEMEN...

...YET SO SOFTLY THAT IT FADES AWAY TO NOTHING.

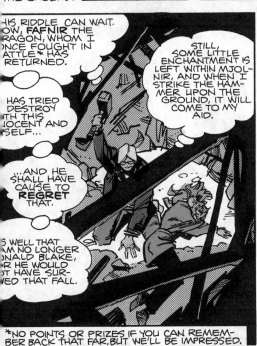

THIS RIDDLE CAN WAIT. NOW, FAFNIR THE DRAGON, WHOM I ONCE FOUGHT IN BATTLE* HAS RETURNED.

HE HAS TRIED TO DESTROY BOTH THIS INNOCENT AND HIMSELF...

...AND HE SHALL HAVE CAUSE TO REGRET THAT.

IS WELL THAT I AM NO LONGER DONALD BLAKE, FOR HE WOULD NOT HAVE SURVIVED THAT FALL.

STILL, SOME LITTLE ENCHANTMENT IS LEFT WITHIN MJOLNIR, AND WHEN I STRIKE THE HAMMER UPON THE GROUND, IT WILL COME TO MY AID.

*NO POINTS OR PRIZES IF YOU CAN REMEMBER BACK THAT FAR, BUT WE'LL BE IMPRESSED.

SO DIES THE MIGHTY THOR, A VICTIM OF AN EVEN MIGHTIER--

KRACKE!

WHAT WAS THAT?

SURELY NOT EVEN THOR COULD HAVE SURVIVED THAT FALL, BUT I SHALL NOT UNDERESTIMATE HIM.

I SHALL FIND HIS BODY AND BURN IT TO A CINDER!

THEN WILL ODIN KNOW AND FEAR ME.

SCION OF EVIL! MY FATHER FEARS **NO** GOD OR DRAGON, WHATEVER HIS POWER!

UGGH!

WHARRODDMM!

NOW SPEAK BEFORE I UNLEASH MY FURY! HOW CAME YOU HERE AND WHAT DO YOU SEEK?

TALK NOT TO ME OF FURY, SON OF AN AC-CURSED LINE! THE WRATH OF GODS COUNTS FOR **NOTHING** BESIDE THE TERRIBLE **ANGER** OF THE **DRAGON!**

AND YET I THANK BOTH YOU AND YOUR FATHER.

WHERE I WAS ONCE A MORTA KING WHO DALLIED WITH PALTR EVILS, NOW, BECAUSE OF ODI I AM AN INVINCIBLE CREATUR OF **HATE!**

FOR ODIN HIMSELF DESTROYED MY PEOPLE AND FORCED ME INTO THE WEARI-SOME EXILE...

...WHEREIN I DISCOVERED THE SECRET OF MY TRANSFORMATION!

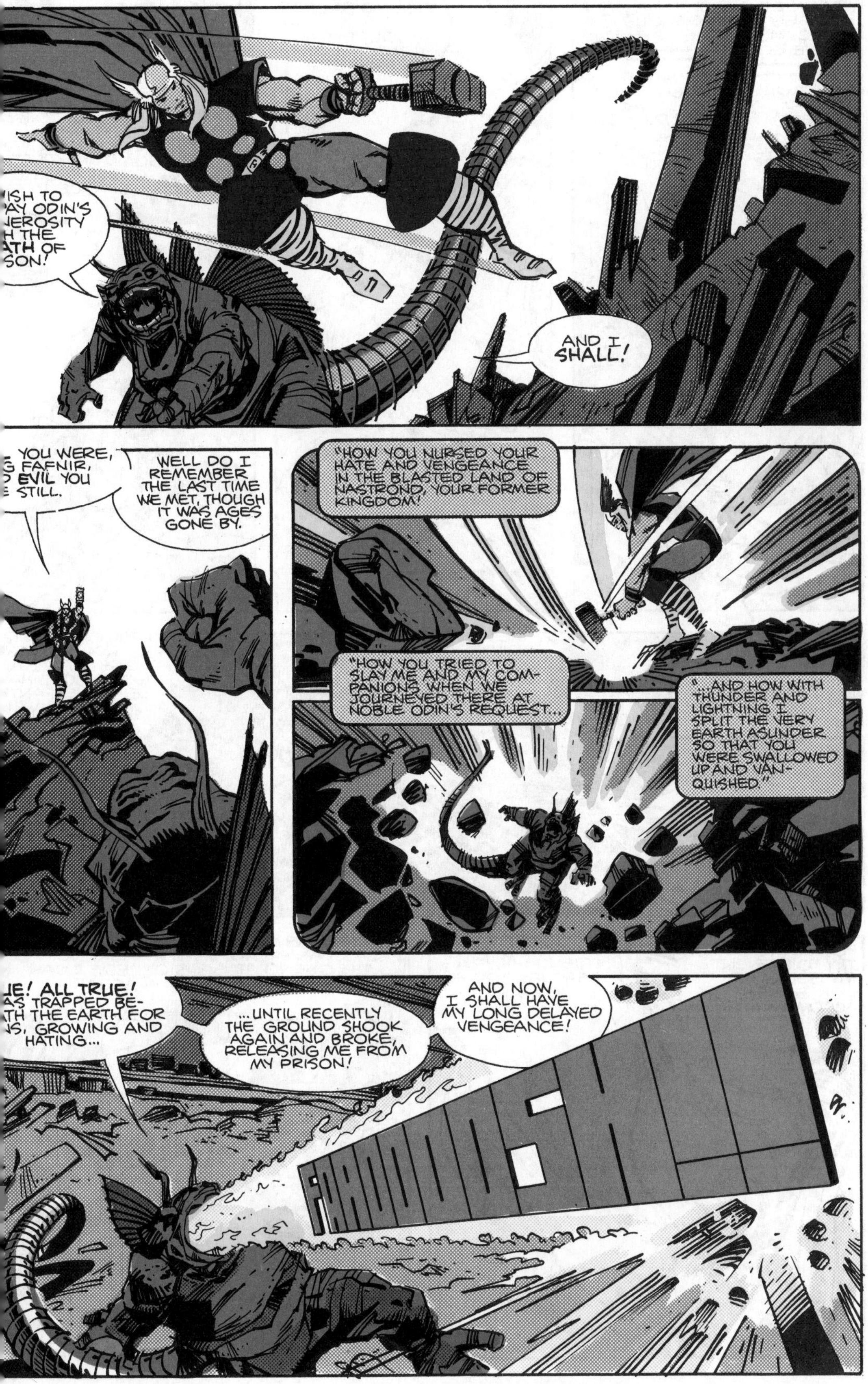
WISH TO
AY ODIN'S
NEROSITY
H THE
ATH OF
SON!
AND I SHALL!
YOU WERE,
G FAFNIR,
D EVIL YOU
E STILL.
WELL DO I REMEMBER THE LAST TIME WE MET, THOUGH IT WAS AGES GONE BY.
"HOW YOU NURSED YOUR HATE AND VENGEANCE IN THE BLASTED LAND OF NASTROND, YOUR FORMER KINGDOM!
"HOW YOU TRIED TO SLAY ME AND MY COMPANIONS WHEN WE JOURNEYED THERE AT NOBLE ODIN'S REQUEST...
"...AND HOW WITH THUNDER AND LIGHTNING I SPLIT THE VERY EARTH ASUNDER SO THAT YOU WERE SWALLOWED UP AND VANQUISHED."
UE! ALL TRUE!
AS TRAPPED BE-
TH THE EARTH FOR
NS, GROWING AND
HATING...
...UNTIL RECENTLY THE GROUND SHOOK AGAIN AND BROKE, RELEASING ME FROM MY PRISON!
AND NOW, I SHALL HAVE MY LONG DELAYED VENGEANCE!
FAROOOOOSH

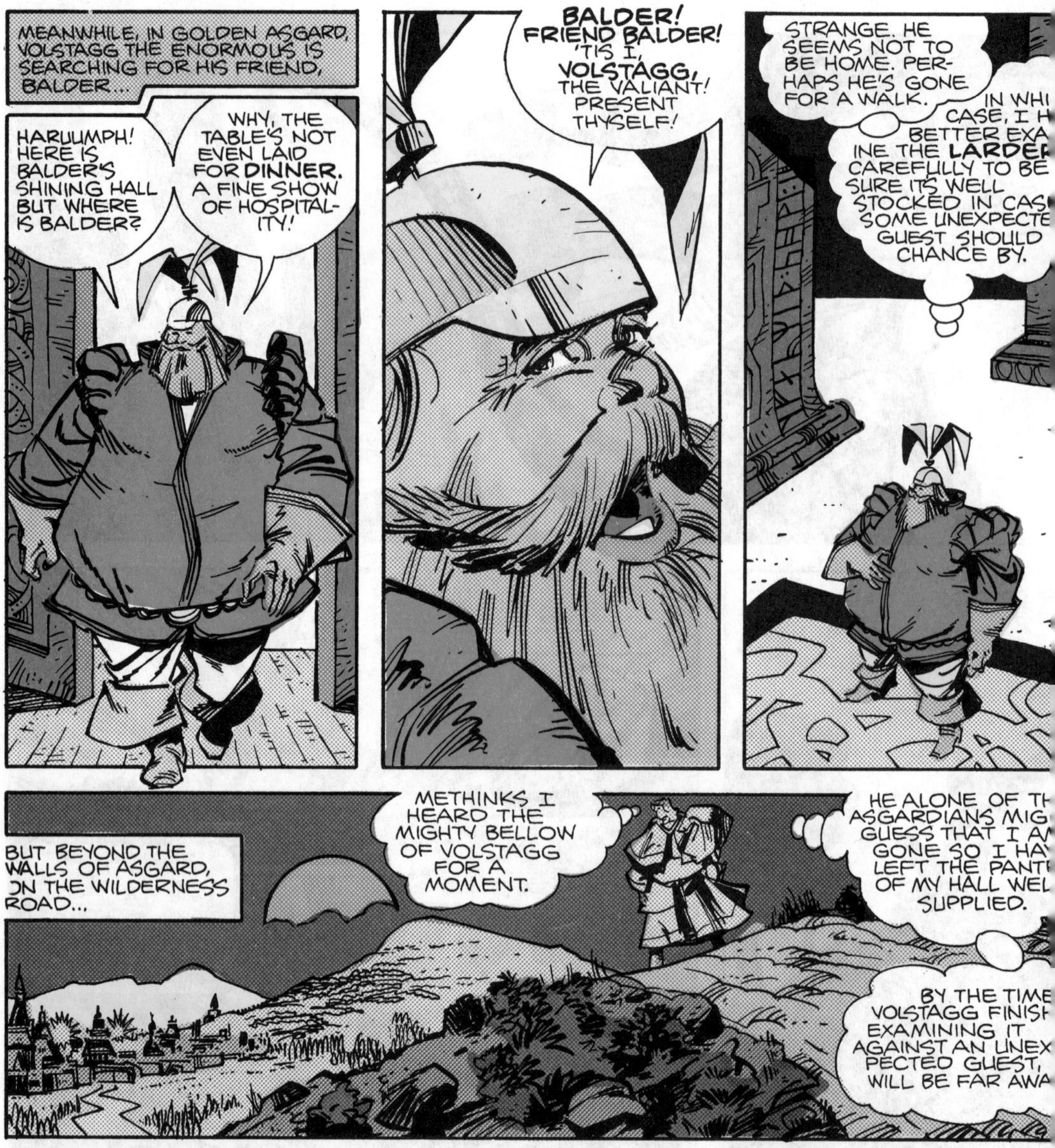
MEANWHILE, IN GOLDEN ASGARD, VOLSTAGG THE ENORMOUS IS SEARCHING FOR HIS FRIEND, BALDER...
HARUUMPH! HERE IS BALDER'S SHINING HALL BUT WHERE IS BALDER?
WHY, THE TABLE'S NOT EVEN LAID FOR **DINNER.** A FINE SHOW OF HOSPITALITY!
BALDER! FRIEND BALDER! 'TIS I, **VOLSTAGG,** THE VALIANT! PRESENT THYSELF!
STRANGE. HE SEEMS NOT TO BE HOME. PERHAPS HE'S GONE FOR A WALK.
IN WHI CASE, I H BETTER EXA INE THE **LARDER** CAREFULLY TO BE SURE IT'S WELL STOCKED IN CAS SOME UNEXPECTE GUEST SHOULD CHANCE BY.
BUT BEYOND THE WALLS OF ASGARD, ON THE WILDERNESS ROAD...
METHINKS I HEARD THE MIGHTY BELLOW OF VOLSTAGG FOR A MOMENT.
HE ALONE OF TH ASGARDIANS MIG GUESS THAT I AM GONE SO I HA LEFT THE PANT OF MY HALL WEL SUPPLIED.
BY THE TIME VOLSTAGG FINISH EXAMINING IT AGAINST AN UNEX PECTED GUEST, WILL BE FAR AWA
FOR HE MIGHT TRY TO PREVENT MY GOING, OR WORSE, INSIST ON ACCOMPANYING ME.
AND THOUGH HIS FRIENDSHIP IS A TREASURE TO ME, ALL COMPANY HAS NOW BECOME A BURDEN.
WHEN THE MERE MEMORY OF WHAT I WAS CAN PROVOKE AN ATTACK SUCH AS THE ONE VOLSTAGG STOPPED,* I CAN NO LONGER REMAIN IN ASGARD.
I MUST CLOSE MY HEART TILL ALL THAT I WAS IS LESS THAN THE SHADOW OF A MEMORY...
...AND ASGAR HERSELF REMEMBER ME NO MORE.
*THOR 338.

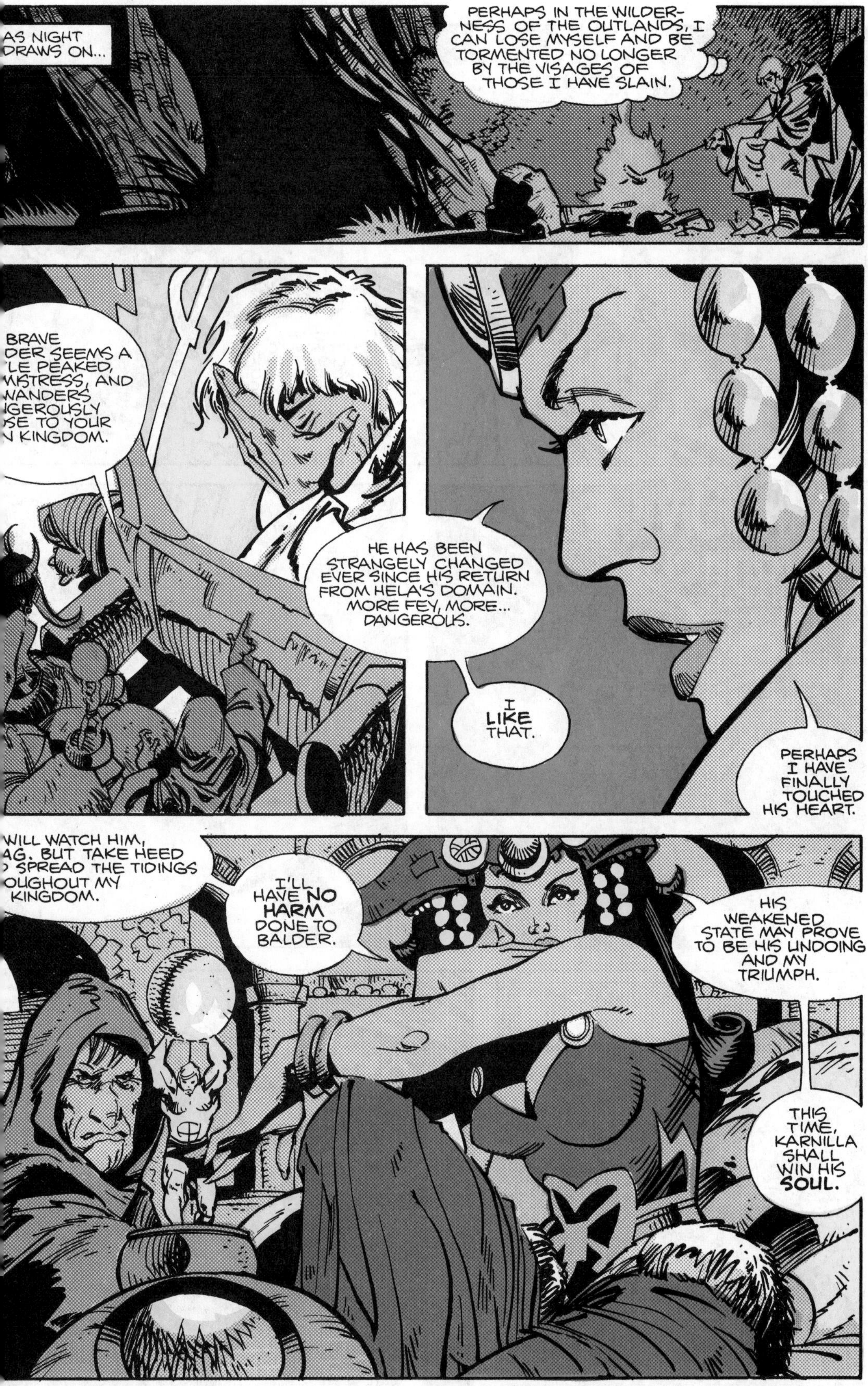

AS NIGHT DRAWS ON...
PERHAPS IN THE WILDERNESS OF THE OUTLANDS, I CAN LOSE MYSELF AND BE TORMENTED NO LONGER BY THE VISAGES OF THOSE I HAVE SLAIN.
BRAVE DER SEEMS A LE PEAKED, MISTRESS, AND WANDERS IGEROUSLY SE TO YOUR N KINGDOM.
HE HAS BEEN STRANGELY CHANGED EVER SINCE HIS RETURN FROM HELA'S DOMAIN. MORE FEY, MORE... DANGEROUS.
I LIKE THAT.
PERHAPS I HAVE FINALLY TOUCHED HIS HEART.
WILL WATCH HIM, AG. BUT TAKE HEED SPREAD THE TIDINGS OUGHOUT MY KINGDOM.
I'LL HAVE NO HARM DONE TO BALDER.
HIS WEAKENED STATE MAY PROVE TO BE HIS UNDOING AND MY TRIUMPH.
THIS TIME, KARNILLA SHALL WIN HIS SOUL.

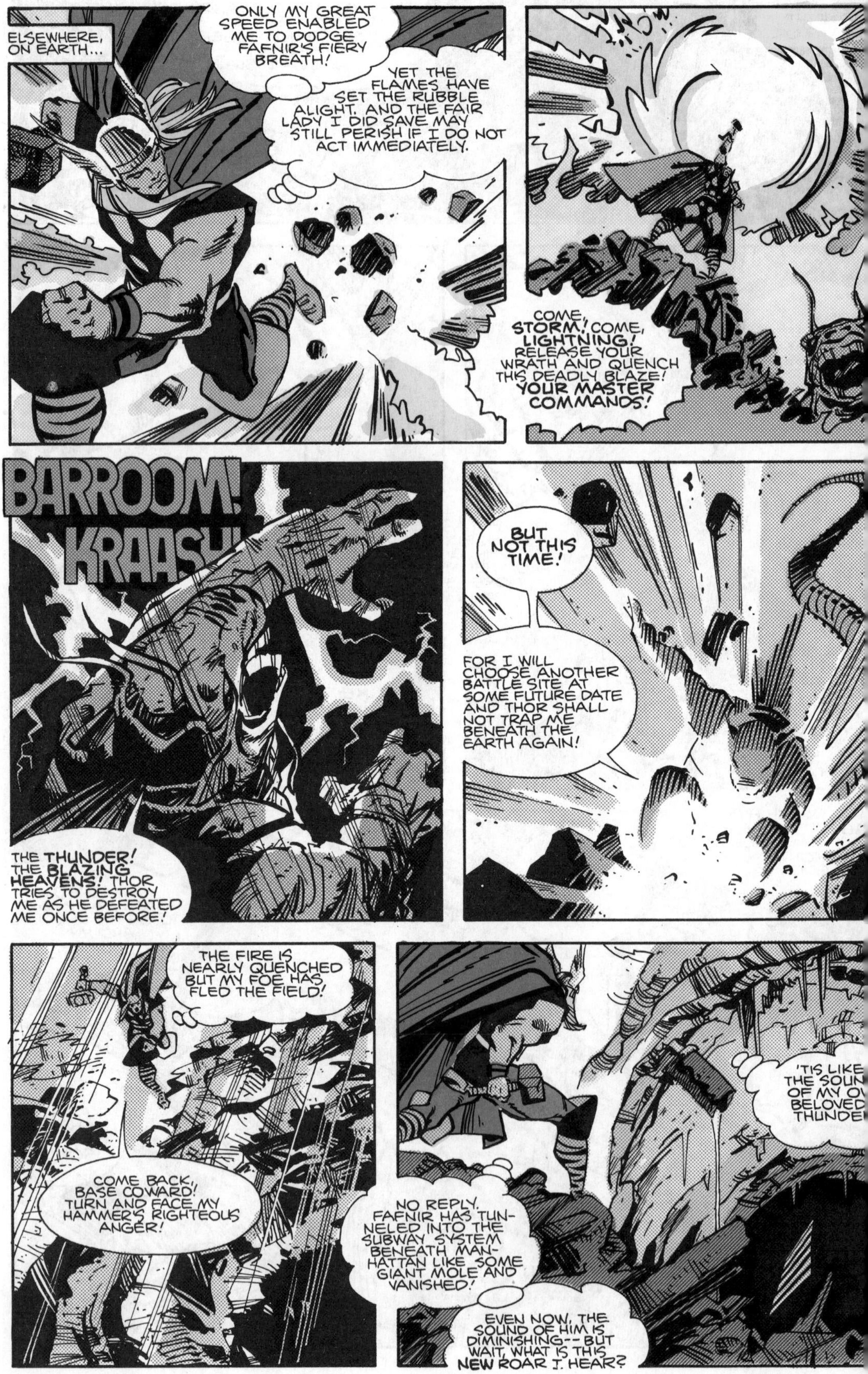
ELSEWHERE, ON EARTH...
ONLY MY GREAT SPEED ENABLED ME TO DODGE FAFNIR'S FIERY BREATH!
YET THE FLAMES HAVE SET THE RUBBLE ALIGHT. AND THE FAIR LADY I DID SAVE MAY STILL PERISH IF I DO NOT ACT IMMEDIATELY.
COME, STORM! COME, LIGHTNING! RELEASE YOUR WRATH AND QUENCH THIS DEADLY BLAZE! YOUR MASTER COMMANDS!
BARROOM!
KRAASH!
THE THUNDER! THE BLAZING HEAVENS! THOR TRIES TO DESTROY ME AS HE DEFEATED ME ONCE BEFORE!
BUT NOT THIS TIME!
FOR I WILL CHOOSE ANOTHER BATTLE SITE AT SOME FUTURE DATE AND THOR SHALL NOT TRAP ME BENEATH THE EARTH AGAIN!
THE FIRE IS NEARLY QUENCHED BUT MY FOE HAS FLED THE FIELD!
COME BACK, BASE COWARD! TURN AND FACE MY HAMMER'S RIGHTEOUS ANGER!
NO REPLY. FAFNIR HAS TUNNELED INTO THE SUBWAY SYSTEM BENEATH MANHATTAN LIKE SOME GIANT MOLE AND VANISHED!
EVEN NOW, THE SOUND OF HIM IS DIMINISHING-- BUT WAIT, WHAT IS THIS NEW ROAR I HEAR?
'TIS LIKE THE SOUN OF MY OV BELOVED THUNDE

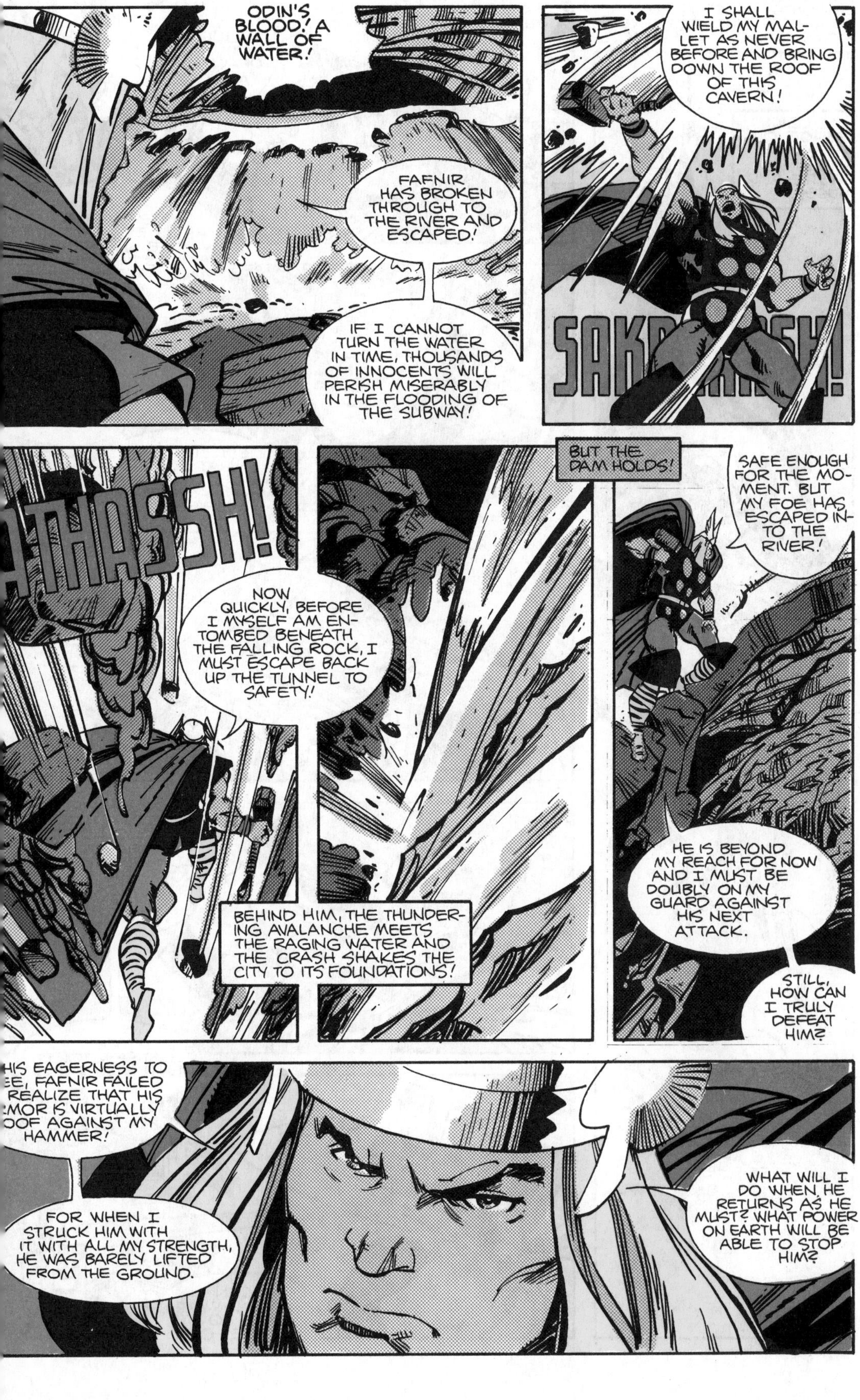
ODIN'S BLOOD! A WALL OF WATER!
FAFNIR HAS BROKEN THROUGH TO THE RIVER AND ESCAPED!
IF I CANNOT TURN THE WATER IN TIME, THOUSANDS OF INNOCENTS WILL PERISH MISERABLY IN THE FLOODING OF THE SUBWAY!
I SHALL WIELD MY MALLET AS NEVER BEFORE AND BRING DOWN THE ROOF OF THIS CAVERN!
SAKR—SH!
—ATHASSH!
NOW QUICKLY, BEFORE I MYSELF AM ENTOMBED BENEATH THE FALLING ROCK, I MUST ESCAPE BACK UP THE TUNNEL TO SAFETY!
BEHIND HIM, THE THUNDERING AVALANCHE MEETS THE RAGING WATER AND THE CRASH SHAKES THE CITY TO ITS FOUNDATIONS!
BUT THE DAM HOLDS!
SAFE ENOUGH FOR THE MOMENT. BUT MY FOE HAS ESCAPED INTO THE RIVER!
HE IS BEYOND MY REACH FOR NOW AND I MUST BE DOUBLY ON MY GUARD AGAINST HIS NEXT ATTACK.
STILL, HOW CAN I TRULY DEFEAT HIM?
HIS EAGERNESS TO EE, FAFNIR FAILED REALIZE THAT HIS MOR IS VIRTUALLY OOF AGAINST MY HAMMER!
FOR WHEN I STRUCK HIM WITH IT WITH ALL MY STRENGTH, HE WAS BARELY LIFTED FROM THE GROUND.
WHAT WILL I DO WHEN HE RETURNS AS HE MUST? WHAT POWER ON EARTH WILL BE ABLE TO STOP HIM?

AND INDEED, THE SELFSAME THOUGHTS ARE CROSSING ANOTHER'S MIND AT THAT VERY MOMENT A LONG WAY AWAY...

...AS LOKI, PRINCE OF ASGARD, SITS IN HIS CASTLE AND MUSES.

AH, MY BROTHER, IT MAY HAVE BEEN WORTH MY LIFE JUST TO SEE YOU WEARING A PONY TAIL!

BUT IT IS **YOUR** LIFE THAT IS DRAWING TO A CLOSE.

WHEN FAFNIR RECOVERS WHAT LITTLE WITS HE HAS, HE MAY REALIZE THAT HE COULD HAVE MASTERED THE FIGHT AGAINST YOU.

WHAT A FOOL! BLESSED WITH POWER LIKE THAT AND NOT AN OUNCE OF BRAIN IN HIS ENTIRE BODY.

STILL, POWER IS WHAT COUNTS AGAINST THOR AND FAFNIR HAS PLENTY TO SPARE.

PITY ABOUT LORELEI. BUT I SUPPOSE SHE'LL FIND SOME OTHER MALE TO PURSUE SHOULD THOR FINALLY HAVE MET HIS MATCH.

AND HOW RARE A TREAT TO WATCH HER HANG HERSELF FROM THE CRANE WHILE UNDER THE DRAGON'S SPELL.

FOOLISH GIRL! TO BELIEVE THAT HER SIMPLE WILES COULD SEDUCE A DRAGON TO HER WILL WHEN EVERYONE KNOWS THAT THE DRAGON IS THE MOST IRRESISTIBLE SEDUCER OF ALL.

A MOST SATISFACTORY ENTERTAINMENT.

SHATTER!

I CAN HARDLY WAIT TO SEE HOW IT COMES OUT!

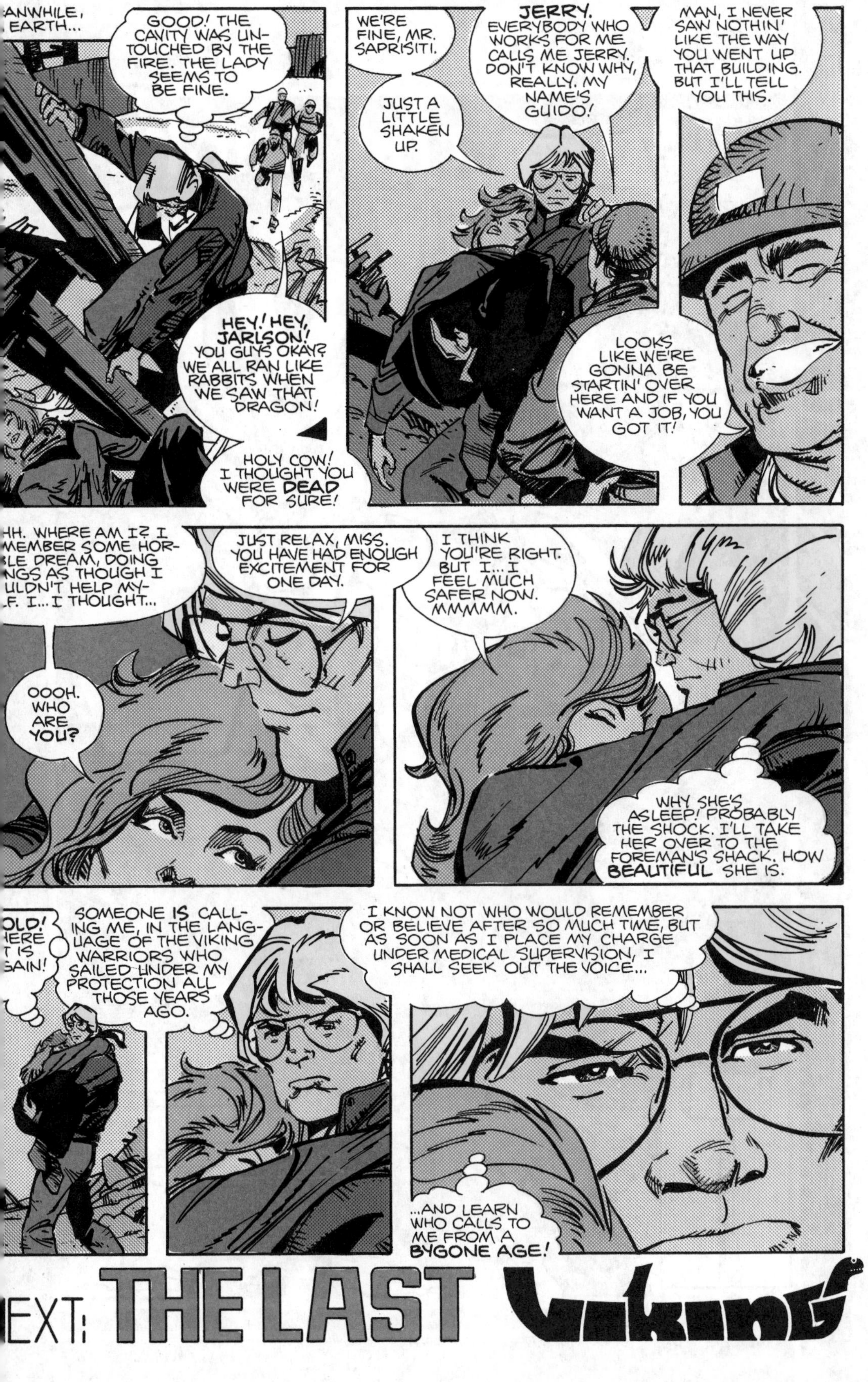

...ANWHILE, ...EARTH...
GOOD! THE CAVITY WAS UNTOUCHED BY THE FIRE. THE LADY SEEMS TO BE FINE.
HEY! HEY, JARLSON! YOU GUYS OKAY? WE ALL RAN LIKE RABBITS WHEN WE SAW THAT DRAGON!
HOLY COW! I THOUGHT YOU WERE DEAD FOR SURE!
WE'RE FINE, MR. SAPRISITI.
JUST A LITTLE SHAKEN UP.
JERRY. EVERYBODY WHO WORKS FOR ME CALLS ME JERRY. DON'T KNOW WHY, REALLY. MY NAME'S GUIDO!
MAN, I NEVER SAW NOTHIN' LIKE THE WAY YOU WENT UP THAT BUILDING. BUT I'LL TELL YOU THIS.
LOOKS LIKE WE'RE GONNA BE STARTIN' OVER HERE AND IF YOU WANT A JOB, YOU GOT IT!
...HH. WHERE AM I? I ...EMEMBER SOME HOR...LE DREAM, DOING ...NGS AS THOUGH I ...ULDN'T HELP MY...LF. I... I THOUGHT...
OOOH. WHO ARE YOU?
JUST RELAX, MISS. YOU HAVE HAD ENOUGH EXCITEMENT FOR ONE DAY.
I THINK YOU'RE RIGHT. BUT I... I FEEL MUCH SAFER NOW. MMMMM.
WHY SHE'S ASLEEP! PROBABLY THE SHOCK. I'LL TAKE HER OVER TO THE FOREMAN'S SHACK. HOW BEAUTIFUL SHE IS.
...OLD! ...HERE ...T IS ...GAIN!
SOMEONE IS CALLING ME, IN THE LANGUAGE OF THE VIKING WARRIORS WHO SAILED UNDER MY PROTECTION ALL THOSE YEARS AGO.
I KNOW NOT WHO WOULD REMEMBER OR BELIEVE AFTER SO MUCH TIME, BUT AS SOON AS I PLACE MY CHARGE UNDER MEDICAL SUPERVISION, I SHALL SEEK OUT THE VOICE...
...AND LEARN WHO CALLS TO ME FROM A BYGONE AGE!
...EXT: THE LAST VIKING

CHAPTER SIX

MARVEL

60¢
U.K. 25p
CAN. 75¢

342 APR

THE MIGHTY THOR

STAN LEE PRESENTS: the MIGHTY THOR®

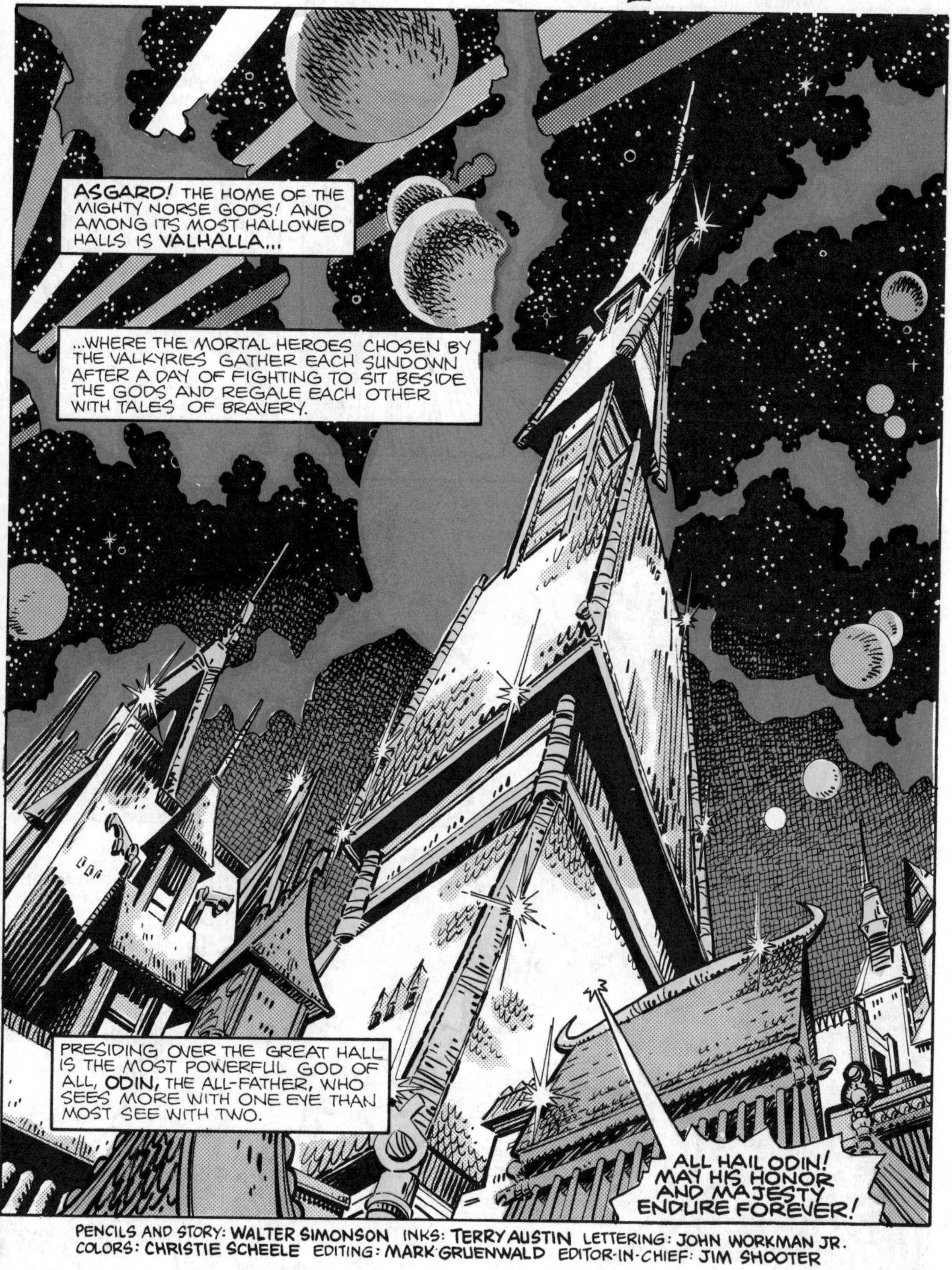
ASGARD! THE HOME OF THE MIGHTY NORSE GODS! AND AMONG ITS MOST HALLOWED HALLS IS VALHALLA...
...WHERE THE MORTAL HEROES CHOSEN BY THE VALKYRIES GATHER EACH SUNDOWN AFTER A DAY OF FIGHTING TO SIT BESIDE THE GODS AND REGALE EACH OTHER WITH TALES OF BRAVERY.
PRESIDING OVER THE GREAT HALL IS THE MOST POWERFUL GOD OF ALL, ODIN, THE ALL-FATHER, WHO SEES MORE WITH ONE EYE THAN MOST SEE WITH TWO.
ALL HAIL ODIN! MAY HIS HONOR AND MAJESTY ENDURE FOREVER!

PENCILS AND STORY: WALTER SIMONSON INKS: TERRY AUSTIN LETTERING: JOHN WORKMAN JR.
COLORS: CHRISTIE SCHEELE EDITING: MARK GRUENWALD EDITOR-IN-CHIEF: JIM SHOOTER

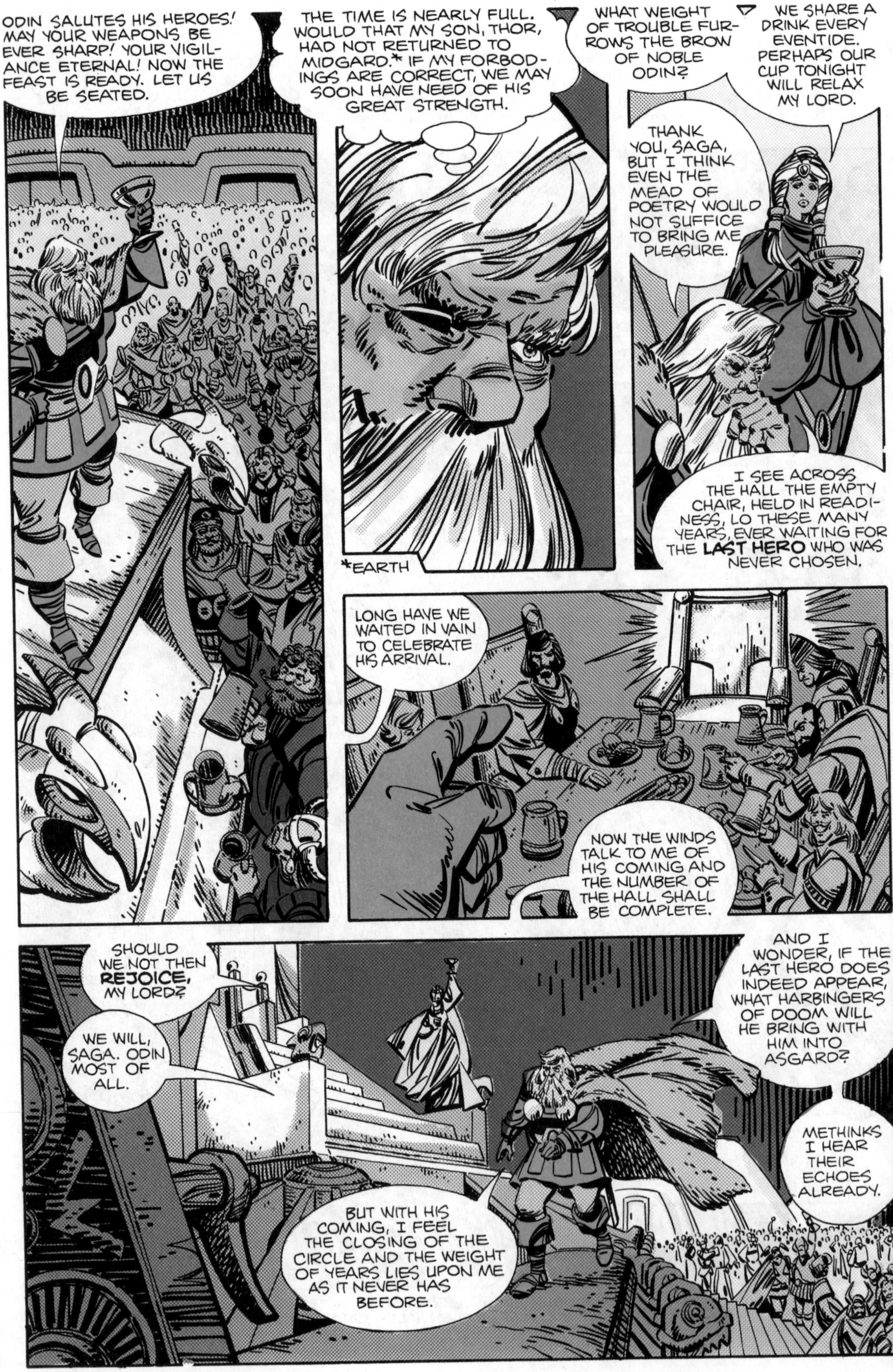
ODIN SALUTES HIS HEROES! MAY YOUR WEAPONS BE EVER SHARP! YOUR VIGILANCE ETERNAL! NOW THE FEAST IS READY. LET US BE SEATED.
THE TIME IS NEARLY FULL. WOULD THAT MY SON, THOR, HAD NOT RETURNED TO MIDGARD.* IF MY FORBODINGS ARE CORRECT, WE MAY SOON HAVE NEED OF HIS GREAT STRENGTH.
*EARTH
WHAT WEIGHT OF TROUBLE FURROWS THE BROW OF NOBLE ODIN?
WE SHARE A DRINK EVERY EVENTIDE. PERHAPS OUR CUP TONIGHT WILL RELAX MY LORD.
THANK YOU, SAGA, BUT I THINK EVEN THE MEAD OF POETRY WOULD NOT SUFFICE TO BRING ME PLEASURE.
I SEE ACROSS THE HALL THE EMPTY CHAIR, HELD IN READINESS, LO THESE MANY YEARS, EVER WAITING FOR THE LAST HERO WHO WAS NEVER CHOSEN.
LONG HAVE WE WAITED IN VAIN TO CELEBRATE HIS ARRIVAL.
NOW THE WINDS TALK TO ME OF HIS COMING AND THE NUMBER OF THE HALL SHALL BE COMPLETE.
SHOULD WE NOT THEN REJOICE, MY LORD?
WE WILL, SAGA. ODIN MOST OF ALL.
BUT WITH HIS COMING, I FEEL THE CLOSING OF THE CIRCLE AND THE WEIGHT OF YEARS LIES UPON ME AS IT NEVER HAS BEFORE.
AND I WONDER, IF THE LAST HERO DOES INDEED APPEAR, WHAT HARBINGERS OF DOOM WILL HE BRING WITH HIM INTO ASGARD?
METHINKS I HEAR THEIR ECHOES ALREADY.

ELSEWHERE, ON MANHATTAN ISLAND, AT THE CONSTRUCTION SITE DECIMATED BY THE DRAGON FAFNIR*...

ALL LAST ISSUE.

WELL, I SURE HOPE THE BUILDER HAS INSURANCE THAT'LL COVER AGAINST DESTRUCTION BY DRAGONS. WADDA MESS.

WE WERE LUCKY THOR WAS IN THE NEIGHBORHOOD AND SCARED HIM OFF.

I THOUGHT GOLDILOCKS WAS IN CHICAGO THESE DAYS.

PERHAPS HE IS REALLY A METS FAN AND RETURNED.

HEY, MISTER! YOU WITH THE GLASSES!

JARLSON. SIGURD JARLSON.

I DOUBT IT. GUYS LIKE HIM, THEY DON'T GET THE SAME WORRIES GUYS LIKE YOU 'N' ME DO. BESIDES, IT AIN'T BASEBALL SEASON!

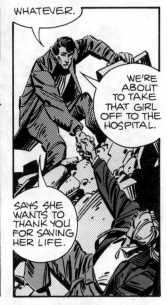

WHATEVER.

WE'RE ABOUT TO TAKE THAT GIRL OFF TO THE HOSPITAL.

SAYS SHE WANTS TO THANK YOU FOR SAVING HER LIFE.

I'M PRETTY SURE SHE'S OKAY. JUST A LITTLE SHOCK, BUT YOU CAN'T BE TOO CAREFUL, YOU KNOW?

BROTHER, SHE, SURE IS A LOOKER! YOU OUGHT TO GET HER PHONE NUMBER.

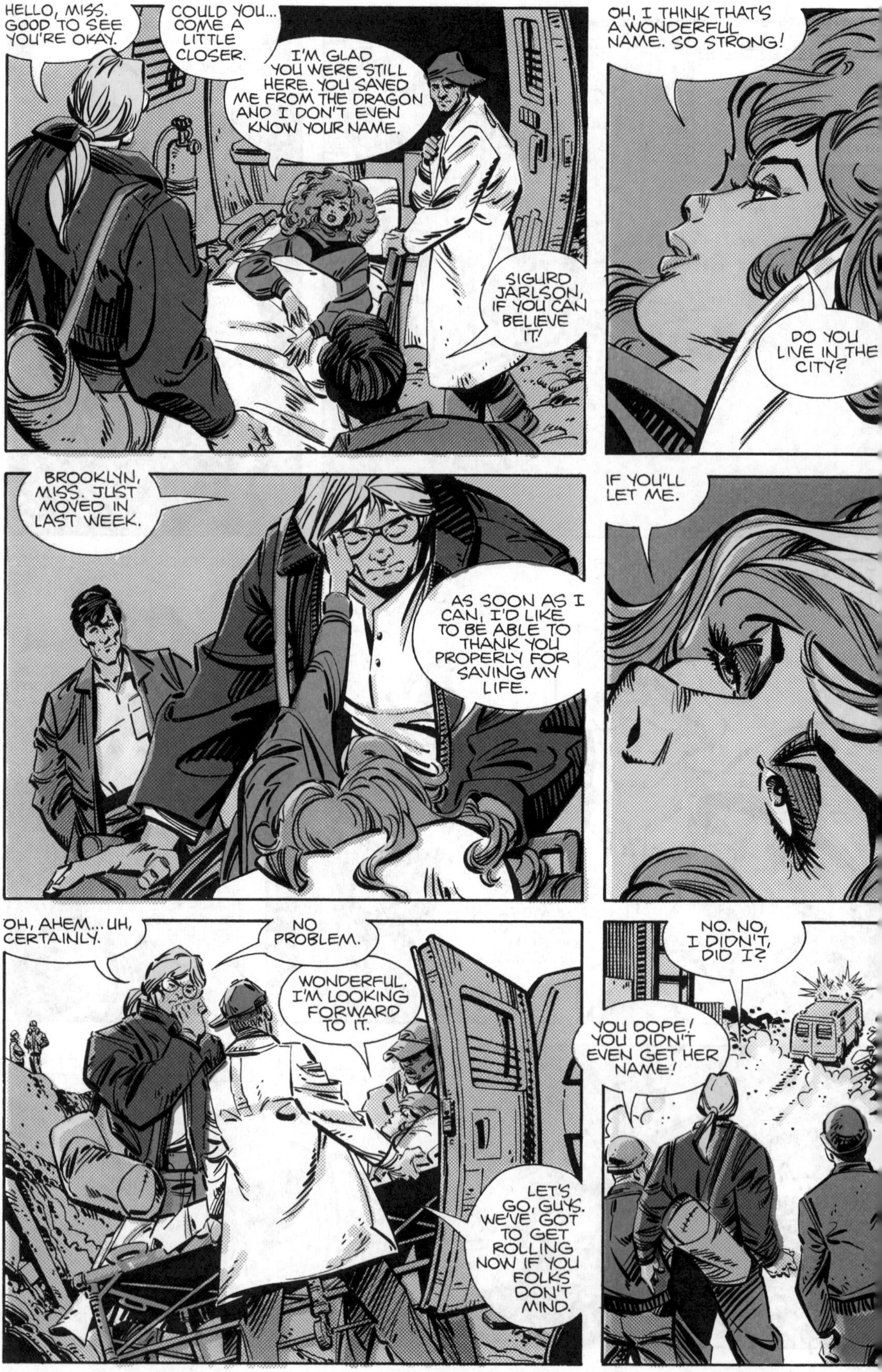
HELLO, MISS. GOOD TO SEE YOU'RE OKAY.
COULD YOU... COME A LITTLE CLOSER.
I'M GLAD YOU WERE STILL HERE. YOU SAVED ME FROM THE DRAGON AND I DON'T EVEN KNOW YOUR NAME.
SIGURD JARLSON, IF YOU CAN BELIEVE IT!
OH, I THINK THAT'S A WONDERFUL NAME. SO STRONG!
DO YOU LIVE IN THE CITY?
BROOKLYN, MISS. JUST MOVED IN LAST WEEK.
AS SOON AS I CAN, I'D LIKE TO BE ABLE TO THANK YOU PROPERLY FOR SAVING MY LIFE.
IF YOU'LL LET ME.
OH, AHEM... UH, CERTAINLY.
NO PROBLEM.
WONDERFUL. I'M LOOKING FORWARD TO IT.
LET'S GO, GUYS. WE'VE GOT TO GET ROLLING NOW IF YOU FOLKS DON'T MIND.
NO. NO, I DIDN'T, DID I?
YOU DOPE! YOU DIDN'T EVEN GET HER NAME!

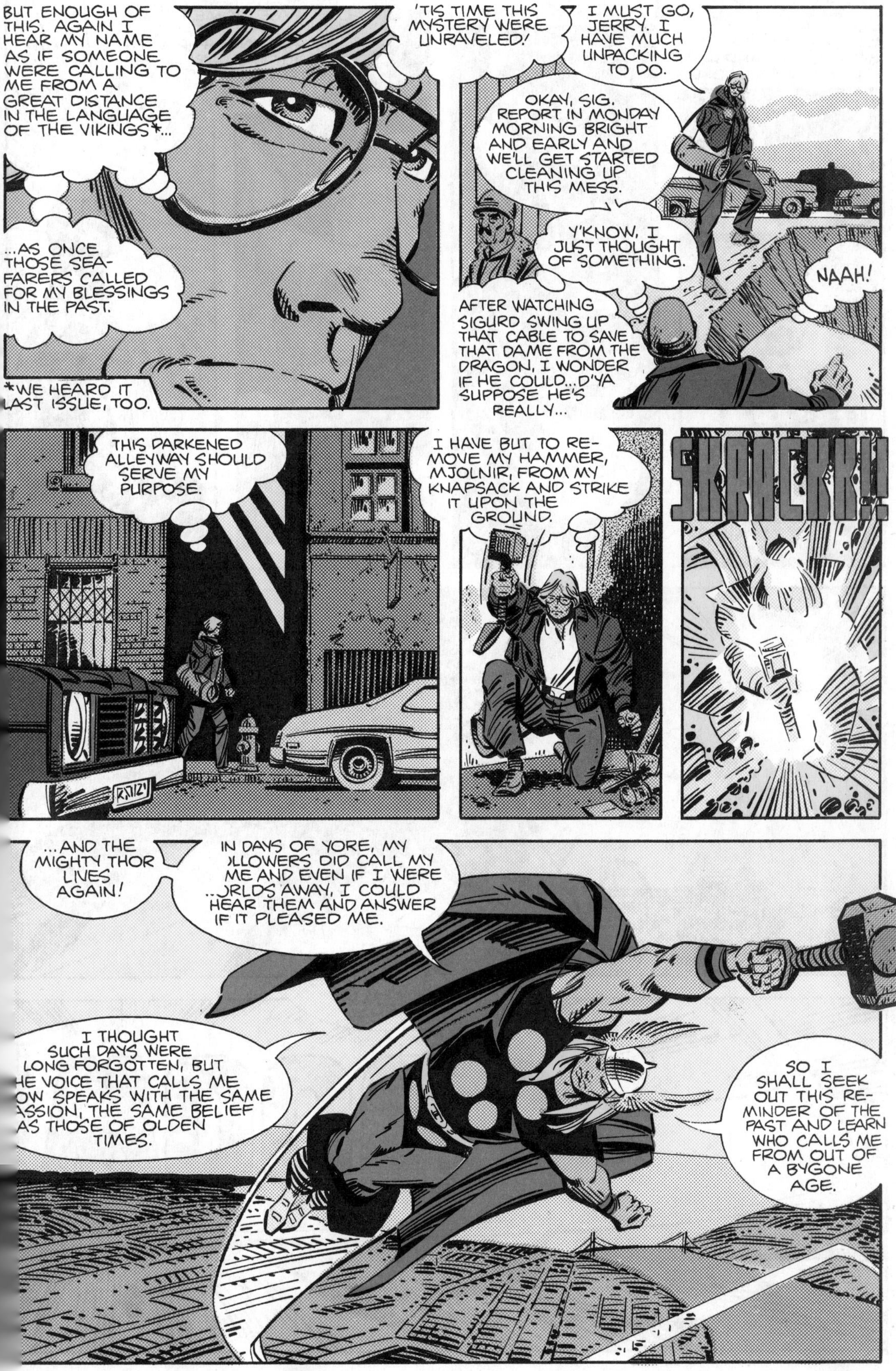
BUT ENOUGH OF THIS. AGAIN I HEAR MY NAME AS IF SOMEONE WERE CALLING TO ME FROM A GREAT DISTANCE IN THE LANGUAGE OF THE VIKINGS*...
...AS ONCE THOSE SEA-FARERS CALLED FOR MY BLESSINGS IN THE PAST.
*WE HEARD IT LAST ISSUE, TOO.
'TIS TIME THIS MYSTERY WERE UNRAVELED!
I MUST GO, JERRY. I HAVE MUCH UNPACKING TO DO.
OKAY, SIG. REPORT IN MONDAY MORNING BRIGHT AND EARLY AND WE'LL GET STARTED CLEANING UP THIS MESS.
Y'KNOW, I JUST THOUGHT OF SOMETHING.
AFTER WATCHING SIGURD SWING UP THAT CABLE TO SAVE THAT DAME FROM THE DRAGON, I WONDER IF HE COULD...D'YA SUPPOSE HE'S REALLY...
NAAH!
THIS DARKENED ALLEYWAY SHOULD SERVE MY PURPOSE.
I HAVE BUT TO RE-MOVE MY HAMMER, MJOLNIR, FROM MY KNAPSACK AND STRIKE IT UPON THE GROUND.
SKRACKK!!
...AND THE MIGHTY THOR LIVES AGAIN!
IN DAYS OF YORE, MY OLLOWERS DID CALL MY ME AND EVEN IF I WERE ORLDS AWAY, I COULD HEAR THEM AND ANSWER IF IT PLEASED ME.
I THOUGHT SUCH DAYS WERE LONG FORGOTTEN, BUT HE VOICE THAT CALLS ME OW SPEAKS WITH THE SAME ASSION, THE SAME BELIEF AS THOSE OF OLDEN TIMES.
SO I SHALL SEEK OUT THIS RE-MINDER OF THE PAST AND LEARN WHO CALLS ME FROM OUT OF A BYGONE AGE.

ELSEWHERE, BEYOND THE FIELDS WE KNOW, A MASSIVE FIGURE STANDS BEFORE A MIGHTY ANVIL AND A HALF FINISHED SWORD...

...AS A GREAT HOST MURMURS WITH ANTICIPATION...

...WHEN SUDDENLY...

LET ALL NOW BE SILENT.

THE BLACK RAVENS OF ODIN HAVE COME HIDING IN THE NIGHT, SEEKING ANSWERS FOR THEIR MASTER. BUT THE DARKNESS WILL NOT PROTECT THEM.

AND WITHOUT THE DARK TO HIDE THEM, THE RAVENS WILL DIE WITH THE KNOWLEDGE THEY HAVE OBTAINED.

LET THIS, THEN, BE THE FIRST BLOW AGAINST THE POWER OF ASGARD!

DOOM!

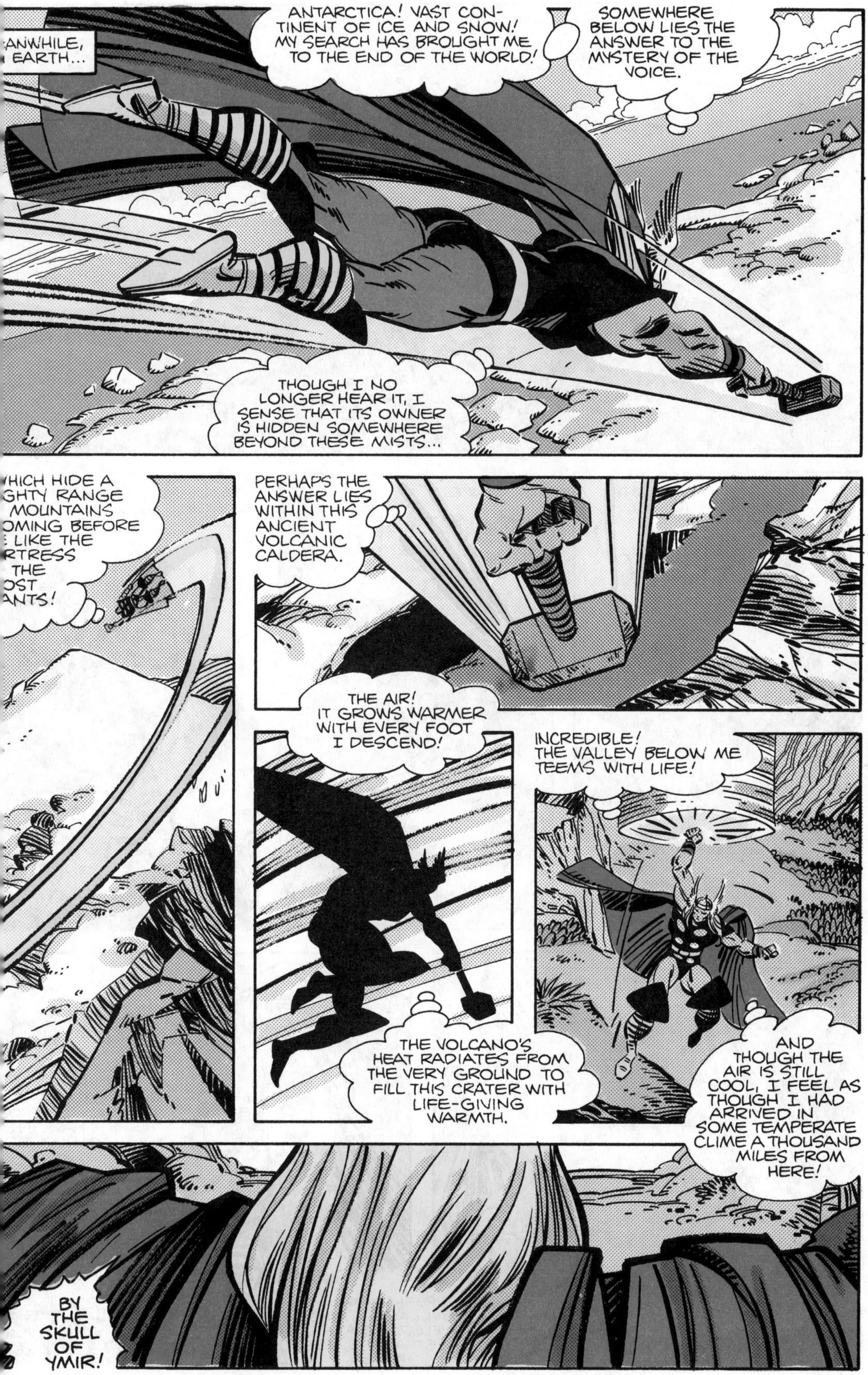
ANWHILE,
EARTH...
ANTARCTICA! VAST CONTINENT OF ICE AND SNOW! MY SEARCH HAS BROUGHT ME TO THE END OF THE WORLD!
SOMEWHERE BELOW LIES THE ANSWER TO THE MYSTERY OF THE VOICE.
THOUGH I NO LONGER HEAR IT, I SENSE THAT ITS OWNER IS HIDDEN SOMEWHERE BEYOND THESE MISTS...
HICH HIDE A GHTY RANGE MOUNTAINS OMING BEFORE LIKE THE RTRESS THE OST ANTS!
PERHAPS THE ANSWER LIES WITHIN THIS ANCIENT VOLCANIC CALDERA.
THE AIR! IT GROWS WARMER WITH EVERY FOOT I DESCEND!
THE VOLCANO'S HEAT RADIATES FROM THE VERY GROUND TO FILL THIS CRATER WITH LIFE-GIVING WARMTH.
INCREDIBLE! THE VALLEY BELOW ME TEEMS WITH LIFE!
AND THOUGH THE AIR IS STILL COOL, I FEEL AS THOUGH I HAD ARRIVED IN SOME TEMPERATE CLIME A THOUSAND MILES FROM HERE!
BY THE SKULL OF YMIR!

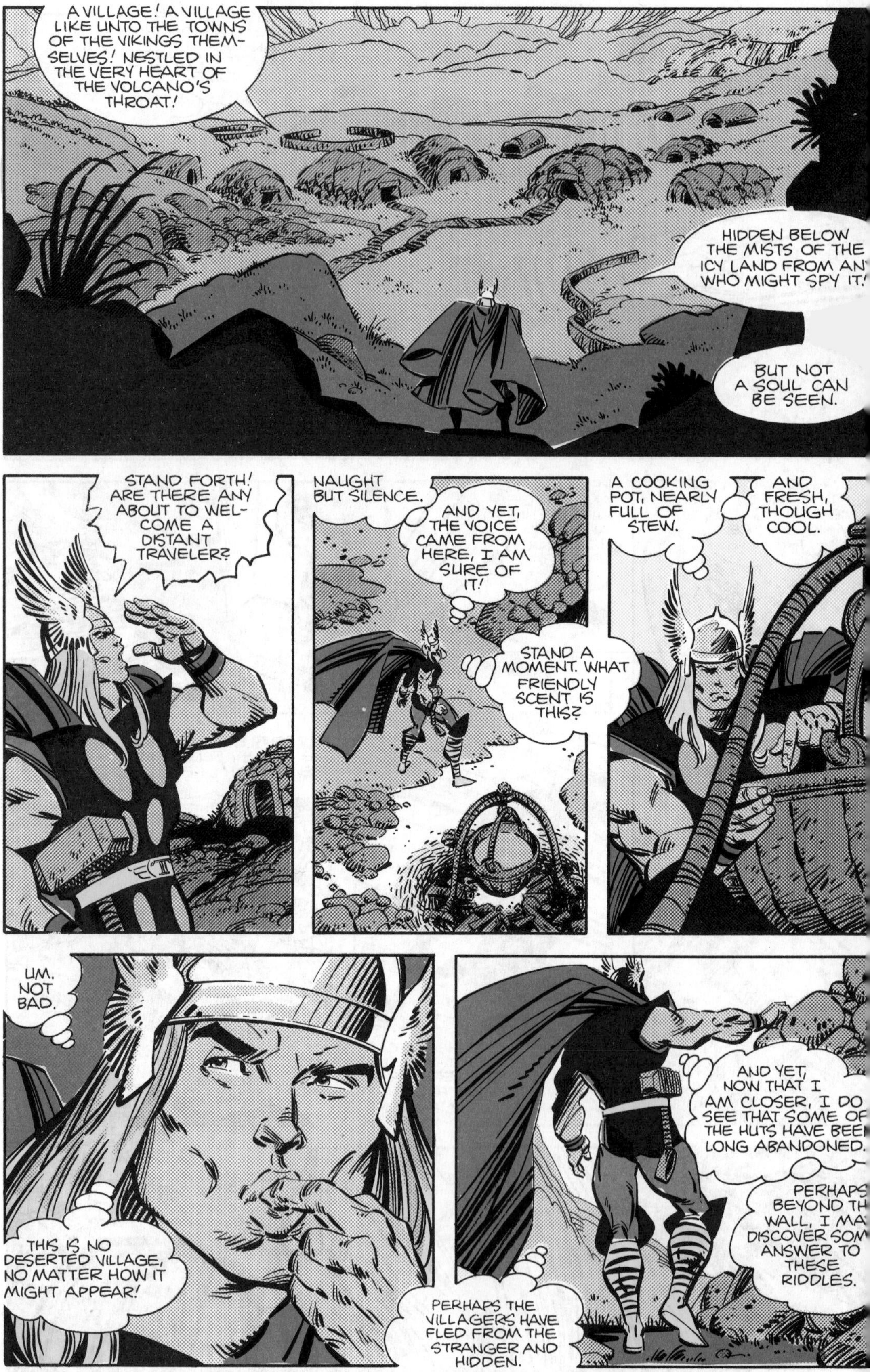
A VILLAGE! A VILLAGE LIKE UNTO THE TOWNS OF THE VIKINGS THEMSELVES! NESTLED IN THE VERY HEART OF THE VOLCANO'S THROAT!
HIDDEN BELOW THE MISTS OF THE ICY LAND FROM AN WHO MIGHT SPY IT!
BUT NOT A SOUL CAN BE SEEN.
STAND FORTH! ARE THERE ANY ABOUT TO WELCOME A DISTANT TRAVELER?
NAUGHT BUT SILENCE.
AND YET, THE VOICE CAME FROM HERE, I AM SURE OF IT!
STAND A MOMENT. WHAT FRIENDLY SCENT IS THIS?
A COOKING POT, NEARLY FULL OF STEW.
AND FRESH, THOUGH COOL.
UM. NOT BAD.
THIS IS NO DESERTED VILLAGE, NO MATTER HOW IT MIGHT APPEAR!
PERHAPS THE VILLAGERS HAVE FLED FROM THE STRANGER AND HIDDEN.
AND YET, NOW THAT I AM CLOSER, I DO SEE THAT SOME OF THE HUTS HAVE BEE LONG ABANDONED.
PERHAPS BEYOND TH WALL, I MA DISCOVER SOM ANSWER TO THESE RIDDLES.

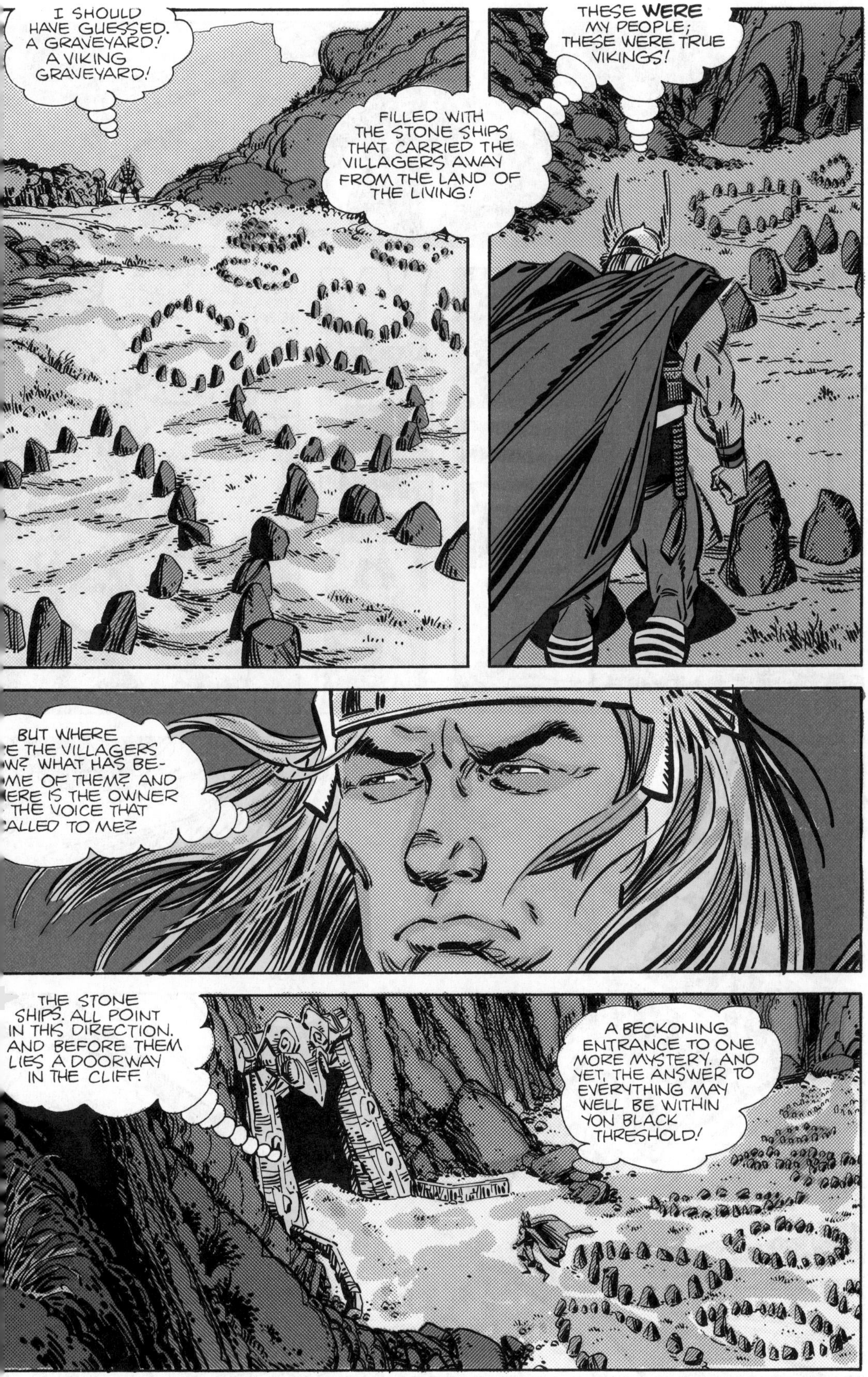
I SHOULD HAVE GUESSED. A GRAVEYARD! A VIKING GRAVEYARD!
FILLED WITH THE STONE SHIPS THAT CARRIED THE VILLAGERS AWAY FROM THE LAND OF THE LIVING!
THESE WERE MY PEOPLE; THESE WERE TRUE VIKINGS!
BUT WHERE E THE VILLAGERS W? WHAT HAS BE- ME OF THEM? AND ERE IS THE OWNER THE VOICE THAT ALLED TO ME?
THE STONE SHIPS. ALL POINT IN THIS DIRECTION. AND BEFORE THEM LIES A DOORWAY IN THE CLIFF.
A BECKONING ENTRANCE TO ONE MORE MYSTERY. AND YET, THE ANSWER TO EVERYTHING MAY WELL BE WITHIN YON BLACK THRESHOLD!

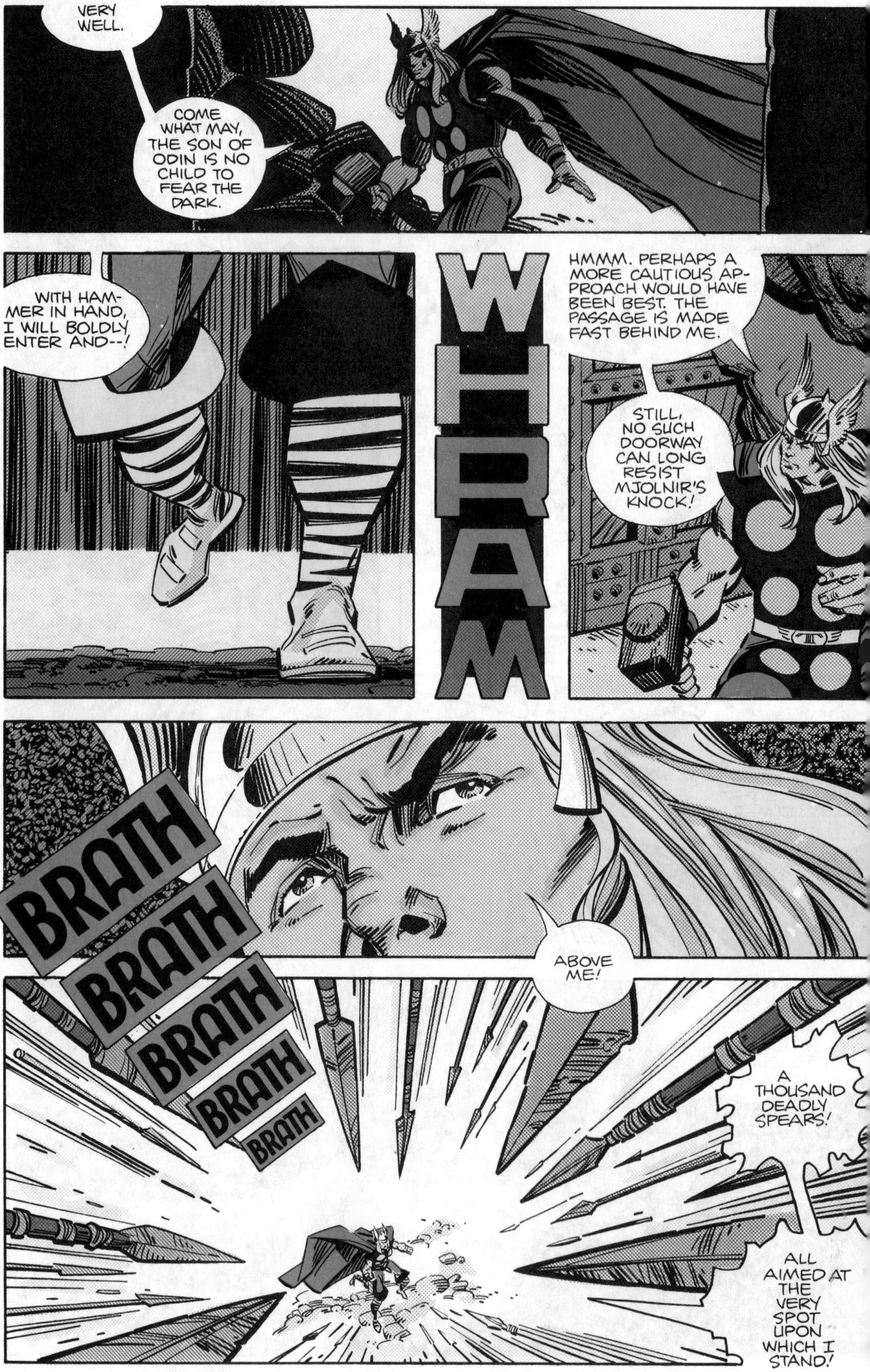
VERY WELL.
COME WHAT MAY, THE SON OF ODIN IS NO CHILD TO FEAR THE DARK.
WITH HAMMER IN HAND, I WILL BOLDLY ENTER AND--!
WHRAM
HMMM. PERHAPS A MORE CAUTIOUS APPROACH WOULD HAVE BEEN BEST. THE PASSAGE IS MADE FAST BEHIND ME.
STILL, NO SUCH DOORWAY CAN LONG RESIST MJOLNIR'S KNOCK!
BRATH BRATH BRATH BRATH BRATH BRATH
ABOVE ME!
A THOUSAND DEADLY SPEARS!
ALL AIMED AT THE VERY SPOT UPON WHICH I STAND!

...T WHILE THOR STANDS BENEATH A VERITABLE
...N OF DEATH, WE FIND THE BRAVE BALDER,
...ONE IN THE WILDERNESS FAR BEYOND THE
...LLS OF ASGARD...

...R PERHAPS,
...T SO ALONE.

COME OUT OF
THE SHADOWS, WAY-
FARER, AND REST BE-
SIDE THE FIRE. THERE
IS WARMTH ENOUGH
HERE FOR TWO.

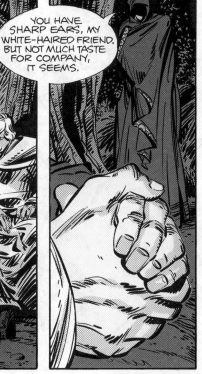

YOU HAVE
SHARP EARS, MY
WHITE-HAIRED FRIEND.
BUT NOT MUCH TASTE
FOR COMPANY,
IT SEEMS.

YOU ARE FAR
FROM ANYWHERE
IN THESE
WILDS.

PERHAPS
MY PRES-
ENCE IS AN
UNWELCOME
INTRUSION.

I HAVE
SOUGHT
SOLITUDE AND
THE BEAUTY OF
EMPTINESS. IT
HAS ELUDED ME
THUS FAR, EVEN
HERE.

BUT I HAVE
...OT FORSAKEN
...SPITALITY. AND
...RHAPS I HAVE
...T LOST MY TASTE
...R COMPANY AS
...ICH AS I HAD
...OUGHT THESE
...LAST FEW
WEEKS.

DO YOU
SEEK COM-
PANIONSHIP
NOW?

I CAN SCARCELY AVOID
IT, IT SEEMS. I HEAR
THE SOUND OF YOUR
MEN AT ARMS IN THE
WOODS. WILL THEY
CARRY ME OFF IF
YOUR BEAUTY FAILS
TO MOVE ME?

YOU WERE
ALWAYS LOVELY,
KARNILLA. BUT
I NEVER FOUND
BEAUTY AND EVIL
SEDUCTIVE.

WHAT DO YOU
KNOW OF EVIL,
BALDER? YOU
WHOM THE VERY
GODS ENVY FOR
YOUR GOOD-
NESS.

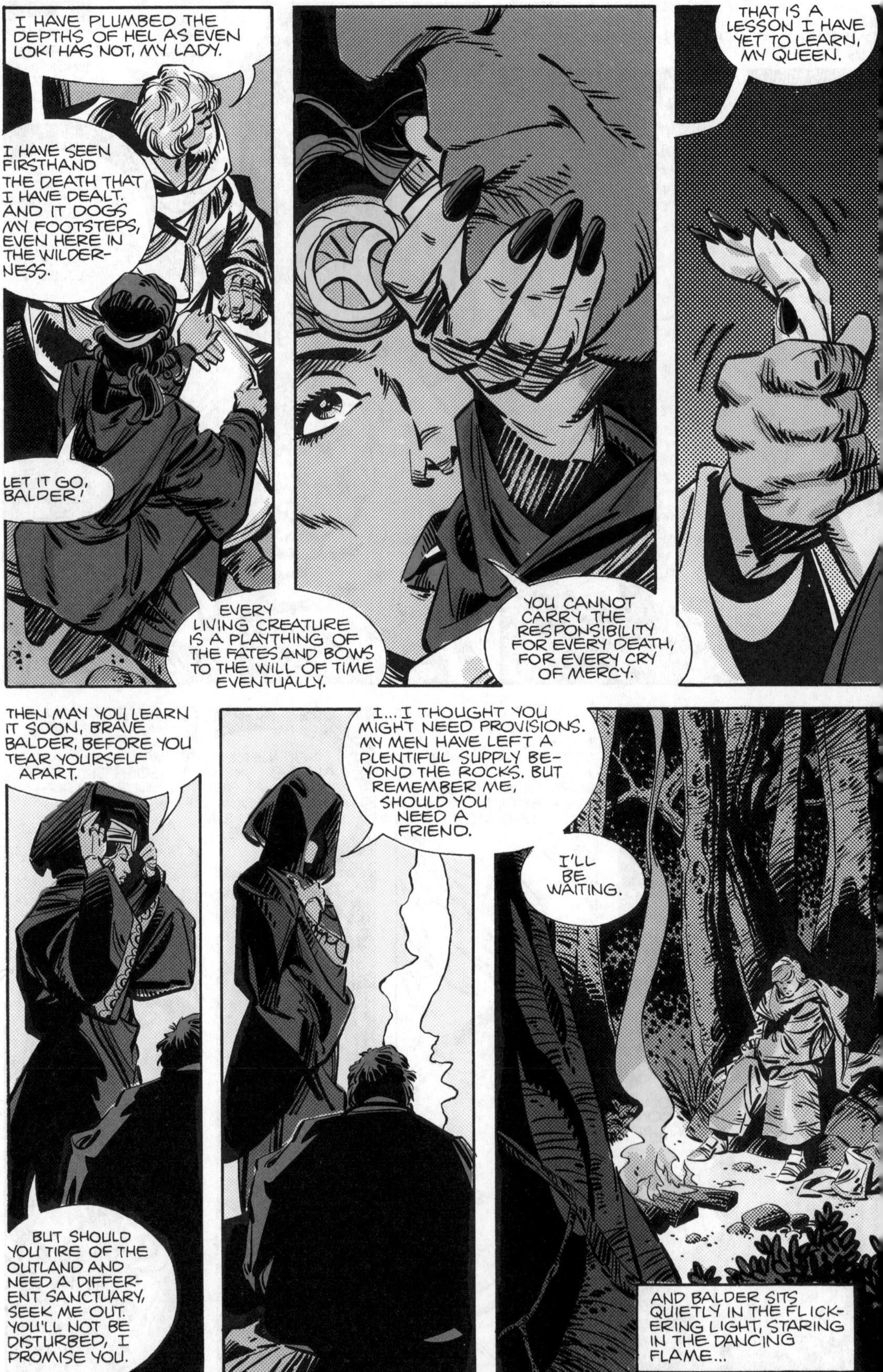
I HAVE PLUMBED THE DEPTHS OF HEL AS EVEN LOKI HAS NOT, MY LADY.
I HAVE SEEN FIRSTHAND THE DEATH THAT I HAVE DEALT. AND IT DOGS MY FOOTSTEPS, EVEN HERE IN THE WILDER-NESS.
LET IT GO, BALDER!
EVERY LIVING CREATURE IS A PLAYTHING OF THE FATES AND BOWS TO THE WILL OF TIME EVENTUALLY.
YOU CANNOT CARRY THE RESPONSIBILITY FOR EVERY DEATH, FOR EVERY CRY OF MERCY.
THAT IS A LESSON I HAVE YET TO LEARN, MY QUEEN.
THEN MAY YOU LEARN IT SOON, BRAVE BALDER, BEFORE YOU TEAR YOURSELF APART.
BUT SHOULD YOU TIRE OF THE OUTLAND AND NEED A DIFFER-ENT SANCTUARY, SEEK ME OUT. YOU'LL NOT BE DISTURBED, I PROMISE YOU.
I... I THOUGHT YOU MIGHT NEED PROVISIONS. MY MEN HAVE LEFT A PLENTIFUL SUPPLY BE-YOND THE ROCKS. BUT REMEMBER ME, SHOULD YOU NEED A FRIEND.
I'LL BE WAITING.
AND BALDER SITS QUIETLY IN THE FLICK-ERING LIGHT, STARING IN THE DANCING FLAME...

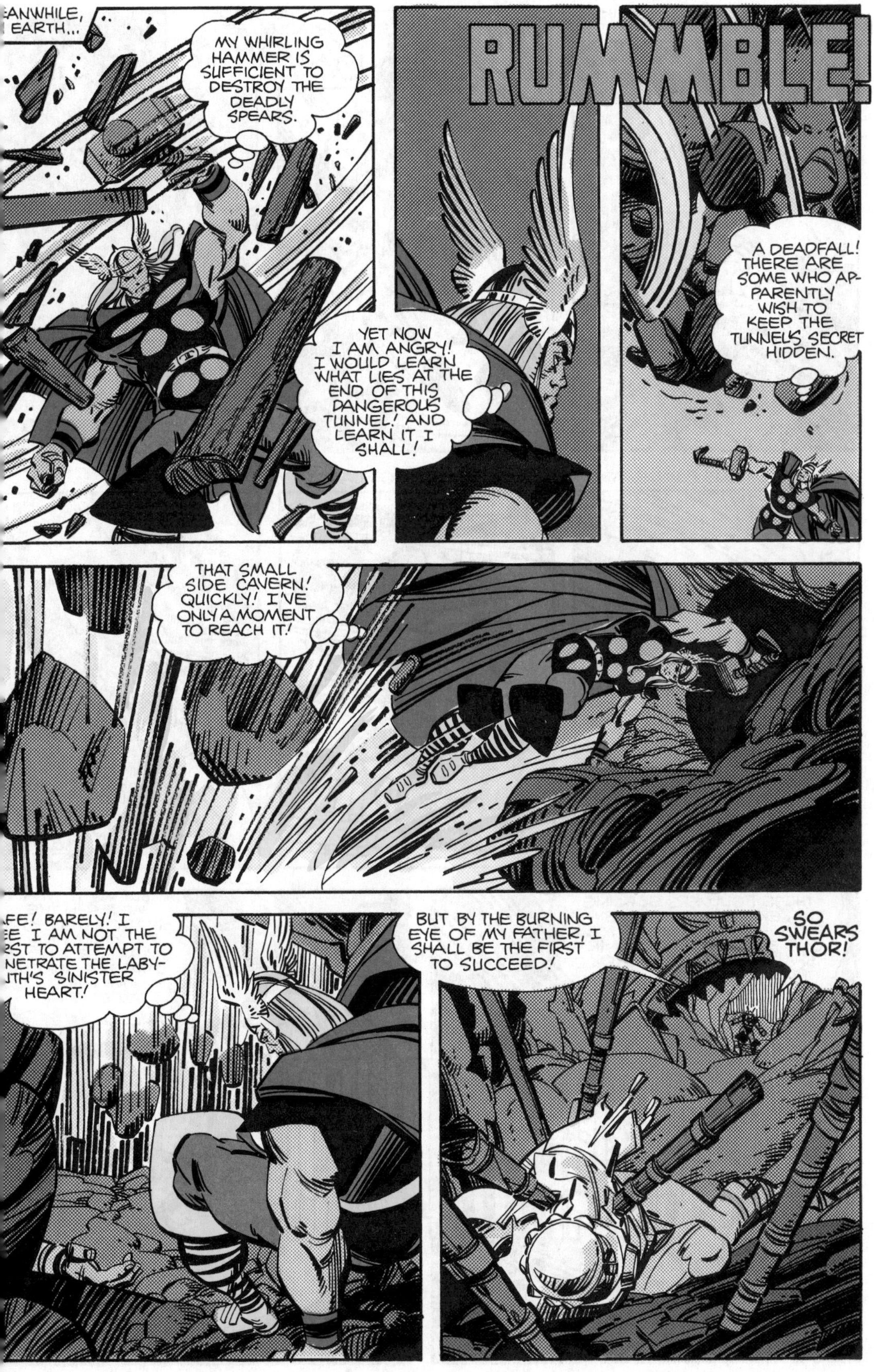

EANWHILE, EARTH...
MY WHIRLING HAMMER IS SUFFICIENT TO DESTROY THE DEADLY SPEARS.
YET NOW I AM ANGRY! I WOULD LEARN WHAT LIES AT THE END OF THIS DANGEROUS TUNNEL! AND LEARN IT, I SHALL!
RUMMBLE!
A DEADFALL! THERE ARE SOME WHO APPARENTLY WISH TO KEEP THE TUNNEL'S SECRET HIDDEN.
THAT SMALL SIDE CAVERN! QUICKLY! I'VE ONLY A MOMENT TO REACH IT!
AFE! BARELY! I EE I AM NOT THE RST TO ATTEMPT TO NETRATE THE LABY-NTH'S SINISTER HEART!
BUT BY THE BURNING EYE OF MY FATHER, I SHALL BE THE FIRST TO SUCCEED!
SO SWEARS THOR!

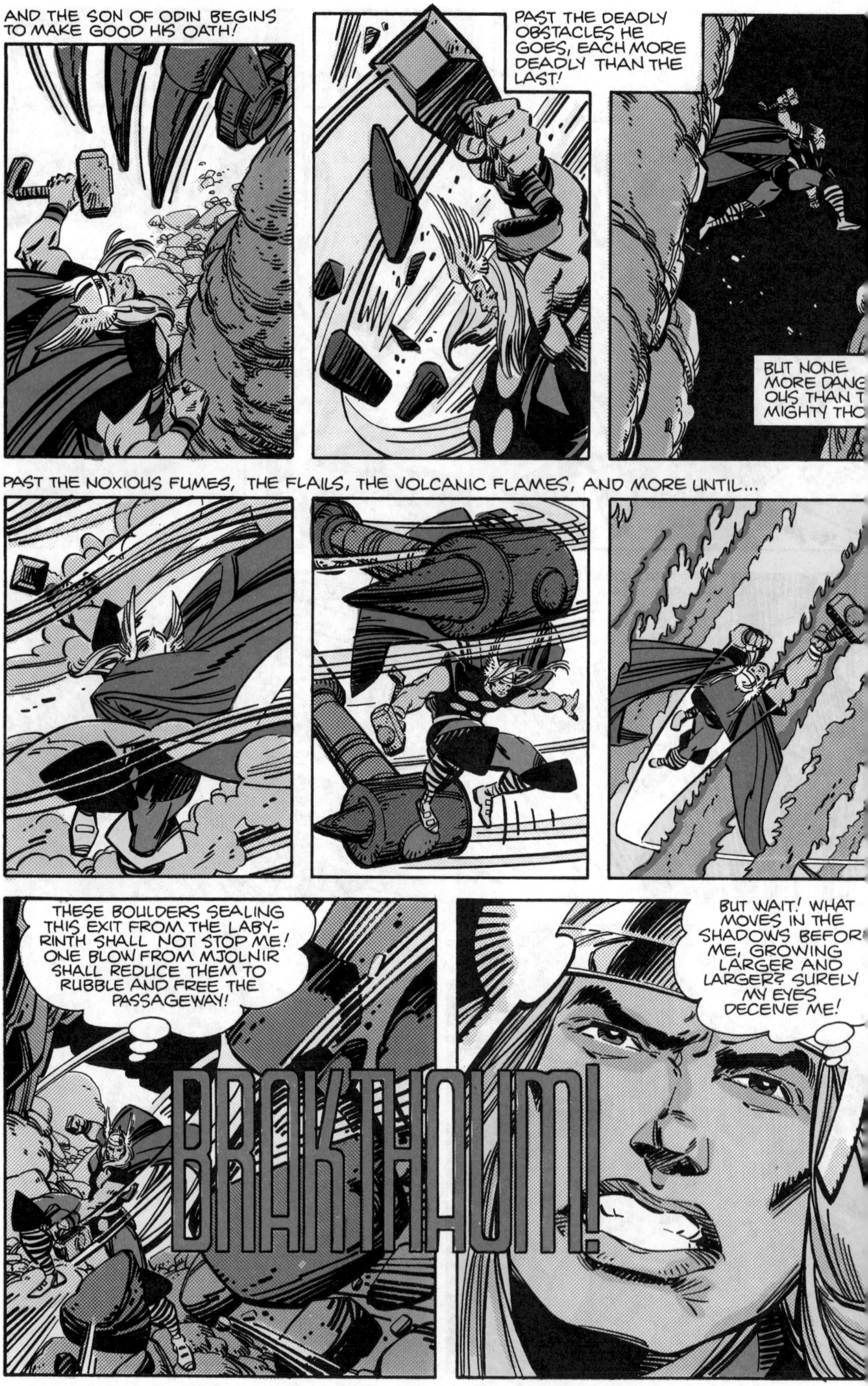
AND THE SON OF ODIN BEGINS TO MAKE GOOD HIS OATH!
PAST THE DEADLY OBSTACLES HE GOES, EACH MORE DEADLY THAN THE LAST!
BUT NONE MORE DANG OUS THAN T MIGHTY THO
PAST THE NOXIOUS FUMES, THE FLAILS, THE VOLCANIC FLAMES, AND MORE UNTIL...
THESE BOULDERS SEALING THIS EXIT FROM THE LABY-RINTH SHALL NOT STOP ME! ONE BLOW FROM MJOLNIR SHALL REDUCE THEM TO RUBBLE AND FREE THE PASSAGEWAY!
BRAKTHAUM!
BUT WAIT! WHAT MOVES IN THE SHADOWS BEFOR ME, GROWING LARGER AND LARGER? SURELY MY EYES DECEIVE ME!

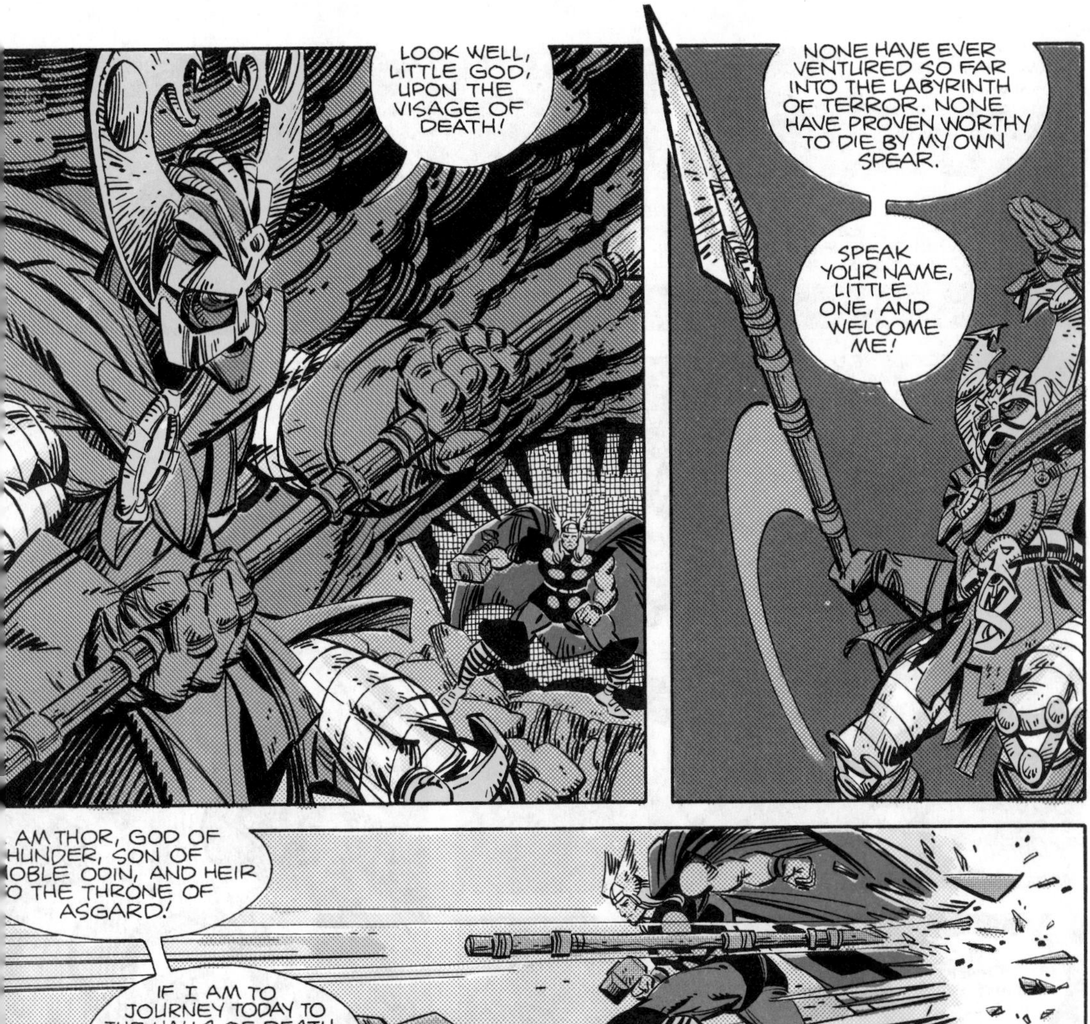
LOOK WELL, LITTLE GOD, UPON THE VISAGE OF DEATH!
NONE HAVE EVER VENTURED SO FAR INTO THE LABYRINTH OF TERROR. NONE HAVE PROVEN WORTHY TO DIE BY MY OWN SPEAR.
SPEAK YOUR NAME, LITTLE ONE, AND WELCOME ME!
AM THOR, GOD OF HUNDER, SON OF OBLE ODIN, AND HEIR O THE THRONE OF ASGARD!
IF I AM TO JOURNEY TODAY TO THE HALLS OF DEATH, THEN LET IT BE IN THE FIGHTING FURY OF MY WARRIOR'S WRATH.
HAVE AT YOU, VILLAIN. WERE YOU HELA'S OWN KIN, YOU WOULD NOT FIND ME SIMPLE PREY.
THRAKKSH!
WHA--! MY FOE'S HELMET! IT HAS COME LOOSE, FALLING AWAY TO REVEAL HIS FACE!
BY THE GODS... I CANNOT BELIEVE IT!

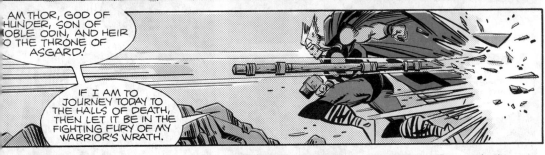

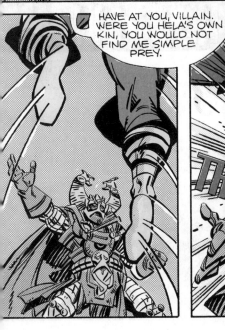

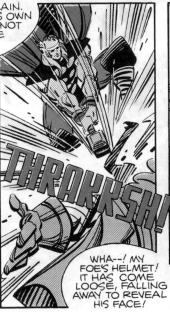

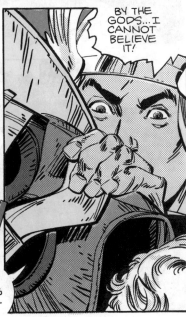

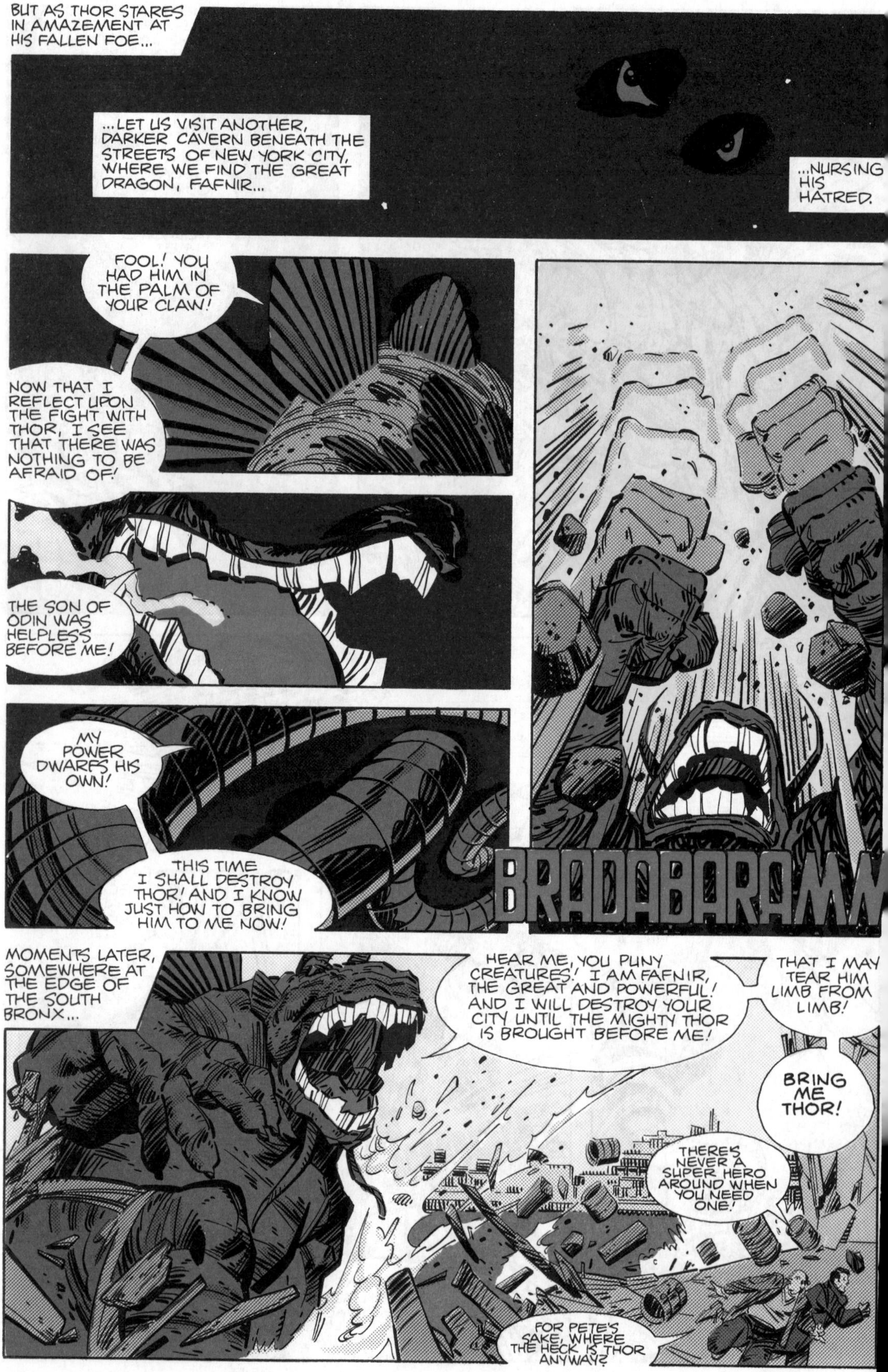

BUT AS THOR STARES IN AMAZEMENT AT HIS FALLEN FOE...
...LET US VISIT ANOTHER, DARKER CAVERN BENEATH THE STREETS OF NEW YORK CITY, WHERE WE FIND THE GREAT DRAGON, FAFNIR...
...NURSING HIS HATRED.
FOOL! YOU HAD HIM IN THE PALM OF YOUR CLAW!
NOW THAT I REFLECT UPON THE FIGHT WITH THOR, I SEE THAT THERE WAS NOTHING TO BE AFRAID OF!
THE SON OF ODIN WAS HELPLESS BEFORE ME!
MY POWER DWARFS HIS OWN!
THIS TIME I SHALL DESTROY THOR! AND I KNOW JUST HOW TO BRING HIM TO ME NOW!
BRADABARAMM
MOMENTS LATER, SOMEWHERE AT THE EDGE OF THE SOUTH BRONX...
HEAR ME, YOU PUNY CREATURES! I AM FAFNIR, THE GREAT AND POWERFUL! AND I WILL DESTROY YOUR CITY UNTIL THE MIGHTY THOR IS BROUGHT BEFORE ME!
THAT I MAY TEAR HIM LIMB FROM LIMB!
BRING ME THOR!
THERE'S NEVER A SUPER HERO AROUND WHEN YOU NEED ONE!
FOR PETE'S SAKE, WHERE THE HECK IS THOR ANYWAY?

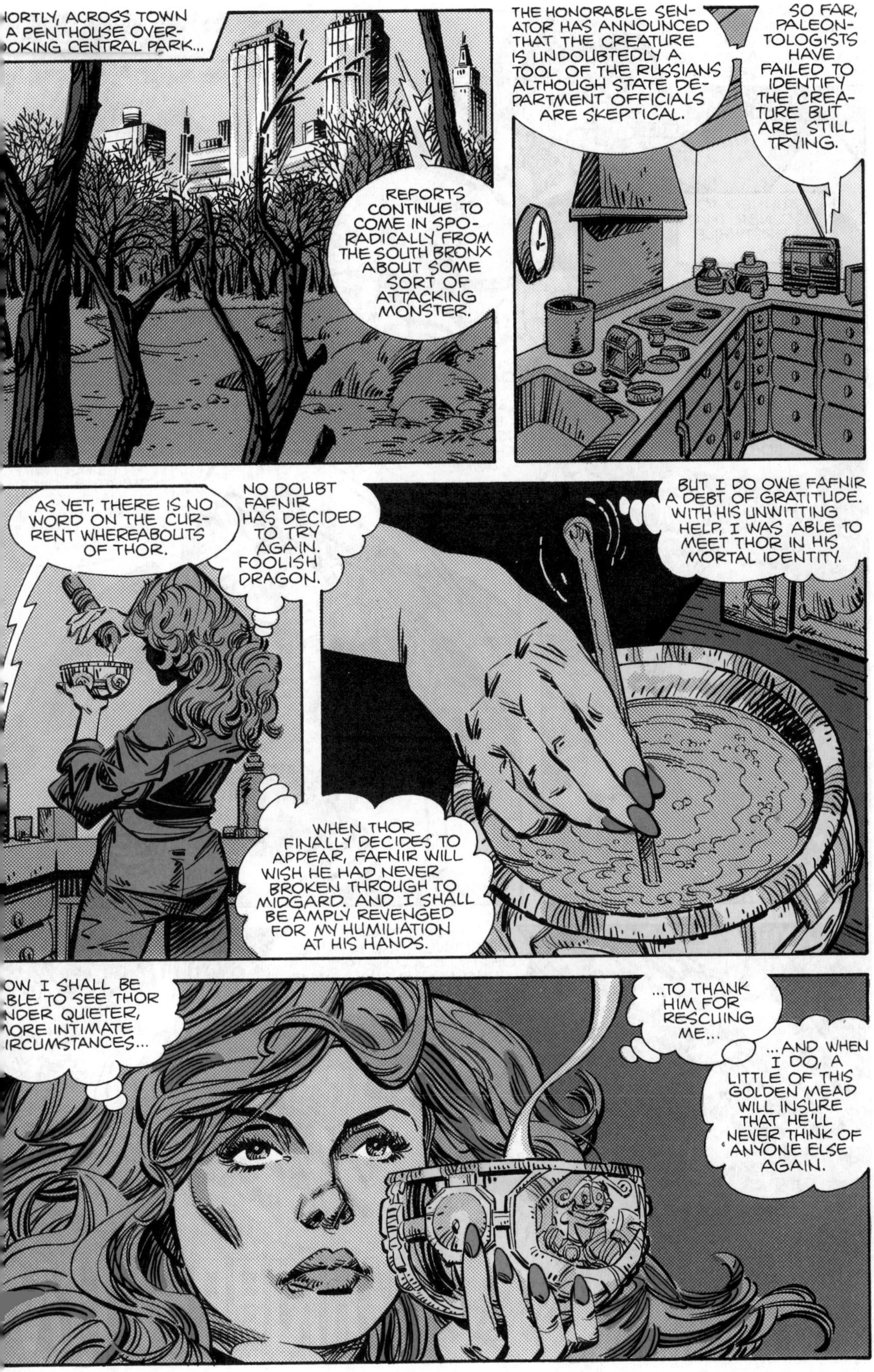

HORTLY, ACROSS TOWN A PENTHOUSE OVER-LOOKING CENTRAL PARK...
REPORTS CONTINUE TO COME IN SPORADICALLY FROM THE SOUTH BRONX ABOUT SOME SORT OF ATTACKING MONSTER.
THE HONORABLE SENATOR HAS ANNOUNCED THAT THE CREATURE IS UNDOUBTEDLY A TOOL OF THE RUSSIANS ALTHOUGH STATE DEPARTMENT OFFICIALS ARE SKEPTICAL.
SO FAR, PALEONTOLOGISTS HAVE FAILED TO IDENTIFY THE CREATURE BUT ARE STILL TRYING.
AS YET, THERE IS NO WORD ON THE CURRENT WHEREABOUTS OF THOR.
NO DOUBT FAFNIR HAS DECIDED TO TRY AGAIN. FOOLISH DRAGON.
BUT I DO OWE FAFNIR A DEBT OF GRATITUDE. WITH HIS UNWITTING HELP, I WAS ABLE TO MEET THOR IN HIS MORTAL IDENTITY.
WHEN THOR FINALLY DECIDES TO APPEAR, FAFNIR WILL WISH HE HAD NEVER BROKEN THROUGH TO MIDGARD. AND I SHALL BE AMPLY REVENGED FOR MY HUMILIATION AT HIS HANDS.
OW I SHALL BE BLE TO SEE THOR NDER QUIETER, MORE INTIMATE IRCUMSTANCES...
...TO THANK HIM FOR RESCUING ME...
...AND WHEN I DO, A LITTLE OF THIS GOLDEN MEAD WILL INSURE THAT HE'LL NEVER THINK OF ANYONE ELSE AGAIN.

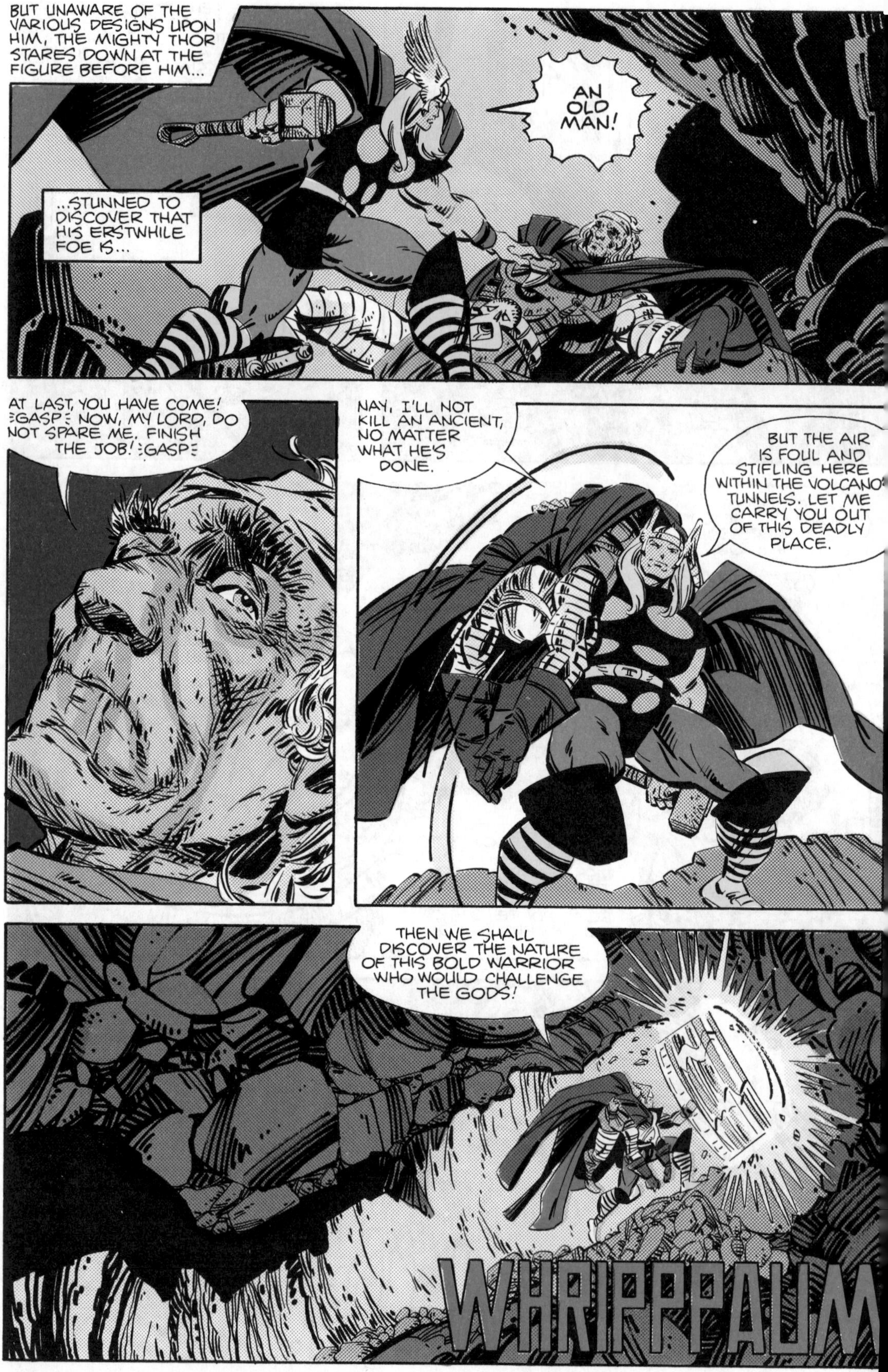
BUT UNAWARE OF THE VARIOUS DESIGNS UPON HIM, THE MIGHTY THOR STARES DOWN AT THE FIGURE BEFORE HIM...
...STUNNED TO DISCOVER THAT HIS ERSTWHILE FOE IS...
AN OLD MAN!
AT LAST, YOU HAVE COME! =GASP= NOW, MY LORD, DO NOT SPARE ME. FINISH THE JOB! =GASP=
NAY, I'LL NOT KILL AN ANCIENT, NO MATTER WHAT HE'S DONE.
BUT THE AIR IS FOUL AND STIFLING HERE WITHIN THE VOLCANO TUNNELS. LET ME CARRY YOU OUT OF THIS DEADLY PLACE.
THEN WE SHALL DISCOVER THE NATURE OF THIS BOLD WARRIOR WHO WOULD CHALLENGE THE GODS!
WHRIPPPAUM

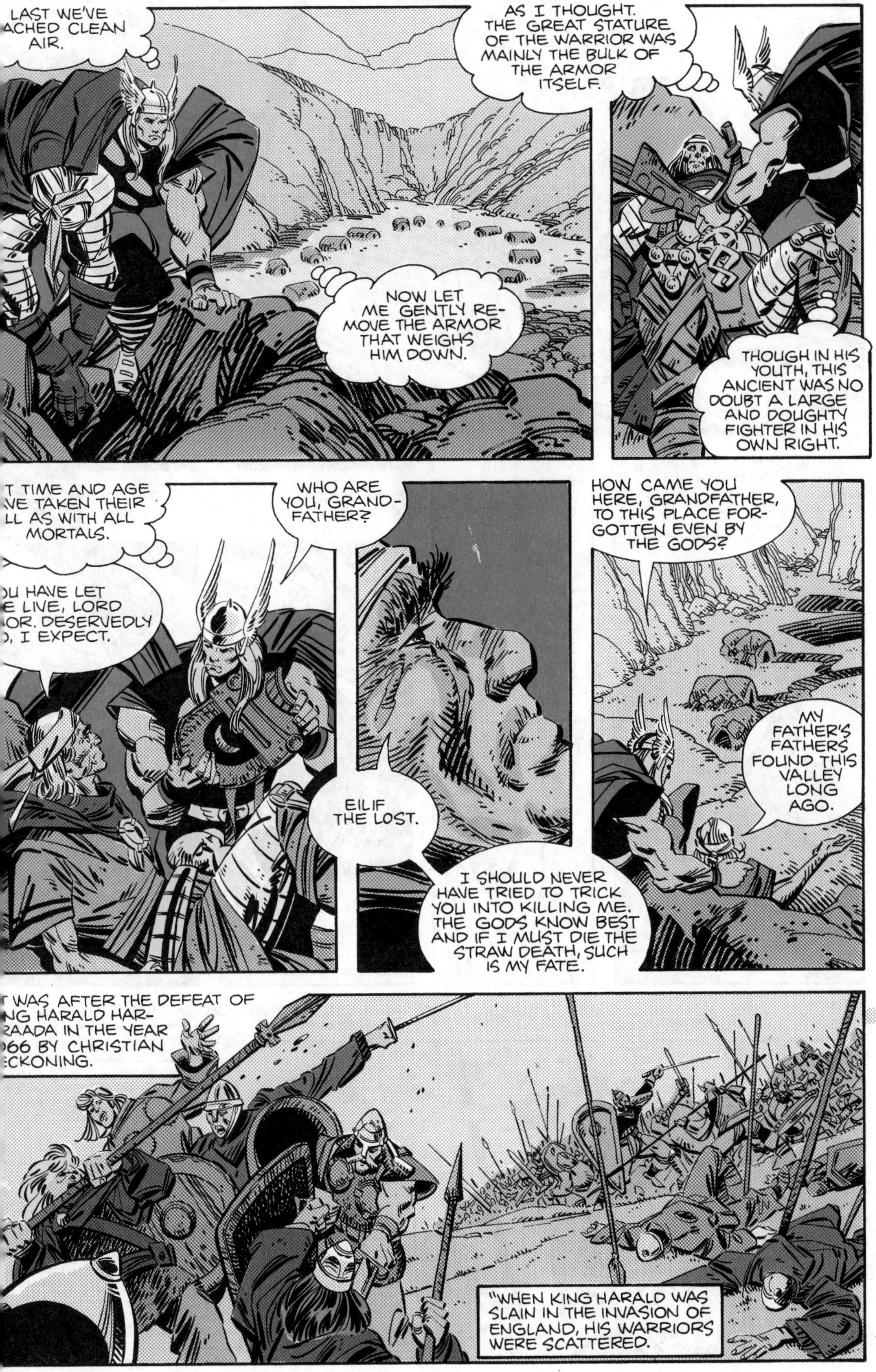
LAST WE'VE
ACHED CLEAN
AIR.
NOW LET
ME GENTLY RE-
MOVE THE ARMOR
THAT WEIGHS
HIM DOWN.
AS I THOUGHT.
THE GREAT STATURE
OF THE WARRIOR WAS
MAINLY THE BULK OF
THE ARMOR
ITSELF.
THOUGH IN HIS
YOUTH, THIS
ANCIENT WAS NO
DOUBT A LARGE
AND DOUGHTY
FIGHTER IN HIS
OWN RIGHT.
T TIME AND AGE
VE TAKEN THEIR
LL AS WITH ALL
MORTALS.
WHO ARE
YOU, GRAND-
FATHER?
OU HAVE LET
E LIVE, LORD
OR. DESERVEDLY
D, I EXPECT.
EILIF
THE LOST.
I SHOULD NEVER
HAVE TRIED TO TRICK
YOU INTO KILLING ME.
THE GODS KNOW BEST
AND IF I MUST DIE THE
STRAW DEATH, SUCH
IS MY FATE.
HOW CAME YOU
HERE, GRANDFATHER,
TO THIS PLACE FOR-
GOTTEN EVEN BY
THE GODS?
MY
FATHER'S
FATHERS
FOUND THIS
VALLEY
LONG
AGO.
T WAS AFTER THE DEFEAT OF
NG HARALD HAR-
RAADA IN THE YEAR
066 BY CHRISTIAN
ECKONING.
"WHEN KING HARALD WAS
SLAIN IN THE INVASION OF
ENGLAND, HIS WARRIORS
WERE SCATTERED.

"SOME TOOK THEIR FAMILIES AND FLED FAR ALONG THE SOUTHERN COASTS, RAIDING WHERE THEY COULD, LIVING OFF THE LAND.

"THEY SAY THERE WERE SEVEN DRAGON SHIPS BUT THAT STORMS AND FIGHTING CUT THEM DOWN...

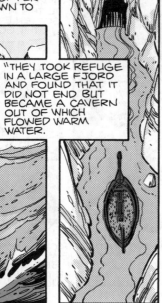

"...UNTIL ONE SHIP WAS DRIVEN BY MONSTROUS WAVES TO A LAND OF PERPETUAL ICE, UNKNOWN TO THEM.

"THEY TOOK REFUGE IN A LARGE FJORD AND FOUND THAT IT DID NOT END BUT BECAME A CAVERN OUT OF WHICH FLOWED WARM WATER.

"THEY FOLLOWED THE CAVERN THROUGH TO DAYLIGHT, THE SHIP STRUCK A HIDDEN ROCK AND WAS LOST.

"THE SURVIVORS, MEN AND WOMEN, SALVAGED WHAT THEY COULD AND FOUND THAT THEY HAD EMERGED IN A LARGE VALLEY SURROUNDED BY IMPASSIBLE WALLS.

"AND THERE THEY STAYED AS DID THEIR CHILDREN NOW I, WHO WAS THE LAST CHIEFTAIN, AM ALSO THE LAST SURVIVOR.

"AND MY DAYS ARE NUMBERED."

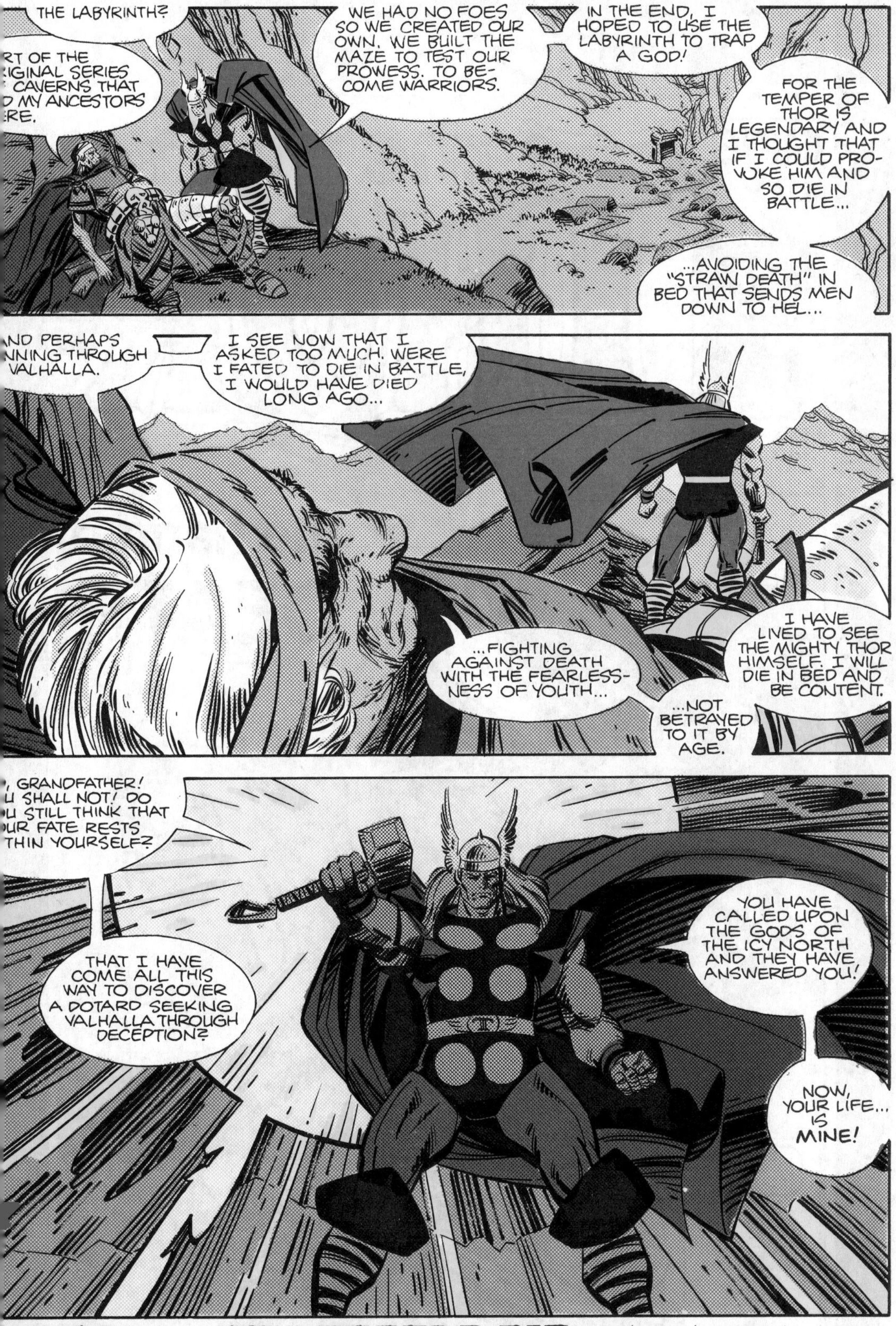
THE LABYRINTH?
RT OF THE RIGINAL SERIES CAVERNS THAT D MY ANCESTORS ERE.
WE HAD NO FOES SO WE CREATED OUR OWN. WE BUILT THE MAZE TO TEST OUR PROWESS. TO BE-COME WARRIORS.
IN THE END, I HOPED TO USE THE LABYRINTH TO TRAP A GOD!
FOR THE TEMPER OF THOR IS LEGENDARY AND I THOUGHT THAT IF I COULD PRO-VOKE HIM AND SO DIE IN BATTLE...
...AVOIDING THE "STRAW DEATH" IN BED THAT SENDS MEN DOWN TO HEL...
ND PERHAPS NNING THROUGH VALHALLA.
I SEE NOW THAT I ASKED TOO MUCH. WERE I FATED TO DIE IN BATTLE, I WOULD HAVE DIED LONG AGO...
...FIGHTING AGAINST DEATH WITH THE FEARLESS-NESS OF YOUTH...
...NOT BETRAYED TO IT BY AGE.
I HAVE LIVED TO SEE THE MIGHTY THOR HIMSELF. I WILL DIE IN BED AND BE CONTENT.
, GRANDFATHER! U SHALL NOT! DO U STILL THINK THAT UR FATE RESTS THIN YOURSELF?
THAT I HAVE COME ALL THIS WAY TO DISCOVER A DOTARD SEEKING VALHALLA THROUGH DECEPTION?
YOU HAVE CALLED UPON THE GODS OF THE ICY NORTH AND THEY HAVE ANSWERED YOU!
NOW, YOUR LIFE... IS MINE!

NEXT: IF I SHOULD DIE BEFORE I WAKE...

THOR! EILIF! LORELEI! FAFNIR! ODIN! DOOM! RAVENS? AND EVERYTHING ELSE WE CAN FIT INTO A SINGLE ISSUE!
(OF COURSE, IT WILL ALL BE VERY, VERY TINY.)

Chapter Seven

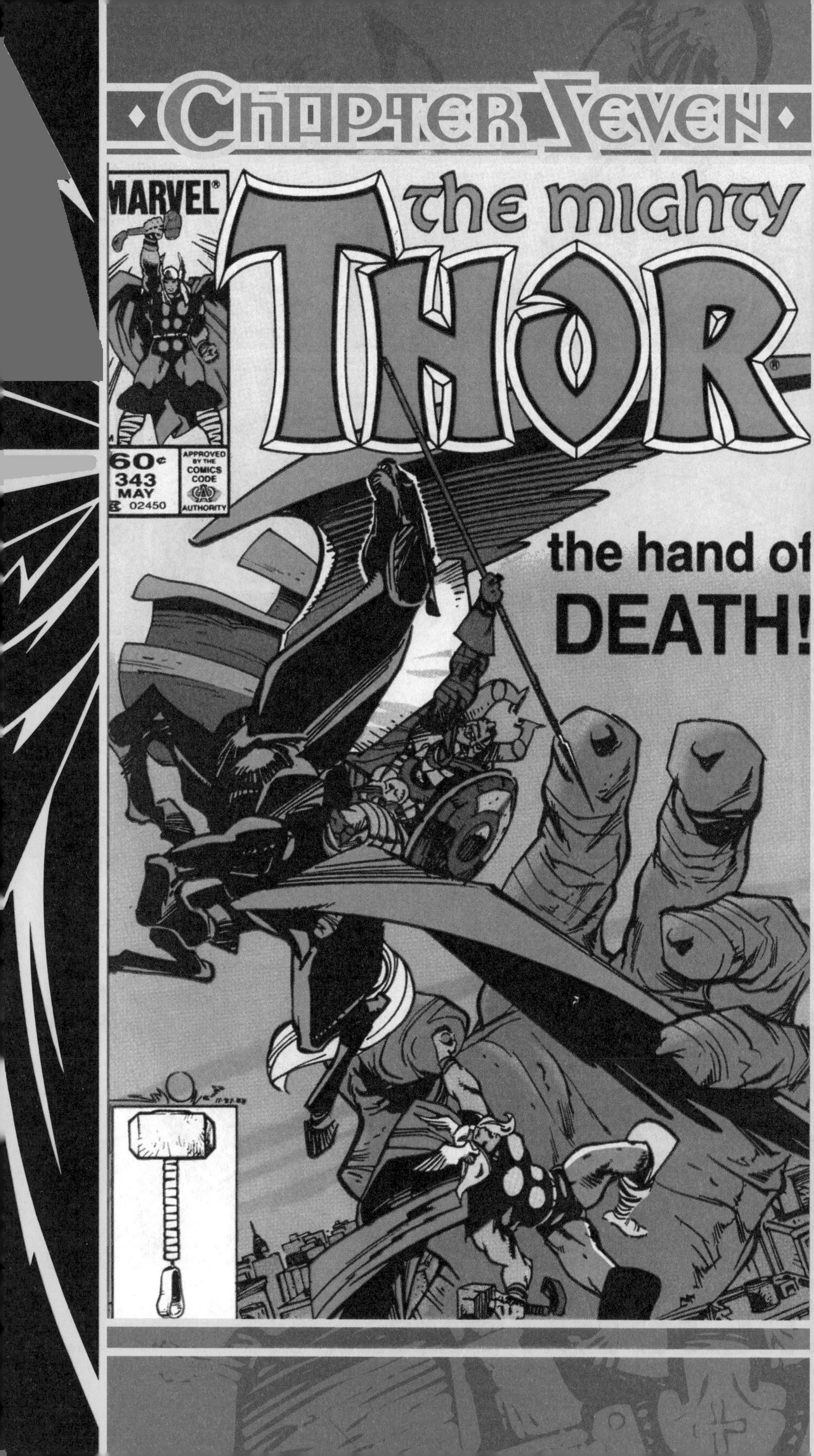
MARVEL®
the mighty
THOR®
60¢
343
MAY
02450
APPROVED BY THE COMICS CODE AUTHORITY
the hand of
DEATH!

TAN LEE
RESENTS: the MIGHTY THOR®

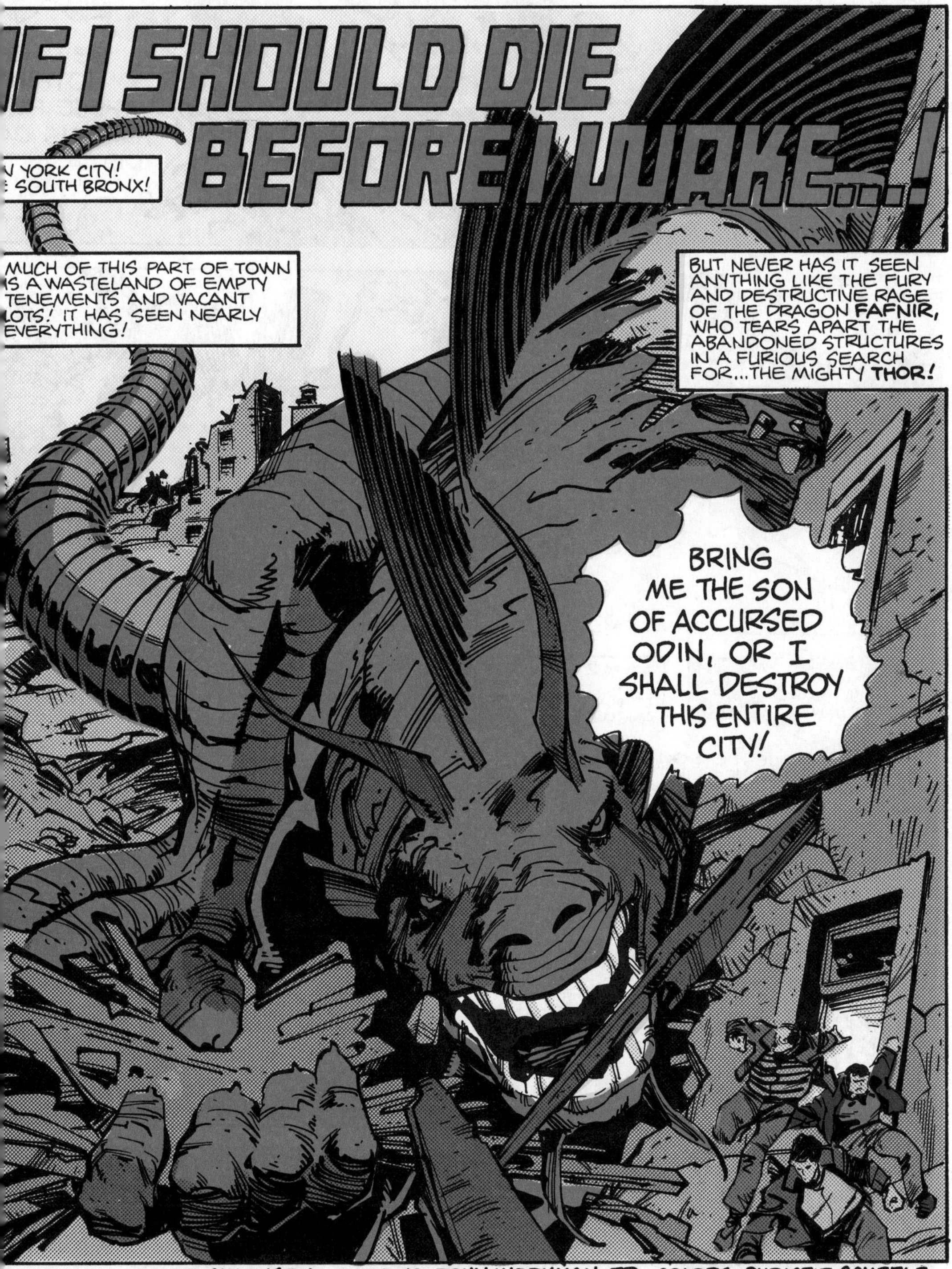

F I SHOULD DIE BEFORE I WAKE...!
V YORK CITY!
E SOUTH BRONX!
MUCH OF THIS PART OF TOWN S A WASTELAND OF EMPTY TENEMENTS AND VACANT LOTS! IT HAS SEEN NEARLY EVERYTHING!
BUT NEVER HAS IT SEEN ANYTHING LIKE THE FURY AND DESTRUCTIVE RAGE OF THE DRAGON **FAFNIR**, WHO TEARS APART THE ABANDONED STRUCTURES IN A FURIOUS SEARCH FOR...THE MIGHTY **THOR!**
BRING ME THE SON OF ACCURSED ODIN, OR I SHALL DESTROY THIS ENTIRE CITY!

T AND STORY: WALTER SIMONSON · LETTERING: JOHN WORKMAN, JR. · COLORS: CHRISTIE SCHEELE
EDITING: MARK GRUENWALD · EDITOR-IN-CHIEF: JIM SHOOTER

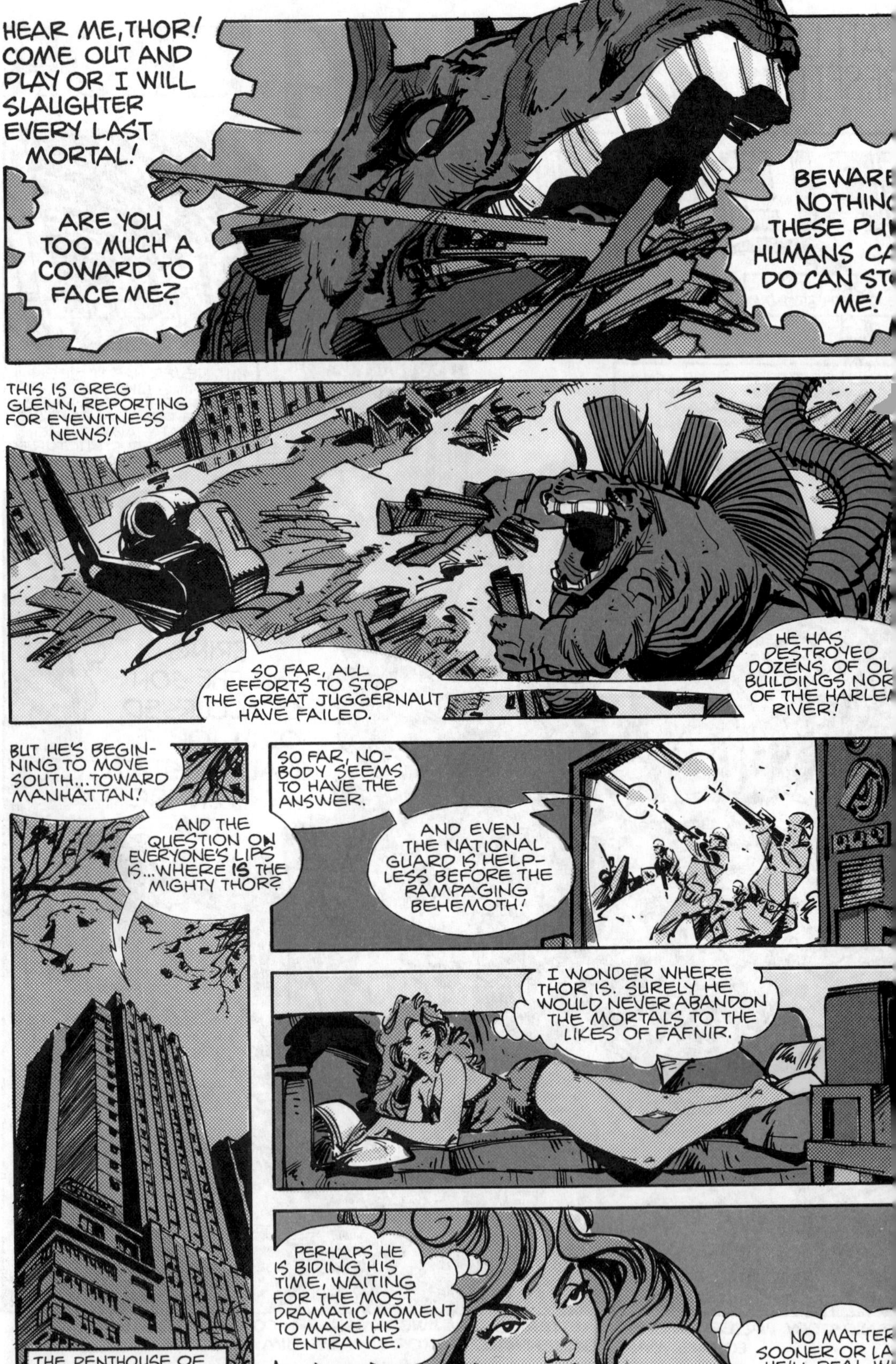
HEAR ME, THOR! COME OUT AND PLAY OR I WILL SLAUGHTER EVERY LAST MORTAL!
ARE YOU TOO MUCH A COWARD TO FACE ME?
BEWARE NOTHIN THESE PU HUMANS CA DO CAN ST ME!
THIS IS GREG GLENN, REPORTING FOR EYEWITNESS NEWS!
SO FAR, ALL EFFORTS TO STOP THE GREAT JUGGERNAUT HAVE FAILED.
HE HAS DESTROYED DOZENS OF OL BUILDINGS NOR OF THE HARLE RIVER!
BUT HE'S BEGINNING TO MOVE SOUTH...TOWARD MANHATTAN!
AND THE QUESTION ON EVERYONE'S LIPS IS...WHERE IS THE MIGHTY THOR?
SO FAR, NOBODY SEEMS TO HAVE THE ANSWER.
AND EVEN THE NATIONAL GUARD IS HELPLESS BEFORE THE RAMPAGING BEHEMOTH!
I WONDER WHERE THOR IS. SURELY HE WOULD NEVER ABANDON THE MORTALS TO THE LIKES OF FAFNIR.
THE PENTHOUSE OF THE SORCERESS LORELEI, OVERLOOKING CENTRAL PARK...
PERHAPS HE IS BIDING HIS TIME, WAITING FOR THE MOST DRAMATIC MOMENT TO MAKE HIS ENTRANCE.
NO MATTER SOONER OR LA HE'LL DEAL W FAFNIR. AND T I SHALL DEAL HIM! I CA HARDLY WA

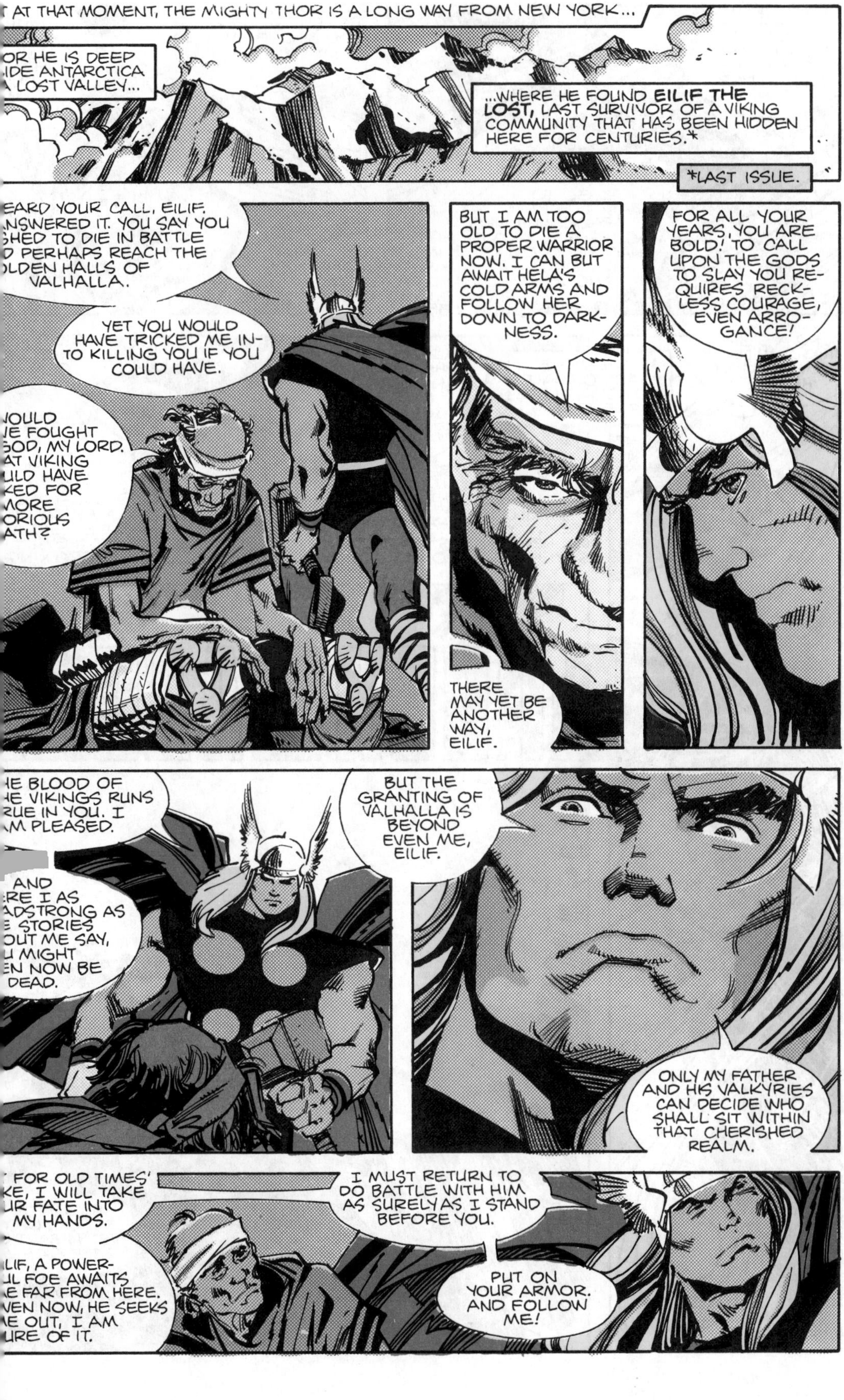
T AT THAT MOMENT, THE MIGHTY THOR IS A LONG WAY FROM NEW YORK...
OR HE IS DEEP
IDE ANTARCTICA
A LOST VALLEY...
...WHERE HE FOUND EILIF THE LOST, LAST SURVIVOR OF A VIKING COMMUNITY THAT HAS BEEN HIDDEN HERE FOR CENTURIES.*
*LAST ISSUE.
EARD YOUR CALL, EILIF. NSWERED IT. YOU SAY YOU SHED TO DIE IN BATTLE D PERHAPS REACH THE OLDEN HALLS OF VALHALLA.
YET YOU WOULD HAVE TRICKED ME INTO KILLING YOU IF YOU COULD HAVE.
WOULD E FOUGHT GOD, MY LORD. AT VIKING ULD HAVE KED FOR MORE ORIOUS ATH?
BUT I AM TOO OLD TO DIE A PROPER WARRIOR NOW. I CAN BUT AWAIT HELA'S COLD ARMS AND FOLLOW HER DOWN TO DARKNESS.
THERE MAY YET BE ANOTHER WAY, EILIF.
FOR ALL YOUR YEARS, YOU ARE BOLD! TO CALL UPON THE GODS TO SLAY YOU REQUIRES RECKLESS COURAGE, EVEN ARROGANCE!
HE BLOOD OF HE VIKINGS RUNS RUE IN YOU. I AM PLEASED.
AND ERE I AS ADSTRONG AS E STORIES OUT ME SAY, U MIGHT EN NOW BE DEAD.
BUT THE GRANTING OF VALHALLA IS BEYOND EVEN ME, EILIF.
ONLY MY FATHER AND HIS VALKYRIES CAN DECIDE WHO SHALL SIT WITHIN THAT CHERISHED REALM.
T FOR OLD TIMES' KE, I WILL TAKE UR FATE INTO MY HANDS.
ILIF, A POWERUL FOE AWAITS E FAR FROM HERE. VEN NOW, HE SEEKS E OUT, I AM URE OF IT.
I MUST RETURN TO DO BATTLE WITH HIM AS SURELY AS I STAND BEFORE YOU.
PUT ON YOUR ARMOR. AND FOLLOW ME!

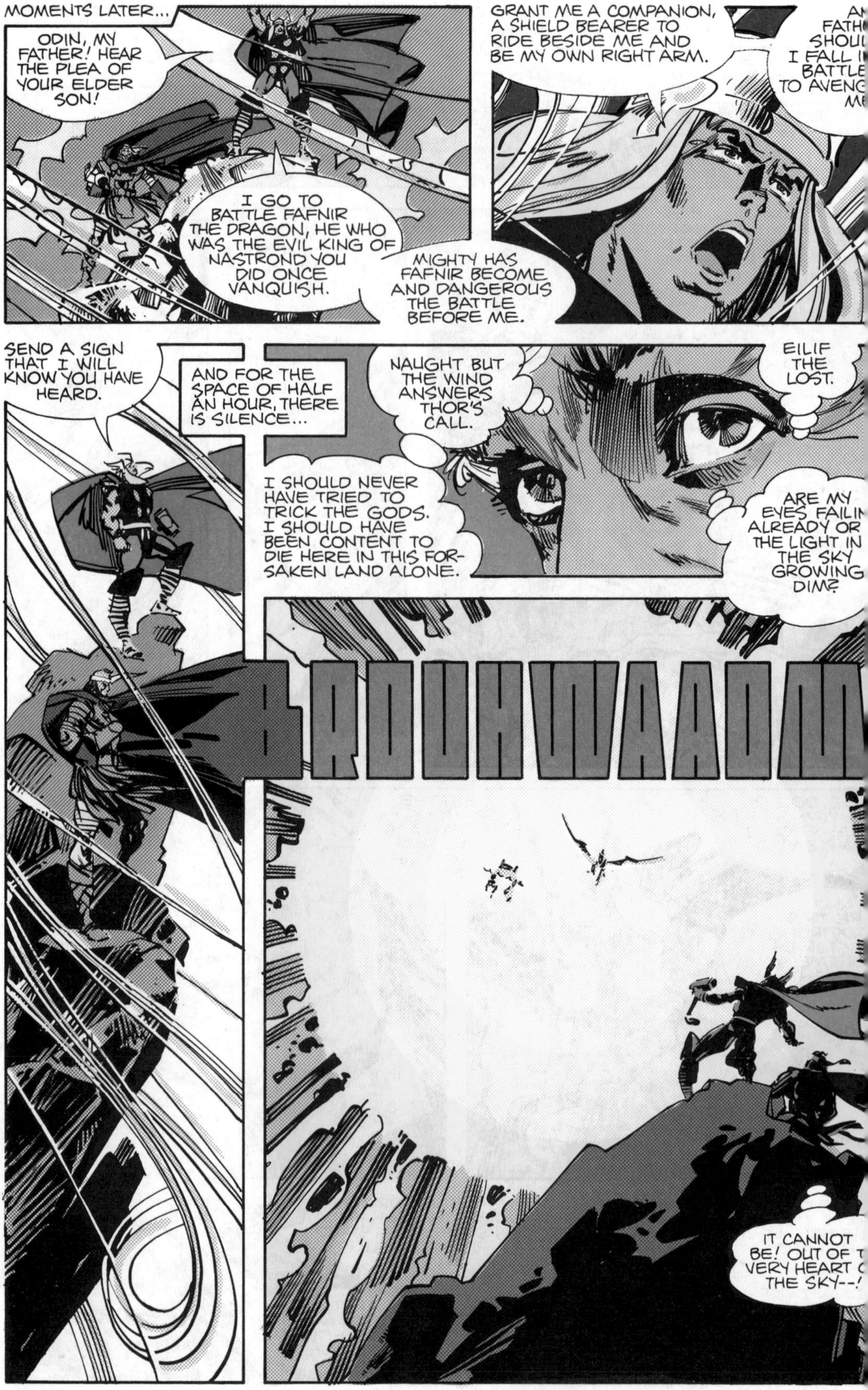
MOMENTS LATER...
ODIN, MY FATHER! HEAR THE PLEA OF YOUR ELDER SON!
I GO TO BATTLE FAFNIR THE DRAGON, HE WHO WAS THE EVIL KING OF NASTROND YOU DID ONCE VANQUISH.
MIGHTY HAS FAFNIR BECOME AND DANGEROUS THE BATTLE BEFORE ME.
GRANT ME A COMPANION, A SHIELD BEARER TO RIDE BESIDE ME AND BE MY OWN RIGHT ARM.
SEND A SIGN THAT I WILL KNOW YOU HAVE HEARD.
AND FOR THE SPACE OF HALF AN HOUR, THERE IS SILENCE...
NAUGHT BUT THE WIND ANSWERS THOR'S CALL.
EILIF THE LOST.
I SHOULD NEVER HAVE TRIED TO TRICK THE GODS. I SHOULD HAVE BEEN CONTENT TO DIE HERE IN THIS FOR-SAKEN LAND ALONE.

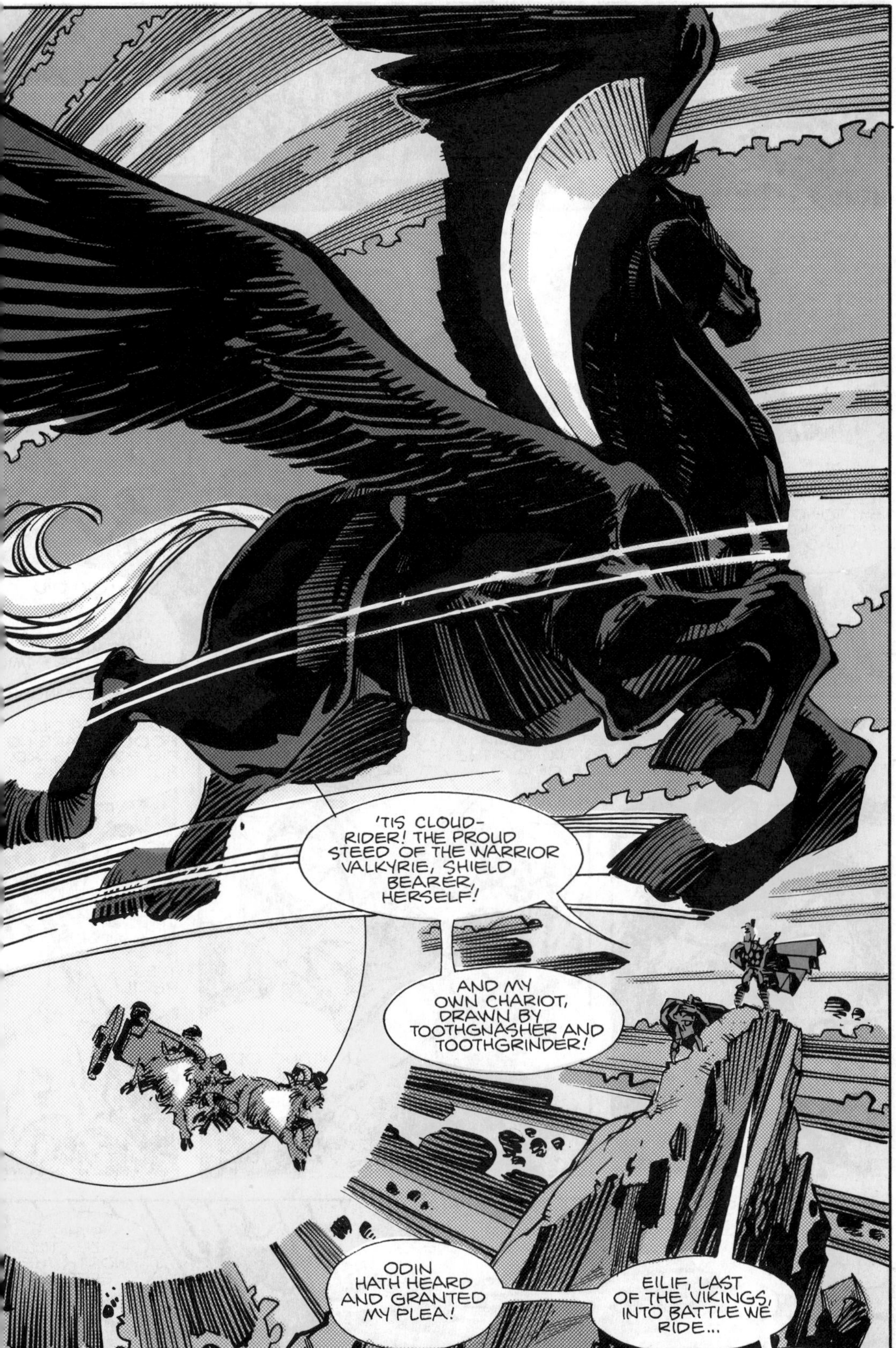
'TIS CLOUD-RIDER! THE PROUD STEED OF THE WARRIOR VALKYRIE, SHIELD BEARER, HERSELF!
AND MY OWN CHARIOT, DRAWN BY TOOTHGNASHER AND TOOTHGRINDER!
ODIN HATH HEARD AND GRANTED MY PLEA!
EILIF, LAST OF THE VIKINGS, INTO BATTLE WE RIDE...
...TOGETHER!

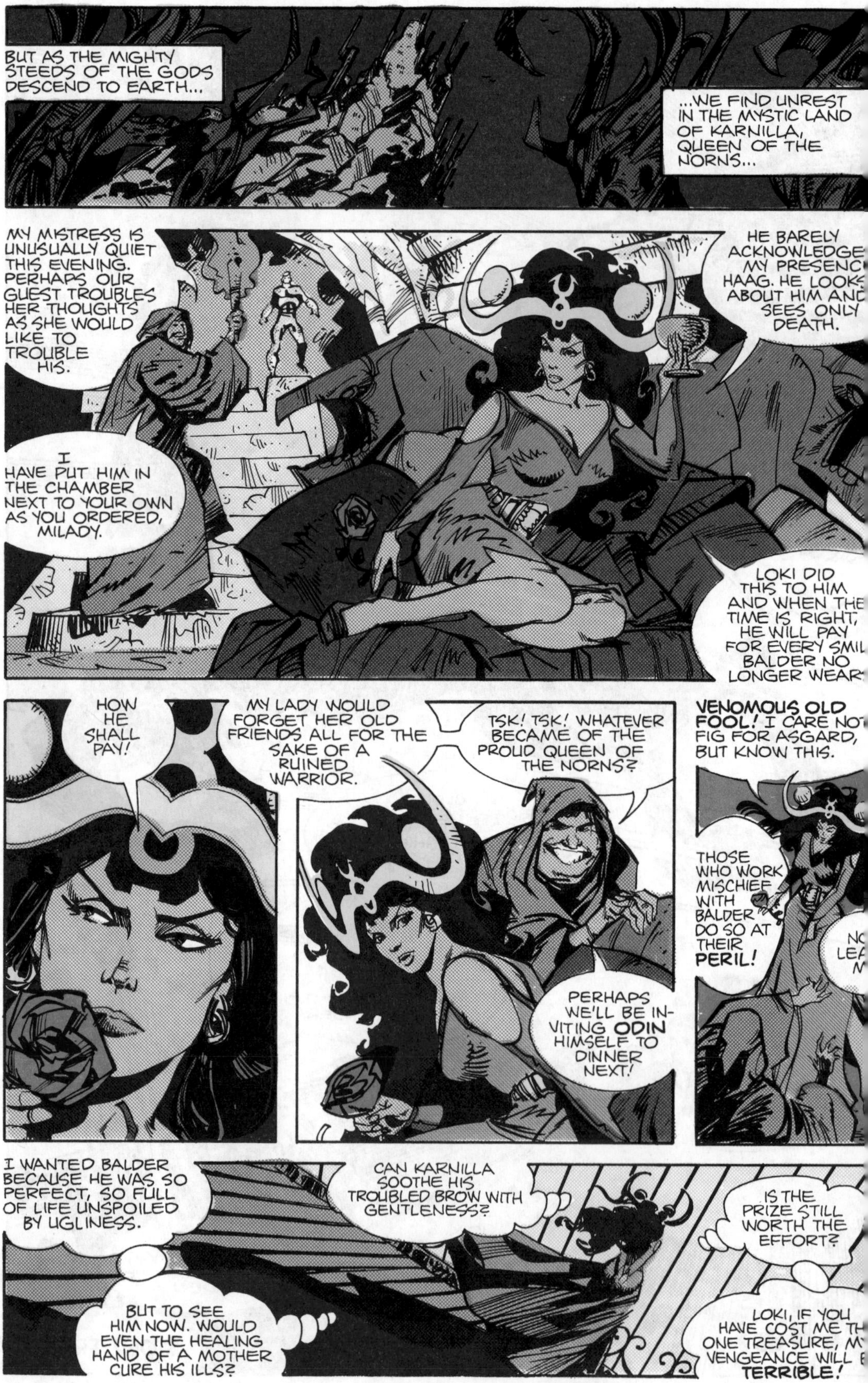

BUT AS THE MIGHTY STEEDS OF THE GODS DESCEND TO EARTH...
...WE FIND UNREST IN THE MYSTIC LAND OF KARNILLA, QUEEN OF THE NORNS...
MY MISTRESS IS UNUSUALLY QUIET THIS EVENING. PERHAPS OUR GUEST TROUBLES HER THOUGHTS AS SHE WOULD LIKE TO TROUBLE HIS.
I HAVE PUT HIM IN THE CHAMBER NEXT TO YOUR OWN AS YOU ORDERED, MILADY.
HE BARELY ACKNOWLEDGE MY PRESENC HAAG. HE LOOKS ABOUT HIM AND SEES ONLY DEATH.
LOKI DID THIS TO HIM AND WHEN THE TIME IS RIGHT, HE WILL PAY FOR EVERY SMIL BALDER NO LONGER WEAR
HOW HE SHALL PAY!
MY LADY WOULD FORGET HER OLD FRIENDS ALL FOR THE SAKE OF A RUINED WARRIOR.
TSK! TSK! WHATEVER BECAME OF THE PROUD QUEEN OF THE NORNS?
PERHAPS WE'LL BE IN-VITING ODIN HIMSELF TO DINNER NEXT!
VENOMOUS OLD FOOL! I CARE NOT FIG FOR ASGARD, BUT KNOW THIS.
THOSE WHO WORK MISCHIEF WITH BALDER DO SO AT THEIR PERIL!
I WANTED BALDER BECAUSE HE WAS SO PERFECT, SO FULL OF LIFE UNSPOILED BY UGLINESS.
CAN KARNILLA SOOTHE HIS TROUBLED BROW WITH GENTLENESS?
IS THE PRIZE STILL WORTH THE EFFORT?
BUT TO SEE HIM NOW. WOULD EVEN THE HEALING HAND OF A MOTHER CURE HIS ILLS?
LOKI, IF YOU HAVE COST ME TH ONE TREASURE, M VENGEANCE WILL TERRIBLE!

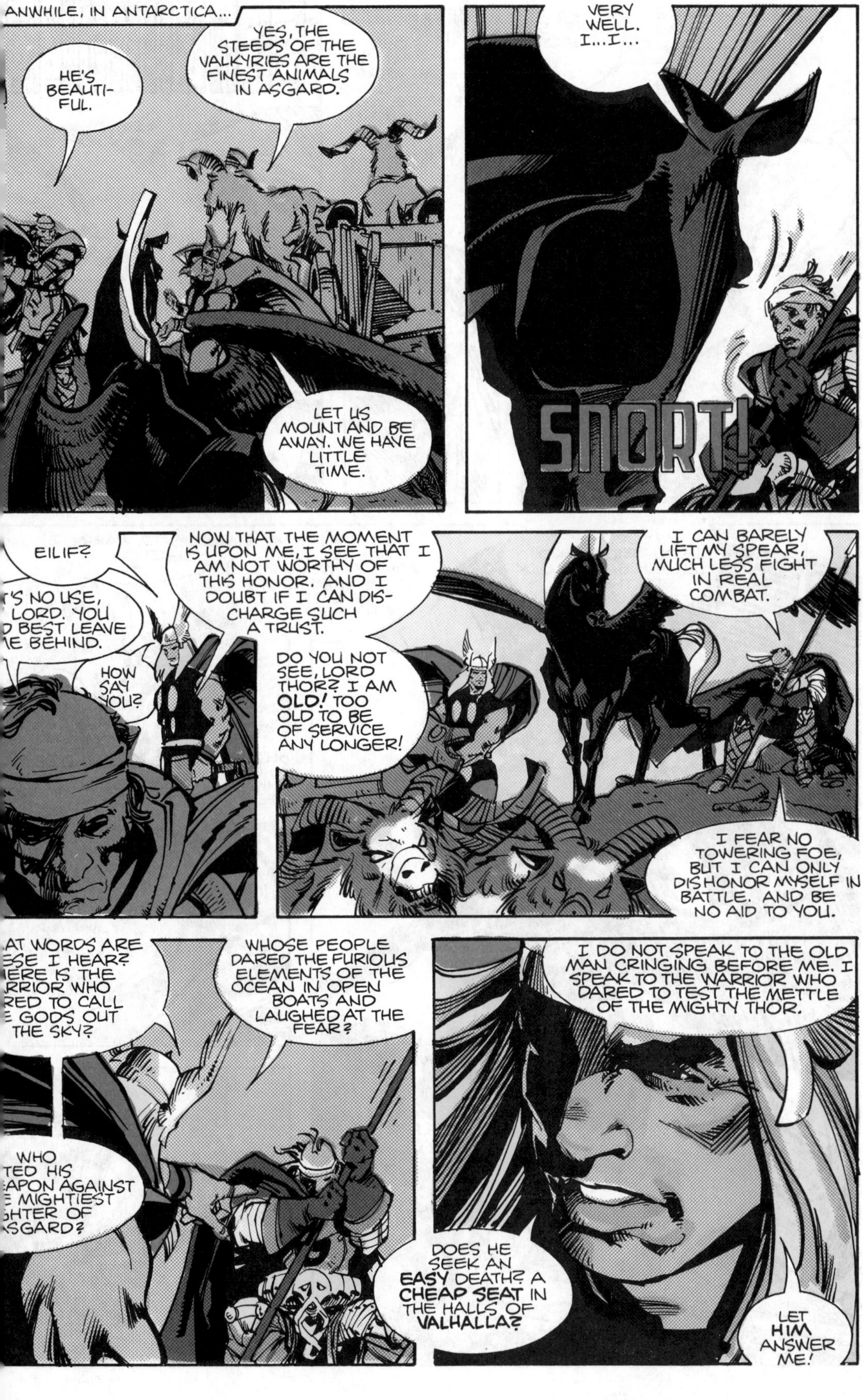
ANWHILE, IN ANTARCTICA...
HE'S BEAUTI-FUL.
YES, THE STEEDS OF THE VALKYRIES ARE THE FINEST ANIMALS IN ASGARD.
LET US MOUNT AND BE AWAY. WE HAVE LITTLE TIME.
VERY WELL. I...I...
SNORT!
EILIF?
T'S NO USE, LORD. YOU D BEST LEAVE E BEHIND.
HOW SAY YOU?
NOW THAT THE MOMENT IS UPON ME, I SEE THAT I AM NOT WORTHY OF THIS HONOR. AND I DOUBT IF I CAN DIS-CHARGE SUCH A TRUST.
DO YOU NOT SEE, LORD THOR? I AM OLD! TOO OLD TO BE OF SERVICE ANY LONGER!
I CAN BARELY LIFT MY SPEAR, MUCH LESS FIGHT IN REAL COMBAT.
I FEAR NO TOWERING FOE, BUT I CAN ONLY DISHONOR MYSELF IN BATTLE. AND BE NO AID TO YOU.
AT WORDS ARE ESE I HEAR? HERE IS THE RRIOR WHO RED TO CALL E GODS OUT THE SKY?
WHOSE PEOPLE DARED THE FURIOUS ELEMENTS OF THE OCEAN IN OPEN BOATS AND LAUGHED AT THE FEAR?
WHO TED HIS EAPON AGAINST E MIGHTIEST GHTER OF SGARD?
I DO NOT SPEAK TO THE OLD MAN CRINGING BEFORE ME. I SPEAK TO THE WARRIOR WHO DARED TO TEST THE METTLE OF THE MIGHTY THOR.
DOES HE SEEK AN EASY DEATH? A CHEAP SEAT IN THE HALLS OF VALHALLA?
LET HIM ANSWER ME!

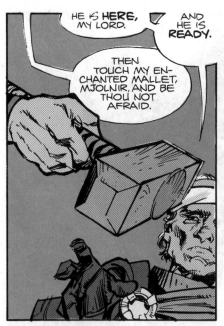

HE IS **HERE**, MY LORD. AND HE IS **READY**.

THEN TOUCH MY ENCHANTED MALLET, MJOLNIR, AND BE THOU NOT AFRAID.

OUR FATES, EILIF, WERE WRITTEN LONG BEFORE WE WERE BORN.

SCHRAKKLE!

NOW, RISE UP AND MOUNT THE STEED THAT AWAITS YOU!

MY LIMBS! MY SINEWS!

I FEEL THE VERY FIRE OF **YOUTH** COURSING THROUGH

MY LORD THOR, LET US **RIDE**. AND LET THE BARDS LOOK TO THEIR BALLADS.

FOR OUR DEEDS SHALL RESOUND ACROSS MIDGARD TO THE VERY ROOTS OF THE WORLD ASH ITSELF!

WELL SAID, WARRIOR. LEAD ON.

BUT WAIT! WHO IS THIS I SEE?

ANOTHER IN THE VALLEY OF THE LOST?

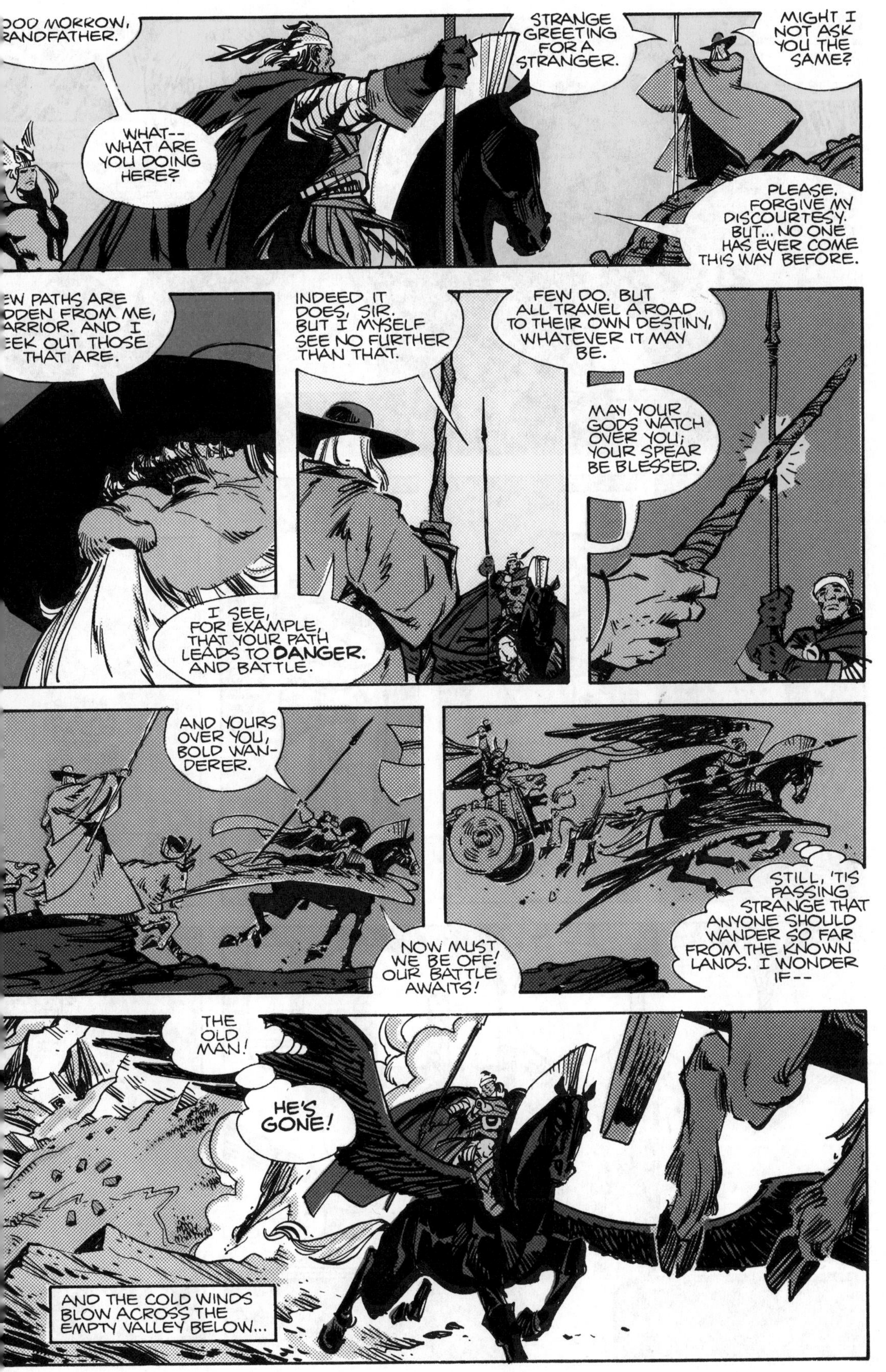
OOD MORROW,
RANDFATHER.
WHAT--
WHAT ARE
YOU DOING
HERE?
STRANGE
GREETING
FOR A
STRANGER.
MIGHT I
NOT ASK
YOU THE
SAME?
PLEASE.
FORGIVE MY
DISCOURTESY.
BUT... NO ONE
HAS EVER COME
THIS WAY BEFORE.
EW PATHS ARE
DDEN FROM ME,
ARRIOR. AND I
EEK OUT THOSE
THAT ARE.
I SEE,
FOR EXAMPLE,
THAT YOUR PATH
LEADS TO DANGER.
AND BATTLE.
INDEED IT
DOES, SIR.
BUT I MYSELF
SEE NO FURTHER
THAN THAT.
FEW DO. BUT
ALL TRAVEL A ROAD
TO THEIR OWN DESTINY,
WHATEVER IT MAY
BE.
MAY YOUR
GODS WATCH
OVER YOU;
YOUR SPEAR
BE BLESSED.
AND YOURS
OVER YOU,
BOLD WAN-
DERER.
NOW MUST
WE BE OFF!
OUR BATTLE
AWAITS!
STILL, 'TIS
PASSING
STRANGE THAT
ANYONE SHOULD
WANDER SO FAR
FROM THE KNOWN
LANDS. I WONDER
IF--
THE
OLD
MAN!
HE'S
GONE!
AND THE COLD WINDS
BLOW ACROSS THE
EMPTY VALLEY BELOW...

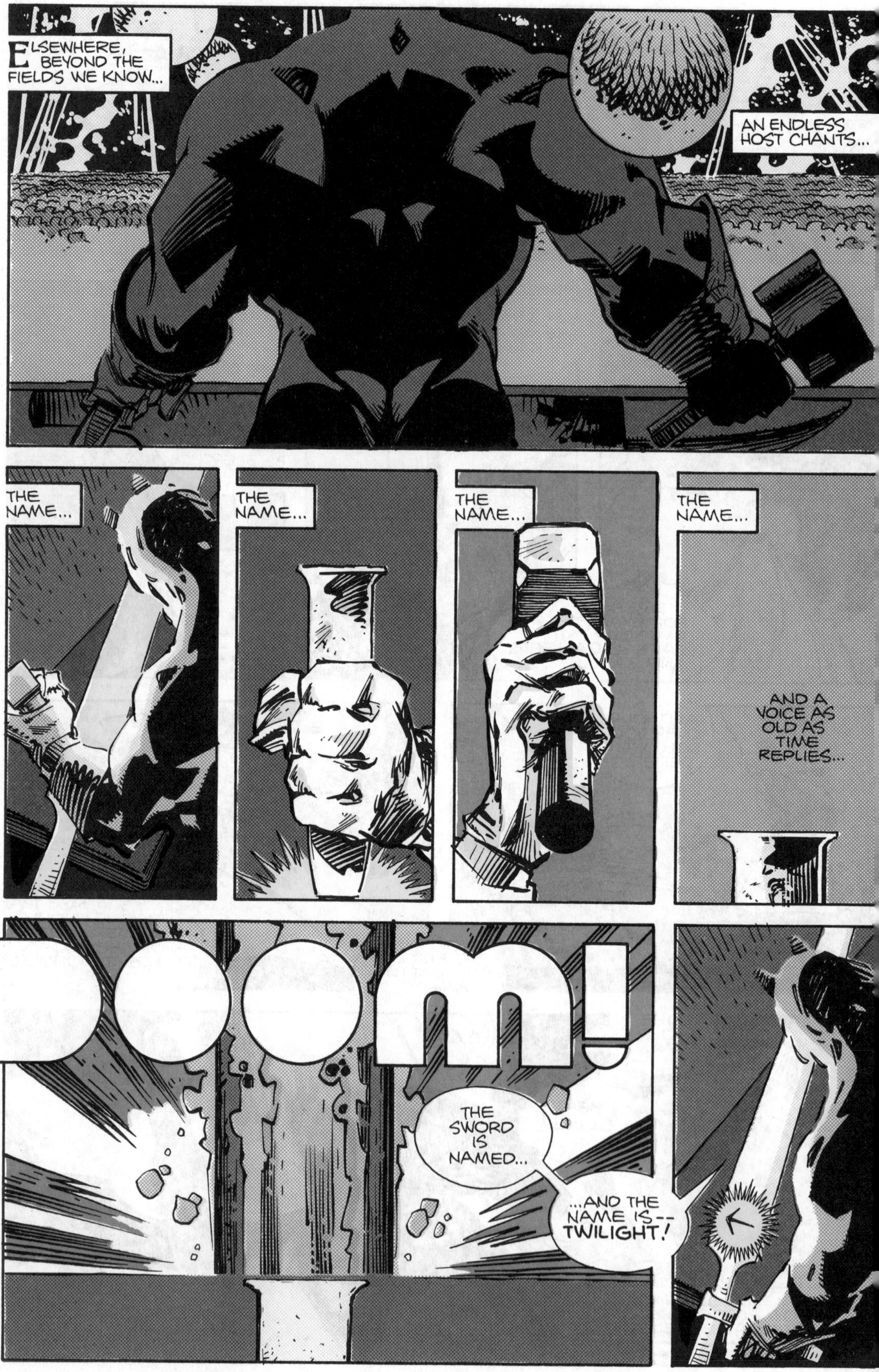
ELSEWHERE, BEYOND THE FIELDS WE KNOW...
AN ENDLESS HOST CHANTS...
THE NAME...
THE NAME...
THE NAME...
THE NAME...
AND A VOICE AS OLD AS TIME REPLIES...
DOOM!
THE SWORD IS NAMED...
...AND THE NAME IS-- TWILIGHT!

MEANWHILE, IN THE SOUTH BRONX, THINGS HAVE GOTTEN OUT OF HAND...

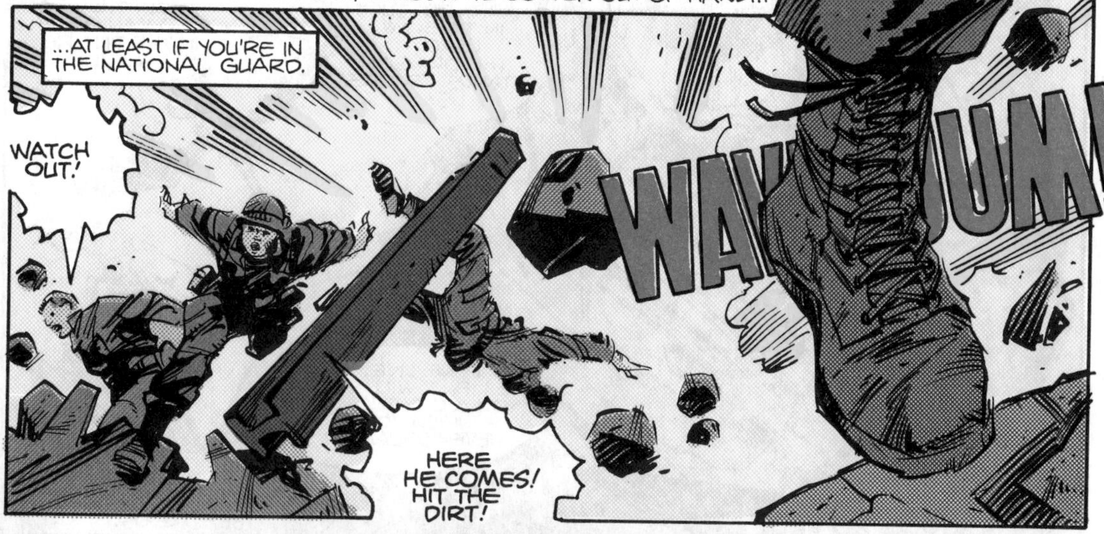
...AT LEAST IF YOU'RE IN THE NATIONAL GUARD.
WATCH OUT!
HERE HE COMES! HIT THE DIRT!

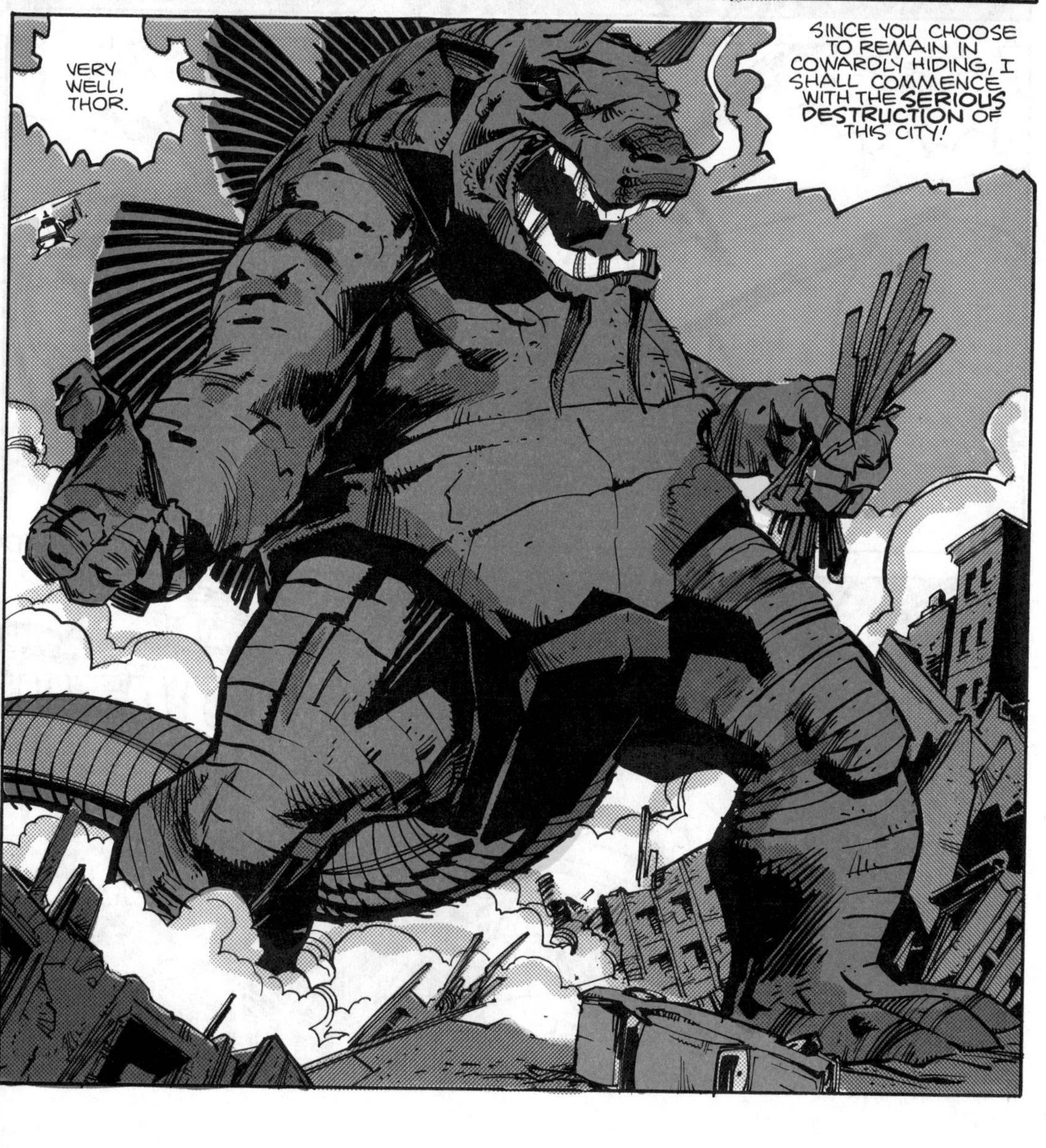
VERY WELL, THOR.
SINCE YOU CHOOSE TO REMAIN IN COWARDLY HIDING, I SHALL COMMENCE WITH THE **SERIOUS DESTRUCTION** OF THIS CITY!

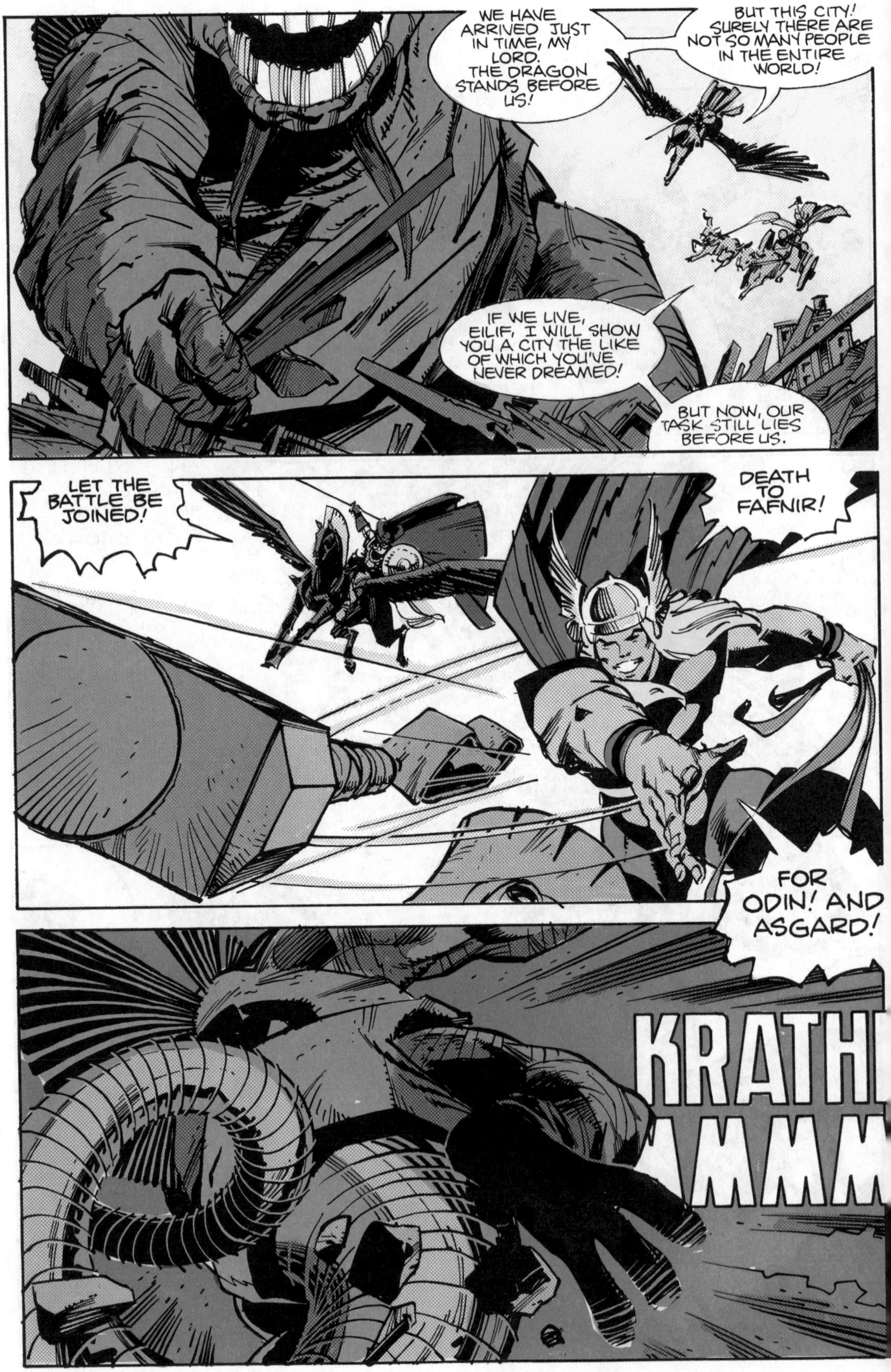
WE HAVE ARRIVED JUST IN TIME, MY LORD. THE DRAGON STANDS BEFORE US!
BUT THIS CITY! SURELY THERE ARE NOT SO MANY PEOPLE IN THE ENTIRE WORLD!
IF WE LIVE, EILIF, I WILL SHOW YOU A CITY THE LIKE OF WHICH YOU'VE NEVER DREAMED!
BUT NOW, OUR TASK STILL LIES BEFORE US.
LET THE BATTLE BE JOINED!
DEATH TO FAFNIR!
FOR ODIN! AND ASGARD!
KRATH
AMMM

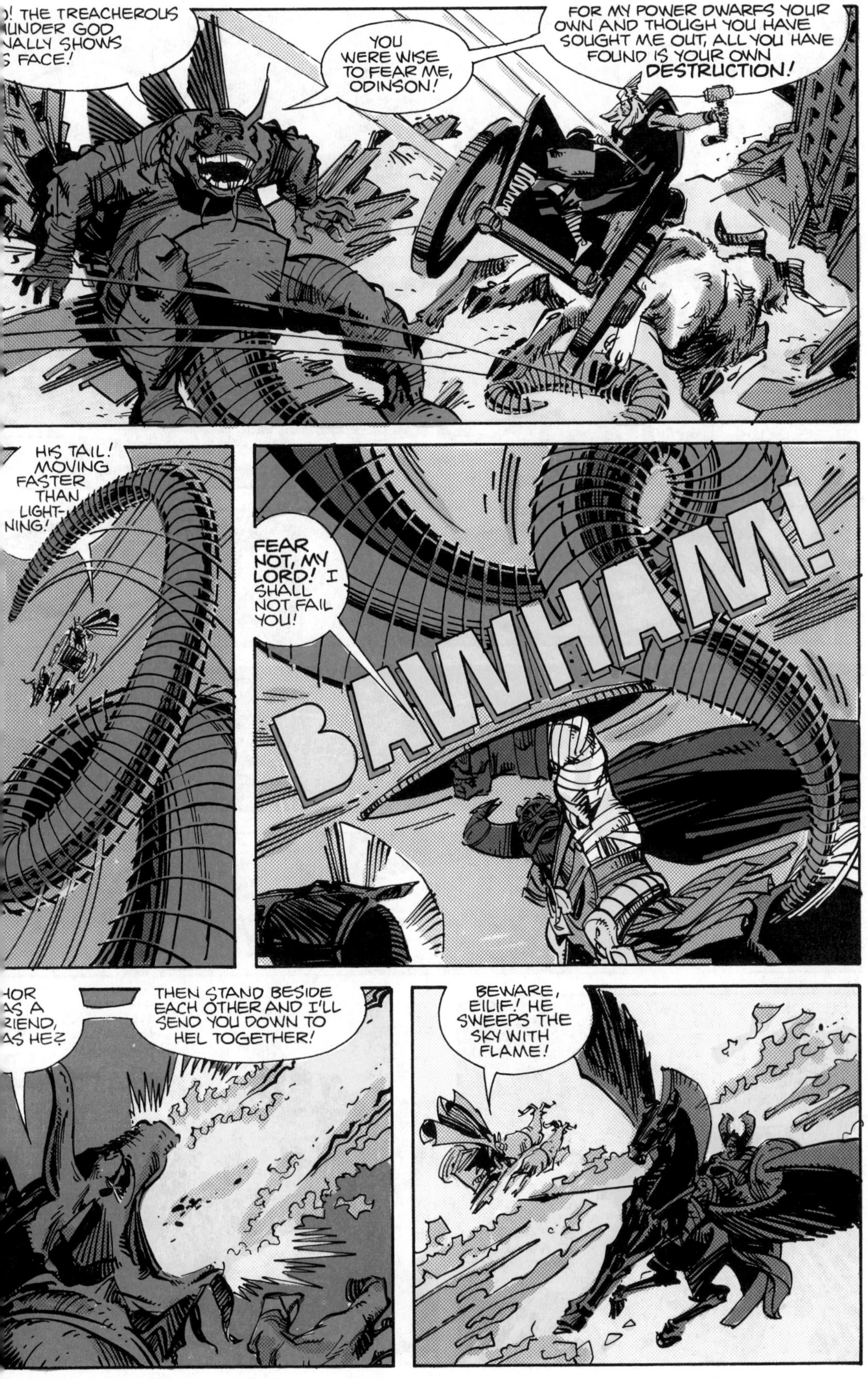

O! THE TREACHEROUS
UNDER GOD
NALLY SHOWS
S FACE!
YOU WERE WISE TO FEAR ME, ODINSON!
FOR MY POWER DWARFS YOUR OWN AND THOUGH YOU HAVE SOUGHT ME OUT, ALL YOU HAVE FOUND IS YOUR OWN DESTRUCTION!
HIS TAIL! MOVING FASTER THAN LIGHT-NING!
FEAR NOT, MY LORD! I SHALL NOT FAIL YOU!
BAWHAM!
HOR
AS A
RIEND,
AS HE?
THEN STAND BESIDE EACH OTHER AND I'LL SEND YOU DOWN TO HEL TOGETHER!
BEWARE, EILIF! HE SWEEPS THE SKY WITH FLAME!

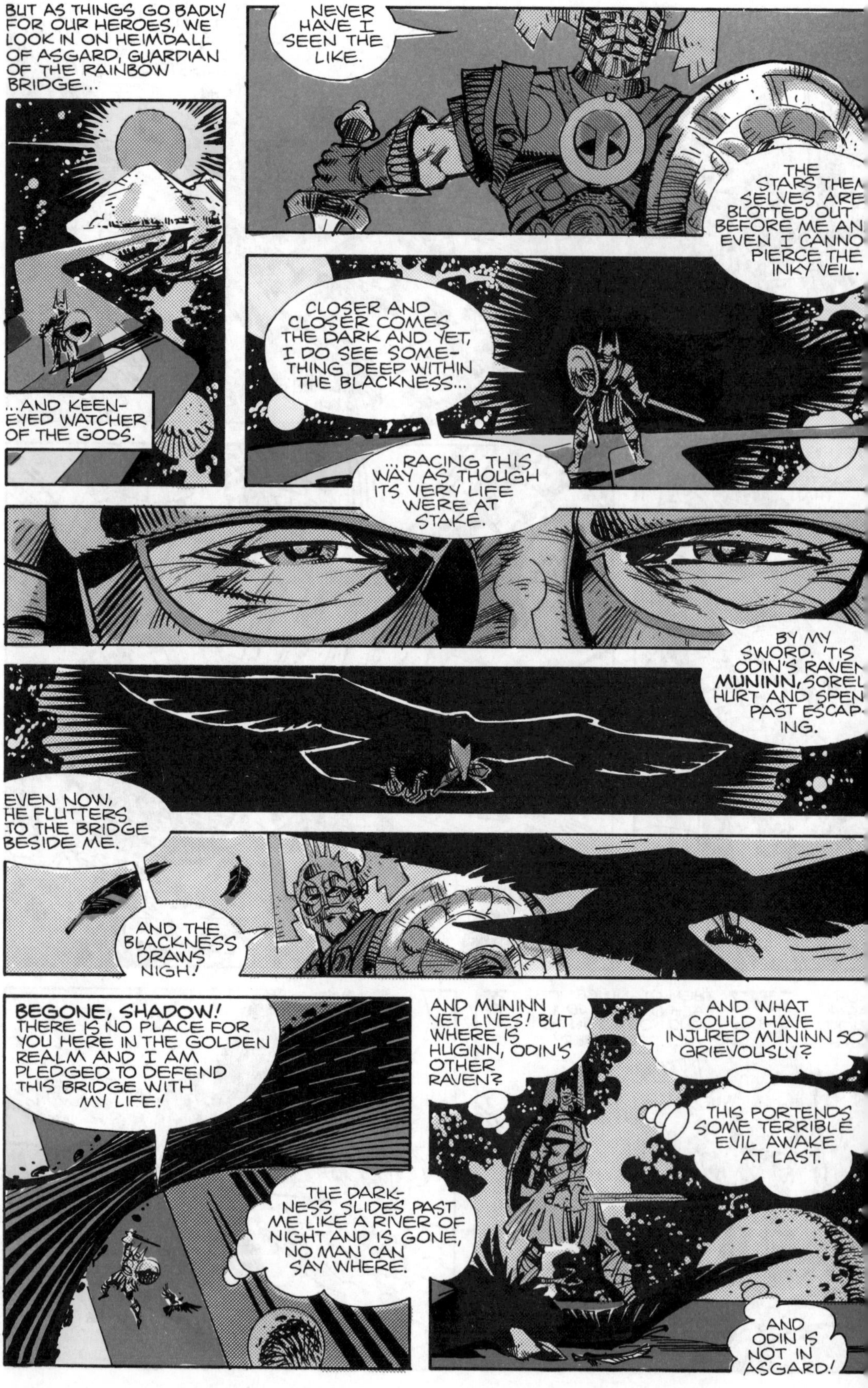

BUT AS THINGS GO BADLY FOR OUR HEROES, WE LOOK IN ON HEIMDALL OF ASGARD, GUARDIAN OF THE RAINBOW BRIDGE...
...AND KEEN-EYED WATCHER OF THE GODS.
NEVER HAVE I SEEN THE LIKE.
THE STARS THEM SELVES ARE BLOTTED OUT BEFORE ME AN EVEN I CANNO PIERCE THE INKY VEIL.
CLOSER AND CLOSER COMES THE DARK AND YET, I DO SEE SOMETHING DEEP WITHIN THE BLACKNESS...
...RACING THIS WAY AS THOUGH ITS VERY LIFE WERE AT STAKE.
BY MY SWORD. 'TIS ODIN'S RAVEN MUNINN, SOREL HURT AND SPEN PAST ESCAPING.
EVEN NOW, HE FLUTTERS TO THE BRIDGE BESIDE ME.
AND THE BLACKNESS DRAWS NIGH!
BEGONE, SHADOW! THERE IS NO PLACE FOR YOU HERE IN THE GOLDEN REALM AND I AM PLEDGED TO DEFEND THIS BRIDGE WITH MY LIFE!
THE DARKNESS SLIDES PAST ME LIKE A RIVER OF NIGHT AND IS GONE, NO MAN CAN SAY WHERE.
AND MUNINN YET LIVES! BUT WHERE IS HUGINN, ODIN'S OTHER RAVEN?
AND WHAT COULD HAVE INJURED MUNINN SO GRIEVOUSLY?
THIS PORTENDS SOME TERRIBLE EVIL AWAKE AT LAST.
AND ODIN IS NOT IN ASGARD!

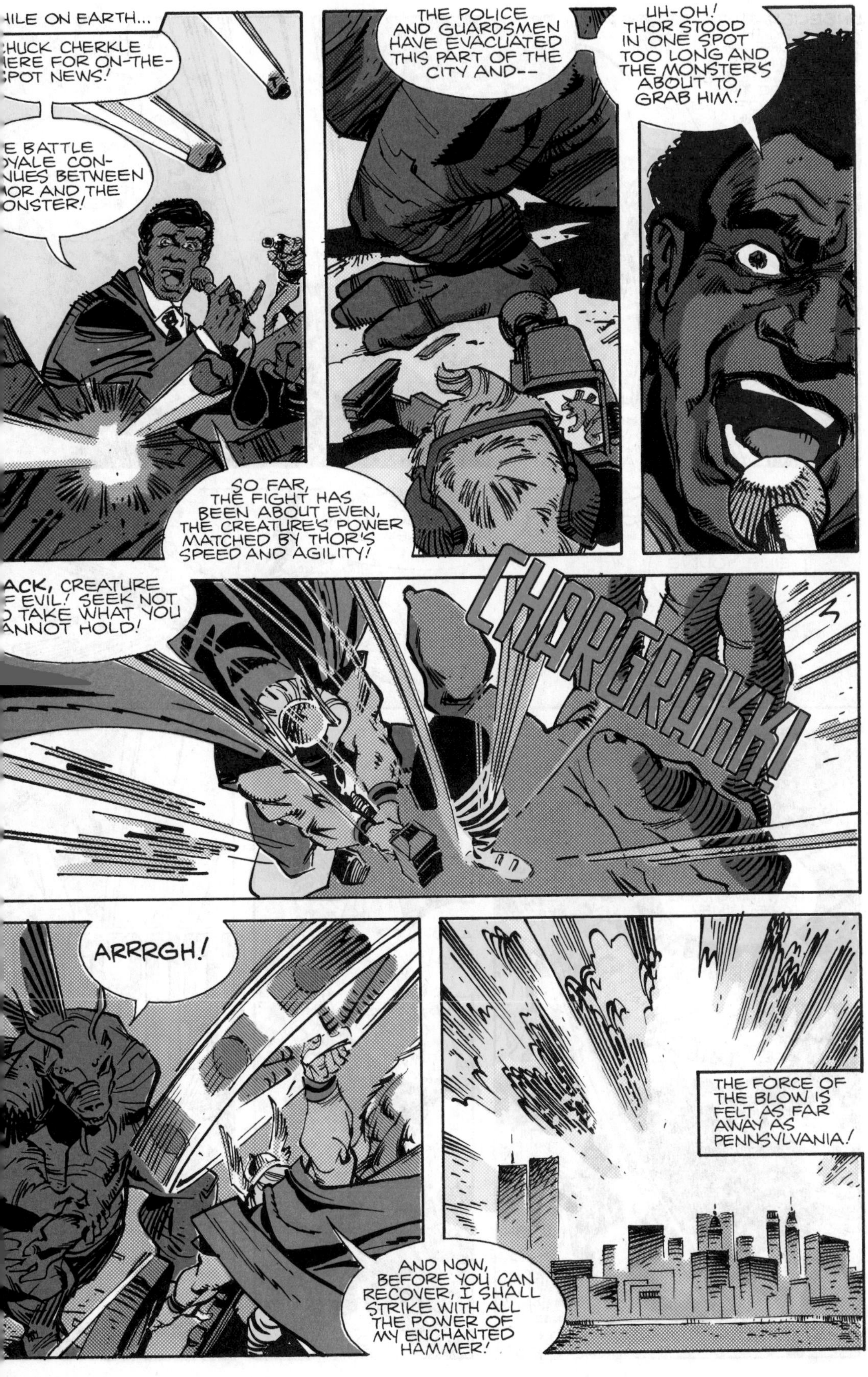

HILE ON EARTH...
CHUCK CHERKLE HERE FOR ON-THE-SPOT NEWS!
E BATTLE OYALE CONNUES BETWEEN HOR AND THE MONSTER!
SO FAR, THE FIGHT HAS BEEN ABOUT EVEN, THE CREATURE'S POWER MATCHED BY THOR'S SPEED AND AGILITY!
THE POLICE AND GUARDSMEN HAVE EVACUATED THIS PART OF THE CITY AND--
UH-OH! THOR STOOD IN ONE SPOT TOO LONG AND THE MONSTER'S ABOUT TO GRAB HIM!
ACK, CREATURE F EVIL! SEEK NOT O TAKE WHAT YOU ANNOT HOLD!
CHARGRAKK!
ARRRGH!
AND NOW, BEFORE YOU CAN RECOVER, I SHALL STRIKE WITH ALL THE POWER OF MY ENCHANTED HAMMER!
THE FORCE OF THE BLOW IS FELT AS FAR AWAY AS PENNSYLVANIA!

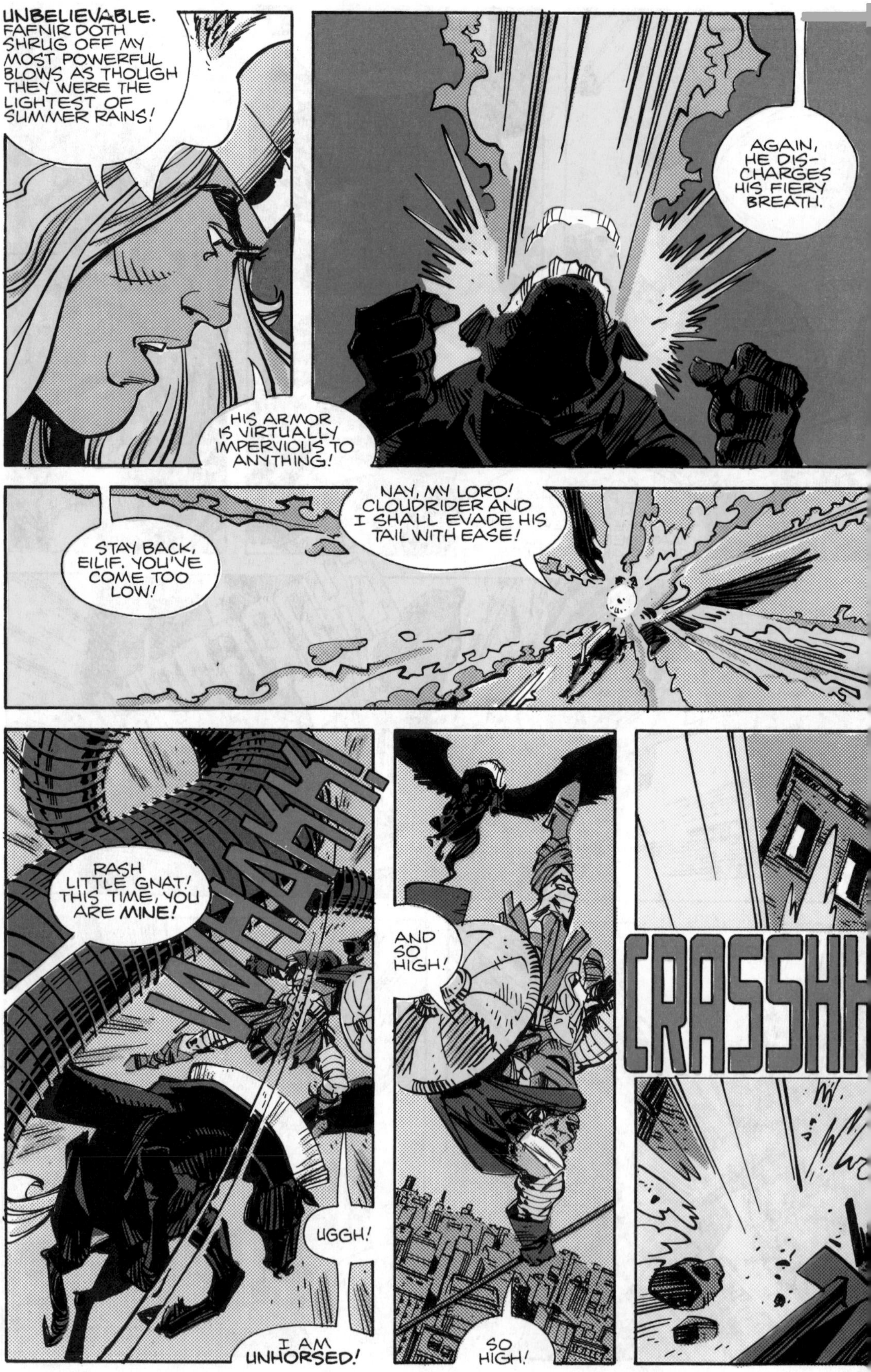
UNBELIEVABLE. FAFNIR DOTH SHRUG OFF MY MOST POWERFUL BLOWS AS THOUGH THEY WERE THE LIGHTEST OF SUMMER RAINS!
AGAIN, HE DIS-CHARGES HIS FIERY BREATH.
HIS ARMOR IS VIRTUALLY IMPERVIOUS TO ANYTHING!
STAY BACK, EILIF. YOU'VE COME TOO LOW!
NAY, MY LORD! CLOUDRIDER AND I SHALL EVADE HIS TAIL WITH EASE!
RASH LITTLE GNAT! THIS TIME, YOU ARE MINE!
WHAAK!
UGGH!
I AM UNHORSED!
AND SO HIGH!
SO HIGH!
CRASSHH

EILIF!!

WELL SAID, GODLING! I KNEW YOUR CONCERN FOR THE MORTAL WOULD UNDO YOU SOONER OR LATER!

SMMMSH!

THIS COULD BE IT, FOLKS! THE DRAGON'S REALLY LAYING INTO THOR NOW!

AND WITH-OUT HIS CHARIOT, THOR CAN'T GET CLEAR!

KA-WHAM! WHAODOOM!

UH, FOLKS, WE'RE GOING TO RETURN YOU TO THE STUDIO NOW SO THAT WE CAN...RELOCATE...OUR REMOTE FACILITIES AT A...A... BETTER VANTAGE POINT!

WE'LL BE BACK WITH YOU AS SOON AS WE CAN!

LET'S GET THE HECK OUT OF HERE, CLANCY!

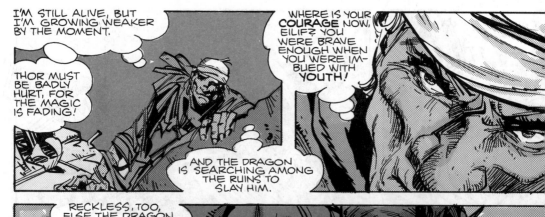

I'M STILL ALIVE, BUT I'M GROWING WEAKER BY THE MOMENT.

THOR MUST BE BADLY HURT, FOR THE MAGIC IS FADING!

WHERE IS YOUR **COURAGE** NOW, EILIF? YOU WERE BRAVE ENOUGH WHEN YOU WERE IMBUED WITH **YOUTH!**

AND THE DRAGON IS SEARCHING AMONG THE RUINS TO SLAY HIM.

RECKLESS, TOO, ELSE THE DRAGON WOULD NEVER HAVE CAUGHT YOU.

THE SON...

...OF ODIN...

...MUST NOT...

...PERISH...

...BECAUSE EILIF...

...FAILED IN HIS DUTY!

WHAT LITTLE STRENGTH IS MINE BY BIRTH IS WANING RAPIDLY. I AM DYING!

BUT I AM ABOVE THE GREAT BEAST NOW...

...AND I STILL HAVE MY SPEAR!

NOT EVEN VOICE LEFT TO SHOUT WITH.

BUT I WILL BE THE WEAPON...

FOR
ĐIN, FOR
ŌR, AND
ŚGARD!

ARRROOOO!

WHO HAS DARED TO **WOUND** ME?

ACCURSED MORTAL! THOR CAN WAIT! ONLY YOUR **DEATH** WILL SATISFY ME NOW!

HILE UNDER THE RUBBLE...

EILIF'S
PEAR! IT
ATH PIERCED
AFNIR'S IM-
ENETRABLE
HIDE!

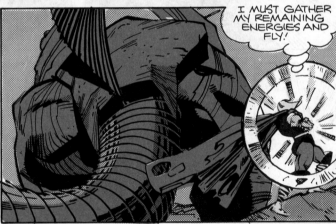

I MUST GATHER MY REMAINING ENERGIES AND FLY!

FOR EILIF HATH SHOWED ME THE WAY AND WHAT I COULD NOT DO ALONE...

...MAY YET BE ACCOMPLISHED! EILIF'S WEAPON SHALL BE THE DRAGON'S BANE!

NOW BY ALL THE STRENGTH OF MY HERITAGE, BY THE POWER OF MJOLNIR, LET EVIL PERISH!

AAAHHHFEE!

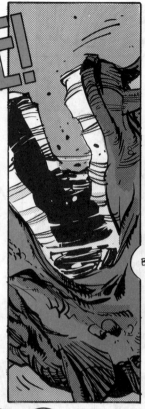

'TIS DONE! THE SPEAR HATH BEEN DRIVEN INTO THE BEAST FULL FORCE!

AND HE BEGINS TO TOPPLE!

THE DRAGON'S FIRE...

BOOOOM!

...IS QUENCHE

BUT WHAT OF VALIANT EILIF?

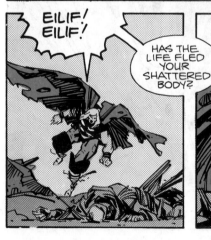

EILIF! EILIF!

HAS THE LIFE FLED YOUR SHATTERED BODY?

CAN YOU NO LONGER HEAR EVEN THE VOICES OF THE GODS?

A TRUER COMPANION HATH NO MORTAL BEEN TO ME!

OH, EILIF, MY SHIELD BEARER EILIF!

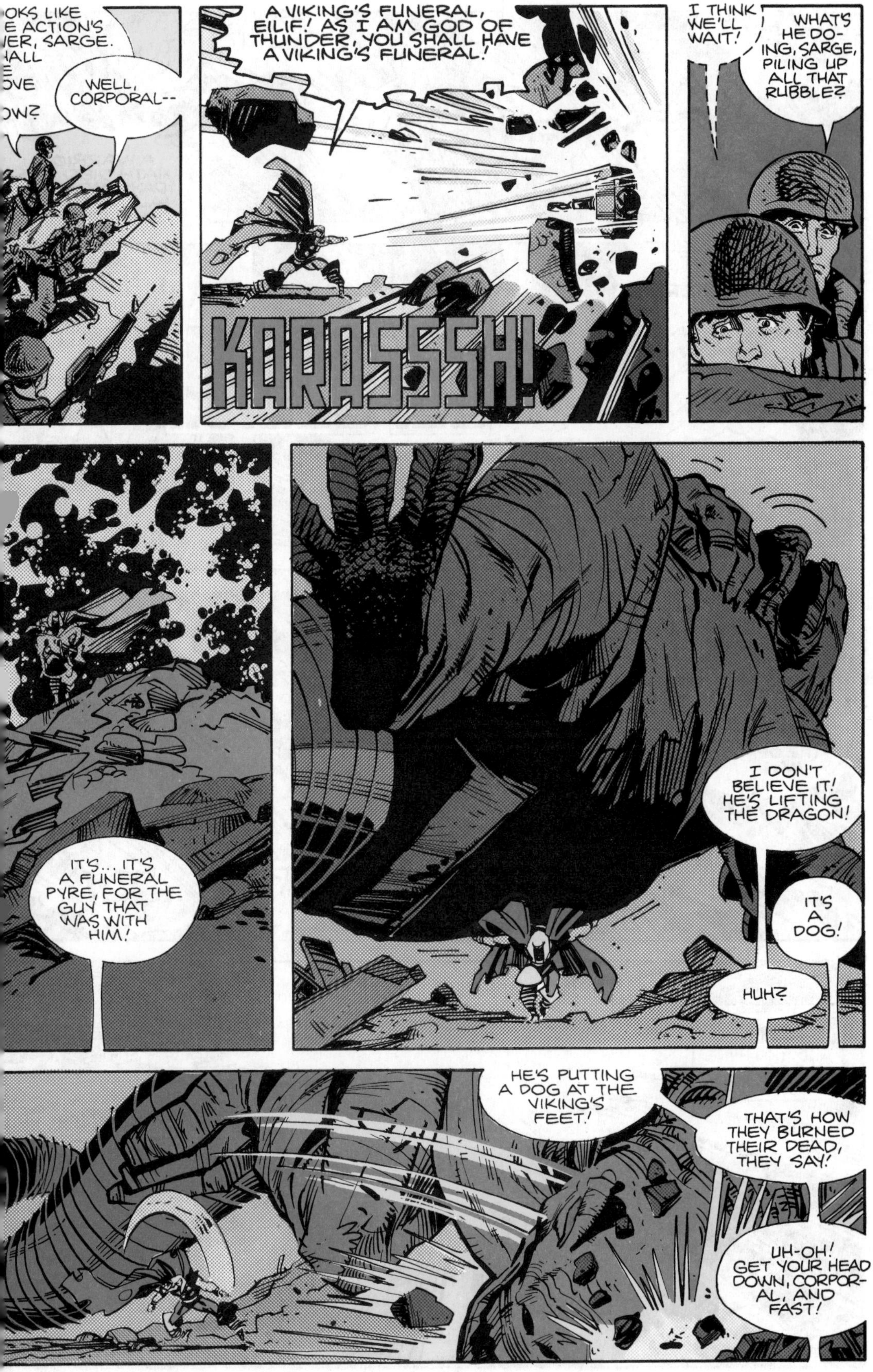
OKS LIKE E ACTION'S VER, SARGE. HALL E OVE OW?
WELL, CORPORAL--
A VIKING'S FUNERAL, EILIF! AS I AM GOD OF THUNDER, YOU SHALL HAVE A VIKING'S FUNERAL!
KARASSSH!
I THINK WE'LL WAIT!
WHAT'S HE DOING, SARGE, PILING UP ALL THAT RUBBLE?
IT'S... IT'S A FUNERAL PYRE, FOR THE GUY THAT WAS WITH HIM!
I DON'T BELIEVE IT! HE'S LIFTING THE DRAGON!
IT'S A DOG!
HUH?
HE'S PUTTING A DOG AT THE VIKING'S FEET!
THAT'S HOW THEY BURNED THEIR DEAD, THEY SAY!
UH-OH! GET YOUR HEAD DOWN, CORPORAL, AND FAST!

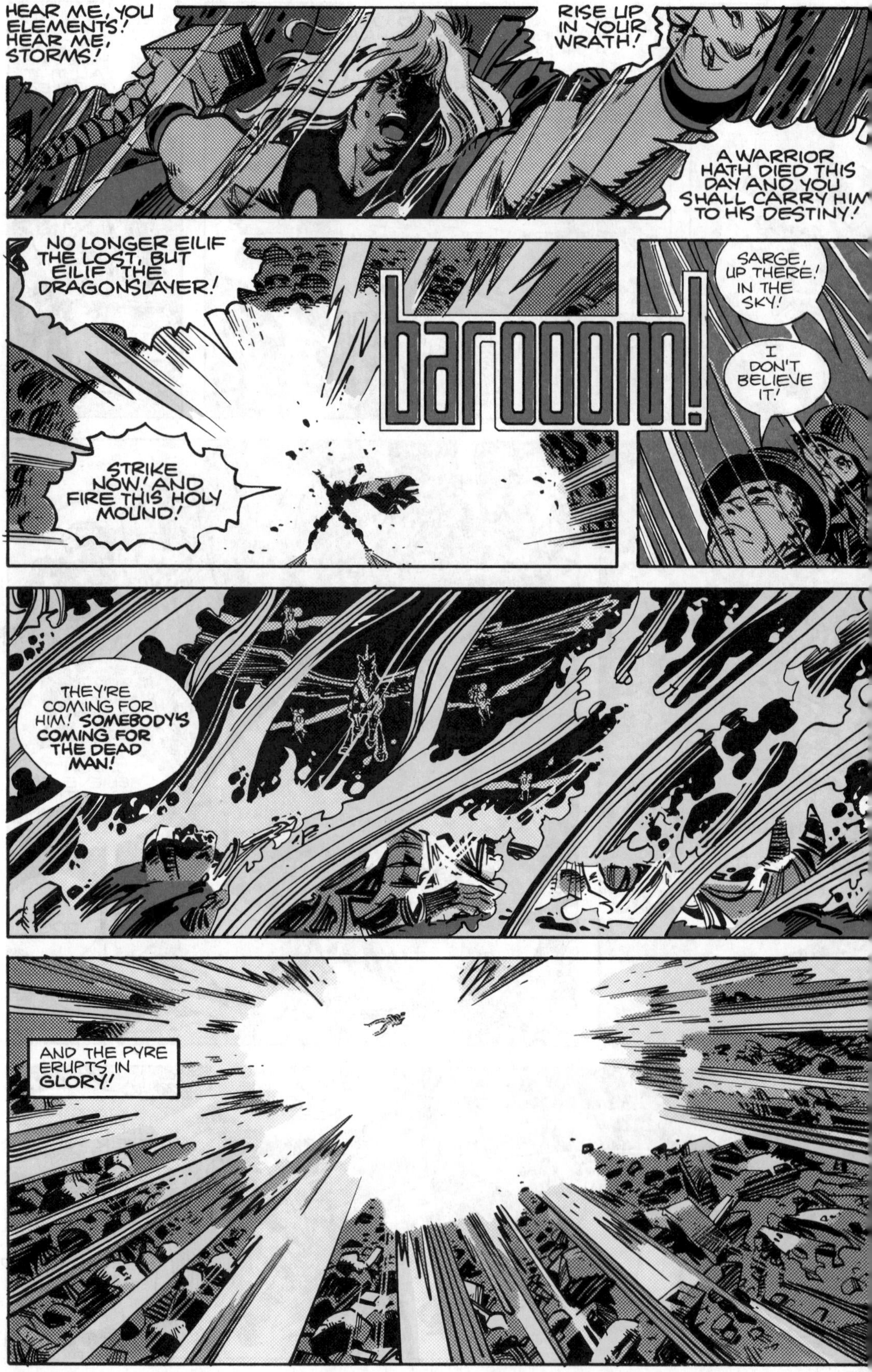

HEAR ME, YOU ELEMENTS! HEAR ME, STORMS!
RISE UP IN YOUR WRATH!
A WARRIOR HATH DIED THIS DAY AND YOU SHALL CARRY HIM TO HIS DESTINY!
NO LONGER EILIF THE LOST, BUT EILIF THE DRAGONSLAYER!
STRIKE NOW! AND FIRE THIS HOLY MOUND!
barooom!
SARGE, UP THERE! IN THE SKY!
I DON'T BELIEVE IT!
THEY'RE COMING FOR HIM! SOMEBODY'S COMING FOR THE DEAD MAN!
AND THE PYRE ERUPTS IN GLORY!

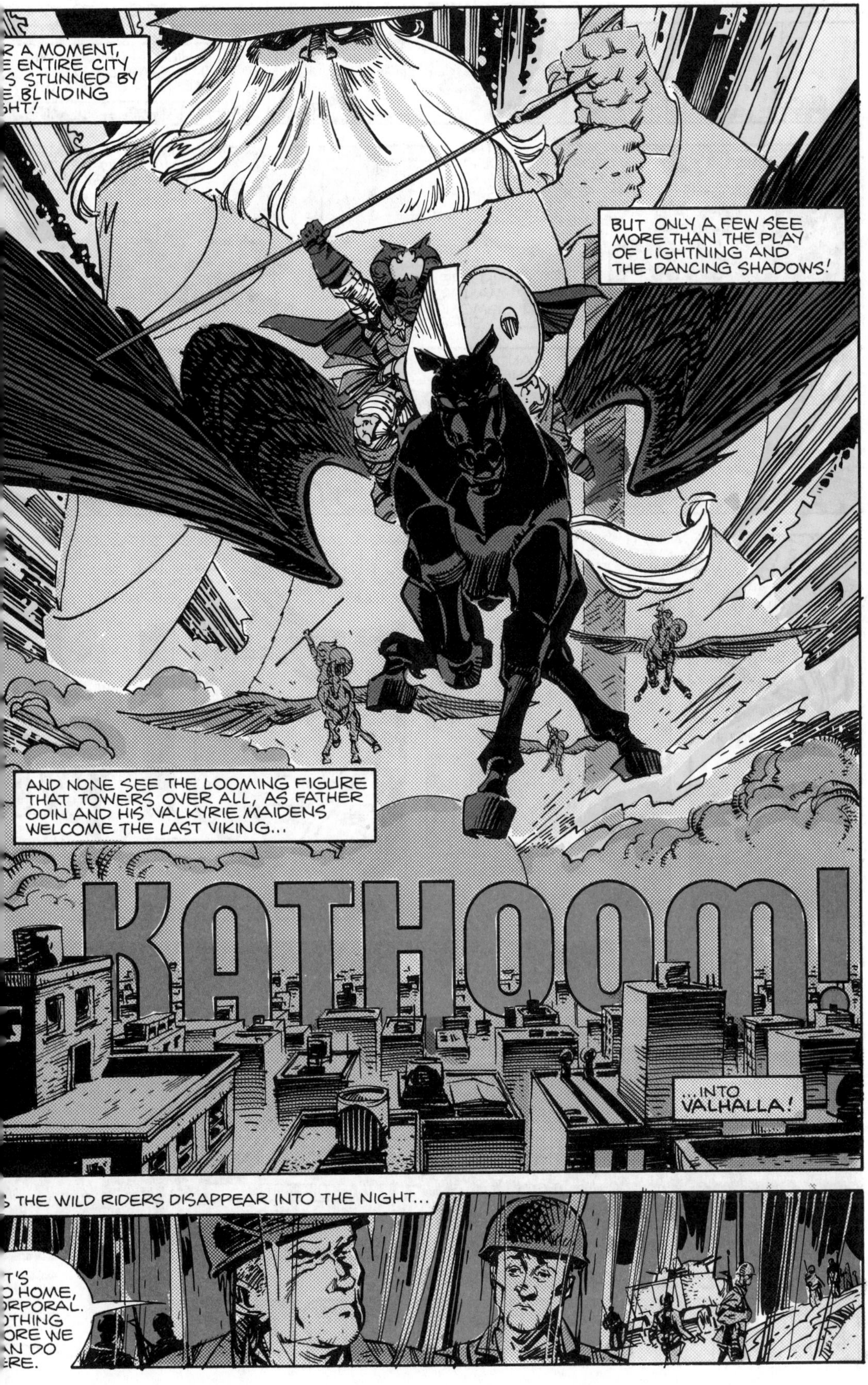

R A MOMENT, E ENTIRE CITY S STUNNED BY E BLINDING GHT!
BUT ONLY A FEW SEE MORE THAN THE PLAY OF LIGHTNING AND THE DANCING SHADOWS!
AND NONE SEE THE LOOMING FIGURE THAT TOWERS OVER ALL, AS FATHER ODIN AND HIS VALKYRIE MAIDENS WELCOME THE LAST VIKING...
KATHOOM!
...INTO VALHALLA!
S THE WILD RIDERS DISAPPEAR INTO THE NIGHT...
T'S O HOME, ORPORAL. OTHING ORE WE AN DO ERE.

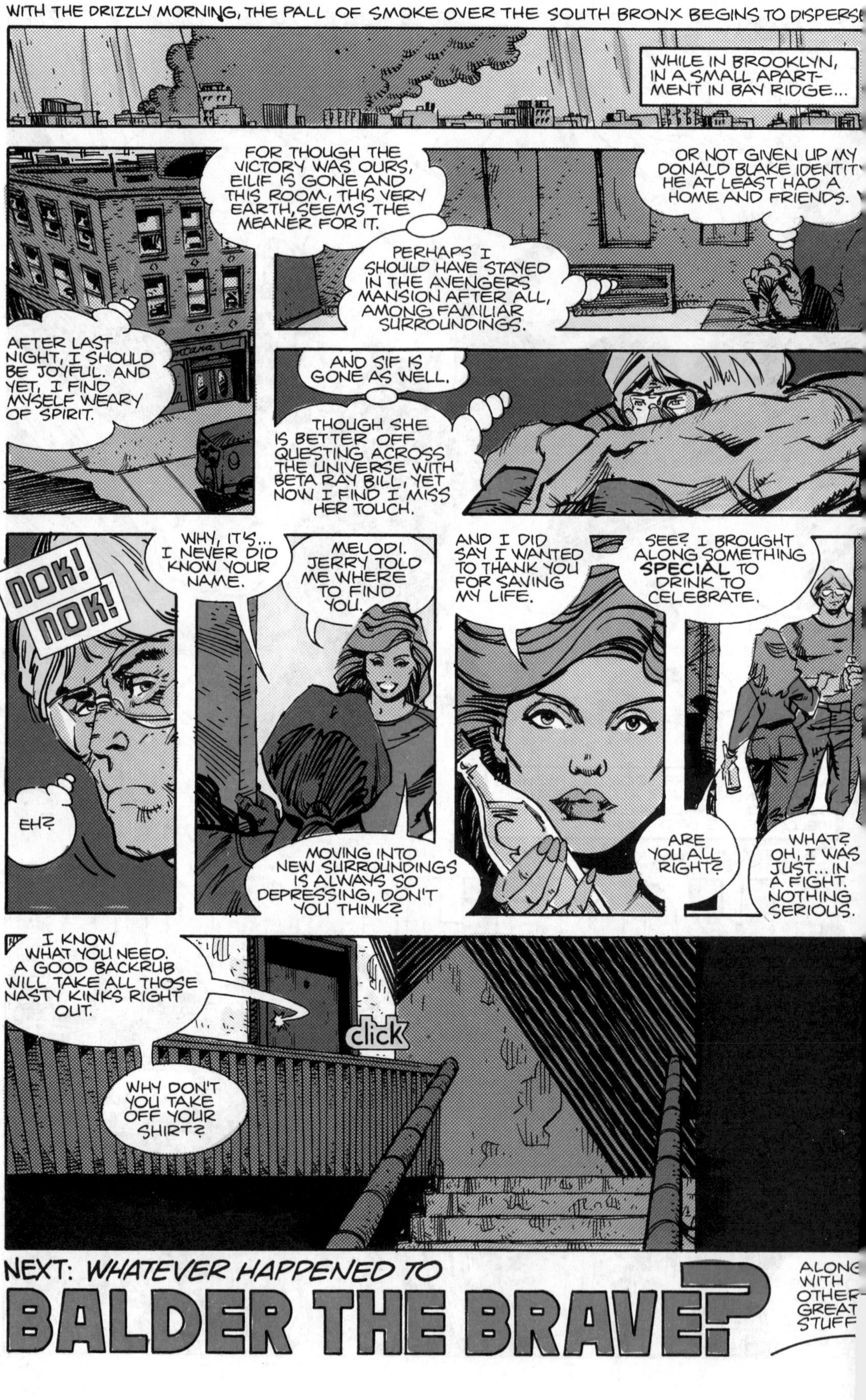
WITH THE DRIZZLY MORNING, THE PALL OF SMOKE OVER THE SOUTH BRONX BEGINS TO DISPERSE
WHILE IN BROOKLYN, IN A SMALL APARTMENT IN BAY RIDGE...
AFTER LAST NIGHT, I SHOULD BE JOYFUL. AND YET, I FIND MYSELF WEARY OF SPIRIT.
FOR THOUGH THE VICTORY WAS OURS, EILIF IS GONE AND THIS ROOM, THIS VERY EARTH, SEEMS THE MEANER FOR IT.
PERHAPS I SHOULD HAVE STAYED IN THE AVENGERS MANSION AFTER ALL, AMONG FAMILIAR SURROUNDINGS.
OR NOT GIVEN UP MY DONALD BLAKE IDENTITY. HE AT LEAST HAD A HOME AND FRIENDS.
AND SIF IS GONE AS WELL.
THOUGH SHE IS BETTER OFF QUESTING ACROSS THE UNIVERSE WITH BETA RAY BILL, YET NOW I FIND I MISS HER TOUCH.
NOK! NOK!
EH?
WHY, IT'S... I NEVER DID KNOW YOUR NAME.
MELODI. JERRY TOLD ME WHERE TO FIND YOU.
MOVING INTO NEW SURROUNDINGS IS ALWAYS SO DEPRESSING, DON'T YOU THINK?
AND I DID SAY I WANTED TO THANK YOU FOR SAVING MY LIFE.
SEE? I BROUGHT ALONG SOMETHING SPECIAL TO DRINK TO CELEBRATE.
ARE YOU ALL RIGHT?
WHAT? OH, I WAS JUST... IN A FIGHT. NOTHING SERIOUS.
I KNOW WHAT YOU NEED. A GOOD BACKRUB WILL TAKE ALL THOSE NASTY KINKS RIGHT OUT.
click
WHY DON'T YOU TAKE OFF YOUR SHIRT?
NEXT: WHATEVER HAPPENED TO BALDER THE BRAVE?
ALONG WITH OTHER GREAT STUFF

Chapter Eight

MARVEL
the mighty
THOR
60¢
344
JUNE
02450
APPROVED BY THE COMICS CODE AUTHORITY
BALDER--
THE BRAVE?

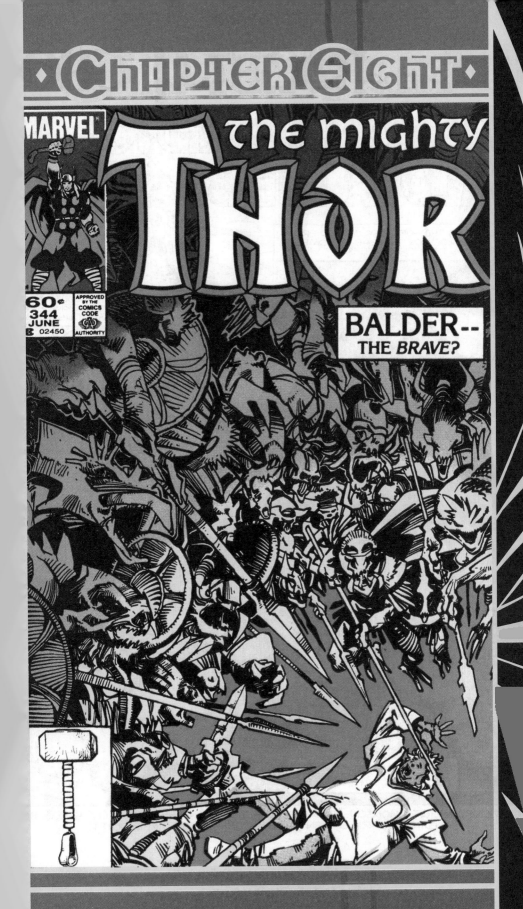

STAN LEE PRESENTS: the MIGHTY THOR

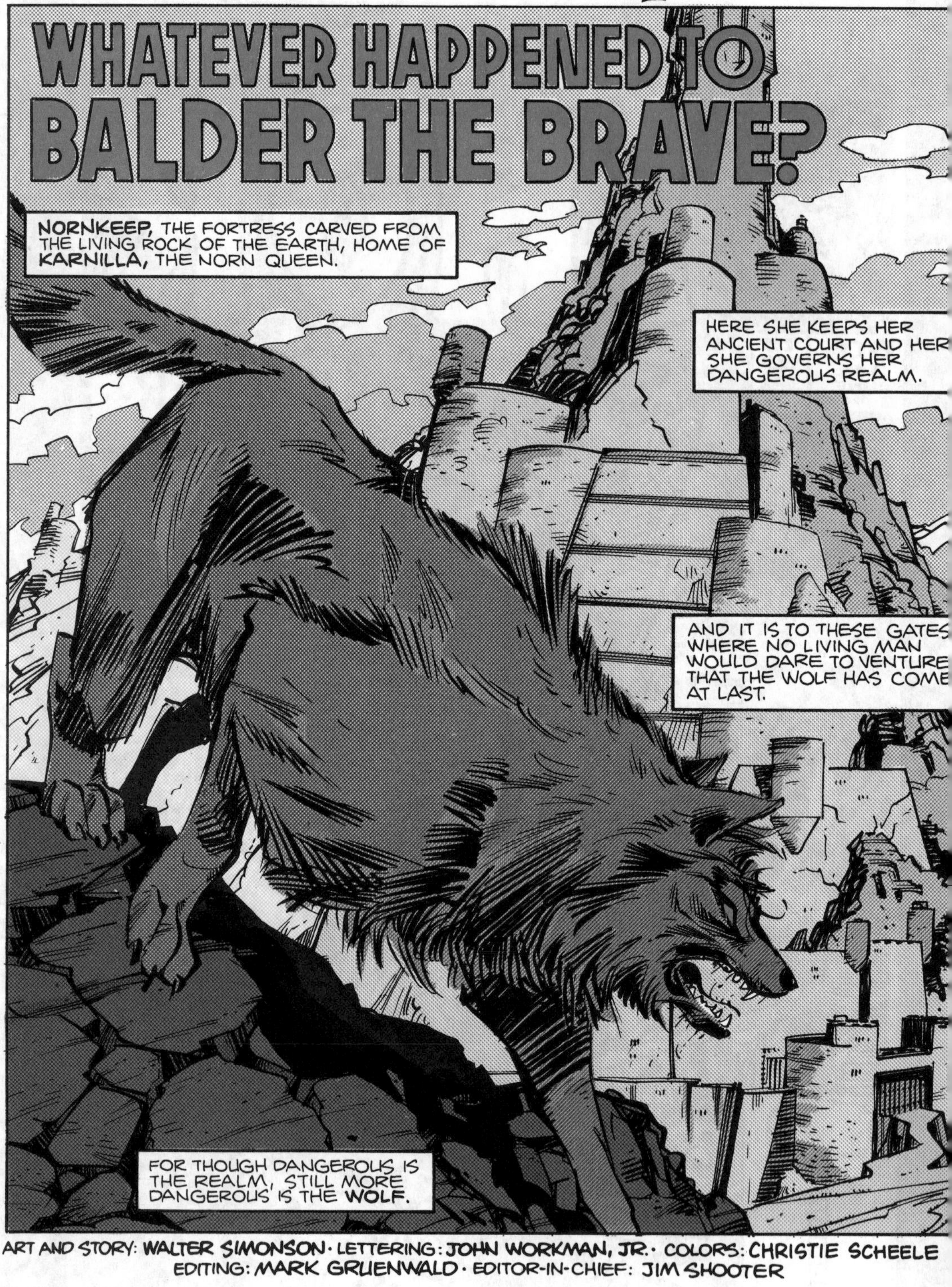

WHATEVER HAPPENED TO BALDER THE BRAVE?
NORNKEEP, THE FORTRESS CARVED FROM THE LIVING ROCK OF THE EARTH, HOME OF KARNILLA, THE NORN QUEEN.
HERE SHE KEEPS HER ANCIENT COURT AND HER SHE GOVERNS HER DANGEROUS REALM.
AND IT IS TO THESE GATES WHERE NO LIVING MAN WOULD DARE TO VENTURE THAT THE WOLF HAS COME AT LAST.
FOR THOUGH DANGEROUS IS THE REALM, STILL MORE DANGEROUS IS THE WOLF.

ART AND STORY: WALTER SIMONSON · LETTERING: JOHN WORKMAN, JR. · COLORS: CHRISTIE SCHEELE
EDITING: MARK GRUENWALD · EDITOR-IN-CHIEF: JIM SHOOTER

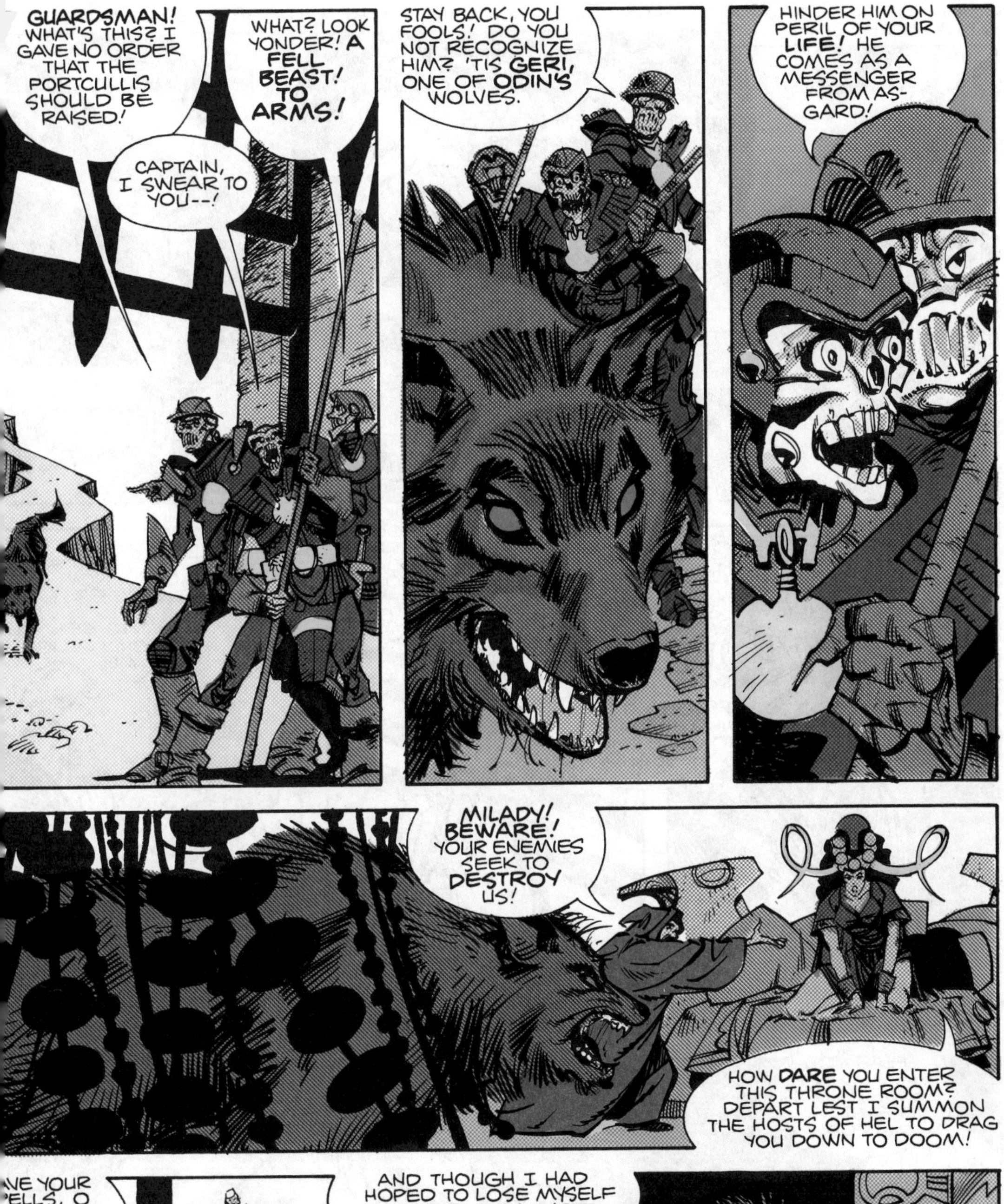

GUARDSMAN! WHAT'S THIS? I GAVE NO ORDER THAT THE PORTCULLIS SHOULD BE RAISED!
WHAT? LOOK YONDER! A FELL BEAST! TO ARMS!
CAPTAIN, I SWEAR TO YOU--!
STAY BACK, YOU FOOLS! DO YOU NOT RECOGNIZE HIM? 'TIS GERI, ONE OF ODIN'S WOLVES.
HINDER HIM ON PERIL OF YOUR LIFE! HE COMES AS A MESSENGER FROM AS-GARD!
MILADY! BEWARE! YOUR ENEMIES SEEK TO DESTROY US!
HOW DARE YOU ENTER THIS THRONE ROOM? DEPART LEST I SUMMON THE HOSTS OF HEL TO DRAG YOU DOWN TO DOOM!
VE YOUR PELLS, O UEEN, FOR HEY WOULD AIL YOU UGHT.
THE CHILDREN F ODIN TRAVEL NDER HIS PRO-ECTION AND ARE ENT TO SUMMON HOSE THE ALL-ATHER WISHES TO ASGARD.
AS GERI HAS BEEN SENT TO SUMMON ME.
AND THOUGH I HAD HOPED TO LOSE MYSELF FOREVER, I CANNOT DISOBEY MY LIEGE.
FAITHFUL GERI, I WILL COME WITH YOU.

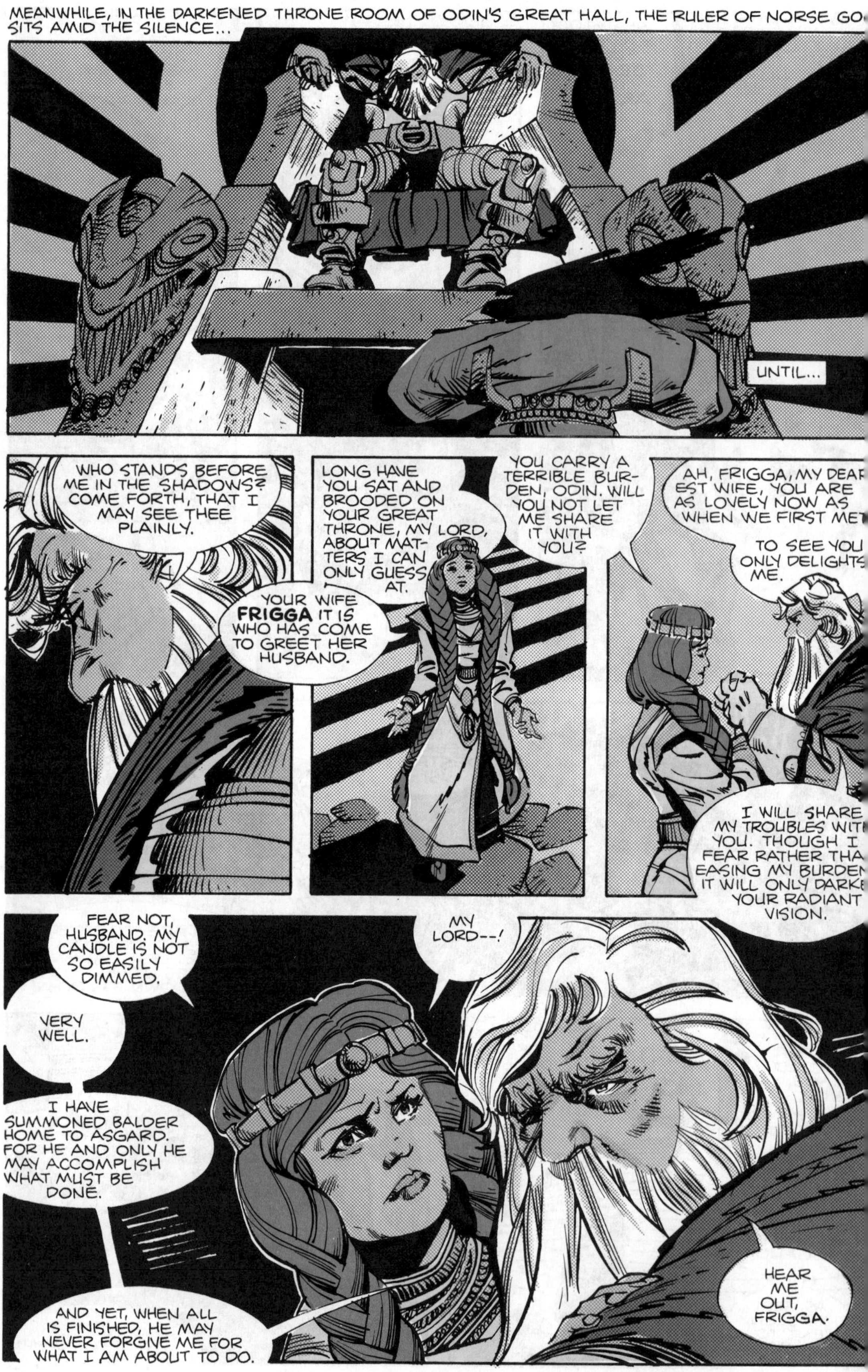

MEANWHILE, IN THE DARKENED THRONE ROOM OF ODIN'S GREAT HALL, THE RULER OF NORSE GO
SITS AMID THE SILENCE...
UNTIL...
WHO STANDS BEFORE ME IN THE SHADOWS? COME FORTH, THAT I MAY SEE THEE PLAINLY.
LONG HAVE YOU SAT AND BROODED ON YOUR GREAT THRONE, MY LORD, ABOUT MATTERS I CAN ONLY GUESS AT.
YOUR WIFE **FRIGGA** IT IS WHO HAS COME TO GREET HER HUSBAND.
YOU CARRY A TERRIBLE BURDEN, ODIN. WILL YOU NOT LET ME SHARE IT WITH YOU?
AH, FRIGGA, MY DEAR EST WIFE, YOU ARE AS LOVELY NOW AS WHEN WE FIRST ME
TO SEE YOU ONLY DELIGHTS ME.
I WILL SHARE MY TROUBLES WIT YOU. THOUGH I FEAR RATHER THA EASING MY BURDE IT WILL ONLY DARK YOUR RADIANT VISION.
FEAR NOT, HUSBAND. MY CANDLE IS NOT SO EASILY DIMMED.
MY LORD--!
VERY WELL.
I HAVE SUMMONED BALDER HOME TO ASGARD. FOR HE AND ONLY HE MAY ACCOMPLISH WHAT MUST BE DONE.
AND YET, WHEN ALL IS FINISHED, HE MAY NEVER FORGIVE ME FOR WHAT I AM ABOUT TO DO.
HEAR ME OUT, FRIGGA.

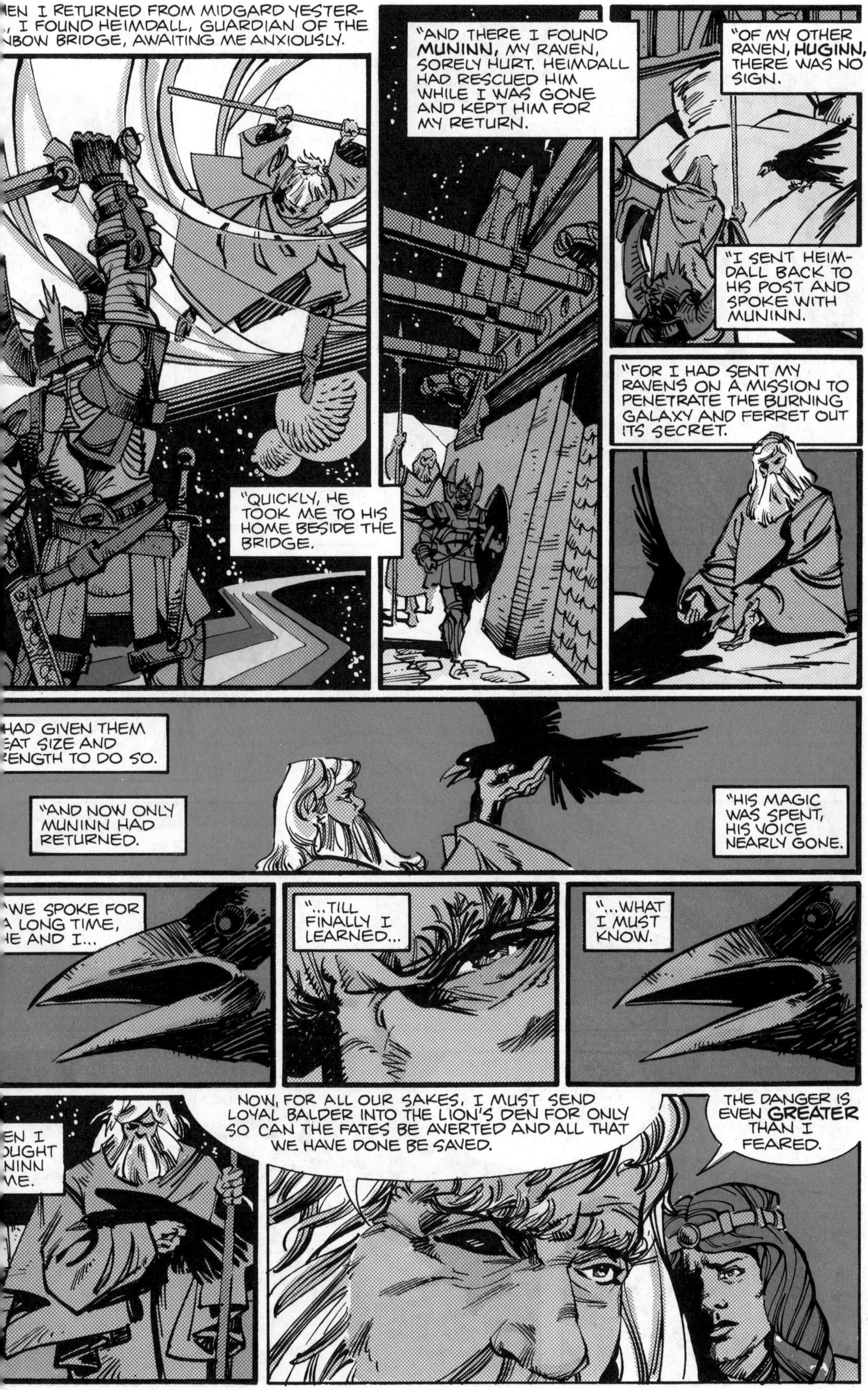

EN I RETURNED FROM MIDGARD YESTER-, I FOUND HEIMDALL, GUARDIAN OF THE NBOW BRIDGE, AWAITING ME ANXIOUSLY.
"QUICKLY, HE TOOK ME TO HIS HOME BESIDE THE BRIDGE.
"AND THERE I FOUND MUNINN, MY RAVEN, SORELY HURT. HEIMDALL HAD RESCUED HIM WHILE I WAS GONE AND KEPT HIM FOR MY RETURN.
"OF MY OTHER RAVEN, HUGINN, THERE WAS NO SIGN.
"I SENT HEIMDALL BACK TO HIS POST AND SPOKE WITH MUNINN.
"FOR I HAD SENT MY RAVENS ON A MISSION TO PENETRATE THE BURNING GALAXY AND FERRET OUT ITS SECRET.
HAD GIVEN THEM EAT SIZE AND RENGTH TO DO SO.
"AND NOW ONLY MUNINN HAD RETURNED.
"HIS MAGIC WAS SPENT, HIS VOICE NEARLY GONE.
WE SPOKE FOR A LONG TIME, HE AND I...
"...TILL FINALLY I LEARNED...
"...WHAT I MUST KNOW.
EN I OUGHT NINN ME.
NOW, FOR ALL OUR SAKES, I MUST SEND LOYAL BALDER INTO THE LION'S DEN FOR ONLY SO CAN THE FATES BE AVERTED AND ALL THAT WE HAVE DONE BE SAVED.
THE DANGER IS EVEN GREATER THAN I FEARED.

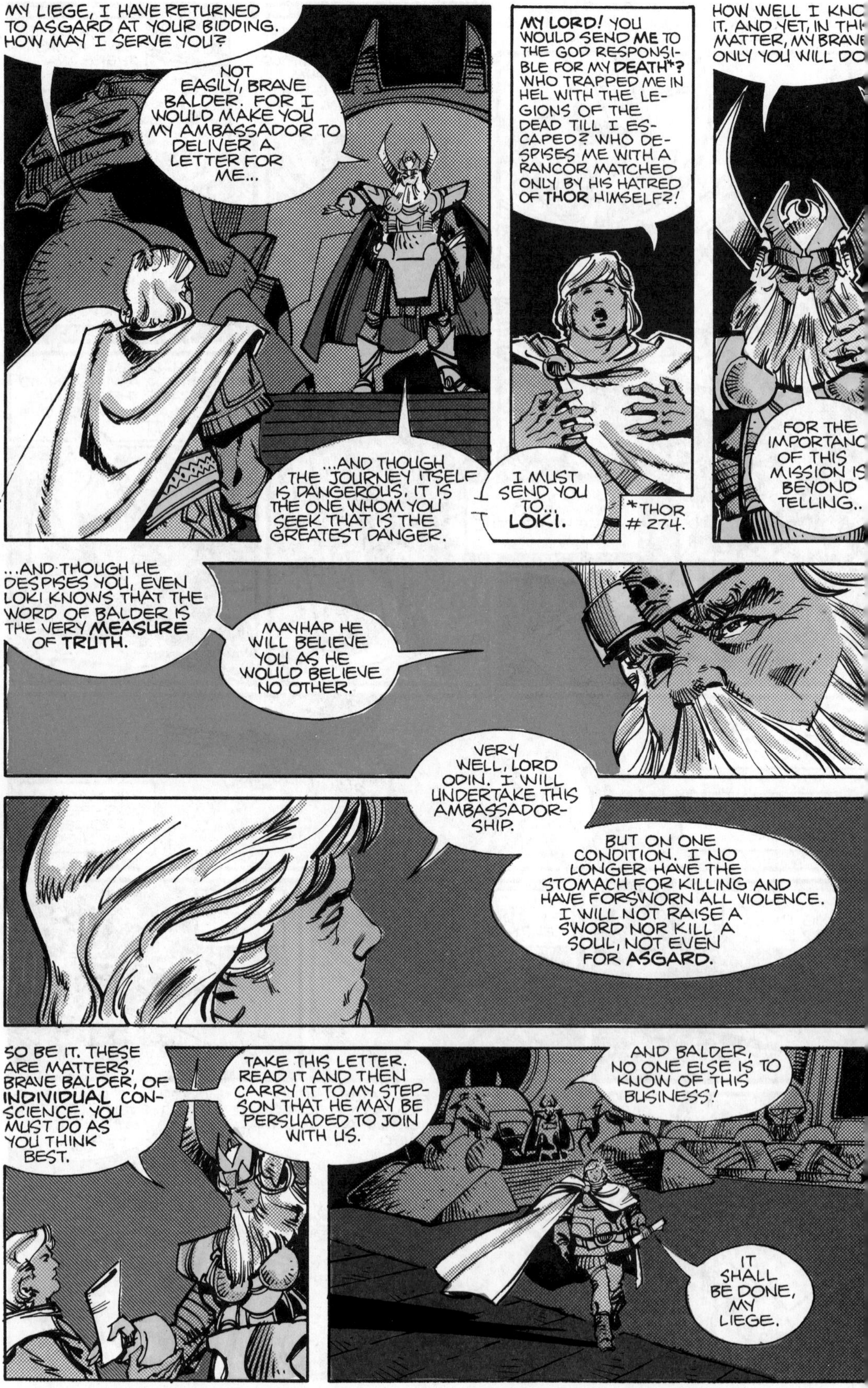
MY LIEGE, I HAVE RETURNED TO ASGARD AT YOUR BIDDING. HOW MAY I SERVE YOU?
NOT EASILY, BRAVE BALDER. FOR I WOULD MAKE YOU MY AMBASSADOR TO DELIVER A LETTER FOR ME...
...AND THOUGH THE JOURNEY ITSELF IS DANGEROUS, IT IS THE ONE WHOM YOU SEEK THAT IS THE GREATEST DANGER.
I MUST SEND YOU TO... LOKI.
MY LORD! YOU WOULD SEND ME TO THE GOD RESPONSIBLE FOR MY DEATH*? WHO TRAPPED ME IN HEL WITH THE LEGIONS OF THE DEAD TILL I ESCAPED? WHO DESPISES ME WITH A RANCOR MATCHED ONLY BY HIS HATRED OF THOR HIMSELF?!
*THOR # 274.
HOW WELL I KNO IT. AND YET, IN THI MATTER, MY BRAVE ONLY YOU WILL DO
FOR THE IMPORTANC OF THIS MISSION IS BEYOND TELLING..
...AND THOUGH HE DESPISES YOU, EVEN LOKI KNOWS THAT THE WORD OF BALDER IS THE VERY MEASURE OF TRUTH.
MAYHAP HE WILL BELIEVE YOU AS HE WOULD BELIEVE NO OTHER.
VERY WELL, LORD ODIN. I WILL UNDERTAKE THIS AMBASSADORSHIP.
BUT ON ONE CONDITION. I NO LONGER HAVE THE STOMACH FOR KILLING AND HAVE FORSWORN ALL VIOLENCE. I WILL NOT RAISE A SWORD NOR KILL A SOUL, NOT EVEN FOR ASGARD.
SO BE IT. THESE ARE MATTERS, BRAVE BALDER, OF INDIVIDUAL CONSCIENCE. YOU MUST DO AS YOU THINK BEST.
TAKE THIS LETTER. READ IT AND THEN CARRY IT TO MY STEPSON THAT HE MAY BE PERSUADED TO JOIN WITH US.
AND BALDER, NO ONE ELSE IS TO KNOW OF THIS BUSINESS!
IT SHALL BE DONE, MY LIEGE.

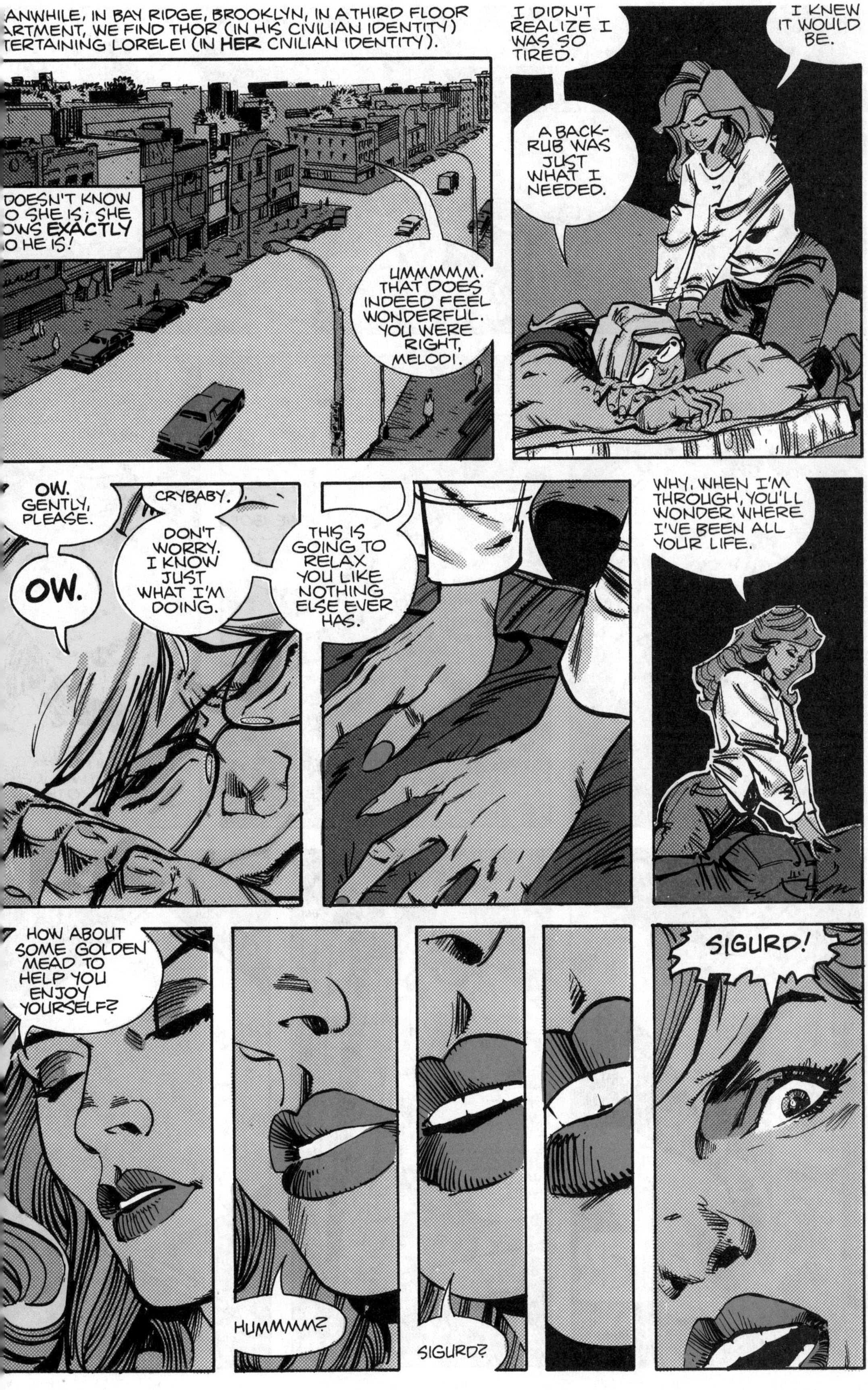
ANWHILE, IN BAY RIDGE, BROOKLYN, IN A THIRD FLOOR
ARTMENT, WE FIND THOR (IN HIS CIVILIAN IDENTITY)
TERTAINING LORELEI (IN HER CIVILIAN IDENTITY).
DOESN'T KNOW
O SHE IS; SHE
OWS EXACTLY
O HE IS!
UMMMMM. THAT DOES INDEED FEEL WONDERFUL. YOU WERE RIGHT, MELODI.
I DIDN'T REALIZE I WAS SO TIRED.
A BACK-RUB WAS JUST WHAT I NEEDED.
I KNEW IT WOULD BE.
OW. GENTLY, PLEASE.
OW.
CRYBABY.
DON'T WORRY. I KNOW JUST WHAT I'M DOING.
THIS IS GOING TO RELAX YOU LIKE NOTHING ELSE EVER HAS.
WHY, WHEN I'M THROUGH, YOU'LL WONDER WHERE I'VE BEEN ALL YOUR LIFE.
HOW ABOUT SOME GOLDEN MEAD TO HELP YOU ENJOY YOURSELF?
HUMMMM?
SIGURD?
SIGURD!

I DON'T BELIEVE IT. HE'S ASLEEP.

AND AFTER ALL THE TROUBLE I WENT TO TO BREW THE ENCHANTED MEAD.

A FEW SIPS AND HE WOULD HAVE BEEN MINE FOREVER!

I'VE GOT A GOOD MIND TO...

IT IS FUNNY, THOUGH. AFTER ALL, I FELL ASLEEP ON HIM THE FIRST TIME WE MET.

AND THIS WON'T BE THE LAST TIME WE'S EACH OTHER, MY HANDSOME THOR.

CLiiCK

NEXT TIME, THE GAME WILL BE MINE. AND SO WILL YOU.

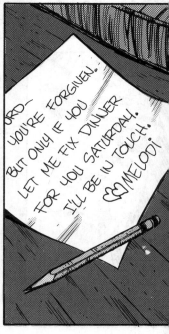

'ORD—
YOU'RE FORGIVEN.
BUT ONLY IF YOU
LET ME FIX DINNER
FOR YOU SATURDAY.
I'LL BE IN TOUCH.
♥ MELODI

MEANWHILE, FAR BEYOND THE GREEN FIELDS OF ASGARD...

FAITHFUL STEED, OUR JOURNEY IS NEARLY AT AN END. BEYOND THE FAR MOUNTAINS LIES THE LONELY DWELL-ING OF LOKI.

FORWARD, NOBLE SILVER-HOOF, AND GALLOP AS THE WIND!

STILL, THE GREAT-EST DANGERS ARE YET TO COME.

FOR IF THE LEGENDS ARE TRUE, NOW THE CHASE BE-GINS!

AND SUDDENLY, FROM THE HILLS ON EITHER SIDE OF THE TRAIL, A THUNDEROUS ROAR IS HEARD AS THE MOUNTAINSIDES BEGIN TO TREMBLE.

THRUMMBLE!

THE LIVING LAND-SLIDE! THE DEADLY BOULDERS THAT CAN CRUSH THE LIFE OUT OF ANY UNWARY PASSERBY, BE HE MORTAL OR GOD!

FASTER, SILVERHOOF! FASTER!

THE ROCKS OVERTAKE US AND OUR MISSION MUST NOT FAIL!

BADOOM! BADOOM!

JUST AHEAD! THE CLIFF THAT MARKS THE END OF THE LANDSLIDE'S TREACHEROUS REALM!

UP, NOBLE STEED! AND LEAP FOR YOUR LIFE! THE BOULDERS ARE UPON US!

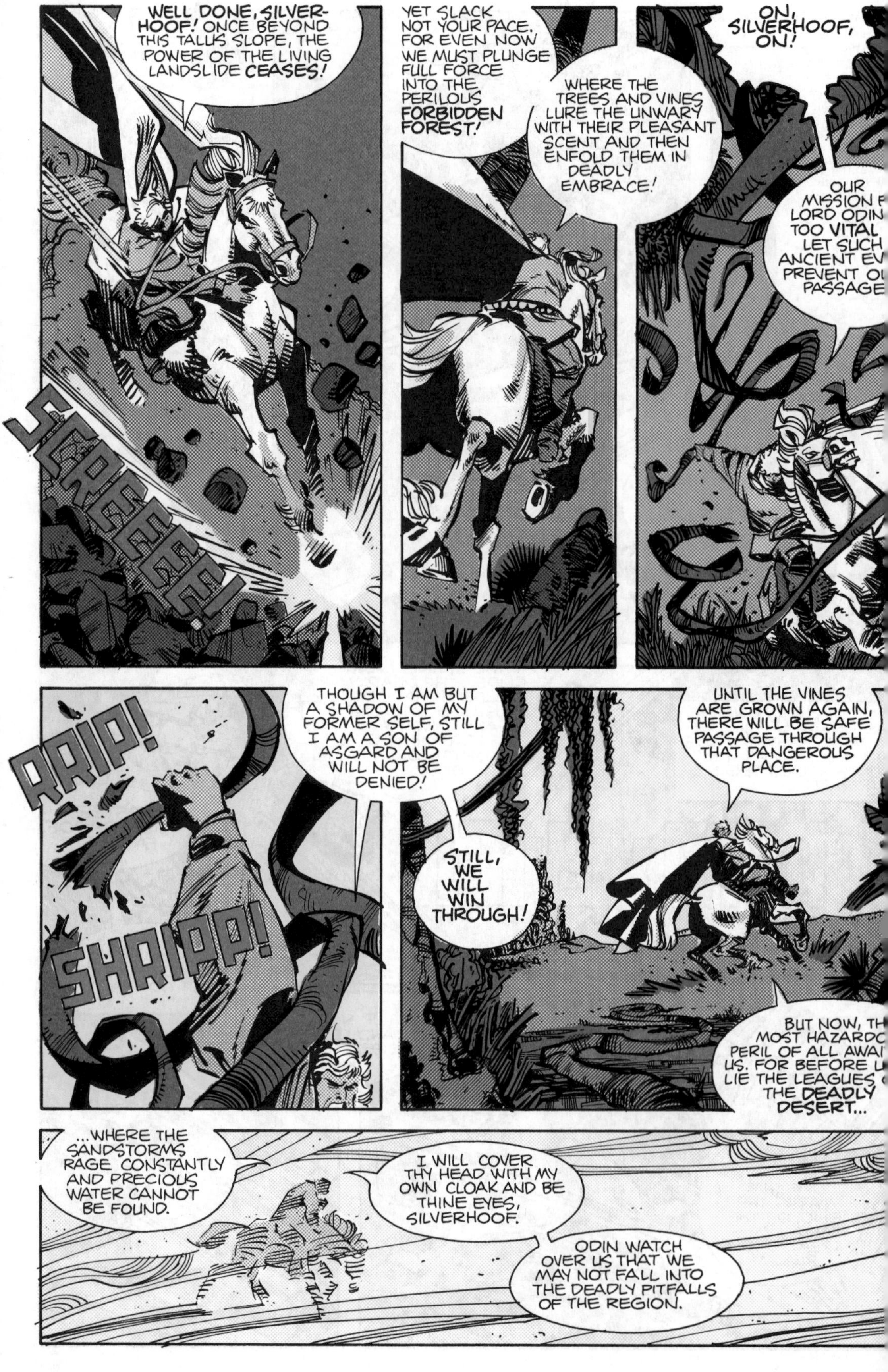
WELL DONE, SILVERHOOF! ONCE BEYOND THIS TALUS SLOPE, THE POWER OF THE LIVING LANDSLIDE CEASES!
SCREEEE!
YET SLACK NOT YOUR PACE. FOR EVEN NOW WE MUST PLUNGE FULL FORCE INTO THE PERILOUS FORBIDDEN FOREST!
WHERE THE TREES AND VINES LURE THE UNWARY WITH THEIR PLEASANT SCENT AND THEN ENFOLD THEM IN DEADLY EMBRACE!
ON, SILVERHOOF, ON!
OUR MISSION LORD ODIN TOO VITAL LET SUCH ANCIENT EV PREVENT O PASSAGE
ARRIP!
SHRIPP!
THOUGH I AM BUT A SHADOW OF MY FORMER SELF, STILL I AM A SON OF ASGARD AND WILL NOT BE DENIED!
STILL, WE WILL WIN THROUGH!
UNTIL THE VINES ARE GROWN AGAIN, THERE WILL BE SAFE PASSAGE THROUGH THAT DANGEROUS PLACE.
BUT NOW, TH MOST HAZARDO PERIL OF ALL AWAI US. FOR BEFORE L LIE THE LEAGUES THE DEADLY DESERT...
...WHERE THE SANDSTORMS RAGE CONSTANTLY AND PRECIOUS WATER CANNOT BE FOUND.
I WILL COVER THY HEAD WITH MY OWN CLOAK AND BE THINE EYES, SILVERHOOF.
ODIN WATCH OVER US THAT WE MAY NOT FALL INTO THE DEADLY PITFALLS OF THE REGION.

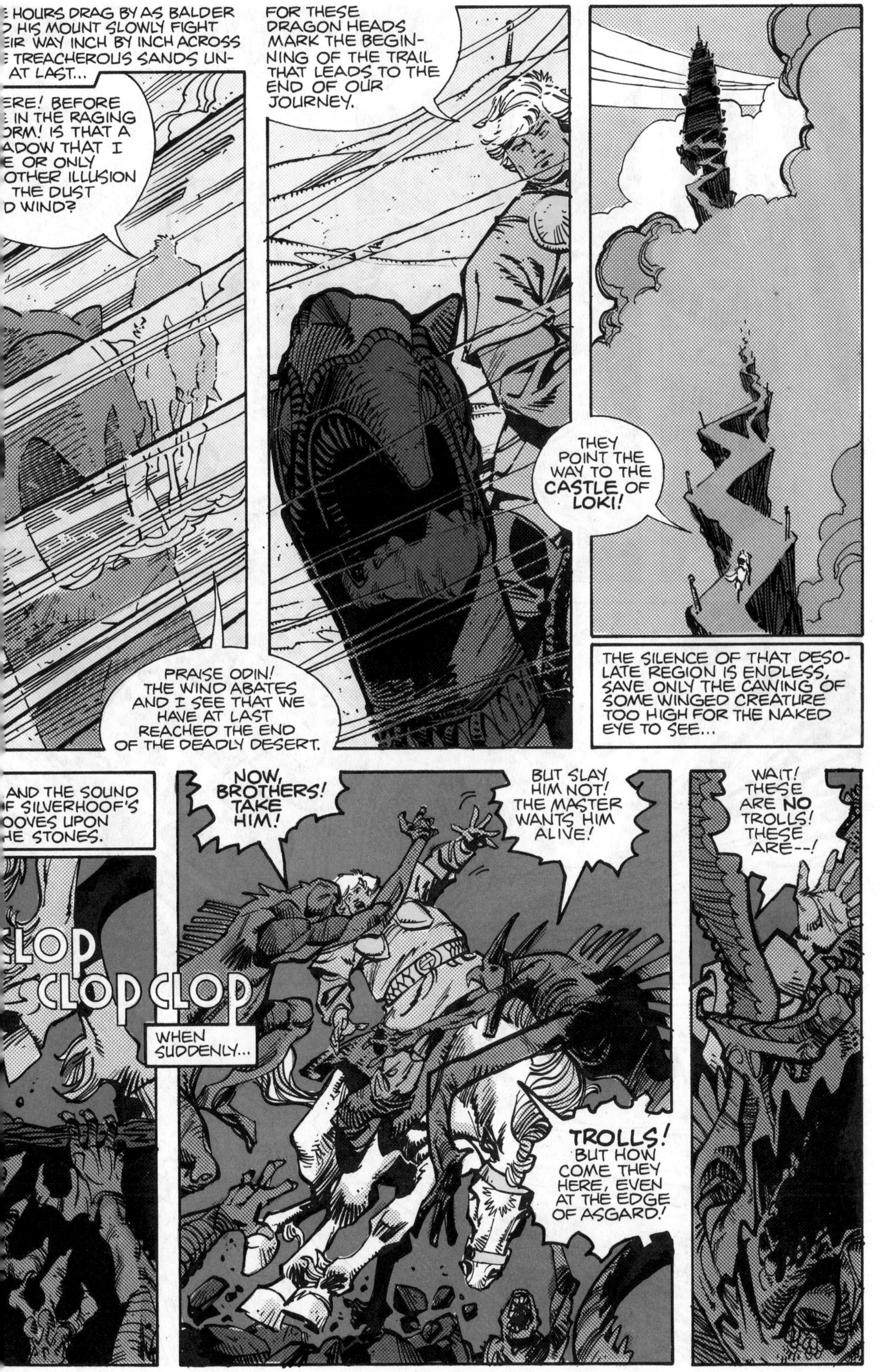
E HOURS DRAG BY AS BALDER D HIS MOUNT SLOWLY FIGHT EIR WAY INCH BY INCH ACROSS E TREACHEROUS SANDS UN- AT LAST...
ERE! BEFORE E IN THE RAGING ORM! IS THAT A ADOW THAT I E OR ONLY OTHER ILLUSION THE DUST D WIND?
PRAISE ODIN! THE WIND ABATES AND I SEE THAT WE HAVE AT LAST REACHED THE END OF THE DEADLY DESERT.
FOR THESE DRAGON HEADS MARK THE BEGIN- NING OF THE TRAIL THAT LEADS TO THE END OF OUR JOURNEY.
THEY POINT THE WAY TO THE CASTLE OF LOKI!
THE SILENCE OF THAT DESO- LATE REGION IS ENDLESS, SAVE ONLY THE CAWING OF SOME WINGED CREATURE TOO HIGH FOR THE NAKED EYE TO SEE...
...AND THE SOUND F SILVERHOOF'S OOVES UPON HE STONES.
CLOP CLOP CLOP
WHEN SUDDENLY...
NOW, BROTHERS! TAKE HIM!
BUT SLAY HIM NOT! THE MASTER WANTS HIM ALIVE!
TROLLS! BUT HOW COME THEY HERE, EVEN AT THE EDGE OF ASGARD!
WAIT! THESE ARE NO TROLLS! THESE ARE--!

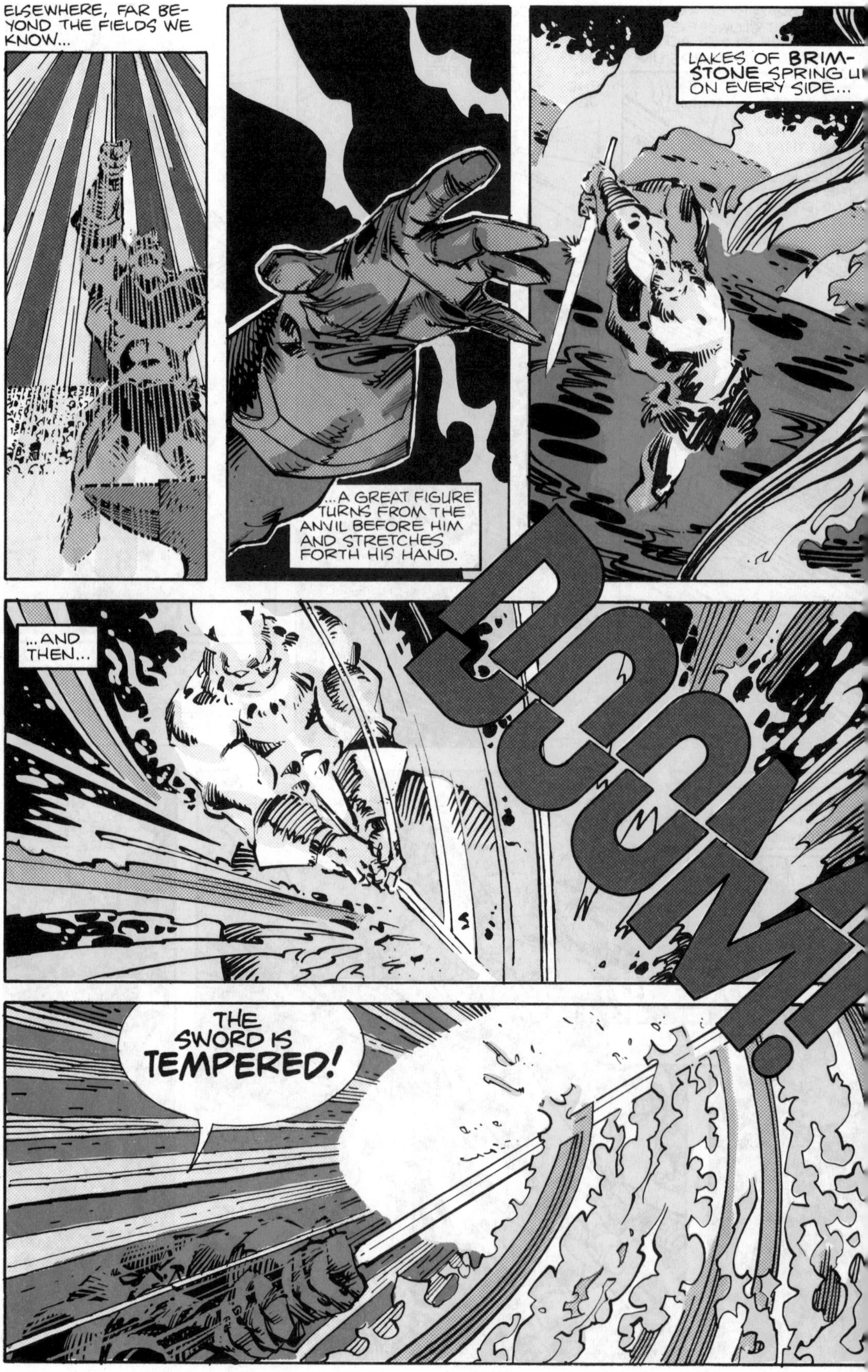

ELSEWHERE, FAR BEYOND THE FIELDS WE KNOW...
...A GREAT FIGURE TURNS FROM THE ANVIL BEFORE HIM AND STRETCHES FORTH HIS HAND.
LAKES OF BRIMSTONE SPRING U
ON EVERY SIDE...
...AND THEN...
THE SWORD IS TEMPERED!

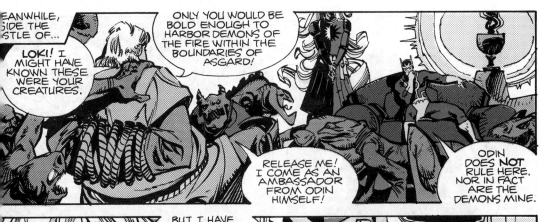

MEANWHILE, ~~SIDE~~ THE ~~STLE~~ OF...

LOKI! I MIGHT HAVE KNOWN THESE WERE YOUR CREATURES.

ONLY YOU WOULD BE BOLD ENOUGH TO HARBOR DEMONS OF THE FIRE WITHIN THE BOUNDARIES OF ASGARD!

RELEASE ME! I COME AS AN AMBASSADOR FROM ODIN HIMSELF!

ODIN DOES **NOT** RULE HERE. NOR IN FACT ARE THE DEMONS MINE.

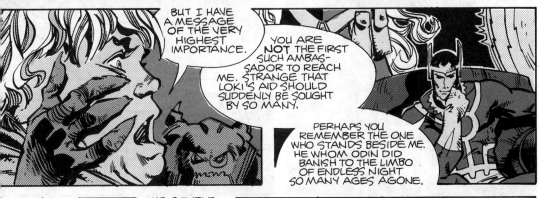

BUT I HAVE A MESSAGE OF THE VERY HIGHEST IMPORTANCE.

YOU ARE **NOT** THE FIRST SUCH AMBASSADOR TO REACH ME. STRANGE THAT LOKI'S AID SHOULD SUDDENLY BE SOUGHT BY SO MANY.

PERHAPS YOU REMEMBER THE ONE WHO STANDS BESIDE ME. HE WHOM ODIN DID BANISH TO THE LIMBO OF ENDLESS NIGHT SO MANY AGES AGONE.

MAY I PRESENT MALEKITH, THE DARK ELF.

THE GENTLE-MEN HOLDING YOU ARE PART OF HIS ENTOURAGE.

THIS UNSEEMLY OUTBURST DIS-PLEASES US, MY DEMONS. GAG HIM!

LOK-- MMMMPH!

MALEKITH! BUT 'TIS HE AND HIS MASTER WHO WOULD DESTROY US ALL!

LOKI, YOU MUST LISTEN TO ME!

AH, BALDER, EVER THE TOOTHLESS UNDERSTRAP-PER OF THE NOBILITY OF ASGARD.

THE YEARS HAVE NOT BEEN KIND TO YOU, BRAVE BALDER. YOU WERE HAND-SOME ONCE.

IS THIS THE BEST THAT ODIN CAN DO?

SEND A SPINELESS, OVERWEIGHT FLUNKY TO CURRY THE FAVOR OF HIS STEP-SON...

...WHEN ALL KNOW THAT ODIN REGRETS EVER HAVING ADOPTED LOKI IN THE FIRST PLACE!

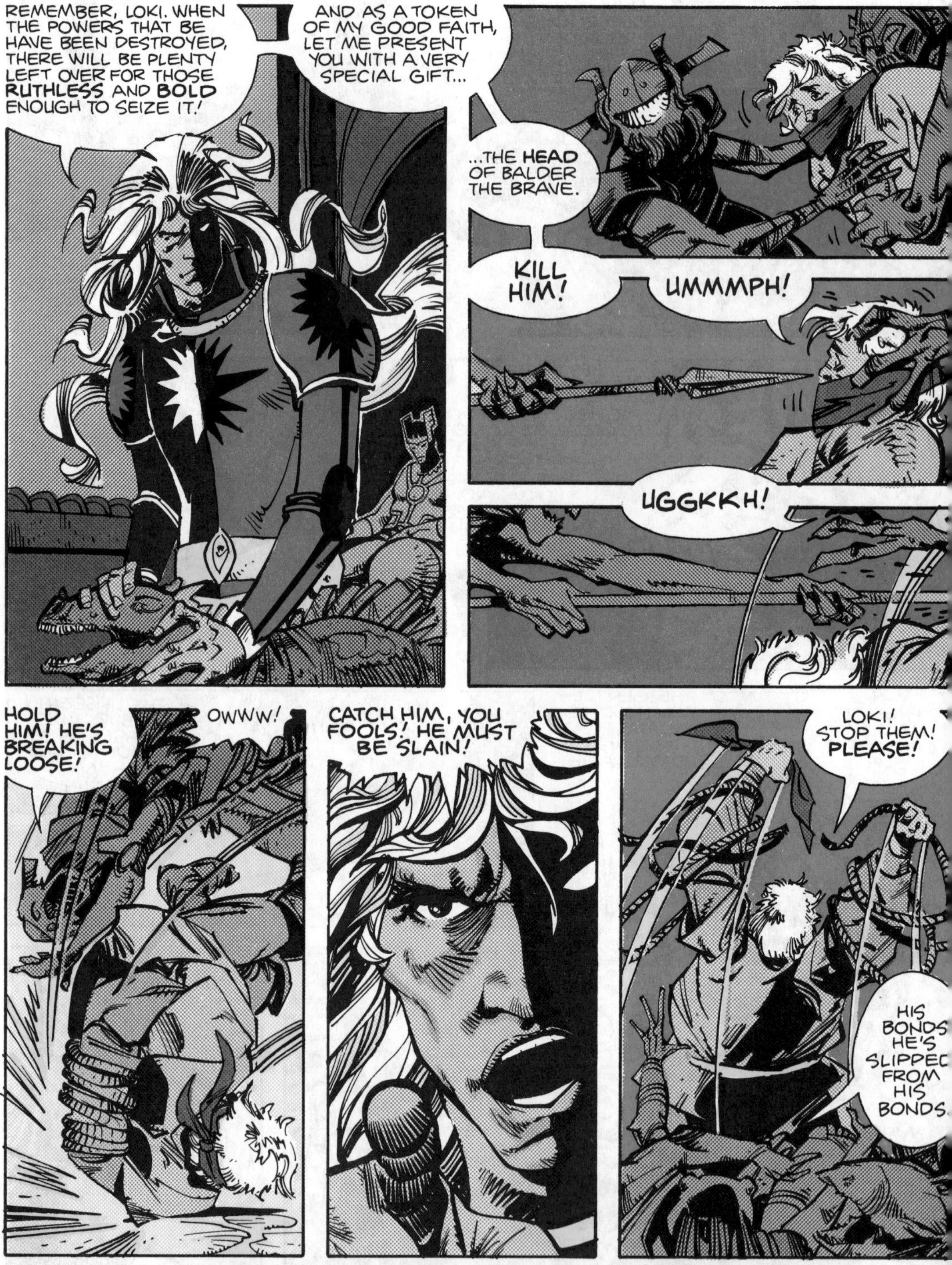

REMEMBER, LOKI. WHEN THE POWERS THAT BE HAVE BEEN DESTROYED, THERE WILL BE PLENTY LEFT OVER FOR THOSE **RUTHLESS** AND **BOLD** ENOUGH TO SEIZE IT!
AND AS A TOKEN OF MY GOOD FAITH, LET ME PRESENT YOU WITH A VERY SPECIAL GIFT...
...THE **HEAD** OF BALDER THE BRAVE.
KILL HIM!
UMMMPH!
UGGKKH!
HOLD HIM! HE'S BREAKING LOOSE!
OWWW!
CATCH HIM, YOU FOOLS! HE MUST BE SLAIN!
LOKI! STOP THEM! **PLEASE!**
HIS BONDS HE'S SLIPPED FROM HIS BONDS.
AFTER HIM! HE LEAPS INTO THE COURT-YARD!
LOKI! HEAR ME OUT YOU KNOW I CANNO **FIGHT** THESE DEMONS!
HE CAN'T ESCAPE US ALL!

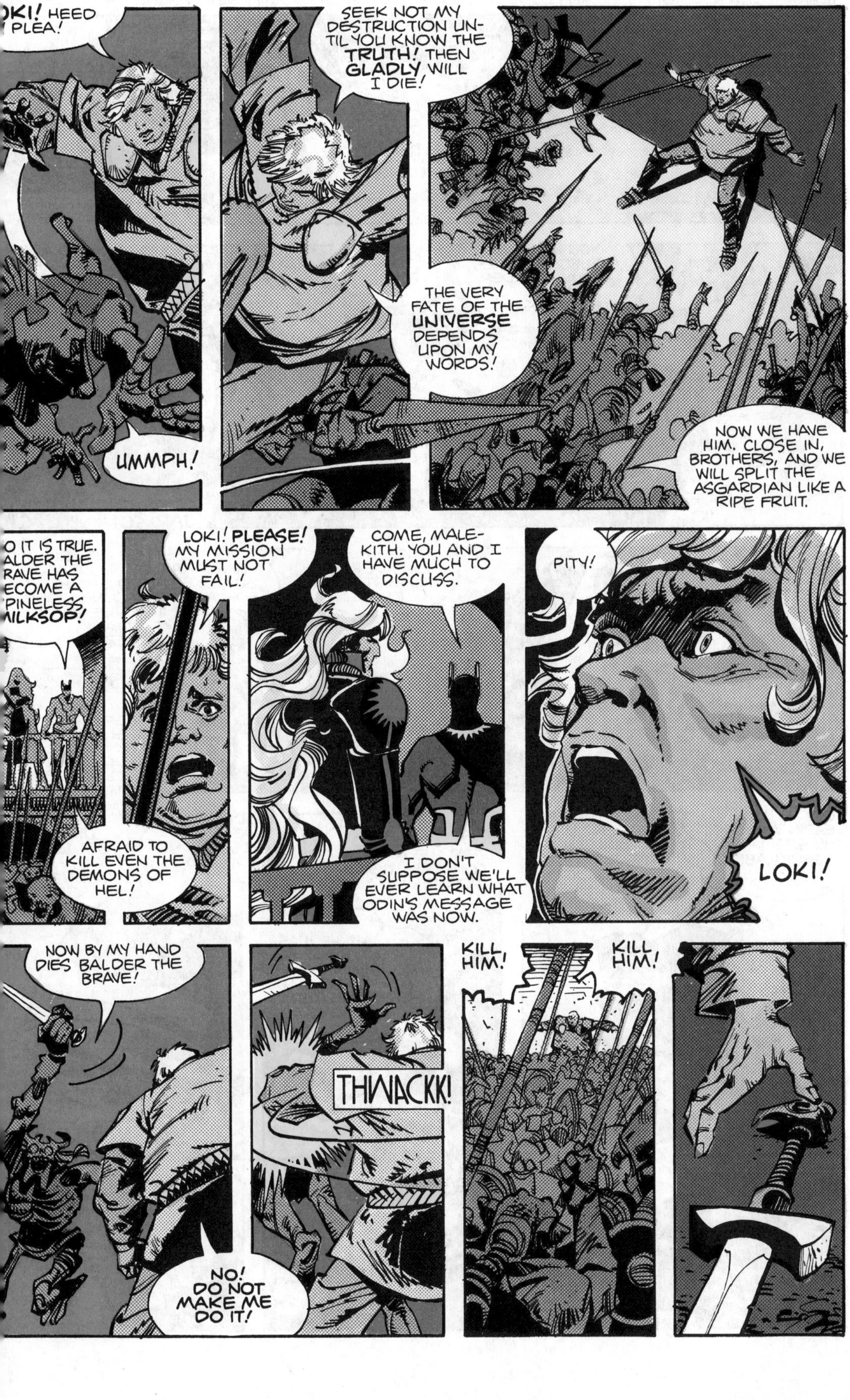

OKI! HEED
PLEA!
SEEK NOT MY DESTRUCTION UNTIL YOU KNOW THE TRUTH! THEN GLADLY, WILL I DIE!
THE VERY FATE OF THE UNIVERSE DEPENDS UPON MY WORDS!
UMMPH!
NOW WE HAVE HIM. CLOSE IN, BROTHERS, AND WE WILL SPLIT THE ASGARDIAN LIKE A RIPE FRUIT.
O IT IS TRUE. ALDER THE RAVE HAS ECOME A PINELESS MILKSOP!
AFRAID TO KILL EVEN THE DEMONS OF HEL!
LOKI! PLEASE! MY MISSION MUST NOT FAIL!
COME, MALEKITH. YOU AND I HAVE MUCH TO DISCUSS.
I DON'T SUPPOSE WE'LL EVER LEARN WHAT ODIN'S MESSAGE WAS NOW.
PITY!
LOKI!
NOW BY MY HAND DIES BALDER THE BRAVE!
NO! DO NOT MAKE ME DO IT!
THWACKK!
KILL HIM!
KILL HIM!

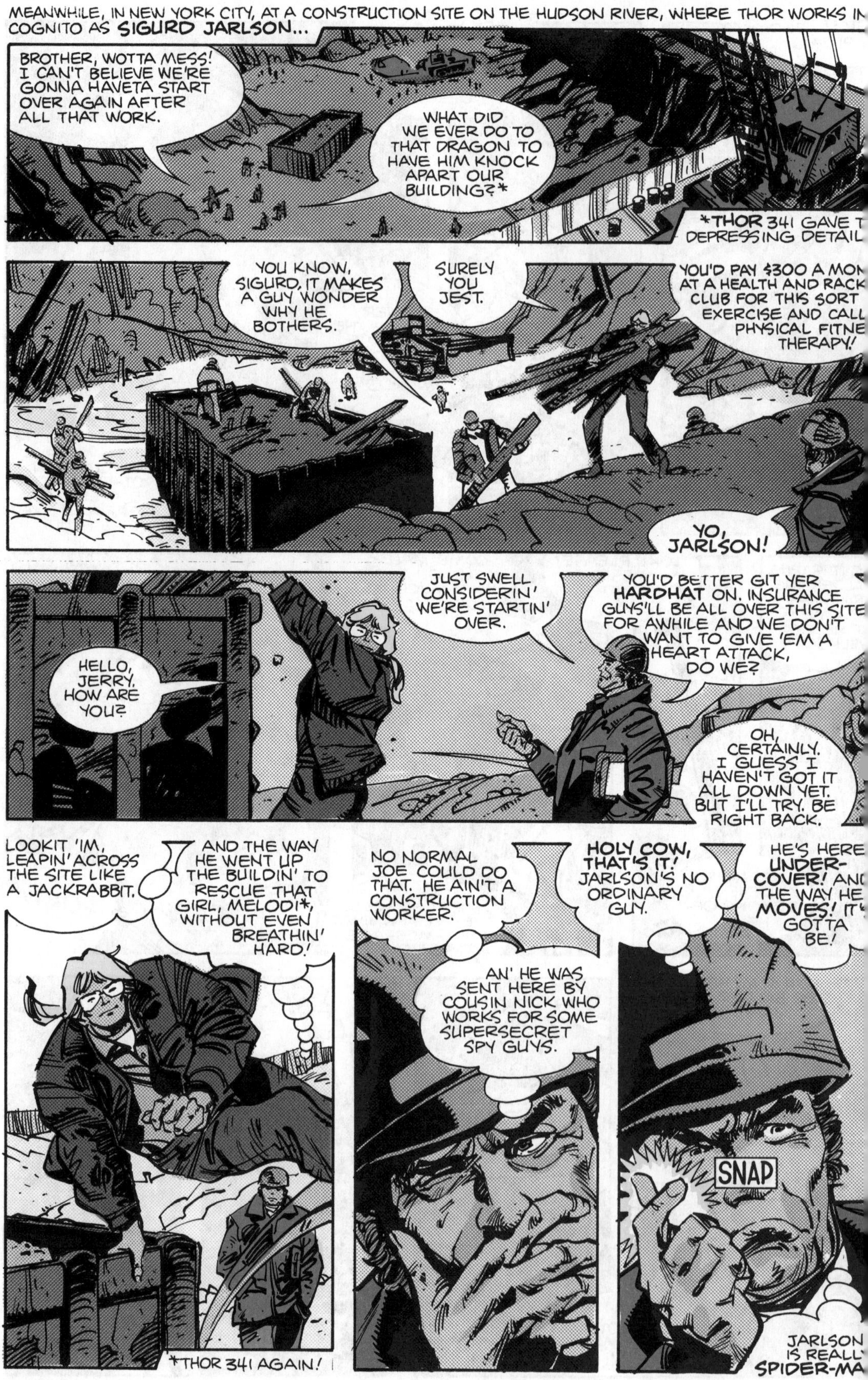
MEANWHILE, IN NEW YORK CITY, AT A CONSTRUCTION SITE ON THE HUDSON RIVER, WHERE THOR WORKS INCOGNITO AS SIGURD JARLSON...
BROTHER, WOTTA MESS! I CAN'T BELIEVE WE'RE GONNA HAVETA START OVER AGAIN AFTER ALL THAT WORK.
WHAT DID WE EVER DO TO THAT DRAGON TO HAVE HIM KNOCK APART OUR BUILDING?*
*THOR 341 GAVE T DEPRESSING DETAIL
YOU KNOW, SIGURD, IT MAKES A GUY WONDER WHY HE BOTHERS.
SURELY YOU JEST.
YOU'D PAY $300 A MON AT A HEALTH AND RACK CLUB FOR THIS SORT EXERCISE AND CALL PHYSICAL FITNE THERAPY!
YO, JARLSON!
HELLO, JERRY. HOW ARE YOU?
JUST SWELL CONSIDERIN' WE'RE STARTIN' OVER.
YOU'D BETTER GIT YER HARDHAT ON. INSURANCE GUYS'LL BE ALL OVER THIS SITE FOR AWHILE AND WE DON'T WANT TO GIVE 'EM A HEART ATTACK, DO WE?
OH, CERTAINLY. I GUESS I HAVEN'T GOT IT ALL DOWN YET. BUT I'LL TRY. BE RIGHT BACK.
LOOKIT 'IM, LEAPIN' ACROSS THE SITE LIKE A JACKRABBIT.
AND THE WAY HE WENT UP THE BUILDIN' TO RESCUE THAT GIRL, MELODI*, WITHOUT EVEN BREATHIN' HARD!
*THOR 341 AGAIN!
NO NORMAL JOE COULD DO THAT. HE AIN'T A CONSTRUCTION WORKER.
AN' HE WAS SENT HERE BY COUSIN NICK WHO WORKS FOR SOME SUPERSECRET SPY GUYS.
HOLY COW, THAT'S IT! JARLSON'S NO ORDINARY GUY.
HE'S HERE UNDER-COVER! AN THE WAY HE MOVES! IT' GOTTA BE!
SNAP
JARLSON IS REALL SPIDER-MA

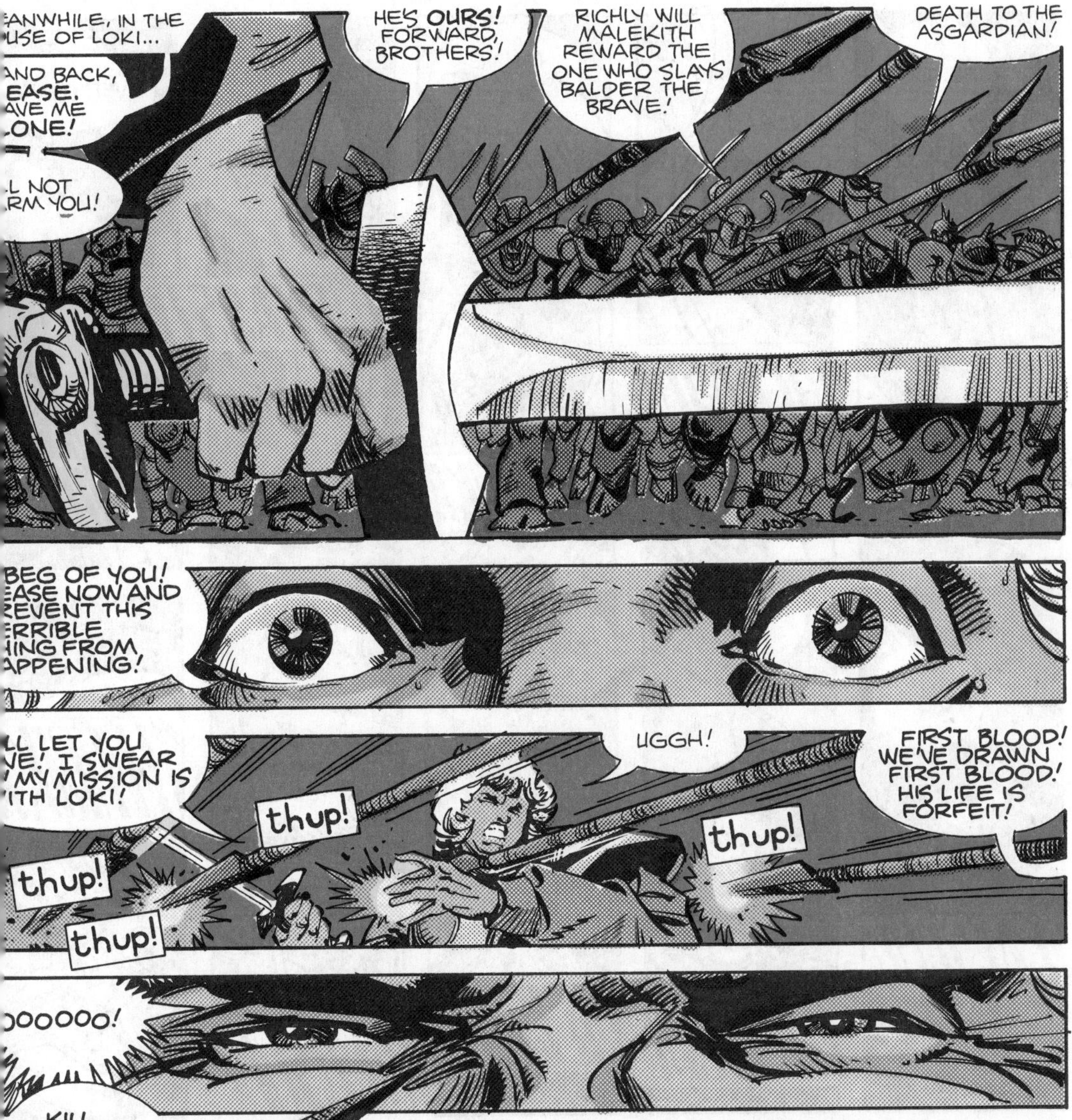
EANWHILE, IN THE USE OF LOKI...
AND BACK, EASE. AVE ME ONE!
L NOT RM YOU!
HE'S **OURS!** FORWARD, BROTHERS!
RICHLY WILL MALEKITH REWARD THE ONE WHO SLAYS BALDER THE BRAVE!
DEATH TO THE ASGARDIAN!
BEG OF YOU! EASE NOW AND REVENT THIS ERRIBLE HING FROM APPENING!
LL LET YOU VE! I SWEAR MY MISSION IS ITH LOKI!
thup!
thup!
thup!
UGGH!
thup!
FIRST BLOOD! WE'VE DRAWN FIRST BLOOD! HIS LIFE IS FORFEIT!
OOOOOO!
KILL HIM! FOR MALEKITH! AND THE BURNING FLAMES!
DEMONS! I FORESWORE THE SWORD FOREVER!
BUT BILLIONS OF INNOCENTS WILL **PERISH** IF MY MISSION FAILS!
CONSCIENCE, I CAST THEE ASIDE! DEATH SHALL BE MY HELPMEET!

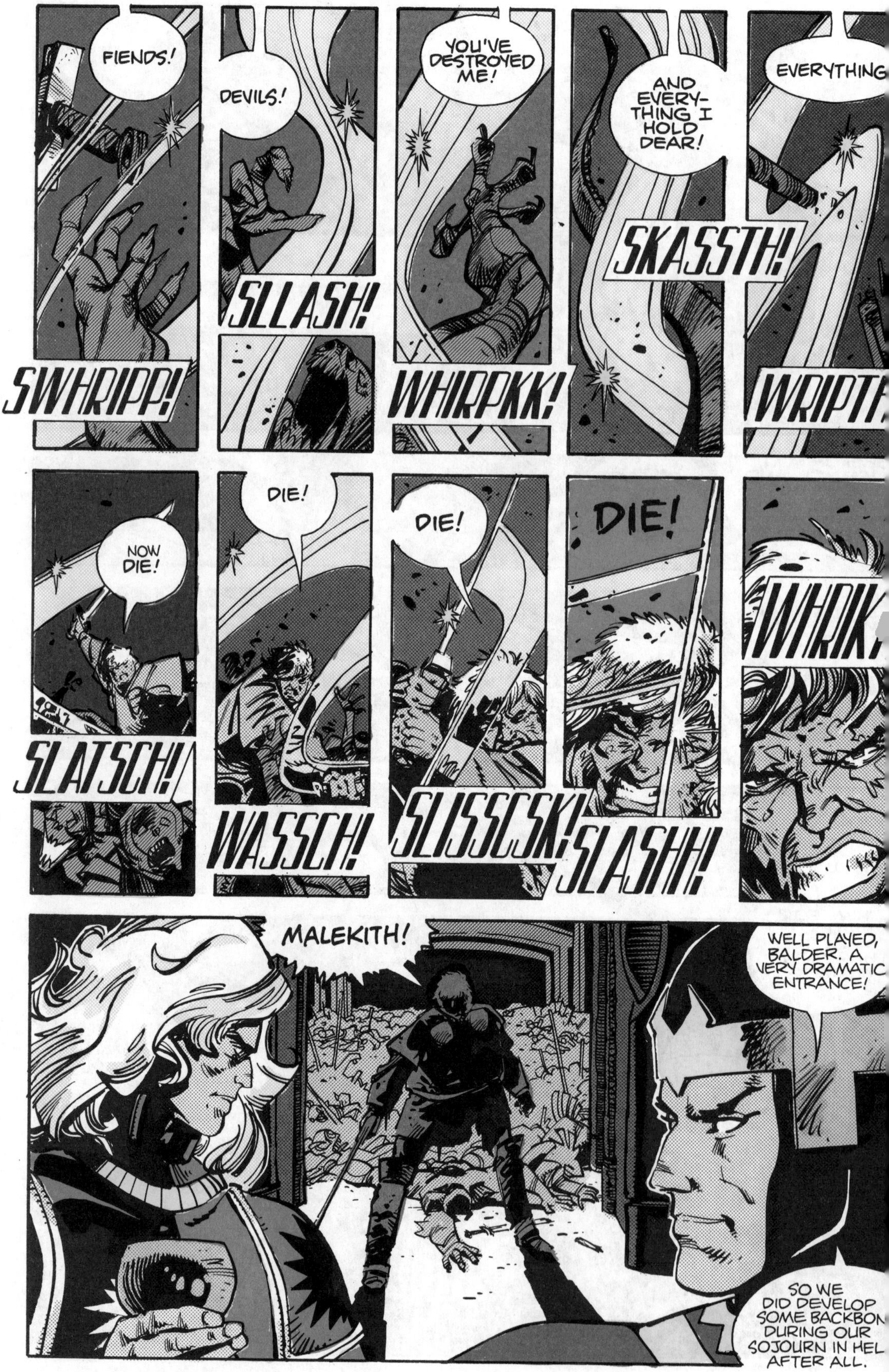
FIENDS!
SWHRIPP!
DEVILS!
SLLASH!
YOU'VE DESTROYED ME!
WHIRPKK!
AND EVERY-THING I HOLD DEAR!
SKASSTH!
EVERYTHING
WRIPT
NOW DIE!
SLATSCH!
DIE!
WASSCH!
DIE!
SLISSCSK!
DIE!
SLASHH!
WHRIK
MALEKITH!
WELL PLAYED, BALDER. A VERY DRAMATIC ENTRANCE!
SO WE DID DEVELOP SOME BACKBON DURING OUR SOJOURN IN HEL AFTER ALL.

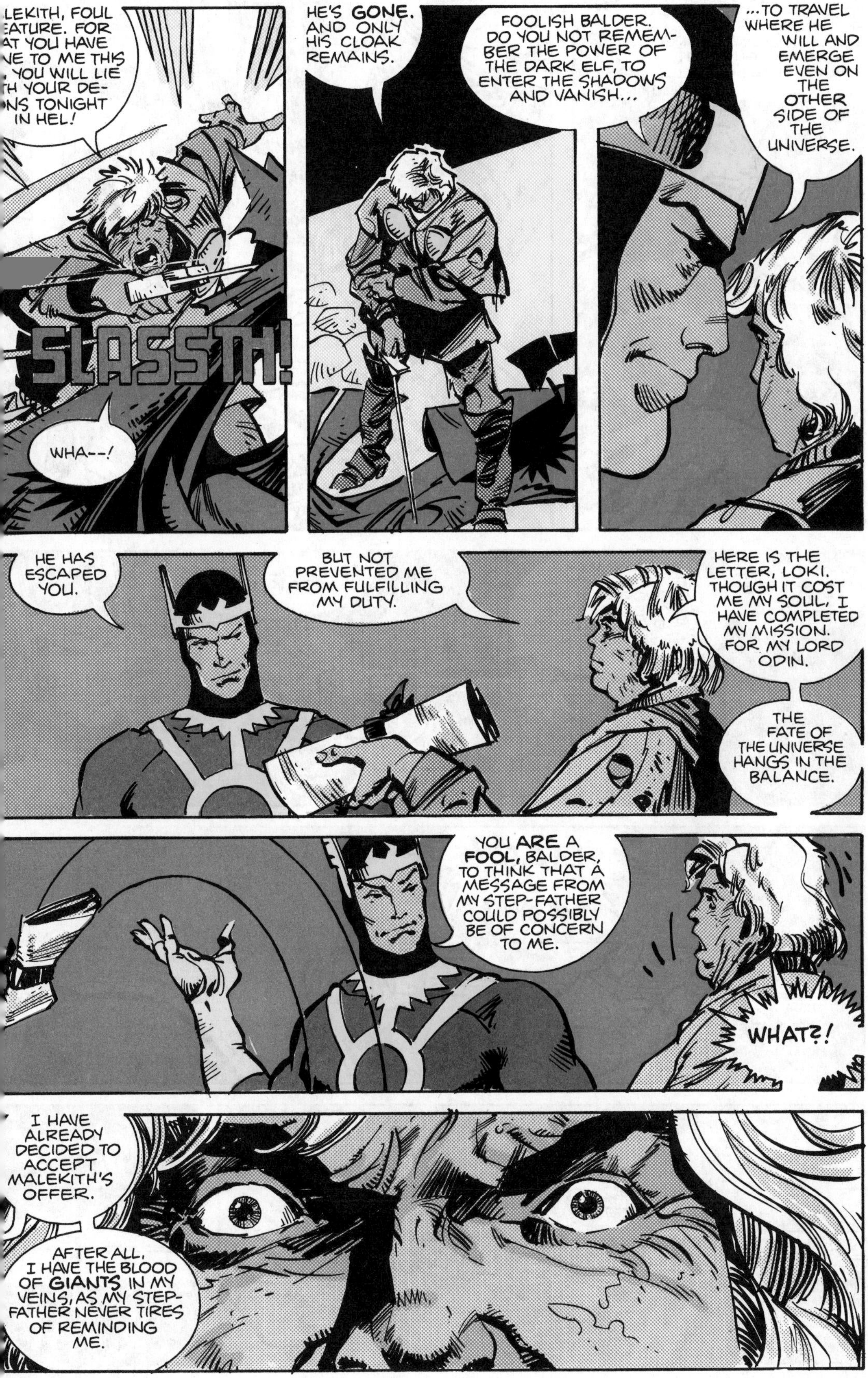
LEKITH, FOUL
EATURE. FOR
AT YOU HAVE
NE TO ME THIS
, YOU WILL LIE
TH YOUR DE-
NS TONIGHT
IN HEL!
SLASSTH!
WHA--!
HE'S **GONE**. AND ONLY HIS CLOAK REMAINS.
FOOLISH BALDER. DO YOU NOT REMEMBER THE POWER OF THE DARK ELF, TO ENTER THE SHADOWS AND VANISH...
...TO TRAVEL WHERE HE WILL AND EMERGE EVEN ON THE OTHER SIDE OF THE UNIVERSE.
HE HAS ESCAPED YOU.
BUT NOT PREVENTED ME FROM FULFILLING MY DUTY.
HERE IS THE LETTER, LOKI. THOUGH IT COST ME MY SOUL, I HAVE COMPLETED MY MISSION. FOR MY LORD ODIN.
THE FATE OF THE UNIVERSE HANGS IN THE BALANCE.
YOU **ARE** A **FOOL**, BALDER, TO THINK THAT A MESSAGE FROM MY STEP-FATHER COULD POSSIBLY BE OF CONCERN TO ME.
WHAT?!
I HAVE ALREADY DECIDED TO ACCEPT MALEKITH'S OFFER.
AFTER ALL, I HAVE THE BLOOD OF **GIANTS** IN MY VEINS, AS MY STEP-FATHER NEVER TIRES OF REMINDING ME.

BUT IT WAS SO DELIGHTFUL TO WATCH A PACIFIST SLAY HIS THOUSANDS THAT I SIMPLY COULDN'T BRING MYSELF TO MENTION IT BEFORE THIS.

WHY, IT WOULD HAVE SPOILED THE FUN.

DEVILSPAWN! WAS IT NOT ENOUGH THAT YOU KILL ME AND SEND ME DOWN TO HEL?

NOW YOU DESTROY WHAT LITTLE LIFE I HAD LEFT!

ASGARD MAY YET PERISH BY THE SWORD BUT NOT BEFORE I RID THE WORLD OF THE DEAD-LIEST SERPENT IN HER HALLS!

THREATEN ME NOT, THOU SAPLESS WEAKLING.

THOU HAST NOT THE METTLE FOR THE DEED!

LIAR!

SHLIKKK!

THUD

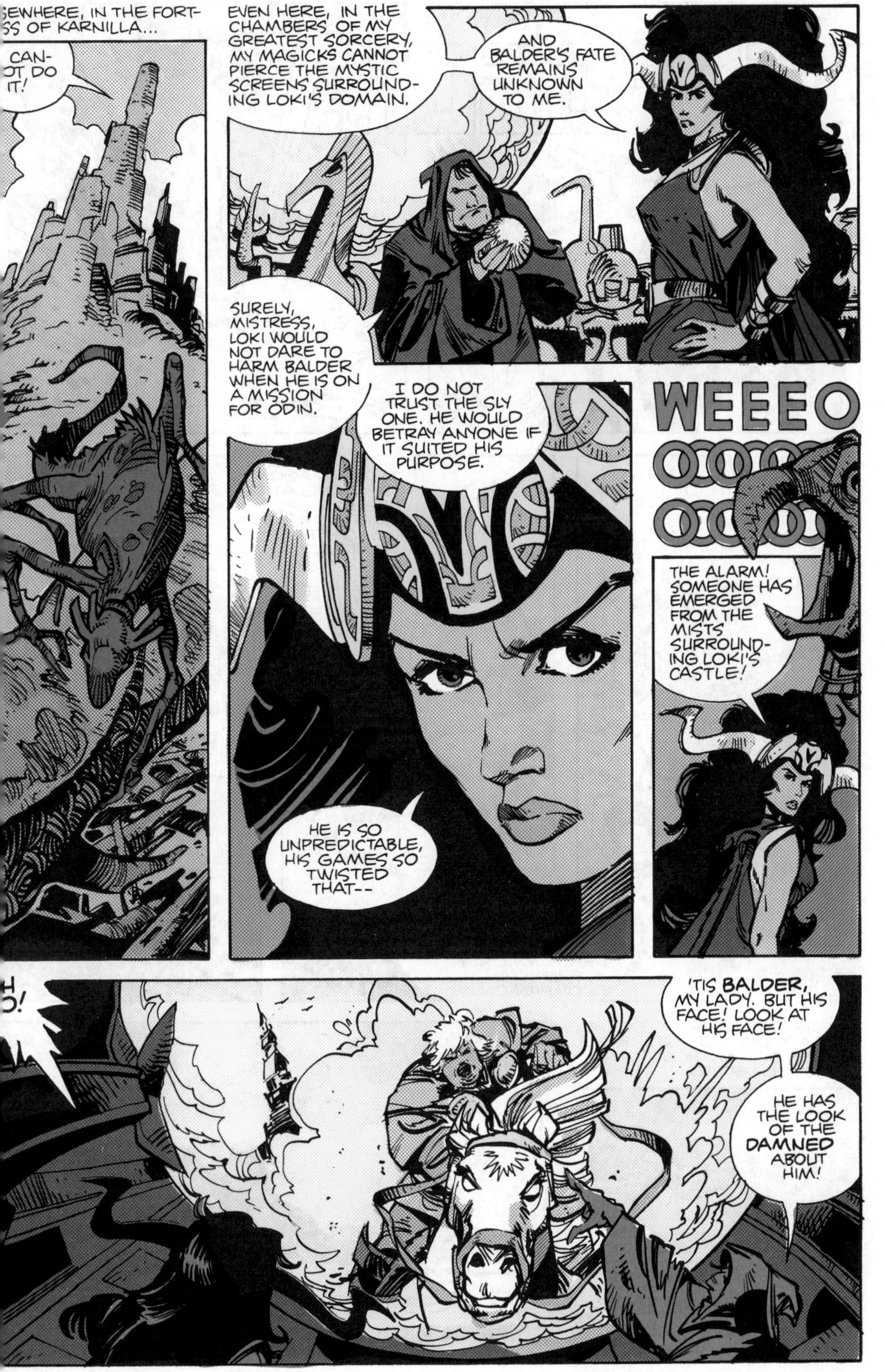

...EWHERE, IN THE FORT-
...SS OF KARNILLA...
...CAN-
...OT DO
...IT!
EVEN HERE, IN THE CHAMBERS OF MY GREATEST SORCERY, MY MAGICKS CANNOT PIERCE THE MYSTIC SCREENS SURROUNDING LOKI'S DOMAIN.
AND BALDER'S FATE REMAINS UNKNOWN TO ME.
SURELY, MISTRESS, LOKI WOULD NOT DARE TO HARM BALDER WHEN HE IS ON A MISSION FOR ODIN.
I DO NOT TRUST THE SLY ONE. HE WOULD BETRAY ANYONE IF IT SUITED HIS PURPOSE.
HE IS SO UNPREDICTABLE, HIS GAMES SO TWISTED THAT--
WEEEO
OOOOO
OOOOO
THE ALARM! SOMEONE HAS EMERGED FROM THE MISTS SURROUNDING LOKI'S CASTLE!
'TIS BALDER, MY LADY. BUT HIS FACE! LOOK AT HIS FACE!
HE HAS THE LOOK OF THE DAMNED ABOUT HIM!

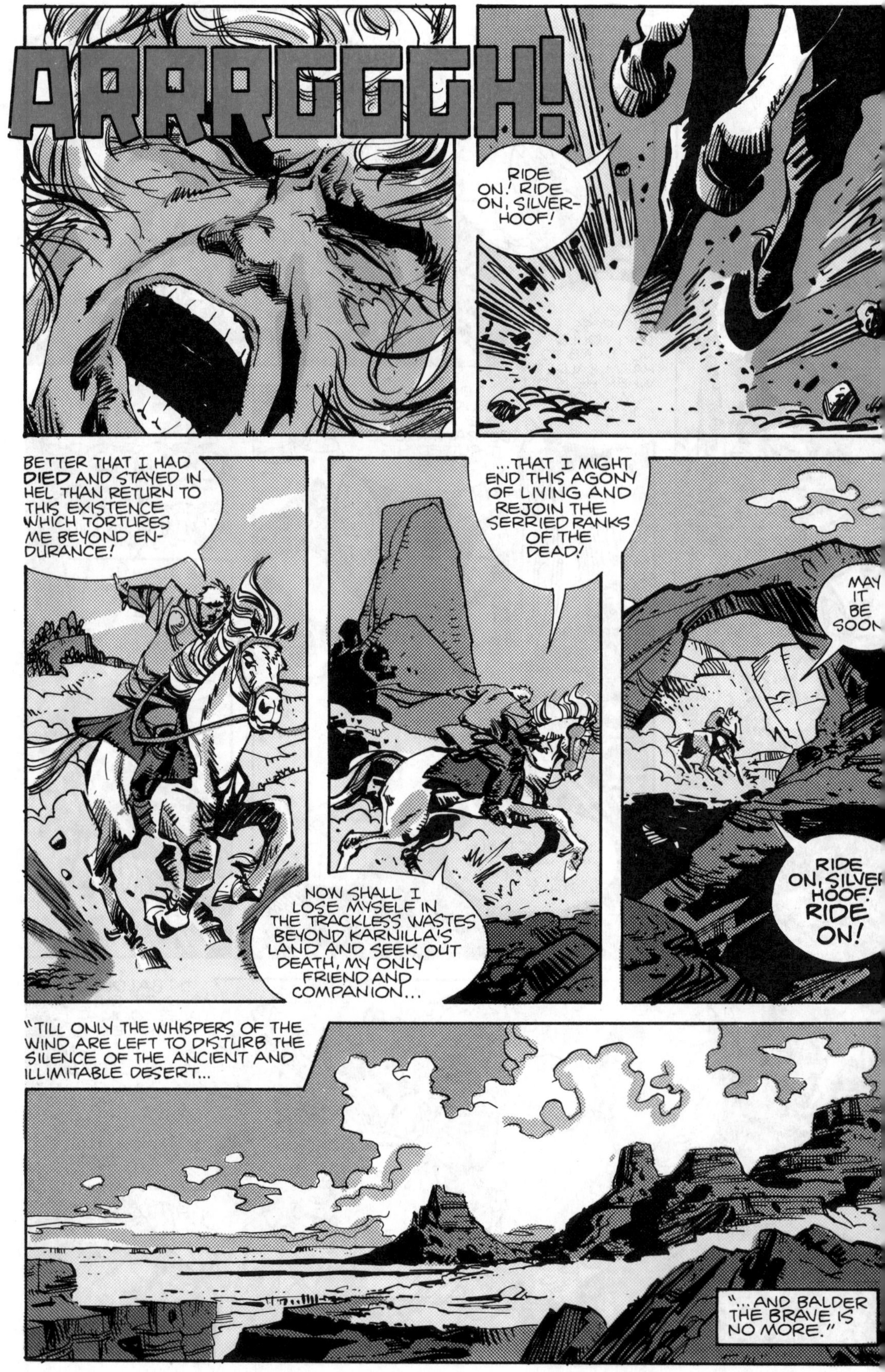
ARRRGGGH!
RIDE ON! RIDE ON, SILVER-HOOF!
BETTER THAT I HAD DIED AND STAYED IN HEL THAN RETURN TO THIS EXISTENCE WHICH TORTURES ME BEYOND ENDURANCE!
...THAT I MIGHT END THIS AGONY OF LIVING AND REJOIN THE SERRIED RANKS OF THE DEAD!
NOW SHALL I LOSE MYSELF IN THE TRACKLESS WASTES BEYOND KARNILLA'S LAND AND SEEK OUT DEATH, MY ONLY FRIEND AND COMPANION...
MAY IT BE SOON
RIDE ON, SILVER HOOF! RIDE ON!
"TILL ONLY THE WHISPERS OF THE WIND ARE LEFT TO DISTURB THE SILENCE OF THE ANCIENT AND ILLIMITABLE DESERT...
"...AND BALDER THE BRAVE IS NO MORE."

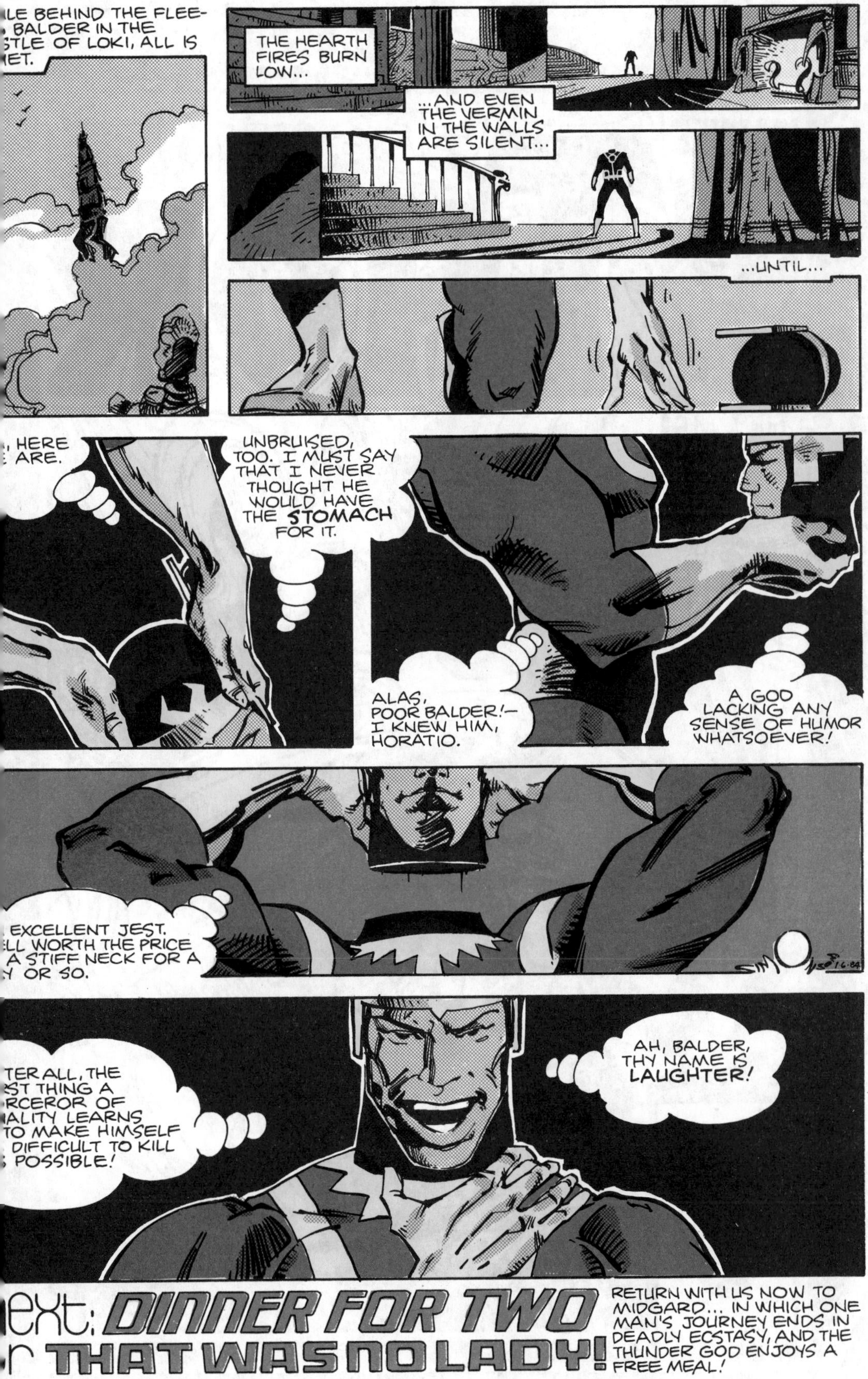

LE BEHIND THE FLEE-
BALDER IN THE
STLE OF LOKI, ALL IS
IET.
THE HEARTH FIRES BURN LOW...
...AND EVEN THE VERMIN IN THE WALLS ARE SILENT...
...UNTIL...
, HERE
ARE.
UNBRUISED, TOO. I MUST SAY THAT I NEVER THOUGHT HE WOULD HAVE THE STOMACH FOR IT.
ALAS, POOR BALDER!— I KNEW HIM, HORATIO.
A GOD LACKING ANY SENSE OF HUMOR WHATSOEVER!
EXCELLENT JEST.
LL WORTH THE PRICE
A STIFF NECK FOR A
OR SO.
TER ALL, THE
ST THING A
RCEROR OF
ALITY LEARNS
TO MAKE HIMSELF
DIFFICULT TO KILL
POSSIBLE!
AH, BALDER, THY NAME IS LAUGHTER!

ext: DINNER FOR TWO
r THAT WAS NO LADY!

RETURN WITH US NOW TO MIDGARD... IN WHICH ONE MAN'S JOURNEY ENDS IN DEADLY ECSTASY, AND THE THUNDER GOD ENJOYS A FREE MEAL!

Chapter Nine

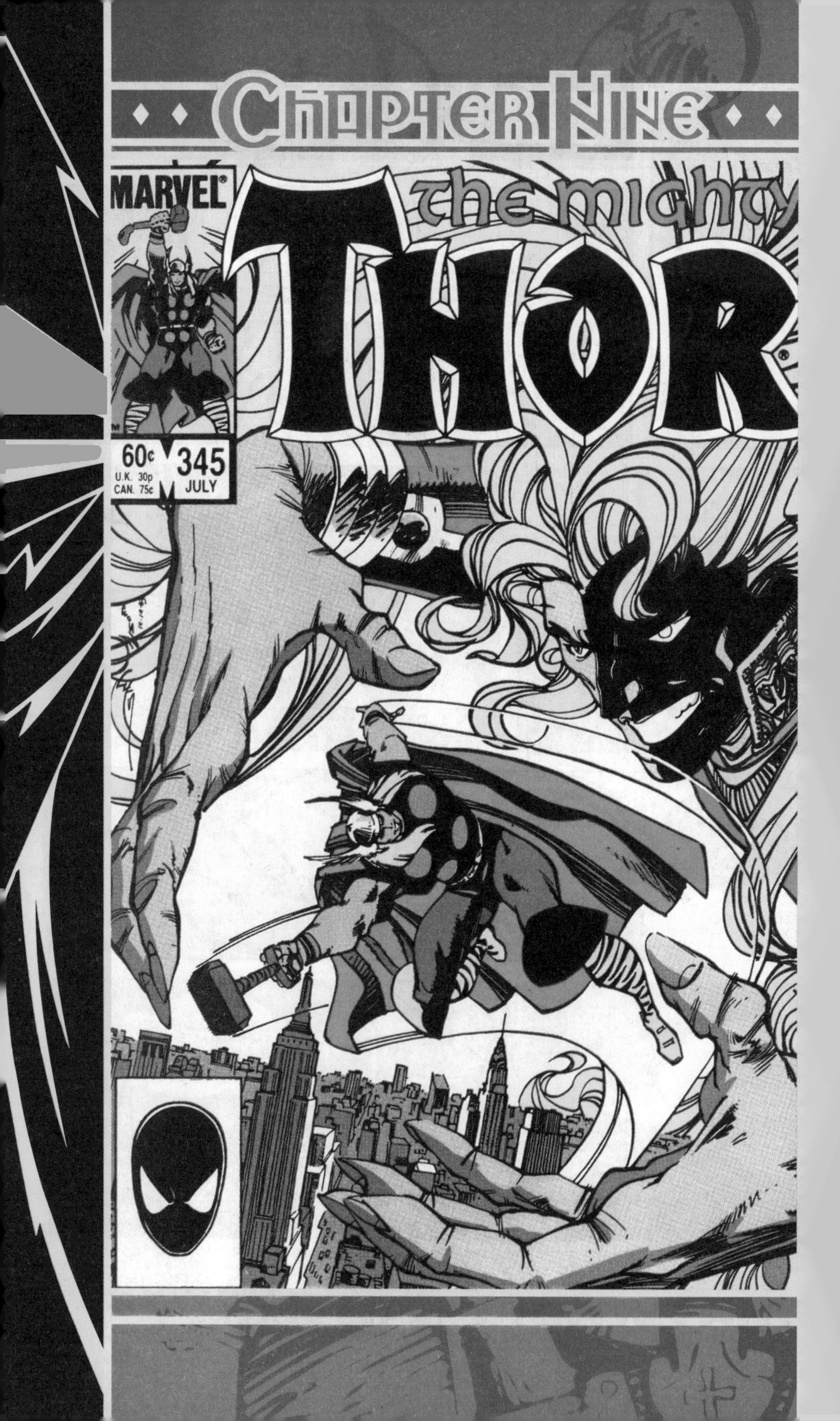
MARVEL
the mighty
THOR
60¢
345
U.K. 30p
CAN. 75¢
JULY

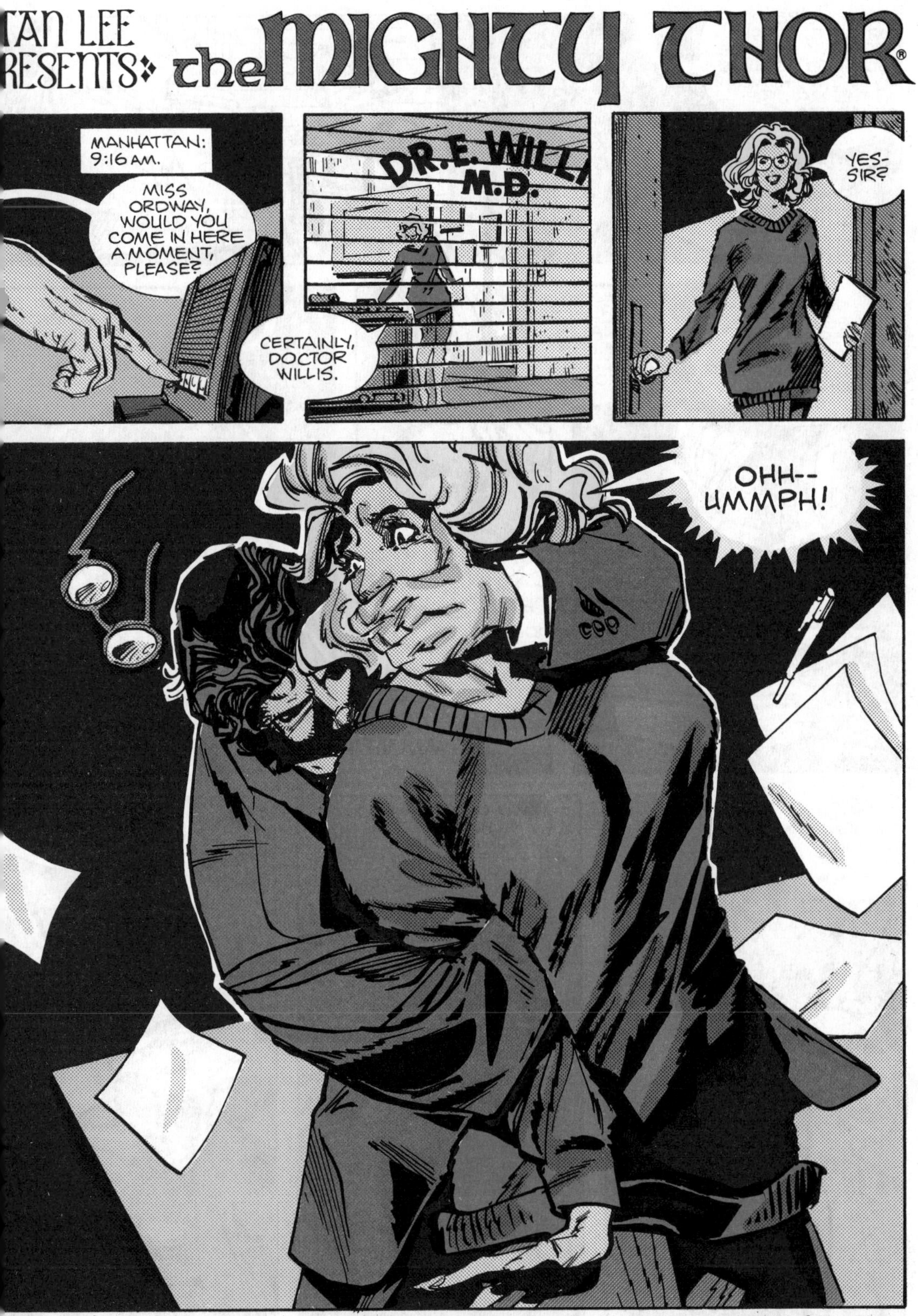

TAN LEE PRESENTS: the MIGHTY THOR®
MANHATTAN: 9:16 AM.
MISS ORDWAY, WOULD YOU COME IN HERE A MOMENT, PLEASE?
DR. E. WILLI M.D.
CERTAINLY, DOCTOR WILLIS.
YES-SIR?
OHH-- UMMPH!

RT AND STORY: WALTER SIMONSON · LETTERING: JOHN WORKMAN, JR. · COLORS: CHRISTIE SCHEELE
EDITING: MARK GRUENWALD · EDITOR-IN-CHIEF: JIM SHOOTER

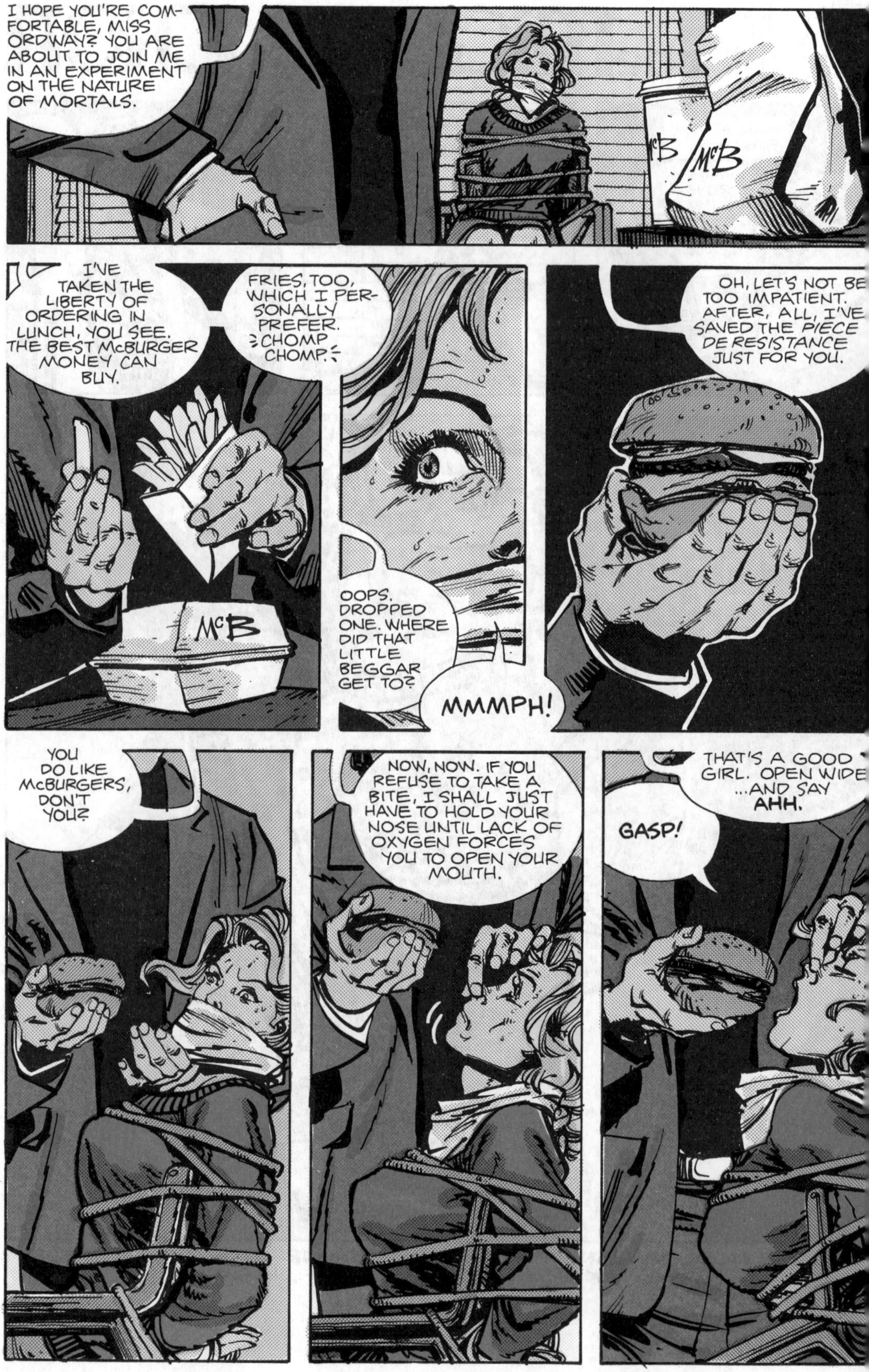
I HOPE YOU'RE COMFORTABLE, MISS ORDWAY? YOU ARE ABOUT TO JOIN ME IN AN EXPERIMENT ON THE NATURE OF MORTALS.
I'VE TAKEN THE LIBERTY OF ORDERING IN LUNCH, YOU SEE. THE BEST McBURGER MONEY CAN BUY.
FRIES, TOO, WHICH I PERSONALLY PREFER. CHOMP CHOMP.
OOPS. DROPPED ONE. WHERE DID THAT LITTLE BEGGAR GET TO?
MMMPH!
OH, LET'S NOT BE TOO IMPATIENT. AFTER, ALL, I'VE SAVED THE PIECE DE RESISTANCE JUST FOR YOU.
YOU DO LIKE McBURGERS, DON'T YOU?
NOW, NOW. IF YOU REFUSE TO TAKE A BITE, I SHALL JUST HAVE TO HOLD YOUR NOSE UNTIL LACK OF OXYGEN FORCES YOU TO OPEN YOUR MOUTH.
THAT'S A GOOD GIRL. OPEN WIDE ...AND SAY AHH.
GASP!

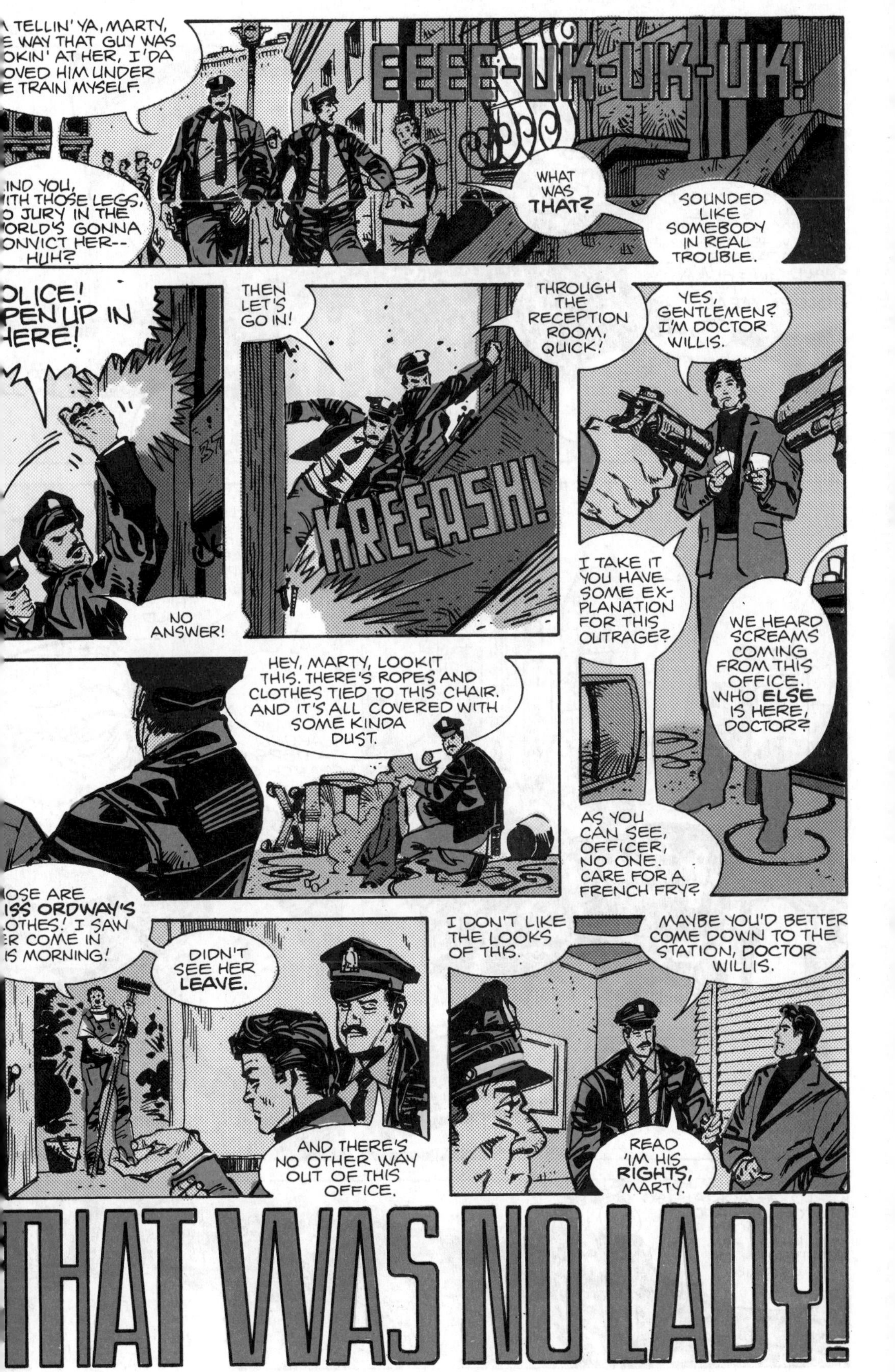

TELLIN' YA, MARTY, E WAY THAT GUY WAS OKIN' AT HER, I'DA OVED HIM UNDER E TRAIN MYSELF.
IND YOU, WITH THOSE LEGS, O JURY IN THE ORLD'S GONNA ONVICT HER-- HUH?
EEEE-UK-UK-UK!
WHAT WAS THAT?
SOUNDED LIKE SOMEBODY IN REAL TROUBLE.
OLICE! PEN UP IN HERE!
NO ANSWER!
THEN LET'S GO IN!
KREEASH!
THROUGH THE RECEPTION ROOM, QUICK!
YES, GENTLEMEN? I'M DOCTOR WILLIS.
I TAKE IT YOU HAVE SOME EXPLANATION FOR THIS OUTRAGE?
WE HEARD SCREAMS COMING FROM THIS OFFICE. WHO ELSE IS HERE, DOCTOR?
HEY, MARTY, LOOKIT THIS. THERE'S ROPES AND CLOTHES TIED TO THIS CHAIR. AND IT'S ALL COVERED WITH SOME KINDA DUST.
AS YOU CAN SEE, OFFICER, NO ONE. CARE FOR A FRENCH FRY?
OSE ARE ISS ORDWAY'S LOTHES! I SAW R COME IN S MORNING!
DIDN'T SEE HER LEAVE.
AND THERE'S NO OTHER WAY OUT OF THIS OFFICE.
I DON'T LIKE THE LOOKS OF THIS.
MAYBE YOU'D BETTER COME DOWN TO THE STATION, DOCTOR WILLIS.
READ 'IM HIS RIGHTS, MARTY.
THAT WAS NO LADY!

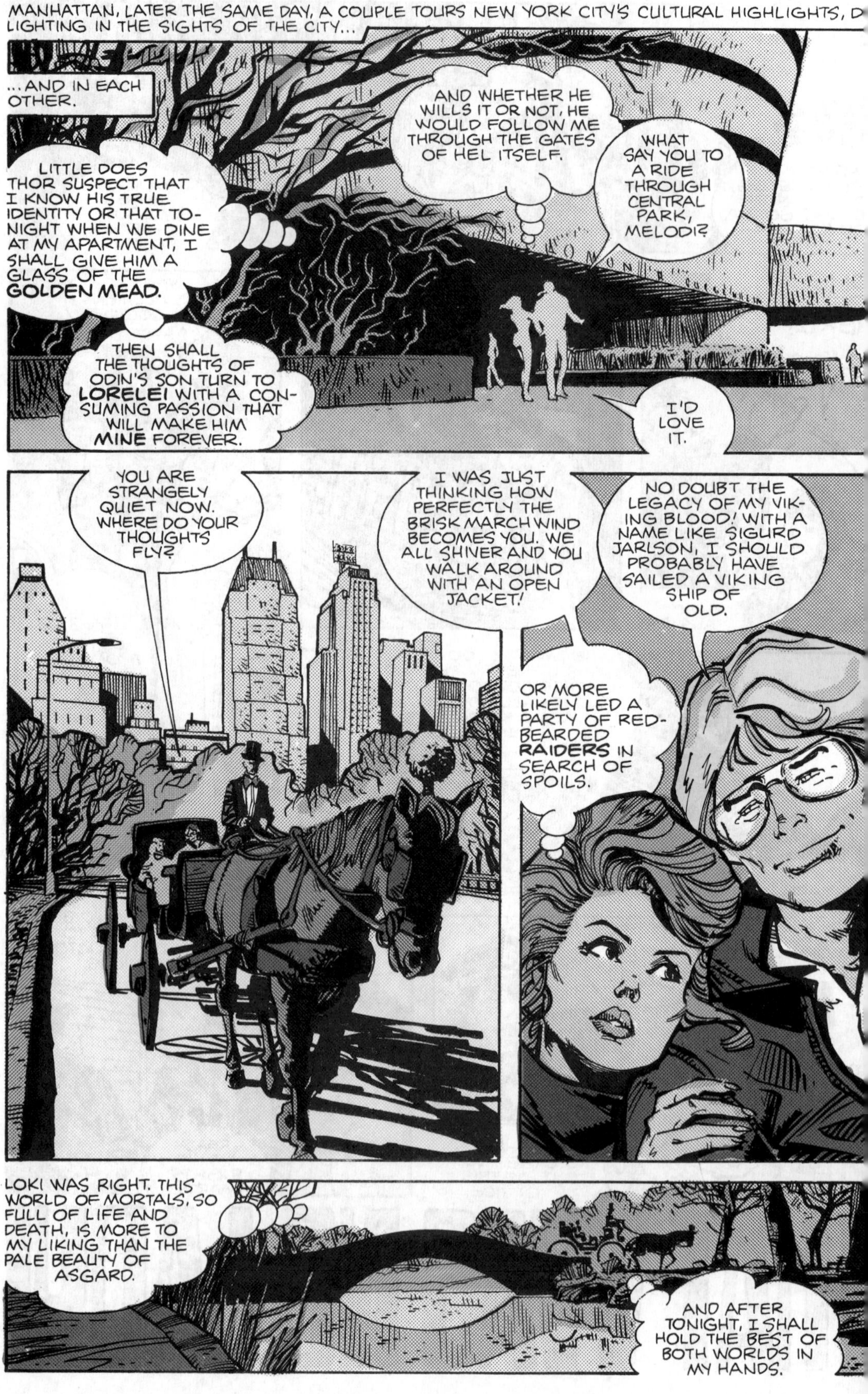

MANHATTAN, LATER THE SAME DAY, A COUPLE TOURS NEW YORK CITY'S CULTURAL HIGHLIGHTS, DE-LIGHTING IN THE SIGHTS OF THE CITY...
...AND IN EACH OTHER.
LITTLE DOES THOR SUSPECT THAT I KNOW HIS TRUE IDENTITY OR THAT TO-NIGHT WHEN WE DINE AT MY APARTMENT, I SHALL GIVE HIM A GLASS OF THE GOLDEN MEAD.
AND WHETHER HE WILLS IT OR NOT, HE WOULD FOLLOW ME THROUGH THE GATES OF HEL ITSELF.
THEN SHALL THE THOUGHTS OF ODIN'S SON TURN TO LORELEI WITH A CON-SUMING PASSION THAT WILL MAKE HIM MINE FOREVER.
WHAT SAY YOU TO A RIDE THROUGH CENTRAL PARK, MELODI?
I'D LOVE IT.
YOU ARE STRANGELY QUIET NOW. WHERE DO YOUR THOUGHTS FLY?
I WAS JUST THINKING HOW PERFECTLY THE BRISK MARCH WIND BECOMES YOU. WE ALL SHIVER AND YOU WALK AROUND WITH AN OPEN JACKET!
NO DOUBT THE LEGACY OF MY VIK-ING BLOOD! WITH A NAME LIKE SIGURD JARLSON, I SHOULD PROBABLY HAVE SAILED A VIKING SHIP OF OLD.
OR MORE LIKELY LED A PARTY OF RED-BEARDED RAIDERS IN SEARCH OF SPOILS.
LOKI WAS RIGHT. THIS WORLD OF MORTALS, SO FULL OF LIFE AND DEATH, IS MORE TO MY LIKING THAN THE PALE BEAUTY OF ASGARD.
AND AFTER TONIGHT, I SHALL HOLD THE BEST OF BOTH WORLDS IN MY HANDS.

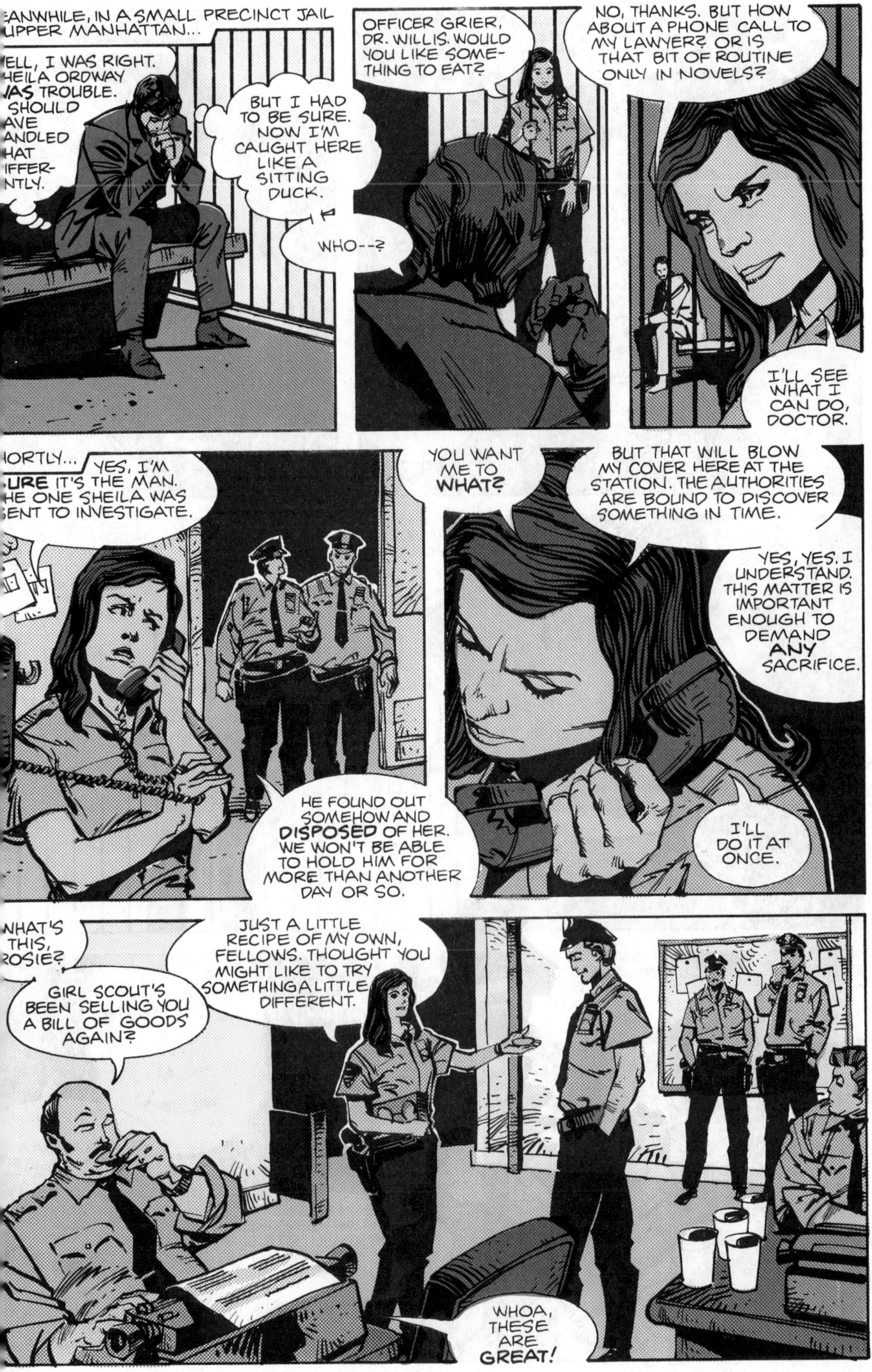

EANWHILE, IN A SMALL PRECINCT JAIL
UPPER MANHATTAN...
ELL, I WAS RIGHT. HEILA ORDWAY WAS TROUBLE. SHOULD AVE ANDLED HAT IFFER- NTLY.
BUT I HAD TO BE SURE. NOW I'M CAUGHT HERE LIKE A SITTING DUCK.
WHO--?
OFFICER GRIER, DR. WILLIS. WOULD YOU LIKE SOME- THING TO EAT?
NO, THANKS. BUT HOW ABOUT A PHONE CALL TO MY LAWYER? OR IS THAT BIT OF ROUTINE ONLY IN NOVELS?
I'LL SEE WHAT I CAN DO, DOCTOR.
HORTLY...
YES, I'M SURE IT'S THE MAN. HE ONE SHEILA WAS SENT TO INVESTIGATE.
HE FOUND OUT SOMEHOW AND DISPOSED OF HER. WE WON'T BE ABLE TO HOLD HIM FOR MORE THAN ANOTHER DAY OR SO.
YOU WANT ME TO WHAT?
BUT THAT WILL BLOW MY COVER HERE AT THE STATION. THE AUTHORITIES ARE BOUND TO DISCOVER SOMETHING IN TIME.
YES, YES. I UNDERSTAND. THIS MATTER IS IMPORTANT ENOUGH TO DEMAND ANY SACRIFICE.
I'LL DO IT AT ONCE.
WHAT'S THIS, ROSIE?
GIRL SCOUT'S BEEN SELLING YOU A BILL OF GOODS AGAIN?
JUST A LITTLE RECIPE OF MY OWN, FELLOWS. THOUGHT YOU MIGHT LIKE TO TRY SOMETHING A LITTLE DIFFERENT.
WHOA, THESE ARE GREAT!

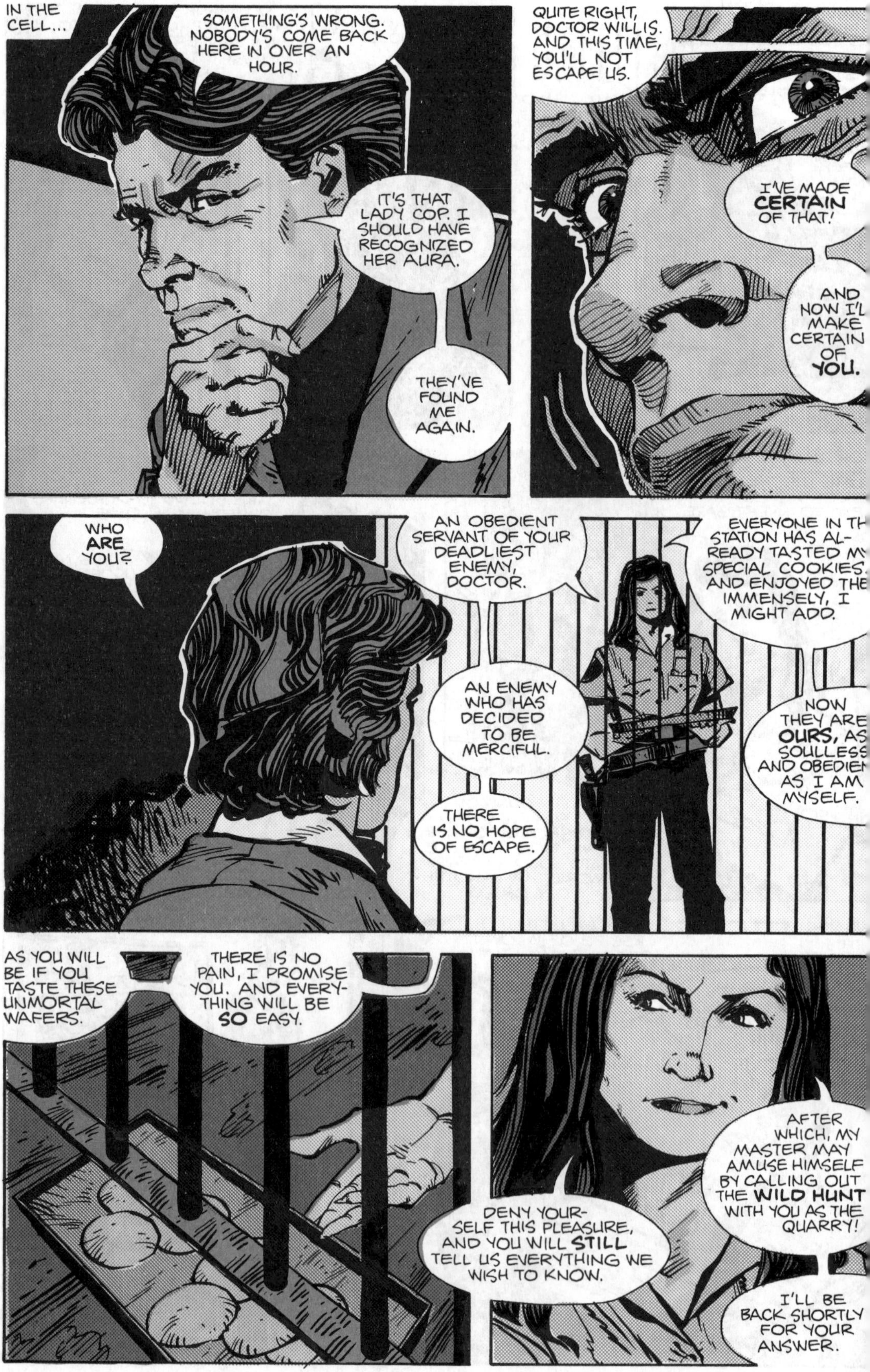
IN THE CELL...
SOMETHING'S WRONG. NOBODY'S COME BACK HERE IN OVER AN HOUR.
IT'S THAT LADY COP. I SHOULD HAVE RECOGNIZED HER AURA.
THEY'VE FOUND ME AGAIN.
QUITE RIGHT, DOCTOR WILLIS. AND THIS TIME, YOU'LL NOT ESCAPE US.
I'VE MADE CERTAIN OF THAT!
AND NOW I'L MAKE CERTAIN OF YOU.
WHO ARE YOU?
AN OBEDIENT SERVANT OF YOUR DEADLIEST ENEMY, DOCTOR.
AN ENEMY WHO HAS DECIDED TO BE MERCIFUL.
THERE IS NO HOPE OF ESCAPE.
EVERYONE IN TH STATION HAS AL-READY TASTED M SPECIAL COOKIES. AND ENJOYED THE IMMENSELY, I MIGHT ADD.
NOW THEY ARE OURS, AS SOULLESS AND OBEDIEN AS I AM MYSELF.
AS YOU WILL BE IF YOU TASTE THESE UNMORTAL WAFERS.
THERE IS NO PAIN, I PROMISE YOU. AND EVERY-THING WILL BE SO EASY.
DENY YOUR-SELF THIS PLEASURE, AND YOU WILL STILL TELL US EVERYTHING WE WISH TO KNOW.
AFTER WHICH, MY MASTER MAY AMUSE HIMSELF BY CALLING OUT THE WILD HUNT WITH YOU AS THE QUARRY!
I'LL BE BACK SHORTLY FOR YOUR ANSWER.

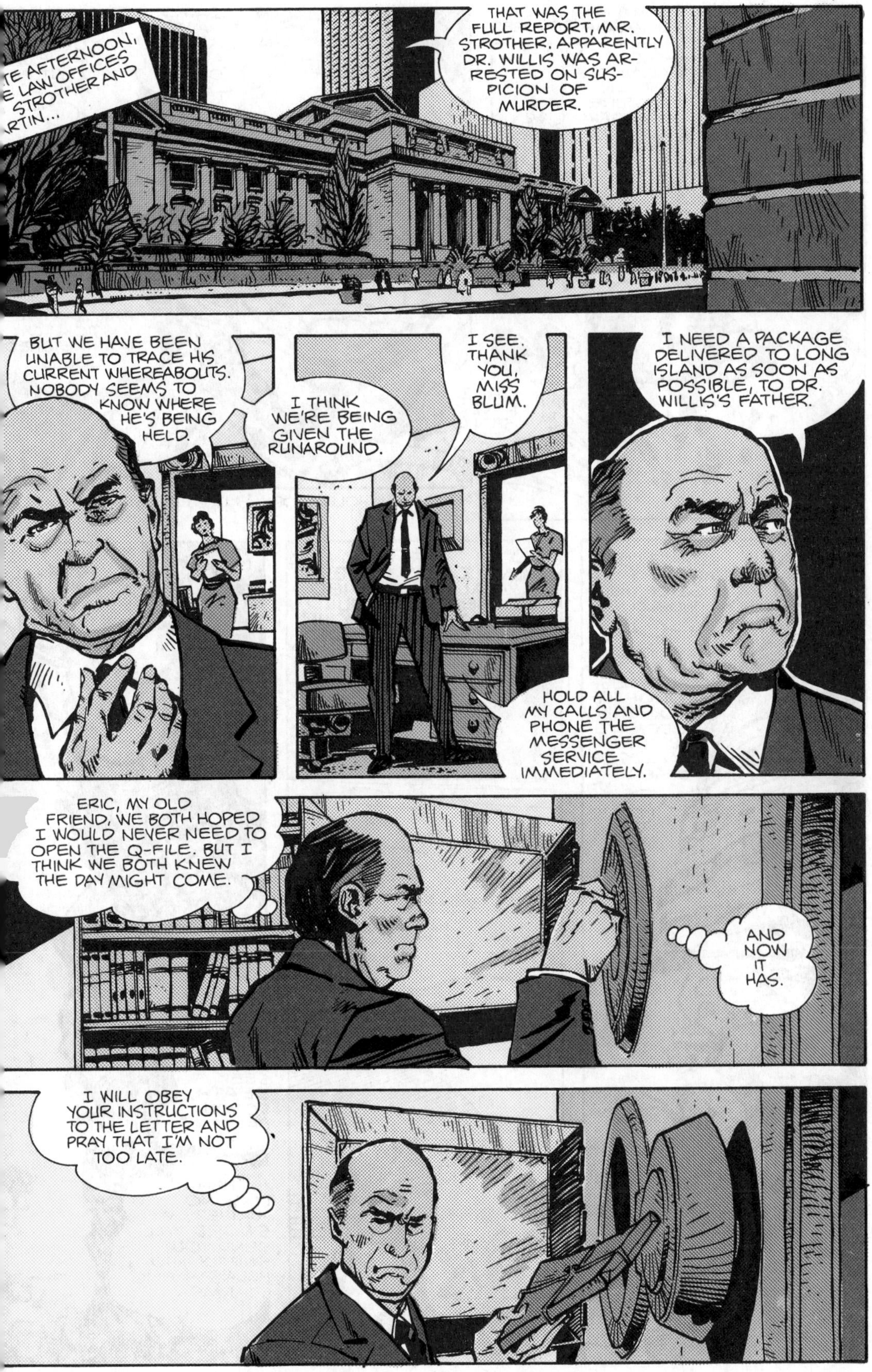
TE AFTERNOON, E LAW OFFICES STROTHER AND ARTIN...
THAT WAS THE FULL REPORT, MR. STROTHER. APPARENTLY DR. WILLIS WAS ARRESTED ON SUSPICION OF MURDER.
BUT WE HAVE BEEN UNABLE TO TRACE HIS CURRENT WHEREABOUTS. NOBODY SEEMS TO KNOW WHERE HE'S BEING HELD.
I THINK WE'RE BEING GIVEN THE RUNAROUND.
I SEE. THANK YOU, MISS BLUM.
I NEED A PACKAGE DELIVERED TO LONG ISLAND AS SOON AS POSSIBLE, TO DR. WILLIS'S FATHER.
HOLD ALL MY CALLS AND PHONE THE MESSENGER SERVICE IMMEDIATELY.
ERIC, MY OLD FRIEND, WE BOTH HOPED I WOULD NEVER NEED TO OPEN THE Q-FILE. BUT I THINK WE BOTH KNEW THE DAY MIGHT COME.
AND NOW IT HAS.
I WILL OBEY YOUR INSTRUCTIONS TO THE LETTER AND PRAY THAT I'M NOT TOO LATE.

MEANWHILE, IN A FAR DISTANT CORNER OF THE FABULOUS REALM OF **ASGARD**, DEEP IN THE VAST WASTES...

HOME, NOBLE SILVERHOOF, HOME! YOU HAVE SERVED ME WELL AND SHOULD NOT SHARE MY FATE.

SEEK AGAIN THE GREEN PASTURES OF ASGARD AND LIVE FREE...

...AS I NEVER SHALL.

I, WHO HAVE **BROKEN** ALL MY OATHS...

...WHO, AGAIN, TOOK THE LIVES OF COUNTLESS DEMONS...

...AND WHO, IN MY TRUST AS AN AMBASSADOR, **SLEW** THE ADOPTED SON OF ODIN, **LOKI**...

...WHEN I FAILED IN MY MISSION TO THAT WRETCHED GOD.*

*NOT THE WHOLE STORY, BUT A FAIR SUMMATION OF THOR #344!

...I HAVE COME TO THE VERY EDGE OF THE WORLD.

BEYOND THIS LAST MOUNTAINOUS BASTION OF THE NORN QUEEN'S KINGDOM LIE ONLY ENDLESS LEAGUES OF DESERT.

AND THERE SHALL THE FATE OF BALDER BE DECIDED.

DEATH! I, WHO HAVE ALREADY DIED BEFORE, WOULD GAZE UPON YOUR VISAGE ONCE MORE!

SO YOU SEEK **DEATH**, DO YOU, BALDER?

THEN LOOK NO FURTHER! MY **SWORD** WILL SEND YOU SWIFTLY INTO HELA'S WAITING ARMS!

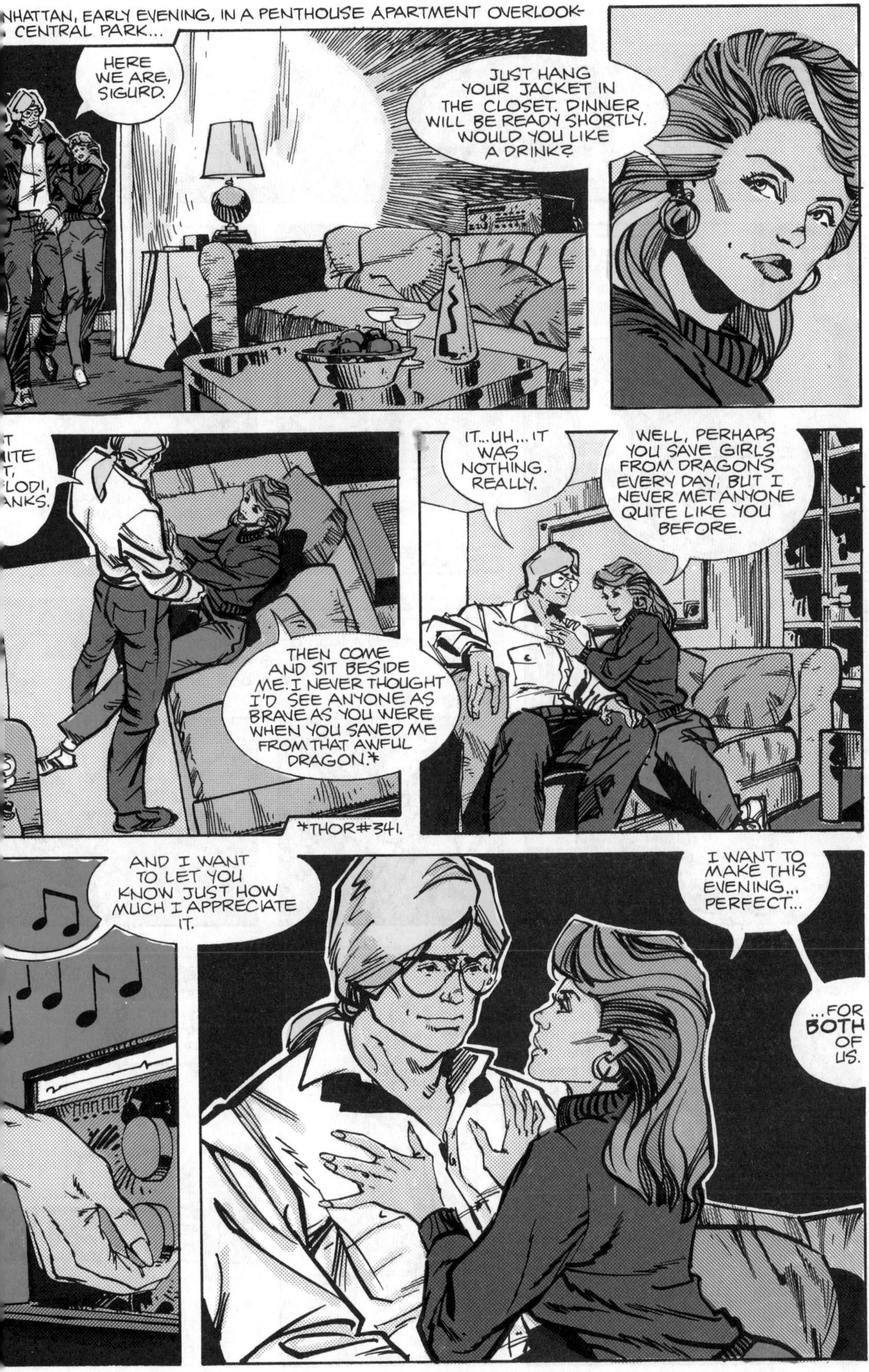

NHATTAN, EARLY EVENING, IN A PENTHOUSE APARTMENT OVERLOOK- CENTRAL PARK...
HERE WE ARE, SIGURD.
JUST HANG YOUR JACKET IN THE CLOSET. DINNER WILL BE READY SHORTLY. WOULD YOU LIKE A DRINK?
T ITE T, LODI, ANKS.
THEN COME AND SIT BESIDE ME. I NEVER THOUGHT I'D SEE ANYONE AS BRAVE AS YOU WERE WHEN YOU SAVED ME FROM THAT AWFUL DRAGON.*
*THOR #341.
IT...UH... IT WAS NOTHING. REALLY.
WELL, PERHAPS YOU SAVE GIRLS FROM DRAGONS EVERY DAY, BUT I NEVER MET ANYONE QUITE LIKE YOU BEFORE.
AND I WANT TO LET YOU KNOW JUST HOW MUCH I APPRECIATE IT.
I WANT TO MAKE THIS EVENING... PERFECT...
...FOR BOTH OF US.

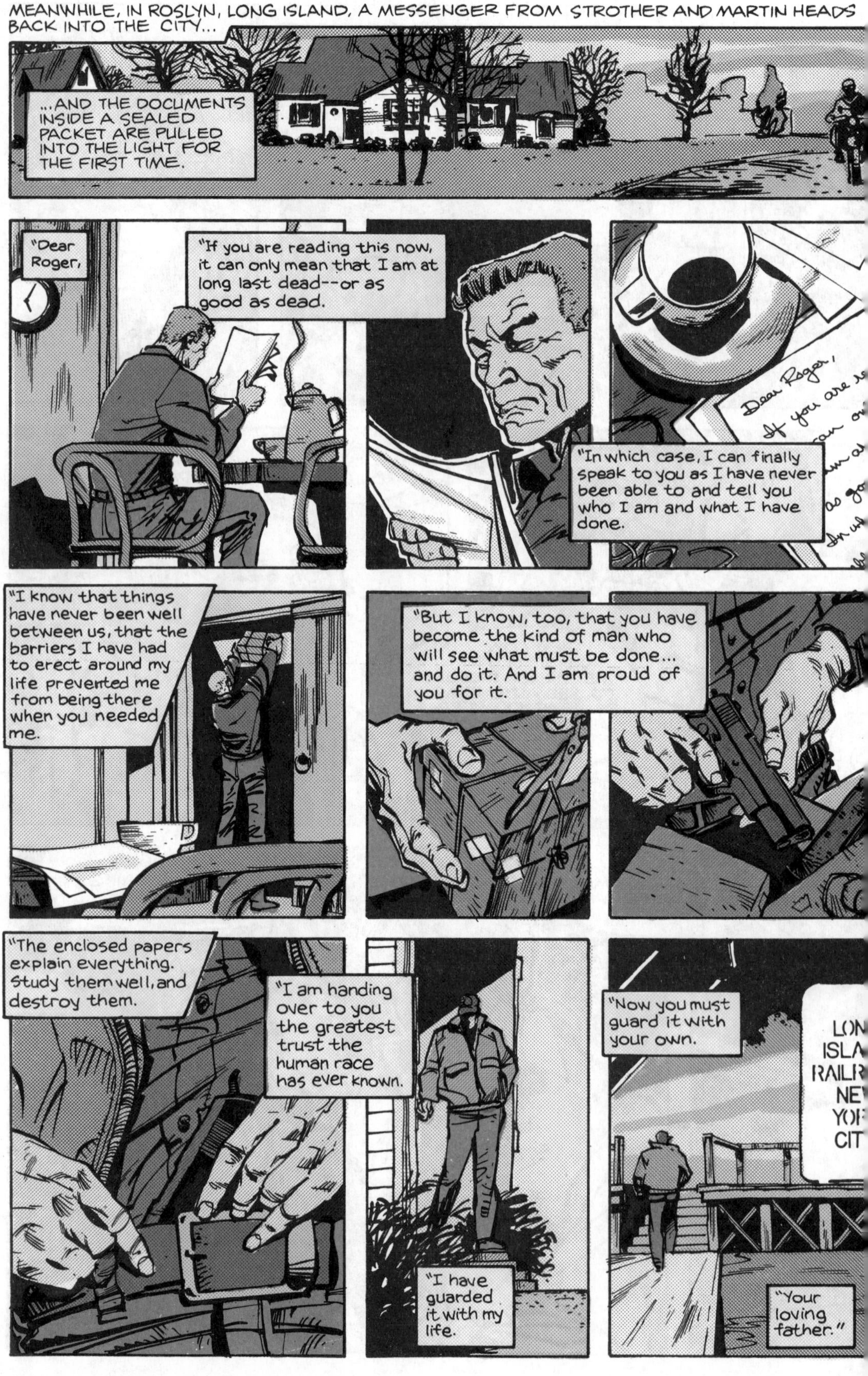
MEANWHILE, IN ROSLYN, LONG ISLAND, A MESSENGER FROM STROTHER AND MARTIN HEADS BACK INTO THE CITY...
...AND THE DOCUMENTS INSIDE A SEALED PACKET ARE PULLED INTO THE LIGHT FOR THE FIRST TIME.
"Dear Roger,
"If you are reading this now, it can only mean that I am at long last dead--or as good as dead.
"In which case, I can finally speak to you as I have never been able to and tell you who I am and what I have done.
"I know that things have never been well between us, that the barriers I have had to erect around my life prevented me from being there when you needed me.
"But I know, too, that you have become the kind of man who will see what must be done... and do it. And I am proud of you for it.
"The enclosed papers explain everything. Study them well, and destroy them.
"I am handing over to you the greatest trust the human race has ever known.
"I have guarded it with my life.
"Now you must guard it with your own.
"Your loving father."

...SEWHERE, IN [A] CELL IN [M]ANHATTAN...

[A]NYTIME NOW, [T]HEY'LL COME [F]OR ME, AND [W]HEN THEY DO, [I]'LL TELL THEM [E]VERYTHING.

I'LL BE FORCED [T]O EVEN IF I DON'T [E]AT THE FOOD.

IF ONLY-- WHAT'S THIS?

A FRENCH FRY! THE ONE I DROPPED THIS MORNING! MAYBE I'VE GOT A CHANCE AFTER ALL.

FIRST, I'LL GET RID OF THESE COOKIES.

[S]HORTLY...

[I] SEE YOU'VE [E]ATEN YOUR SNACK. [E]XCELLENT. STAND [U]P AND COME [O]VER HERE.

NOW THAT YOU'RE ONE OF US, PERHAPS YOU FEEL LIKE TALKING.

I...I DON'T KNOW WHERE TO BEGIN.

WHY NOT START WITH THE CASKET'S LOCATION.

I'D RATHER START WITH BREAKFAST! I HAD FRIES!

WHAT?!

HERE, TRY ONE! THEY'RE DELICIOUS!

MUMPH!

GONE! JUST LIKE ALL OF THEM! AND NOTHING LEFT BUT THE CLOTHES OFF HER BACK...

FAWHAAHHH!

...ALONG WITH MY TICKET OUT OF HERE!

SOON, ON A ROSLYN-BOUND BUS ON THE LONG ISLAND EXPRESSWAY...

NOBODY HOME AT EITHER STROTHER'S OR ROGER'S.

LUCKY OFFICER GRIER HAD ENOUGH MONEY ON HER TO COVER BUS FARE.

IF I CAN JUST REACH ROGER IN TIME, MAYBE TOGETHER WE CAN ESCAPE THE PURSUIT THAT'S CERTAIN TO FOLLOW.

I'VE NO WHERE ELSE TO TURN.

THIS IS IT!

IF THEY CALL OUT THE WILD HUNT WHEN THEY'RE THIS CLOSE, WE'RE BOTH DEAD!

BUS STOP

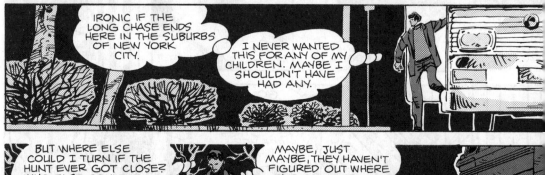

IRONIC IF THE LONG CHASE ENDS HERE IN THE SUBURBS OF NEW YORK CITY.

I NEVER WANTED THIS FOR ANY OF MY CHILDREN. MAYBE I SHOULDN'T HAVE HAD ANY.

BUT WHERE ELSE COULD I TURN IF THE HUNT EVER GOT CLOSE? WHO ELSE COULD I DEPEND UPON TO BECOME THE GUARDIAN OF THE CASKET?

MAYBE, JUST MAYBE, THEY HAVEN'T FIGURED OUT WHERE I'VE GONE YET.

OR MAYBE THEY HAVE!

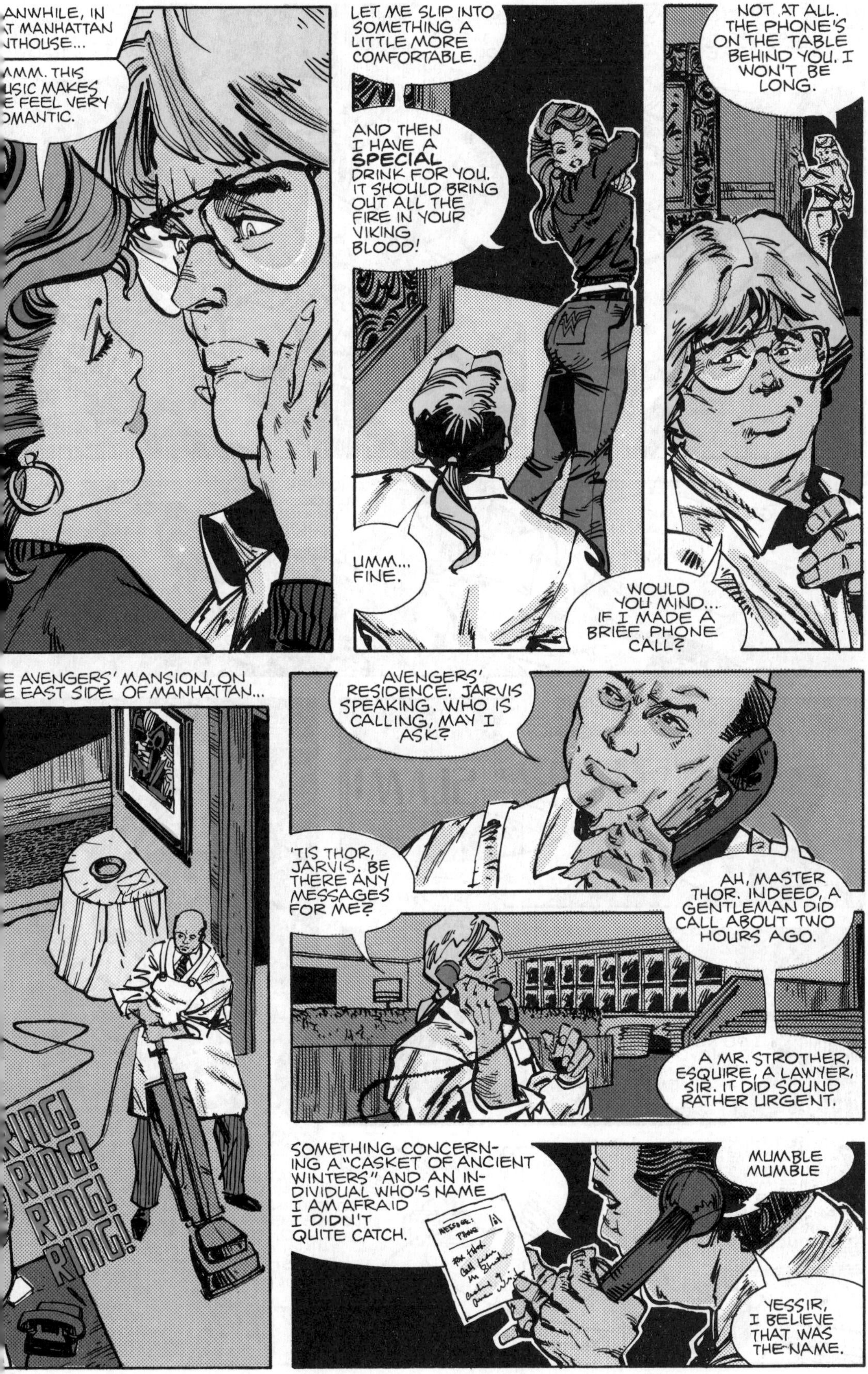
ANWHILE, IN
T MANHATTAN
NTHOUSE...
AMM. THIS
USIC MAKES
E FEEL VERY
OMANTIC.
LET ME SLIP INTO SOMETHING A LITTLE MORE COMFORTABLE.
AND THEN I HAVE A SPECIAL DRINK FOR YOU. IT SHOULD BRING OUT ALL THE FIRE IN YOUR VIKING BLOOD!
UMM... FINE.
WOULD YOU MIND... IF I MADE A BRIEF PHONE CALL?
NOT AT ALL. THE PHONE'S ON THE TABLE BEHIND YOU. I WON'T BE LONG.
E AVENGERS' MANSION, ON
E EAST SIDE OF MANHATTAN...
RING! RING! RING! RING!
AVENGERS' RESIDENCE. JARVIS SPEAKING. WHO IS CALLING, MAY I ASK?
'TIS THOR, JARVIS. BE THERE ANY MESSAGES FOR ME?
AH, MASTER THOR. INDEED, A GENTLEMAN DID CALL ABOUT TWO HOURS AGO.
A MR. STROTHER, ESQUIRE, A LAWYER, SIR. IT DID SOUND RATHER URGENT.
SOMETHING CONCERNING A "CASKET OF ANCIENT WINTERS" AND AN INDIVIDUAL WHO'S NAME I AM AFRAID I DIDN'T QUITE CATCH.
MUMBLE MUMBLE
YESSIR, I BELIEVE THAT WAS THE NAME.

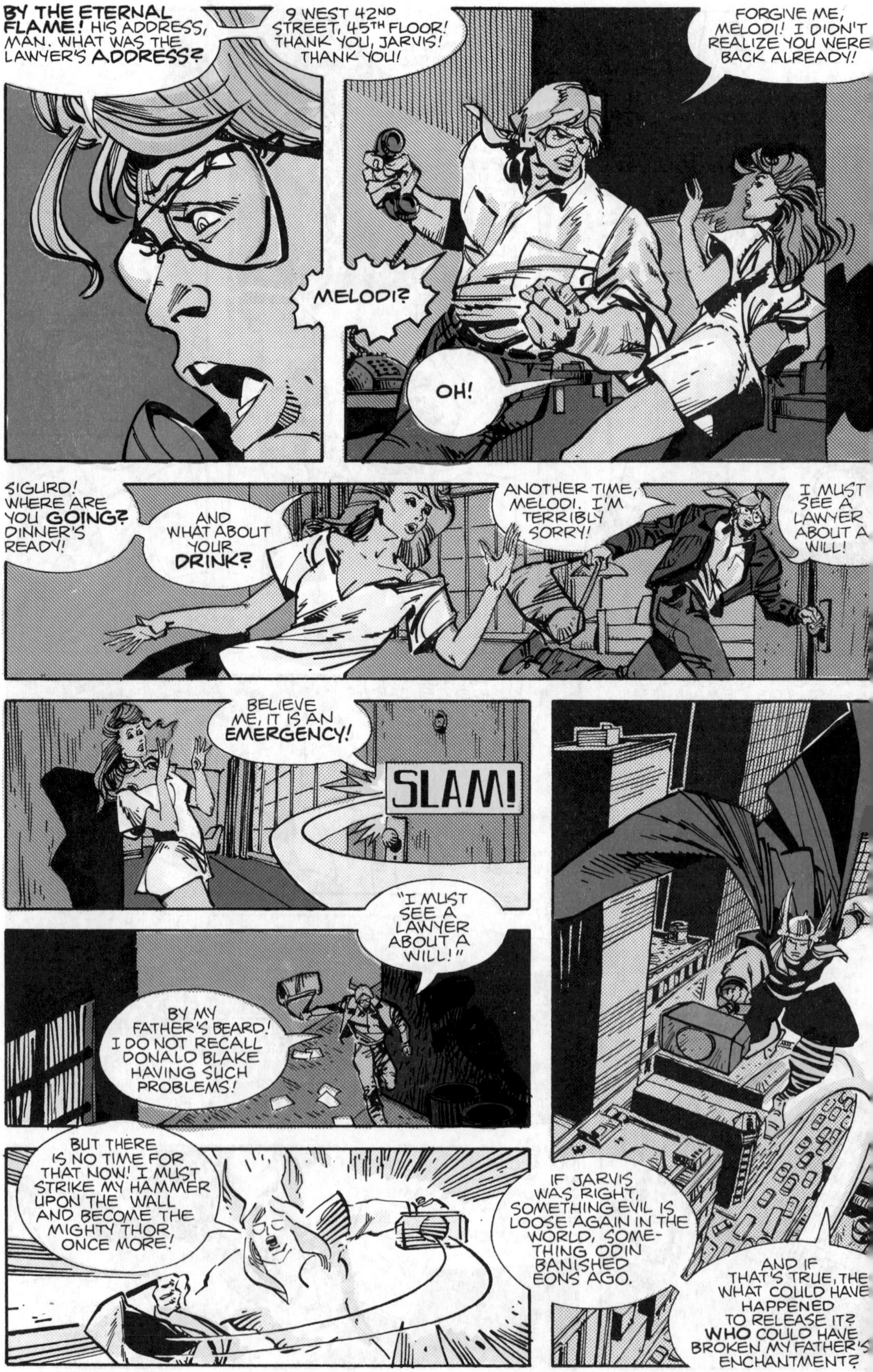
BY THE ETERNAL FLAME! HIS ADDRESS, MAN. WHAT WAS THE LAWYER'S ADDRESS?
9 WEST 42ND STREET, 45TH FLOOR! THANK YOU, JARVIS! THANK YOU!
FORGIVE ME, MELODI! I DIDN'T REALIZE YOU WERE BACK ALREADY!
MELODI?
OH!
SIGURD! WHERE ARE YOU GOING? DINNER'S READY!
AND WHAT ABOUT YOUR DRINK?
ANOTHER TIME, MELODI. I'M TERRIBLY SORRY!
I MUST SEE A LAWYER ABOUT A WILL!
BELIEVE ME, IT IS AN EMERGENCY!
SLAM!
"I MUST SEE A LAWYER ABOUT A WILL!"
BY MY FATHER'S BEARD! I DO NOT RECALL DONALD BLAKE HAVING SUCH PROBLEMS!
BUT THERE IS NO TIME FOR THAT NOW! I MUST STRIKE MY HAMMER UPON THE WALL AND BECOME THE MIGHTY THOR ONCE MORE!
IF JARVIS WAS RIGHT, SOMETHING EVIL IS LOOSE AGAIN IN THE WORLD, SOMETHING ODIN BANISHED EONS AGO.
AND IF THAT'S TRUE, THE WHAT COULD HAVE HAPPENED TO RELEASE IT? WHO COULD HAVE BROKEN MY FATHER'S ENCHANTMENT?

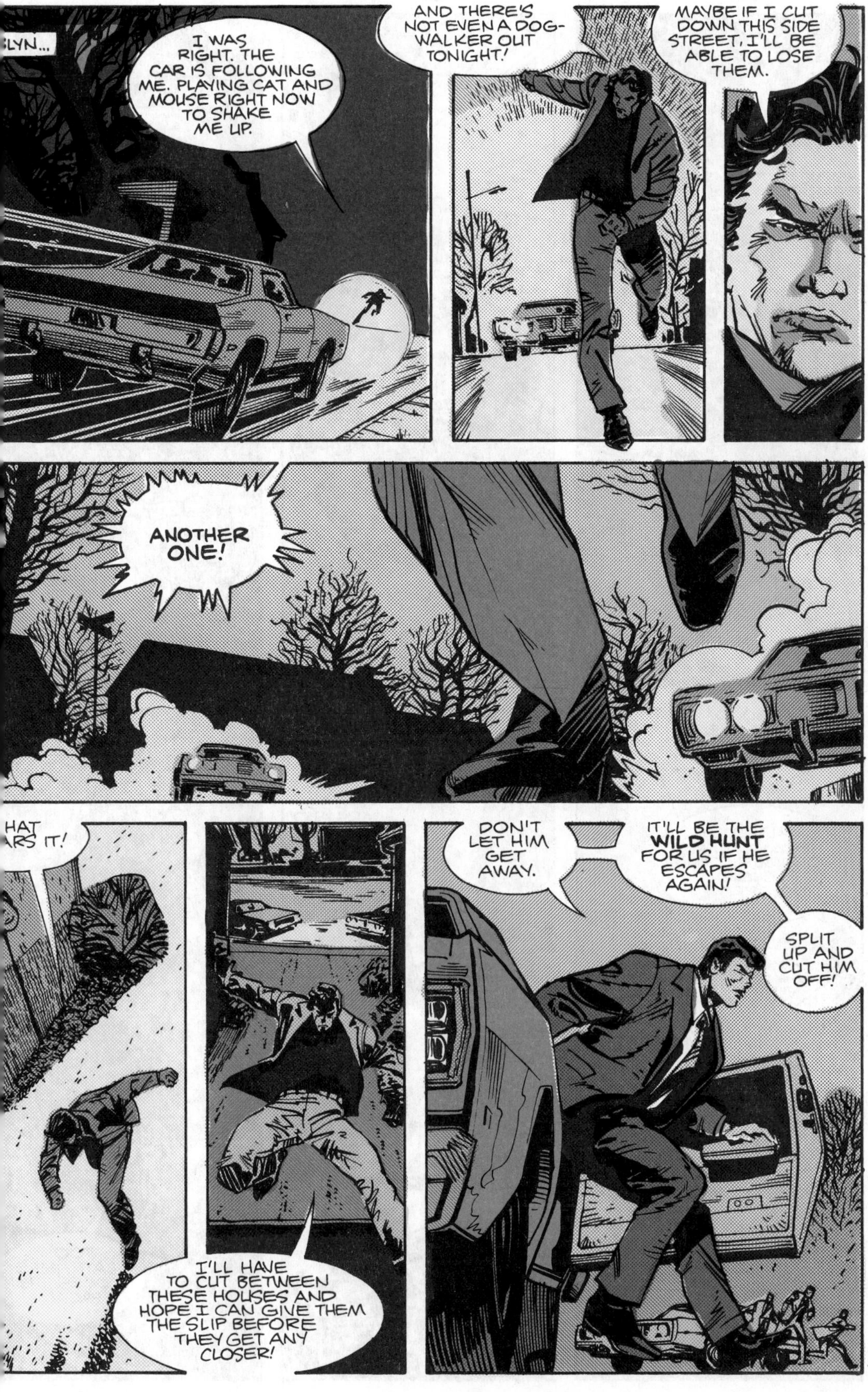

LYN...
I WAS RIGHT. THE CAR IS FOLLOWING ME. PLAYING CAT AND MOUSE RIGHT NOW TO SHAKE ME UP.
AND THERE'S NOT EVEN A DOG-WALKER OUT TONIGHT!
MAYBE IF I CUT DOWN THIS SIDE STREET, I'LL BE ABLE TO LOSE THEM.
ANOTHER ONE!
HAT ARS IT!
I'LL HAVE TO CUT BETWEEN THESE HOUSES AND HOPE I CAN GIVE THEM THE SLIP BEFORE THEY GET ANY CLOSER!
DON'T LET HIM GET AWAY.
IT'LL BE THE **WILD HUNT** FOR US IF HE ESCAPES AGAIN!
SPLIT UP AND CUT HIM OFF!

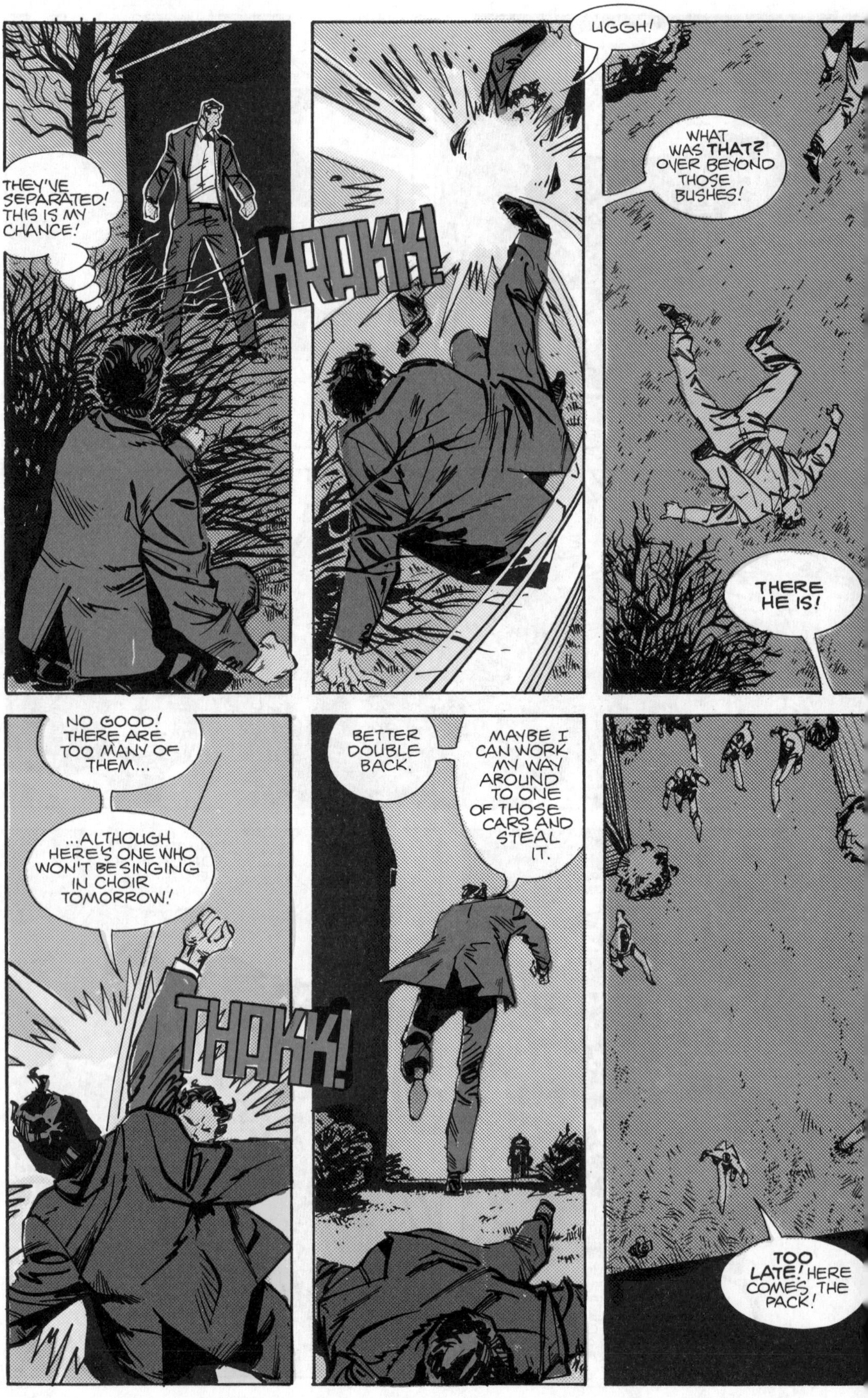

THEY'VE SEPARATED! THIS IS MY CHANCE!
KRAKK!
UGGH!
WHAT WAS THAT? OVER BEYOND THOSE BUSHES!
THERE HE IS!
NO GOOD! THERE ARE TOO MANY OF THEM...
...ALTHOUGH HERE'S ONE WHO WON'T BE SINGING IN CHOIR TOMORROW!
THAKK!
BETTER DOUBLE BACK.
MAYBE I CAN WORK MY WAY AROUND TO ONE OF THOSE CARS AND STEAL IT.
TOO LATE! HERE COMES THE PACK!

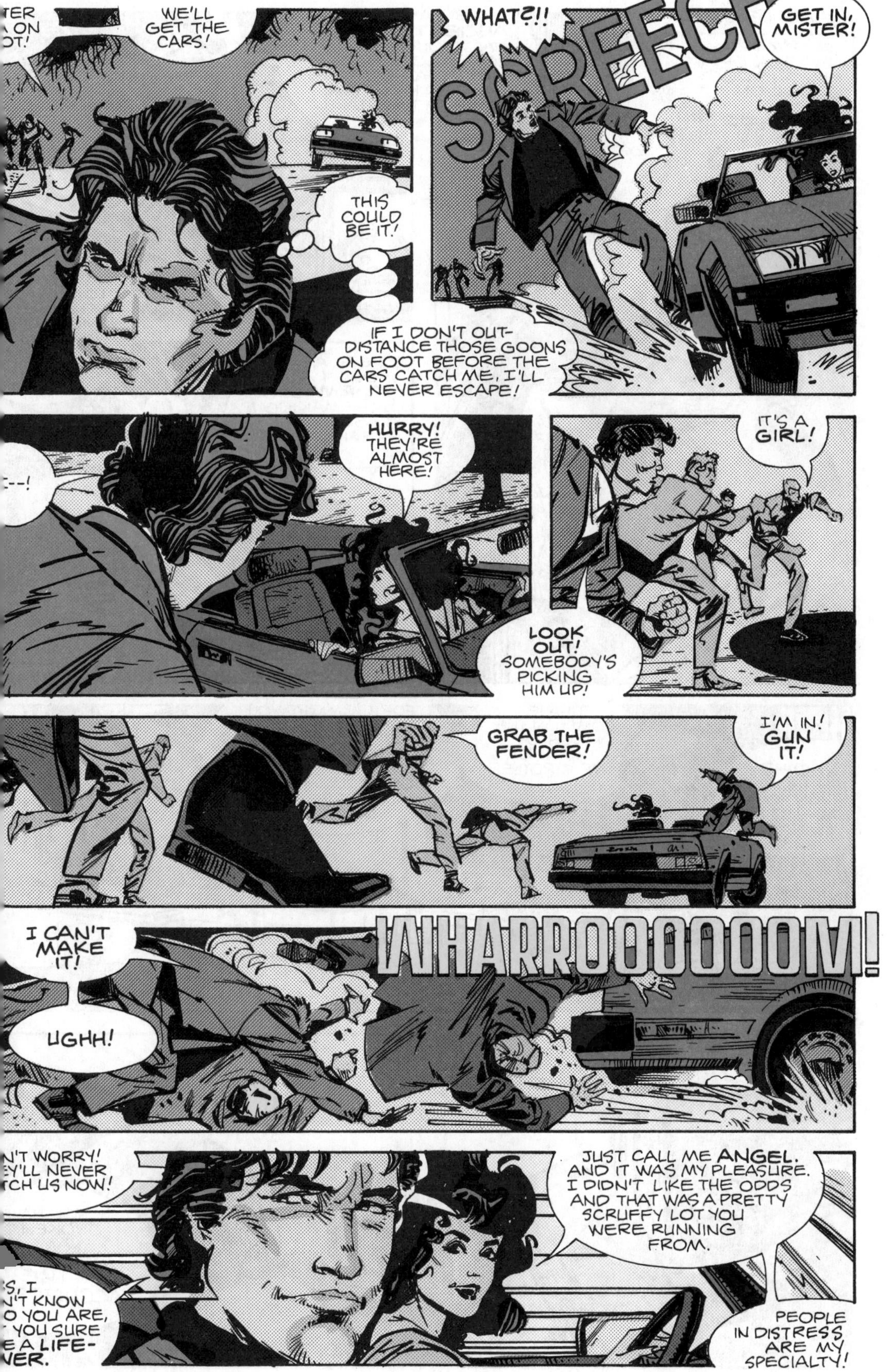
WE'LL GET THE CARS!
THIS COULD BE IT!
IF I DON'T OUT-DISTANCE THOSE GOONS ON FOOT BEFORE THE CARS CATCH ME, I'LL NEVER ESCAPE!
WHAT?!!
SCREECH
GET IN, MISTER!
HURRY! THEY'RE ALMOST HERE!
IT'S A GIRL!
LOOK OUT! SOMEBODY'S PICKING HIM UP!
GRAB THE FENDER!
I'M IN! GUN IT!
WHARROOOOOOOM!
I CAN'T MAKE IT!
UGHH!
N'T WORRY! EY'LL NEVER TCH US NOW!
JUST CALL ME ANGEL. AND IT WAS MY PLEASURE. I DIDN'T LIKE THE ODDS AND THAT WAS A PRETTY SCRUFFY LOT YOU WERE RUNNING FROM.
S, I N'T KNOW O YOU ARE, YOU SURE E A LIFE-VER.
PEOPLE IN DISTRESS ARE MY SPECIALTY!

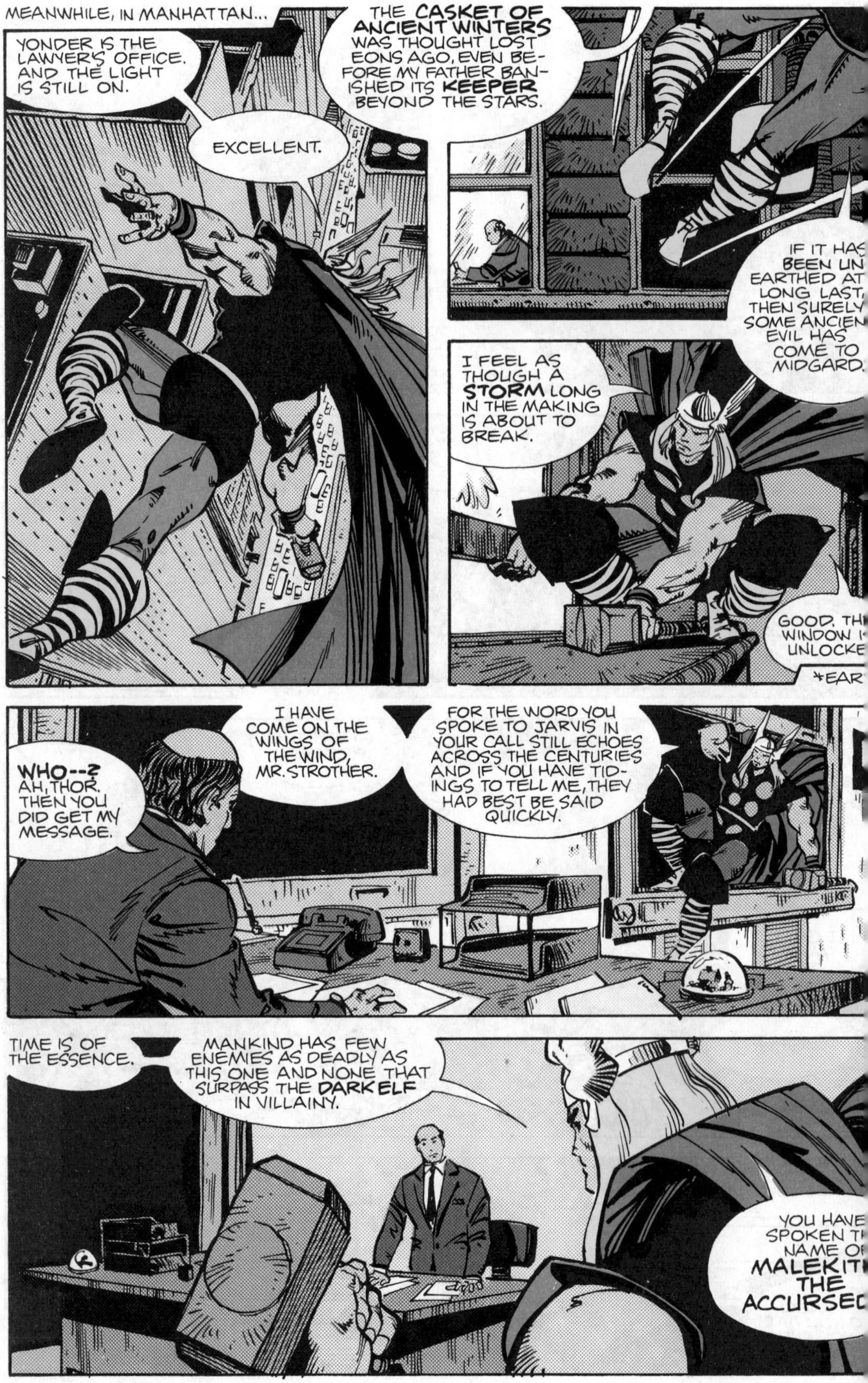

MEANWHILE, IN MANHATTAN...
YONDER IS THE LAWYER'S OFFICE. AND THE LIGHT IS STILL ON.
EXCELLENT.
THE CASKET OF ANCIENT WINTERS WAS THOUGHT LOST EONS AGO, EVEN BEFORE MY FATHER BANISHED ITS KEEPER BEYOND THE STARS.
I FEEL AS THOUGH A STORM LONG IN THE MAKING IS ABOUT TO BREAK.
WHO--? AH, THOR. THEN YOU DID GET MY MESSAGE.
I HAVE COME ON THE WINGS OF THE WIND, MR. STROTHER.
FOR THE WORD YOU SPOKE TO JARVIS IN YOUR CALL STILL ECHOES ACROSS THE CENTURIES AND IF YOU HAVE TIDINGS TO TELL ME, THEY HAD BEST BE SAID QUICKLY.
TIME IS OF THE ESSENCE.
MANKIND HAS FEW ENEMIES AS DEADLY AS THIS ONE AND NONE THAT SURPASS THE DARK ELF IN VILLAINY.

MEANWHILE, ROSLYN...

CAN'T BELIEVE HOW RELAXED I FEEL, ESPECIALLY AFTER SUCH A NARROW ESCAPE.

AND THAT MUSIC ON THE RADIO. IT SEEMS TO FLOW RIGHT THROUGH ME. WHAT STATION IS THAT?

IT IS MUSIC TO SOOTH THE SOUL. TO HELP A PERSON GENTLY SAIL AWAY ON THE WINGS OF DREAMS.

IT'S STRANGE, ANGEL. I FEEL AT PEACE WITH YOU, AS IF I'VE KNOWN YOU ALL MY LIFE.

WE'VE... WE'VE NEVER MET BEFORE, HAVE WE?

PERHAPS WE **HAVE**, ERIC, IN DREAMS.

I HAVE BEEN WAITING TO MEET YOU FOR A LONG TIME.

AND YOU HAVE BEEN WAITING TO MEET ME.

I FEEL DIZZY?

WHEN I LOOK AT YOU, I...I THINK YOU'RE RIGHT.

THERE'S SOMETHING ABOUT YOU THAT'S FAMILIAR.

MAYBE IT'S THE MUSIC. IT'S WEAVING THROUGH MY BRAIN. I CAN'T SEEM TO HOLD ONTO MY THOUGHTS...

...BUT I'VE NEVER SEEN A WOMAN MORE BEAUTIFUL.

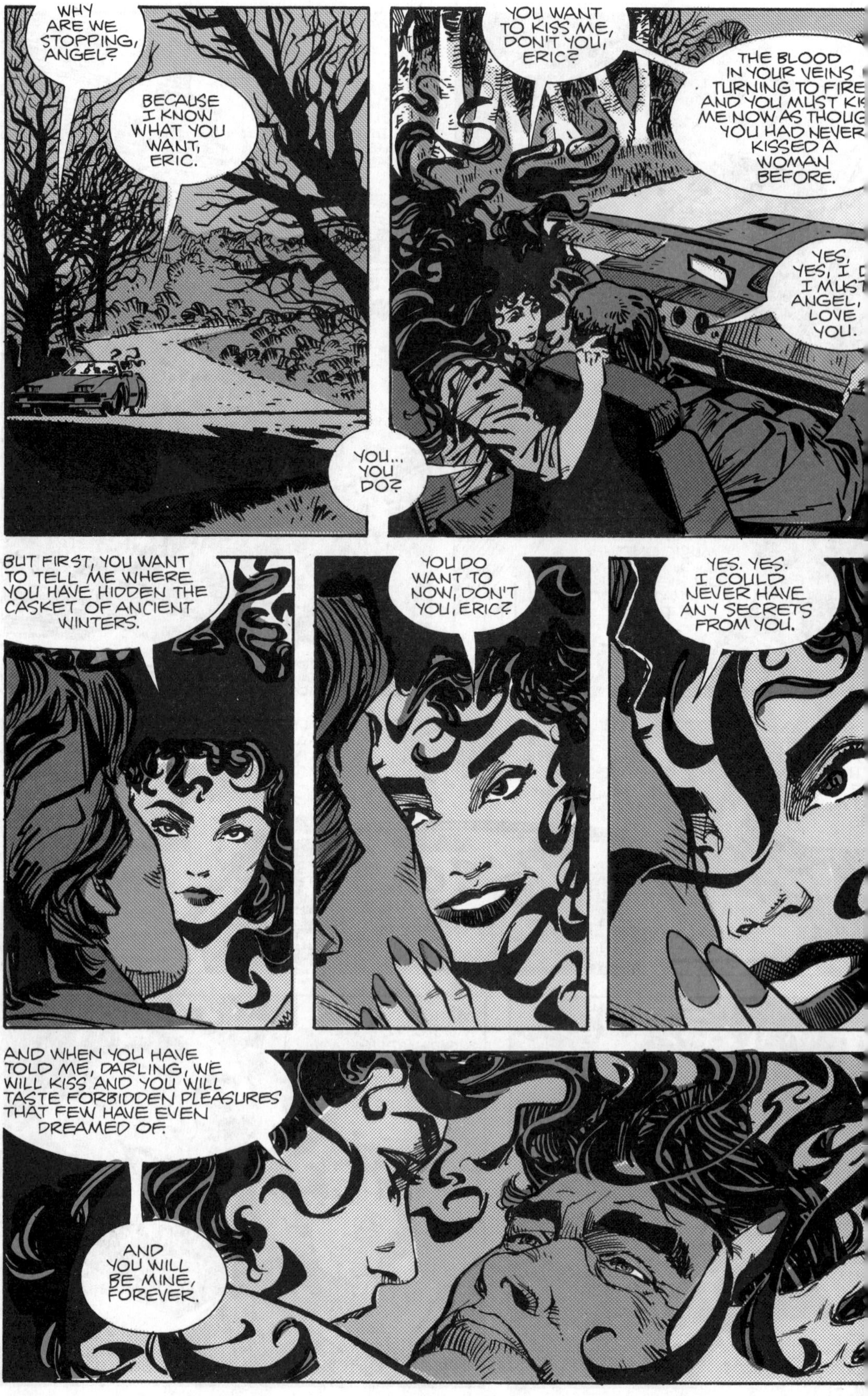
WHY ARE WE STOPPING, ANGEL?
BECAUSE I KNOW WHAT YOU WANT, ERIC.
YOU WANT TO KISS ME, DON'T YOU, ERIC?
THE BLOOD IN YOUR VEINS TURNING TO FIRE AND YOU MUST KI ME NOW AS THOUG YOU HAD NEVER KISSED A WOMAN BEFORE.
YES, YES, I I MUST ANGEL, LOVE YOU.
YOU... YOU DO?
BUT FIRST, YOU WANT TO TELL ME WHERE YOU HAVE HIDDEN THE CASKET OF ANCIENT WINTERS.
YOU DO WANT TO NOW, DON'T YOU, ERIC?
YES. YES. I COULD NEVER HAVE ANY SECRETS FROM YOU.
AND WHEN YOU HAVE TOLD ME, DARLING, WE WILL KISS AND YOU WILL TASTE FORBIDDEN PLEASURES THAT FEW HAVE EVEN DREAMED OF.
AND YOU WILL BE MINE, FOREVER.

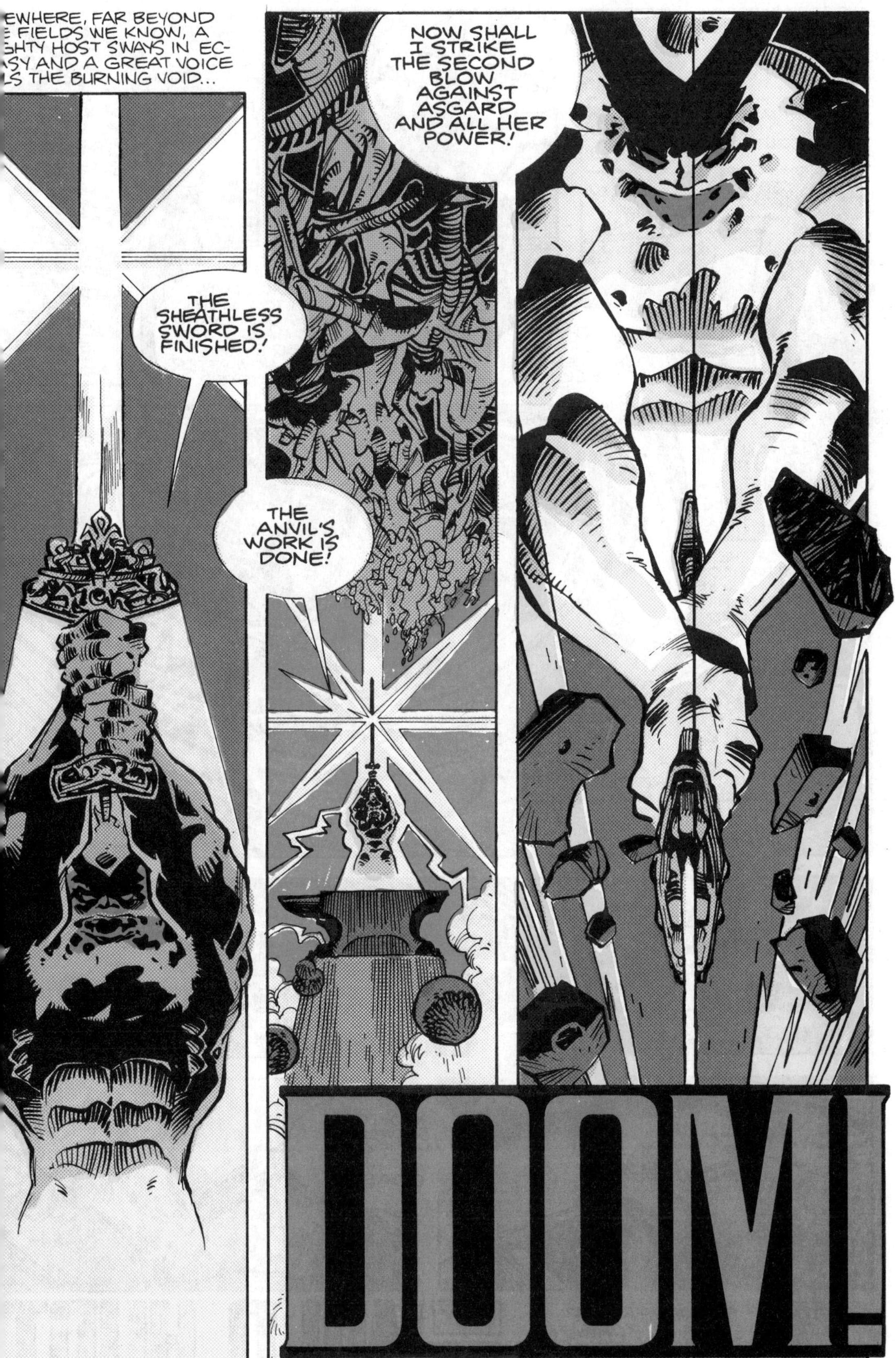
EWHERE, FAR BEYOND
E FIELDS WE KNOW, A
GHTY HOST SWAYS IN EC-
SY AND A GREAT VOICE
S THE BURNING VOID...
THE SHEATHLESS SWORD IS FINISHED!
THE ANVIL'S WORK IS DONE!
NOW SHALL I STRIKE THE SECOND BLOW AGAINST ASGARD AND ALL HER POWER!
DOOM!

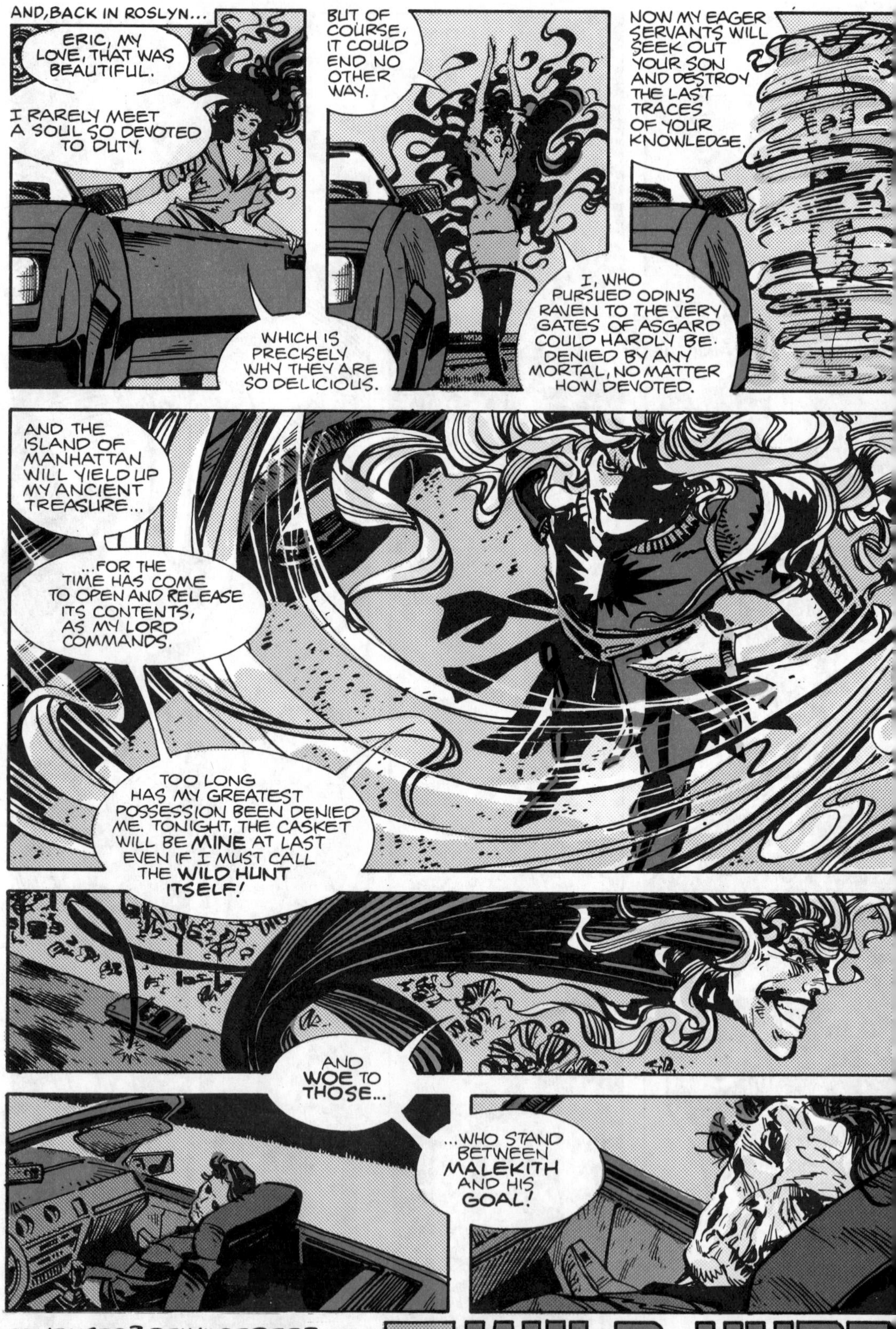
AND, BACK IN ROSLYN...
ERIC, MY LOVE, THAT WAS BEAUTIFUL.
I RARELY MEET A SOUL SO DEVOTED TO DUTY.
WHICH IS PRECISELY WHY THEY ARE SO DELICIOUS.
BUT OF COURSE, IT COULD END NO OTHER WAY.
I, WHO PURSUED ODIN'S RAVEN TO THE VERY GATES OF ASGARD COULD HARDLY BE DENIED BY ANY MORTAL, NO MATTER HOW DEVOTED.
NOW MY EAGER SERVANTS WILL SEEK OUT YOUR SON AND DESTROY THE LAST TRACES OF YOUR KNOWLEDGE.
AND THE ISLAND OF MANHATTAN WILL YIELD UP MY ANCIENT TREASURE...
...FOR THE TIME HAS COME TO OPEN AND RELEASE ITS CONTENTS, AS MY LORD COMMANDS.
TOO LONG HAS MY GREATEST POSSESSION BEEN DENIED ME. TONIGHT, THE CASKET WILL BE MINE AT LAST EVEN IF I MUST CALL THE WILD HUNT ITSELF!
AND WOE TO THOSE...
...WHO STAND BETWEEN MALEKITH AND HIS GOAL!
CONFUSED? BEWILDERED? AFRAID TO EAT A McBURGER AGAIN? DON'T BE! ALL WILL BE EXPLAINED NEXT ISSUE (IF WE CAN FIGURE IT OUT IN TIME)!
NEXT: THE WILD HUNT

Chapter Ten

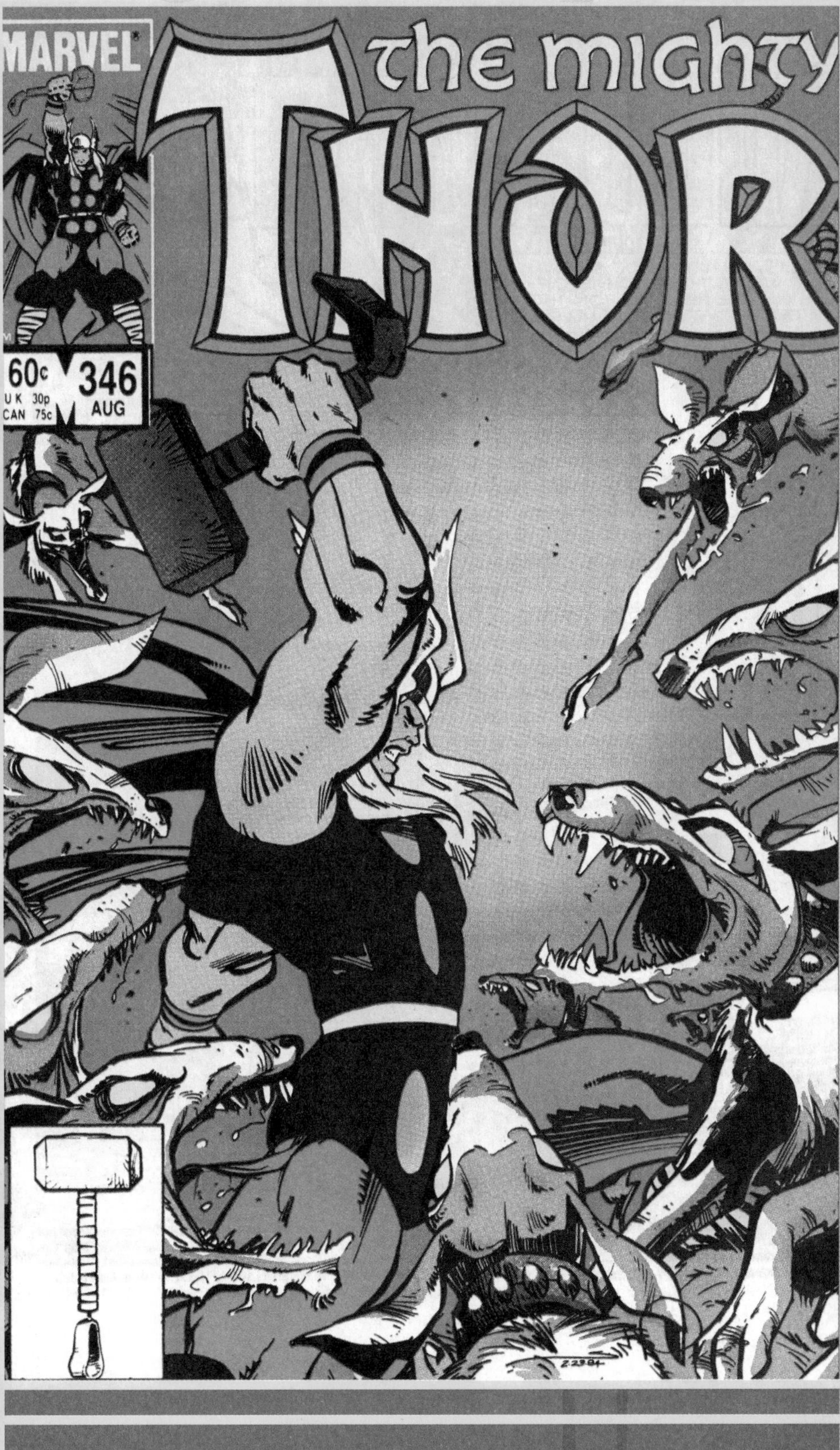
MARVEL
the mighty THOR
60¢ 346 AUG
U K 30p
CAN 75c

STAN LEE PRESENTS: the MIGHTY THOR®

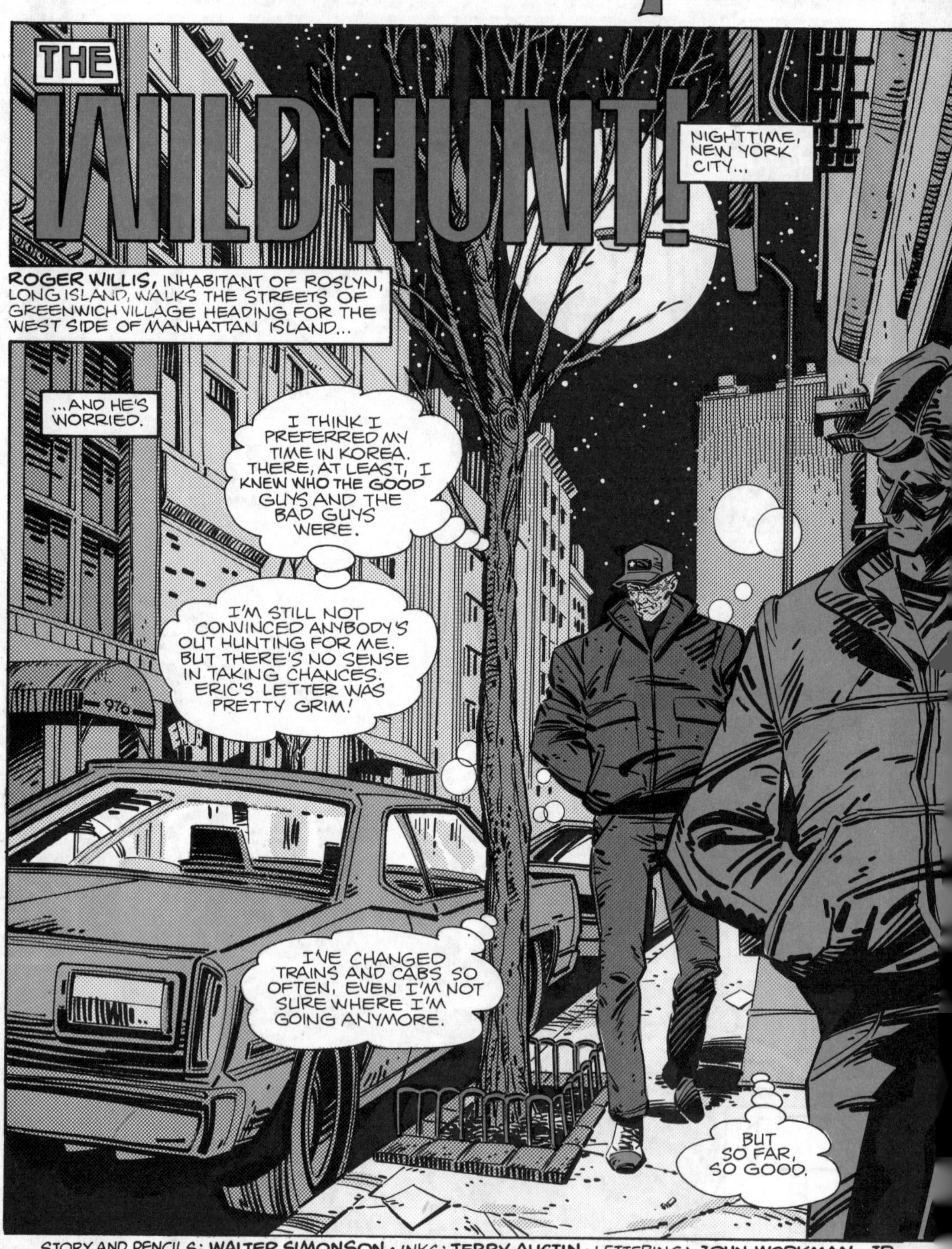
THE WILD HUNT!
NIGHTTIME, NEW YORK CITY...
ROGER WILLIS, INHABITANT OF ROSLYN, LONG ISLAND, WALKS THE STREETS OF GREENWICH VILLAGE HEADING FOR THE WEST SIDE OF MANHATTAN ISLAND...
...AND HE'S WORRIED.
I THINK I PREFERRED MY TIME IN KOREA. THERE, AT LEAST, I KNEW WHO THE GOOD GUYS AND THE BAD GUYS WERE.
I'M STILL NOT CONVINCED ANYBODY'S OUT HUNTING FOR ME. BUT THERE'S NO SENSE IN TAKING CHANCES. ERIC'S LETTER WAS PRETTY GRIM!
I'VE CHANGED TRAINS AND CABS SO OFTEN, EVEN I'M NOT SURE WHERE I'M GOING ANYMORE.
BUT SO FAR, SO GOOD.

STORY AND PENCILS: WALTER SIMONSON • INKS: TERRY AUSTIN • LETTERING: JOHN WORKMAN, JR.
COLORING: CHRISTIE SCHEELE • EDITING: MARK GRUENWALD • EDITOR IN CHIEF: JIM SHOOTER

HEY, MAC!
GOTTA LIGHT?
WHAT?
OH, SURE.
NDA
ARM OUT
NIGHT,
N'T IT?
YEAH, I GUESS SO.
IT'S ABOUT TO GET A LOT HOTTER!
WHA--!
GET HIM! THIS IS THE ONE THE MASTER WANTS!
UHHH!

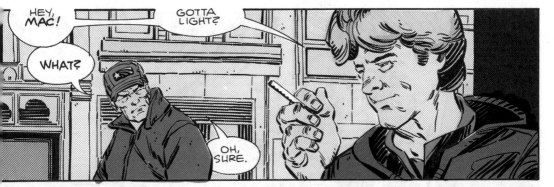

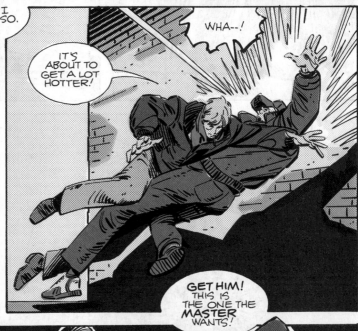

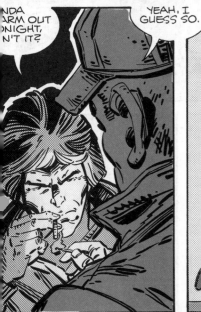

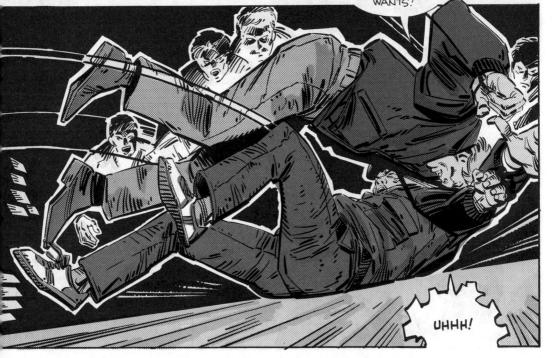

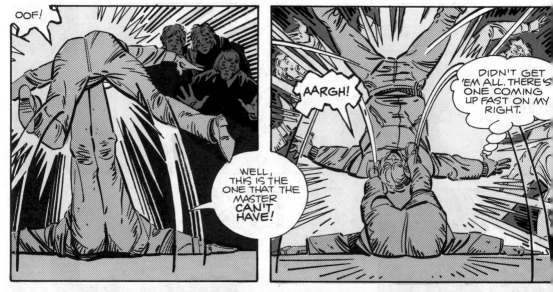

OOF!

WELL, THIS IS THE ONE THAT THE MASTER CAN'T HAVE!

AARGH!

DIDN'T GET 'EM ALL. THERE'S ONE COMING UP FAST ON MY RIGHT.

GAK!

THAT OUGHT TO HOLD 'EM FOR A SECOND.

NOW BEFORE THEY CAN UNTANGLE THEM-SELVES, I'D BETTER SEE ABOUT GETTING SOMEWHERE ELSE FAST!

CAB!

SCREECH

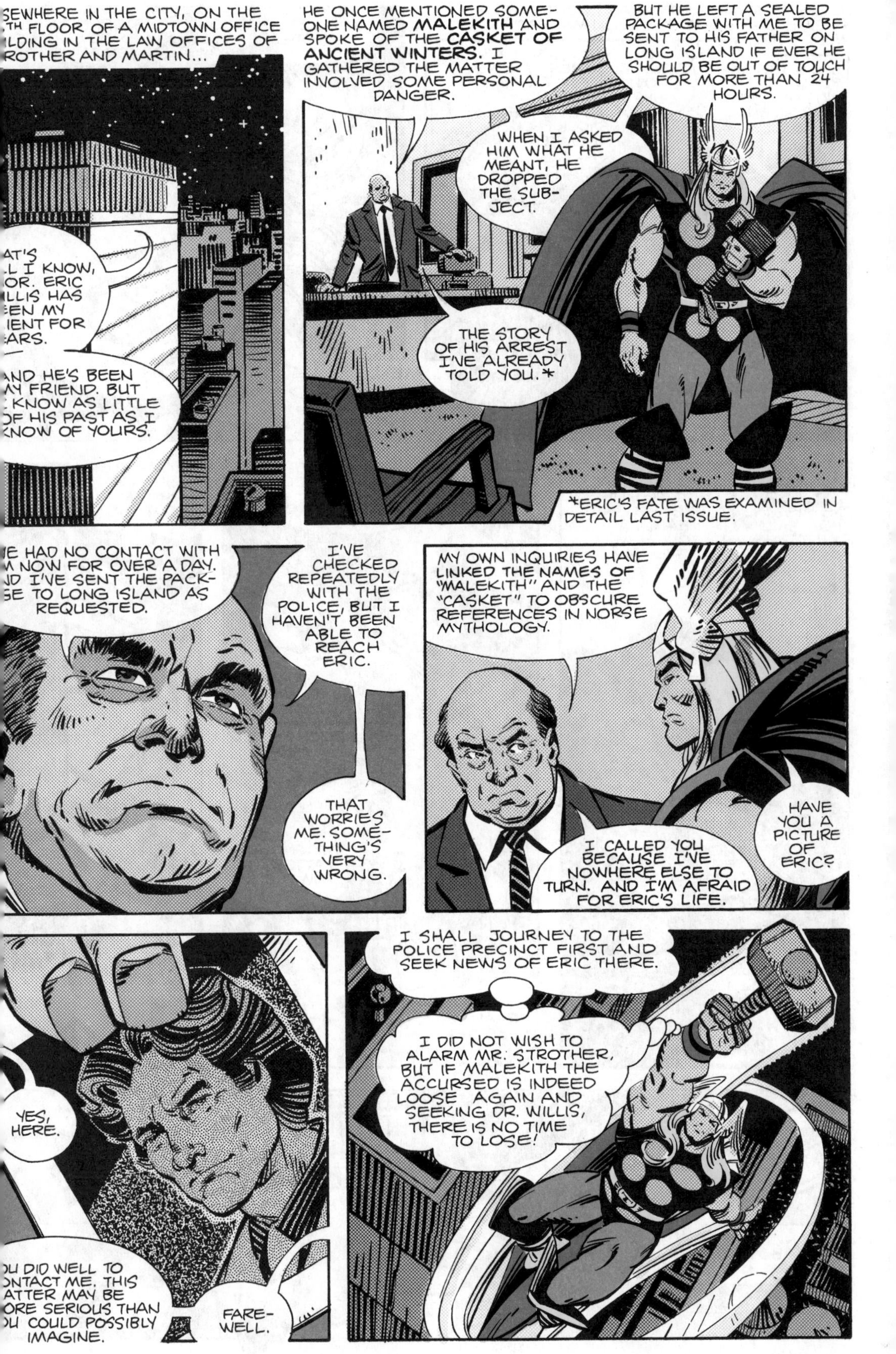
SEWHERE IN THE CITY, ON THE TH FLOOR OF A MIDTOWN OFFICE ILDING IN THE LAW OFFICES OF ROTHER AND MARTIN...
AT'S L I KNOW, OR. ERIC ILLIS HAS EEN MY IENT FOR EARS.
AND HE'S BEEN MY FRIEND. BUT I KNOW AS LITTLE OF HIS PAST AS I KNOW OF YOURS.
HE ONCE MENTIONED SOMEONE NAMED **MALEKITH** AND SPOKE OF THE **CASKET OF ANCIENT WINTERS**. I GATHERED THE MATTER INVOLVED SOME PERSONAL DANGER.
BUT HE LEFT A SEALED PACKAGE WITH ME TO BE SENT TO HIS FATHER ON LONG ISLAND IF EVER HE SHOULD BE OUT OF TOUCH FOR MORE THAN 24 HOURS.
WHEN I ASKED HIM WHAT HE MEANT, HE DROPPED THE SUBJECT.
THE STORY OF HIS ARREST I'VE ALREADY TOLD YOU.*
*ERIC'S FATE WAS EXAMINED IN DETAIL LAST ISSUE.
E HAD NO CONTACT WITH M NOW FOR OVER A DAY. D I'VE SENT THE PACKGE TO LONG ISLAND AS REQUESTED.
I'VE CHECKED REPEATEDLY WITH THE POLICE, BUT I HAVEN'T BEEN ABLE TO REACH ERIC.
THAT WORRIES ME. SOMETHING'S VERY WRONG.
MY OWN INQUIRIES HAVE LINKED THE NAMES OF "MALEKITH" AND THE "CASKET" TO OBSCURE REFERENCES IN NORSE MYTHOLOGY.
I CALLED YOU BECAUSE I'VE NOWHERE ELSE TO TURN. AND I'M AFRAID FOR ERIC'S LIFE.
HAVE YOU A PICTURE OF ERIC?
YES, HERE.
OU DID WELL TO ONTACT ME. THIS ATTER MAY BE ORE SERIOUS THAN OU COULD POSSIBLY IMAGINE.
FAREWELL.
I SHALL JOURNEY TO THE POLICE PRECINCT FIRST AND SEEK NEWS OF ERIC THERE.
I DID NOT WISH TO ALARM MR. STROTHER, BUT IF MALEKITH THE ACCURSED IS INDEED LOOSE AGAIN AND SEEKING DR. WILLIS, THERE IS NO TIME TO LOSE!

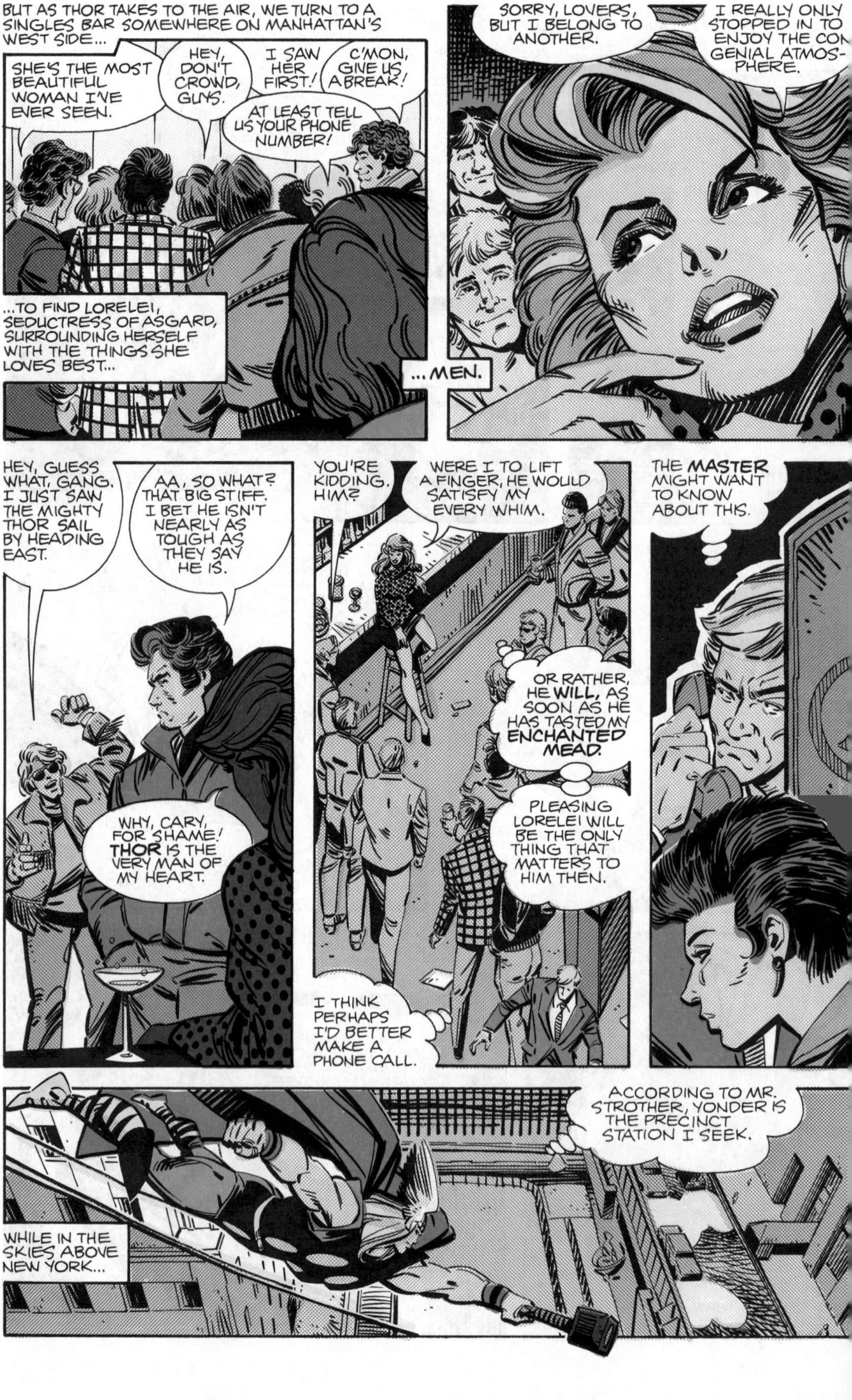

BUT AS THOR TAKES TO THE AIR, WE TURN TO A SINGLES BAR SOMEWHERE ON MANHATTAN'S WEST SIDE...
SHE'S THE MOST BEAUTIFUL WOMAN I'VE EVER SEEN.
HEY, DON'T CROWD, GUYS.
I SAW HER FIRST!
C'MON, GIVE US A BREAK!
AT LEAST TELL US YOUR PHONE NUMBER!
...TO FIND LORELEI, SEDUCTRESS OF ASGARD, SURROUNDING HERSELF WITH THE THINGS SHE LOVES BEST...
...MEN.
SORRY, LOVERS, BUT I BELONG TO ANOTHER.
I REALLY ONLY STOPPED IN TO ENJOY THE CON GENIAL ATMOS- PHERE.
HEY, GUESS WHAT, GANG. I JUST SAW THE MIGHTY THOR SAIL BY HEADING EAST.
AA, SO WHAT? THAT BIG STIFF. I BET HE ISN'T NEARLY AS TOUGH AS THEY SAY HE IS.
WHY, CARY, FOR SHAME! THOR IS THE VERY MAN OF MY HEART.
YOU'RE KIDDING. HIM?
WERE I TO LIFT A FINGER, HE WOULD SATISFY MY EVERY WHIM.
OR RATHER, HE WILL, AS SOON AS HE HAS TASTED MY ENCHANTED MEAD.
PLEASING LORELEI WILL BE THE ONLY THING THAT MATTERS TO HIM THEN.
I THINK PERHAPS I'D BETTER MAKE A PHONE CALL.
THE MASTER MIGHT WANT TO KNOW ABOUT THIS.
WHILE IN THE SKIES ABOVE NEW YORK...
ACCORDING TO MR. STROTHER, YONDER IS THE PRECINCT STATION I SEEK.

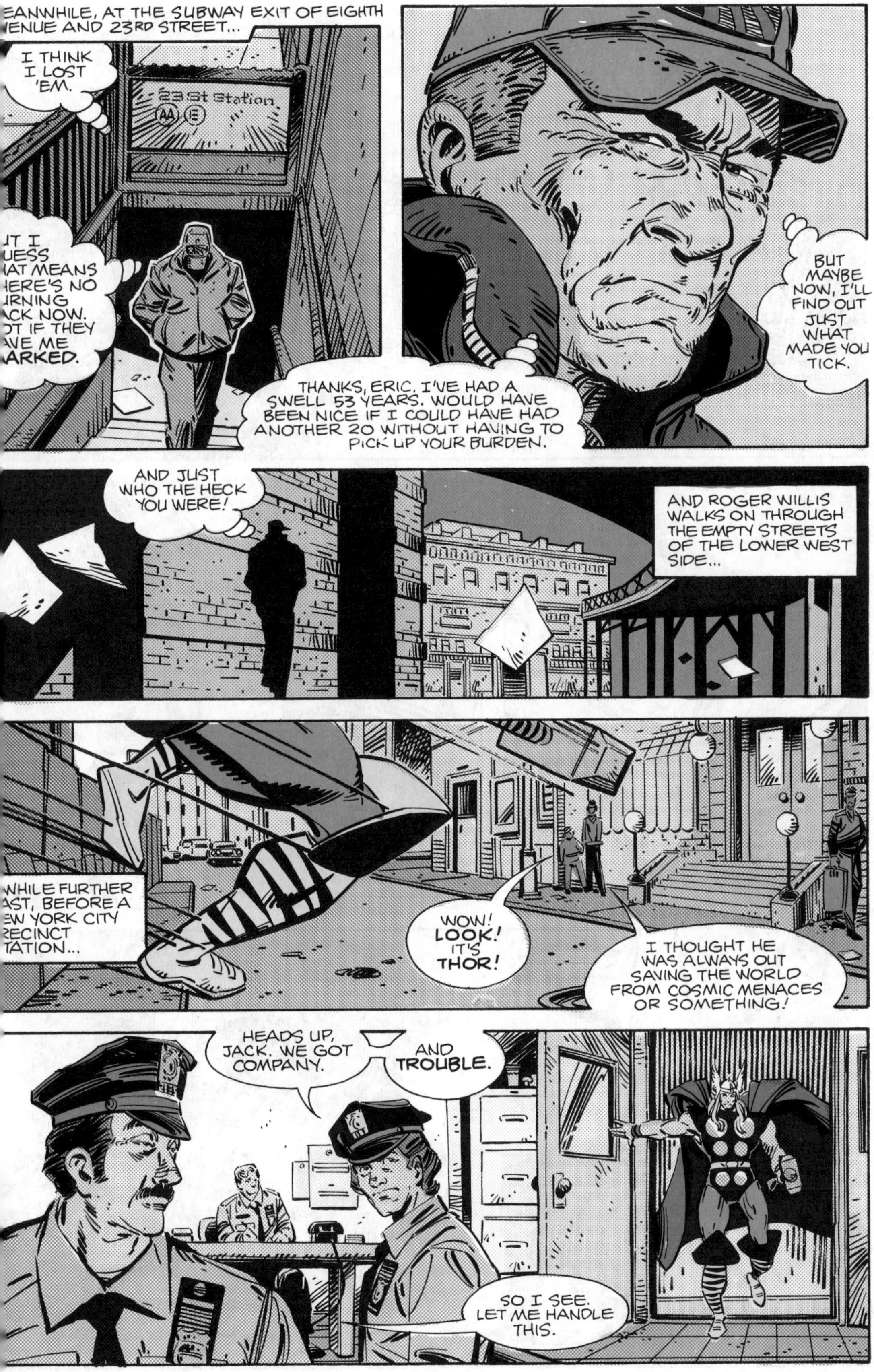
EANWHILE, AT THE SUBWAY EXIT OF EIGHTH
VENUE AND 23RD STREET...
I THINK I LOST 'EM.
23 St Station
AA E
UT I UESS HAT MEANS HERE'S NO URNING ACK NOW. OT IF THEY AVE ME ARKED.
THANKS, ERIC. I'VE HAD A SWELL 53 YEARS. WOULD HAVE BEEN NICE IF I COULD HAVE HAD ANOTHER 20 WITHOUT HAVING TO PICK UP YOUR BURDEN.
BUT MAYBE NOW, I'LL FIND OUT JUST WHAT MADE YOU TICK.
AND JUST WHO THE HECK YOU WERE!
AND ROGER WILLIS WALKS ON THROUGH THE EMPTY STREETS OF THE LOWER WEST SIDE...
WHILE FURTHER AST, BEFORE A EW YORK CITY RECINCT TATION...
WOW! LOOK! IT'S THOR!
I THOUGHT HE WAS ALWAYS OUT SAVING THE WORLD FROM COSMIC MENACES OR SOMETHING!
HEADS UP, JACK. WE GOT COMPANY.
AND TROUBLE.
SO I SEE. LET ME HANDLE THIS.

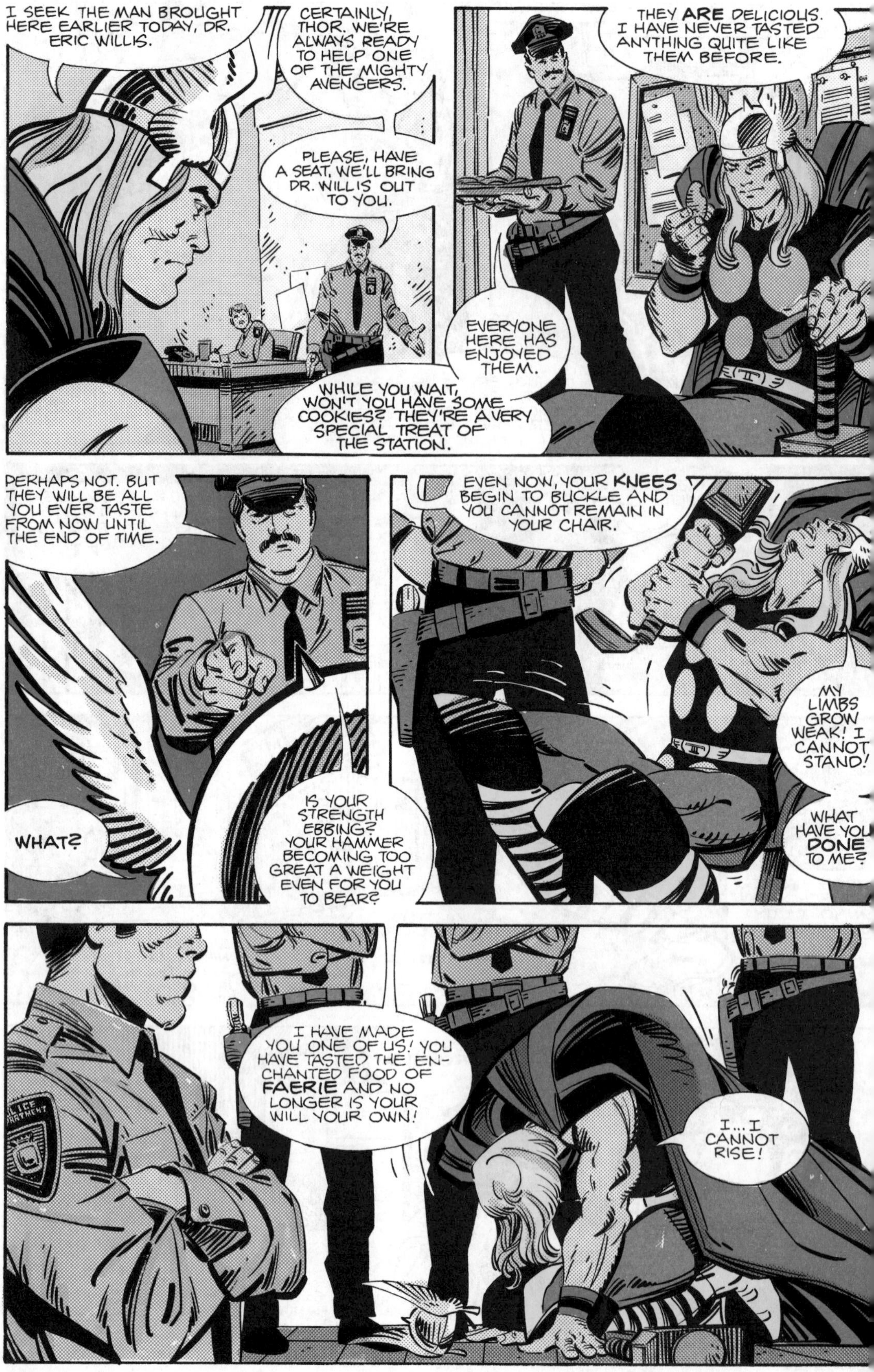
I SEEK THE MAN BROUGHT HERE EARLIER TODAY, DR. ERIC WILLIS.
CERTAINLY, THOR. WE'RE ALWAYS READY TO HELP ONE OF THE MIGHTY AVENGERS.
PLEASE, HAVE A SEAT. WE'LL BRING DR. WILLIS OUT TO YOU.
WHILE YOU WAIT, WON'T YOU HAVE SOME COOKIES? THEY'RE A VERY SPECIAL TREAT OF THE STATION.
THEY ARE DELICIOUS. I HAVE NEVER TASTED ANYTHING QUITE LIKE THEM BEFORE.
EVERYONE HERE HAS ENJOYED THEM.
PERHAPS NOT. BUT THEY WILL BE ALL YOU EVER TASTE FROM NOW UNTIL THE END OF TIME.
WHAT?
IS YOUR STRENGTH EBBING? YOUR HAMMER BECOMING TOO GREAT A WEIGHT EVEN FOR YOU TO BEAR?
EVEN NOW, YOUR KNEES BEGIN TO BUCKLE AND YOU CANNOT REMAIN IN YOUR CHAIR.
MY LIMBS GROW WEAK! I CANNOT STAND!
WHAT HAVE YOU DONE TO ME?
I HAVE MADE YOU ONE OF US! YOU HAVE TASTED THE EN-CHANTED FOOD OF FAERIE AND NO LONGER IS YOUR WILL YOUR OWN!
I... I CANNOT RISE!

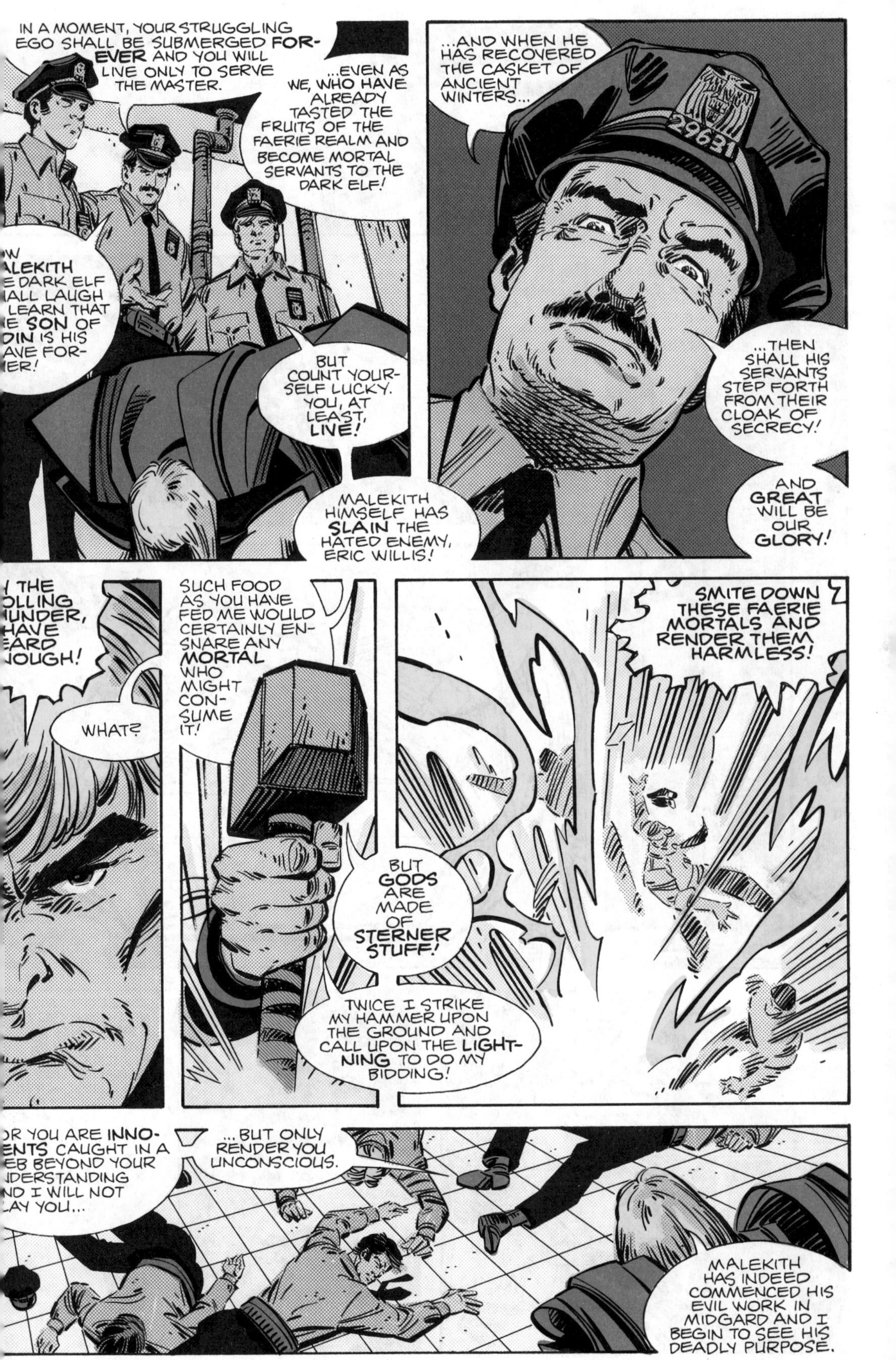
IN A MOMENT, YOUR STRUGGLING EGO SHALL BE SUBMERGED FOR-EVER AND YOU WILL LIVE ONLY TO SERVE THE MASTER.
...EVEN AS WE, WHO HAVE ALREADY TASTED THE FRUITS OF THE FAERIE REALM AND BECOME MORTAL SERVANTS TO THE DARK ELF!
W ALEKITH E DARK ELF ALL LAUGH LEARN THAT E SON OF DIN IS HIS AVE FOR-ER!
BUT COUNT YOUR-SELF LUCKY. YOU, AT LEAST, LIVE!
MALEKITH HIMSELF HAS SLAIN THE HATED ENEMY, ERIC WILLIS!
...AND WHEN HE HAS RECOVERED THE CASKET OF ANCIENT WINTERS...
29631
...THEN SHALL HIS SERVANTS STEP FORTH FROM THEIR CLOAK OF SECRECY!
AND GREAT WILL BE OUR GLORY!
THE OLLING UNDER, HAVE EARD NOUGH!
WHAT?
SUCH FOOD AS YOU HAVE FED ME WOULD CERTAINLY EN-SNARE ANY MORTAL WHO MIGHT CON-SUME IT!
BUT GODS ARE MADE OF STERNER STUFF!
TWICE I STRIKE MY HAMMER UPON THE GROUND AND CALL UPON THE LIGHT-NING TO DO MY BIDDING!
SMITE DOWN THESE FAERIE MORTALS AND RENDER THEM HARMLESS!
OR YOU ARE INNO-ENTS CAUGHT IN A EB BEYOND YOUR NDERSTANDING ND I WILL NOT LAY YOU...
...BUT ONLY RENDER YOU UNCONSCIOUS.
MALEKITH HAS INDEED COMMENCED HIS EVIL WORK IN MIDGARD AND I BEGIN TO SEE HIS DEADLY PURPOSE.

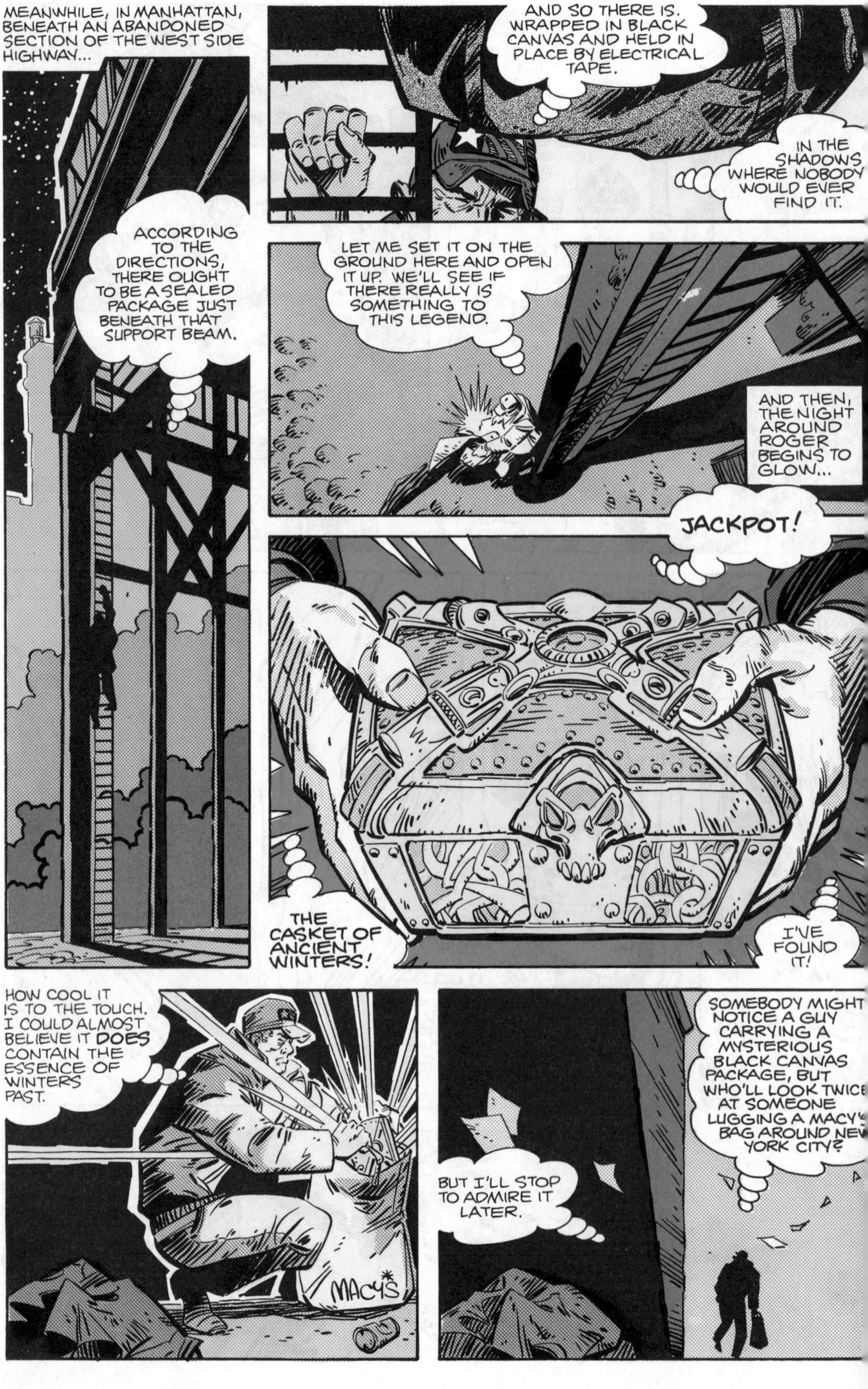
MEANWHILE, IN MANHATTAN, BENEATH AN ABANDONED SECTION OF THE WEST SIDE HIGHWAY...
ACCORDING TO THE DIRECTIONS, THERE OUGHT TO BE A SEALED PACKAGE JUST BENEATH THAT SUPPORT BEAM.
AND SO THERE IS. WRAPPED IN BLACK CANVAS AND HELD IN PLACE BY ELECTRICAL TAPE.
IN THE SHADOWS WHERE NOBODY WOULD EVER FIND IT.
LET ME SET IT ON THE GROUND HERE AND OPEN IT UP. WE'LL SEE IF THERE REALLY IS SOMETHING TO THIS LEGEND.
AND THEN, THE NIGHT AROUND ROGER BEGINS TO GLOW...
JACKPOT!
THE CASKET OF ANCIENT WINTERS!
I'VE FOUND IT!
HOW COOL IT IS TO THE TOUCH. I COULD ALMOST BELIEVE IT DOES CONTAIN THE ESSENCE OF WINTERS PAST.
MACY'S
SOMEBODY MIGHT NOTICE A GUY CARRYING A MYSTERIOUS BLACK CANVAS PACKAGE, BUT WHO'LL LOOK TWICE AT SOMEONE LUGGING A MACY'S BAG AROUND NEW YORK CITY?
BUT I'LL STOP TO ADMIRE IT LATER.

BUT NO SOONER
AS ROGER
TURNED THE
CORNER ON
7TH STREET,
HEADING FOR
THE SUBWAY
STATION...

AT LAST! THE CASKET IS NEARLY MINE AGAIN!

NOW SHALL ALL MANKIND RUE THE DAY WHEN IT WAS STOLEN FROM ME SO LONG AGO!

WAIT! WHAT'S THIS I'VE FOUND?

BLACK CANVAS! THE CASKET'S PROTECTIVE SHEATH!

SOMEONE HAS BEEN HERE BEFORE ME AND SNATCHED THE CASKET FROM MY GRASP ONCE AGAIN!

STILL, THE FAMILY OF ERIC LIVES ON TO PLAGUE ME.

BUT THE CANVAS IS COOL! THE CASKET WAS HERE ONLY MOMENTS AGO!

AND THIS TIME, IT SHALL NOT ELUDE ME! FOR THE SCENT ON THE CANVAS IS FRESH!

NOW SHALL THE HUNTING HORN BE SOUNDED!

TONIGHT, THE WILD HUNT WILL RIDE AND THE CASKET SHALL AT LAST BE MINE!

AND A SINGLE NOTE, UNHEARD BY HUMAN EARS, RINGS IN THE NIGHT AIR.

WHILE AT THAT SELFSAME MOMENT IN THE PRECINCT HOUSE...

I HAVE NOTIFIED THE PROPER AUTHORITIES CONCERNING THESE MORTALS WHO HAVE BEEN LOST TO THE DARK ELF.

I SWEAR THAT WHEN THIS PRESENT BUSINESS IS CONCLUDED...

...I SHALL LEARN THE SECRET OF THE FAERIE ENCHANTMENT AND FREE THESE POOR SOULS FROM BONDAGE...

...BUT NOTHING HERE INDICATES THE WHEREABOUTS OF ROGER WILLIS.

PERHAPS--!

HARK! WHAT IS THIS MY EARS DO HEAR? SOME TRICK OF THE WIND?

NAY! I KNOW THAT SOUND! 'TIS THE HUNTING HORN OF FAERIE!

SOMEONE HATH CALLED THE WILD HUNT! IT CAN ONLY BE MALEKITH!

THEN HIS PREY MUST SURELY BE WITHIN HIS GRASP!

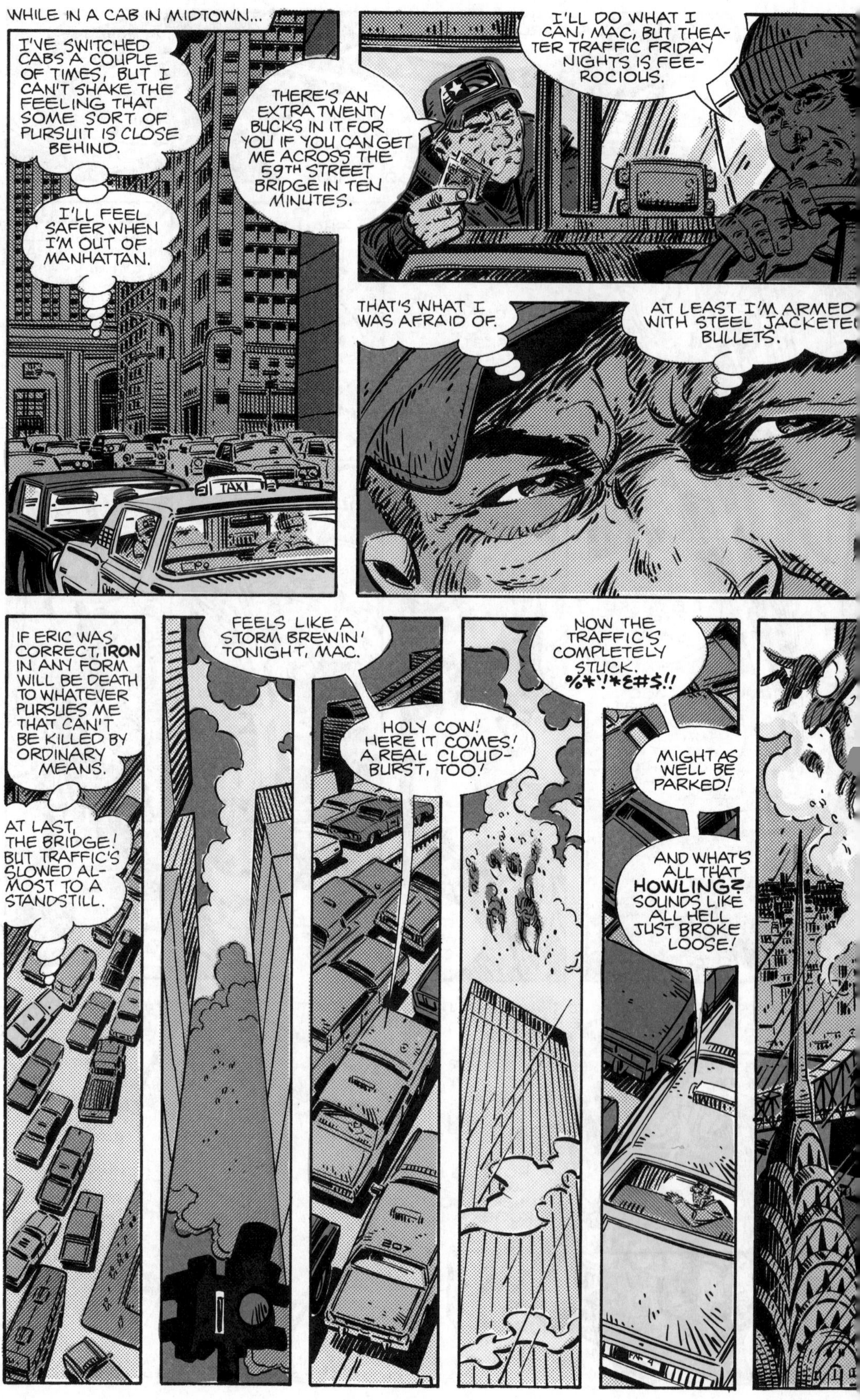
WHILE IN A CAB IN MIDTOWN...
I'VE SWITCHED CABS A COUPLE OF TIMES, BUT I CAN'T SHAKE THE FEELING THAT SOME SORT OF PURSUIT IS CLOSE BEHIND.
I'LL FEEL SAFER WHEN I'M OUT OF MANHATTAN.
TAXI
THERE'S AN EXTRA TWENTY BUCKS IN IT FOR YOU IF YOU CAN GET ME ACROSS THE 59TH STREET BRIDGE IN TEN MINUTES.
I'LL DO WHAT I CAN, MAC, BUT THEATER TRAFFIC FRIDAY NIGHTS IS FEE-ROCIOUS.
THAT'S WHAT I WAS AFRAID OF.
AT LEAST I'M ARMED WITH STEEL JACKETED BULLETS.
IF ERIC WAS CORRECT, IRON IN ANY FORM WILL BE DEATH TO WHATEVER PURSUES ME THAT CAN'T BE KILLED BY ORDINARY MEANS.
AT LAST, THE BRIDGE! BUT TRAFFIC'S SLOWED ALMOST TO A STANDSTILL.
FEELS LIKE A STORM BREWIN' TONIGHT, MAC.
HOLY COW! HERE IT COMES! A REAL CLOUD-BURST, TOO!
NOW THE TRAFFIC'S COMPLETELY STUCK. %*!*£#$!!
MIGHT AS WELL BE PARKED!
AND WHAT'S ALL THAT HOWLING? SOUNDS LIKE ALL HELL JUST BROKE LOOSE!

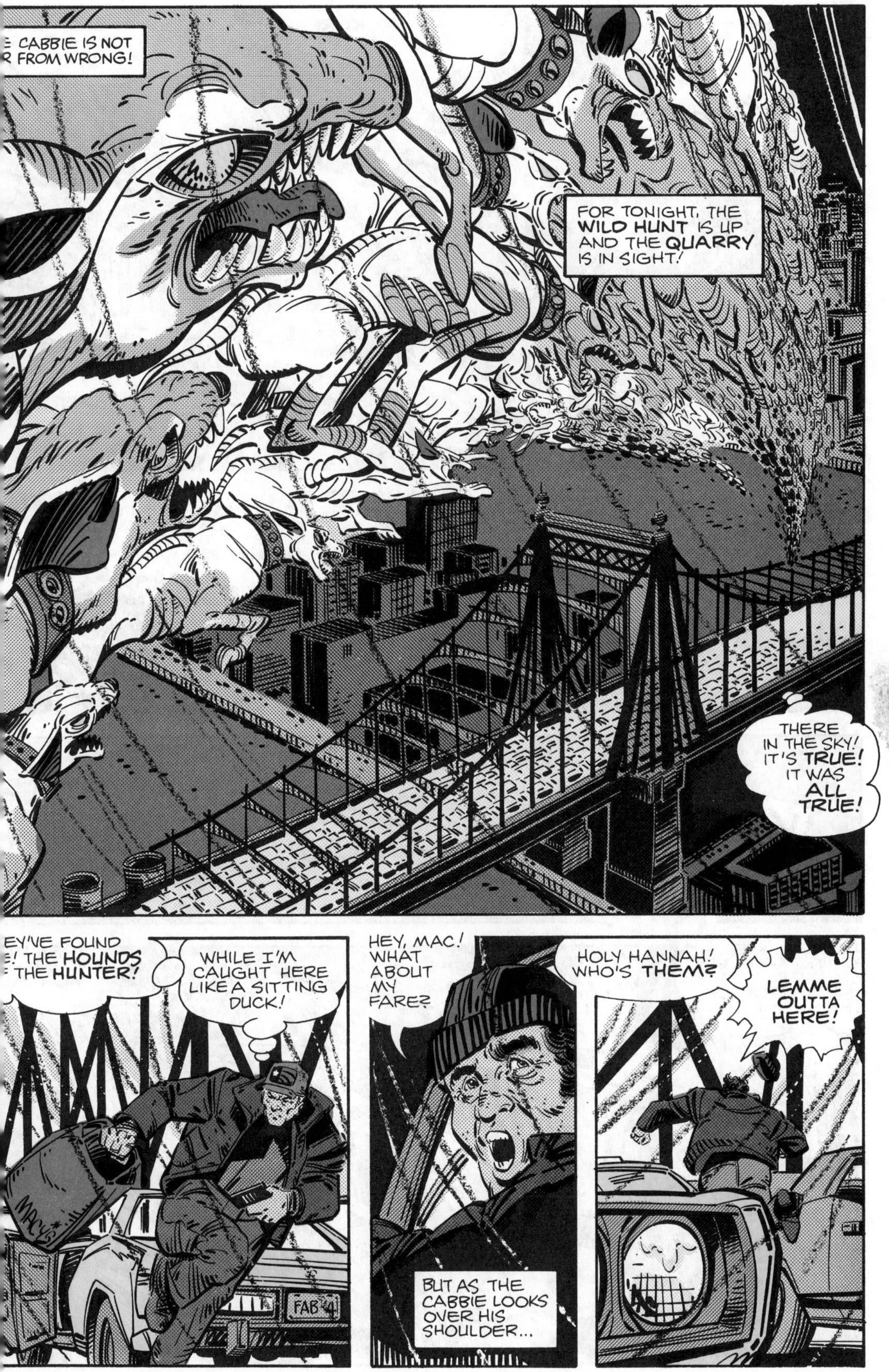
E CABBIE IS NOT
R FROM WRONG!
FOR TONIGHT, THE **WILD HUNT** IS UP AND THE **QUARRY** IS IN SIGHT!
THERE IN THE SKY! IT'S **TRUE!** IT WAS **ALL TRUE!**
EY'VE FOUND E! THE **HOUNDS** F THE **HUNTER!**
WHILE I'M CAUGHT HERE LIKE A SITTING DUCK!
HEY, MAC! WHAT ABOUT MY FARE?
BUT AS THE CABBIE LOOKS OVER HIS SHOULDER...
HOLY HANNAH! WHO'S **THEM?**
LEMME OUTTA HERE!

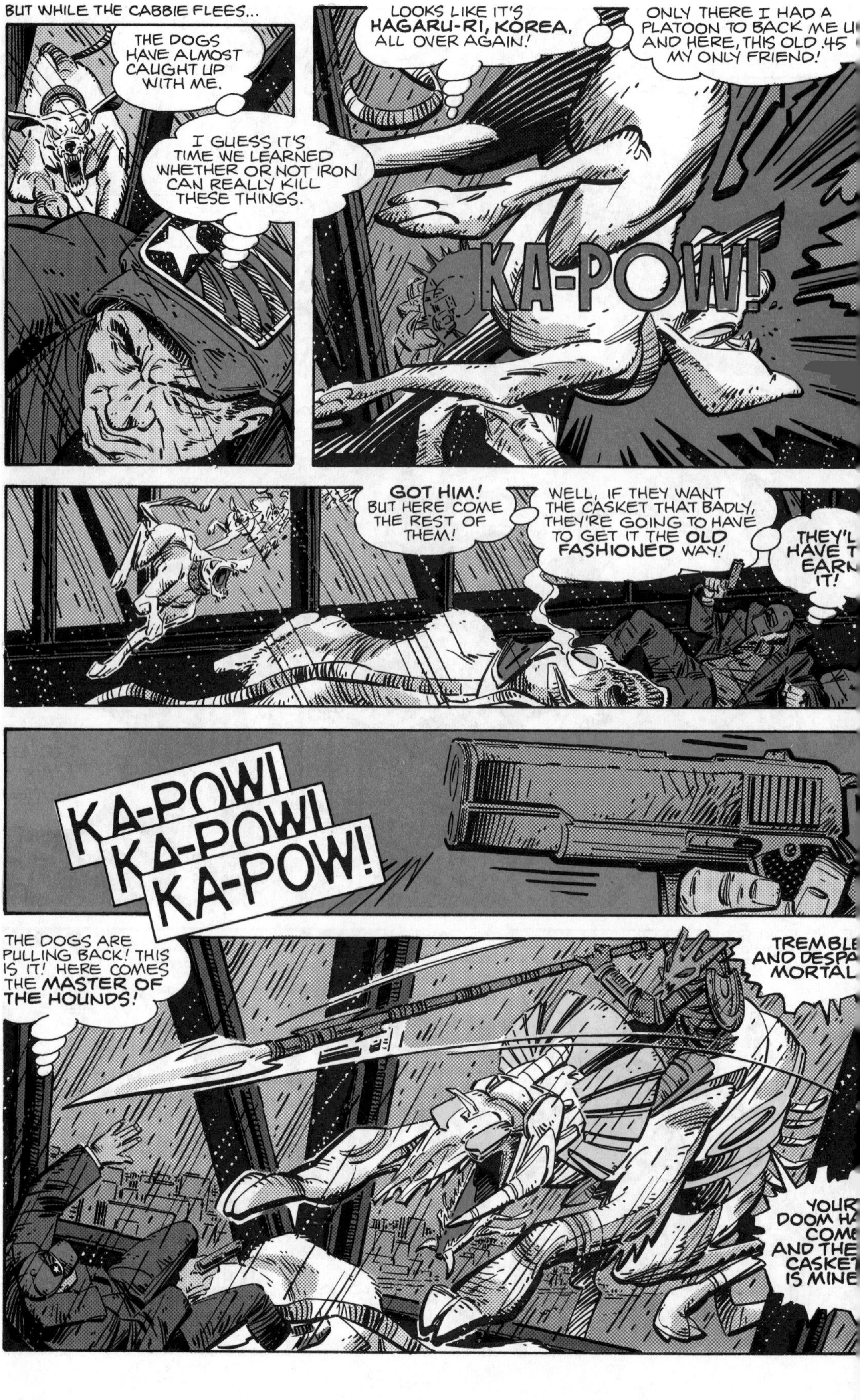
BUT WHILE THE CABBIE FLEES...
THE DOGS HAVE ALMOST CAUGHT UP WITH ME.
I GUESS IT'S TIME WE LEARNED WHETHER OR NOT IRON CAN REALLY KILL THESE THINGS.
LOOKS LIKE IT'S HAGARU-RI, KOREA, ALL OVER AGAIN!
ONLY THERE I HAD A PLATOON TO BACK ME U
AND HERE, THIS OLD .45
MY ONLY FRIEND!
KA-POW!
GOT HIM! BUT HERE COME THE REST OF THEM!
WELL, IF THEY WANT THE CASKET THAT BADLY, THEY'RE GOING TO HAVE TO GET IT THE OLD FASHIONED WAY!
KA-POW! KA-POW! KA-POW!
THE DOGS ARE PULLING BACK! THIS IS IT! HERE COMES THE MASTER OF THE HOUNDS!

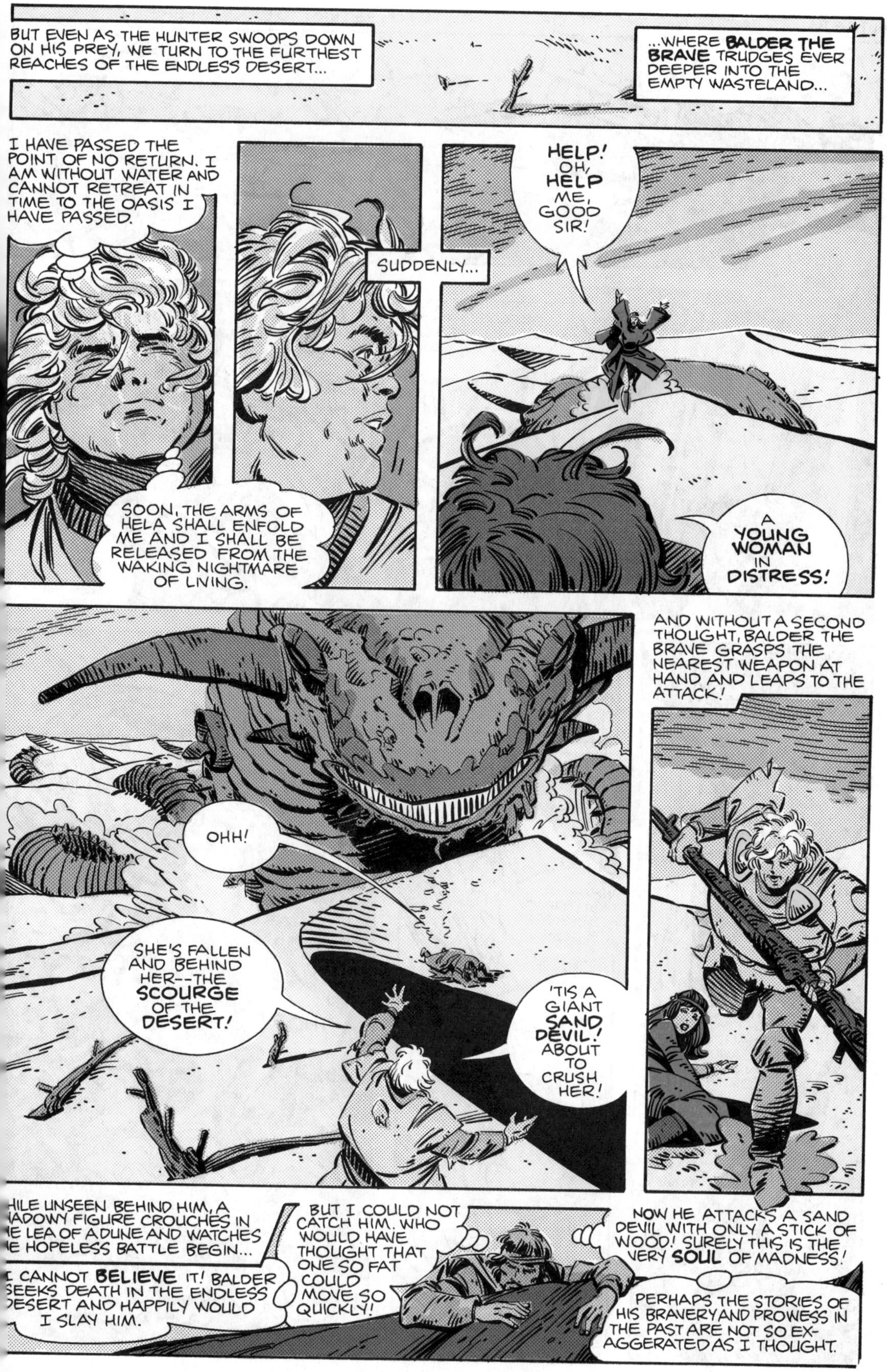

BUT EVEN AS THE HUNTER SWOOPS DOWN ON HIS PREY, WE TURN TO THE FURTHEST REACHES OF THE ENDLESS DESERT...
...WHERE BALDER THE BRAVE TRUDGES EVER DEEPER INTO THE EMPTY WASTELAND...
I HAVE PASSED THE POINT OF NO RETURN. I AM WITHOUT WATER AND CANNOT RETREAT IN TIME TO THE OASIS I HAVE PASSED.
SOON, THE ARMS OF HELA SHALL ENFOLD ME AND I SHALL BE RELEASED FROM THE WAKING NIGHTMARE OF LIVING.
SUDDENLY...
HELP! OH, HELP ME, GOOD SIR!
A YOUNG WOMAN IN DISTRESS!
OHH!
SHE'S FALLEN AND BEHIND HER--THE SCOURGE OF THE DESERT!
'TIS A GIANT SAND DEVIL! ABOUT TO CRUSH HER!
AND WITHOUT A SECOND THOUGHT, BALDER THE BRAVE GRASPS THE NEAREST WEAPON AT HAND AND LEAPS TO THE ATTACK!
HILE UNSEEN BEHIND HIM, A HADOWY FIGURE CROUCHES IN E LEA OF A DUNE AND WATCHES E HOPELESS BATTLE BEGIN...
I CANNOT BELIEVE IT! BALDER SEEKS DEATH IN THE ENDLESS DESERT AND HAPPILY WOULD I SLAY HIM.
BUT I COULD NOT CATCH HIM. WHO WOULD HAVE THOUGHT THAT ONE SO FAT COULD MOVE SO QUICKLY!
NOW HE ATTACKS A SAND DEVIL WITH ONLY A STICK OF WOOD! SURELY THIS IS THE VERY SOUL OF MADNESS!
PERHAPS THE STORIES OF HIS BRAVERY AND PROWESS IN THE PAST ARE NOT SO EXAGGERATED AS I THOUGHT.

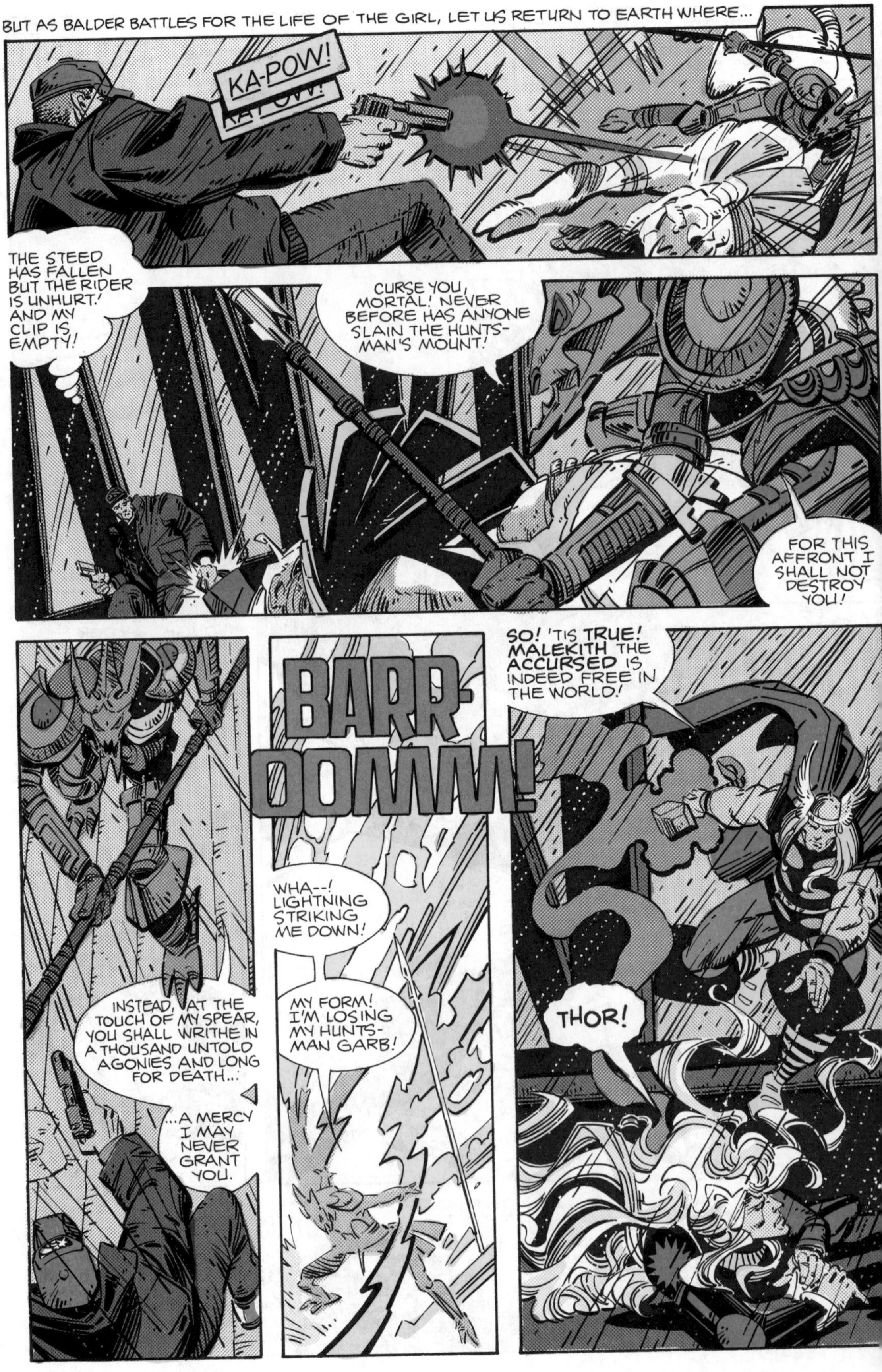
BUT AS BALDER BATTLES FOR THE LIFE OF THE GIRL, LET US RETURN TO EARTH WHERE...
KA-POW!
KA-POW!
THE STEED HAS FALLEN BUT THE RIDER IS UNHURT! AND MY CLIP IS EMPTY!
CURSE YOU, MORTAL! NEVER BEFORE HAS ANYONE SLAIN THE HUNTS-MAN'S MOUNT!
FOR THIS AFFRONT I SHALL NOT DESTROY YOU!
INSTEAD, AT THE TOUCH OF MY SPEAR, YOU SHALL WRITHE IN A THOUSAND UNTOLD AGONIES AND LONG FOR DEATH...
...A MERCY I MAY NEVER GRANT YOU.
BARR-OOMM!
WHA--! LIGHTNING STRIKING ME DOWN!
MY FORM! I'M LOSING MY HUNTS-MAN GARB!
SO! 'TIS TRUE! MALEKITH THE ACCURSED IS INDEED FREE IN THE WORLD!
THOR!

WN ONDER- L!

EIZE IM, MY OUNDS, ND TEAR M LIMB ROM MB!

THUS DO WE SERVE THE SONS OF AS- GARD!

LET THOR'S END BE THE HARBINGER OF THE DOOM TO COME!

BACK! BACK, YOU SCURRILOUS DOGS OF DEATH!

THE BEASTS OF MALEKITH FIND AT ODIN'S SON IS NO SIMPLE EY AS HE MEETS THEIR ATTACK TH A FEROCITY THAT MORE THAN UALS THEIR OWN.

YOUR SLAVERING ANGER IS AS NOTH- ING COMPARED TO THE WRATH OF THE GOD OF THUNDER!

MORTAL, HOW FARE YOU?

N'T WORRY OUT ME! E HAD A ANCE TO LOAD!

BUT WATCH YOUR BACK, THOR!

A-POW! KATOW!

THEN COMMEND YOUR SPIRIT TO ODIN AND WE SHALL SHOW THESE BEASTS THE VERY HEART OF THE STORM UN- LEASHED!

E CREATURES TACK OM BOTH ES OF THE IDGE!

THROO BOOMM!

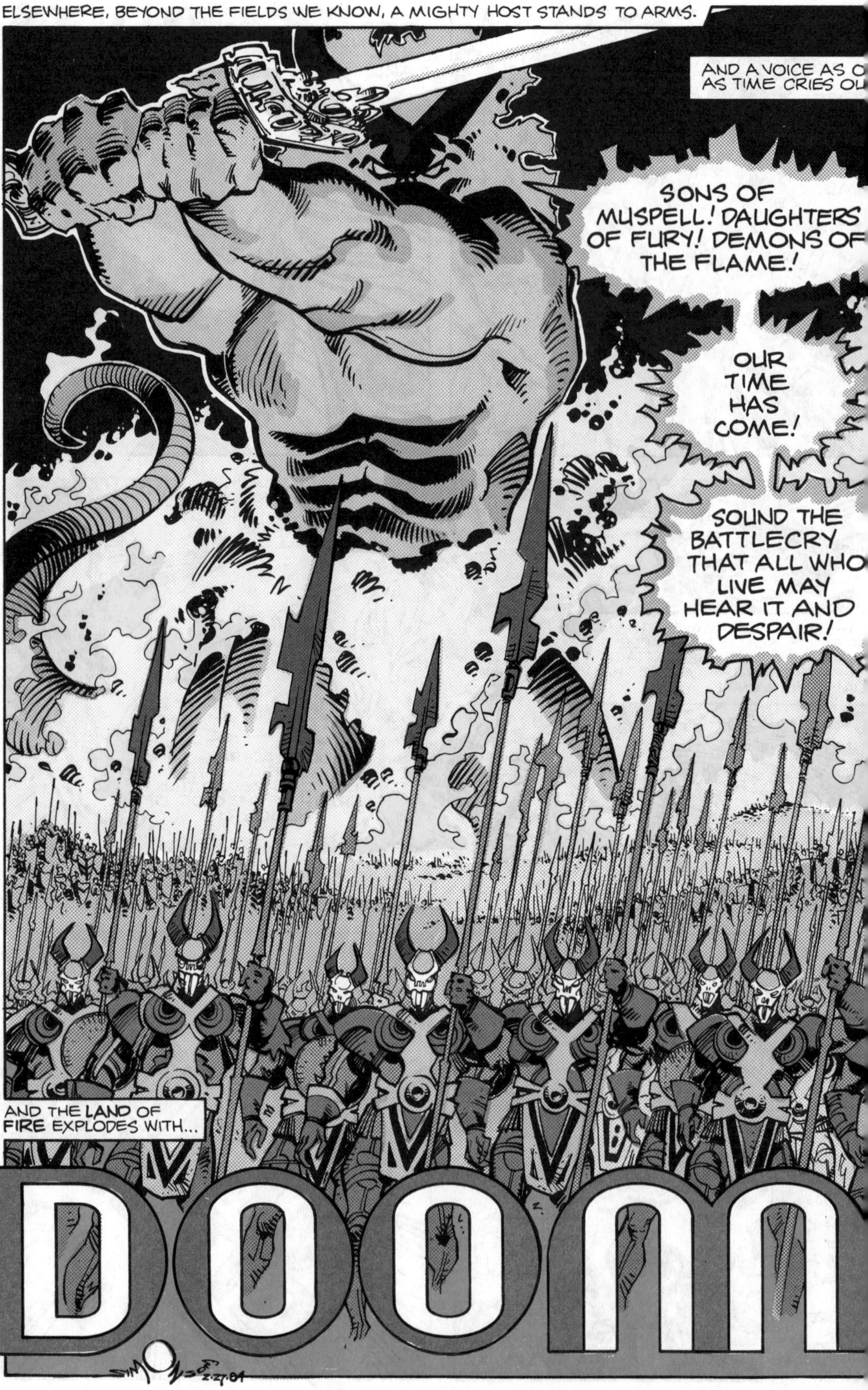
ELSEWHERE, BEYOND THE FIELDS WE KNOW, A MIGHTY HOST STANDS TO ARMS.
AND A VOICE AS O
AS TIME CRIES OU
SONS OF MUSPELL! DAUGHTERS OF FURY! DEMONS OF THE FLAME!
OUR TIME HAS COME!
SOUND THE BATTLECRY THAT ALL WHO LIVE MAY HEAR IT AND DESPAIR!
AND THE LAND OF FIRE EXPLODES WITH...
DOOM
SIMONSON 2.27.84

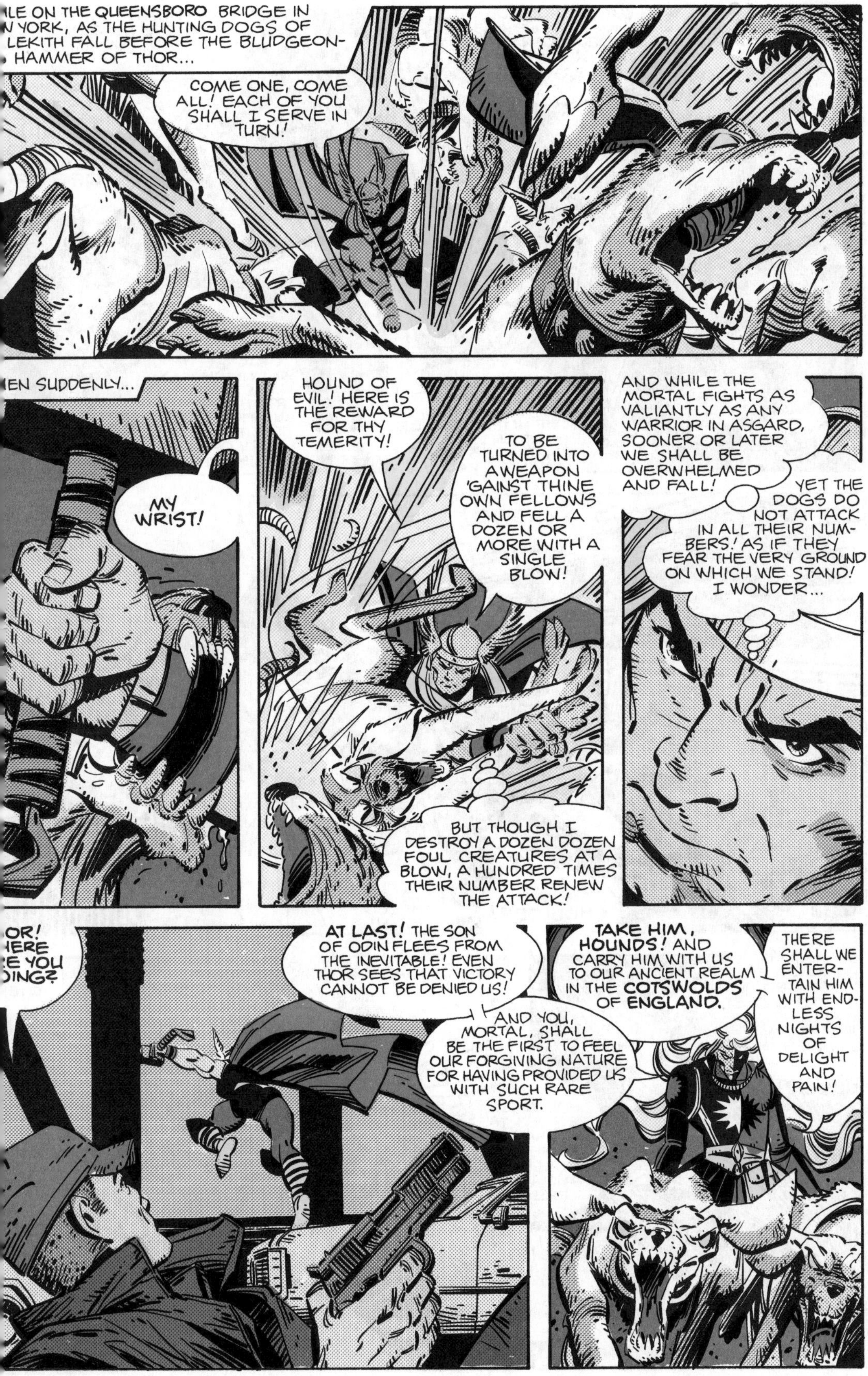
ILE ON THE QUEENSBORO BRIDGE IN N YORK, AS THE HUNTING DOGS OF LEKITH FALL BEFORE THE BLUDGEON- HAMMER OF THOR...
COME ONE, COME ALL! EACH OF YOU SHALL I SERVE IN TURN!
EN SUDDENLY...
MY WRIST!
HOUND OF EVIL! HERE IS THE REWARD FOR THY TEMERITY!
TO BE TURNED INTO A WEAPON 'GAINST THINE OWN FELLOWS AND FELL A DOZEN OR MORE WITH A SINGLE BLOW!
BUT THOUGH I DESTROY A DOZEN DOZEN FOUL CREATURES AT A BLOW, A HUNDRED TIMES THEIR NUMBER RENEW THE ATTACK!
AND WHILE THE MORTAL FIGHTS AS VALIANTLY AS ANY WARRIOR IN ASGARD, SOONER OR LATER WE SHALL BE OVERWHELMED AND FALL!
YET THE DOGS DO NOT ATTACK IN ALL THEIR NUMBERS! AS IF THEY FEAR THE VERY GROUND ON WHICH WE STAND! I WONDER...
OR! HERE E YOU DING?
AT LAST! THE SON OF ODIN FLEES FROM THE INEVITABLE! EVEN THOR SEES THAT VICTORY CANNOT BE DENIED US!
AND YOU, MORTAL, SHALL BE THE FIRST TO FEEL OUR FORGIVING NATURE FOR HAVING PROVIDED US WITH SUCH RARE SPORT.
TAKE HIM, HOUNDS! AND CARRY HIM WITH US TO OUR ANCIENT REALM IN THE COTSWOLDS OF ENGLAND.
THERE SHALL WE ENTERTAIN HIM WITH ENDLESS NIGHTS OF DELIGHT AND PAIN!

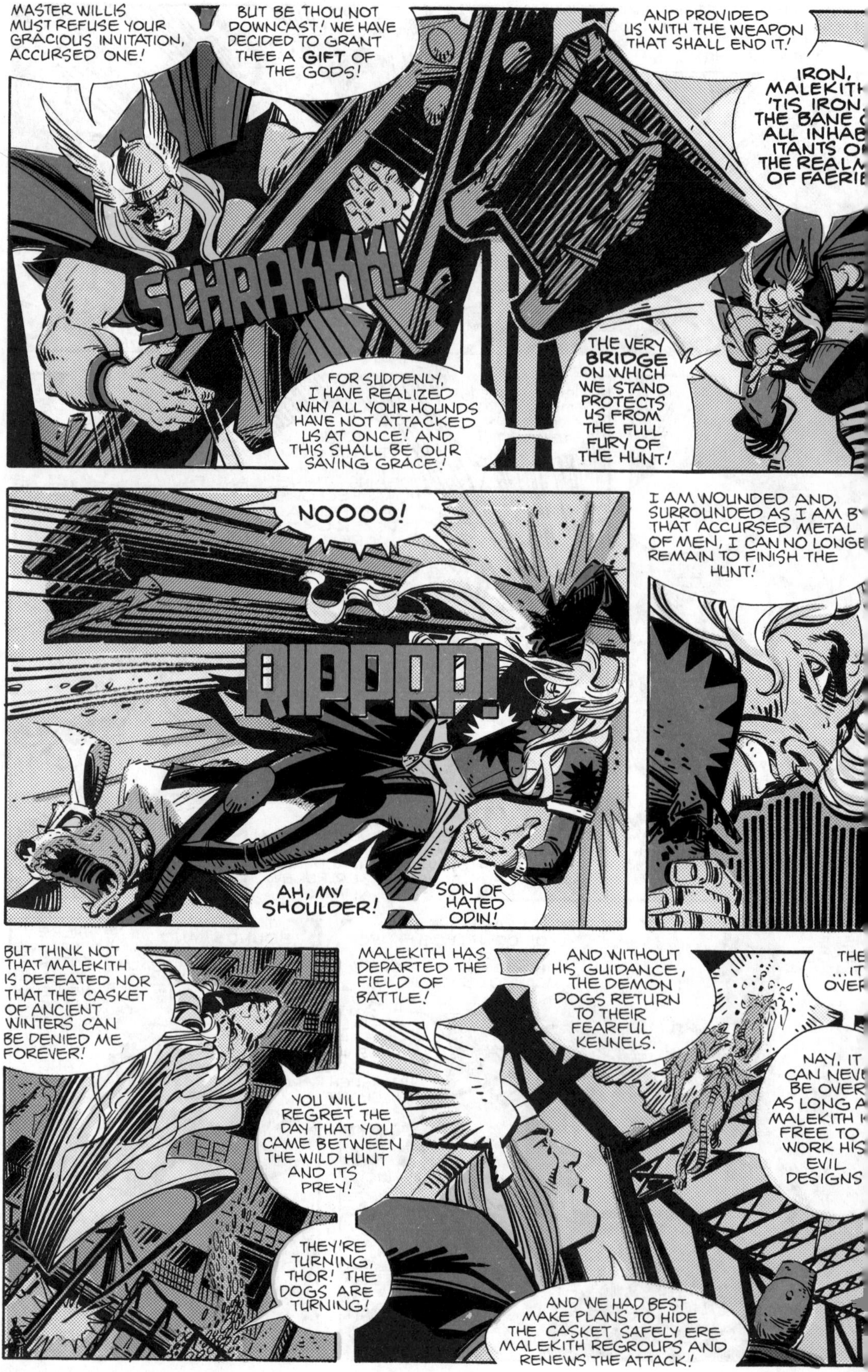
MASTER WILLIS MUST REFUSE YOUR GRACIOUS INVITATION, ACCURSED ONE!
BUT BE THOU NOT DOWNCAST! WE HAVE DECIDED TO GRANT THEE A **GIFT** OF THE GODS!
SCHRAKKK!
FOR SUDDENLY, I HAVE REALIZED WHY ALL YOUR HOUNDS HAVE NOT ATTACKED US AT ONCE! AND THIS SHALL BE OUR SAVING GRACE!
THE VERY **BRIDGE** ON WHICH WE STAND PROTECTS US FROM THE FULL FURY OF THE HUNT!
AND PROVIDED US WITH THE WEAPON THAT SHALL END IT!
IRON, MALEKITH 'TIS IRON, THE BANE ALL INHAB ITANTS O THE REALM OF FAERIE
NOOOO!
RIPPPP!
AH, MY SHOULDER!
SON OF HATED ODIN!
I AM WOUNDED AND, SURROUNDED AS I AM B THAT ACCURSED METAL OF MEN, I CAN NO LONGE REMAIN TO FINISH THE HUNT!
BUT THINK NOT THAT MALEKITH IS DEFEATED NOR THAT THE CASKET OF ANCIENT WINTERS CAN BE DENIED ME FOREVER!
YOU WILL REGRET THE DAY THAT YOU CAME BETWEEN THE WILD HUNT AND ITS PREY!
THEY'RE TURNING, THOR! THE DOGS ARE TURNING!
MALEKITH HAS DEPARTED THE FIELD OF BATTLE!
AND WITHOUT HIS GUIDANCE, THE DEMON DOGS RETURN TO THEIR FEARFUL KENNELS.
THE ...IT OVER
NAY, IT CAN NEVE BE OVER AS LONG A MALEKITH I FREE TO WORK HIS EVIL DESIGNS
AND WE HAD BEST MAKE PLANS TO HIDE THE CASKET SAFELY ERE MALEKITH REGROUPS AND RENEWS THE ATTACK!

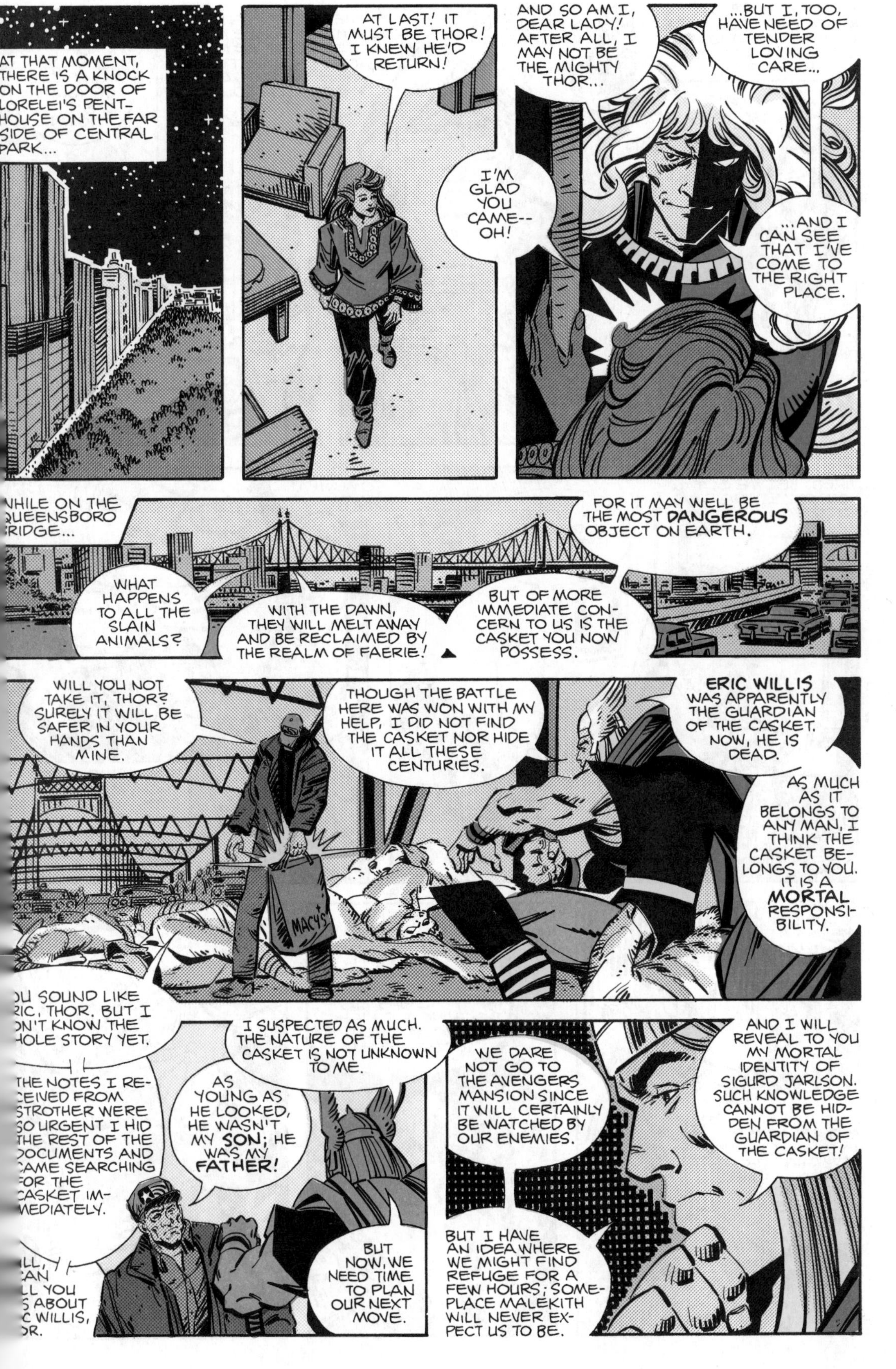
AT THAT MOMENT, THERE IS A KNOCK ON THE DOOR OF LORELEI'S PENT-HOUSE ON THE FAR SIDE OF CENTRAL PARK...
AT LAST! IT MUST BE THOR! I KNEW HE'D RETURN!
I'M GLAD YOU CAME--OH!
AND SO AM I, DEAR LADY! AFTER ALL, I MAY NOT BE THE MIGHTY THOR...
...BUT I, TOO, HAVE NEED OF TENDER LOVING CARE...
...AND I CAN SEE THAT I'VE COME TO THE RIGHT PLACE.
WHILE ON THE QUEENSBORO BRIDGE...
WHAT HAPPENS TO ALL THE SLAIN ANIMALS?
WITH THE DAWN, THEY WILL MELT AWAY AND BE RECLAIMED BY THE REALM OF FAERIE!
BUT OF MORE IMMEDIATE CON-CERN TO US IS THE CASKET YOU NOW POSSESS.
FOR IT MAY WELL BE THE MOST DANGEROUS OBJECT ON EARTH.
WILL YOU NOT TAKE IT, THOR? SURELY IT WILL BE SAFER IN YOUR HANDS THAN MINE.
THOUGH THE BATTLE HERE WAS WON WITH MY HELP, I DID NOT FIND THE CASKET NOR HIDE IT ALL THESE CENTURIES.
ERIC WILLIS WAS APPARENTLY THE GUARDIAN OF THE CASKET. NOW, HE IS DEAD.
AS MUCH AS IT BELONGS TO ANY MAN, I THINK THE CASKET BE-LONGS TO YOU. IT IS A MORTAL RESPONSI-BILITY.
MACY'S
OU SOUND LIKE RIC, THOR. BUT I ON'T KNOW THE HOLE STORY YET.
THE NOTES I RE-CEIVED FROM STROTHER WERE SO URGENT I HID THE REST OF THE DOCUMENTS AND CAME SEARCHING FOR THE CASKET IM-MEDIATELY.
ILL, CAN LL YOU S ABOUT C WILLIS, OR.
I SUSPECTED AS MUCH. THE NATURE OF THE CASKET IS NOT UNKNOWN TO ME.
AS YOUNG AS HE LOOKED, HE WASN'T MY SON; HE WAS MY FATHER!
BUT NOW, WE NEED TIME TO PLAN OUR NEXT MOVE.
WE DARE NOT GO TO THE AVENGERS MANSION SINCE IT WILL CERTAINLY BE WATCHED BY OUR ENEMIES.
BUT I HAVE AN IDEA WHERE WE MIGHT FIND REFUGE FOR A FEW HOURS; SOME-PLACE MALEKITH WILL NEVER EX-PECT US TO BE.
AND I WILL REVEAL TO YOU MY MORTAL IDENTITY OF SIGURD JARLSON. SUCH KNOWLEDGE CANNOT BE HID-DEN FROM THE GUARDIAN OF THE CASKET!

SHORTLY, THERE IS A KNOCK ON THE DOOR OF LORELEI'S PENTHOUSE ON THE FAR SIDE OF CENTRAL PARK...

SIGURD! I CAN'T TELL YOU HOW GLAD I AM TO SEE YOU.

I WAS HOPING YOU'D COME BY.

I'VE BROUGHT A FRIEND OF MINE, MELODI.

WE'RE... HAVING A LITTLE TROUBLE AND WONDERED IF WE MIGHT STOP BY FOR A LITTLE WHILE TO DECIDE WHAT TO DO ABOUT IT.

OF COURSE. ANY FRIEND OF YOURS. SIT DOWN.

YOU BOTH LOOK TIRED. LET ME GET YOU SOMETHING TO DRINK.

A LITTLE GOLDEN MEAD IS JUST WHAT YOU NEED.

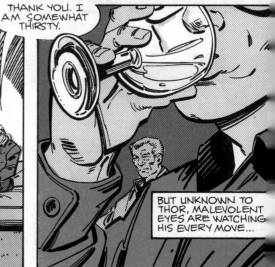

THANK YOU. I AM SOMEWHAT THIRSTY.

BUT UNKNOWN TO THOR, MALEVOLENT EYES ARE WATCHING HIS EVERY MOVE...

AH, HE DRINKS! **HE DRINKS!**

THAT WAS SUPERBLY DONE, MY DEAR. I SHOULD NEVER HAVE THOUGHT OF SUCH A SIMPLE DEVICE AS AN ENCHANTED DRINK!

WHY, WHEN I DETECTED THE MAGICAL EMANATIONS OF THE MEAD IN YOUR APARTMENT, I KNEW INSTANTLY THAT HERE WAS JUST THE THING I SOUGHT TO MAKE MY DREAMS COME TRUE!

THOR IS THE FISH AND YOU, MY BEAUTY, ARE THE **BAIT!**

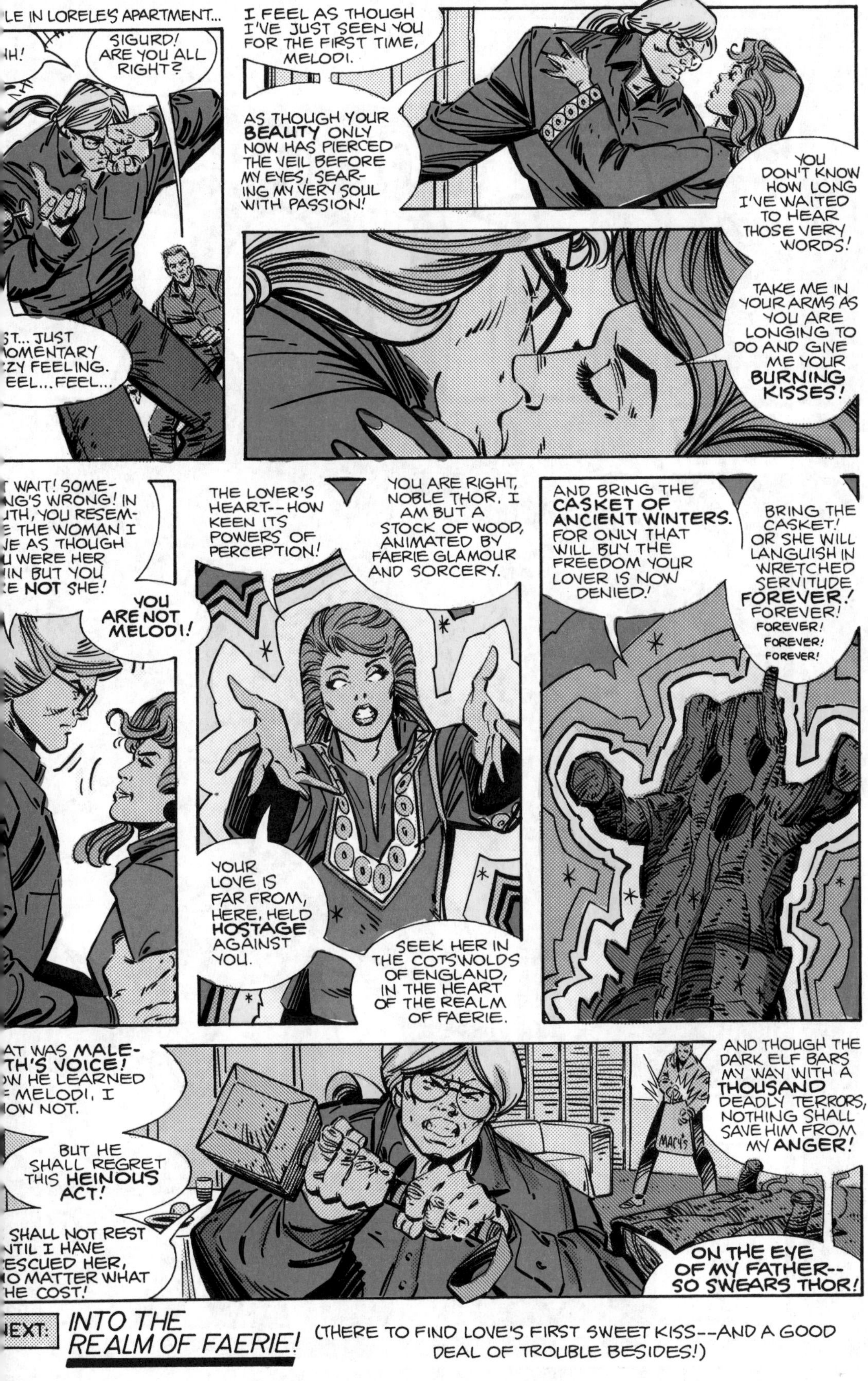
LE IN LORELE'S APARTMENT...
IH!
SIGURD! ARE YOU ALL RIGHT?
ST... JUST OMENTARY ZZY FEELING. EEL... FEEL...
I FEEL AS THOUGH I'VE JUST SEEN YOU FOR THE FIRST TIME, MELODI.
AS THOUGH YOUR BEAUTY ONLY NOW HAS PIERCED THE VEIL BEFORE MY EYES, SEARING MY VERY SOUL WITH PASSION!
YOU DON'T KNOW HOW LONG I'VE WAITED TO HEAR THOSE VERY WORDS!
TAKE ME IN YOUR ARMS AS YOU ARE LONGING TO DO AND GIVE ME YOUR BURNING KISSES!
T WAIT! SOME-NG'S WRONG! IN UTH, YOU RESEM-E THE WOMAN I VE AS THOUGH U WERE HER IN BUT YOU E NOT SHE!
YOU ARE NOT MELODI!
THE LOVER'S HEART--HOW KEEN ITS POWERS OF PERCEPTION!
YOU ARE RIGHT, NOBLE THOR. I AM BUT A STOCK OF WOOD, ANIMATED BY FAERIE GLAMOUR AND SORCERY.
YOUR LOVE IS FAR FROM, HERE, HELD HOSTAGE AGAINST YOU.
SEEK HER IN THE COTSWOLDS OF ENGLAND, IN THE HEART OF THE REALM OF FAERIE.
AND BRING THE CASKET OF ANCIENT WINTERS. FOR ONLY THAT WILL BUY THE FREEDOM YOUR LOVER IS NOW DENIED!
BRING THE CASKET! OR SHE WILL LANGUISH IN WRETCHED SERVITUDE FOREVER! FOREVER! FOREVER! FOREVER! FOREVER!
AT WAS MALE-TH'S VOICE! OW HE LEARNED F MELODI, I OW NOT.
BUT HE SHALL REGRET THIS HEINOUS ACT!
SHALL NOT REST NTIL I HAVE ESCUED HER, O MATTER WHAT HE COST!
AND THOUGH THE DARK ELF BARS MY WAY WITH A THOUSAND DEADLY TERRORS, NOTHING SHALL SAVE HIM FROM MY ANGER!
ON THE EYE OF MY FATHER-- SO SWEARS THOR!
MACY'S
NEXT: INTO THE REALM OF FAERIE!
(THERE TO FIND LOVE'S FIRST SWEET KISS--AND A GOOD DEAL OF TROUBLE BESIDES!)

Chapter Eleven

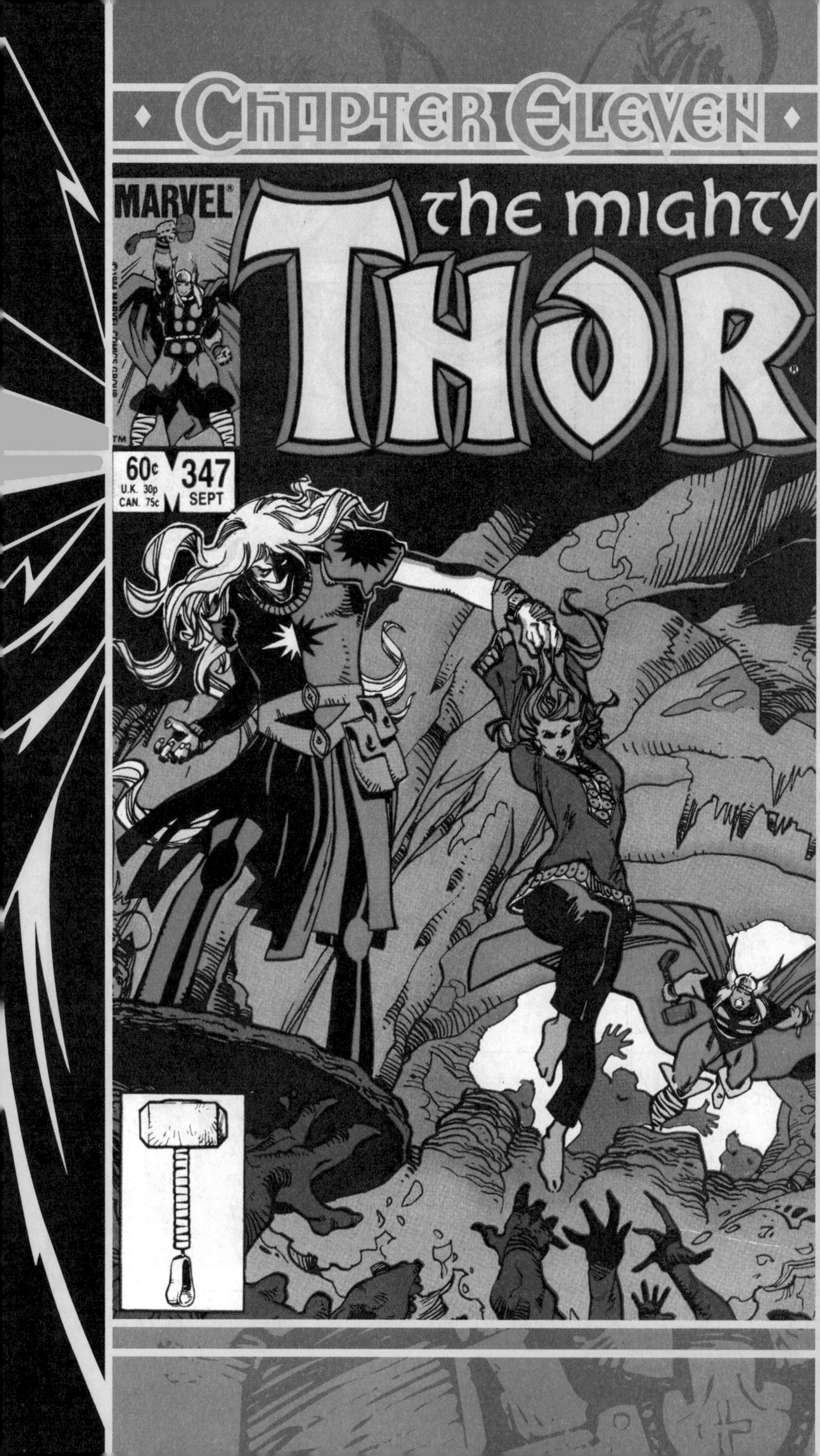
MARVEL
the mighty
THOR
60¢
U.K. 30p
CAN. 75c
347
SEPT

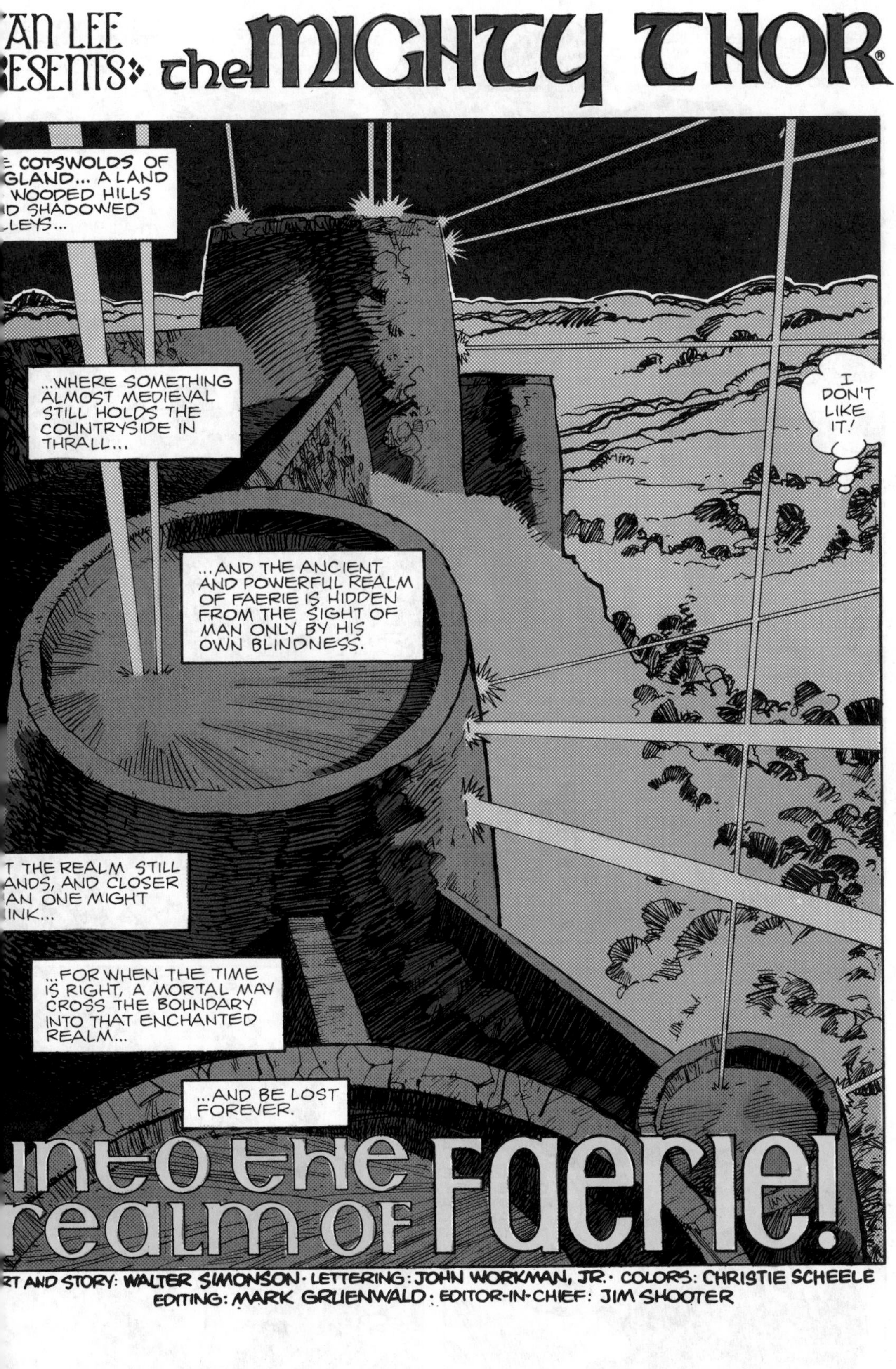

AN LEE
ESENTS: the MIGHTY THOR®
E COTSWOLDS OF
GLAND... A LAND
WOODED HILLS
D SHADOWED
LEYS...
...WHERE SOMETHING ALMOST MEDIEVAL STILL HOLDS THE COUNTRYSIDE IN THRALL...
I DON'T LIKE IT!
...AND THE ANCIENT AND POWERFUL REALM OF FAERIE IS HIDDEN FROM THE SIGHT OF MAN ONLY BY HIS OWN BLINDNESS.
T THE REALM STILL
ANDS, AND CLOSER
AN ONE MIGHT
INK...
...FOR WHEN THE TIME IS RIGHT, A MORTAL MAY CROSS THE BOUNDARY INTO THAT ENCHANTED REALM...
...AND BE LOST FOREVER.
NTO THE
REALM OF FAERIE!
RT AND STORY: WALTER SIMONSON · LETTERING: JOHN WORKMAN, JR. · COLORS: CHRISTIE SCHEELE
EDITING: MARK GRUENWALD · EDITOR-IN-CHIEF: JIM SHOOTER

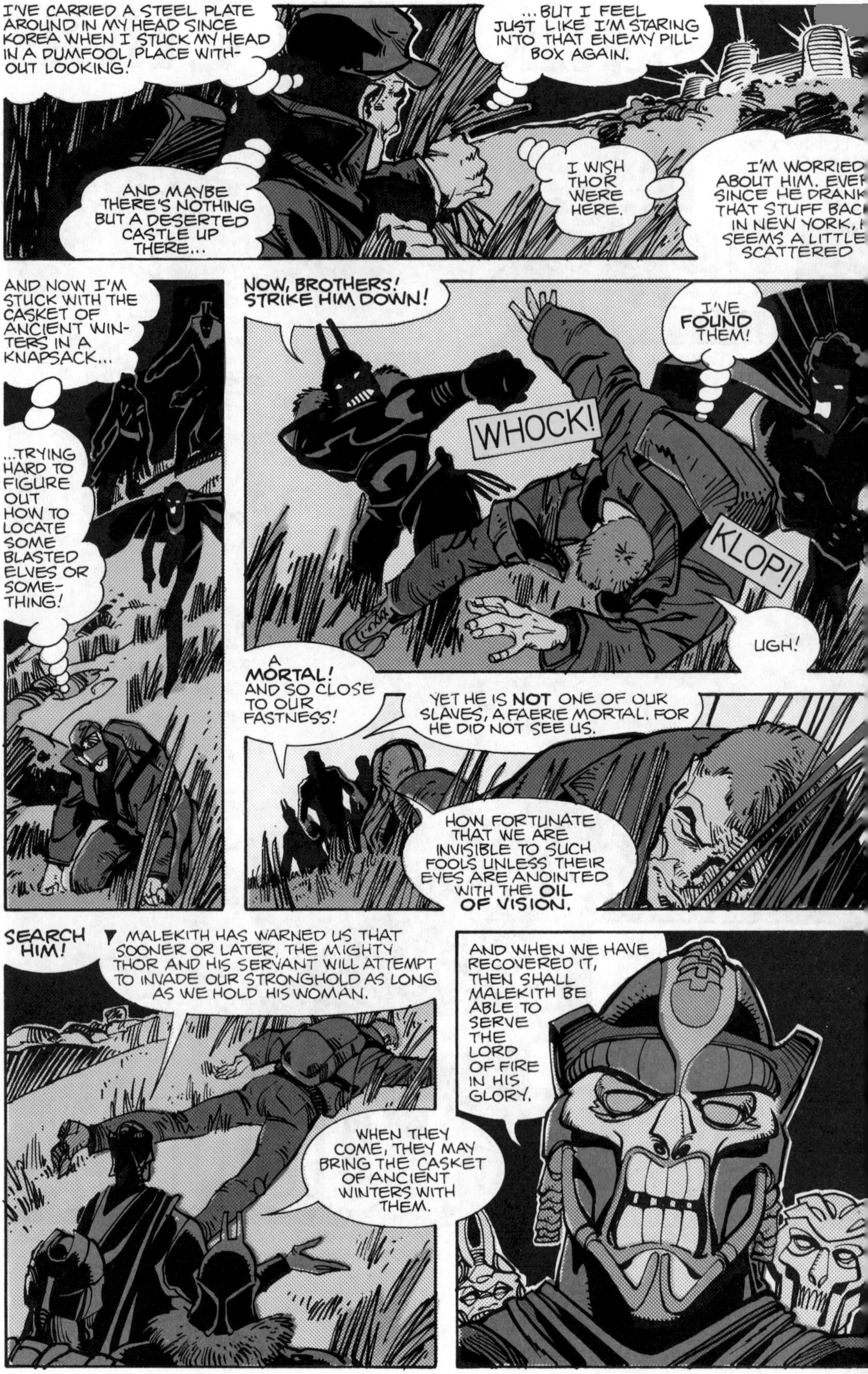
I'VE CARRIED A STEEL PLATE AROUND IN MY HEAD SINCE KOREA WHEN I STUCK MY HEAD IN A DUMFOOL PLACE WITH-OUT LOOKING!
...BUT I FEEL JUST LIKE I'M STARING INTO THAT ENEMY PILL-BOX AGAIN.
AND MAYBE THERE'S NOTHING BUT A DESERTED CASTLE UP THERE...
I WISH THOR WERE HERE.
I'M WORRIED ABOUT HIM. EVER SINCE HE DRANK THAT STUFF BACK IN NEW YORK, HE SEEMS A LITTLE SCATTERED
AND NOW I'M STUCK WITH THE CASKET OF ANCIENT WIN-TERS IN A KNAPSACK...
...TRYING HARD TO FIGURE OUT HOW TO LOCATE SOME BLASTED ELVES OR SOME-THING!
NOW, BROTHERS! STRIKE HIM DOWN!
I'VE FOUND THEM!
WHOCK!
KLOP!
UGH!
A MORTAL! AND SO CLOSE TO OUR FASTNESS!
YET HE IS NOT ONE OF OUR SLAVES, A FAERIE MORTAL. FOR HE DID NOT SEE US.
HOW FORTUNATE THAT WE ARE INVISIBLE TO SUCH FOOLS UNLESS THEIR EYES ARE ANOINTED WITH THE OIL OF VISION.
SEARCH HIM!
MALEKITH HAS WARNED US THAT SOONER OR LATER, THE MIGHTY THOR AND HIS SERVANT WILL ATTEMPT TO INVADE OUR STRONGHOLD AS LONG AS WE HOLD HIS WOMAN.
WHEN THEY COME, THEY MAY BRING THE CASKET OF ANCIENT WINTERS WITH THEM.
AND WHEN WE HAVE RECOVERED IT, THEN SHALL MALEKITH BE ABLE TO SERVE THE LORD OF FIRE IN HIS GLORY.

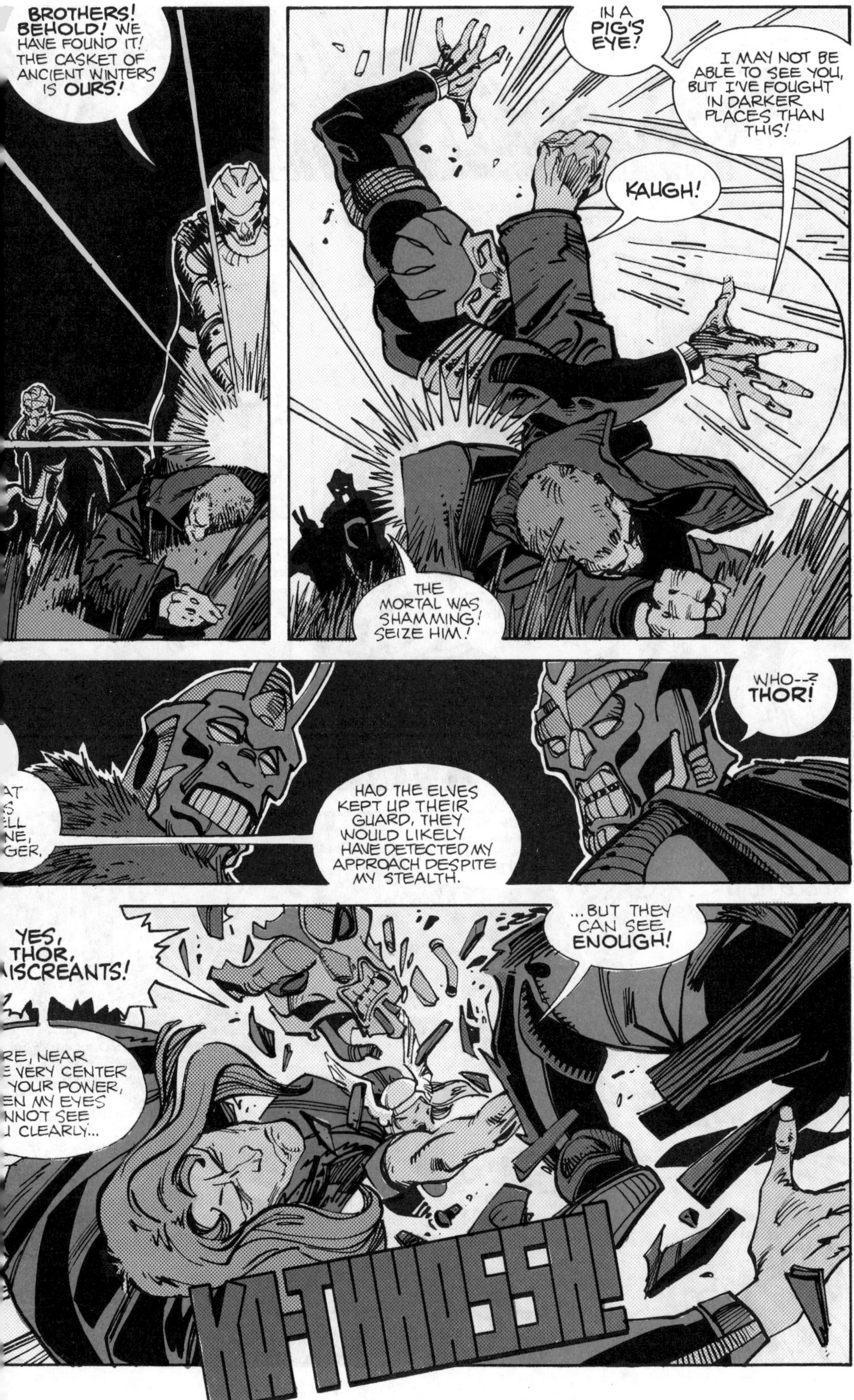
BROTHERS! BEHOLD! WE HAVE FOUND IT! THE CASKET OF ANCIENT WINTERS IS OURS!
IN A PIG'S EYE!
I MAY NOT BE ABLE TO SEE YOU, BUT I'VE FOUGHT IN DARKER PLACES THAN THIS!
KAUGH!
THE MORTAL WAS SHAMMING! SEIZE HIM!
AT
S
ELL
NE,
GER.
HAD THE ELVES KEPT UP THEIR GUARD, THEY WOULD LIKELY HAVE DETECTED MY APPROACH DESPITE MY STEALTH.
WHO--? THOR!
YES, THOR,
ISCREANTS!
RE, NEAR
E VERY CENTER
YOUR POWER,
EN MY EYES
NNOT SEE
U CLEARLY...
...BUT THEY CAN SEE ENOUGH!
KA-THWASSH!

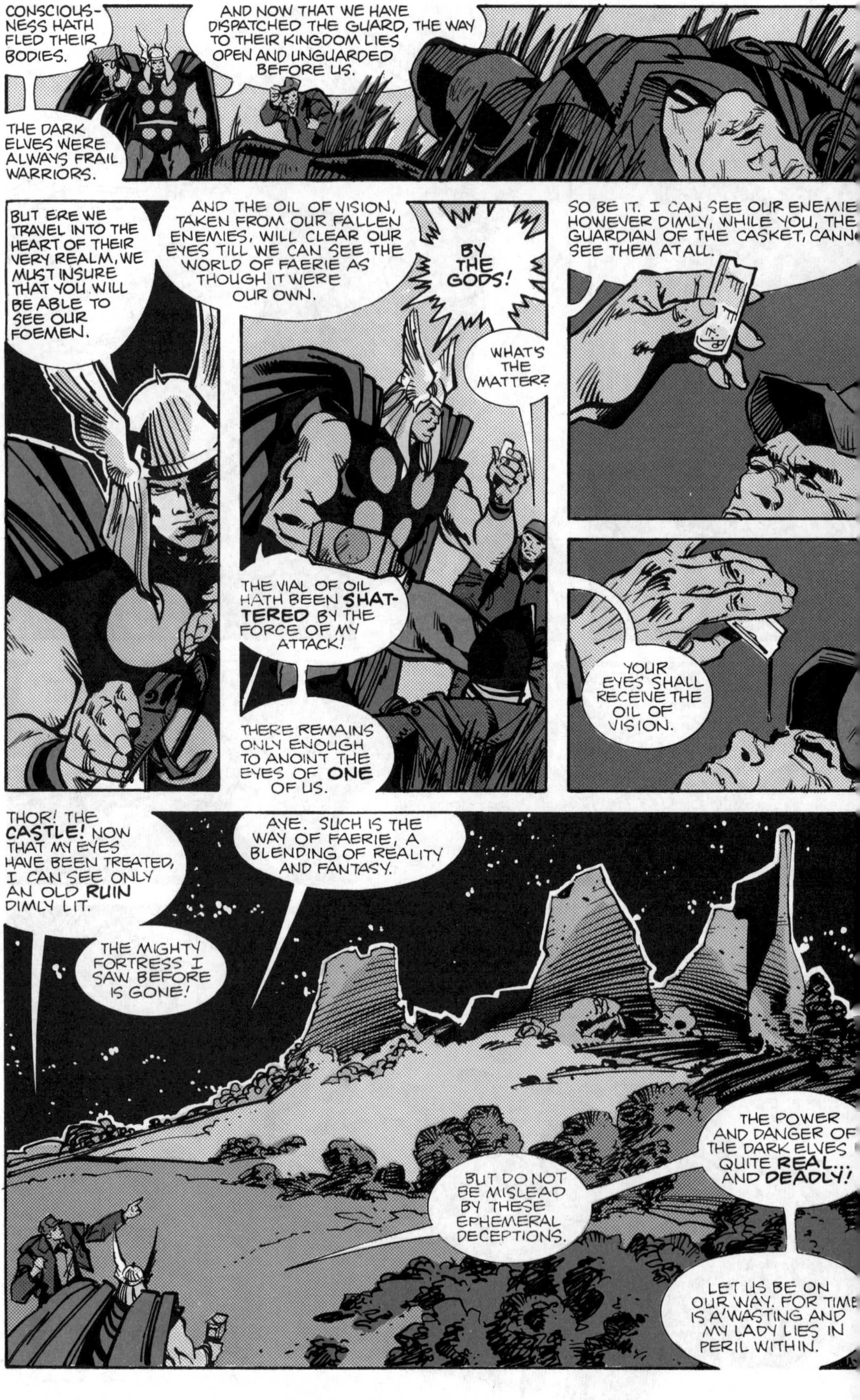
CONSCIOUS-NESS HATH FLED THEIR BODIES.
THE DARK ELVES WERE ALWAYS FRAIL WARRIORS.
AND NOW THAT WE HAVE DISPATCHED THE GUARD, THE WAY TO THEIR KINGDOM LIES OPEN AND UNGUARDED BEFORE US.
BUT ERE WE TRAVEL INTO THE HEART OF THEIR VERY REALM, WE MUST INSURE THAT YOU WILL BE ABLE TO SEE OUR FOEMEN.
AND THE OIL OF VISION, TAKEN FROM OUR FALLEN ENEMIES, WILL CLEAR OUR EYES TILL WE CAN SEE THE WORLD OF FAERIE AS THOUGH IT WERE OUR OWN.
BY THE GODS!
WHAT'S THE MATTER?
THE VIAL OF OIL HATH BEEN SHAT-TERED BY THE FORCE OF MY ATTACK!
THERE REMAINS ONLY ENOUGH TO ANOINT THE EYES OF ONE OF US.
SO BE IT. I CAN SEE OUR ENEMIE HOWEVER DIMLY, WHILE YOU, THE GUARDIAN OF THE CASKET, CANN SEE THEM AT ALL.
YOUR EYES SHALL RECEIVE THE OIL OF VISION.
THOR! THE CASTLE! NOW THAT MY EYES HAVE BEEN TREATED, I CAN SEE ONLY AN OLD RUIN DIMLY LIT.
THE MIGHTY FORTRESS I SAW BEFORE IS GONE!
AYE. SUCH IS THE WAY OF FAERIE, A BLENDING OF REALITY AND FANTASY.
BUT DO NOT BE MISLEAD BY THESE EPHEMERAL DECEPTIONS.
THE POWER AND DANGER OF THE DARK ELVES QUITE REAL... AND DEADLY!
LET US BE ON OUR WAY. FOR TIME IS A'WASTING AND MY LADY LIES IN PERIL WITHIN.

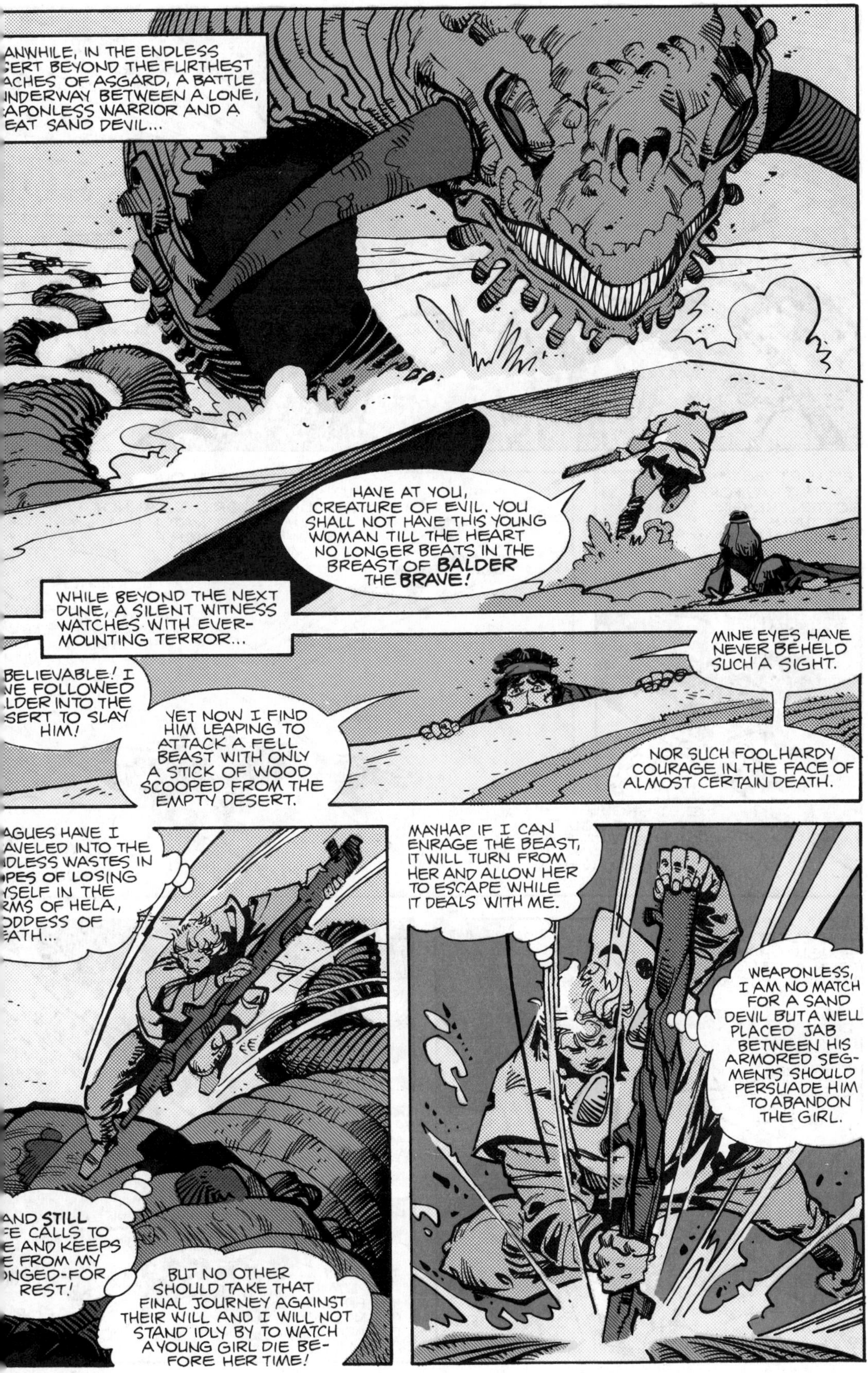
ANWHILE, IN THE ENDLESS
ERT BEYOND THE FURTHEST
ACHES OF ASGARD, A BATTLE
UNDERWAY BETWEEN A LONE,
APONLESS WARRIOR AND A
EAT SAND DEVIL...
HAVE AT YOU, CREATURE OF EVIL. YOU SHALL NOT HAVE THIS YOUNG WOMAN TILL THE HEART NO LONGER BEATS IN THE BREAST OF **BALDER** THE **BRAVE!**
WHILE BEYOND THE NEXT DUNE, A SILENT WITNESS WATCHES WITH EVER-MOUNTING TERROR...
BELIEVABLE! I VE FOLLOWED LDER INTO THE SERT TO SLAY HIM!
YET NOW I FIND HIM LEAPING TO ATTACK A FELL BEAST WITH ONLY A STICK OF WOOD SCOOPED FROM THE EMPTY DESERT.
MINE EYES HAVE NEVER BEHELD SUCH A SIGHT.
NOR SUCH FOOLHARDY COURAGE IN THE FACE OF ALMOST CERTAIN DEATH.
AGUES HAVE I AVELED INTO THE DLESS WASTES IN PES OF LOSING YSELF IN THE RMS OF HELA, ODDESS OF EATH...
AND **STILL** FE CALLS TO E AND KEEPS E FROM MY ONGED-FOR REST!
BUT NO OTHER SHOULD TAKE THAT FINAL JOURNEY AGAINST THEIR WILL AND I WILL NOT STAND IDLY BY TO WATCH A YOUNG GIRL DIE BEFORE HER TIME!
MAYHAP IF I CAN ENRAGE THE BEAST, IT WILL TURN FROM HER AND ALLOW HER TO ESCAPE WHILE IT DEALS WITH ME.
WEAPONLESS, I AM NO MATCH FOR A SAND DEVIL BUT A WELL PLACED JAB BETWEEN HIS ARMORED SEGMENTS SHOULD PERSUADE HIM TO ABANDON THE GIRL.

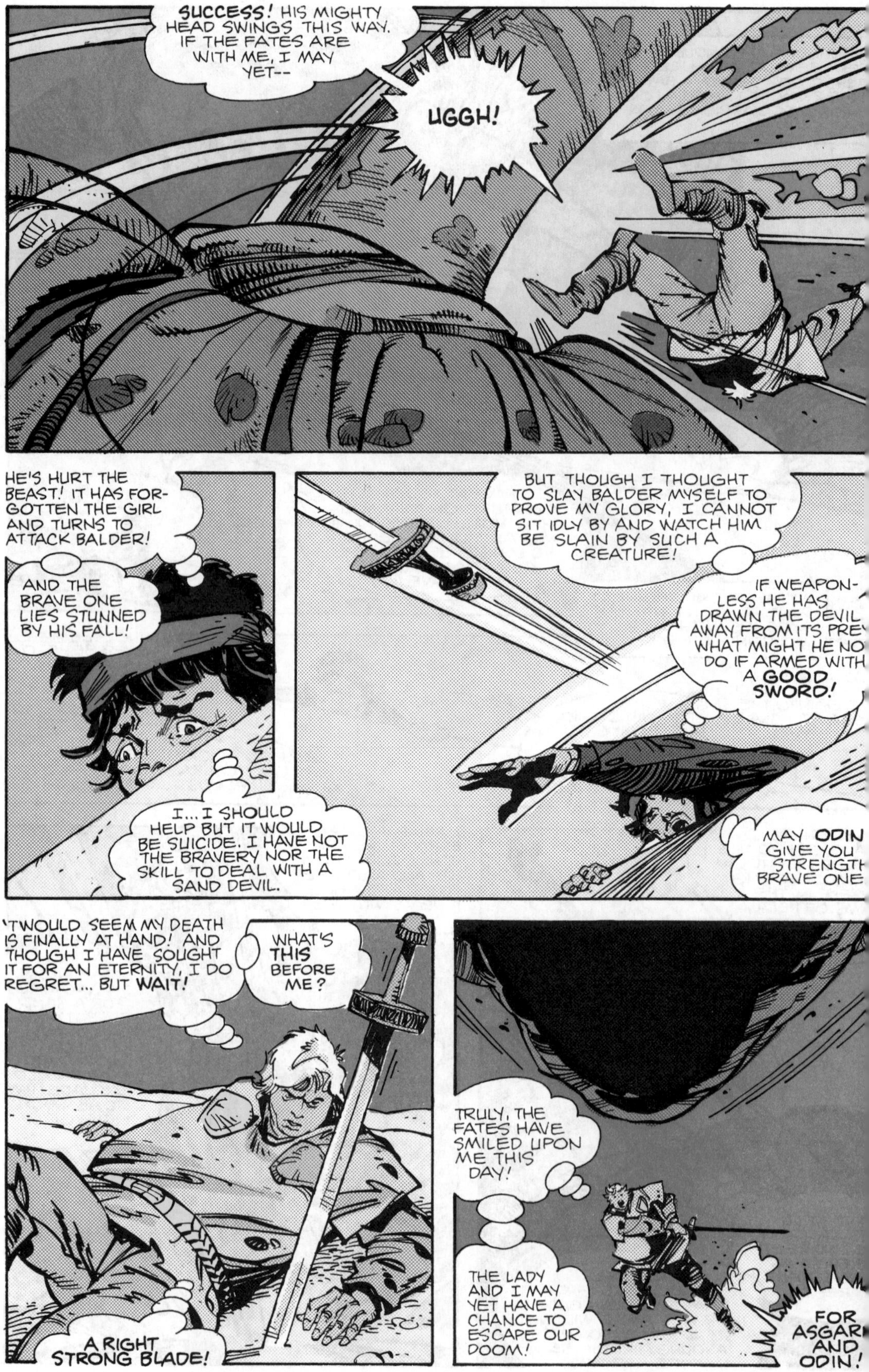
SUCCESS! HIS MIGHTY HEAD SWINGS THIS WAY. IF THE FATES ARE WITH ME, I MAY YET--
UGGH!
HE'S HURT THE BEAST! IT HAS FORGOTTEN THE GIRL AND TURNS TO ATTACK BALDER!
AND THE BRAVE ONE LIES STUNNED BY HIS FALL!
I... I SHOULD HELP BUT IT WOULD BE SUICIDE. I HAVE NOT THE BRAVERY NOR THE SKILL TO DEAL WITH A SAND DEVIL.
BUT THOUGH I THOUGHT TO SLAY BALDER MYSELF TO PROVE MY GLORY, I CANNOT SIT IDLY BY AND WATCH HIM BE SLAIN BY SUCH A CREATURE!
IF WEAPONLESS HE HAS DRAWN THE DEVIL AWAY FROM ITS PREY
MAY ODIN GIVE YOU STRENGTH
'TWOULD SEEM MY DEATH IS FINALLY AT HAND! AND THOUGH I HAVE SOUGHT IT FOR AN ETERNITY, I DO REGRET... BUT WAIT!
WHAT'S THIS BEFORE ME?
A RIGHT STRONG BLADE!
TRULY, THE FATES HAVE SMILED UPON ME THIS DAY!
THE LADY AND I MAY YET HAVE A CHANCE TO ESCAPE OUR DOOM!
AND ODIN!

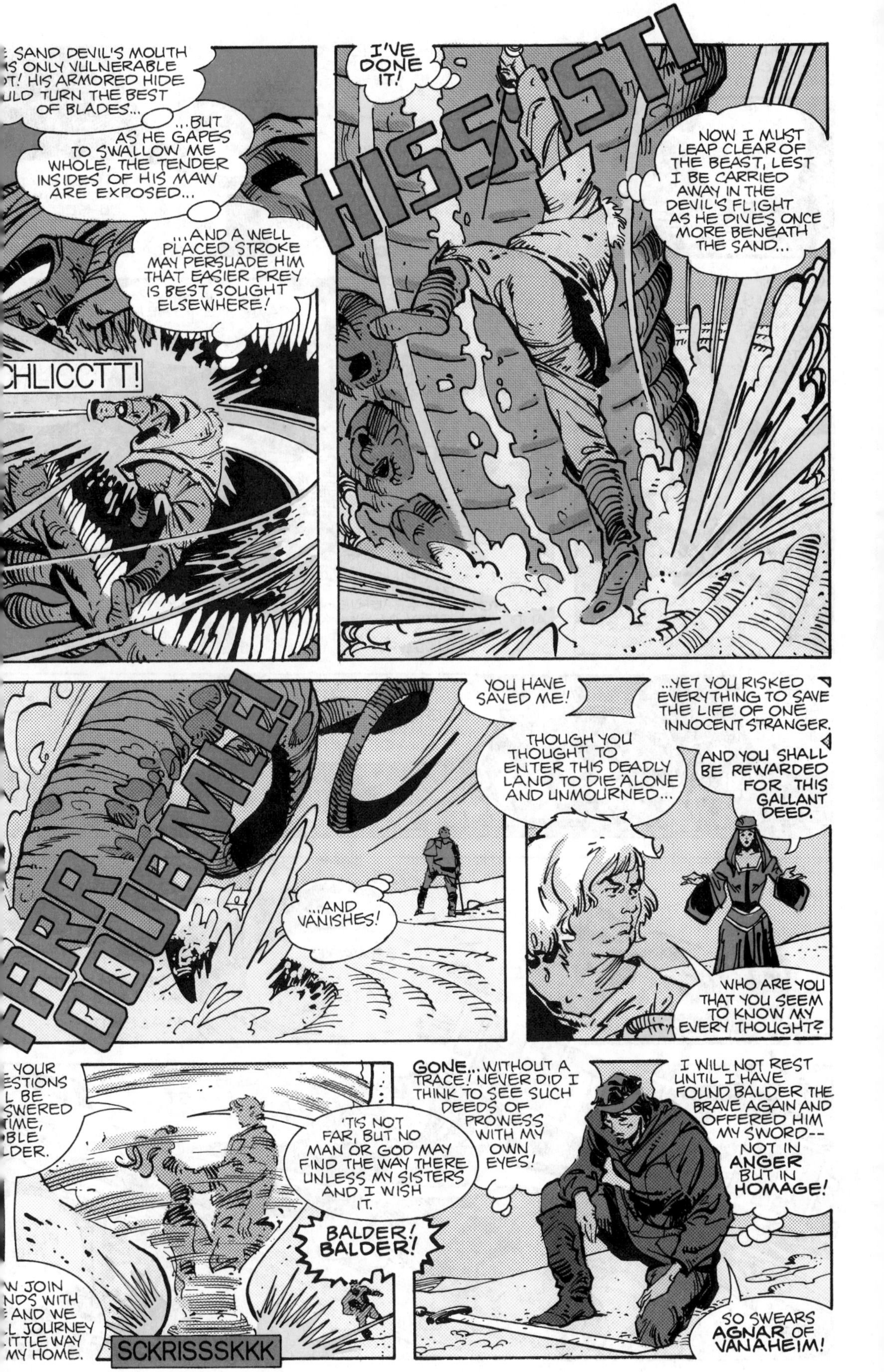

E SAND DEVIL'S MOUTH IS ONLY VULNERABLE OT! HIS ARMORED HIDE ULD TURN THE BEST OF BLADES...
...BUT AS HE GAPES TO SWALLOW ME WHOLE, THE TENDER INSIDES OF HIS MAW ARE EXPOSED...
...AND A WELL PLACED STROKE MAY PERSUADE HIM THAT EASIER PREY IS BEST SOUGHT ELSEWHERE!
CHLICCTT!
I'VE DONE IT!
HISSSST!
NOW I MUST LEAP CLEAR OF THE BEAST, LEST I BE CARRIED AWAY IN THE DEVIL'S FLIGHT AS HE DIVES ONCE MORE BENEATH THE SAND...
FARR DOUBMLE!
...AND VANISHES!
YOU HAVE SAVED ME!
THOUGH YOU THOUGHT TO ENTER THIS DEADLY LAND TO DIE ALONE AND UNMOURNED...
...YET YOU RISKED EVERYTHING TO SAVE THE LIFE OF ONE INNOCENT STRANGER.
AND YOU SHALL BE REWARDED FOR THIS GALLANT DEED.
WHO ARE YOU THAT YOU SEEM TO KNOW MY EVERY THOUGHT?
YOUR ESTIONS L BE SWERED TIME, BLE LDER.
'TIS NOT FAR, BUT NO MAN OR GOD MAY FIND THE WAY THERE UNLESS MY SISTERS AND I WISH IT.
W JOIN NDS WITH E AND WE L JOURNEY LITTLE WAY MY HOME.
BALDER! BALDER!
SCKRISSSKKK
GONE... WITHOUT A TRACE! NEVER DID I THINK TO SEE SUCH DEEDS OF PROWESS WITH MY OWN EYES!
I WILL NOT REST UNTIL I HAVE FOUND BALDER THE BRAVE AGAIN AND OFFERED HIM MY SWORD-- NOT IN ANGER BUT IN HOMAGE!
SO SWEARS AGNAR OF VANAHEIM!

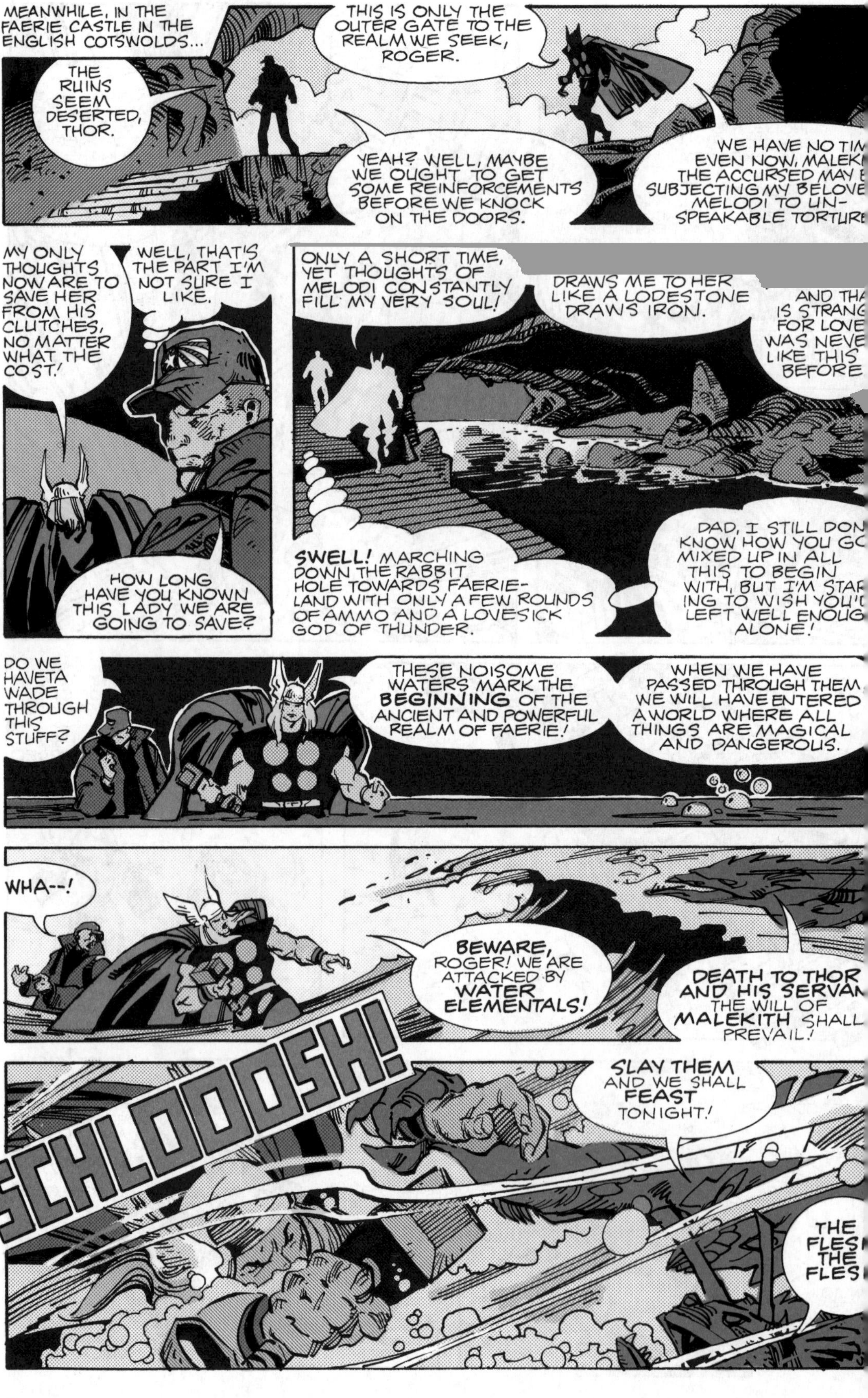
MEANWHILE, IN THE FAERIE CASTLE IN THE ENGLISH COTSWOLDS...
THE RUINS SEEM DESERTED, THOR.
THIS IS ONLY THE OUTER GATE TO THE REALM WE SEEK, ROGER.
YEAH? WELL, MAYBE WE OUGHT TO GET SOME REINFORCEMENTS BEFORE WE KNOCK ON THE DOORS.
WE HAVE NO TIM EVEN NOW, MALEK THE ACCURSED MAY SUBJECTING MY BELOVE MELODI TO UN- SPEAKABLE TORTUR
MY ONLY THOUGHTS NOW ARE TO SAVE HER FROM HIS CLUTCHES, NO MATTER WHAT THE COST!
WELL, THAT'S THE PART I'M NOT SURE I LIKE.
HOW LONG HAVE YOU KNOWN THIS LADY WE ARE GOING TO SAVE?
ONLY A SHORT TIME, YET THOUGHTS OF MELODI CONSTANTLY FILL MY VERY SOUL!
DRAWS ME TO HER LIKE A LODESTONE DRAWS IRON.
AND TH IS STRANG FOR LOVE WAS NEVE LIKE THIS BEFORE
SWELL! MARCHING DOWN THE RABBIT HOLE TOWARDS FAERIE-LAND WITH ONLY A FEW ROUNDS OF AMMO AND A LOVESICK GOD OF THUNDER.
DAD, I STILL DON KNOW HOW YOU G MIXED UP IN ALL THIS TO BEGIN WITH, BUT I'M STA ING TO WISH YOU LEFT WELL ENOUG ALONE!
DO WE HAVETA WADE THROUGH THIS STUFF?
THESE NOISOME WATERS MARK THE BEGINNING OF THE ANCIENT AND POWERFUL REALM OF FAERIE!
WHEN WE HAVE PASSED THROUGH THEM, WE WILL HAVE ENTERED A WORLD WHERE ALL THINGS ARE MAGICAL AND DANGEROUS.
WHA--!
BEWARE, ROGER! WE ARE ATTACKED BY WATER ELEMENTALS!
DEATH TO THOR AND HIS SERVA THE WILL OF MALEKITH SHALL PREVAIL!
SCHLOOOSH!
SLAY THEM AND WE SHALL FEAST TONIGHT!
THE FLES THE FLES

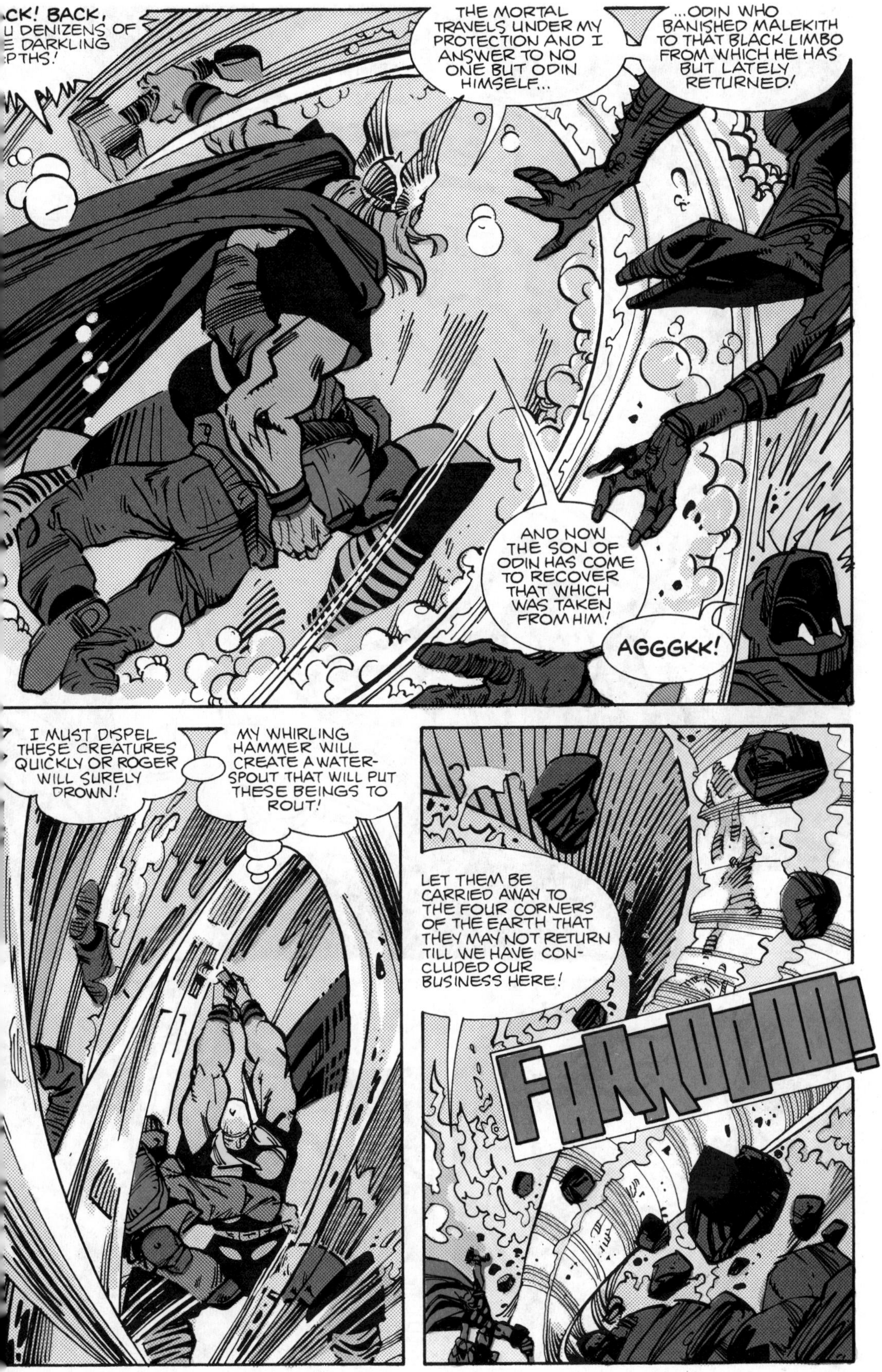

CK! BACK, U DENIZENS OF E DARKLING EPTHS!
THE MORTAL TRAVELS UNDER MY PROTECTION AND I ANSWER TO NO ONE BUT ODIN HIMSELF...
...ODIN WHO BANISHED MALEKITH TO THAT BLACK LIMBO FROM WHICH HE HAS BUT LATELY RETURNED!
AND NOW THE SON OF ODIN HAS COME TO RECOVER THAT WHICH WAS TAKEN FROM HIM!
AGGGKK!
I MUST DISPEL THESE CREATURES QUICKLY OR ROGER WILL SURELY DROWN!
MY WHIRLING HAMMER WILL CREATE A WATER-SPOUT THAT WILL PUT THESE BEINGS TO ROUT!
LET THEM BE CARRIED AWAY TO THE FOUR CORNERS OF THE EARTH THAT THEY MAY NOT RETURN TILL WE HAVE CON-CLUDED OUR BUSINESS HERE!
FARROOOM!

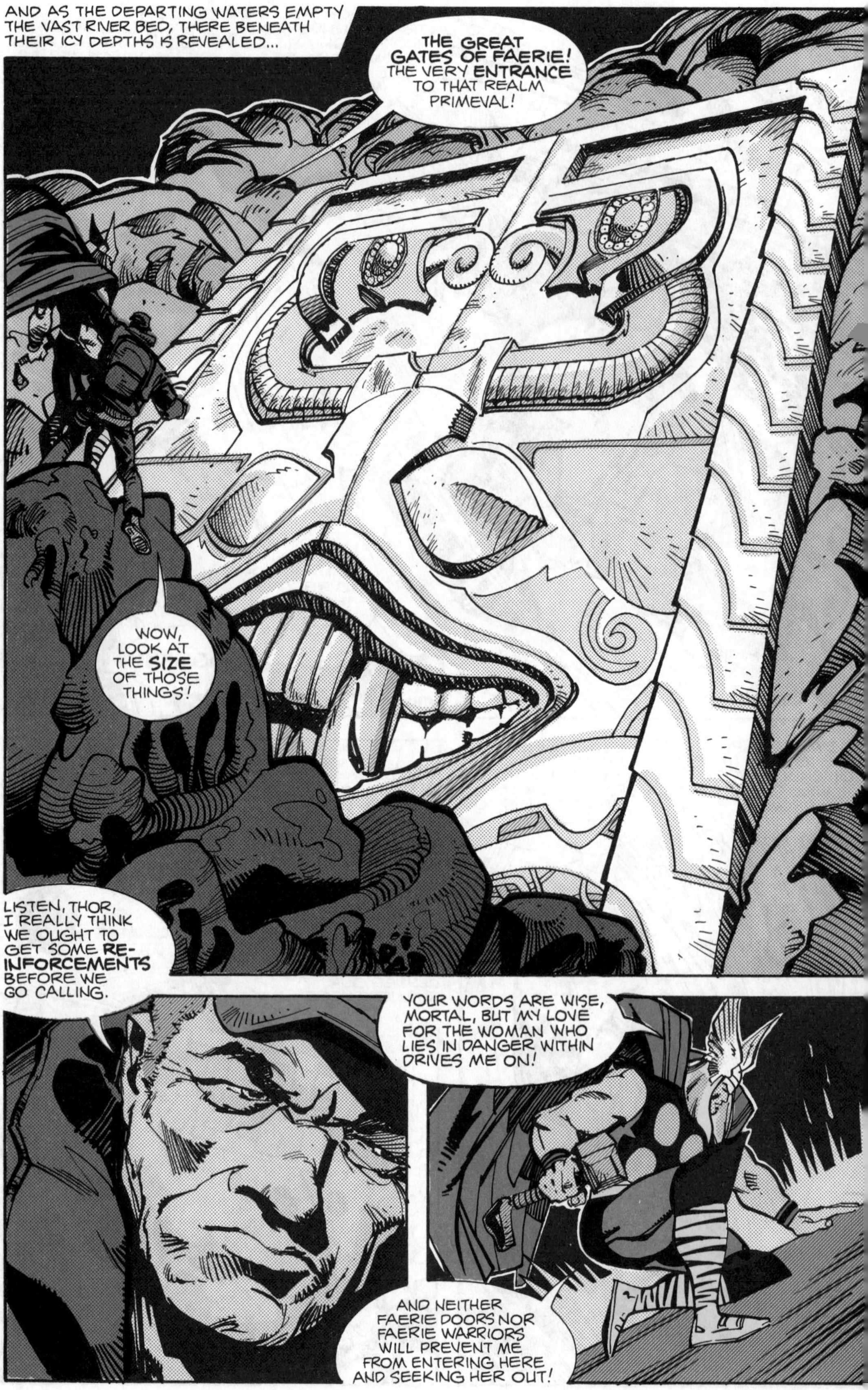
AND AS THE DEPARTING WATERS EMPTY THE VAST RIVER BED, THERE BENEATH THEIR ICY DEPTHS IS REVEALED...
THE GREAT GATES OF FAERIE! THE VERY ENTRANCE TO THAT REALM PRIMEVAL!
WOW, LOOK AT THE SIZE OF THOSE THINGS!
LISTEN, THOR, I REALLY THINK WE OUGHT TO GET SOME RE-INFORCEMENTS BEFORE WE GO CALLING.
YOUR WORDS ARE WISE, MORTAL, BUT MY LOVE FOR THE WOMAN WHO LIES IN DANGER WITHIN DRIVES ME ON!
AND NEITHER FAERIE DOORS NOR FAERIE WARRIORS WILL PREVENT ME FROM ENTERING HERE AND SEEKING HER OUT!

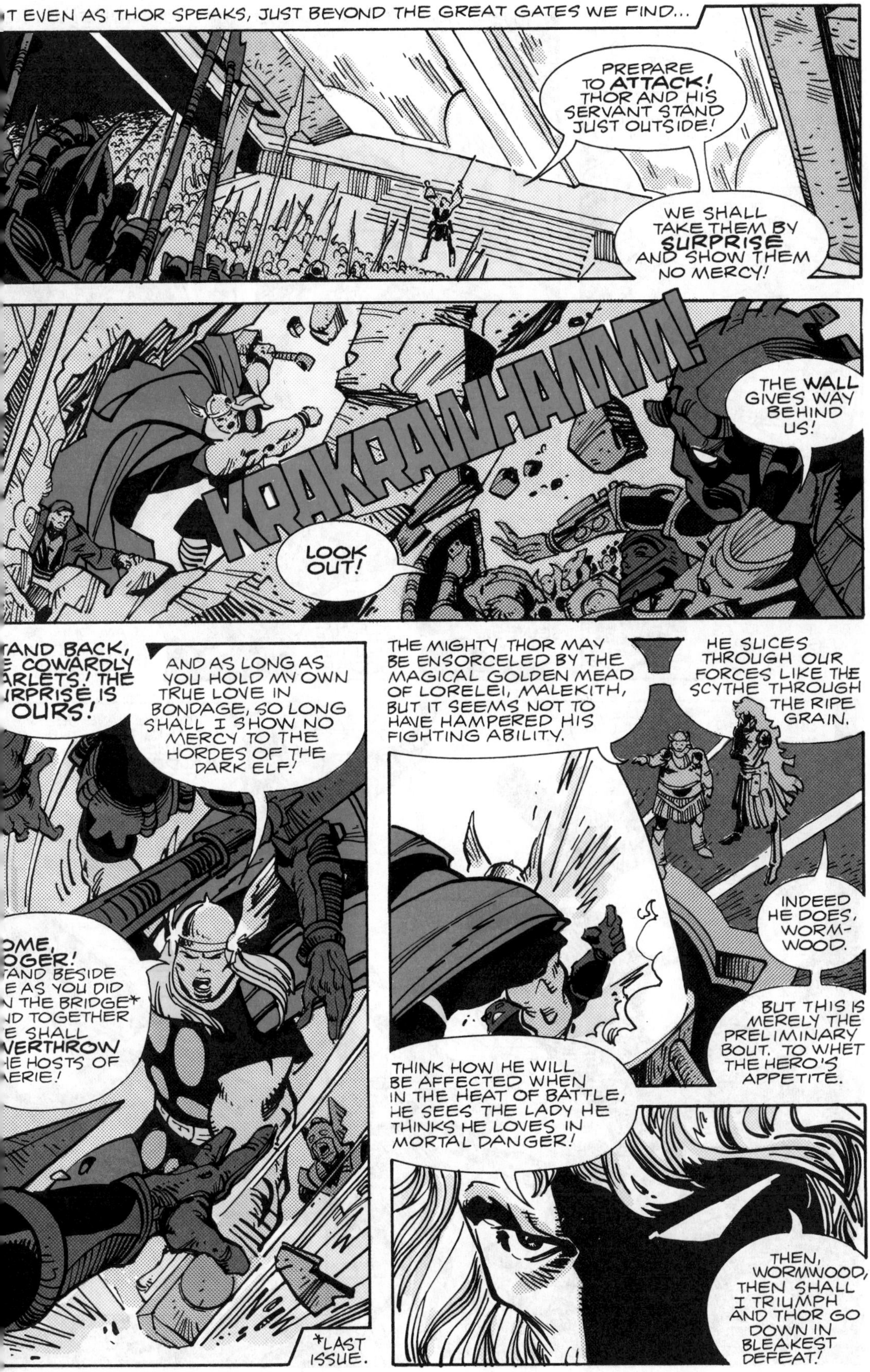
T EVEN AS THOR SPEAKS, JUST BEYOND THE GREAT GATES WE FIND...
PREPARE TO ATTACK! THOR AND HIS SERVANT STAND JUST OUTSIDE!
WE SHALL TAKE THEM BY SURPRISE AND SHOW THEM NO MERCY!
KRAKRAWHAMM!
THE WALL GIVES WAY BEHIND US!
LOOK OUT!
TAND BACK, E COWARDLY ARLETS! THE URPRISE IS OURS!
AND AS LONG AS YOU HOLD MY OWN TRUE LOVE IN BONDAGE, SO LONG SHALL I SHOW NO MERCY TO THE HORDES OF THE DARK ELF!
OME, OGER! TAND BESIDE E AS YOU DID N THE BRIDGE* ND TOGETHER E SHALL VERTHROW HE HOSTS OF ERIE!
*LAST ISSUE.
THE MIGHTY THOR MAY BE ENSORCELED BY THE MAGICAL GOLDEN MEAD OF LORELEI, MALEKITH, BUT IT SEEMS NOT TO HAVE HAMPERED HIS FIGHTING ABILITY.
HE SLICES THROUGH OUR FORCES LIKE THE SCYTHE THROUGH THE RIPE GRAIN.
INDEED HE DOES, WORM-WOOD.
BUT THIS IS MERELY THE PRELIMINARY BOUT, TO WHET THE HERO'S APPETITE.
THINK HOW HE WILL BE AFFECTED WHEN IN THE HEAT OF BATTLE, HE SEES THE LADY HE THINKS HE LOVES IN MORTAL DANGER!
THEN, WORMWOOD, THEN SHALL I TRIUMPH AND THOR GO DOWN IN BLEAKEST DEFEAT!

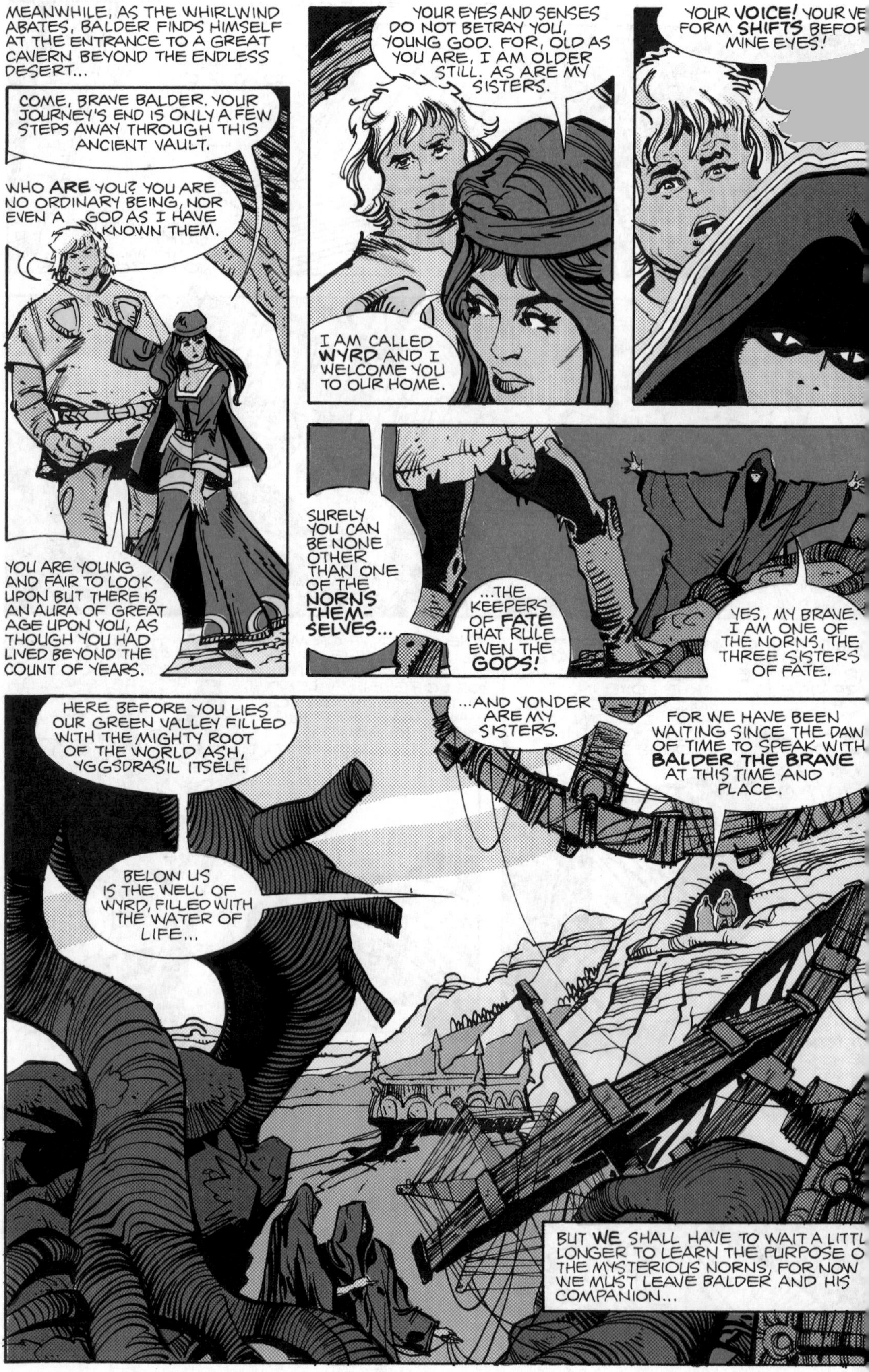
MEANWHILE, AS THE WHIRLWIND ABATES, BALDER FINDS HIMSELF AT THE ENTRANCE TO A GREAT CAVERN BEYOND THE ENDLESS DESERT...
COME, BRAVE BALDER. YOUR JOURNEY'S END IS ONLY A FEW STEPS AWAY THROUGH THIS ANCIENT VAULT.
WHO ARE YOU? YOU ARE NO ORDINARY BEING, NOR EVEN A GOD AS I HAVE KNOWN THEM.
YOU ARE YOUNG AND FAIR TO LOOK UPON BUT THERE IS AN AURA OF GREAT AGE UPON YOU, AS THOUGH YOU HAD LIVED BEYOND THE COUNT OF YEARS.
YOUR EYES AND SENSES DO NOT BETRAY YOU, YOUNG GOD. FOR, OLD AS YOU ARE, I AM OLDER STILL. AS ARE MY SISTERS.
I AM CALLED WYRD AND I WELCOME YOU TO OUR HOME.
YOUR VOICE! YOUR VE FORM SHIFTS BEFOR MINE EYES!
SURELY YOU CAN BE NONE OTHER THAN ONE OF THE NORNS THEM-SELVES...
...THE KEEPERS OF FATE THAT RULE EVEN THE GODS!
YES, MY BRAVE. I AM ONE OF THE NORNS, THE THREE SISTERS OF FATE.
HERE BEFORE YOU LIES OUR GREEN VALLEY FILLED WITH THE MIGHTY ROOT OF THE WORLD ASH, YGGSDRASIL ITSELF.
BELOW US IS THE WELL OF WYRD, FILLED WITH THE WATER OF LIFE...
...AND YONDER ARE MY SISTERS.
FOR WE HAVE BEEN WAITING SINCE THE DAW OF TIME TO SPEAK WITH BALDER THE BRAVE AT THIS TIME AND PLACE.
BUT WE SHALL HAVE TO WAIT A LITTL LONGER TO LEARN THE PURPOSE O THE MYSTERIOUS NORNS, FOR NOW WE MUST LEAVE BALDER AND HIS COMPANION...

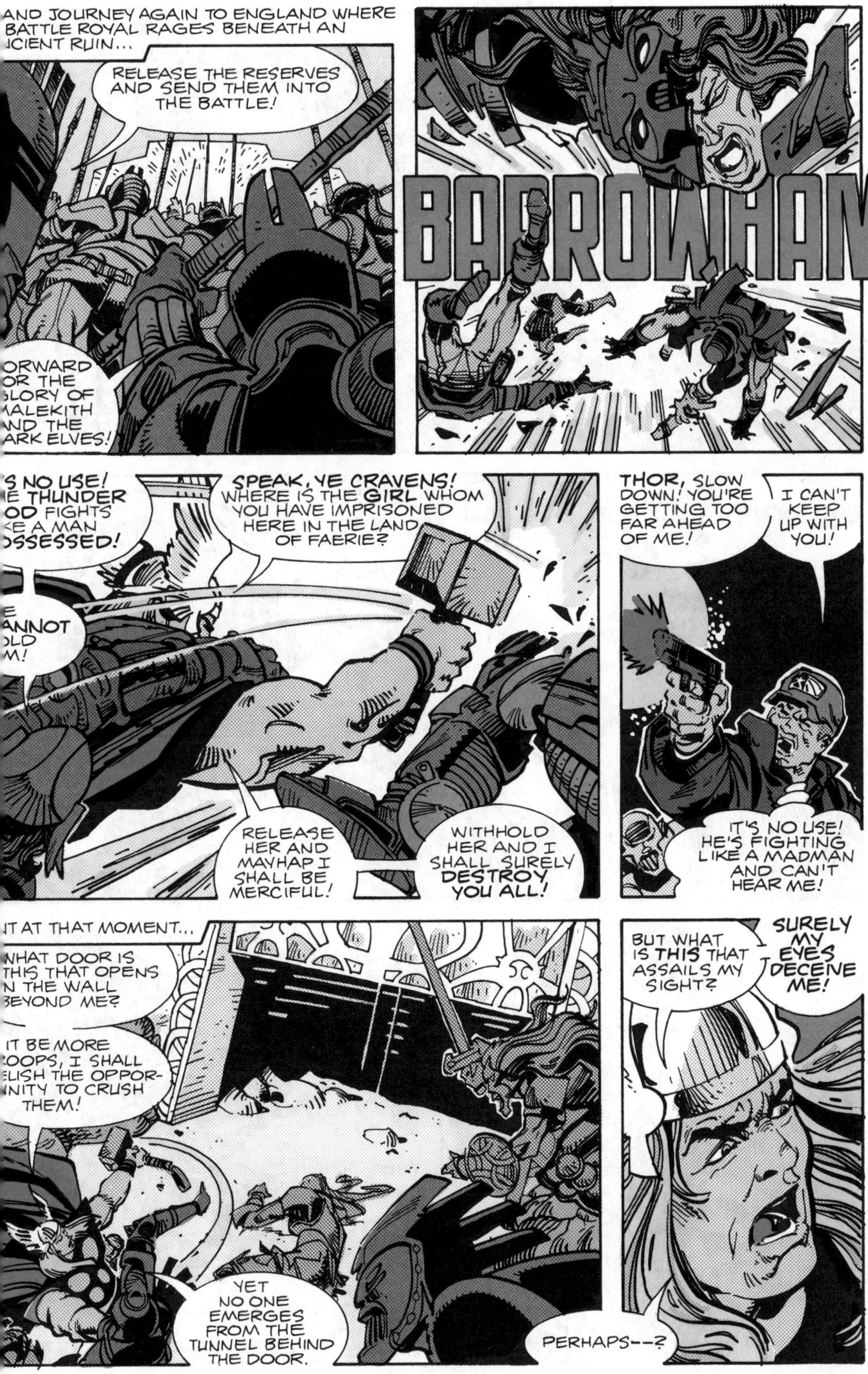
AND JOURNEY AGAIN TO ENGLAND WHERE BATTLE ROYAL RAGES BENEATH AN CIENT RUIN...
RELEASE THE RESERVES AND SEND THEM INTO THE BATTLE!
ORWARD OR THE LORY OF ALEKITH ND THE ARK ELVES!
BARROWHAM
S NO USE! E THUNDER OD FIGHTS E A MAN OSSESSED!
SPEAK, YE CRAVENS! WHERE IS THE GIRL WHOM YOU HAVE IMPRISONED HERE IN THE LAND OF FAERIE?
E ANNOT OLD M!
RELEASE HER AND MAYHAP I SHALL BE MERCIFUL!
WITHHOLD HER AND I SHALL SURELY DESTROY YOU ALL!
THOR, SLOW DOWN! YOU'RE GETTING TOO FAR AHEAD OF ME!
I CAN'T KEEP UP WITH YOU!
IT'S NO USE! HE'S FIGHTING LIKE A MADMAN AND CAN'T HEAR ME!
T AT THAT MOMENT...
WHAT DOOR IS THIS THAT OPENS N THE WALL BEYOND ME?
IT BE MORE ROOPS, I SHALL ELISH THE OPPOR- NITY TO CRUSH THEM!
YET NO ONE EMERGES FROM THE TUNNEL BEHIND THE DOOR.
BUT WHAT IS THIS THAT ASSAILS MY SIGHT?
SURELY MY EYES DECEIVE ME!
PERHAPS--?

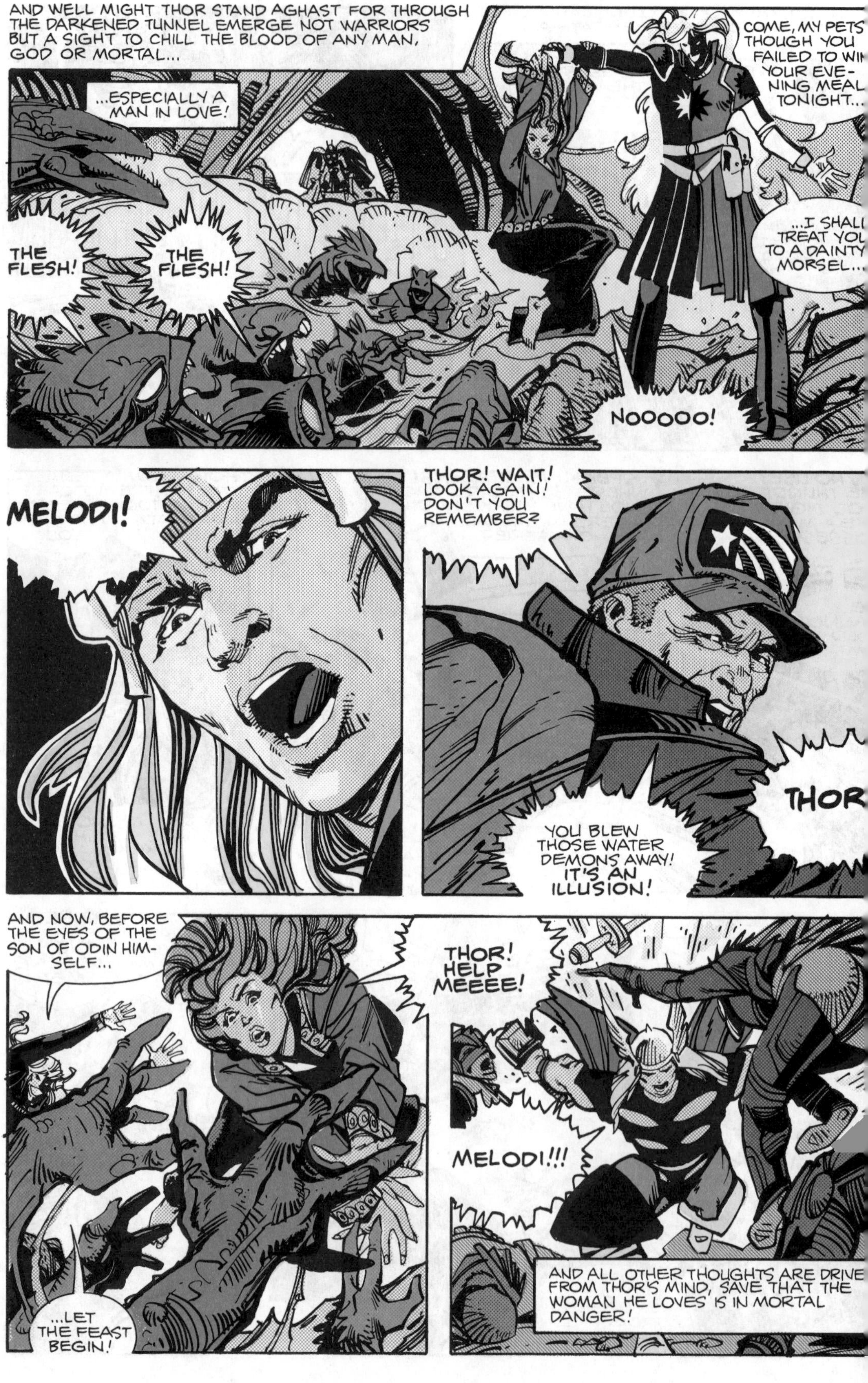

AND WELL MIGHT THOR STAND AGHAST FOR THROUGH THE DARKENED TUNNEL EMERGE NOT WARRIORS BUT A SIGHT TO CHILL THE BLOOD OF ANY MAN, GOD OR MORTAL...
...ESPECIALLY A MAN IN LOVE!
COME, MY PETS THOUGH YOU FAILED TO WI YOUR EVE-NING MEAL TONIGHT...
THE FLESH!
THE FLESH!
...I SHAL TREAT YO TO A DAINTY MORSEL...
NOOOOO!
MELODI!
THOR! WAIT! LOOK AGAIN! DON'T YOU REMEMBER?
THOR
YOU BLEW THOSE WATER DEMONS AWAY! IT'S AN ILLUSION!
AND NOW, BEFORE THE EYES OF THE SON OF ODIN HIM-SELF...
THOR! HELP MEEEE!
MELODI!!!
...LET THE FEAST BEGIN!
AND ALL OTHER THOUGHTS ARE DRIVE FROM THOR'S MIND, SAVE THAT THE WOMAN HE LOVES IS IN MORTAL DANGER!

OR! COME BACK! CAN'T HOLD THEM F WITHOUT YOU!

DON'T FORGET THE CAS--

BUT ROGER'S CRY GOES UNHEEDED AS THOR RACES INTO THE TUNNEL...

MALEKITH WAS RIGHT! THE THUNDERER IS OBLIVIOUS TO EVERYTHING BUT THE WOMAN!

HE FAILED TO SEE ME IN THE SHADOWS IN MY EBONY ARMOR...

...BUT I CAN SEE HIM!

THRAKT!

UHHH!

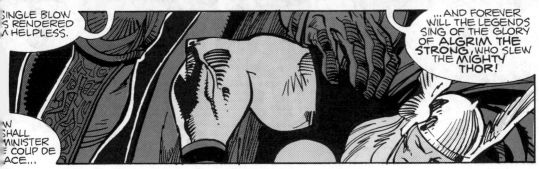

INGLE BLOW S RENDERED A HELPLESS.

W SHALL MINISTER E COUP DE ACE...

...AND FOREVER WILL THE LEGENDS SING OF THE GLORY OF ALGRIM THE STRONG, WHO SLEW THE MIGHTY THOR!

BUT AS ALGRIM PREPARES TO DELIVER THAT BLOW, LET US LOOK FOR A MOMENT AT FABLED ASGARD WHERE ODIN, RULER OF THE GODS, SITS ON HIS GOLDEN THRONE...

HAIL, SIRE! YOU HAVE CALLED AND THE **WARRIORS THREE** HAVE ANSWERED.

HOW MAY THE KINGDOM'S DOUGHTIEST FIGHTERS SERVE THEIR LIEGE?

WELL MET, BRAVE WARRIORS. HEAR NOW THE WORDS OF YOUR LORD.

A STORM IS ABOUT TO BREAK AGAINST ASGARD AND ALL THAT SHE HOLDS DEAR.

AND IF SHE WILL WEATHER THE STORM, NONE CAN SAY.

BUT NOW THE TIME IS RIPE WHEN WE MUST PREPARE THE ARMED MIGHT OF THE GOLDEN REALM AGAINST A SEA OF ENEMIES.

THEREFORE I CHARGE THE WARRIORS THREE WITH THE TASK OF GATHERING AND ORDERING THE FIGHTING MEN OF ASGARD AND HER ALLIES.

TO EVERY CORNER OF THE KINGDOM LET THE WORD GO FORTH THE HOSTING OF ASGARD SHALL BEGIN!

SO BE IT!

AND EVEN VOLSTAGG IS SILENT AS THE SOLDIERS THREE PASS OUT OF THE HALL INTO THE SUNLIGHT BEYOND...

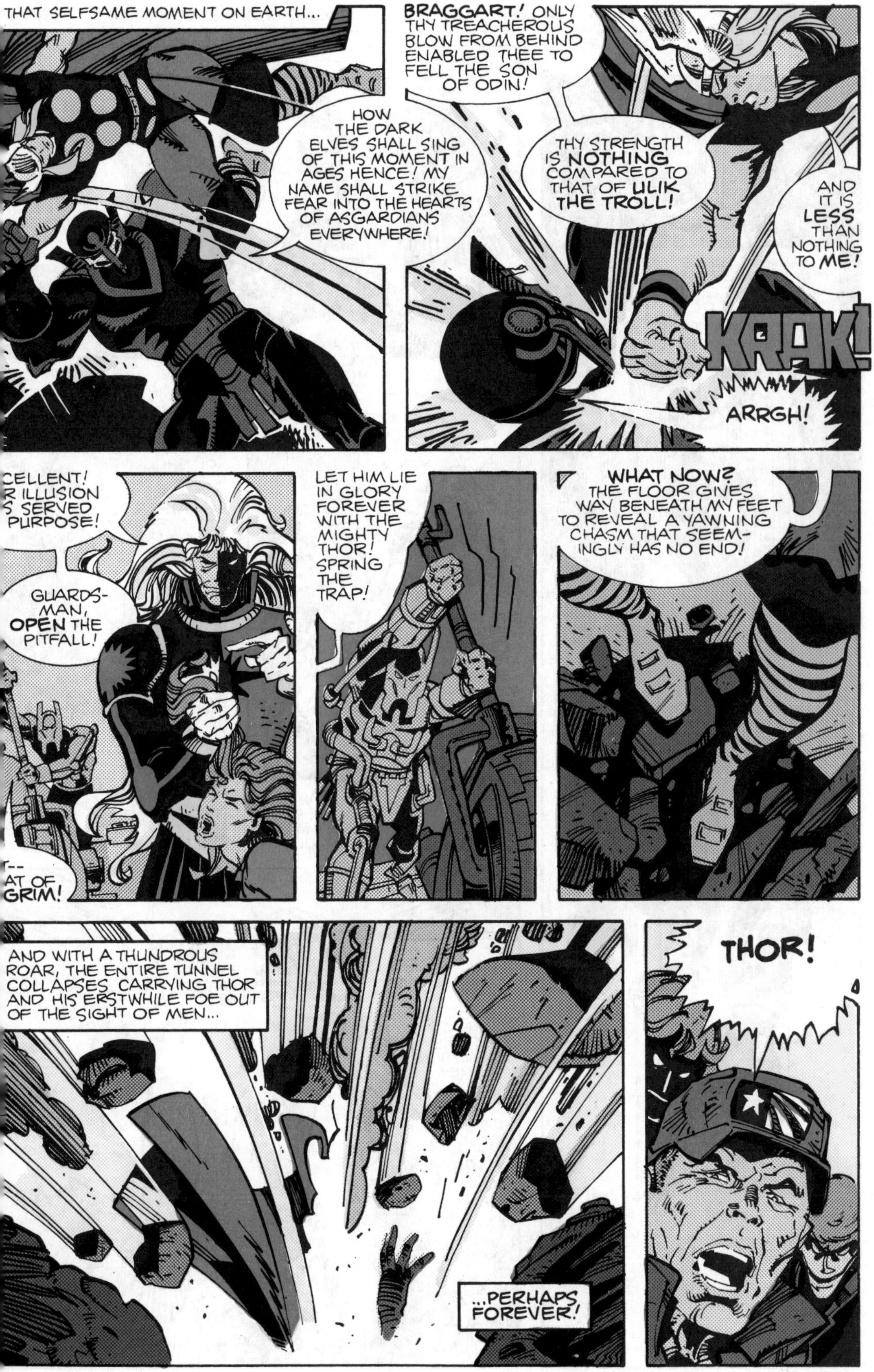

THAT SELFSAME MOMENT ON EARTH...
HOW THE DARK ELVES SHALL SING OF THIS MOMENT IN AGES HENCE! MY NAME SHALL STRIKE FEAR INTO THE HEARTS OF ASGARDIANS EVERYWHERE!
BRAGGART! ONLY THY TREACHEROUS BLOW FROM BEHIND ENABLED THEE TO FELL THE SON OF ODIN!
THY STRENGTH IS NOTHING COMPARED TO THAT OF ULIK THE TROLL!
AND IT IS LESS THAN NOTHING TO ME!
KRAK!
ARRGH!
CELLENT! R ILLUSION S SERVED PURPOSE!
GUARDS-MAN, OPEN THE PITFALL!
T-- AT OF GRIM!
LET HIM LIE IN GLORY FOREVER WITH THE MIGHTY THOR! SPRING THE TRAP!
WHAT NOW? THE FLOOR GIVES WAY BENEATH MY FEET TO REVEAL A YAWNING CHASM THAT SEEM-INGLY HAS NO END!
AND WITH A THUNDROUS ROAR, THE ENTIRE TUNNEL COLLAPSES CARRYING THOR AND HIS ERSTWHILE FOE OUT OF THE SIGHT OF MEN...
...PERHAPS FOREVER!
THOR!

ROGER'S CALL IS ALL BUT DROWNED OUT BY THE ROARING AVALANCHE THAT FOLLOWS THOR AND ALGRIM INTO THE BOTTOMLESS CHASM...

...UNTIL THE LAST ECHOES HAVE DIED AWAY AND ONLY SILENC REMAINS.

AT LAST I AM REVENGED UPON ODIN FOR MY BANISHMENT. FAREWELL, THOR.

YOU WER NO MATCH FO MALEKIT THE ACCURSEC

...AN AVALANCHE THAT SHAKES THE VERY ROOTS OF THE FAERIE KINGDOM...

WHAT ABOUT THE WOMAN, LORD?

SHE'S YOURS, WORMWOOD. DO WITH HER WHAT YOU WILL.

BUT TREAT HER AS SHE DESERVES. AFTER ALL, HER GOLDEN MEAD ENABLED US TO DEFEAT THE GOD OF THUNDER.

I WISH TO SEE OUR OTHER MORTAL GUEST.

SO YOU ARE ERIC'S WHELP, EH?

HOW APPROPRIATE THAT THE SON SHOULD RECOVER THE TREASURE WHICH HIS FATHER STOLE FROM ME SO MANY EONS AGO.

OPEN HIS KNAPSACK.

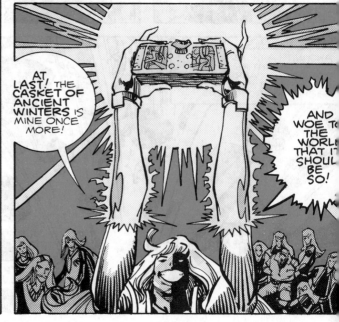

AT LAST! THE CASKET OF ANCIENT WINTERS IS MINE ONCE MORE!

AND WOE TO THE WORL THAT IT SHOUL BE SO!

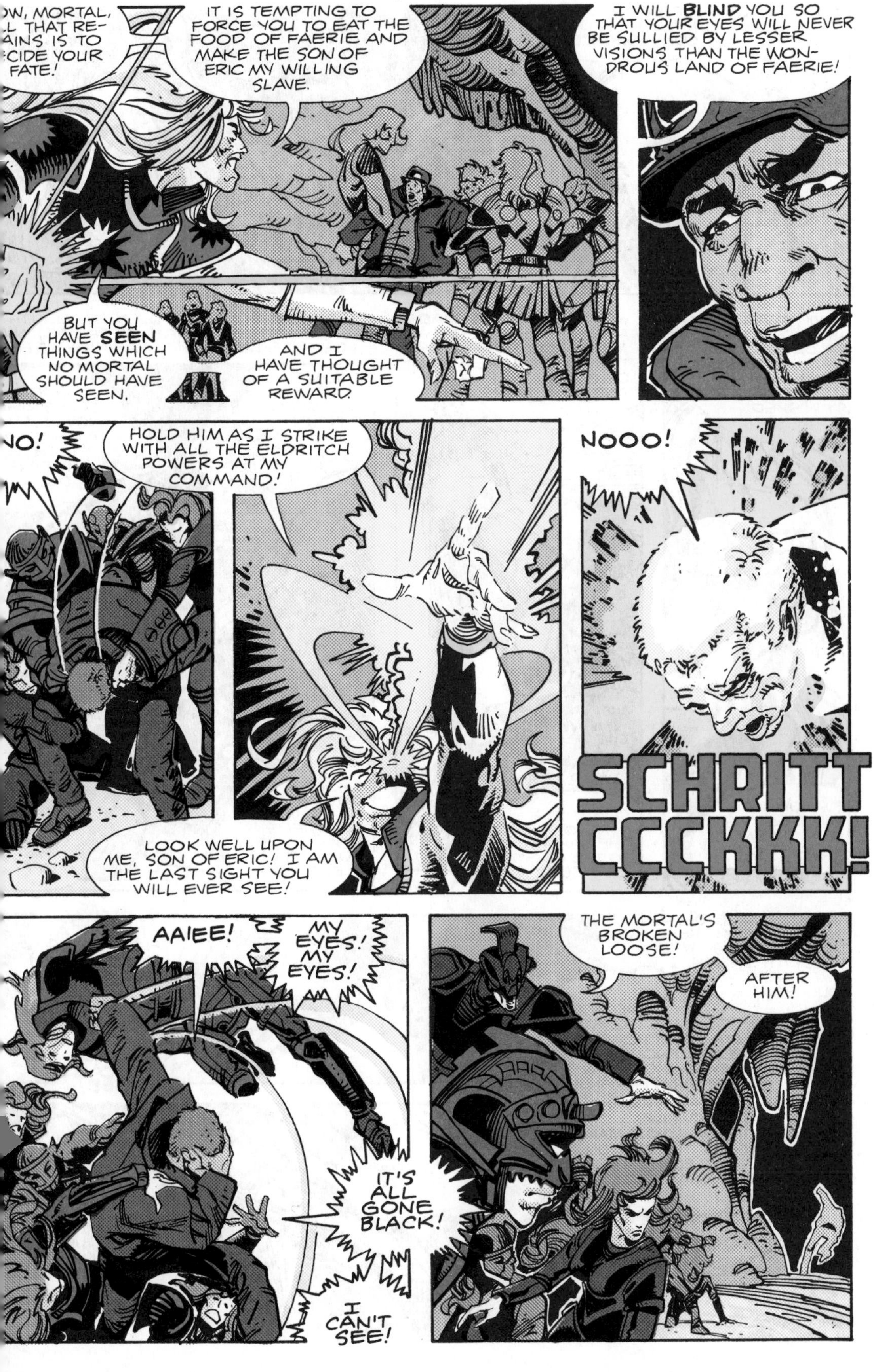

OW, MORTAL, LL THAT RE- AINS IS TO CIDE YOUR FATE!
IT IS TEMPTING TO FORCE YOU TO EAT THE FOOD OF FAERIE AND MAKE THE SON OF ERIC MY WILLING SLAVE.
BUT YOU HAVE SEEN THINGS WHICH NO MORTAL SHOULD HAVE SEEN.
AND I HAVE THOUGHT OF A SUITABLE REWARD.
I WILL BLIND YOU SO THAT YOUR EYES WILL NEVER BE SULLIED BY LESSER VISIONS THAN THE WONDROUS LAND OF FAERIE!
NO!
HOLD HIM AS I STRIKE WITH ALL THE ELDRITCH POWERS AT MY COMMAND!
LOOK WELL UPON ME, SON OF ERIC! I AM THE LAST SIGHT YOU WILL EVER SEE!
NOOO!
SCHRITT CCCKKK!
AAIEE!
MY EYES! MY EYES!
IT'S ALL GONE BLACK!
I CAN'T SEE!
THE MORTAL'S BROKEN LOOSE!
AFTER HIM!

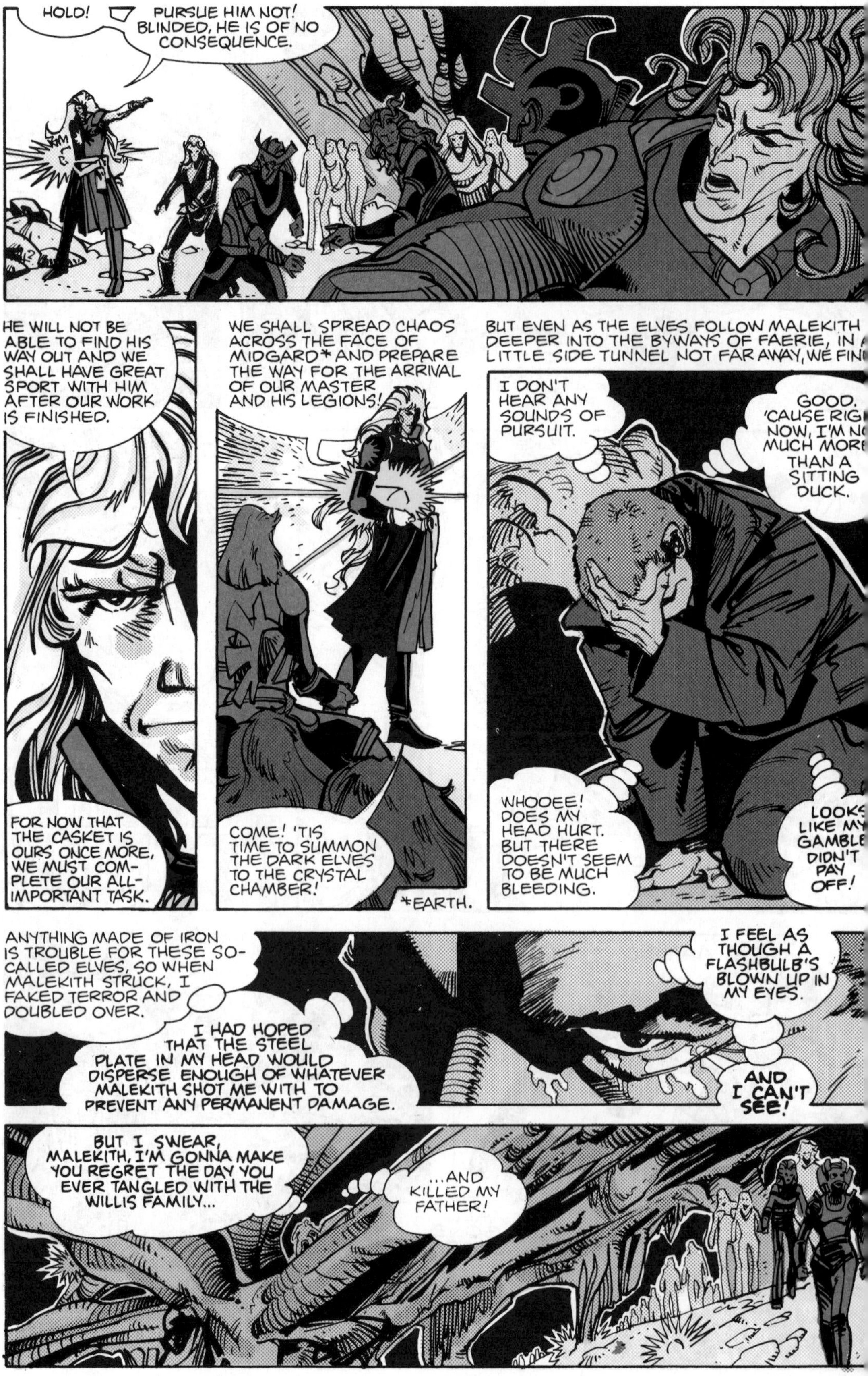
HOLD!
PURSUE HIM NOT! BLINDED, HE IS OF NO CONSEQUENCE.
HE WILL NOT BE ABLE TO FIND HIS WAY OUT AND WE SHALL HAVE GREAT SPORT WITH HIM AFTER OUR WORK IS FINISHED.
FOR NOW THAT THE CASKET IS OURS ONCE MORE, WE MUST COMPLETE OUR ALL-IMPORTANT TASK.
WE SHALL SPREAD CHAOS ACROSS THE FACE OF MIDGARD* AND PREPARE THE WAY FOR THE ARRIVAL OF OUR MASTER AND HIS LEGIONS!
COME! 'TIS TIME TO SUMMON THE DARK ELVES TO THE CRYSTAL CHAMBER!
*EARTH.
BUT EVEN AS THE ELVES FOLLOW MALEKITH DEEPER INTO THE BYWAYS OF FAERIE, IN A LITTLE SIDE TUNNEL NOT FAR AWAY, WE FIN
I DON'T HEAR ANY SOUNDS OF PURSUIT.
GOOD. 'CAUSE RIG NOW, I'M N MUCH MORE THAN A SITTING DUCK.
WHOOEE! DOES MY HEAD HURT. BUT THERE DOESN'T SEEM TO BE MUCH BLEEDING.
LOOK LIKE MY GAMBLE DIDN'T PAY OFF!
ANYTHING MADE OF IRON IS TROUBLE FOR THESE SO-CALLED ELVES, SO WHEN MALEKITH STRUCK, I FAKED TERROR AND DOUBLED OVER.
I HAD HOPED THAT THE STEEL PLATE IN MY HEAD WOULD DISPERSE ENOUGH OF WHATEVER MALEKITH SHOT ME WITH TO PREVENT ANY PERMANENT DAMAGE.
I FEEL AS THOUGH A FLASHBULB'S BLOWN UP IN MY EYES.
AND I CAN'T SEE!
BUT I SWEAR, MALEKITH, I'M GONNA MAKE YOU REGRET THE DAY YOU EVER TANGLED WITH THE WILLIS FAMILY...
...AND KILLED MY FATHER!

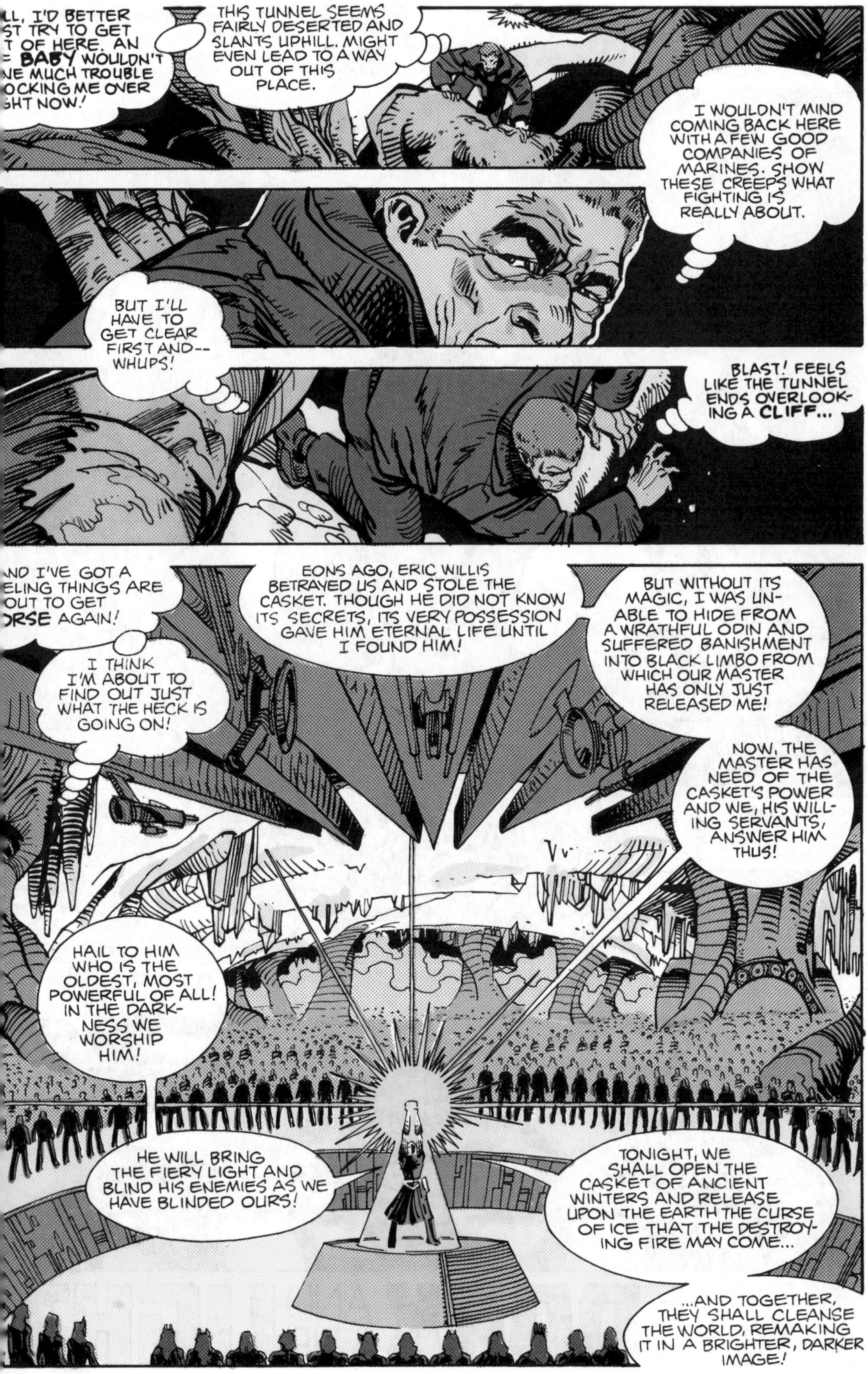

LL, I'D BETTER ST TRY TO GET T OF HERE. AN BABY WOULDN'T VE MUCH TROUBLE OCKING ME OVER GHT NOW!
THIS TUNNEL SEEMS FAIRLY DESERTED AND SLANTS UPHILL. MIGHT EVEN LEAD TO A WAY OUT OF THIS PLACE.
I WOULDN'T MIND COMING BACK HERE WITH A FEW GOOD COMPANIES OF MARINES. SHOW THESE CREEPS WHAT FIGHTING IS REALLY ABOUT.
BUT I'LL HAVE TO GET CLEAR FIRST AND-- WHUPS!
BLAST! FEELS LIKE THE TUNNEL ENDS OVERLOOKING A CLIFF...
ND I'VE GOT A ELING THINGS ARE OUT TO GET RSE AGAIN!
I THINK I'M ABOUT TO FIND OUT JUST WHAT THE HECK IS GOING ON!
EONS AGO, ERIC WILLIS BETRAYED US AND STOLE THE CASKET. THOUGH HE DID NOT KNOW ITS SECRETS, ITS VERY POSSESSION GAVE HIM ETERNAL LIFE UNTIL I FOUND HIM!
BUT WITHOUT ITS MAGIC, I WAS UNABLE TO HIDE FROM A WRATHFUL ODIN AND SUFFERED BANISHMENT INTO BLACK LIMBO FROM WHICH OUR MASTER HAS ONLY JUST RELEASED ME!
NOW, THE MASTER HAS NEED OF THE CASKET'S POWER AND WE, HIS WILLING SERVANTS, ANSWER HIM THUS!
HAIL TO HIM WHO IS THE OLDEST, MOST POWERFUL OF ALL! IN THE DARKNESS WE WORSHIP HIM!
HE WILL BRING THE FIERY LIGHT AND BLIND HIS ENEMIES AS WE HAVE BLINDED OURS!
TONIGHT, WE SHALL OPEN THE CASKET OF ANCIENT WINTERS AND RELEASE UPON THE EARTH THE CURSE OF ICE THAT THE DESTROYING FIRE MAY COME...
...AND TOGETHER, THEY SHALL CLEANSE THE WORLD, REMAKING IT IN A BRIGHTER, DARKER IMAGE!

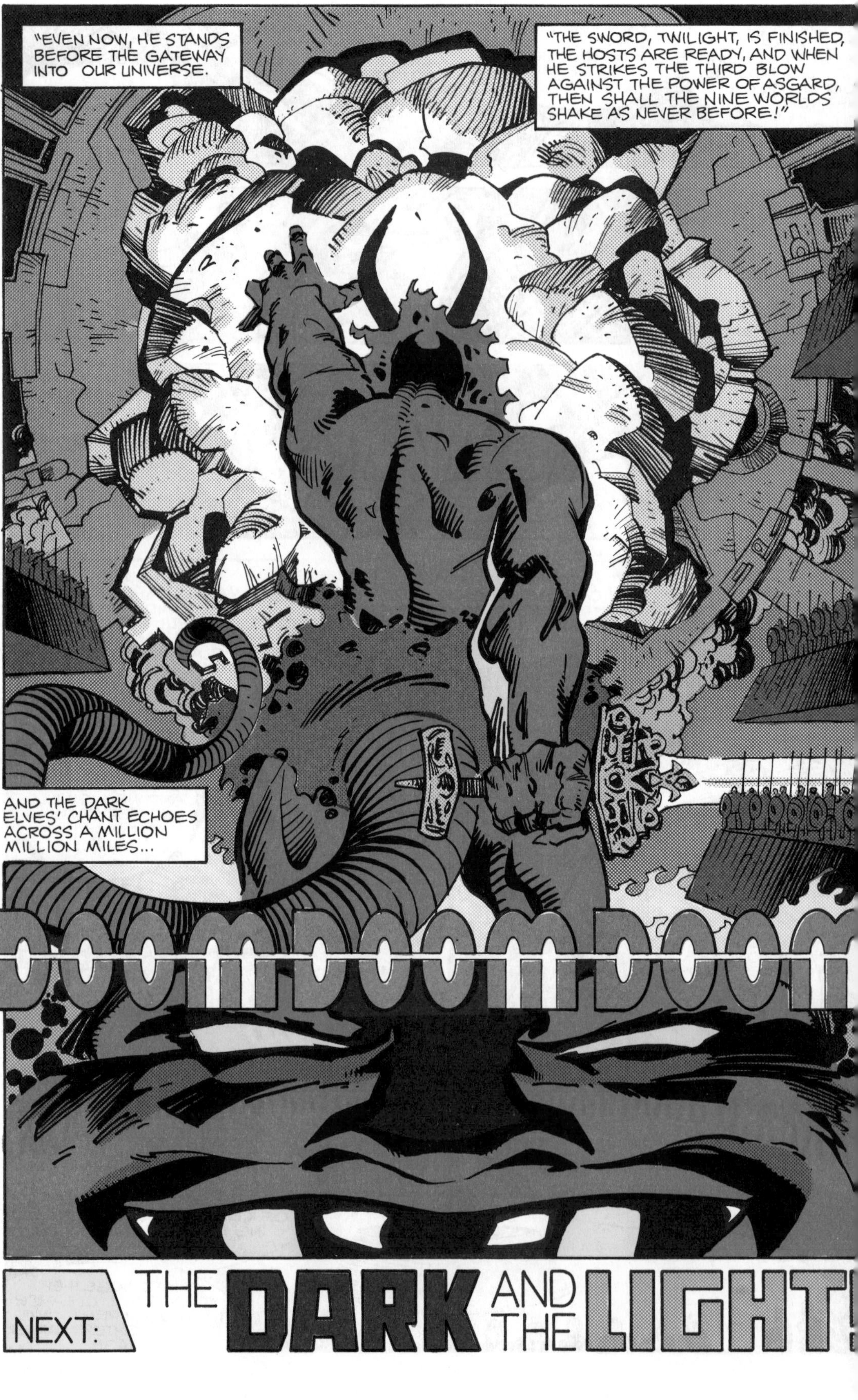
"EVEN NOW, HE STANDS BEFORE THE GATEWAY INTO OUR UNIVERSE.
"THE SWORD, TWILIGHT, IS FINISHED, THE HOSTS ARE READY, AND WHEN HE STRIKES THE THIRD BLOW AGAINST THE POWER OF ASGARD, THEN SHALL THE NINE WORLDS SHAKE AS NEVER BEFORE!"
AND THE DARK ELVES' CHANT ECHOES ACROSS A MILLION MILLION MILES...
DOOM DOOM DOOM
NEXT: THE DARK AND THE LIGHT!

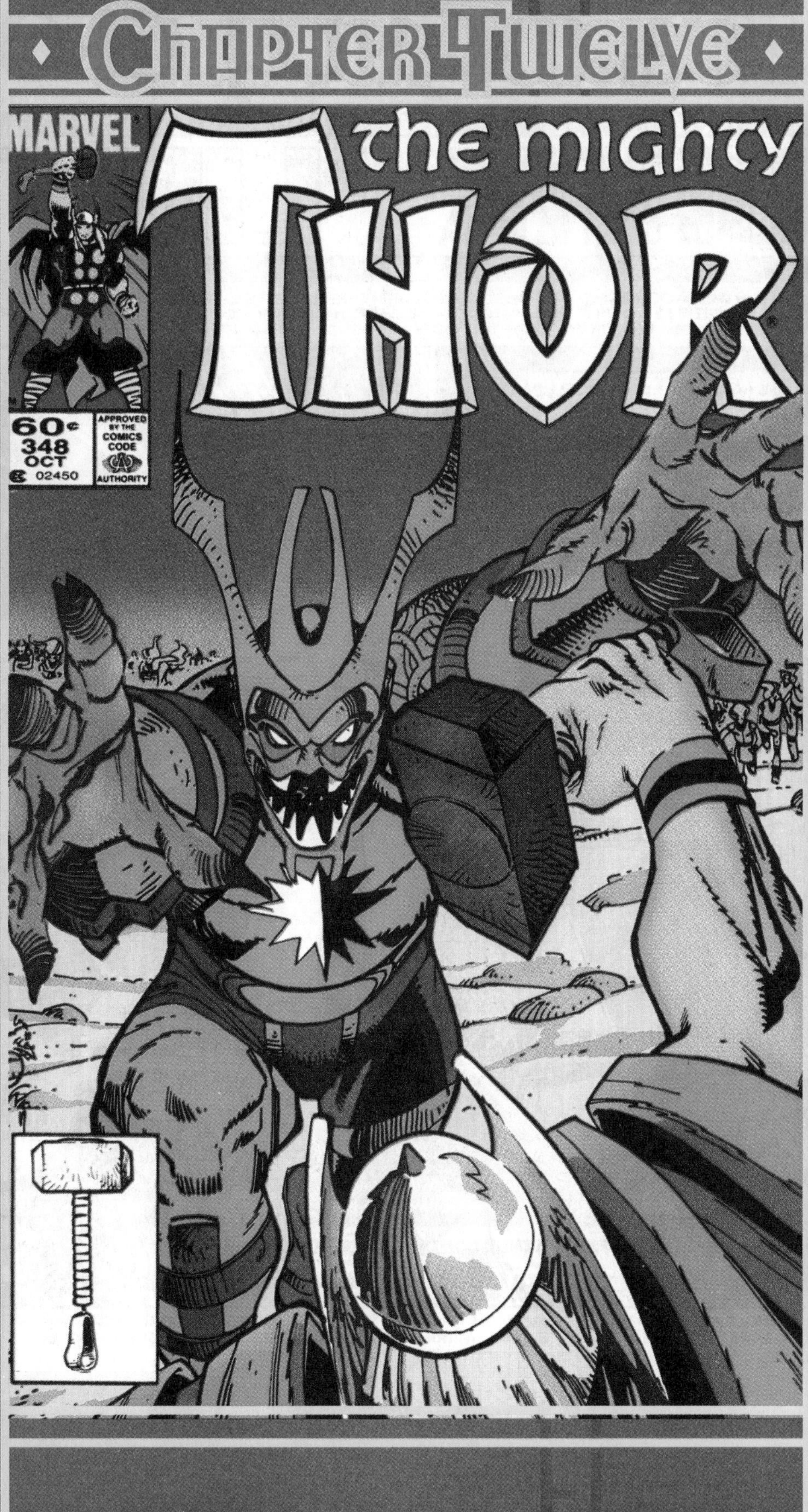
Chapter Twelve
MARVEL
the mighty
THOR
60¢
348
OCT
02450
APPROVED BY THE COMICS CODE AUTHORITY

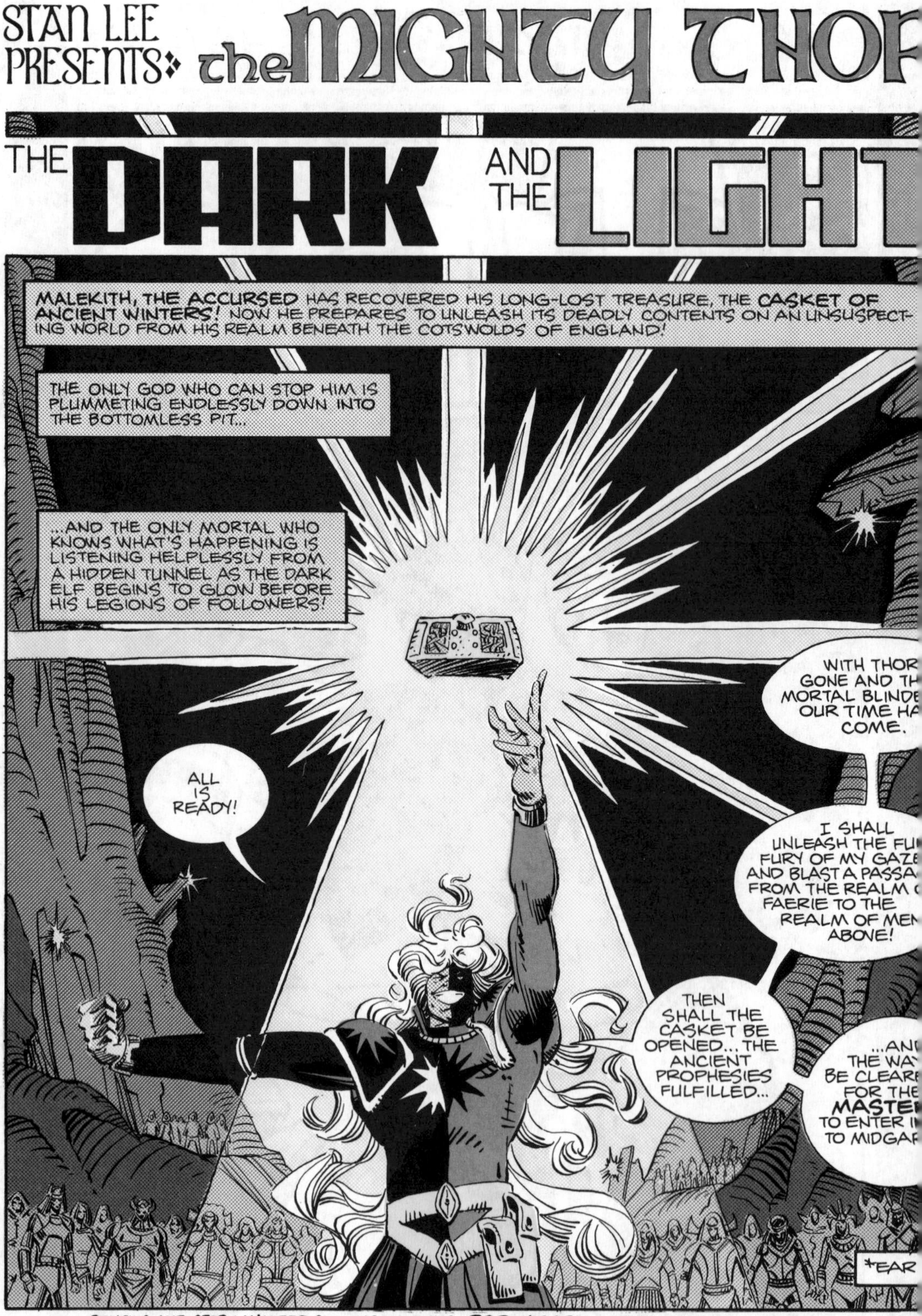
STAN LEE PRESENTS: the MIGHTY THOR
THE DARK AND THE LIGHT
MALEKITH, THE ACCURSED HAS RECOVERED HIS LONG-LOST TREASURE, THE CASKET OF ANCIENT WINTERS! NOW HE PREPARES TO UNLEASH ITS DEADLY CONTENTS ON AN UNSUSPECTING WORLD FROM HIS REALM BENEATH THE COTSWOLDS OF ENGLAND!
THE ONLY GOD WHO CAN STOP HIM IS PLUMMETING ENDLESSLY DOWN INTO THE BOTTOMLESS PIT...
...AND THE ONLY MORTAL WHO KNOWS WHAT'S HAPPENING IS LISTENING HELPLESSLY FROM A HIDDEN TUNNEL AS THE DARK ELF BEGINS TO GLOW BEFORE HIS LEGIONS OF FOLLOWERS!
ALL IS READY!
WITH THOR GONE AND TH MORTAL BLINDE OUR TIME HA COME.
I SHALL UNLEASH THE FU FURY OF MY GAZE AND BLAST A PASSA FROM THE REALM FAERIE TO THE REALM OF MEN ABOVE!
THEN SHALL THE CASKET BE OPENED... THE ANCIENT PROPHESIES FULFILLED...
...AN THE WA BE CLEAR FOR THE MASTE TO ENTER I TO MIDGAR
*EAR

PENCILS AND STORY: WALTER SIMONSON INKS: BOB WIACEK LETTERING: JOHN WORKMAN JR.
COLORS: CHRISTIE SCHEELE EDITING: MARK GRUENWALD EDITOR-IN-CHIEF: JIM SHOOTER

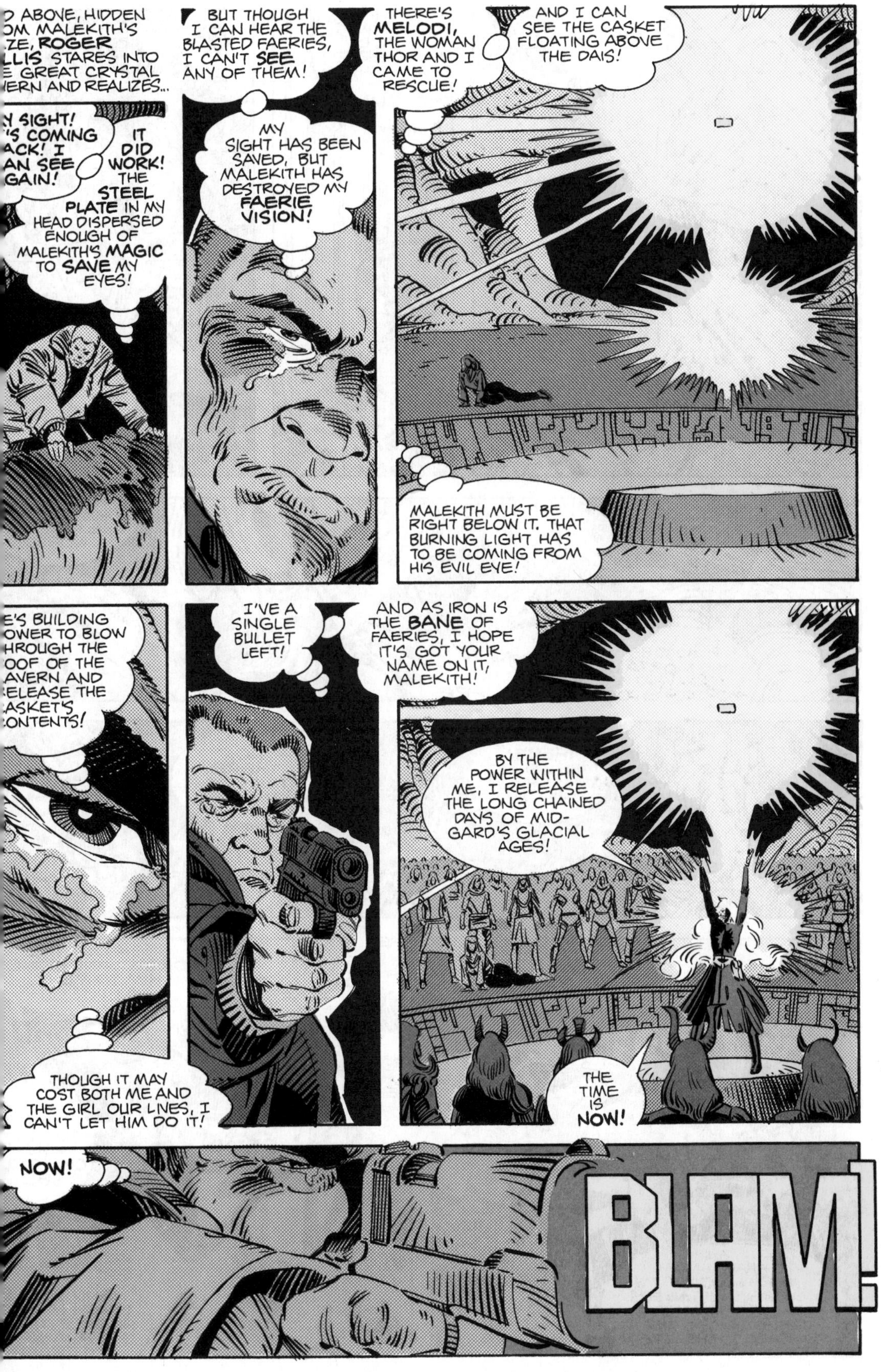

D ABOVE, HIDDEN OM MALEKITH'S ZE, ROGER LLIS STARES INTO E GREAT CRYSTAL VERN AND REALIZES...
Y SIGHT! 'S COMING ACK! I AN SEE GAIN!
IT DID WORK! THE STEEL PLATE IN MY HEAD DISPERSED ENOUGH OF MALEKITH'S MAGIC TO SAVE MY EYES!
BUT THOUGH I CAN HEAR THE BLASTED FAERIES, I CAN'T SEE ANY OF THEM!
MY SIGHT HAS BEEN SAVED, BUT MALEKITH HAS DESTROYED MY FAERIE VISION!
THERE'S MELODI, THE WOMAN THOR AND I CAME TO RESCUE!
AND I CAN SEE THE CASKET FLOATING ABOVE THE DAIS!
MALEKITH MUST BE RIGHT BELOW IT. THAT BURNING LIGHT HAS TO BE COMING FROM HIS EVIL EYE!
E'S BUILDING OWER TO BLOW HROUGH THE OOF OF THE AVERN AND ELEASE THE ASKET'S ONTENTS!
THOUGH IT MAY COST BOTH ME AND THE GIRL OUR LIVES, I CAN'T LET HIM DO IT!
I'VE A SINGLE BULLET LEFT!
AND AS IRON IS THE BANE OF FAERIES, I HOPE IT'S GOT YOUR NAME ON IT, MALEKITH!
BY THE POWER WITHIN ME, I RELEASE THE LONG CHAINED DAYS OF MID-GARD'S GLACIAL AGES!
THE TIME IS NOW!
NOW!
BLAM!

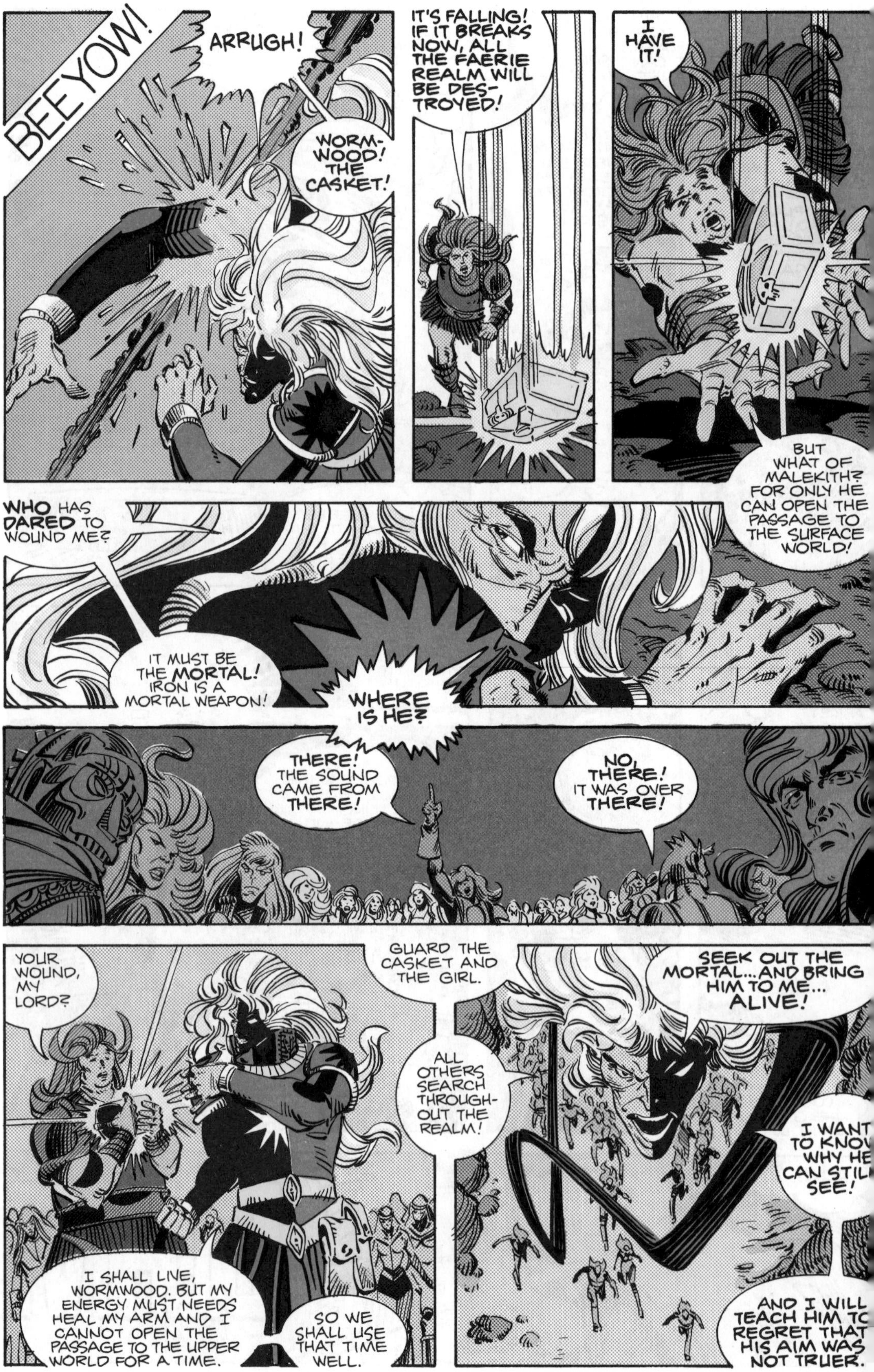
BEEYOW!
ARRUGH!
WORM-WOOD! THE CASKET!
IT'S FALLING! IF IT BREAKS NOW, ALL THE FAERIE REALM WILL BE DES-TROYED!
I HAVE IT!
BUT WHAT OF MALEKITH? FOR ONLY HE CAN OPEN THE PASSAGE TO THE SURFACE WORLD!
WHO HAS DARED TO WOUND ME?
IT MUST BE THE MORTAL! IRON IS A MORTAL WEAPON!
WHERE IS HE?
THERE! THE SOUND CAME FROM THERE!
NO, THERE! IT WAS OVER THERE!
YOUR WOUND, MY LORD?
I SHALL LIVE, WORMWOOD. BUT MY ENERGY MUST NEEDS HEAL MY ARM AND I CANNOT OPEN THE PASSAGE TO THE UPPER WORLD FOR A TIME.
SO WE SHALL USE THAT TIME WELL.
GUARD THE CASKET AND THE GIRL.
ALL OTHERS SEARCH THROUGH-OUT THE REALM!
SEEK OUT THE MORTAL... AND BRING HIM TO ME... ALIVE!
AND I WILL TEACH HIM TO REGRET THAT HIS AIM WAS NOT TRUER.

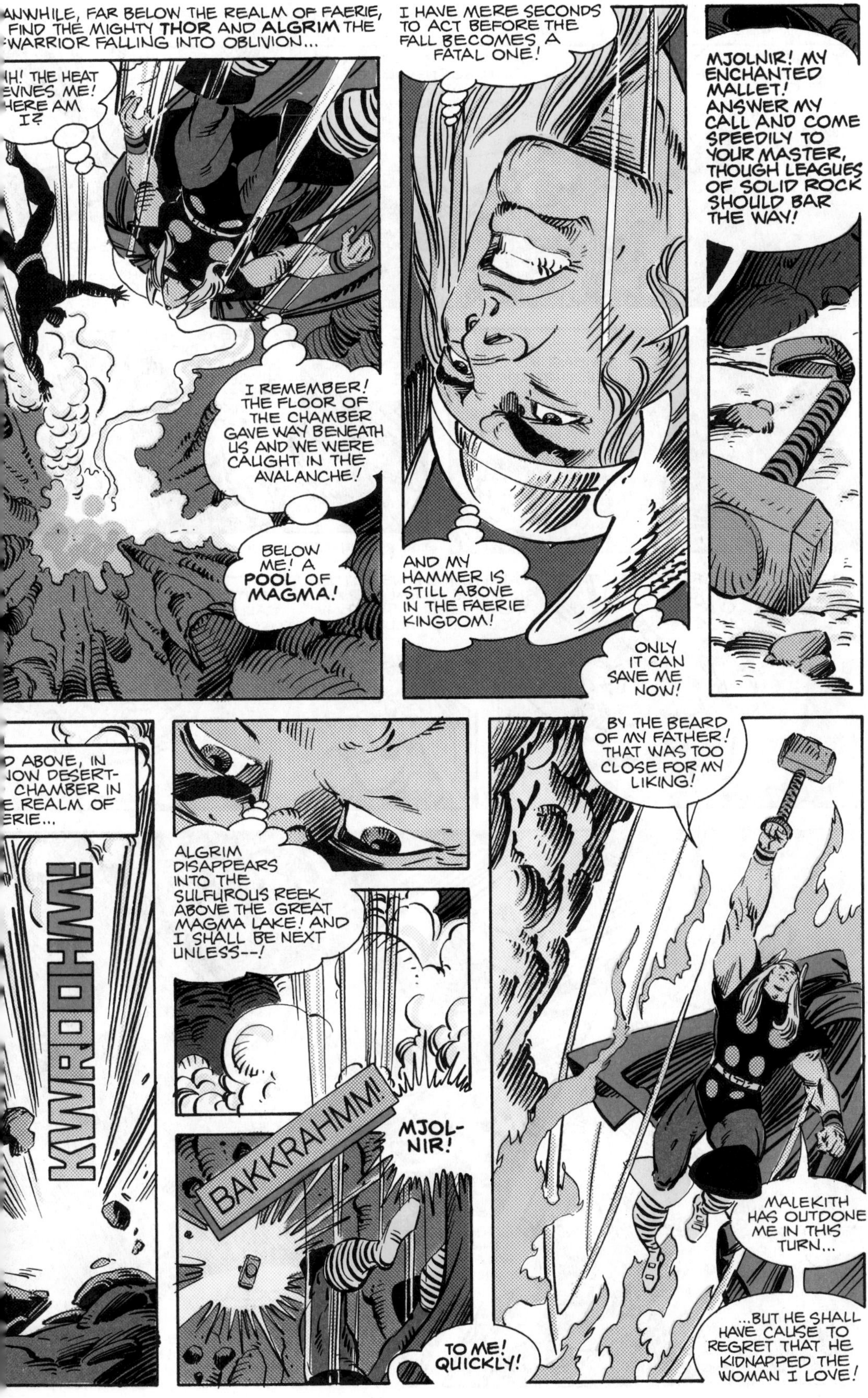
ANWHILE, FAR BELOW THE REALM OF FAERIE, FIND THE MIGHTY THOR AND ALGRIM THE WARRIOR FALLING INTO OBLIVION...
H! THE HEAT EVNES ME! HERE AM I?
I REMEMBER! THE FLOOR OF THE CHAMBER GAVE WAY BENEATH US AND WE WERE CAUGHT IN THE AVALANCHE!
BELOW ME! A POOL OF MAGMA!
I HAVE MERE SECONDS TO ACT BEFORE THE FALL BECOMES A FATAL ONE!
AND MY HAMMER IS STILL ABOVE IN THE FAERIE KINGDOM!
ONLY IT CAN SAVE ME NOW!
MJOLNIR! MY ENCHANTED MALLET! ANSWER MY CALL AND COME SPEEDILY TO YOUR MASTER, THOUGH LEAGUES OF SOLID ROCK SHOULD BAR THE WAY!
D ABOVE, IN NOW DESERT- CHAMBER IN E REALM OF ERIE...
KWROOHM!
ALGRIM DISAPPEARS INTO THE SULFUROUS REEK ABOVE THE GREAT MAGMA LAKE! AND I SHALL BE NEXT UNLESS--!
BAKKRAHMM!
MJOL- NIR!
TO ME! QUICKLY!
BY THE BEARD OF MY FATHER! THAT WAS TOO CLOSE FOR MY LIKING!
MALEKITH HAS OUTDONE ME IN THIS TURN...
...BUT HE SHALL HAVE CAUSE TO REGRET THAT HE KIDNAPPED THE WOMAN I LOVE!

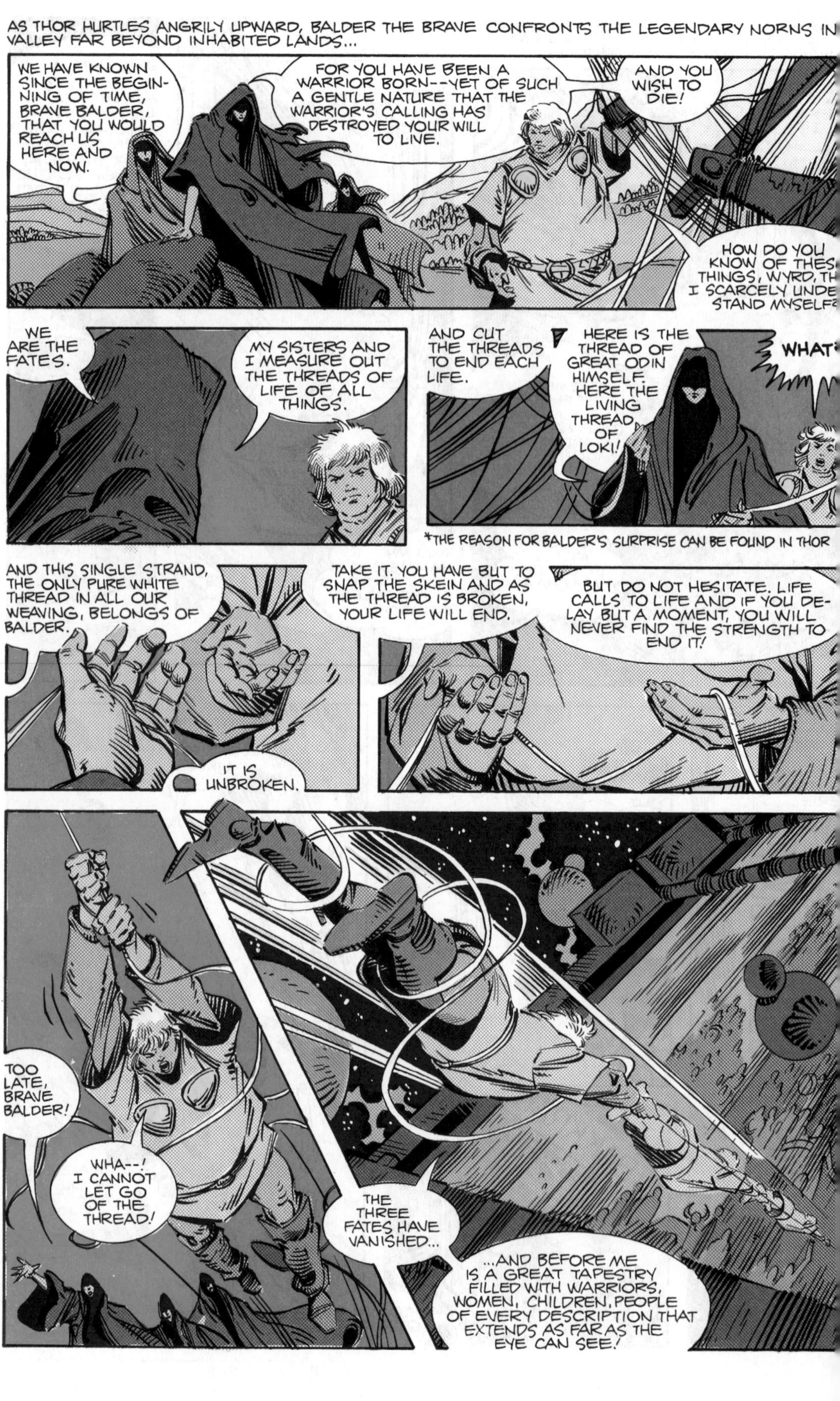
AS THOR HURTLES ANGRILY UPWARD, BALDER THE BRAVE CONFRONTS THE LEGENDARY NORNS IN VALLEY FAR BEYOND INHABITED LANDS...
WE HAVE KNOWN SINCE THE BEGINNING OF TIME, BRAVE BALDER, THAT YOU WOULD REACH US HERE AND NOW.
FOR YOU HAVE BEEN A WARRIOR BORN--YET OF SUCH A GENTLE NATURE THAT THE WARRIOR'S CALLING HAS DESTROYED YOUR WILL TO LIVE.
AND YOU WISH TO DIE!
HOW DO YOU KNOW OF THES THINGS, WYRD, TH I SCARCELY UNDE STAND MYSELF?
WE ARE THE FATES.
MY SISTERS AND I MEASURE OUT THE THREADS OF LIFE OF ALL THINGS.
AND CUT THE THREADS TO END EACH LIFE.
HERE IS THE THREAD OF GREAT ODIN HIMSELF. HERE THE LIVING THREAD OF LOKI!
WHAT
*THE REASON FOR BALDER'S SURPRISE CAN BE FOUND IN THOR
AND THIS SINGLE STRAND, THE ONLY PURE WHITE THREAD IN ALL OUR WEAVING, BELONGS OF BALDER.
TAKE IT. YOU HAVE BUT TO SNAP THE SKEIN AND AS THE THREAD IS BROKEN, YOUR LIFE WILL END.
BUT DO NOT HESITATE. LIFE CALLS TO LIFE AND IF YOU DELAY BUT A MOMENT, YOU WILL NEVER FIND THE STRENGTH TO END IT!
IT IS UNBROKEN.
TOO LATE, BRAVE BALDER!
WHA--! I CANNOT LET GO OF THE THREAD!
THE THREE FATES HAVE VANISHED...
...AND BEFORE ME IS A GREAT TAPESTRY FILLED WITH WARRIORS, WOMEN, CHILDREN, PEOPLE OF EVERY DESCRIPTION THAT EXTENDS AS FAR AS THE EYE CAN SEE!

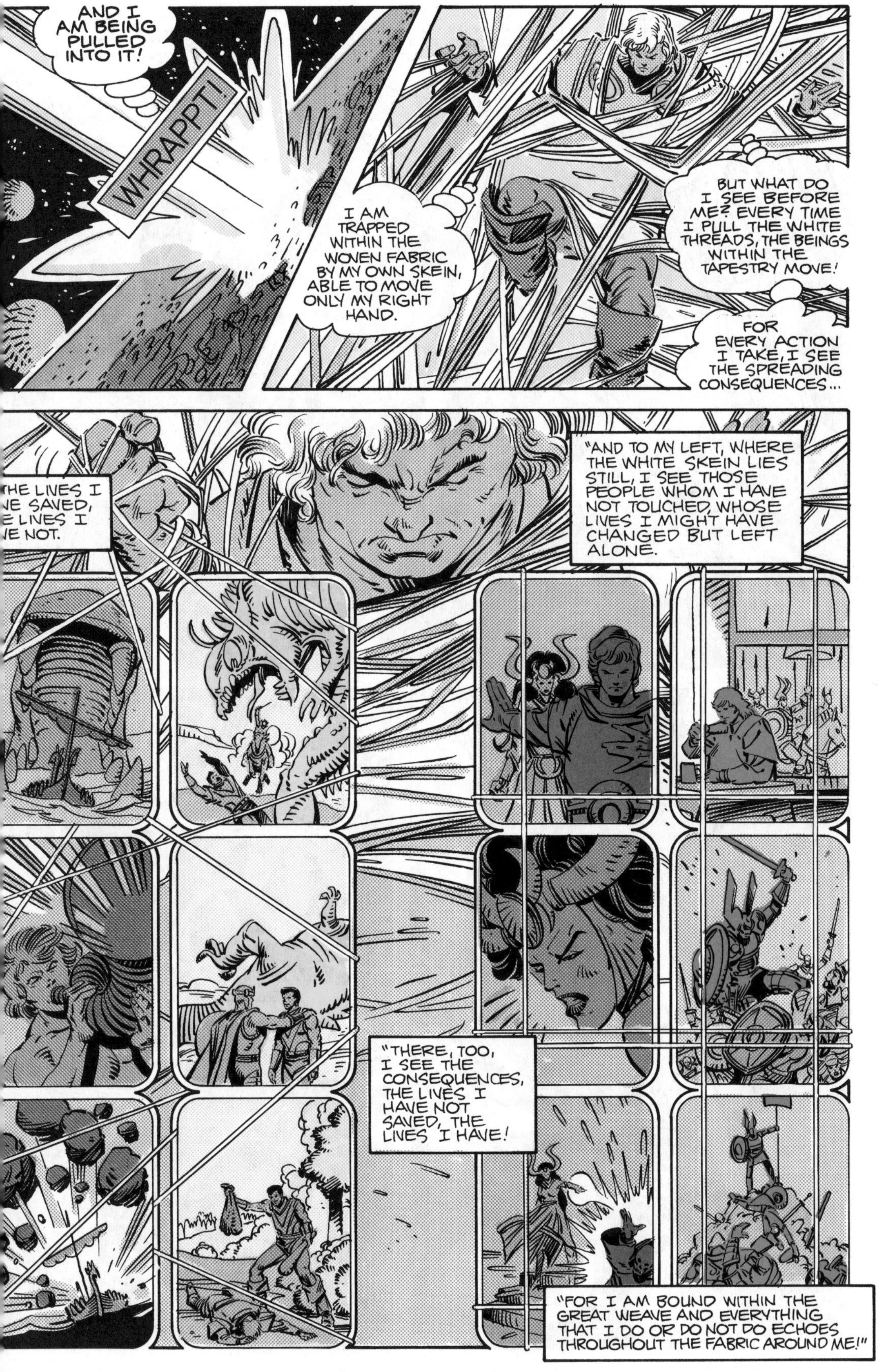
AND I AM BEING PULLED INTO IT!
WHRAPPT!
I AM TRAPPED WITHIN THE WOVEN FABRIC BY MY OWN SKEIN, ABLE TO MOVE ONLY MY RIGHT HAND.
BUT WHAT DO I SEE BEFORE ME? EVERY TIME I PULL THE WHITE THREADS, THE BEINGS WITHIN THE TAPESTRY MOVE!
FOR EVERY ACTION I TAKE, I SEE THE SPREADING CONSEQUENCES...
THE LIVES I VE SAVED, E LIVES I VE NOT.
"AND TO MY LEFT, WHERE THE WHITE SKEIN LIES STILL, I SEE THOSE PEOPLE WHOM I HAVE NOT TOUCHED, WHOSE LIVES I MIGHT HAVE CHANGED BUT LEFT ALONE.
"THERE, TOO, I SEE THE CONSEQUENCES, THE LIVES I HAVE NOT SAVED, THE LIVES I HAVE!
"FOR I AM BOUND WITHIN THE GREAT WEAVE AND EVERYTHING THAT I DO OR DO NOT DO ECHOES THROUGHOUT THE FABRIC AROUND ME!"

I CAN BEAR NO MORE! I WILL TEAR MYSELF AWAY FROM THIS DANCING PLAY AND QUIT THE MADNESS OF LIVING!

AND ALL WHO ARE BOUND WITHIN ITS WEAVE FALL WITH ME!

THI' MUS' NOT BE!

BUT EVEN AS I FALL INTO THE DARK, THE TAPESTRY BEGINS TO UNRAVEL!

NO MAN OR GOD CAN SET ASIDE THE FATE OF SO MANY AS I HAVE TRIED TO DO!

RRIPPP!

THERE AHEAD OF ME-- THE TORN ENDS OF THE WHITE THREAD.

AND BEYOND THAT, SOME GREAT SHADOW FLICKERING AS IF WRAPPED IN A DARK FLAME WAITING TO CATCH THE FALLING TAPESTRY AND DESTROY IT!

AS THOUGH MY DEATH HERALDS THE END OF A UNIVERSE!

I HAVE BUT ONE CHANC' TO GRAB THE ENDS'

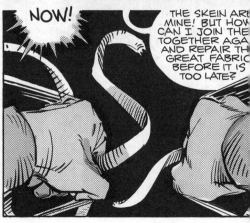

NOW!

THE SKEIN ARE MINE! BUT HOW CAN I JOIN THE TOGETHER AGA' AND REPAIR TH' GREAT FABRIC BEFORE IT IS TOO LATE?

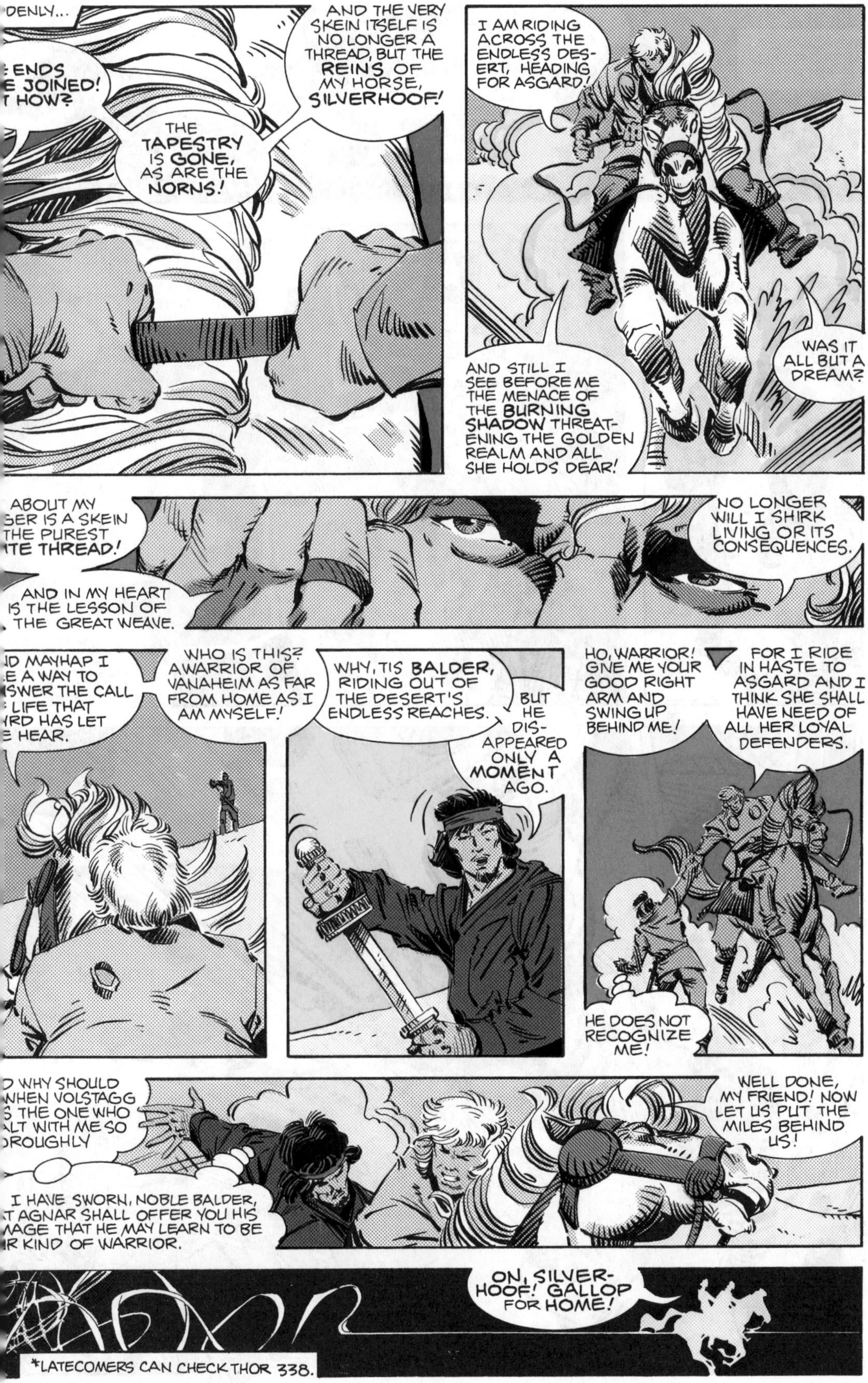

DENLY...
E ENDS
E JOINED!
T HOW?
THE TAPESTRY IS GONE, AS ARE THE NORNS!
AND THE VERY SKEIN ITSELF IS NO LONGER A THREAD, BUT THE REIN'S OF MY HORSE, SILVERHOOF!
I AM RIDING ACROSS THE ENDLESS DESERT, HEADING FOR ASGARD!
AND STILL I SEE BEFORE ME THE MENACE OF THE BURNING SHADOW THREATENING THE GOLDEN REALM AND ALL SHE HOLDS DEAR!
WAS IT ALL BUT A DREAM?
ABOUT MY
GER IS A SKEIN
THE PUREST
TE THREAD!
AND IN MY HEART IS THE LESSON OF THE GREAT WEAVE.
NO LONGER WILL I SHIRK LIVING OR ITS CONSEQUENCES.
D MAYHAP I
E A WAY TO
SWER THE CALL
LIFE THAT
RD HAS LET
E HEAR.
WHO IS THIS? A WARRIOR OF VANAHEIM AS FAR FROM HOME AS I AM MYSELF!
WHY, TIS BALDER, RIDING OUT OF THE DESERT'S ENDLESS REACHES.
BUT HE DISAPPEARED ONLY A MOMENT AGO.
HO, WARRIOR! GIVE ME YOUR GOOD RIGHT ARM AND SWING UP BEHIND ME!
FOR I RIDE IN HASTE TO ASGARD AND I THINK SHE SHALL HAVE NEED OF ALL HER LOYAL DEFENDERS.
HE DOES NOT RECOGNIZE ME!
D WHY SHOULD
WHEN VOLSTAGG
S THE ONE WHO
ALT WITH ME SO
OROUGHLY
I HAVE SWORN, NOBLE BALDER,
T AGNAR SHALL OFFER YOU HIS
MAGE THAT HE MAY LEARN TO BE
R KIND OF WARRIOR.
WELL DONE, MY FRIEND! NOW LET US PUT THE MILES BEHIND US!
ON, SILVERHOOF! GALLOP FOR HOME!
*LATECOMERS CAN CHECK THOR 338.

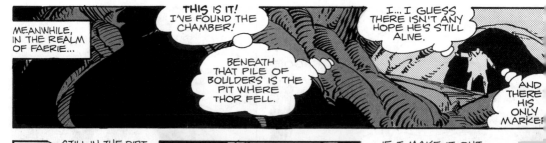

MEANWHILE, IN THE REALM OF FAERIE...

THIS IS IT! I'VE FOUND THE CHAMBER!

BENEATH THAT PILE OF BOULDERS IS THE PIT WHERE THOR FELL.

I...I GUESS THERE ISN'T ANY HOPE HE'S STILL ALIVE.

AND THERE HIS ONLY MARKER

MY HAT.

STILL IN THE DIRT WHERE IT FELL DURING OUR STRUGGLE WITH THE ELVISH WARRIORS OF MALEKITH.

IF I MAKE IT OUT, THOR, I'LL COME BACK AND WIPE THIS PLACE OFF THE FACE OF THE EARTH, I PROMISE YOU.

SLEEP WELL.

UH-OH! I HEAR A RUMBLE OFF IN THE DISTANCE. TIME TO GET ROLLING AND HEAD FOR HOME!

I DON'T WANT TO RUN INTO ANY OF THESE GUYS WHEN I CAN'T SEE THE

BRA-TOOOM!

HOLY--!

THOR!

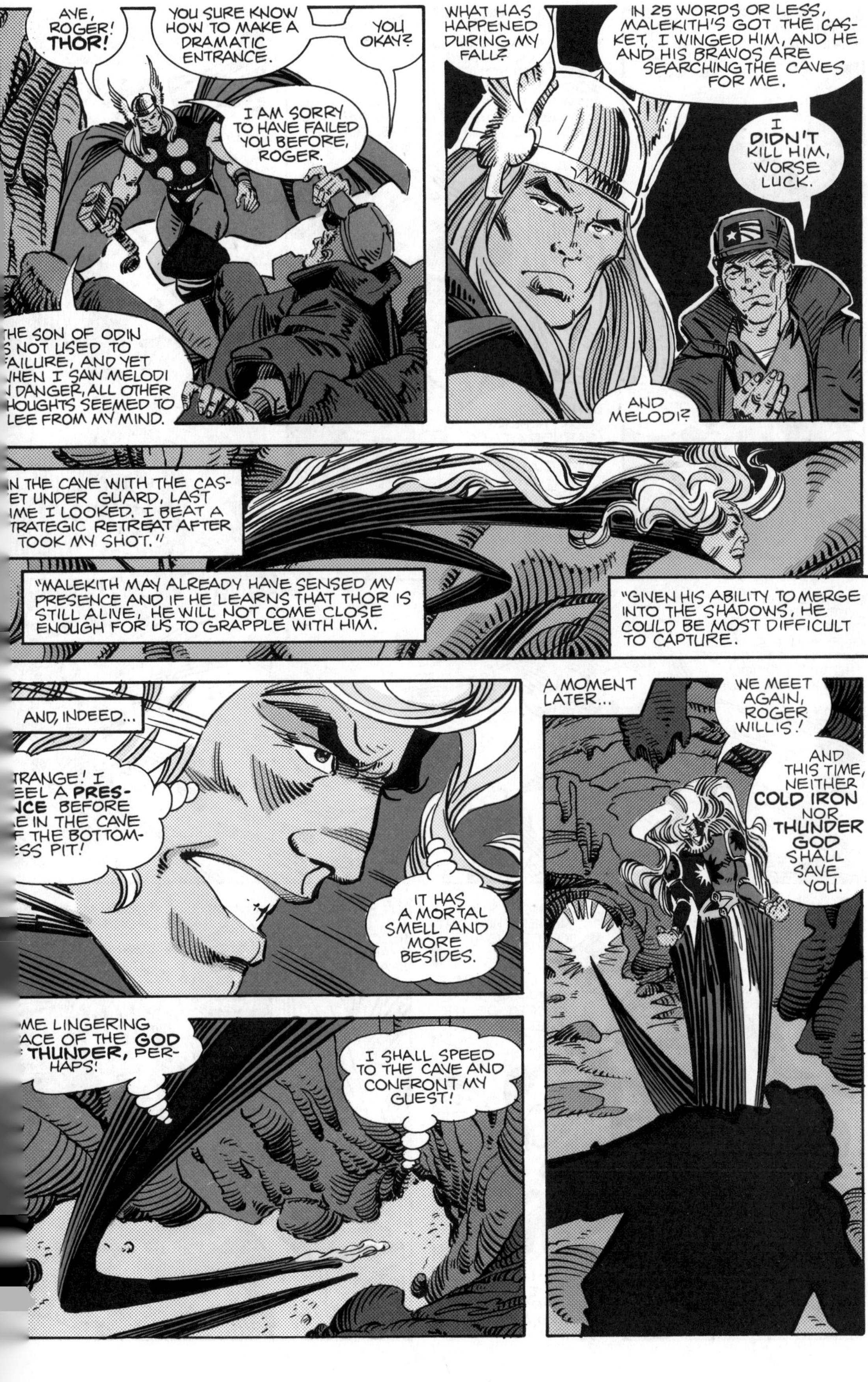

AYE, ROGER! THOR!
YOU SURE KNOW HOW TO MAKE A DRAMATIC ENTRANCE.
YOU OKAY?
I AM SORRY TO HAVE FAILED YOU BEFORE, ROGER.
THE SON OF ODIN IS NOT USED TO FAILURE, AND YET WHEN I SAW MELODI IN DANGER, ALL OTHER THOUGHTS SEEMED TO FLEE FROM MY MIND.
WHAT HAS HAPPENED DURING MY FALL?
IN 25 WORDS OR LESS, MALEKITH'S GOT THE CASKET, I WINGED HIM, AND HE AND HIS BRAVOS ARE SEARCHING THE CAVES FOR ME.
I DIDN'T KILL HIM, WORSE LUCK.
AND MELODI?
IN THE CAVE WITH THE CASKET UNDER GUARD, LAST TIME I LOOKED. I BEAT A STRATEGIC RETREAT AFTER I TOOK MY SHOT."
"MALEKITH MAY ALREADY HAVE SENSED MY PRESENCE AND IF HE LEARNS THAT THOR IS STILL ALIVE, HE WILL NOT COME CLOSE ENOUGH FOR US TO GRAPPLE WITH HIM.
"GIVEN HIS ABILITY TO MERGE INTO THE SHADOWS, HE COULD BE MOST DIFFICULT TO CAPTURE.
AND, INDEED...
STRANGE! I FEEL A PRESENCE BEFORE ME IN THE CAVE OF THE BOTTOMLESS PIT!
IT HAS A MORTAL SMELL AND MORE BESIDES.
SOME LINGERING TRACE OF THE GOD OF THUNDER, PERHAPS!
I SHALL SPEED TO THE CAVE AND CONFRONT MY GUEST!
A MOMENT LATER...
WE MEET AGAIN, ROGER WILLIS!
AND THIS TIME, NEITHER COLD IRON NOR THUNDER GOD SHALL SAVE YOU.

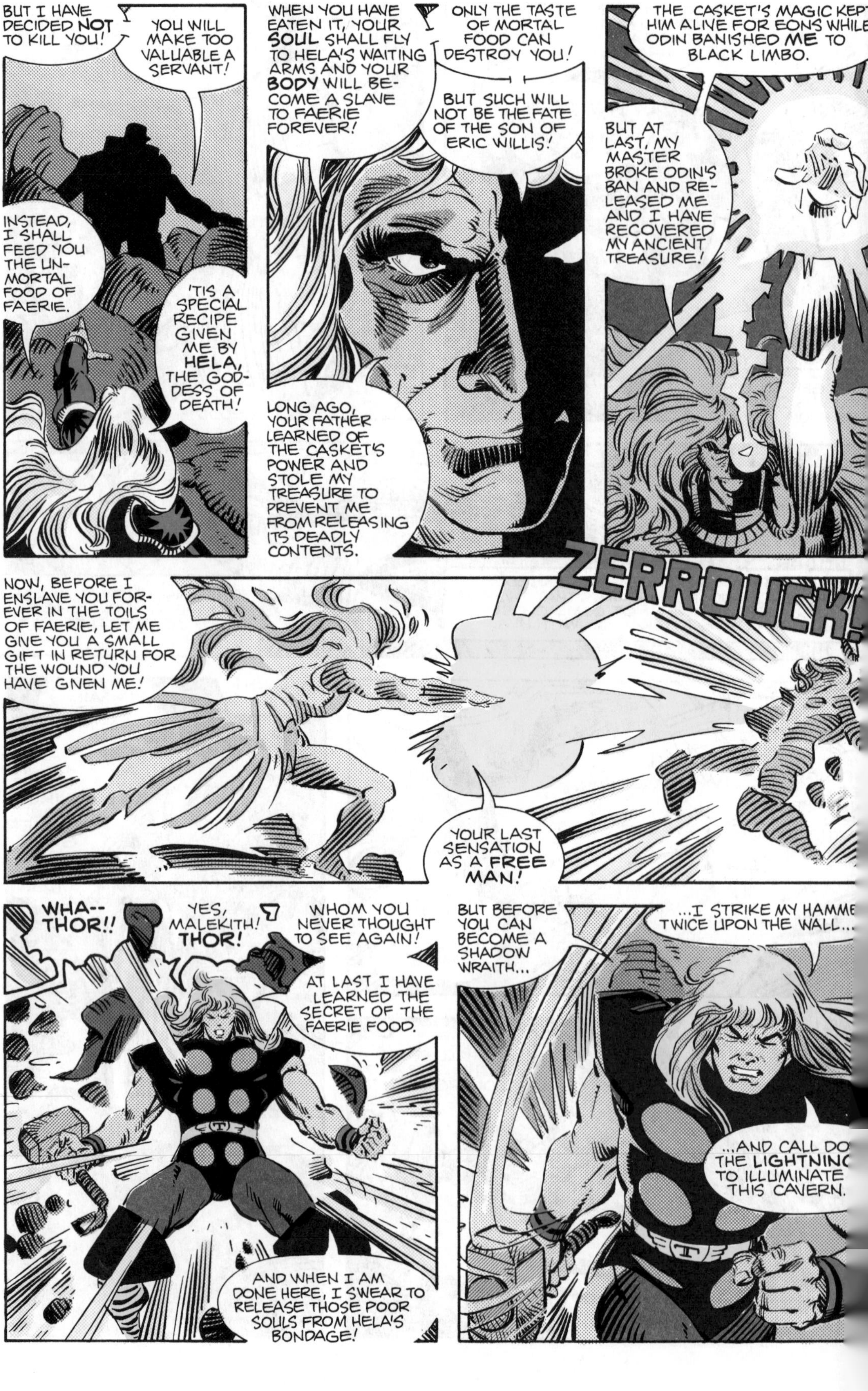
BUT I HAVE DECIDED NOT TO KILL YOU!
YOU WILL MAKE TOO VALUABLE A SERVANT!
INSTEAD, I SHALL FEED YOU THE UN-MORTAL FOOD OF FAERIE.
'TIS A SPECIAL RECIPE GIVEN ME BY HELA, THE GOD-DESS OF DEATH!
WHEN YOU HAVE EATEN IT, YOUR SOUL SHALL FLY TO HELA'S WAITING ARMS AND YOUR BODY WILL BE-COME A SLAVE TO FAERIE FOREVER!
ONLY THE TASTE OF MORTAL FOOD CAN DESTROY YOU!
BUT SUCH WILL NOT BE THE FATE OF THE SON OF ERIC WILLIS!
LONG AGO, YOUR FATHER LEARNED OF THE CASKET'S POWER AND STOLE MY TREASURE TO PREVENT ME FROM RELEASING ITS DEADLY CONTENTS.
THE CASKET'S MAGIC KEPT HIM ALIVE FOR EONS WHILE ODIN BANISHED ME TO BLACK LIMBO.
BUT AT LAST, MY MASTER BROKE ODIN'S BAN AND RE-LEASED ME AND I HAVE RECOVERED MY ANCIENT TREASURE!
NOW, BEFORE I ENSLAVE YOU FOR-EVER IN THE TOILS OF FAERIE, LET ME GIVE YOU A SMALL GIFT IN RETURN FOR THE WOUND YOU HAVE GIVEN ME!
ZERROUCK!
YOUR LAST SENSATION AS A FREE MAN!
WHA-- THOR!!
YES, MALEKITH! THOR!
WHOM YOU NEVER THOUGHT TO SEE AGAIN!
AT LAST I HAVE LEARNED THE SECRET OF THE FAERIE FOOD.
AND WHEN I AM DONE HERE, I SWEAR TO RELEASE THOSE POOR SOULS FROM HELA'S BONDAGE!
BUT BEFORE YOU CAN BECOME A SHADOW WRAITH...
...I STRIKE MY HAMME TWICE UPON THE WALL...
...AND CALL DO THE LIGHTNIN TO ILLUMINATE THIS CAVERN.

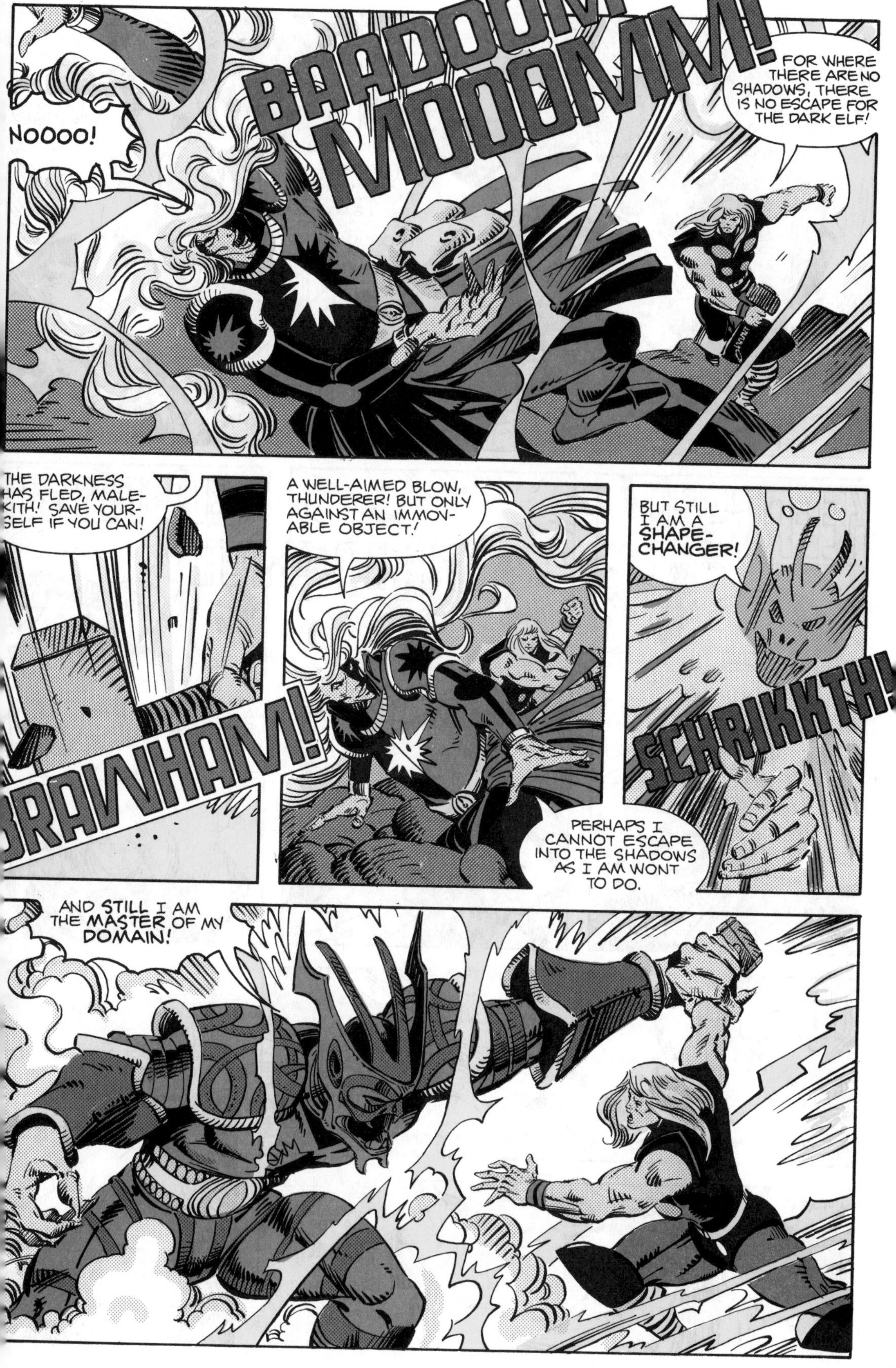
NOOOO!
BAADOOM MOOOMM!
FOR WHERE THERE ARE NO SHADOWS, THERE IS NO ESCAPE FOR THE DARK ELF!
THE DARKNESS HAS FLED, MALEKITH! SAVE YOURSELF IF YOU CAN!
BRAWHAM!
A WELL-AIMED BLOW, THUNDERER! BUT ONLY AGAINST AN IMMOVABLE OBJECT!
PERHAPS I CANNOT ESCAPE INTO THE SHADOWS AS I AM WONT TO DO.
BUT STILL I AM A SHAPE-CHANGER!
SCHRIKKTH!
AND STILL I AM THE MASTER OF MY DOMAIN!

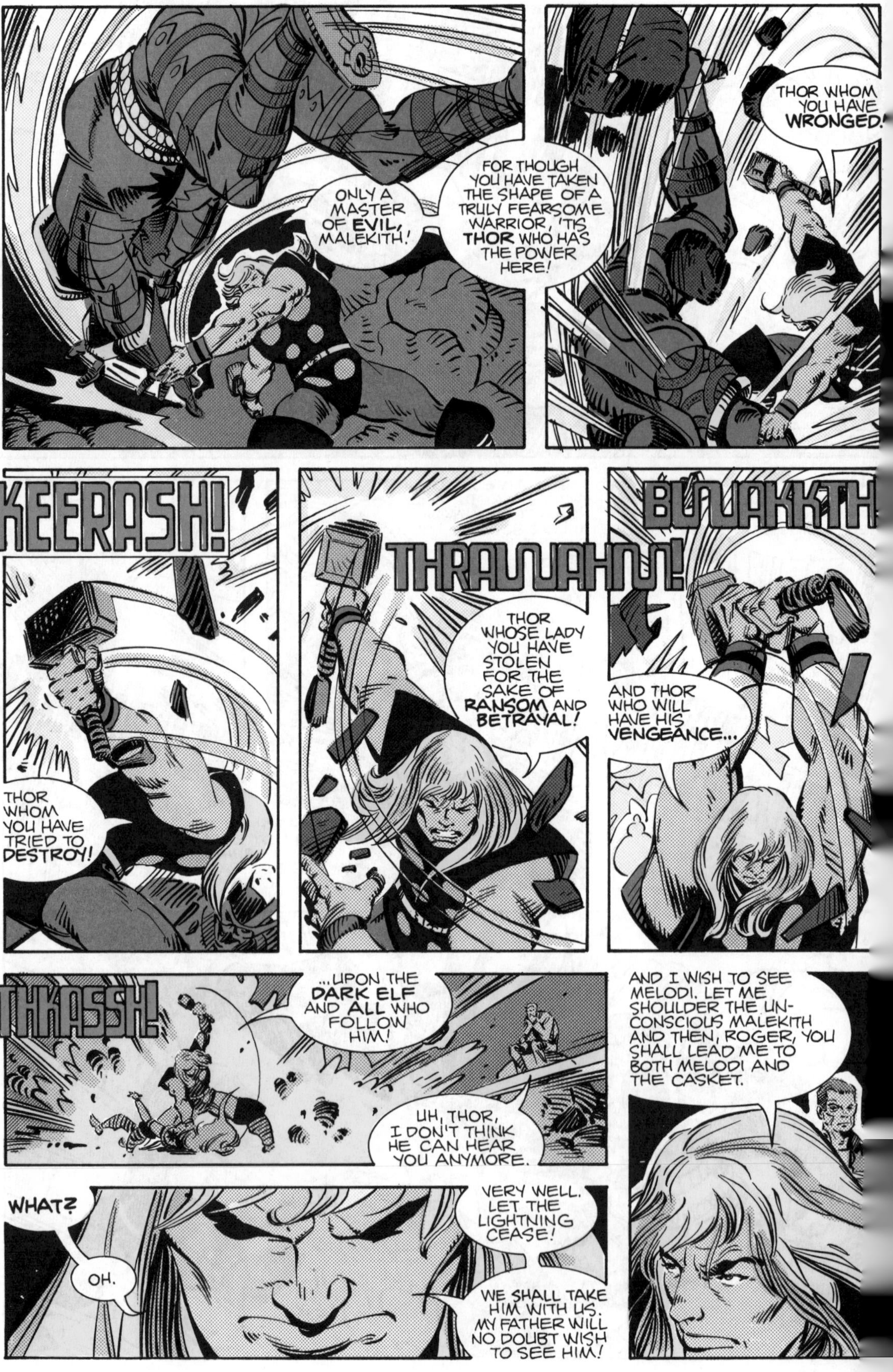

ONLY A MASTER OF EVIL, MALEKITH!
FOR THOUGH YOU HAVE TAKEN THE SHAPE OF A TRULY FEARSOME WARRIOR, 'TIS THOR WHO HAS THE POWER HERE!
THOR WHOM YOU HAVE WRONGED!
KEERASH!
THOR WHOM YOU HAVE TRIED TO DESTROY!
THRAWAHNN!
THOR WHOSE LADY YOU HAVE STOLEN FOR THE SAKE OF RANSOM AND BETRAYAL!
BLWAKKTH
AND THOR WHO WILL HAVE HIS VENGEANCE...
THKASSH!
...UPON THE DARK ELF AND ALL WHO FOLLOW HIM!
UH, THOR, I DON'T THINK HE CAN HEAR YOU ANYMORE.
WHAT?
OH.
VERY WELL. LET THE LIGHTNING CEASE!
WE SHALL TAKE HIM WITH US. MY FATHER WILL NO DOUBT WISH TO SEE HIM!
AND I WISH TO SEE MELODI. LET ME SHOULDER THE UNCONSCIOUS MALEKITH AND THEN, ROGER, YOU SHALL LEAD ME TO BOTH MELODI AND THE CASKET.

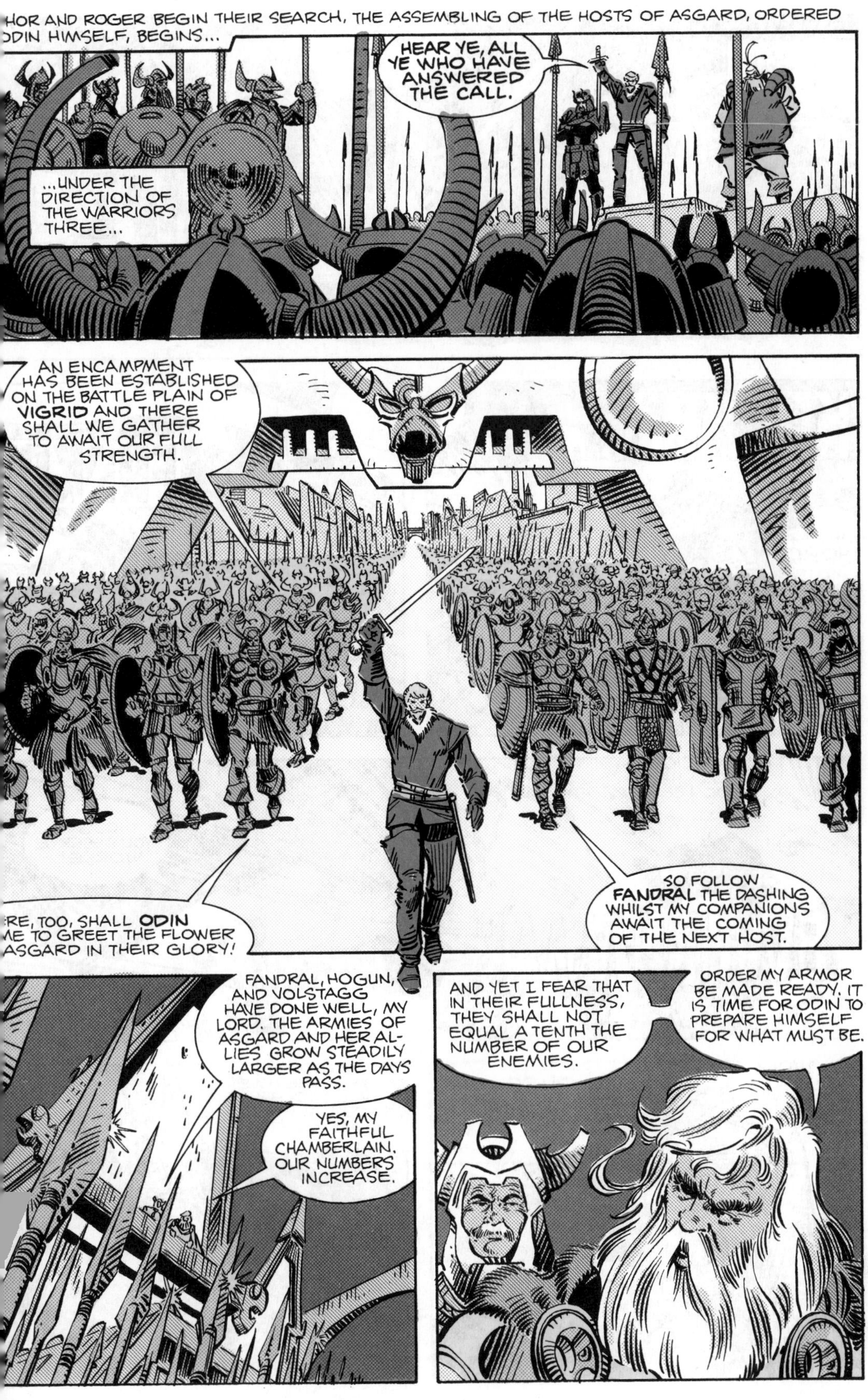
HOR AND ROGER BEGIN THEIR SEARCH, THE ASSEMBLING OF THE HOSTS OF ASGARD, ORDERED
ODIN HIMSELF, BEGINS...
HEAR YE, ALL YE WHO HAVE ANSWERED THE CALL.
...UNDER THE DIRECTION OF THE WARRIORS THREE...
AN ENCAMPMENT HAS BEEN ESTABLISHED ON THE BATTLE PLAIN OF VIGRID AND THERE SHALL WE GATHER TO AWAIT OUR FULL STRENGTH.
RE, TOO, SHALL ODIN ME TO GREET THE FLOWER ASGARD IN THEIR GLORY!
SO FOLLOW FANDRAL THE DASHING WHILST MY COMPANIONS AWAIT THE COMING OF THE NEXT HOST.
FANDRAL, HOGUN, AND VOLSTAGG HAVE DONE WELL, MY LORD. THE ARMIES OF ASGARD AND HER ALLIES GROW STEADILY LARGER AS THE DAYS PASS.
YES, MY FAITHFUL CHAMBERLAIN. OUR NUMBERS INCREASE.
AND YET I FEAR THAT IN THEIR FULLNESS, THEY SHALL NOT EQUAL A TENTH THE NUMBER OF OUR ENEMIES.
ORDER MY ARMOR BE MADE READY. IT IS TIME FOR ODIN TO PREPARE HIMSELF FOR WHAT MUST BE.

MEANWHILE, IN THE CRYSTAL CAVERN...

MALEKITH SHOULD HAVE RETURNED BY NOW.

HE HAS RETURNED, VILLAINS!

KROKKT!

WHAT--? THOR!!

AND I HAVE BROUGHT HIM!

FRAKAT!

UNCONSCIOUS! AS YOU SHALL SOON BE!

THOUGH YOU DESERVE WORSE!

BVVHRAMM!

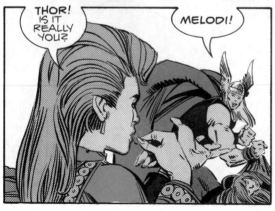

THOR! IS IT REALLY YOU?

MELODI!

MELODI, MY OWN TRUE LOVE! HAVE THEY HARMED YOU? ARE YOU ALL RIGHT?

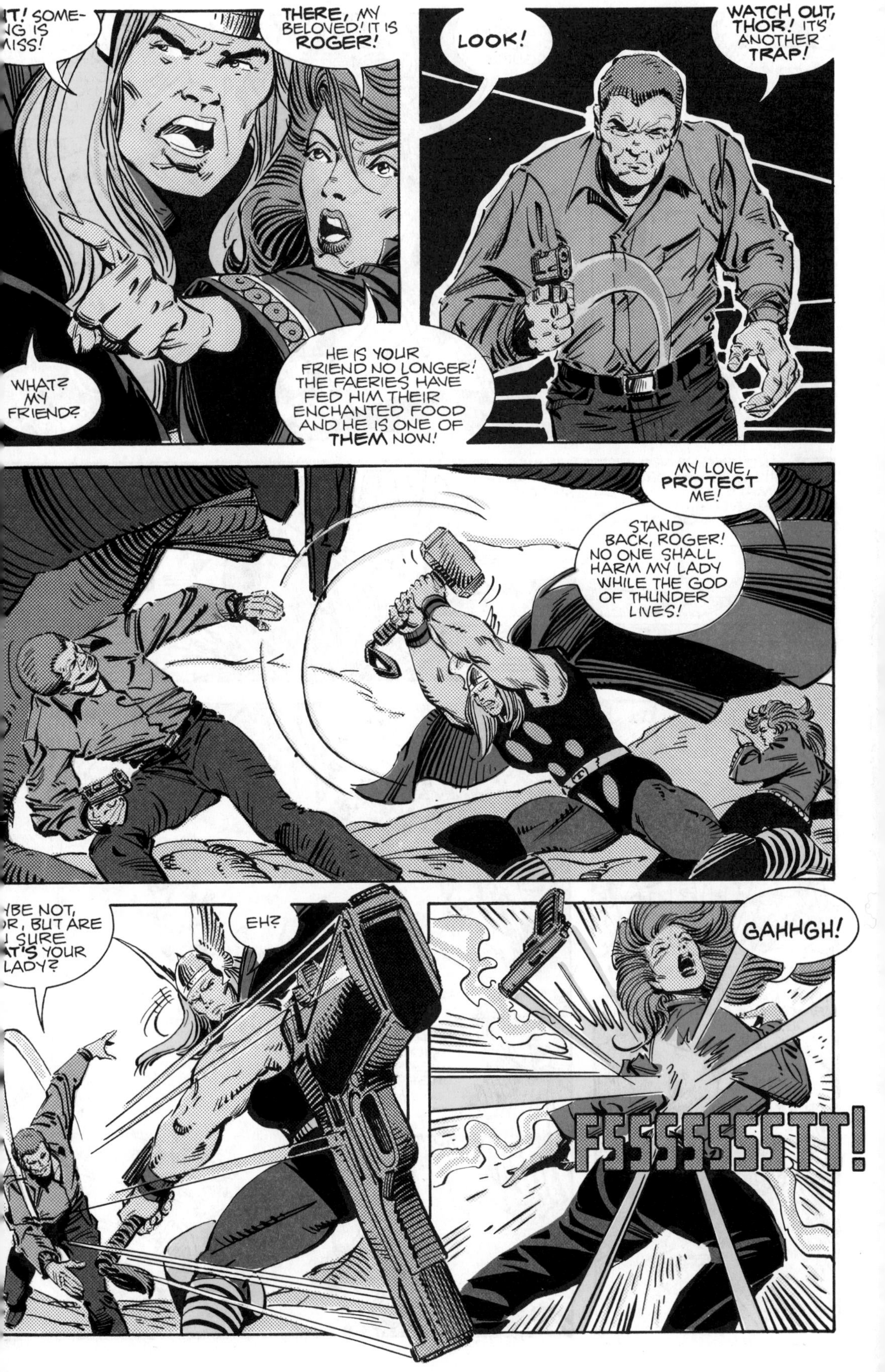
IT! SOME- NG IS MISS!
THERE, MY BELOVED! IT IS ROGER!
WHAT? MY FRIEND?
HE IS YOUR FRIEND NO LONGER! THE FAERIES HAVE FED HIM THEIR ENCHANTED FOOD AND HE IS ONE OF THEM NOW!
LOOK!
WATCH OUT, THOR! IT'S ANOTHER TRAP!
MY LOVE, PROTECT ME!
STAND BACK, ROGER! NO ONE SHALL HARM MY LADY WHILE THE GOD OF THUNDER LIVES!
YBE NOT, R, BUT ARE U SURE AT'S YOUR LADY?
EH?
GAHHGH!
FSSSSSSSTT!

MELODI'S FORM! IT SHIFTS LIKE A MIRAGE IN THE DESERT!

OH, NO! THE CURSED IRON HAS DISRUPTED MY DISGUISE!

SO!

WITHOUT THE FAERIE VISION THAT MALEKITH DESTROYED, I COULDN'T SEE ANYONE, BUT I COULD STILL HEAR 'IM.

SO I THREW MY GUN AT THE SOUND.

AND I'VE HEARD THIS ONE BEFORE. MALEKITH CALLED HIM WORMWOOD!

HE WAS GUARDING MELODI!

WHAKKKK!

BY GOADING YOU TO ATTACK ME, HE FIGURED HE'D DISTRACT YOU FROM PENETRATING HIS DISGUISE AND PREVENT ME FROM REVEALING IT.

NO DOUBT THE KNIFE WAS MEANT FOR YOU.

MELODI!

THOR! LOOK! THAT BOULDER!

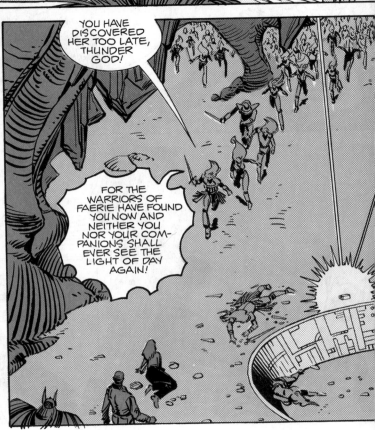

YOU HAVE DISCOVERED HER TOO LATE, THUNDER GOD!

FOR THE WARRIORS OF FAERIE HAVE FOUND YOU NOW AND NEITHER YOU NOR YOUR COMPANIONS SHALL EVER SEE THE LIGHT OF DAY AGAIN!

KRATHOOMM!

PHAPS, LET US THE THE SUN ETHER O SEE O IS THE RONGER!

WE CANNOT STAND THE **LIGHT!**

FLEE, BROTHERS, FLEE!

INTO THE CAVES OF NIGHT!

OVE! E BLUE Y!

HIS HAMMER HAS DESTROYED THE ROOF OF FAERIE!

CK! CK! S THE WNING OUR!

OHHH.

THOR, WHAT'S HAPPENED? I FEEL AS THOUGH I'VE JUST AWAKENED FROM A DEEP SLEEP!

INDEED YOU HAVE, MY LOVE. A LONG NIGHTMARE THAT HAS ENDED.

THOR! YOU'VE NEVER LOOKED AT ME LIKE THAT BEFORE! DOES THIS MEAN...?

I AM YOURS NOW AND FOREVER!

INTERESTING. THOR WENT TO SEE MELODI IN HIS CIVILIAN DISGUISE OF "SIGURD JARLSON."

I DIDN'T GET THE IMPRESSION THAT HE THOUGHT SHE KNEW WHO HE WAS FOR REAL.

BUT AS ROGER RUMINATES, A FEW FEET AWAY, UNNOTICED BY OUR HEROES...

SO ALL MY PLANS HAVE COME TO NAUGHT. THOR AND THE MORTAL STILL LIVE AND MY WARRIORS HAVE BEEN DEFEATED.

I AM TOO WEAK TO ESCAPE, BUT THOR'S ENCHANTED LOVE FOR THE WOMAN SHALL YET BE HIS UNDOING!

IN HER EMBRACE HE HAS FORGOTTEN ME...FOR THE LAST TIME!

ARGGHH!

WHAT--?

OH!

THOR! LOOK OUT! MALEKITH'S AWAKE AND HE'S PICKED UP MY GUN!

TOO LATE, MORTAL! NEITHER YOU NOR THOR CAN STOP ME FROM COMPLETING MY APPOINTED TASK!

THOUGH THE COLD IRON BURNS MY FLESH, YOUR WEAPON SHALL SERVE ME EVEN AS IT HAS SERVED YOU!

YOU HAVE WON THE BATTLE BUT YOU HAVE LOST THE WAR!

UGGH!

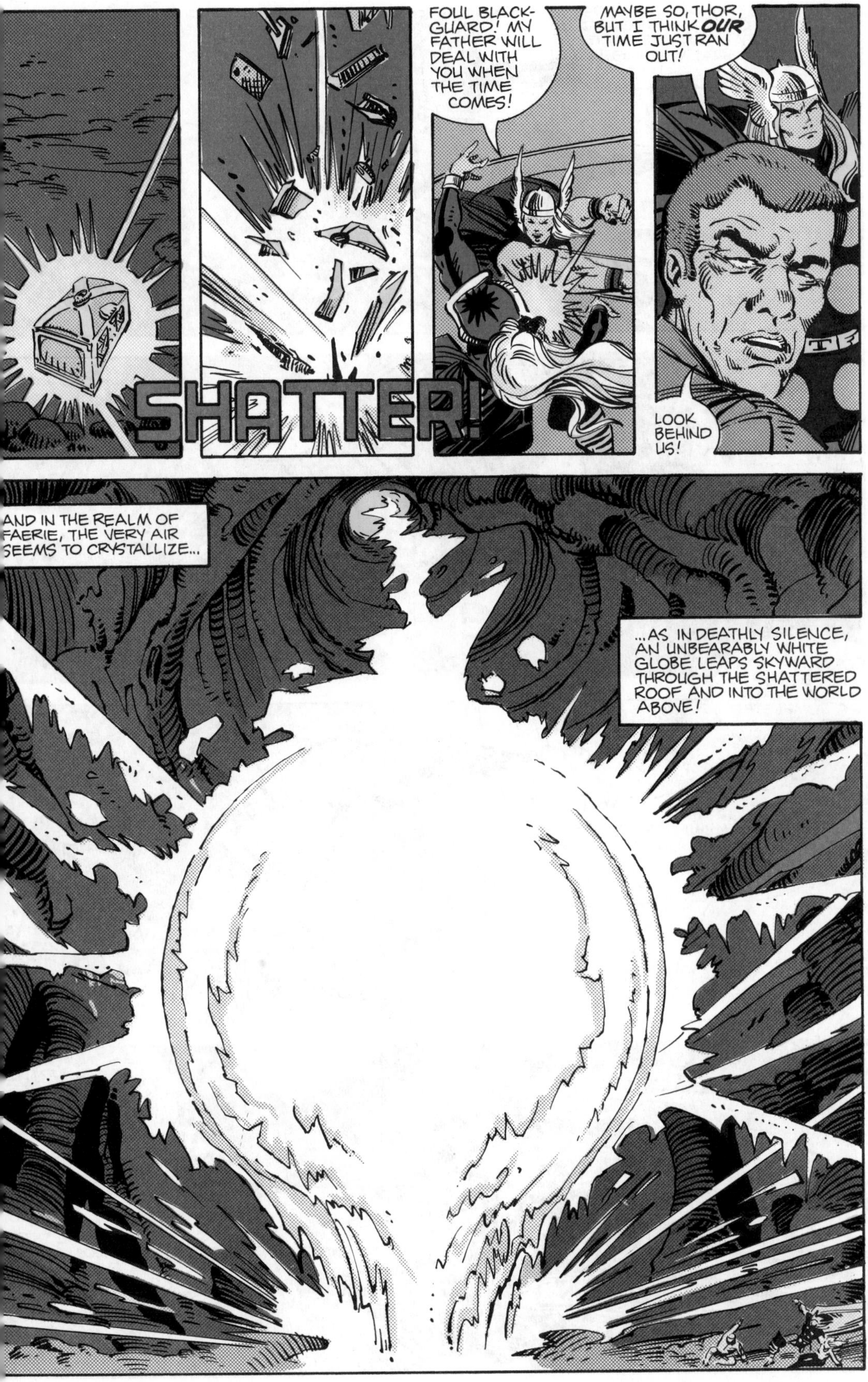
SHATTER!
FOUL BLACK-GUARD! MY FATHER WILL DEAL WITH YOU WHEN THE TIME COMES!
MAYBE SO, THOR, BUT I THINK OUR TIME JUST RAN OUT!
LOOK BEHIND US!
AND IN THE REALM OF FAERIE, THE VERY AIR SEEMS TO CRYSTALLIZE...
...AS IN DEATHLY SILENCE, AN UNBEARABLY WHITE GLOBE LEAPS SKYWARD THROUGH THE SHATTERED ROOF AND INTO THE WORLD ABOVE!

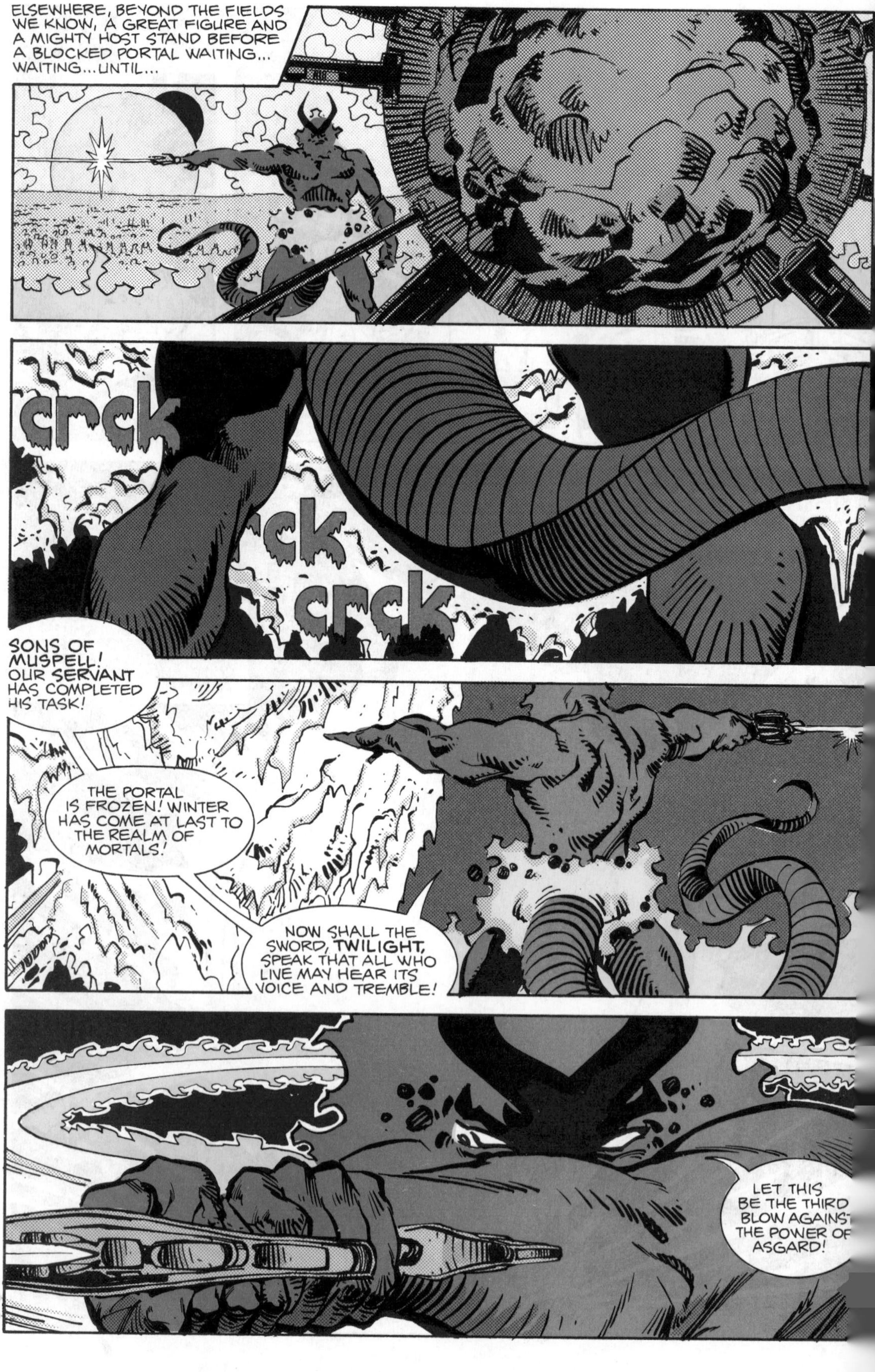
ELSEWHERE, BEYOND THE FIELDS WE KNOW, A GREAT FIGURE AND A MIGHTY HOST STAND BEFORE A BLOCKED PORTAL WAITING... WAITING... UNTIL...
crck
crck
crck
SONS OF MUSPELL! OUR SERVANT HAS COMPLETED HIS TASK!
THE PORTAL IS FROZEN! WINTER HAS COME AT LAST TO THE REALM OF MORTALS!
NOW SHALL THE SWORD, TWILIGHT, SPEAK THAT ALL WHO LIVE MAY HEAR ITS VOICE AND TREMBLE!
LET THIS BE THE THIRD BLOW AGAINST THE POWER OF ASGARD!

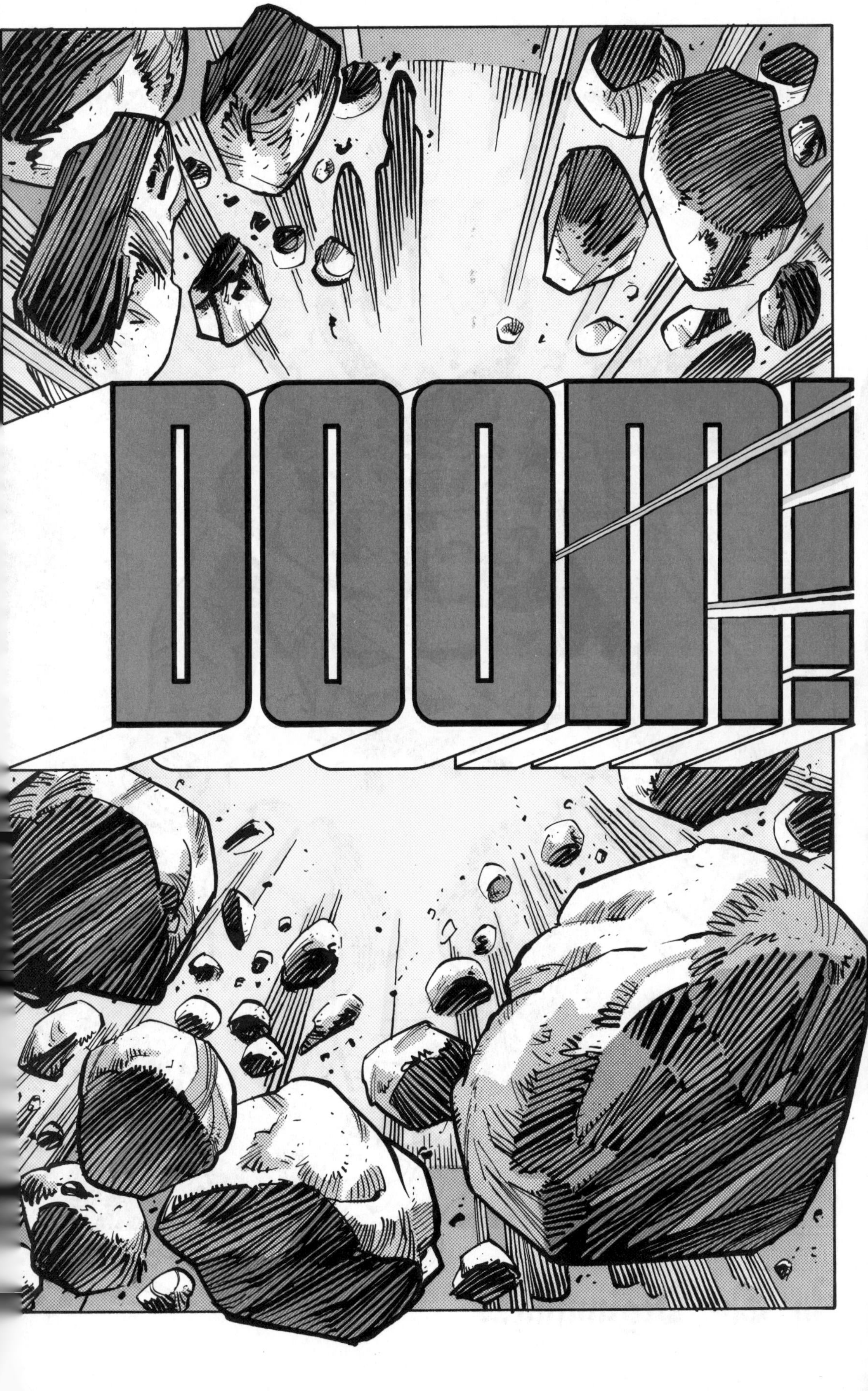
DOOM!

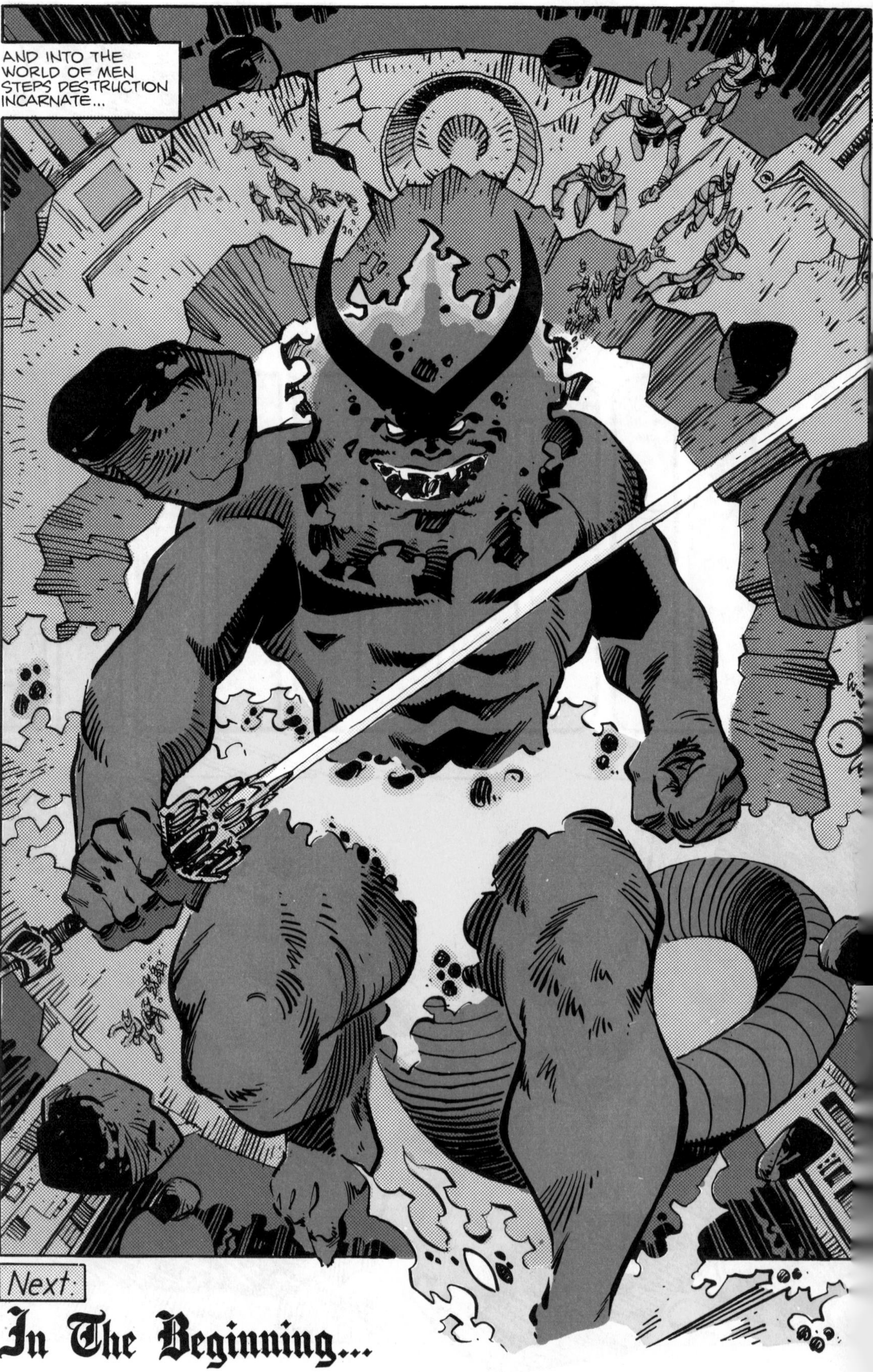
AND INTO THE WORLD OF MEN STEPS DESTRUCTION INCARNATE...

Next:

In The Beginning...

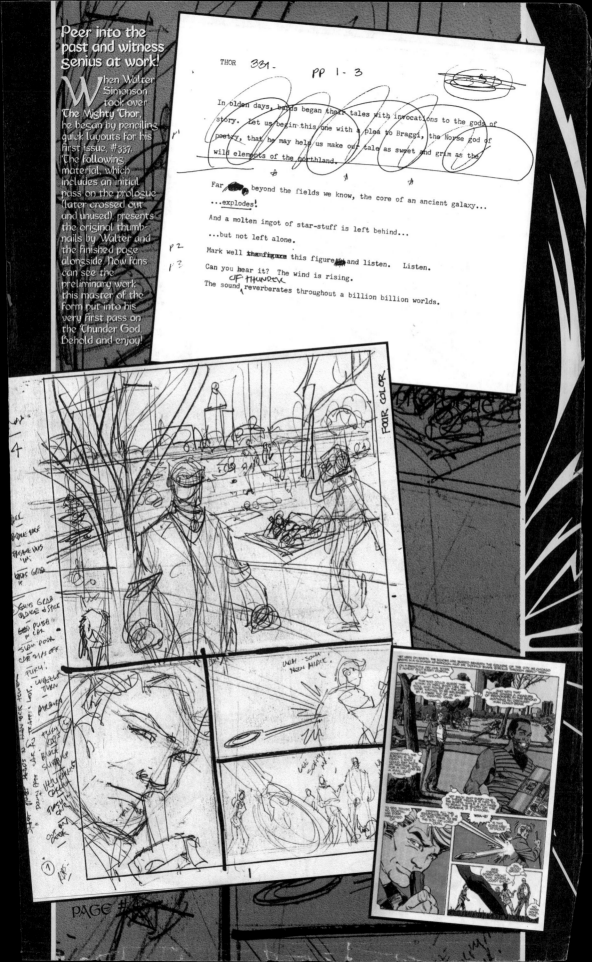

Peer into the past and witness genius at work!

When Walter Simonson took over *The Mighty Thor*, he began by penciling quick layouts for his first issue, #337. The following material, which includes an initial pass on the prologue (later crossed out and unused), presents the original thumbnails by Walter and the finished page alongside. Now fans can see the preliminary work this master of the form put into his very first pass on the Thunder God. Behold and enjoy!

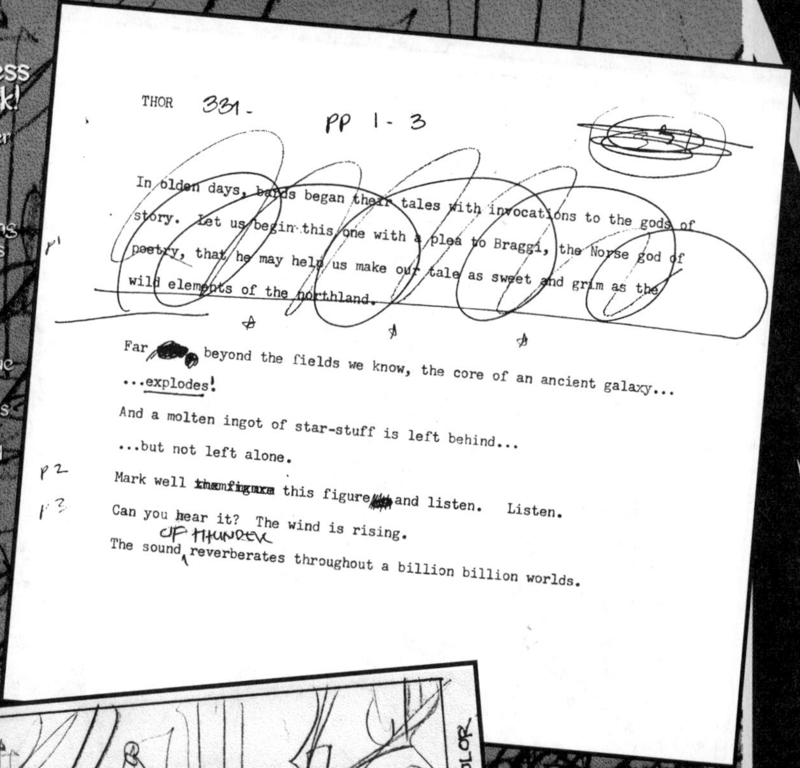

THOR 331- PP 1-3

In olden days, bards began their tales with invocations to the gods of story. Let us begin this one with a plea to Braggi, the Norse god of poetry, that he may help us make our tale as sweet and grim as the wild elements of the northland.

Far beyond the fields we know, the core of an ancient galaxy...

...explodes!

And a molten ingot of star-stuff is left behind...

...but not left alone.

P2 Mark well ~~the figure~~ this figure and listen. Listen.

P3 Can you hear it? The wind is rising.

The sound OF THUNDER reverberates throughout a billion billion worlds.

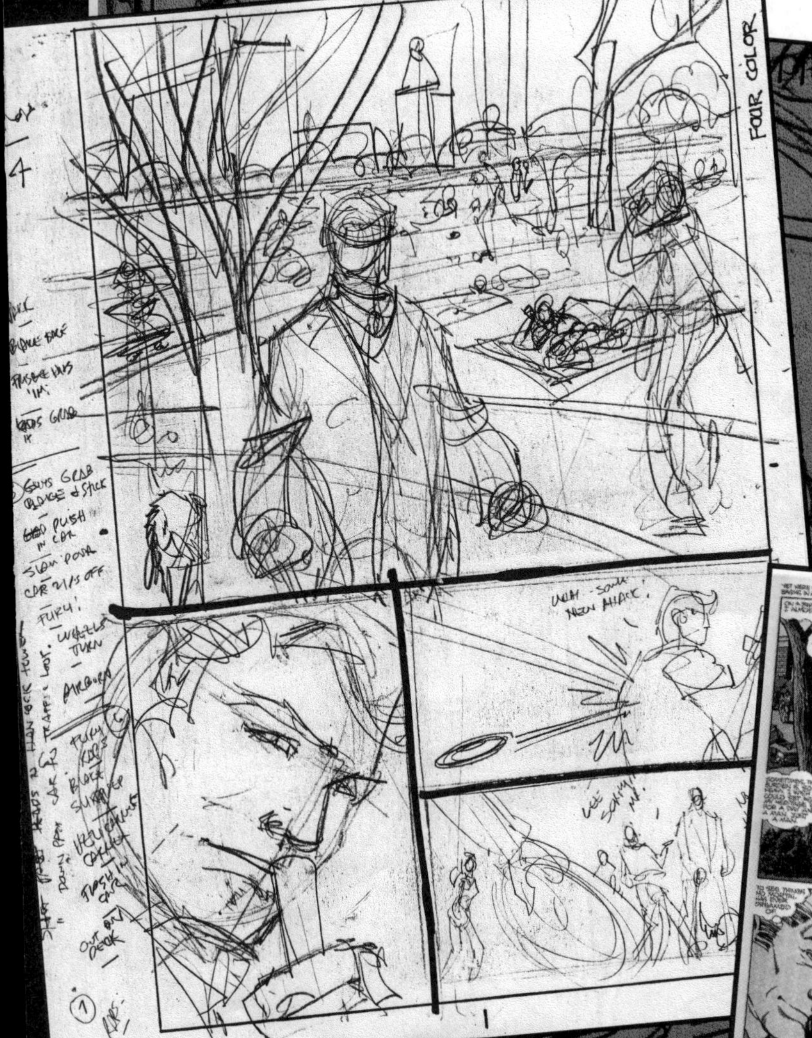
FOUR COLOR

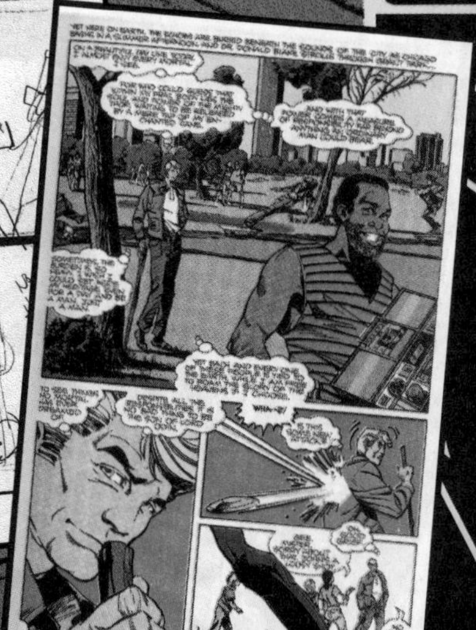

PAGE #

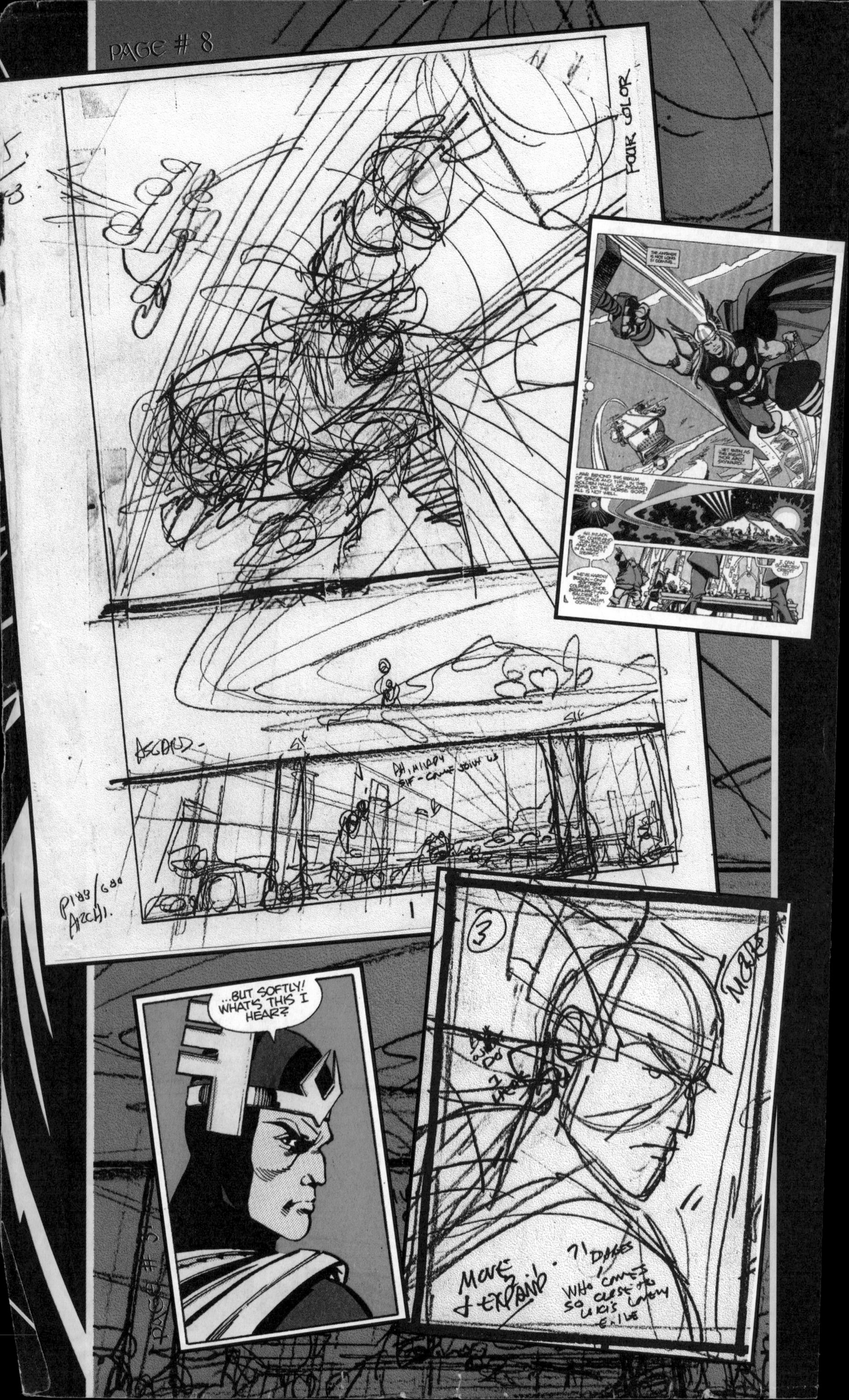
PAGE # 8
FOUR COLOR
ASGARD-
...BUT SOFTLY! WHAT'S THIS I HEAR?
MOVE & EXPAND

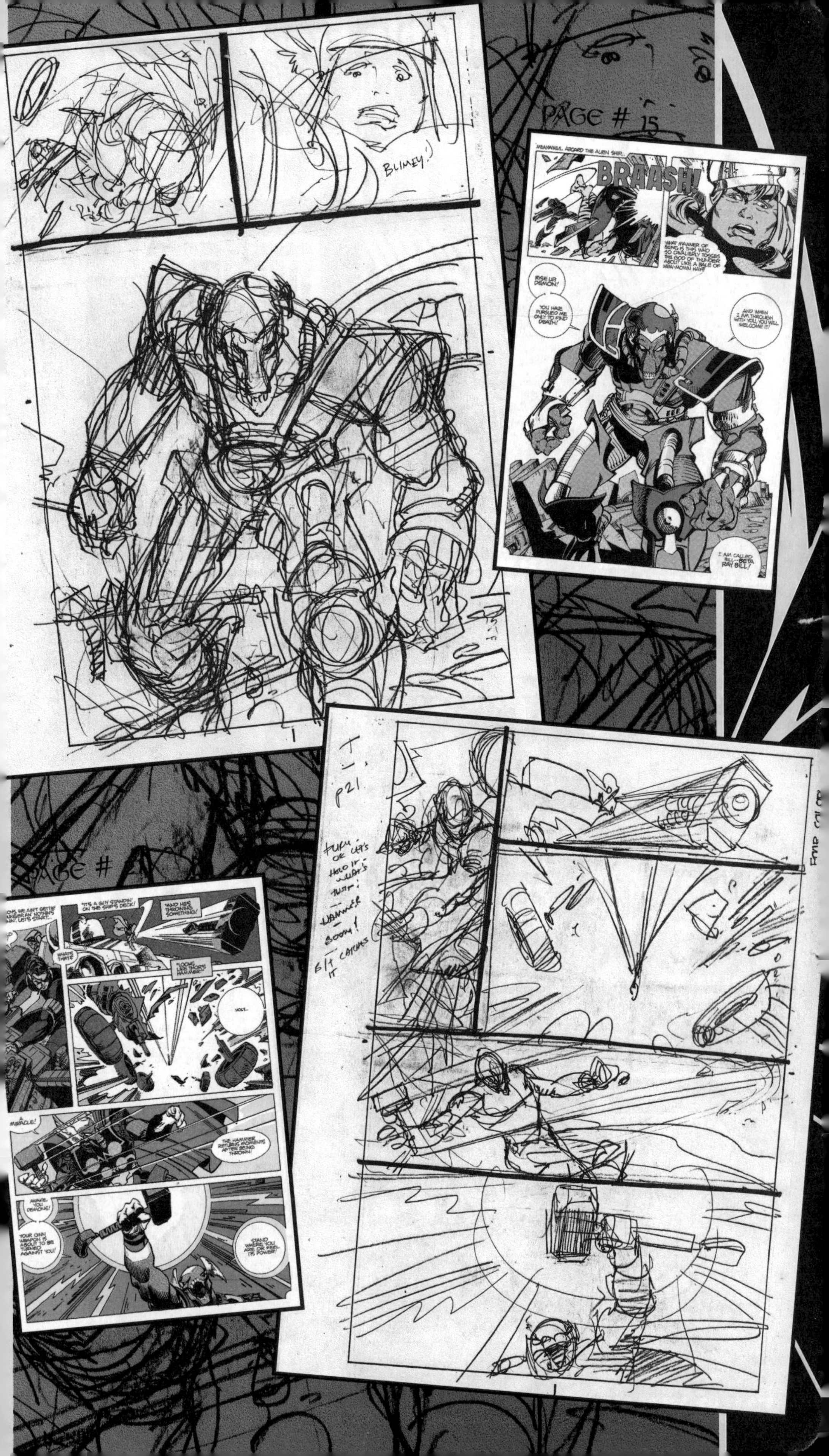
BLIMEY!
PAGE # 15
MEANWHILE, ABOARD THE ALIEN SHIP...
BRAASH!
WHAT MANNER OF BEING IS THIS WHO SO CAVALIERLY TOSSES THE GOD OF THUNDER ABOUT LIKE A BALE OF NEW-MOWN HAY?
RISE UP, DEMON!
YOU HAVE PURSUED ME ONLY TO FIND DEATH!
AND WHEN I AM THROUGH WITH YOU, YOU WILL WELCOME IT!
I AM CALLED BILL-- BETA RAY BILL!
PAGE #
"IT'S A GUY STANDIN' ON THE SHIP'S DECK!
"AND HE'S THROWING SOMETHING!
WHAT'S THAT?
"LOOKS LIKE THOR'S HAMMER!"
HOLY...
A MIRACLE!
THE HAMMER RETURNS MOMENTS AFTER BEING THROWN!
AWAKE, YOU DEMONS!
YOUR OWN WEAPON IS ABOUT TO BE TURNED AGAINST YOU!
STAND WHERE YOU ARE OR FEEL ITS POWER!
P21
BOOM!

VISIONARIES

Daredevil Visionaries:
Frank Miller Vol. 1
$17.95 US $27.50 CAN
ISBN # 07851-0757-6

Daredevil Visionaries:
Frank Miller Vol. 2
$24.95 US $37.95 CAN
ISBN # 07851-0771-1

Daredevil Visionaries:
Kevin Smith
$19.95 US $29.95 CAN
ISBN # 07851-0737-1

X-Men Visionaries:
Neal Adams
$24.95 US $37.95 CAN
ISBN # 07851-0198-5

X-Men Visionaries:
Joe Madureira
$17.95 US $27.50 CAN
ISBN # 07851-0748-7

X-Men Visionaries:
Chris Claremont
$24.95 US $35.00 CAN
ISBN # 07851-0598-0

Avengers Visionaries:
George Perez
$16.95 US $24.95 CAN

Thor Visionaries:
Walter Simonson
$24.95 US $37.95 CAN

COMING SOON
Daredevil Visionaries:
Frank Miller Vol. 3
November 2001

Spider-Man Visionaries
John Romita Sr.
Fall 2001